DATE DUE

3/25/99RL			

DEMCO 38-297

Second Edition

Introduction to the Counseling Profession

David Capuzzi
Douglas R. Gross

Allyn and Bacon

Boston   London   Toronto   Sydney   Tokyo   Singapore

Vice President, Education: Nancy Forsyth
Series Editor: Ray Short
Series Editorial Assistant: Christine Svitila
Marketing Manager: Kris Farnsworth
Production Coordinator: Thomas E. Dorsaneo
Editorial Production Service: Melanie Field, Strawberry Field Publishing
Composition: TBH/Typecast, Inc.
Composition and Prepress Buyer: Linda Cox
Manufacturing Buyer: Suzanne Lareau
Cover Administrator: Suzanne Harbison

Library of Congress Cataloging-in-Publication Data

Introduction to the counseling profession / David Capuzzi, Douglas R.
   Gross, [editors]. — 2nd ed.
       p.   cm.
   Rev ed. of: Introduction to counseling. 1991.
   Includes bibliographical references and index.
   ISBN 0-205-26535-9
    1. Counseling. I. Capuzzi, Dave. II. Gross, Douglas R.
  III. Introduction to counseling.
  BF637.C6I535 1997
  158'.3 — dc21   96-46277
                                            CIP

Printed in the United States of America

10 9 8 7 6 5 4 3 2 1 01 00 99 98 97 96

Contents

Conrad Sieber, Ph.D.
Postdoctoral Fellow, Counselor Education
Portland State University
Portland, Oregon

David Capuzzi, Ph.D.
Professor, Counselor Education
Portland State University
Portland, Oregon
Douglas R. Gross, Ph.D.
Professor, Division of Psychology in Education
Arizona State University
Tempe, Arizona

Ellen Hawley McWhirter, Ph.D.
Assistant Professor, Educational Psychology
University of Nebraska–Lincoln
Lincoln, Nebraska

Larry C. Loesch, Ph.D., NCC
Professor, Counselor Education
University of Florida
Gainesville, Florida
Nicholas A. Vacc, Ed.D., NCC
Professor and Chairperson, Counselor Education
University of Florida
Gainesville, Florida

Linda Seligman, Ph.D., LPC
Professor, Counseling and Development
George Mason University
Fairfax, Virginia

Ann Vernon, Ph.D.
Professor and Coordinator, Counselor Education
University of Northern Iowa
Cedar Falls, Iowa

Claire Cole Vaught, Ed.D.
Associate Professor, Counselor Education
Virginia Tech
Blacksburg, Virginia

Preface

The profession of counseling is best described as one through which counselors interact with clients to assist these individuals in learning about and dealing with themselves and their environment and the roles and responsibilities inherent in this interactive process. Individuals who are exploring counseling as a career choice need to be aware of the personal, professional, and societal demands that are placed on the professional counselor. The role of the professional counselor calls for individuals who are skilled and knowledgeable in the process and theory that undergird the profession, who are able and willing to reach deep levels of self-understanding, and who are able to integrate this skill, knowledge, and self-understanding to provide the effective counseling interaction to which clients are entitled. Individuals attempting to decide whether this is the right career choice for them will find the information contained in this text helpful in the decision-making process.

The book is unique both in its format and in its content. The contributing authors format provides state-of-the-art information by experts in their respective fields. The content provides readers with information on areas not often addressed in introductory texts. Examples include a chapter devoted to counseling from a rehabilitative perspective, a chapter devoted to brief therapies, a chapter devoted to client diagnosis and assessment that includes an introduction to the DSM-IV, a chapter that takes a comprehensive look at mental health counseling, and a number of chapters that discuss counseling special populations. Both format and content enhance the readability of the book and should increase student interest in the material.

The book is designed for students who are taking a preliminary course in the counseling field and who are trying to determine whether they are well matched to the profession of counseling; it provides an orientation to the profession. The book presents a comprehensive overview of the major aspects of counseling as a profession and provides its reader with insight into the myriad of issues that surround not only the process of counseling and its many populations but also the personal dynamics of the counselor that have an impact on this process. We know that one text cannot adequately address all the elements that make up this complex profession. We have, however, attempted to provide our readers with a broad perspective on the profession of counseling. The following overview highlights the major features of the text.

Overview

The format for this coedited/coauthored text is based on the contributions of thirty authors selected for their expertise in various areas of counseling. With few exceptions, each chapter contains information specific to a topic and uses case examples to demonstrate the various concepts within the chapter. The text is divided into the following four parts: "Counseling Foundations," "Counseling Skills," "Counseling in Specific Settings," and "Counseling Special Populations."

Part 1—"Counseling Foundations" (Chapters 1 through 5)—begins with information dealing with the philosophical and historical perspectives that serve as the foundation of the counseling profession and builds on this foundation, providing the reader with current information regarding legislation, professional associations, certification, licensure, accreditation, and current issues and trends related to counseling. The five chapters are entitled "The Counseling Profession: A Historical Perspective," "What Does It Mean to Be Psychologically Healthy?" "The Helping Relationship," "Ethical and Legal Considerations in Counseling: What Beginning Counselors Should Know," and "Counseling Theory: A Rationale and a Framework for an Eclectic Approach."

Part 2—"Counseling Skills" (Chapters 6 through 12)—presents information relative to the skills counselors must acquire through a combination of education, supervision, and practice. These chapters are entitled "Individual Counseling: Traditional Approaches," "Individual Counseling: Brief Approaches," "Group Counseling," "Career Counseling: Counseling for Life," "Counseling Uses of Tests," "Diagnosis in Counseling," and "Specialized Approaches to Counseling." All these chapters provide overviews and introduce readers to roles that cut across a variety of work settings.

Part 3—"Counseling in Specific Settings" (Chapters 13 and 14)—presents information relative to counseling not only in educational settings but also in mental health and private practice settings. These chapters—"School Counseling" and "Counseling in Mental Health and Private Practice Settings"—highlight specific processes and procedures that have applications to these diverse settings.

Part 4—"Counseling Special Populations" (Chapters 15 through 20)—covers the wide spectrum of clients who present for the services of the counselor. Included in this section are special approaches for dealing with children and adolescents, older adults, couples and families, gay, lesbian, and bisexual clients, minorities, and clients with disabilities. Each chapter includes not only a discussion of the special needs of these populations but also specialized approaches and techniques that have been found to be effective with these groups.

Every attempt has been made by the editors and contributors to provide the reader with current information in each of the twenty areas of focus. It is our hope that *Introduction to the Counseling Profession* will provide the neophyte with the foundation needed to make a decision regarding future study in the professional arena of counseling.

Acknowledgments

We would like to thank the thirty authors who contributed their time, expertise, and experience to the development of this textbook for the beginning professional. We would also like to thank our families, who provided the support to make our writing and editing efforts possible, as well as the counselor education faculties at Portland State and Arizona State universities. Our thanks are also directed to Ray Short and other staff of Allyn and Bacon for their encouragement and editing skills. Special recognition is given to Nila Epstein, graduate assistant at Portland State University, who worked so diligently and so competently to make this second edition a reality.

Special acknowledgment must be given to the Department of Special and Counselor Education of Portland State University. A special faculty development grant to the senior author/editor facilitated the employment of Nila Epstein to assist with the development of *Introduction to the Counseling Profession*.

Meet the Editors

David Capuzzi, Ph.D., NCC, LPC, is a past president of the American Counseling Association, or ACA (formerly the American Association for Counseling and Development), and professor of counselor education in the school of education at Portland State University in Portland, Oregon.

From 1980 to 1984, Dr. Capuzzi was editor of *The School Counselor*. He has authored a number of textbook chapters and monographs on the topic of preventing adolescent suicide and is coeditor and author, with Dr. Larry Golden, of *Helping Families Help Children: Family Interventions with School Related Problems* (1986) and *Preventing Adolescent Suicide* (1988). He has coauthored and coedited, with Douglas R. Gross, the following textbooks: *Youth at Risk: A Prevention Resource for Counselors, Teachers and Parents* (1996); *Counseling and Psychotherapy: Theories and Interventions* (1995), and *Introduction to Group Counseling* (1992). Dr. Capuzzi published *Suicide Prevention in the Schools: Guidelines for Middle and High School Settings* in 1994. He has authored or coauthored articles in a number of ACA and related journals.

A frequent speaker and keynoter at professional conferences and institutes, Dr. Capuzzi has also consulted with a variety of school districts and community agencies interested in initiating counseling and intervention strategies for adolescents at risk for suicide. He has facilitated the development of suicide prevention, crisis management, and postvention programs in communities in twenty-four states. He also provides trainings on the topics of youth at risk and counseling and teaching youth at risk.

Douglas R. Gross, Ph.D., NCC, CPC, has been a faculty member in the counseling program at Arizona State University in Tempe for twenty-eight years. His professional work history includes public school teaching, counseling, and administration. He has been president of the Arizona Counselors Association, president of the Western Association for Counselor Education and Supervision, chair of the Western Regional Branch Assembly of the American Counseling Association (formerly the American Association for Counseling and Development), president of the Association for Humanistic Education and Development, and treasurer and parliamentarian of the ACA.

Dr. Gross has coauthored and coedited four textbooks and has contributed chapters in *Foundations of Mental Health Counseling* (1986); *Counseling: Theory, Process and Practice* (1977); and *The Counselor's Handbook* (1974). His research has appeared in *The Journal of Counseling Psychology, The Journal of Counseling and Development, The Association for Counselor Education and Supervision Journal, The Journal of Educational Research, Counseling and Human Development, The Arizona Counselors Journal, The Texas Counseling Journal,* and *The AMHCA Journal.*

Dr. Gross also serves as a consultant to several alcohol and drug programs in the state of Arizona.

Meet the Contributors

Donald R Atkinson, Ph.D., is a professor of education in the combined counseling, clinical, and school psychology program at the University of California, Santa Barbara. He received his Ph.D. from the University of Wisconsin in 1970. Professor Atkinson is a fellow in the American Psychological Society and Divisions 17 and 45 of the American Psychological Association. He is a co-author of *Counseling American Minorities: A Cross-Cultural Perspective* (now in its fourth edition), *Counseling Non-Ethnic American Minorities*, and *Counseling Diverse Populations*. He is also author or co-author of over a hundred journal articles, most of which report the results of research on cultural variables in counseling.

David D. Brooks, Jr., Ph.D., is a member of the counseling and human development services department at the College of Education, Kent State University. He received his doctorate in counseling from the University of Georgia in 1984. He has served as president of the American Mental Health Counselors Association and as a member of both the governing council and the executive committee of the American Counseling Association. He has served as a member of the board of the Council for Accreditation of Counseling and Related Educational Programs. Dr. Brooks received the Carl D. Perkins Government Relations Award from ACA in 1989 in recognition of his contributions to the counselor licensure movement. His professional interests include counselor identity, role, and function; life skills training; and counseling supervision.

Carol A. Burden, Ed.D., serves as coordinator of the counselor education program at Portland State University. She supervises students during the clinical components of their studies. In addition to her focus on school counseling, she has an interest in eating disorders, career counseling, and in helping schools cope with change.

Cass Dykeman, Ph.D., NCC, NCSC, MAC, is an associate professor of applied psychology at Eastern Washington University in Spokane. At Eastern, he serves as the director of the school counseling program. Dr. Dykeman received a master's degree in counseling from the University of Washington and a doctorate in counselor education from the University of Virginia. He holds national certification in both addictions counseling and school counseling. His research interests include the use of family counseling in addictions treatment. He has authored numerous articles that have appeared in journals such as *Social Work in Education, Journal of Thought,* and *The School Counselor.*

Harriet L. Glosoff, Ph.D., LPC, NCC, is an assistant professor of counseling and counseling psychology at the University of Southern Mississippi (USM). She received a Ph.D. in counseling and development from the American University, Washington, D.C., and an M.A. in counseling and personnel services from the University of Maryland. Prior to joining the faculty at USM, Dr. Glosoff served as the assistant executive director for the American Counseling Association, and she remains active in ACA at the state and national levels. Dr. Glosoff's multifaceted professional background has included teaching, supervision, research, and counseling in diverse settings such as universities, community agencies, psychiatric facilities, public schools, and the private sector. Her current professional and research interests are in the areas of ethical and legal issues in counseling, parental adjustment to children's disability, and clinical supervision.

Larry Golden, Ph.D., is an associate professor and coordinator of the counseling and guidance program at the University of Texas at San Antonio. Dr. Golden is also a psychologist and specializes in counseling children and families. He received a Ph.D. in counseling psychology from Arizona State University, an M.S. in child counseling from the City University of New York, and a B.Ed. in elementary education from the University of Miami. Dr. Golden's published books are *Psychotherapeutic Techniques in School Psychology; Helping Families Help Children: Family Interventions with School Related Problems; Preventing Adolescent Suicide; ACA Ethical Standards Casebook,* fourth edition; and *Case Studies in Child Counseling.*

D. Scott Herrmann, M.C., is a doctoral student in the program of counseling psychology at Arizona State University. He has a master's degree in counseling from Arizona State University, and a bachelor's degree in psychology from the University of California, Los Angeles. His work has appeared in scholarly journals published in the United States, Canada, and Great Britain; and he has addressed professional audiences during speaking engagements in several different states. He holds student affiliate memberships with the American Psychological Association and the American Counseling Association. His current research interests include forensic psychology, counseling theory, and cognitive-behavioral interventions.

Reese M. House, Ed.D., is a professor of education at Oregon State University. He specializes in AIDS education and prevention strategies. He was the co-founder of the Cascade AIDS Project and has been active in the gay, lesbian, and bisexual community. He is interested in social change and justice issues.

Richard T. Kinnier, Ph.D., is an associate professor in the counseling psychology program at Arizona State University (ASU). He received a B.A. in psychology from Boston College, an M.Ed. in counseling from Teachers College, Columbia University, and a Ph.D. in counseling psychology from Stanford University in 1982. Dr. Kinnier has worked in a variety of settings, including a state hospital, a psychiatric out-patient program, and a university counseling center. He currently teaches a variety of counseling courses at ASU. His research interests include issues related to values and meaning in life.

Sharon E. Robinson Kurpius, Ph.D., received her doctorate from Indiana University in 1978 and has been a member of the counseling faculty at ASU since that time. She holds fellow status in the Counseling Psychology and the Consulting Psychology divisions of APA. She has been active at both state and national levels of ACA and most recently was the associate editor for the *Journal for Counseling and Development*. Professional areas of interest include at-risk youth, ethics, consultation, and health counseling. She recently co-authored (with Neil Weiner) a new book: *Shattered Innocence: A Practical Guide for Counseling Women Survivors of Childhood Sexual Abuse.*

Rolla E. Lewis, Ed.D., is an assistant professor in counselor and teacher education at Portland State University. He received his doctorate from the University of San Francisco. In addition to an interest in normative and brief approaches, Dr. Lewis's research focuses on using programmed writing interventions to help students make successful transitions into high school. With colleagues at Portland State University, Dr. Lewis is collaborating to integrate structuring and relationship skills into an innovative teacher education program.

Hanoch Livneh, Ph.D., is professor of counselor education and coordinator of the rehabilitation counseling specialization at Portland State University, Portland, Oregon. He received his M.A. and Ph.D. degrees in rehabilitation counseling psychology from the University of Wisconsin at Madison. Before joining the faculty at Portland State University, he served as the director of the rehabilitation counseling program, Department of Counseling and Educational Psychology, at Rhode Island College, Providence, Rhode Island.

Larry C. Loesch, Ph.D., is a professor in the department of counselor education at the University of Florida, a National Certified Counselor, and a research and evaluation consultant for the National Board for Certified Counselors. He was a co-recipient of the 1983 APGA Research Award, the 1985 AMECD Exemplary Practices Award, and the 1992 AACD Arthur A. Hitchcock Distinguished Professional Service Award. He was president of the Florida Association for Counseling and Development (1992–1993), the Association for Measurement and Evaluation in Counseling and Development (1982–1983), Chi Sigma Iota (International) (1991–1992), and Southern Association for Counselor Education and Supervision (1995–1996).

Gary J. Loya, M.S., is a doctoral student in counseling psychology at the University of Nebraska–Lincoln. He received his B.A. from California State University, Dominguez Hills, and his master of science degree in counseling psychology from Eastern Washington University. Gary Loya's heritage is biracial, born of a mixed Mexican American/Anglo parentage. His research interests include multicultural counseling competencies, with an emphasis on biracial identity and bicultural issues and substance abuse counseling.

Linda G. Matthews, M.A., is a doctoral candidate in the counseling/clinical/school psychology program at the University of California at Santa Barbara. She obtained a B.A. in psychology from UCLA and an M.A. in counseling psychology from UCSB. Her primary research interests include cross-cultural counseling process and outcome, as well as career development among ethnic minorities.

Benedict T. McWhirter, Ph.D., is an assistant professor in the counseling psychology program at the University of Nebraska–Lincoln and a licensed psychologist in the state of Nebraska. He received his B.A. from the University of Notre Dame and both his master's in counseling and his Ph.D. in counseling psychology from Arizona State University. Part of his education has also included work and study in Latin America, Asia Minor, and Australia. He currently teaches counseling practica, school counseling and guidance techniques, and counseling supervision. His research focuses on loneliness and social support, intervention strategies for youth at-risk, and experiential learning. He is a member of the American Psychological Association, the American Counseling Association, and the American Association of Applied and Preventive Psychology. He has published numerous articles in refereed journals, book chapters, and recently coauthored with his family the text: *At-Risk Youth: A Comprehensive Response* (1993).

Ellen Hawley McWhirter, Ph.D., is an assistant professor in the counseling psychology program in the Department of Educational Psychology at the University of Nebraska-Lincoln. She received her B.A. from the University of Notre Dame and her master of counseling and Ph.D. in counseling psychology from Arizona State University. Dr. McWhirter recently authored *Counseling for Empowerment* and is a coauthor of *At-Risk Youth: A Comprehensive Response*. Her scholarly interests focus on ethnic minority and female adolescent perceptions of career and educational barriers, youth at risk, and applications of empowerment as a framework for counseling. Her publications appear in such journals as the *Journal of Counseling and Development, Journal of Career Development*, and *Journal of Mental Health Counseling*. Dr. McWhirter received the O'Hana Honor Award for contributions to the profession in the areas of diversity and multicultural counseling from the American Counseling Association in 1995.

J. Jeffries McWhirter, Ph.D., ABPP, is a professor in the counseling and counseling psychology programs at Arizona State University. He has had over thirty years experience as a teacher, counselor, and university professor and has served as a consultant to school and mental health personnel on a variety of topics. He is the author of sixteen books, monographs, and training manuals and over a hundred chapters and articles that have been published in professional journals. He is the senior author of *At-Risk Youth: A Comprehensive Response*. He has been a visiting professor to twenty universities, including two Fulbright grants to Turkey and Australia. In addition to his work in counseling theories, Dr. McWhirter's areas of special interest include small-group research, family counseling and parent education, learning disabilities, international aspects of counseling, and at-risk children, youth, and families.

Russell D. Miars, Ph.D., is an assistant professor in the counselor education program at Portland State University. Previously Dr. Miars was director of the Counseling and Student Development Center and adjunct associate professor in clinical psychology at Indiana University of Pennsylvania. His research and scholarly interests include counselor supervision, legal and ethical issues, life span human development, career development, and assessment in counseling. He currently maintains a part-time private practice as a licensed psychologist in Oregon.

Jennie L. Miller, M.A., NCC, is a doctoral student in counselor education at Oregon State University. She received her master of arts from Chadron State College and her bachelor of arts from the University of Wyoming. Prior to entering the doctoral program, she worked as a mental health counselor and also an educator at the secondary and college levels. Her research interests include gay/lesbian/bisexual issues, gender issues, multicultural issues, and counselor education.

Margaret M. Pedersen, M.S., M.B.A., LPC, is a counselor and instructor at Clackamas Community College. She received her M.S. degree in counselor education from Portland State University. Her M.B.A. degree with a specialization in organizational behavior is from the University of Michigan. In addition to her work at the community college, Ms. Pedersen is an adjunct faculty member in counselor education at Portland State University and in counseling psychology at Lewis and Clark College in Portland, Oregon. She has worked as a counselor, consultant, instructor, and education coordinator in a variety of settings, including universities, medical school, an employee assistance program, private practice, and community college. Her areas of special interest are life span development, communication, and adult learning.

Perry Rockwell, Jr., Ph.D., is professor emeritus of counselor education at the University of Wisconsin at Platteville. He received his B.S., M.S., and Ph.D. degrees from the University of Wisconsin at Madison. Dr. Rockwell has both taught and counseled in a variety of schools and colleges in several states. He has a continuing interest in the social effects of guidance and counseling on society and of social pressures on the profession. He has been active in the ACA at local, state, and national levels since 1958.

Linda Seligman, Ph.D., is a professor at George Mason University in Fairfax, Virginia, where she is in charge of the graduate program in community agency counseling. Dr. Seligman also is a licensed psychologist and licensed professional counselor with experience in a variety of clinical settings. She is currently the director of the Center for Counseling and Consultation, a group private practice with offices in Fairfax, Virginia, and Bethesda, Maryland. Dr. Seligman received the Ph.D. degree in counseling psychology from Columbia University. Her research interests include diagnosis and treatment planning, counseling people with cancer, and career counseling. She has written six books and over forty professional articles and book chapters, has served as editor of the *Journal of Mental Health Counseling*, and in 1990 was selected as Researcher of the Year by the American Mental Health Counselors Association.

Ardis Sherwood-Hawes, M.S., is a counselor in private practice in Beaverton, Oregon, and instructor for human development at Clark College, Vancouver, Washington. She received her masters in counseling degree from the counselor education program at Portland State University. Her professional interests and expertise include issues related to women, survivors of sexual abuse, life skills training, parent skills training, and adolescent pregnancy and parenthood. Her publication history includes chapters on adolescent pregnancy and childbearing, suicide, counseling children and adolescents, group therapy, and nontraditional approaches to counseling and psychotherapy.

Conrad Sieber, Ph.D., is a postdoctoral fellow in the counselor education program at Portland State University and is involved in teaching courses as well as the training and supervision of graduate students. Dr. Sieber received his doctoral degree from Colorado State University and completed an internship at The Ohio

State University's counseling and consultation services. He has five years experience in university counseling centers, where he coordinated and developed group programs, provided program evaluation of clinical services, and was actively involved in the training and supervision of graduate student trainees.

Nicholas A. Vacc, Ed.D., is professor and chairperson of the department of counseling and educational development at the University of North Carolina at Greensboro. He received his doctorate in counseling from the State University of New York at Albany. He is a National Certified Counselor, an examination consultant for the National Board for Certified Counselors, a member of the American Counseling Association, a fellow in the American Orthopsychiatric Association, and past president of the Association for Assessment in Counseling. Dr. Vacc's prior employment experience includes work in residence life, counseling with veterans and their dependents, and directing a university counseling center. He is former editor of *Measurement and Evaluation in Counseling and Development* (formerly known as *Measurement and Evaluation in Guidance*), past chair of the ACA Council of Journal Editors, and former president of the North Carolina Association of Measurement and Evaluation in Counseling and Development. He is currently a member of the Joint Committee on Testing Practices, a group that develops and recommends policy and practices concerning testing.

Claire Cole Vaught, Ed.D., is currently associate professor of counselor education at Virginia Tech. Dr. Cole Vaught is a former middle school counselor, high school counselor, and central office administrator. She is past editor of *The School Counselor* and co-author of *Helping Relationships and Strategies*. She has written numerous articles and monographs on middle school counseling and teacher advisory programs. She believes strongly in the value of school counseling for all children.

Ann Vernon, Ph.D., is professor and coordinator of counseling in the department of educational administration and counseling at the University of Northern Iowa. In addition, she maintains a private practice where she works primarily with children, adolescents, and their parents. Dr. Vernon presents workshops in the United States and Canada on a variety of topics such as counseling techniques with children and adolescents, effective parenting, and rational emotive therapy. Dr. Vernon is the author of numerous books and articles, including *Thinking, Feeling, Behaving, Counseling Children and Adolescents, Developmental Assessment, Intervention with Children and Adolescents*, and *What Growing Up Is All About: A Parents' Guide to Child and Adolescent Development*.

Elizabeth Wosley-George, Ph.D., is an assistant professor of counselor education at Portland State University in Portland, Oregon. She was formerly director of Emergency Services of North Central Mental Health in Columbus, Ohio. She has teaching and research interests in the areas of diagnosis and treatment planning, psychopharmacology, multicultural perspectives in counseling, and mental health service delivery systems. Dr. Wosley-George has extensive emergency room and community involvement and experience with individuals who have psychiatric disabilities.

Counseling Foundations

Counseling as a profession has an interesting history and encompasses a number of basic premises and foundational perspectives in which the counselor needs to be educated. This section provides the beginning counseling student with an overview of both the historical context of counseling and the philosophical basis on which the counselor operates.

The development of counseling as a distinct profession is outlined in Chapter 1, "The Counseling Profession: A Historical Perspective." The roots of counseling are traced from the vocational guidance movement at the beginning of this century to the current status of professional associations, legislation, certification, licensure, accreditation, and current issues and trends related to counseling.

The context and assumptions within which counselors and mental health professionals operate are examined in Chapter 2, "What Does It Mean to Be Psychologically Healthy?" The author discusses how cultural values have influenced the "standard" criteria for mental health in our society. A possible model for viewing positive mental health is described, in which self-acceptance, self-awareness, and a clear sense of reality are basic components. The chapter discusses the need for individuals to experience a sense of balance and a feeling of purpose in their lives, whatever their cultural context.

Chapter 3, "The Helping Relationship," presents to students the characteristics and qualities that distinguish helping professionals. Personal qualities that effective helpers possess are described, as well as such basic skills as the counselor's reflecting and listening skills, attention to nonverbal cues, and the ability to observe and follow perceptively a client's patterns of speech and behavior. These core skills provide a foundation for the beginning counselor to both understand the counseling process and become more self-aware about his or her own interpersonal interactions.

The relationship between the client and the counselor does not exist in a vacuum; rather, it is interlineated into the personal, legal, and ethical context of our society. Counselors are often called on to make decisions regarding clients in which the "correct" mode of action may not be immediately clear. There may be two contradictory obligations—for example, the obligation to respect the confidentiality of a client and the obligation to protect the client from self-harm or the harming of others. When faced with such situations, the counselor cannot simply rely on personal judgment but instead needs to act from the basis of the professional guidelines and codes of ethics of the counseling and human development professions. Chapter 4, "Ethical and Legal Considerations in Counseling: What Beginning Counselors Should Know," provides an overview of the ethical and legal guidelines on which counselors must base their decisions. It discusses the role of personal values versus professional ethics; the question of counselor competence, clients' rights, confidentiality, and informed consent; and the practicalities of dealing with legal issues and client-related litigation. Such concepts are essential for the beginning counselor to understand and incorporate in gaining a sense of the professional status of the counselor.

Theory provides a framework to understand human behavior and assists the counselor in making decisions regarding the course of therapy. In its essence, theory is highly practical, since it enables the counselor to maintain a consistent and conscious therapeutic relationship with the client and to use interventions that are solidly anchored to the particular client's goals. Chapter 5, "Counseling Theory: A Rationale and a Framework for an Eclectic Approach," outlines the importance of theory in counseling and gives an overview of the major schools of counseling and psychotherapy. The authors discuss the value of an informed, eclectic approach in which the counselor consciously and carefully selects an approach that is most likely to be effective and constructive with a particular client or situation. The chapter stresses the responsibility of counselors today to integrate and synthesize counseling theories into their own personalized approach.

C h a p t e r 1

The Counseling Profession
A Historical Perspective

Harriet L. Glosoff, Ph.D., LPC, NCC   *Perry J. Rockwell, Jr., Ph.D.*

If one assumes that counseling is advising, counselors have existed since people have appeared on earth. Mothers, fathers, friends, lovers, clergy, and social leaders all provide such counsel—whether sought after or not. The idea of a professionally trained counselor is relatively new. This idea did not, however, emerge due to the recognition of a "deep need within human development" (Stripling, 1983, p. 206). The counseling profession evolved in response to meet the demands made by the industrialization and urbanization of the United States. At the turn of the twentieth century, America faced a confluence of social and economic problems such as the proper distribution of a growing work force, dealing with an increasingly educated population, meeting the needs of immigrants, and the preservation of social values as family connections were weakened (Aubrey, 1982; Herr, 1985).

A representative democracy demands an educated citizenry taking responsibility for the government itself. As the new democracy developed, so did the ideal of education for all citizens. Toward the end of the nineteenth century, the curriculum of schools began to change and choices among school subjects became available. Help with such choices was necessary. Jessie Davis, one of the pioneers in counseling, declared in his autobiography that he had graduated from school "fairly well prepared to live in the Middle Ages" (Davis, 1956, p. 57). His experiences led directly to the establishment of guidance and counseling services in schools.

Other factors were providing pressures that made the evolution of professionally training individuals to help people make choices inevitable. The industrial revolution and its attendant job specialization and technologic advances were some of those pressures. There was also an increase in democracy after the Civil War ended in 1865. If the United States had continued to exist as a slave society or a closed class society, there likely would have been little need for the development of counseling services.

The population of the country was on the increase, and the census of 1890 revealed that the frontier was essentially closed. Larger cities were growing increasingly more crowded, and immigrants to the United States and other citizens could no longer move westward or eastward without regard for others. "Free" land was all but gone. It became necessary to remain near the cities to work, to live, and to get along with one's neighbors. Providing assistance in the choices necessary to live in the large industrially based cities became necessary.

During the twentieth century, the development of professional counseling in the United States has been influenced by a variety of factors. The newly developed science of psychology began, and continued, studying the differences among individuals. Instruments for appraising people were in their infancy but were known to pioneers in the field, who noted the need for counseling services. As these tools developed more sophistication, they were adapted and/or adopted by counselors. Other factors contributing to the evolution of counseling included the work of leaders of the early settlement house movement and other social reformers; the mental hygiene movement; the extent to which Americans value personal success; the emphasis placed on the awareness and use of one's talents, interests, and abilities; the ongoing industrialization of the country; the continued growth of career education and career guidance; the development of psychology as a profession; and the rapid changes in all fields due to increased availability of technology (Shertzer & Stone, 1986).

Pressures from various socioeconomic factors also led to the kaleidoscope we know as counseling today. The history of counseling has continued the thread of individual choice in a society that prizes freedom to choose as an ideal. Like a kaleidoscope, the form, emphasis, and brightness of various aspects of counseling have changed as society changes. This chapter examines the following select facets of that kaleidoscope that have shaped the counseling profession:

- The vocational guidance movement
- The mental health counseling movement
- The development of professional identity
- The influence of federal legislation
- The history of the American Counseling Association
- Credentialing and the "professionalization" of counseling

The chapter concludes with a brief review of current issues and trends in the counseling profession.

Beginnings of the Vocational Guidance Movement

Perhaps the earliest notion of professional counseling in response to societal pressures was that of Lysander S. Richards. In 1881 Richards published a slim volume titled *Vocophy*. Vocophy was considered by Richards to be a "new profession, a system enabling a person to name the calling or vocation one is best suited to follow" (Richards, 1881). His work has been dismissed because there is no documented proof that he actually established the services he advocated. Nevertheless, his ideas foreshadowed what was to come. He called his counselors "vocophers" and urged that they study occupations and the people they counseled.

Richards (1881) included letters from various famous people of the day in his book *Vocophy*. He believed that aspirants to particular occupations should consider what successful people had to say about the qualifications for success in that field. Letters from Grant, Longfellow, Westinghouse, and others, which described the ingredients for success in their occupations, were included.

Later, a series of pamphlets published by the Metropolitan Life Insurance Company in the 1960s and used widely by school counselors asked the question, "Should your child be a _____ ?" A famous person in a field would describe what was necessary for success in that field. Using successful people to provide career information is a technique employed by counselors today as well.

Richards also seemed advanced for his time regarding his views of women and youth, and their work. He said that if a woman could do the work "though at present solely followed by man, there can be no objections, whether normally or religiously considered, to her following it" (Richards, 1881, preface). He deplored the drifting of youth from job to job without consideration of what would be best for them and for society.

Whether Richards influenced those who followed is speculative. Influence is the quicksilver of history. He was active in the literary societies in the Boston area, as was Frank Parsons. Did they meet? debate? Richards's *Vocophy* was in the Harvard Library in the 1890s. In an article published in the later 1890s, Parsons (1894) expressed ideas similar to those of Richards. Brewer (1942) noted that Meyer Bloomfield, a colleague of Parsons at the Breadwinners Institute, mentioned Richards in his Harvard courses, as did Henry C. Metcalf of Tufts and Frank Locke of the YMCA in Boston.

Frank Parsons

Regardless of who influenced whom, the need for counseling about vocational choice seems to have permeated American society of the late nineteenth and early twentieth centuries. There is no question of the credit given to Frank Parsons for leading the way to vocational guidance. Parsons had a long history of concern for economic and political reforms that would benefit people. He published books and articles on a wide variety of topics, including taxation, women's suffrage, and education for all people. Of all his endeavors, Parsons was most interested in social reform and especially in assisting people to make sound occupational choices. Other pioneers in the field credited him with being the first counselor (Davis, 1914; Reed, 1944), and he has often been referred to as the "father of guidance." Parsons alone, of those individuals who had some direct connection with the organization and extension of guidance services, had a definite, well-thought-out, and organized social philosophy, which he articulated often and at length (Rockwell, 1958).

Parsons was one of the many in the late nineteenth and early twentieth centuries who was striving to make the world a better place in which to live. These people saw in the growth of large private fortunes, based on industrial might and the resultant political power, a clear danger to the realization of a more perfect society based on the brotherhood of all humankind. They were humanitarians all; each seeking the good things in life for the individual within society. Parsons found himself in the company of such notables of this movement as Henry D. Lloyd, Edward Bellamy, Phillip Brooks, and Benjamin O. Flower (Rockwell, 1958).

Parsons believed it was better to select a vocation scientifically than to drift through a variety of vocations, perhaps never finding one that would be best for the person and thus make society a better place in which to live. Meyer Bloomfield, director of the Civic Service House in Boston, asked Parsons to establish such a service within the Civic Service House. Thus Parsons became director of what was called the Breadwinners Institute from 1905 to 1907 (Brewer, 1942).

Parsons developed a plan for individualized counseling and opened the Vocational Bureau of Boston in January 1908. He served as its director and vocational counselor. The primary goal of the bureau was to develop the potential of Boston's growing immigrant population. Although Parsons was but one of many who were seeking social reforms at this time, he was able to secure the support of the leaders of powerful groups in business, labor, education, and politics. His report to the members of the board controlling the Vocational Bureau was the first recorded instance of the use of the term "vocational guidance." (Brewer, in 1942 published the report as an appendix to his *History*.) Parsons's report emphasized that counseling was not designed to make decisions for counselees. "No attempt is made, of course, to decide FOR (sic) the applicant what his calling should be; but the Bureau tries to help him arrive at a wise, well-founded conclusion for himself" (Brewer, 1942, p. 304). According to Williamson (1965), this was consistent with the moral and intellectual atmosphere of that time. He traced the growth of counseling prior to Parsons's work to the concept of "vocational freedom of choice" (p. 3). He noted that the climate of the late 1800s stimulated practical application of vocational choice or individuals' freedom to pursue choice in personal development.

Parsons also developed a plan for the education of counselors. His plan was outlined in his book, *Choosing a Vocation* (1909), published posthumously. Parsons's prescriptions for how counselees should examine themselves and their lives reflected his political and social philosophy (Rockwell, 1958, pp. 74–130).

Early Ties between Vocational Guidance and School Counseling

Many see educational settings as the first homes to the profession of counseling, especially in terms of vocational guidance. At about the same time that Parsons opened the Vocational Bureau, Jesse Davis began advising students about educational and vocational matters in 1898 (Aubrey, 1982). Jessie B. Davis had been unsure of what he wanted to do with his life throughout his educational career. He was questioned thoroughly by Charles Thurber, one of his professors at Cornell University, and that left a lasting impression on him. He began to use the professor's methods in his work with students at Central High School in Detroit and attempted to incorporate guidance into the normal educational experience of students. In 1907, Davis became principal of the Grand Rapids Michigan Central School and was able to implement his ideas of self-study, occupational study, and examination of self in relation to the chosen occupation throughout the seventh through twelfth grades (Brewer, 1942). This was done primarily through essays written in English classes. Essay topics varied from self-examination of values and ideals to the selection of a vocation by the twelfth grade. Throughout the topics, social and civic ethics were emphasized (Davis, 1914). Just five years later (1912), Grand Rapids established a citywide guidance department.

Grand Rapids was not the only city in the early 1900s that housed newly developed vocational guidance services. Both Anna Y. Reed in Seattle and Eli Weaver in New York established counseling services based on Social Darwinian concepts (Rockwell, 1958). Similar to Darwin's biological theory of "survival of the fittest," Social Darwinism contends that certain groups in a society become powerful because they have adapted best to the evolving requirements of that society. Reed decided that counseling services were needed for America's youth through her study of newsboys, penal institutions, and charity schools. She emphasized that businesspeople were the most successful and that counseling should be designed to help youth emulate them. She equated morality and business ideals and was much concerned that whatever course of action was taken on any social question, it be taken on the basis of social research, of economy, and of how it would be accepted by the business world. Reed urged that schools keep children focused on the potential for making money, which she believed every pupil could understand (Reed, 1916).

The guidance services that Reed developed were similar to those of modern placement agencies that focus on an individual's acceptability to employers. Other programs, she said, "savored too much of a philanthropic or social service proposition and too little of a practical commercial venture" (Reed, 1920, p. 62).

Eli Weaver also believed in working within the framework of the existing society and looked on counseling as a means of keeping the wheels of the machinery well oiled. He was chairman of the Students' Aid Committee of the High School Teachers' Association of New York in 1905. In developing the work of his committee, Weaver concluded that the students were in need of advice and counsel before their entrance into the work-a-day world. He had no funds or active help from school authorities, but was able to secure the volunteer services of teachers to work with young people in New York. By 1910, he was able to report teachers actively attempting to aid boys and girls discover what they could do best and how to secure a job in which their abilities could be used to the fullest advantage (Brewer, 1942; Rockwell, 1958).

Counselors in the school systems of Boston and New York during the 1920s were expected to assist students in making educational and vocational choices. It was during the 1920s that the certification of school counselors began in these two cities. It was also during that decade that the Strong Vocational Interest Inventory was first published (1928) and used by counselors setting the stage for future directions in career counseling (Shertzer & Stone, 1986).

The Creation of the National Vocational Guidance Association

The early pioneers in counseling clearly reflected society's need for workers who were skilled and happy in what they did. A distinct influence in early counseling was the vocational education movement. In 1906, the National Society for the Promotion of Industrial Education (NSPIE) was formed. People who were advocates of vocational counseling served on its board and later on the board of the Vocational Bureau established by Parsons. Ralph Albertson, an employment supervisor at William Filene's Sons Company and confidant of Frank Parsons, became secretary of the board of trustees of the Vocational Bureau (Stephens, 1970). Frank Snedden, a vocational educator from Massachusetts, is given credit for suggesting that a vocational guidance conference separate from the NSPIE be held (Brewer, 1942). Such conferences were held in 1911 and 1912.

At a third national conference in 1913, the National Vocational Guidance Association (NVGA) was formed in Grand Rapids, Michigan (Norris, 1954). Frank Leavitt became the first president and noted the economic, educational, and social demands for guidance and the counseling it entailed. He also felt that it was necessary "for the very preservation of society itself" (Norris, 1954, p. 17). Counseling in regard to career choice remained an integral part of the movement.

Beginnings of the Mental Health Counseling Movement

The economic, educational, and social reform forces that led to the organization of NVGA also led to other movements, which were later incorporated into the kaleidoscope we call counseling today. In the early 1800s, American reformers such as Dorothea Dix advocated for the establishment of institutions that would treat people with emotional disorders in a humane manner. Although these reformers made great strides in accomplishing their goals, following the Civil War there was a rapid decline in the conditions related to the humane treatment of institutionalized individuals (Palmo & Weikel, 1986).

Clifford Beers, who had suffered harsh treatment for mental illness in several psychiatric institutions, published *A Mind That Found Itself*, an autobiography about his experience (Beers, 1908). Publication of this book served as a catalyst for the mental hygiene movement and studies of people with emotional and behavioral problems. Early studies of children with emotional problems supported the concept of providing counseling for all children in schools. Beginning at about the same time as vocational guidance, the mental hygiene movement and the field of psychology have had equally strong influences on the development of professional counseling.

In 1908, the same year Frank Parsons opened the Vocational Bureau, William Healy, M.D., established the first community psychiatric clinic. The Juvenille Psychopathic Institute was founded to provide services to the young people in Chicago who were having problems. The institute used testing, modified psychoanalysis, and involvement of family members. In 1909, leaders of Cook County,

Illinois, deciding that counseling services would benefit children, established coun-tywide child guidance clinics. It was this same year that the U.S. Congress founded the National Committee on Mental Hygiene.

Early Psychologists

It is impossible to discuss any mental health profession without acknowledging the contributions of well-known individuals such as Sigmund Freud, Joseph Breuer, and Alfred Adler. It must, however, be remembered that at about the same time as Freud was developing his theories and the beginnings of psychiatry, the field of psychology was also blossoming. Wilhelm Wundt is typically credited with estab-lishing, in the late 1870s in Germany, the first experimental psychology laboratory. One way that Wundt endeavored to study how the mind is structured was by us-ing a form of introspection or asking subjects to use self-reflection and to verbalize what they were experiencing (Belkin, 1988).

In the United States, William James modified Wundt's introspective base and tried to discover the functions of the mind, rather than focusing primarily on its structure. James believed that individuals function as holistic beings who used thoughts, reasoning, emotions, and behaviors. James and his followers are referred to as "functionalists," and they developed experimental designs to facilitate the understanding of why human beings' minds function as they do (Belkin, 1988). James's interest in the ideas of "adaptive functioning," "free will," and the con-scious functioning of individuals is clearly pertinent to the development of the counseling profession.

A scientific approach to social problems had become popular in the late nine-teenth and early twentieth centuries. Granville Stanley Hall founded what many consider to be the first psychology laboratory in the United States at Johns Hopkins University in 1883, where he focused on collecting data on the mental characteris-tics of children (Belkin, 1988). His efforts in studying the development of children's mental and physical abilities continued under his tenure as president of Clark Uni-versity, where he emphasized graduate study and research. The scientific approach to social problems was based on the assumption that the answer to a social prob-lem could be discovered through objective research. Many consider G. Stanley Hall the "father of American psychology" (Belkin, 1988, p. 15). Even though his work it-self has not endured, in addition to founding one of the first psychology depart-ments G. Stanley Hall was also the primary person to organize the American Psychological Association (APA), and he bestowed the first doctorates in the field of psychology. Of course, the early behaviorists, such as John Watson and B. F. Skinner, and experimental psychologists, such as Max Wetheimer and Wolfgang Kohler, are also associated with the development of the field of psychology.

David Spence Hill, who organized the first guidance and counseling services in New Orleans, was a graduate of Clark University during the presidency of G. Stanley Hall. As director of research for the New Orleans schools, he discovered a need for guidance while researching whether there was a need for a vocational school in his district (Rockwell, 1958). He concluded that there was a need for such a high school, and he also believed it necessary to assist youth in assessing their abilities and in learning about the opportunities that would best help them use those skills. He was aware of the appraisal work being done by Binet and attempted to use the Binet tasks in helping the students in the New Orleans schools. He realized the need for counseling because of his belief that the education of an individual must be of the highest order. Counseling based on scientific research would help secure the best education for each pupil.

If counselors were to help youth know themselves and match their characteristics with qualifications for jobs, it was necessary to have some means of measuring individual characteristics. Counselors relied a great deal on questioning youth about their abilities and their desires. There was the implicit assumption that counselees know themselves and could reason about their reported skills and their qualifications for jobs. A counselor's task was to help them in this process through the use of greater maturity and objective judgment. The development of tests and appraisal instruments lent a scientific air to the process.

During the late 1800s and early 1900s, the testing movement was also taking hold. In the 1890s James Cattell was the first person in this country to focus on ways to measure intelligence. In 1894 he introduced the first mental abilities test, which was administered to freshmen entering Columbia University (Goldenberg, 1973).

At the turn of the twentieth century, the Binet–Simon Test was introduced in France (1905). In 1916 L. M. Terman of Stanford University released a revised version of the Binet–Simon Test he had developed, titled the Stanford–Binet Test. With the release of the Stanford–Binet Test, the term *intelligence quotient* or *IQ* was first used. Although the development of the Stanford–Binet certainly helped spearhead the testing movement in the United States, it was World War I that truly gave flight to the development and use of standardized instruments (Baruth & Robinson, 1987).

Influences of World War I and the Development of Testing

World War I influenced the counseling profession's roots in both the vocational guidance and mental health arenas. The Army, in order to screen personnel, commissioned the development of psychological instruments, including the Army Alpha and Beta IQ tests of intelligence. In the period following World War I, the number and variety of such instruments proliferated, and even though counselors were not the major creators of the instruments, they became users. Counselors began to use standardized instruments as tools for use in military, educational, and clinical settings. These screening tools also supported the development of aptitude and interest tests used by counselors in business and educational settings (Aubrey, 1982). Quantifying a person's intelligence, aptitude, achievement, interest, and personality gave a great deal of credibility to a counselor's judgment about the person (Ginzberg, 1971).

After World War I, psychological testing became pervasive in industrial personnel classification, in education, and in counseling offices. Knowledge about and skill in using standardized tests became part of the education of a counselor. Data derived from appraisal instruments were used to make better judgments about counselees and to advise them about what was the wisest decision to make. Large commercial producers of psychometric devices emerged. The process of developing and marketing tests to industry, education, government, and counselors in private practice became quite sophisticated. Counselors were expected to be experts in selecting and using appropriate instruments from a myriad of those offered. Their use in the counseling process became such that testing and counseling were often considered synonymous.

The practice of using tests in counseling was not without controversy. Criteria for psychometric instruments used in decision making were not published until 1954, with the publication of the American Psychological Association's *Technical Recommendations for Psychological Tests and Diagnostic Techniques* (Stephens, 1954). Publications such as *Testing, Testing, Testing* (Joint Committee on Testing, 1962), *The Educational Decision-Makers* (Cicourel & Kitsuse, 1963), and *The Brain Watchers* (Gross, 1962) are examples of many voices questioning the reliance on test data by counselors and others.

Beginnings of Professional Identity

The Great Depression and the Continuation of the Career Guidance Movement

There was continued progress in the development of career counseling during the 1930s. The Great Depression, with its loss of employment for millions of people, demonstrated the need for career counseling to assist adults as well as youth to identify, develop, and learn to market new vocational skills (Ohlsen, 1983). At the University of Minnesota, E. G. Williamson and colleagues modified the work of Frank Parsons and employed it in working with students. Their work is considered by some to be the first theory of career counseling, and it emphasized a directive, counselor-centered approach known as the "Minnesota point of view." Williamson's approach continued to emphasize matching individuals' traits with those of various jobs and dominated counseling during most of the 1930s and 1940s. The publication of the *Dictionary of Occupational Titles* in 1938 provided counselors with a basic resource to match people with occupations for which they were theoretically well suited (Shertzer & Stone, 1986).

The concept that society would be better if individuals and their occupations were matched for greater efficiency and satisfaction continued to shape the vocational guidance movement. There was a plethora of organizations dedicated to this end. In 1934, a number of them met to form the American Council of Guidance and Personnel Associations, or ACGPA (Brewer, 1942, p. 152), including the American College Personnel Association, the National Association of Deans of Women, the National Federation of Bureau of Occupations, the National Vocational Guidance Association (NVGA), the Personnel Research Foundation, and the Teachers' College Personnel Association. By 1939 the name was changed to the Council of Guidance and Personnel Associations (CGPA), and other groups were added: the Alliance for the Guidance of Rural Youth, the International Association of Altrusa Clubs, the National Federation of Business and Professional Women's Clubs, the Western Personnel Service; the American Association of Collegiate Registrars (withdrew in 1941), and the Institute of Women's Professional Relations; the Kiwanis International and the Association of YMCA Secretaries met with the group from time to time.

Brewer (1942) stated that the October 1938 issue of *Occupations,* the publication of the NVGA, listed ninety-six organizations interested in furthering vocational guidance among the young people of the nation. Counseling, per se, was coming to the forefront of concerns within the vocational guidance movement. All groups seemed dedicated to placing "square pegs in square holes" through the use of tests.

During the 1950s the U.S. government was particularly interested in issues related to vocational or career guidance. In response to the Soviet Union's successful space program (for example, the launching of *Sputnik*), the government became concerned with identifying young people with scientific and mathematical talent. To this end, they passed the National Defense Education Act (NDEA) in 1958. Some contend that the impact of NDEA goes well beyond funding of career guidance programs. Hoyt (1974) stated that NDEA "had a greater impact on counselor education than any other single force" (Hoyt, 1974, p. 504). NDEA funded the training of guidance counselors at both the elementary and secondary levels, and NDEA training programs were established to produce counselors qualified for public schools (Herr, 1985). Although the legislation established counselor education programs specifically to train professionals to identify bright children and steer them into technical fields, these counselors were also trained in other domains of counseling as well.

Influence of World War II

World War II strongly influenced the confluence of the vocational guidance and mental health movements, along with that of rehabilitation counseling. The U.S. government continued to rely on standardized instruments and classification systems during World War II. The government requested that psychologists and counselors aid in selecting and training specialists for the military and industry (Ohlsen, 1983). Prior to and during World War II, millions of men and women were tested and assigned to particular duties according to their test scores and their requests. The armed forces stationed counselors and psychologists at many induction and separation centers. Picchioni and Bonk (1983) quote Mitchell Dreese of the adjutant general's office as saying that counseling "is essentially the same whether it be in the home, the church, the school, industry, business or the Army" (p. 54). The process was certainly an extensive use of the scientific approach to counseling. Society, through its representatives in government, had become embroiled in what counseling should be and what it should become. Society has not relinquished that sense of involvement through all the forms, shapes, and colors of the kaleidoscope counseling has become.

The use of standardized tests is not the only reason World War II had a tremendous influence on the counseling profession. Personnel were also needed on the front lines and in aid stations to help soldiers deal with "battle neuroses." This was accomplished through minimum training and what seemed to be an "overnight" credentialing of new medical school graduates and research-oriented clinical psychologists. Even though poorly trained, their interventions resulted in a significant reduction of chronic battle neuroses (Cummings, 1990).

In 1944, the War Department established the Army Separation-Classification and Counseling Program in response to the emotional and vocational needs of returning soldiers. The Veterans Administration (VA) also established counseling centers within their hospitals (Shertzer & Stone, 1986). The VA coined the term *counseling psychology* and established counseling psychology positions and training programs to fill these positions. The National Institute of Mental Health (NIMH) was established just after World War II and also established a series of training stipends for graduate programs in professional psychology. NIMH reinforced the VA's standard of the doctorate being the entry level into professional psychology by setting up Ph.D. training stipends. The American Psychological Association (APA) was asked to set standards of training for the new programs in university graduate schools. Although the goal of the VA and NIMH was to train counseling psychologists for the public sector, more and more trained psychologists chose to enter private practice.

In addition, during the 1940s a trend toward working with the psychological problems of "normal people" emerged. In reaction to the Nazi movement and World War II, humanistic psychologists and psychiatrists came from Europe to the United States. Their work gradually influenced the strong quantitative leanings in counseling and contributed to the work of well-known psychologists such as Rollo May, Abraham Maslow, and Carl Rogers.

Carl Rogers and the Continuation of the Mental Health Movement

In reviewing a history of what has happened, it is often difficult to know whether events have shaped a leader of an era or whether a person has influenced events. There seems little doubt that Carl R. Rogers, his ideas, and his disciples affected counseling from its core outward. Rogers's idea was that individuals had the capacity to explore themselves and to make decisions without an authoritative judgment from a counselor. He saw little need to make diagnoses of client problems or to provide information or direction to those he called *clients.* He emphasized the importance of the relationship between the counselor and client. In his system, the client rather than the counselor was the most important factor. Since there was no advice given or persuasion used to follow a particular course, Rogers's system became known as *nondirective counseling.*

Rogers became interested in the process of counseling and pioneered the electronic recording and filming of counseling sessions, an unheard-of idea at that time. Working in the academic environment of The Ohio State University and the University of Chicago, Rogers published his ideas in *Counseling and Psychotherapy: Newer Concepts in Practice* in 1942 and *Client-Centered Therapy* in 1951.

It is not the purpose of this chapter to delineate all the postulates of what became known as *client-centered counseling,* and later, *person-centered counseling.* It is important to note, however, the impact that approach had on counseling has continued to the present day. The rise to prominence of Carl Rogers's theory was the first major challenge to the tenets of the Minnesota point of view. In fact, many programs at counseling conventions debated the issue of client-centered versus trait-factored counseling.

Rogers himself remained within the scientific approach to counseling. His concern was to learn what went on in the counseling process, to learn what worked (for him) and what did not. His was a search for necessary and sufficient conditions under which effective counseling could take place.

Whenever research about client-centered counseling was reported by Rogers, it was supported by psychometric data. Certainly one of the effects of Rogers on the profession was to emphasize understanding the counseling process and the need for research. The ensuing debates about the primacy of feeling or rationality as a proper basis of counseling stimulated professional counselors to research their processes and techniques. Theories were refined, and new instruments for determining their efficacy were developed. Counselors-in-training became as familiar with recording devices as they were with textbooks.

Aubrey (1982) noted, "without doubt, the most profound influence in changing the course and direction of the entire guidance movement in the mid and late 1940's was Carl Rogers" (p. 202). Rogers built on the humanistic and individualistic foundations of the education guidance movement in which he was trained at Columbia University by formulating the nondirective client-centered approach to counseling. He brought a psychologically oriented counseling theory into the guidance movement, thus grounding the counseling profession in the broad disciplines of education and psychology (Weikel & Palmo, 1989).

Federal Legislation and Its Influence on the Counseling Profession

The Great Depression prompted the development of government-sponsored programs that included a counseling component with an emphasis on classification. Both the Civilian Conservation Corps (CCC) and the National Youth Administration (NYA) attempted to help youth find themselves in the occupational scene of the 1930s (Miller, 1971). In 1938 the George–Dean Act had appropriated $14 million for vocational education, and by 1938 the Occupational Information and Guidance Services was established. The federal government became influential in the field of counseling and remains so today.

The following list exemplifies how the federal government has influenced the development of the counseling profession by offering examples of governmental actions and legislation (Baruth & Robinson, 1987; Humes, 1987; Vacc & Loesch, 1994; Zunker, 1994). It is not meant to be an exhaustive listing of all legislation that has influenced professional counseling and counseling services.

1917   The Smith–Hughes Act created federal grants to support a nationwide vocational education program.

1933   The Wagner–Peyser Act established the U.S. Employment Services.

1936   The George–Dean Act continued the support established by the Smith–Hughes Act.

1938   The U.S. Office of Education established the Occupational and Information Guidance Services Bureau that, among other things, conducted research on vocational guidance issues. Its publications stressed the need for school counseling.

1944   The Veterans Administration established a nationwide network of guidance services to assist veterans. The services included vocational rehabilitation, counseling, training, and advisement.

1944   The U.S. Employment Service was begun under the influence of the War Manpower Commission. Fifteen hundred offices were established, and employment "counselors" were used.

1946   The George–Barden Act provided government support for establishing training programs for counselors. The emphasis was on vocational guidance and established a precedent for funding of training for counselors.

1946   The National Institute of Mental Health (NIMH) was established just after World War II, and the National Mental Health Act was passed in 1946 authorizing funds for research, demonstration, training, and assistance to states in the use of effective methods of prevention, diagnosis, and treatment of people with mental health disorders.

1949   The U.S. Employment Service published the first edition of the *Dictionary of Occupational Titles*.

1954   The Vocational Rehabilitation ACT (VRA) recognized the needs of people with disabilities. The VRA was a revision of earlier vocational rehabilitation acts and was prompted, in part, by the government's attempts to meet the needs of World War II veterans. It mandated the development of counselors who specialized in assisting people with disabilities and allocated funds for the training of these counselors.

1955   The Mental Health Study Act of 1955 established the Joint Commission on Mental Illness and Health.

1958   As noted previously, the emphasis of the National Defense Education Act (NDEA) was on improving math and science performance in our public schools; counseling in the schools was seen as an important function in helping students explore their abilities, options, and interests in relation to career development. Title V of this act specifically addressed counseling through grants to schools to carry out counseling activities. Title V-D authorized contracts to institutions of higher education to improve the training of counselors in the schools.

1962   The Manpower Development Training Act was enacted and established guidance services to individuals who were underemployed and/or economically disadvantaged.

1963   The Community Mental Health Centers Act, an outgrowth of the Mental Health Study Act, was passed. It is considered by many to be one of the most crucial laws dealing with mental health that has been enacted in the United States. The act mandated the creation of more than 2,000 mental health centers and provided direct counseling services to people in the community as well as providing outreach and coordination of other services. The Community Mental Health Centers Act also provided opportunities for counselors to be employed outside of educational settings.

1964   The NDEA Amendment to the National Defense Education Act of 1958 continued to impact counseling through the addition of counselors in the public schools, especially elementary schools, aimed at reducing the counselor–student ratio.

1965   The Elementary and Secondary Education Act (ESEA) did much to develop and expand the role of the elementary school counseling program and the services provided by the elementary school counselor.

1972   Title IX of the Education Amendments to the 1964 Civil Rights Act, mandated that no one be discriminated against or excluded from participating in any federally funded educational program or activity on the basis of sex. It also prohibited sex-biased appraisal and sex-biased appraisal instruments.

1975   Public Law (P.L.) 94-142, also known as the Education for All Handicapped Children Act, mandated guidelines for the education of exceptional children in public schools. It declared that all children, regardless of their disabilities, were entitled to an appropriate free public education. Counselors became instrumental in designing, implementing, and evaluating the individualized education plans that were required for each student with special needs.

1976   P.L. 94-482 was enacted, extending and revising the Vocational Education Act of 1963 and its 1968 amendments. P.L. 94-482 directed states to develop and implement programs of vocational education specifically to provide equal education opportunities to both sexes and to overcome sex bias and stereotyping. It also specified that funds must be used in vocational education for individuals who are disadvantaged, had limited English proficiency, and/or had handicapping conditions.

1977   Sections 503 and 504 were added to the civil rights law typically known as the Rehabilitation Act of 1973. Section 503 mandates all employers conducting business with the federal government (meeting specific criterion) to take affirmative action in the recruitment, hiring, advancement, and treatment of qualified persons with disabilities. Section 504 notes that no qualified person (spanning all age ranges) who is disabled may be discriminated against in any federally assisted program.

1977   President Carter established the President's Commission on Mental Health.

1979   The Veterans' Health Care Amendments called for the provision of readjustment counseling and related mental health services to Vietnam-era veterans.

1980   The Mental Health Systems Act was passed, stressing the need for balancing services in both preventive and remedial mental health programs. The act required the development of new services for children, youth, minority populations, older people, and people with chronic mental illness. The act was repealed during the same year it was passed, because of the severe federal budget cuts for social programs during the first year of President Reagan's term in office.

1981   The Older Americans Act was enacted to improve the quality of life for many individuals who are 60 years of age or older by authorizing a comprehensive social services program. The act provides assistance for creation and implementation of services, including counseling.

1984   Carl D. Perkins Vocational Education Act amended the Vocational Education Act of 1963. Its primary purpose was to help the states develop, expand, and improve vocational education programs. The act sought to include previously underserved people such as those with disabilities, adults in need of both training and retraining, and single parents, to name a few. The legislation indicated that career guidance and counseling functions should be performed by professionally trained counselors. In addition, the entire act was filled with language that showed how important legislators believed counseling and career development services to be.

1990   Americans with Disabilities Act (ADA) prohibited job discrimination against people with disabilities. It also mandated that individuals with disabilities have the same access to goods, services, facilities, and accommodations afforded to all others.

1990   Carl D. Perkins Vocational Education Act was reauthorized, setting directions for state and local agencies to develop vocational and applied education programs. It targeted single parents, displaced homemakers, and single pregnant women, noting that states were to use a certain percentage of their funds to provide basic academic and occupational skills and materials in preparation for vocational education and training to provide these people with marketable skills.

In addition, states were required to use funds to promote sex equity
by providing programs, services, and comprehensive career guidance, support services, and preparatory services for girls and women.

1994   The School-to-Work Opportunities Act set up partnerships among
educators, businesses, and employers to facilitate the transition of
those students who plan on moving from high school directly to the
world of work.

Continuing Development of Professional Identity

History of the American Counseling Association

Vacc and Loesch (1994) note that one way to understand the evolution of a profession is to study the history of a representative professional organization. The
American Counseling Association (ACA) has a rich history that exemplifies its representation of professional counselors. The philosophical development of the counseling profession can even be seen by simply reviewing the three names by which
ACA has been known along with the times those name changes occurred. From its
founding in 1952 until 1983, ACA was known as the American Personnel and
Guidance Association (APGA). From 1983 until 1992, it was called the American
Association for Counseling and Development (AACD). In 1992 the governing
body of the association renamed it the American Counseling Association. For purposes of simplicity, the association will be referred to as ACA regardless of the time
reference.

Although its official inception is noted as 1952, ACA can trace its organizational beginnings to the turn of the twentieth century with the formation of one of
its founding divisions, the then National Vocational Guidance Association. Having
roots in vocational guidance, education, and psychology has made for an interesting, rich, and often rocky evolution of counseling as a profession unto itself, even
before the founding of ACA. The NVGA had considered changing its name at least
five times between 1922 and 1948 to better reflect the concern members had about
the total adjustment of their clients (Norris, 1954).

Members of the American Council of Guidance and Personnel Associations, a
federation of associations, were also considering whether it was wise or efficient to
attempt to belong to several organizations doing essentially the same thing. Groups
belonging to the federation had the practice of meeting in conventions at the same
time and place. By the late 1940s groups had established their identities in work settings, and members had begun to see commonalities of purpose and function. The
name of the federation had changed from the American Council of Guidance and
Personnel Associations (ACGPA) to the Council of Guidance and Personnel Associations (CGPA) in 1939, so there was precedence for a name change.

In 1948 Daniel Feder, as chair of CGPA and president of NVGA, urged consideration of forming a national organization to include individuals as well as associations. A Committee on Unification was appointed to develop a plan for such an

organization. Its plan was presented at the 1950 convention and forwarded to the organizations concerned (McDaniels, 1964). Both the NVGA and the American College Personnel Association approved the plan and arranged their constitutions to join the new organization as divisions in 1951. At this time the Personnel and Guidance Association (PGA) was born. The following year, 1952, PGA changed its name to the American Personnel and Guidance Association (APGA) so as not to be confused with the Professional Golfers Association (PGA). APGA is now known as the American Counseling Association (ACA). Table 1-1 presents highlights of the ACA's development since its founding.

Professionalism: A Developmental Perspective

A review of Table 1-1 indicates not only the developmental nature of the American Counseling Association (ACA) during the past forty-four years but also the evolving diversity of its divisions and its membership. The concept of unification was a common theme in this country in the 1950s (Vacc & Loesch, 1994). This trend may have been an influencing factor in the four independent founding organizations: NVGA (now NCDA), ACPA (now ACCA), NAGSCT (now ACES), and SPATE (now AHEAD) coming together to work as one federation. The basic format of autonomous divisions working within an umbrella organization has continued to the present time. Divisions have been added as members' interests or counselor work settings changed due to changes in the socioeconomic milieu. (Table 1-2, page 24, indicates the divisional structure of ACA as of August 1996.)

Change is very much reflected in the chronology. For example, the parent organization, APGA, has changed its name twice during the past forty-four years. Prior to 1983, APGA began to feel pressures from its membership for a name change that would accurately reflect the purposes and work activities of its members. The terms *guidance* and *personnel* were onerous to some members. In addition to describing the profession better, the term *counseling* was more prestigious and understood by the public. By 1983 several of the divisions already recognized the terms *counseling* or *counselor* in their titles (ASCA, ARCA, ACES, ARVIC, POCA, NECA, and AMHCA). To appease its growing and diverse membership, to have a clearer identity with counseling, and to attract new members in a changing society, APGA became the American Association for Counseling and Development (AACD). Nine years later in 1992 the name was again changed to the American Counseling Association, removing the word *development* from its title.

Such change was not limited to the parent organization. As can be seen from the chronology, six divisions (NVGA, SPATE, NAGSCT, ANWIC, POCA, and MECA) changed their names at least once and two divisions (AMEG and NCGC) changed their names twice during the same forty-four-year period. Such changes reflected not only the changing nature of the work of the divisions and their members but also brought the divisions' names more in line with the name changes that had occurred within the parent organization.

Beginning in 1952 with four divisions, the first new division to join the parent organization was the American School Counselors Association (ASCA) in 1953,

TABLE 1-1   Organizational Chronology of the American Counseling Association

Year	Division Name	Event
1951	PGA	The Personnel and Guidance Association was formed.
1952	APGA	American Personnel and Guidance Association became the new name for PGA.
1952		*The following divisions became founding partners of APGA:*
	ACPA	American College Personnel Association
	NVGA	National Vocational Guidance Association
	SPATE	Student Personnel Association for Teacher Education
	NAGSCT	National Association of Guidance Supervisors and College Trainers
		The following divisions became part of ACA or changed their names:
1953	ASCA	American School Counselors Association became a division.
1958	DRC	ACA added the Division of Rehabilitation Counseling.
1961	ACES	Association for Counselor Education and Supervision replaced the former NAGSCT.
1962	ARCA	American Rehabilitation Counseling Association became the new name for the former DRC.
1965	AMEG	Association for Measurement and Evaluation in Guidance was established.
1966	NECA	National Employment Counselors Association became a division.
1972	ANWIC	Association for Non-White Concerns in Personnel and Guidance was formed.
1973	ASGW	Association for Specialists in Group Work was established.
1974	NCGC	National Catholic Guidance Conference became a division.
	POCA	Public Offender Counselor Association was established.
1975	AHEAD	Association for Humanistic Education and Development replaced the former SPATE.
1977	ARVIC	Association for Religious Values in Counseling replaced what had been known as NCGA.

which quickly became, and remains, one of the two largest ACA divisions. After World War II, there was a growing recognition in America that people with disabilities had counseling needs. At the same time that the Veterans Administration was attempting to meet the needs of returning World War II servicemen and women, there were a number of ACA members becoming involved in rehabilitation counseling. These factors resulted in the organization of the second new division to join ACA, the American Rehabilitation Counseling Association (ARCA) in 1957 (known as the Division of Rehabilitation Counseling from 1957 to 1962).

Table 1-1 *continued*

Year	Division Name	Event
1978	AMHCA	American Mental Health Counselors Association became a division.
1983	AACD	American Association for Counseling and Development became the new name for what had been called APGA.
1984	AMECD	Association for Measurement and Evaluation in Counseling became the new name for the former AMEG.
	NCDA	National Career Development Association became the new name of the former NVGA.
	AMCD	Association for Multicultural Counseling and Development replaced the former Association for Non-White Concerns in Personnel and Guidance.
	MECA	Military Educators and Counselors Association became an organization affiliate of AACD.
1986	AADA	Association for Adult Development and Aging was formed.
1989	IAMFC	International Association of Marriage and Family Counselors was established.
1990	IAAOC	International Association of Addiction and Offender Counselors replaced the former POCA.
1991	ACCA	American College Counselors Association was formed to replace ACPA, which was in the process of withdrawing from ACA.
1992	ACPA	American College Personnel Association disaffiliated from ACA.
1993	ASERVIC	Association for Spiritual, Ethical and Religious Values in Counseling became the new name for ARVIC.
	AAC	Association for Assessment in Counseling became the new name for AMECD.
1995	ACEG	Association for Counselors and Educators in Government became the new name for MECA.
1996	AGLBIC	Association of Gay, Lesbian, and Bisexual Issues in Counseling became an organizational affiliate.

Seven years passed prior to the addition of two new divisions. In 1965, professionals who used psychometric instruments in their settings needed an organization to help them improve the use of such instruments and to communicate among themselves. The Association for Measurement and Evaluation in Guidance (AMECD) was organized to serve this purpose, although not until 1968 was it formally incorporated as an ACA division. The continued interest in vocational counseling at that same time is evident in the formation of the National Employment Counselors Association (NECA) in 1966. NECA members, who came from both the private and public sectors of counseling, had a strong interest in vocational counseling and focused specifically on employment counseling.

The number of divisions in ACA again remained static for seven years, but the 1970s saw the formation and acceptance of several new divisions. There was increasing concern about minority representation within the structure of ACA. That concern, along with the general social consciousness movement in the 1960s and early 1970s, prompted the development of an interest-based division entitled the Association for Non-White Concerns in Personnel and Guidance (ANWIC), which was added in 1972.

In 1973, based on the growing use of groups as a form of counseling intervention, the Association for Specialists in Group Work (ASGW) became the tenth division of ACA. The following year, 1974, the National Catholic Guidance Conference (NCGC) became the eleventh division of ACA and brought to the parent association its first division with a strong religious orientation. During the last two decades, the focus of this division changed from that of a Catholicism-based organization to a broader examination of spirituality, religious values, and ethical considerations in the field of counseling (Bartlett, Lee, & Doyle, 1985). This shift in focus is reflected in NCGC's changing its name to the Association for Religious Values in Counseling (ARVIC) in 1977, and later (1993) to the Association for Spiritual, Ethical, and Religious Values in Counseling (ASERVIC).

In 1974 the Public Offender Counselor Association (POCA) became the twelfth division and brought into the organization people involved with juvenile and adult probation and those who worked with or within our prison systems. The creation of POCA is one example of how responsive the counseling profession has been to the complex social problems faced by our society. During the 1980s, the correlation between addictive and criminal behaviors became quite clear. Many POCA members became interested in broadening the focus of POCA, and it became the International Association of Addictions and Offenders Counselors (IAAOC) in 1990.

As the demand for school counselors diminished in the early and mid-1970s, a need for counselors in a variety of community agencies developed and counselors found themselves in a variety of noneducational work settings. More nonprofit organizations and services such as crisis centers, hot lines, drop-in clinics, shelters for battered women, rape counseling centers, and clinics for runaway youth emerged. More agencies began to be funded by local governments and began to hire people with master's degrees and experience to run these centers. The profession responded, and in 1978 the American Mental Health Counselors Association (AMHCA) became the thirteenth division of ACA. Between 1976 and the early 1980s, AMHCA's membership expanded more quickly than probably any other mental health organization (Weikel, 1985). It became the largest division within ACA and, along with ASCA, remains one of the two largest ACA groups.

As noted previously, it was in 1983 that APGA changed its name to the American Association for Counseling and Development (AACD). The change symbolized the evolving professional orientation among the association's members, the fact that these members were being found more and more in noneducational work settings, and the concept that what members "did was counseling, not guidance" (Herr, 1985, p. 395).

In 1986, as a reflection of an increasingly larger aging population and problems attendant on growing older in a youth-oriented society, the Association for Adult Development and Aging (AADA) became the fourteenth division of what was now called the American Association for Counseling and Development. The strongest emphasis of AADA has been on gerontological counseling, midlife development, and preretirement planning, but its members have broadened their focus to include the counseling needs of people across the adult life span.

In 1989, based on the growing emphasis on marriage and family counseling and the fact that many ACA members were involved in providing marriage and family counseling, the International Association of Marriage and Family Counselors (IAMFC) became the fifteenth ACA division.

During the later part of the 1980s, ACPA members who served a wide variety of student development needs on college campuses became unhappy with the increasing deemphasis of guidance and personnel issues in ACA and began a movement to disaffiliate from ACA. The withdrawal of ACPA in 1992 led to the formation of its successor, the American College Counseling Association, with a more focused emphasis on counseling college students. At this time AACD became the American Counseling Association. Table 1-2 shows the present ACA structure.

In 1995, the sixteenth division was added to ACA. The Association for Counselors and Educators in Government (ACEG). This professional group was originally formed as an *organizational affiliate* (an interest group with fewer than 1,000 members) in 1984 under the title of Military Educators and Counselors Association (MECA). Members of this division have primary professional affiliations connected to some branch of the military establishment or with various levels of government.

Members of ACA, recognizing the growing numbers of counselors who serve clients dealing with issues associated with their sexual orientation, lobbied for a specialty division that would focus on the needs of these clients and counselors. In April 1996, the Association of Gay, Lesbian, and Bisexual Issues in Counseling (AGLBIC) became an organizational affiliate of ACA. It is anticipated that the AGLBIC will gain the 1,000 members and develop the financial structures needed to become an ACA division by 1998 (Morrissey, 1996a).

It should be noted that the American Counseling Association is much more than a collection of divisions. There is also a geographical regional structure composed of the following four regions: (1) *North Atlantic* (Maine, Massachusetts, New Hampshire, Vermont, Rhode Island, Connecticut, New York, Pennsylvania, Delaware, Maryland, the District of Columbia, New Jersey, and the Virgin Islands); *Southern* (Texas, Kentucky, Georgia, Mississippi, Florida, Tennessee, North Carolina, South Carolina, Virginia, West Virginia, Arkansas, Louisiana, and Alabama); *Midwest* (Michigan, Ohio, Indiana, Illinois, Wisconsin, Minnesota, North Dakota, South Dakota, Kansas, Iowa, Nebraska, Missouri, and Oklahoma); and *Western* (Arizona, California, Oregon, Idaho, Alaska, Hawaii, Nevada, Montana, New Mexico, Colorado, Wyoming, Washington, and Utah). Each region, representing ACA

TABLE 1-2   Divisions of the American Counseling Association as of August 1996

AAC	Association for Assessment in Counseling
AADA	Association for Adult Development and Aging
ACCA	American College Counseling Association
ACES	Association for Counselor Education and Supervision
AGLBIC	Association of Gay, Lesbian, and Bisexual Issues in Counseling (organizational affiliate)
AHEAD	Association for Humanistic Education and Development
AMCD	Association for Multicultural Counseling and Development
AMHCA	American Mental Health Counselors Association
ARCA	American Rehabilitation Counseling Association
ASCA	American School Counselors Association
ASERVIC	Association for Spiritual, Ethical and Religious Values in Counseling
ASGW	Association for Specialists in Group Work
IAAOC	International Association of Addictions and Offenders Counselors
IAMFC	Internal Association of Marriage and Family Counselors
NCDA	National Career Development Association
NECA	National Employment Counseling Association

state branches, was established to provide leadership training, professional development, and continuing education of branch members following the strategic plan adopted by the association.

Through its ACA Press, the association provides its membership with a plethora of books, scholarly journals, and monographs on topics of interest to counselors. Its workshop and home study program and regional and national conventions provide intensive training opportunities that allow members to keep up to date and earn continuing education units necessary in maintaining licensure or certification. Its *Code of Ethics and Standards of Practice* provide members and its publics with both professional direction and guidance. Its legislative arm not only alerts members to current legislation that is either helpful or harmful to counseling but also gives members a voice in policy development at the federal, state, and local levels. The mission of the American Counseling Association is "to enhance human development throughout the life span and to promote public confidence and trust in the counseling profession" (Breasure, 1995, p. 3).

In 1996, with sixteen national divisions, one organizational affiliate, 52 state and territorial branches, four regional associations, a myriad of divisional affiliates in each of the branches, and a membership of more than 56,000, the American Counseling Association remains the strongest organization representing counselors on the national scene. It is not, however, without problems. ACA developed from a "group of groups" and in the 1990s has been faced with ongoing organizational challenges that stem from the continued desire for groups to have independence while working under an umbrella structure. At the time this book went to press, ACA was reported to be back on financial track but was still undergoing organizational upheaval. Two of the largest divisions, the American Mental Health Counseling Association and the American School Counselors Association were considering disaffiliating from ACA and becoming separate, independent national organizations. In early 1996, ACA and these groups were exploring avenues to prevent this move (Morrissey, 1996b).

Credentialing and the "Professionalization" of Counseling

The most commonly noted criteria used to evaluate whether an occupation has evolved to the status of a profession include (1) a specialized body of knowledge and theory-driven research, (2) the establishment of a professional society or association, (3) control of training programs, (4) a code of ethics to guide professional behavior, and (5) standards for admitting and policing practitioners (Caplow, 1966; Glosoff, 1993; Greenwood, 1962). Given these criteria, no historical perspective of the counseling profession can be considered complete without a discussion of the development of standards related to the preparation and practice of professional counselors.

The counseling profession has met the majority of conditions just noted. There is an evolving body of knowledge and systematic theories and a body of literature to provide a forum for such information, ACA serves as the primary professional association for counselors, there are standards for training programs, professional preparation and ethical behavior (see Chapter 4), accredited counselor-training programs have been established, and credentials are granted to individuals demonstrating professional competencies (Glosoff, 1993; Remley, 1991). It should be noted that great progress has been made in establishing licensure and certification regulations, legally validating the profession.

The term *credentialing* was created to represent a broad array of activities pertaining to the establishment of professional training standards and regulations for practice (Bradley, 1991). This term most typically covers three major professional activities: academic program accreditation, certification, and licensure (Loesch, 1984).

Accreditation

Accreditation is one means of providing accountability. The licensed professions in this country began the process of regulation and quality control by developing standards for training programs. One definition of *accreditation* is provided by Altekruse and Wittmer (1991), as follows:

> [a] process by which an association or agency grants public recognition to a
> school, institute, college, university, or specialized program of study that has met

certain established qualifications or standards as determined through initial and periodic evaluations. (p. 53)

The development of standards of preparation for counselors began more than thirty years ago when a joint committee of the ACES and ASCA, divisions of ACA, began two major studies in 1960. More than 700 counselor educators and supervisors and 2,500 practicing counselors participated in the studies over a five-year period (Altekruse and Wittmer, 1991). The results facilitated the creation of the "Standards for Counselor Education in the Preparation of Secondary School Counselors," the first set of standards sanctioned for counselor education, in 1964. After a three-year trial, they were officially adopted by ACES in 1967 (Association for Counselor Education and Supervision, 1967). Shortly after, the "Standards for Preparation of Elementary School Counselors" (1968) and "Guidelines for Graduate Programs in Student Personnel Work in Higher Education" (1969) were established.

The Council on Rehabilitation Education (CORE) was incorporated as a specialized accrediting body with a focus on rehabilitation counseling in 1972 and was a forerunner in setting educational standards and graduate program accreditation in counseling (Sweeney, 1991). The leaders responsible for the creation of the Council for Accreditation of Counseling and Related Educational Programs (CACREP) used CORE as a model. Both councils' basic counseling curricula, which are not focused on specialties, are similar. CORE is comprised of representatives from a number of counseling and rehabilitation organizations such as the American Rehabilitation Counseling Association, the National Rehabilitation Counseling Association, and the National Council on Rehabilitation Education.

According to Altekruse and Wittmer (1991), the "Standards for Entry Preparation of Counselors and Other Personnel-Service Specialists" was developed by ACES in 1973. This document, which merged earlier guidelines, was officially adopted by the ACA governing body in 1979. At that time, ACES was the only association accrediting body using the standards of training. Not until 1981 did ACA's board of directors adopt a resolution to formally oversee the responsibilities of the ACES National Committee on Accreditation. This led to the establishment of the Council for Accreditation of Counseling and Related Educational Programs (CACREP). CACREP was formed as an independently incorporated accrediting body, separate from ACA but sponsored by ACA and several divisions (CACREP, 1987). Since its inception, CACREP has conducted reviews of its accreditation standards. After the initial flurry of changes to the 1981 standards, CACREP declared a five-year time period during which only minor changes would be allowed (Altekruse & Wittmer, 1991). There have been two significant revisions made to the 1981 standards adopted by CACREP, the first in 1988, and the newest set of accreditation standards, which became effective in 1994. These revisions are necessary to keep up with the continually evolving field of counseling.

Currently, CACREP accredits master's degree programs in community counseling, with and without specialization in career counseling or gerontological counseling, marriage and family counseling/therapy, mental health counseling, school counseling, and student affairs practice in higher education (with college counseling or professional practice emphases) and doctoral degree programs in counselor education and supervision (CACREP, 1995). As of August 1996, CACREP had accredited 292 programs in 110 institutions (D. Jacobs, personal communication, August 26, 1996). Of these 292 programs, 34 are doctoral level and 258 accredited master's programs. The majority of the master's programs are in the areas of nonspecialized community counseling (85), school counseling (92), and student affairs practice in higher education (47).

All academic programs accredited by CACREP, regardless of specialty designation, share a common core of curricular requirements. According to the 1994 CACREP *Accreditation Standards and Procedures Manual,* all accredited programs must address the following eight curricular areas: human growth and development, social and cultural foundations, helping relationships, group work, career and lifestyle development, appraisal, research, and professional orientation. Supervised practica and internships are required. In addition to these common core areas, CACREP accredited programs must also offer specific types of curricular experiences related to the specialty accreditation (such as community counseling, school counseling, and mental health counseling).

Currently, CORE has accredited eighty-two master's programs offering a degree in rehabilitation counseling (CORE staff, personal communication, January 12, 1996). All CORE-accredited programs are expected to include courses in the following areas of study: foundations of rehabilitation counseling, counseling services, case management, vocational and career development, assessment, job development and placement, research, and practicum and internship experiences (CORE, 1991).

In addition to CACREP- and CORE-accredited counselor education programs, the American Psychological Association's Committee on Accreditation has been accrediting doctoral-level counseling psychology programs since 1953. According to the APA (1995), there are sixty-seven doctoral counseling psychology programs currently accredited in the United States.

Another professional organization that accredits counseling-related programs is the American Association for Marriage and Family Therapy (AAMFT). Along with CACREP, AAMFT accredits counselor education programs that emphasize marriage and family therapy. Unlike CACREP, however, AAMFT also accredits academic programs in social work and home economics, and nonacademic programs such as agency-based training programs (Everett, 1990).

Certification

It has been noted that *certification* is one of the most confusing of the credentialing terms (Brown & Srebalus, 1988). It is used in reference to (1) the process of becoming qualified to practice in public schools, (2) state laws passed in the same ways as licensure laws, and (3) recognition bestowed on individuals by their professional peers (such as certified public accountants).

Certification is often referred to as a "title control" process because it grants recognition of competence by a professional group or governmental unit but does not confer authority to the holder to practice a profession (Forrest & Stone, 1991; Loesch, 1984). As befits the confusing nature of the term *certification*, there is one exception to this rule. A designated state agency, most typically a state department of education, certifies school personnel. Professional counselors holding positions as public school counselors must be certified by the state to do so. Therefore, school counselor certification regulations are actually practice acts, because they control who may and may not practice as a school counselor (Loesch, 1984).

Types and Purposes of Certification

Certification in Schools.   As noted, state boards or departments of education, by authority of state legislatures, establish certification standards for teachers, counselors, administrators, and other school personnel. Certification of school counselors first began in Boston and New York in the 1920s, but not until the National Defense Education Act (NDEA) was passed in 1958 did this type of certification take hold nationwide. By 1967 more than 24,000 guidance counselors were trained under NDEA funding. The NDEA also mandated the establishment of criteria that would qualify schools to receive funds for the services of school counselors, which led to the rapid growth of certification (Sweeney, 1991).

National Board Certification.   Many professional groups have initiated credentialing efforts, at the national and the state levels, that encourage excellence by promoting high standards of training, knowledge, and supervised experience. These standards promulgated by professional organizations may or may not be considered by governmental agencies, such as state departments of education or mental health, in relation to hiring and promotion requirements (Sweeney, 1991).

The first counseling-related national certification addressed the specialty of rehabilitation counseling. During the late 1960s, rehabilitation counselors belonging to the National Rehabilitation Counselors Association and American Rehabilitation Counselors Association (an ACA division) began to work together toward establishing certification for rehabilitation counseling specialists (Forrest & Stone, 1991). Their efforts bore fruit in 1973 when the Commission on Rehabilitation Counselor Certification, known as CRCC, began to certify rehabilitation counselors (Hedgeman, 1985; Sweeney, 1991; Forrest & Stone, 1991). In addition to a general rehabilitation counselor certification, CRCC also offers specialty certifications in insurance rehabilitation, case management, and, most recently, substance abuse counseling (CRCC, 1994).

Certified Rehabilitation Counselors (CRCs) are required to have a master's or higher degree in rehabilitation counseling; a minimum 600-hour supervised internship; relevant supervised professional experience as a rehabilitation counselor (if the applicant did not graduate from a CORE-accredited program); and successful completion of the CRCC examination. More than 13,000 rehabilitation counselors are designated as CRCs (Leahy & Holt, 1993). Although many of these individuals work in public and private rehabilitation agencies, Hedgeman (1985) noted a growing tendency for private practitioners to apply for certification.

In 1979 the National Academy of Certified Clinical Mental Health Counselors (NACCMHC) was the next national counselor-certifying body to be established. The NACCMHC merged with the National Board for Certified Counselors (NBCC) in 1992. Basic requirements to become a Certified Clinical Mental Health Counselor (CCMHC) include: (1) completion of a minimum of sixty graduate semester hours; (2) graduation with a master's or higher degree from an accredited counselor preparation program encompassing at least two years of postmaster's professional work experience that included a minimum of 3,000 client contact hours and 100 clock hours of individual supervision by a CCMHC, or a professional who holds an equivalent credential; (3) submission of an audio or video tape of a counseling session; and (4) successful completion of the CCMHC's Mental Health Counselor Examination for Specialization in Clinical Counseling (NBCC, 1995a). Palmo and Weikel (1986) noted that the stringent requirements to become a CCMHC may be one reason that there were only slightly more than 1,000 Certified Clinical Mental Health Counselors (CCMHCs) in 1985. The same may continue to be true of the slightly less than 2,000 CCMHCs in existence today.

NBCC is probably the most visible and largest national counselor-certifying body (Sweeney, 1991). Since its establishment by ACA in 1981 as a free-standing corporate body, NBCC today has approximately 24,000 active National Certified Counselors, or NCCs (T. Clawson, letter to all NCCs, December 11, 1995). The founding of NBCC offered the public a way to identify professional counselors who meet knowledge and skills criteria set forth by the counseling profession in the general practice of counseling. This was especially important given the paucity of counselor licensure laws at that time. The concept of a general practice of counseling is in line with CACREP's belief that there is a common core of knowledge that is shared by all professional counselors, regardless of any specific area of specialization. It is assumed that all counselors, regardless of their specialty area(s), must have a shared knowledge base and be able to perform some of the same activities (Forrest & Stone, 1991; Vacc & Loesch, 1987).

In order to be certified by NBCC as a National Certified Counselor (NCC), applicants must hold a minimum of a master's degree in counseling or closely related field; have successfully completed a supervised practicum or internship and graduate coursework in counseling theories and six of the eight core curriculum areas delineated in the CACREP accreditation standards, successfully pass the National Counselor Examination (NCE); and submit letters of reference including ratings of specific skills. Counselors who have not graduated from a CACREP-accredited program must also document the completion of a minimum of two years of postmaster's counseling experience (NBCC, 1995b).

Once counselors have earned the designation of NCC, they can then qualify for specialty certification in addictions, career, clinical mental health, gerontological, and school counseling through NBCC. NBCC and CRCC are not, however, the only bodies that certify specialists in counseling and counseling-related specialties.

IAMFC, in addition to being an ACA division, is an affiliate of the National Academy for Certified Family Therapists, which offers five different options for certification of family therapists. The option most relevant for professional counselors requires professionals who are already NCCs or licensed as professional counselors to document professional training, supervision, and experiences in working with couples and families (Smith, Carlson, Stevens-Smith, & Dennison, 1995). The American Association of Marriage and Family Therapy (AAMFT) also certifies its own members who meet certain criteria and has done so since the 1970s (Everett, 1990). AAFMT's credential is granted to members who have Clinical Member status. The International Certification Reciprocity Consortium (ICRC), the National Association of Alcoholism and Drug Abuse Counselors (NAADAC), and the CRCC (as previously noted) all offer specialty addictions certification. Finally, professionals specializing in the treatment of sexual dysfunction can be certified by the American Association of Sex Educator Counselors and Therapists. Having multiple certifications offered by different associations in the same specialty areas may prove confusing for both professionals and consumers of mental health services.

Licensure

Brown and Srebalus (1988) define a license as "a credential authorized by a state legislature that regulates either the title, practice, or both of an occupational group" (p. 232). Although states enact licensure laws as a means to protect the public from incompetent practitioners, such laws also provide benefits for the profession being regulated. The very fact that a state considers a profession important enough to regulate may lead to an enhanced public image and increased recognition for that profession. Among several types of credentials presented to 1,604 professional counselors surveyed, a license as a professional counselor (or similar title) was considered the most important to hold (Glosoff, 1993). Likewise, licensure has been espoused as the most desirable of the different types of credentials in regard to securing recognition by insurance companies, governmental and private mental health programs, and consumers; being given preferred status in job hiring; and, adding to the qualifications necessary to be seen as an expert witness by authors such as Sweeney (1991); Remley (1991); Throckmorton (1992); Covin (1991); Foos, Ottens, & Hills (1991); and Glosoff (1993).

Just as certification can be confusing, so too can the concept of licensure. Since licensure laws typically delineate a "scope of practice" connected with the profession under consideration, licensing acts are often known as "practice acts" (Shimberg, 1982). States with such laws in place require individuals to be licensed or to meet criteria for exemption of licensing noted in those laws to engage in specified counseling activities. There are, however, licensing laws that dictate who may identify themselves as "licensed counselors" or use other counseling-related titles but do not regulate people who are not licensed. These laws are typically referred to as "title acts." Sweeney (1991) points out that it is essential to examine specific state laws and their accompanying regulations to determine the implications for practice. These authors suggest that practitioners in those states with counselor licensure laws ask the regulatory boards to determine if they need a license to practice, and what they may and may not call themselves. ACA usually publishes an annual list of counseling regulatory boards in the November–December issue of the *Journal of Counseling and Development*.

Licensure of counseling practitioners, separate from psychologists, can be traced to the early 1970s. Prior to 1976, no state law defined or regulated the general profession of counseling. This left the profession in a state of legal limbo—although counseling was not expressly forbidden (except where the laws regulating psychology specifically limited activities of professional counselors), it was not legally recognized as a profession, either (Brooks, 1986).

At that time, the American Psychological Association began to call for stringent psychology licensure laws that would preclude other professionals from rendering any form of "psychological" services. In Virginia this resulted in a cease-and-desist order being served to John Weldon, a counselor in private practice in 1972 (Hosie, 1991; Sweeney, 1991). The Virginia State Board of Psychologist Examiners obtained a court order restraining Weldon from rendering private practice services in career counseling (*Weldon v. Virginia State Board of Psychologist Examiners*, 1972). The board claimed that Weldon was in fact practicing psychology, even though he presented himself as providing guidance and counseling services. In October 1972, Weldon was found to be practicing outside of the law but the court also ruled that the Virginia legislature had created the problem by violating his right to practice his chosen profession of counseling. The court proclaimed that personnel and guidance was a profession separate from psychology and should be recognized and regulated as such (Hosie, 1991). In response to the Weldon case, the Virginia legislature passed a bill certifying Personnel and Guidance Counselors for private practice in March 1975 (Swanson, 1988). This law was amended by the Virginia legislature in 1976 and became the first general practice act for professional counselors.

At about the same time, Dr. Culbreth Cook, an Ohio counselor, faced a challenge similar to that of Weldon. Cook, well known and respected in his community, was employed at a two-year college and provided private educational assessment on a part-time basis. Cook's education and training qualified him to offer the assessment services he rendered, but he was arrested on the felony charge of practicing psychology without a license (Hosie, 1991; Swanson, 1988). Dr. Carl Swanson, an attorney, counselor educator, and ACA Licensure Committee co-chair testified on Cook's behalf (Sweeney, 1991). The Cleveland Municipal Court judge refused to provide a restraining order against Cook, noting that even attorneys used the tools of psychology (*City of Cleveland, Ohio v. Cook*, 1975).

ACA has focused on licensure since the 1970s. It was 1973 when the first ACA licensure committee was created by the Southern Association for Counselor Education and Supervision (Hosie, 1991; Sweeney, 1991). The next year ACA published a position statement on counselor licensure and, in 1975, appointed a special Licensure Commission. The commission distributed an action packet in 1976, including information about counselor licensure, strategies to pursue licensing, and the fourth draft of model state legislation (APGA, 1976).

Model legislation offers a prototype for counselors in states that do not have licensure laws, which are in the process of revising their current laws, and in which credentialing laws face sunset or legislative review (Glosoff, Benshoff, Hosie, & Maki, 1995). It also facilitates the development of uniform standards for the preparation and practice of professional counselors across the United States.

Since the first model legislation for licensed professional counselors was created, ACA has revisited and amended its model on a regular basis (approximately every five to seven years) in order to reflect changes in standards within the profession and experiences in states that have implemented counselor licensure laws. An underlying philosophy of ACA's model legislation is that state licensure laws legalize the general practice of counseling within each state, whereas the credentialing of counseling specialists remains under the purview of professional credentialing organizations such as NBCC and CRCC.

The rate of licensure for counselors during the two decades between the time Virginia passed the first counselor licensure law and the endorsement of ACA's 1994 model legislation is seen by some to be painstakingly slow and by others as quite rapid. Brooks (1986) notes that "legislative successes were distressingly slow in the years following 1974" (p. 253). During the early 1980s, licensure took off when fifteen states passed some form of credentialing acts between 1981 and 1986, fourteen passed laws between 1987 and 1989; and seven passed laws between 1990 and 1994 (Glosoff, 1993; Glosoff et al., 1995). Having counseling licensure laws enacted at that rate of progress is exceptional when compared with the twenty years it took the first eighteen state psychology laws to be passed (Brooks, 1988).

Current Issues and Trends in Counseling

Counselors continue to respond to pressures from various socioeconomic factors—some that led to the kaleidoscope we know as counseling today, others that will shape the future of the profession. These pressures cut across the various specialty areas of counseling and cannot be categorized or delineated as neatly as in a historical review of the profession. For organizational purposes, the current issues and trends will be briefly examined as they relate to the following topics: work settings, licensure, diverse clientele, recognition and reimbursement of professional counselors, and managed care.

Work Settings

Counselors are employed in a wide variety of work settings. They provide services to people who exhibit a full range of functioning from healthy adaptation to pathology—from those seeking assistance with self-exploration to those individuals who are dysfunctional enough to require hospitalization. There is not enough space to comprehensively explore all those work settings and types of services, but we will attempt to briefly review some of the major trends related to work settings where counselors are employed.

School Counseling Services

The establishment of comprehensive, developmental school counseling programs has progressed in a roller coaster way over the past century, following societal trends. Development was strong during the 1920s because of the influence of progressive education, introduced by John Dewey. Progress slowed during the latter part of the 1930s because of mobilized attacks against progressive education and a call for a return to fundamentals in education. As a result, guidance activities deteriorated and did not gain widespread support again until the passage of the National Defense Education Act in 1958.

As noted earlier, NDEA led to a groundswell of school counseling programs, which strongly established the need for professionally trained counselors. These counselors became responsible for attending to the psychosocial factors influencing young people's performance and ability to reach their academic potential. School-based counseling programs continued to grow through the 1970s and the early 1980s. A 1989 survey by Paisley and Hubbard indicated an increase in school counselor positions. They reported that 27 percent of the state departments of education officials indicated having insufficient numbers of counselors to fill positions. This may be because only 32 percent of counselor education programs were offering programs to train school counselors in 1990, as compared to 57 percent of the programs in 1979 (Hollis & Wantz, 1980, 1993).

Over the past forty years, the role of school counselors has broadened from its earlier narrow emphasis on facilitating vocational choices to facilitating students' total development in all areas—personal, social, emotional, career, and cognitive. Today's school counselors develop and implement preventive guidance programs in large groups as well as providing individual and small-group counseling. In addition, they act as coordinators of services, consultants to teachers, administrators, and parents.

Even though the value of having counselors in schools, kindergarten through secondary, has become widely recognized, budget cuts threaten the gains made in implementing comprehensive, developmental school counseling programs. In addition, throughout the history of public education, well-intentioned individuals and groups have questioned or challenged the philosophy, content, and practices of counseling programs and materials. In recent years, the number of such challenges has increased, often resulting in censorship of counseling and guidance materials, activities, and programs. Most recently, these challenges have come from conservative political and religious groups such as the American Family Association, Concerned Women for America, and the Christian Coalition, who contend that school counseling programs usurp parental authority. Concern has been raised that counseling teaches students to make independent decisions and that counselors use "New Age" techniques such as guided imagery. According to Thomas Marino (1995b), at least eighty-two school counseling programs were challenged by conservative groups between 1988 and 1991. The majority of those programs (sixty-six) remain intact today because counselors and supporters of counseling programs mobilized rapidly in response to the challenges.

It is clear that counselors must be able to document that their programs are based on a body of research if they are to combat fears generated by some of the negative literature being distributed by various groups (Marino, 1995b). It is crucial to show the connection between students' psychological well-being and academic performance. In addition, it is critical to recognize that many people do not understand the nature of counseling in general or school counseling specifically. The idea of techniques such as guided imagery can be frightening, evoking thoughts of hypnosis and mind control. Counselors bear the responsibility to communicate effectively and systematically with parents, administrators, and their communities about the services provided by school counselors and their influence on students' learning, behaviors, and relationships with their parents.

Community-Based Services

Since the passage of the Community Mental Health Centers Act in 1963, master's and doctoral-level counselors have found employment in community-based agencies. Many people think only of community mental health centers, typically funded through state and local government dollars, as the primary community-based employer of master's-level counselors. Counselors, however, are employed in a wide variety of government and privately funded agencies such as child abuse agencies, domestic violence facilities (for both victims and perpetrators), residential and outpatient substance abuse programs, programs for people who are HIV positive or have AIDS, vocational rehabilitation facilities, homeless shelters, half-way homes, and crisis intervention programs (Vacc & Loesch, 1994).

Remediation of existing mental health problems remains the focus of the counseling services provided in most community mental health centers. In the past decade, however, preventive services have played a greater role. Health maintenance organizations (HMOs) offer a series of preventive workshops emphasizing everything from deterring back pain to establishing a healthy frame of mind. Because most counselors are trained in group counseling, education, and psychotherapeutic processes, they seem well suited to working in primary and secondary prevention programs such as those offered by HMOs. Similarly, there are increasingly more counselors working in behavioral medicine facilities (Vacc & Loesch, 1994). Mental health counselors have the training to assist individuals in understanding how their own behavior influences health and disease.

Business and Industry

Business and industry settings offer counselors increasing opportunity for employment, most especially in employee assistance programs (EAPs), organizational career development programs, and consultation and training (Lewis & Hayes, 1988). EAPs emphasize very short term treatment and referral of employees to help them address problems that may influence their job performance. Counselors working in EAPs most typically work on issues such as chemical dependence, stress, family concerns, financial problems, and interpersonal difficulties that affect the work setting (Lewis & Hayes, 1988). Counselors may be employed directly by a corporation and have an office within a company. They may also work on a contractual basis to provide services to a corporation's employees. This latter option is a growing trend in EAPs.

As a result of new technology, economic fluctuations, and shifts in services and products, many companies have been forced to lay off or reassign employees. Counselors with expertise in career assessment and development may find themselves very marketable in helping companies provide career development and relocation services to those employees. Counselors can also provide crucial services in developing and implementing orientation programs for new employees as well as helping employees deal with issues related to retirement (Lewis & Hayes, 1988).

Many businesses have also focused on the effective use of their employees. Counselors have been hired or contracted to serve as consultants on organizational development and training issues, both of which typically required strong assessment and group process skills. Team building, stress management, preretirement planning, conflict management, and supervision are just a few examples of the types of training provided by counselors in business and industry (Lewis & Hayes, 1988).

Private Practice

In 1991, Brooks wrote that there were at that time 10,000 ACA members who reported being in private practice. He notes that this is probably only a fraction of the total number of practitioners in either full- or part-time private practice. In a 1993 study, 29 percent of the ACA member participants reported private practice as their primary work setting (Glosoff, 1993). If the 1,604 participants were representative of the full ACA membership, this would equate to between 16,000 and 17,000 counselors in private practice. Although the exact number of counselors in private practice is hard to ascertain, it is clear that this number has increased significantly in the past decade.

The increase is due, at least in part, to the success of counselors in passing counselor credentialing laws in forty-two states and the District of Columbia. These laws have added to counselors' being recognized as competent professionals who have the state's "blessing" to independently offer services to the public. The services offered by counselors in private practice are varied and focus on working with individuals, couples, families, and groups on issues as broad as career and personal adjustment to substance abuse and marital or family problems. Many of these counselors are also involved in consulting and training activities (Vacc & Loesch, 1994).

Although the number of private practitioners has been increasing, the pitfalls faced by these practitioners have also increased. In addition to the feelings of isolation expressed by many private clinicians, the stress of generating and maintaining a paying clientele may be rising as counselors deal more and more with insurance companies. Many clients cannot afford to pay for counseling services out of their own pockets and must rely on insurance benefits. Even those people lucky enough to have comprehensive insurance policies may discover that out-patient mental health therapy is not covered or is covered at only 25–50 percent versus the traditional 80 percent reimbursement for physical health services. Many insurance policies do not pay for marital or family counseling, nor do they pay if the person receiving services is not considered to have a mental disorder. Finally, many HMOs and preferred provider plans do not recognize master's or doctoral-level counselors, licensed or not.

All the problems associated with insurance and managed care may drive many private practitioners, including counselors, to seek employment within agencies and hospitals. According to Psychotherapy Finances (1995), however, private practice is alive and well, with median fees and total incomes holding steady, and direct-pay clients still accounting for a large portion of private practice income. Those persons choosing to stay in private practice may do best in group practice settings where they can share administrative and marketing costs and the responsibility if they are available to handle client emergencies.

Diverse Clientele

The types of clients served by professional counselors are as diverse as the work settings in which counselors are employed. Following are a few examples of the types of clients receiving increasing attention from counselors.

Vacc and Loesch (1994) note that the frequency of abuse of all kinds in our country is astounding. Today's counselors are increasingly serving individuals who are abused, including very young children, adolescents, adults, and elderly clients—both men and women across all races and ethnic groups. In addition, there has been a greater focus of late on treatment of the abuser. This often involves working with people who have been incarcerated for sexual assault, domestic violence, or pedophilia, or those who are on parole. Counselors working with people who are abused, and with those who abuse others, most typically do so in collaboration with other professionals such as attorneys, social workers, and law enforcement personnel (Vacc & Loesch, 1994).

Another subset of clientele groups receiving increased attention from mental health professionals, including counselors, are people who are HIV positive or have AIDS. There is probably not a community in the country that has gone untouched by the AIDS epidemic. The emotional and psychosocial ramifications of this epidemic are staggering for those afflicted, their families and friends, and the communities in which they live. Fear of people with HIV or AIDS has led to a strong sense of isolation, increasing the already difficult task of living with a terminal illness. Counselors are needed to help ease this difficulty, but many may not have the training needed to specialize in assisting people with chronic and terminal diseases. Working with people who have AIDS or are HIV positive also brings up new ethical dilemmas around confidentiality and the application of the duty-to-warn concept. The 1995 ACA *Code of Ethics and Standards of Practice* specifically notes that counselors working with clients with communicable and fatal diseases are "justified in disclosing information to an identifiable third party, who by his or her relationship with the client is at a high risk of contracting the disease" (ACA, 1995, p. 5).

There has also been a marked increase in counseling services targeted to older individuals (Vacc & Loesch, 1994). This makes sense, given the "graying of America" or the steadily increasing average age of the population. In response to the needs of older people, gerontological counseling has, and will continue, to grow as an area of specialization for professional counselors.

People with substance abuse problems comprise yet another group being served by increased numbers of professional counselors. These services focus on the delivery of both prevention and remediation of substance abuse problems with counselors being employed by community mental health agencies, residential treatment programs, schools, and EAPs (Vacc & Loesch, 1994). The expansion of services in this area can be seen in the numbers of professional organizations offering certification to people who specialize in the delivery of substance abuse services. Along with the proliferation of credentials, a variety of therapeutic strategies to effectively treat substance abusers have also appeared, but unfortunately the effectiveness of these strategies remains unclear (Vacc & Loesch, 1994).

Although counselors have traditionally worked with well-functioning individuals, they are increasingly serving people with severe and chronic mental illness in hospital and community settings. Counselors with both master's and doctoral degrees are expected by agencies to provide a variety of assessment and diagnostic services with clients who exhibit a wide range of clinical disorders (West, Hosie, & Mackey, 1987).

Regardless of the functioning level of clients, a "wellness" orientation remains the basis for the work of most counselors. Counselors are working with clients who seek greater physical and mental health by making positive lifestyle choices. As noted earlier, these counselors are working in a variety of settings such as behavioral medicine clinics, HMOs, community centers, and EAPs, delivering a wide range of services from individual and group counseling to workshops on smoking cessation and stress management (Vacc & Loesch, 1994). Unfortunately, many preventive and wellness-oriented programs have focused more on physical than on mental well-being. This is a ripe area for counselors if they choose to market their services in assisting existing wellness programs to expand the mental health component of their interventions (Vacc & Loesch, 1994).

Multicultural Counseling

One of the most significant trends in relation to clients being served by professional counselors is that they reflect the diversity seen in today's society in terms of age, race, ethnicity, gender, and sexual orientation. Sue (1991) wrote that "We are fast becoming a multicultural, multiracial, and multilingual society" (p. 99). He reports that one example of this trend is that 75 percent of people now entering the labor market are minorities and women.

These demographic changes have had a notable impact on society in general as well as on the counseling profession. In fact, many leaders in the field consider multiculturalism to be the *fourth force* in the profession (Pedersen, 1991b). This force calls for the reexamination of assumptions that are inherent in the delivery of traditional mental health services.

It is more likely than not that counselors will work with clients who have different cultural backgrounds from their own. Although people from all cultures may encounter problems that counselors are trained to address, these problems are experienced within a cultural context that may not be understood by counselors (Vacc & Loesch, 1994). The profession must determine the applicability of traditionally taught theories to diverse clientele, as well as explore the effectiveness of *how* services are delivered (for example, fifty-minute sessions, in counselors' offices, that focus on intrapsychic phenomena).

Pedersen (1991a) contends that several changes need to occur if counselors are to effectively provide services to a pluralistic clientele. Counselors need to develop an awareness and understanding of multicultural factors. Counselor educators must prepare the next generation of counselors to work from multicultural perspectives. Counseling-related research must also include recognition of cultural differences and ensure that findings adequately reflect the cultural influences of research participants. Finally, Pedersen asserts that counselors need to "translate the skills, strategies, and techniques of counseling appropriately to many culturally different populations so that the counselor is prepared to match the right approach to each culturally different population" (p. 250). Although Pedersen presents no small challenge, it is clearly one that counselors and counselor educators must accept and make progress on.

Licensure

In the two decades since the passage of the Virginia certification law, a total of forty-two states and the District of Columbia have enacted some form of counselor credentialing legislation. As of May 1996, twenty-three of these states (53.5 percent) regulate both the practice of counseling and the use of related titles ("practice acts"). Twenty of the laws (46.5 percent) were "title acts" that provide title protection only in reference to the use of counseling-related titles (Glosoff et al., 1995).

The model legislation most recently endorsed by ACA's governing body (1994) is clearly a practice act and establishes a comprehensive scope of practice for licensed professional counselors (LPCs). This scope of practice represents the broad continuum of services provided by professional counselors in the general practice of professional counseling and across specialty areas (Glosoff et al., 1995). The broadness of the scope is not meant to imply that all LPCs are experts in the provision of all services. Including a comprehensive scope of practice does, however, legally protect LPCs who are practicing within their scope of expertise. Without this protection, LPCs practicing within their scope of training (for example, career counseling, crisis intervention, or assessment) may find themselves, like John Weldon, legally prevented from rendering the very services for which they have been trained (Glosoff et al., 1995).

The 1994 ACA model legislation for LPCs includes the following requirements for licensure:

(1) completion of a minimum of 60 graduate semester hours in counseling from a regionally accredited institution of higher education, including an earned master's degree in counseling, or an earned doctoral degree in counseling. The master's degree must consist of a minimum of 48 semester hours. Applicants graduating from programs offering at least 48 graduate semester hours but less than 60 can become licensed upon completing post-master's course work to meet the 60 hour requirement.

(2) Applicants must document that their 60 semester hours consisted of study in each of the following areas: (a) helping relationships, including counseling theory and practice; (b) human growth and development; (c) lifestyle and career development; (d) group dynamics, processes, counseling, and consulting; (e) assessment, appraisal, testing of individuals; (f) social and cultural foundation, including multicultural issues; (g) principles of etiology, diagnosis, treatment planning, and prevention of mental and emotional disorders and dysfunctional behavior; (h) marriage and/or family counseling/therapy; (i) research and evaluation; and (j) professional orientation and ethics;

(3) a minimum of 3,000 hours of supervised experience in professional counseling performed over a period of not less than two years under the supervision of an approved supervisor;

(4) documentation that the 3,000 supervised hours included at least 1,200 hours of direct counseling with individuals, couples, families or groups and a minimum of 100 hours spent in direct (face-to-face) supervision with an approved supervisor; and,

(5) successful completion of a written examination as determined by the counseling regulatory board.

Although a great deal has been achieved in the licensing arena and ACA's model legislation has provided counselors with much guidance in the development of counselor-credentialing laws, the statutes are far from uniform in their scope and requirements. This may be due, in part, to the revisions of ACA's model legislation for licensed professional counselors over the years. Licensure laws passed in the 1980s mirror the education, training, and supervision standards that were endorsed by the profession at that time, whereas those passed recently tend to be more comprehensive in the scope of practice and impose more stringent requirements than earlier licensure laws.

Of the forty-three counselor credentialing laws in place, twelve states (28 percent) cite the completion of sixty graduate semester hours as a licensure requirement (as suggested by ACA's 1988 and 1994 models), but education requirements range from a master's degree with no specified number of hours, to sixty semester hours (Glosoff et al., 1995). Some argue that most master's-level professional counselors do not have sixty semester hours, yet close to half (46 percent) of the 1,604 ACA members who participated in a 1993 study reported having earned a minimum of sixty graduate semester hours in counseling (Glosoff, 1993).

Supervision and experience requirements also vary. Although thirty-four states (81 percent) require at least two years of supervised experience for licensure, some states do not specify how many years work experience are required, whereas others designate the number of years but not the number of practice or direct supervision hours needed (Glosoff et al., 1995). Even the titles granted to professional counselors by the regulatory boards vary. "Licensed Professional Counselor" is the most frequently used title; other titles include, but are not limited to, "Licensed Mental Health Counselor," "Licensed Clinical Professional Counselor," "Licensed Clinical Counselor," "Certified Professional Counselor," "Professional Clinical Mental Health Counselor," and "Licensed Mental Health Practitioner." This lack of uniformity has proven to be detrimental to credentialed counselors in their ongoing efforts to gain the same recognition afforded to psychologists and social workers.

In addition to lack of uniformity, or maybe because of it, there have been legal challenges regarding what professional counselors can and cannot do as part of their scope of practice. For example, licensed counselors in states such as Georgia and Louisiana find themselves embroiled in legal battles over their ability to use a variety of assessment instruments (Marino, 1995a). This is ironic given the strong roots that the counseling profession has in testing and assessment. The challenges are driven by efforts on the part of state psychological associations to proclaim that the use of most tests comes under the sole purview of doctoral-level psychologists. The tests noted by psychologists requiring a doctorate in psychology to administer and interpret run the gamut from personality, to psychoeducational and career-related measures.

Counselors will continue to fight for their right to administer and interpret those tests based on education and training rather than on the name of the degree they earned. Legislation proposed by several state psychological associations may serve to bring together master's- and doctoral-level counselors, social workers, marriage and family therapists, and speech therapists, who may all find themselves unable to legally provide testing services for which they are trained. The same challenges have been put forth as to counselors' abilities to diagnose clients, especially those with mental disorders. These efforts to restrain trade require that counselor licensure laws include language similar to the 1994 ACA model legislation, which states that counselors "conduct assessments and diagnoses for the purposes of establishing treatment goals and objectives. . . . Assessment means selecting, administering, scoring and interpreting psychological and educational instruments designed to assess achievements, interests, personal characteristics, disabilities, and mental, emotional and behavioral disorders" (Glosoff et al., 1995, p. 211).

Finally, the struggle to enact counselor licensure laws in the final eight states will be crucial. The primary opposition to counselor licensure has traditionally been, and remains, psychologists. They have often, however, been joined in their opposition by licensed social workers and by groups of paraprofessionals (for example, baccalaureate-level addictions workers). Although we have noted the need to pass comprehensive practice acts, it should also be noted that practice acts, especially those with strong scopes of practice, are perceived by other professional groups as more threatening than title protection acts, and therefore are more strenuously opposed (Glosoff et al., 1995).

Recognition and Reimbursement of Professional Counselors

Credentialing has far-reaching ramifications for the hiring and reimbursement of professional counselors. Contrary to popular belief, credentialing affects the reimbursement of those professionals in settings other than private practice. Administrative rules used by several federal, state, and local agencies specify that only state-licensed practitioners can be employed by these agencies. These same rules often stipulate that only licensed workers can supervise psychological services, and call specifically for licensed psychologists. In the late 1970s, Alabama eliminated all counselor position titles because of this type of thinking. This is also true at many university counseling centers that will only hire licensed psychologists (Sweeney, 1991). These are just a few examples of how credentialing has become strongly related to employment opportunities for counselors. There is an increasing trend in this direction (Glosoff, 1993).

Reimbursement for services rendered has played a strong part in the licensure movement for all mental health practitioners. A motivating force in psychological licensing of the late 1960s and early 1970s was to secure third-party reimbursement and to be included in national health insurance (Hosie, 1991). To facilitate these two goals, in 1975 APA established the *National Register for Health Service Providers in Psychology* as a means of identifying qualified practitioners of psychological services. As of January 1, 1978, to be listed in the *National Register* one was required to have obtained a doctoral degree in psychology from a regionally accredited educational institution. Even though it has been argued that proficiency can be developed just as well in a counselor education department as in a psychology department, criteria for inclusion in the *National Register* clearly do not allow anyone who was trained outside of a psychology department to take the examinations for licensure or certification as psychologists in most states (Rudolph, 1986). This had direct economic consequences for many doctoral-level professional counselors who were previously eligible to be licensed as psychologists.

Even though insurance companies traditionally used inclusion in the *National Register* as a criterion for reimbursement eligibility, that has changed, and counselors have met with limited success in their efforts to be recognized as eligible providers. Professional counselors are included in some federal legislation and federally funded programs (Covin, 1991). For example, licensed counselors and CCMHCs are recognized by the Office of the Civilian Health and Medical Program of the Uniformed Services (CHAMPUS) as meeting standards for third-party payment with a physician's referral. In addition, some licensed counselors are included as clinicians and as administrative staff in managed mental health systems (Throckmorton, 1992).

Yet counselors are not included as recognized providers of Medicare or mental health services paid for through Federal Employee Health Benefit Plans (FEHBP), nor is counseling acknowledged as a professional discipline in the Public Health Service Act (PHSA) for the purposes of clinical training grants. This means that universities cannot receive grants for their graduate programs in counselor education. Although the PHSA was *not* enacted to determine which professional practitioners would be recognized as providers of health or mental health services, it has indirectly led to counselors being excluded as reimbursable providers of service covered through public and private insurance programs. Federal and state laws and regulations related to Medicare, Medicaid, and the Federal Employee Health Benefit Plans, however, used the list of disciplines included in the PHSA as a guideline when developing criteria for reimbursable providers of mental health services. Amending the PHSA will accomplish two primary goals. First, it will change the precedent that has been used in determining provider eligibility for reimbursement purposes under other laws. Second, it will allow counselor education programs to compete for clinical training grants.

The PHSA is reauthorized on a regular basis, and ACA and AMHCA were successful at having the word *counseling* added to Section 303(d)(1) of the PHSA in the reauthorization introduced in the 103rd Congress. Unfortunately, Congress did not pass the bill, for reasons having nothing to do with inclusion of counseling as a core mental health profession. The current Congress (104th) will likely spend the majority of its time dealing with passing a balanced budget, and the PHSA may not be reauthorized.

There have also been attempts made by ACA, AMHCA, and ACA's state branches to change the laws and regulations that have excluded professional counselors as eligible providers of services and paid for through Medicare and Federal Employee Health Benefit Plans. Because professional counselors are not included as Medicare providers in the federal statute, they have been unable to "sign off" on the delivery of mental health services through Medicare. This, in turn, may deter administrators from hiring professional counselors. Many people are not aware that the Medicare policy on the coverage of partial hospitalization services furnished in Community Mental Health Centers (CMHCs) allows for services to be provided by professionals other than physicians and psychologists. This has been used to have CMHCs and other state agencies write regulations and policies to include LPCs as employees. Even so, the law itself needs to be amended to specifically include LPCs *or* do away with the list of providers and include a statement that covered services include "individual and group therapy provided by any licensed mental health professional."

Although the FEHBP is regulated by a federal law, group policies are written across the country by various insurers—most often Blue Cross/Blue Shield. Unless the FEHBP law and/or the regulations are amended to include LPCs, clients who are insured through FEHBP cannot be reimbursed for mental health services provided by LPCs.

Medicaid, which is a federal program, is implemented through state regulations. Once again, most states used the list of core disciplines from the PHSA in determining which mental health practitioners are eligible to provide reimbursable services. At present, this must be changed at the state, not federal, level.

Major criteria for acceptance as reimbursable practitioners include educational degrees and the possession of a license, which allows the mental health provider to practice independently (Bistline, 1991; E. Bongiovanni, personal communication,

April 27, 1993; Throckmorton, 1992). State licensure is also a prerequisite to becoming eligible for third-party reimbursement by insurance companies via any state mandates regulating insurance codes (Covin, 1991; Throckmorton, 1992). Research indicates that LPCs do receive reimbursement from some insurance companies in states that do not legally mandate this (Throckmorton, 1992; Zimpfer, 1992). However, without a state mandate, there are no guarantees that LPCs or their clients will be reimbursed for services rendered.

A number of states have legislated mandates, often called "freedom of choice" (FOC) laws that require the reimbursement for services provided by specific professionals, such as LPCs, if these services are covered by a health plan. FOC laws increase consumers' choice of providers, thereby expanding the markets for mental health providers. According to Covin (1995), at least eleven states have passed FOC mandates. These laws, however, do not regulate managed care companies, employers that set aside money to pay for the medical claims of their employees, or publicly funded (state or federal) insurance programs.

Managed Care

Managed care does much more than influence practitioners' income. The strong movement toward establishment of managed care companies, PPOs, and HMOs is influencing the therapy practices of all mental health practitioners. The majority of 1,700 professional counselors, psychologists, psychiatrists, social workers, and marriage and family therapists surveyed in 1995 reported changing their practices in the following ways: (1) adopting time-limited therapy techniques, (2) attending training workshops on brief therapy, (3) shortening the length of therapy, (4) and having to deal with an increased number of disallowed insurance claims (Psychotherapy Finances, 1995).

This emphasis on brief therapy must be addressed by counseling education programs, many of which continue to teach the application of traditionally based theories. This has ethical implications for both training programs and practitioners. It is considered unethical for practitioners to use modes of treatment in which they are untrained. Counselor educators have a responsibility to provide adequate training appropriate for the work settings in which their graduates will most likely be employed. Readers are referred to Chapter 7 of this text for more information on brief therapy modalities.

Summary

The roots of counseling are deeply embedded in a variety of disciplines that have come together and created different emphases at various points in time. These emphases have led to the development of counseling specialties, counselors working in a wide variety of settings and offering a broad range of services, and the profession struggling with the formation of an identity.

Counselors in the United States, regardless of work setting or theoretical orientation, are linked by the common belief that a person has the capacity and right to choose directions and activities that are most personally satisfying. Choices must be made within the bounds of social and moral value systems that will not bring harm to self or to others. The counselors who were pioneers and the counselors who work now are dedicated to helping individuals find their way in an increasingly complex society.

Counselors are active in dealing with a great number of social problems that affect the populations with which they work. Society is in turmoil trying to deal with the use of illegal drugs, changing family structures, the effect of technology on occupations and employment, immigration issues, and complex pluralism, leading to the development of special populations at risk of being inundated by the majority. There is not space here to discuss each issue and the role of counselors in addressing these and future issues. Counselors must work to ensure that through their systematic, scientific, and professional efforts both individuals and groups will be well served.

References

Altekruse, M., & Wittmer, J. (1991). Accreditation in counselor education. In F. Bradley (Ed.), *Credentialing in counseling* (pp. 53–62). Alexandria, VA: American Association for Counseling and Development.

American Counseling Association (ACA). (1995). *Code of ethics and standards of practice.* Alexandria, VA: Author.

American Personnel and Guidance Association. (1968). *Standards for preparation of elementary school counselors.* Washington, D.C.: Author.

American Personnel and Guidance Association. (1969). *Guidelines for graduate programs in the preparation of student personnel workers in higher education.* Washington, D.C.: Author.

American Personnel and Guidance Association (APGA). (1976). *Model for state legislation concerning the practice of counseling, 1976, draft no. 4.* Alexandria, VA: Author.

American Psychological Association (APA). (1995). APA-accredited doctoral programs in professional psychology: 1995. *American Psychologist, 50*(12), 1069–1081.

Association for Counselor Education and Supervision (ACES). (1967). Standards for the preparation of secondary school counselors. *Personnel and Guidance Journal, 46,* 96–106.

Aubrey, R. F. (1982). A house divided: Guidance and counseling in 20th century America. *Personnel and Guidance Journal, 61,* 198–204.

Bartlett, W. E., Lee, J. E., & Doyle, R. E. (1985). Historical developments of the Association for Religious and Values Issues in Counseling. *Journal of Counseling and Development, 63*(7), 448–451.

Baruth, L. G., & Robinson, E. H., III. (1987). *An introduction to the counseling profession.* Englewood Cliffs, NJ: Prentice Hall.

Beers, C. W. (1908). *A mind that found itself.* New York: Doubleday.

Belkin, G. S. (1988). *Introduction to counseling* (3rd ed.). Dubuque, IA: Brown.

Bistline, J. (1991, Feb.). Self-insured plans and their impact on the counseling profession. *The Advocate,* 10.

Bradley, F. (1991). *Credentialing in counseling.* Alexandria,VA: American Association for Counseling and Development.

Breasure, J. M. (1995). ACA mission and identity: To be or not to be. *Counseling Today, 38*(2), 3.

Brewer, J. M. (1942). *History of vocational guidance.* New York: Harper.

Brooks, D. K. (1986). Credentialing of mental health counselors. In A. J. Palmo & W. J.

Weikel (Eds.), *Foundations of mental health counseling* (pp. 243–261). Springfield, IL: Thomas.

Brooks, D. K., Jr. (1988). Finishing the job. In R. L. Dingman (Ed.), *Licensure for mental health counselors* (pp. 4–7). Alexandria, VA: American Mental Health Counselors Association.

Brooks, D. K., Jr. (1991). The practice of mental health counseling. In D. Capuzzi & D. Gross, *Introduction to Counseling: Perspectives for the 1990s.* Boston: Allyn and Bacon.

Brown, D., & Srebalus, D. (1988). *An introduction to the counseling profession.* Englewood Cliffs, NJ: Prentice Hall.

Caplow, T. (1966). The sequence of professionalization. In H. M. Vollmer & D. L. Mills (Eds.), *Professionalization.* Englewood Cliffs, NJ: Prentice Hall.

Cicourel, A. V., & Kitsuse, J. I. (1963). *The educational decision-makers.* Indianapolis: Bobbs-Merrill.

City of Cleveland, Ohio v. Cook, Municipal Court, Criminal Division, No. 75-CRB 11478, August 12, 1975. (Transcript dated August 19, 1975).

Commission on Rehabilitation Counselor Certification (CRCC). (1994). *CRCC to offer substance abuse specialty ertification—CRC: The counselor.* Rolling Meadows, IL: Author.

Council for Accreditation of Counseling and Related Educational Programs (CACREP). (1987). *Accreditation procedures manual for counseling and related educational programs.* Alexandria, VA: Author.

Council for Accreditation of Counseling and Related Educational Programs (CACREP). (1994). *Accreditation standards and procedures manual.* Alexandria, VA: Author.

Council for Accreditation of Counseling and Related Educational Programs (CACREP). (1995, Summer). *The CACREP Connection.*

Council on Rehabilitation Education, Inc. (CORE). (1991). *CORE policy and procedures manual.* Champaign-Urbana, IL: Author.

Covin, T. M. (1991, January). Freedom of choice and the federal employees health benefits plan—An update. *The Advocate,* 5.

Covin, T. M. (1995, May). Freedom of choice, mental health counseling and clinical social work. *The Advocate,* 4.

Cummings, N. A. (1990). The credentialing of professional psychologists and its implication for the other mental health disciplines.

Davis, J. B. (1914). *Moral and vocational guidance.* Boston: Ginn.

Davis, J. B. (1956). *Saga of a schoolmaster: An autobiography.* Boston: Boston University Press.

Everett, C. A. (1990). The field of marital and family therapy. *Journal of Counseling and Development, 68* (5), 498–502.

Foos, J. A., Ottens, A. J., & Hills, L. K. (1991). Managed mental health: A primer for counselors. *Journal of Counseling & Development, 69*(4), 332–336.

Forrest, D. V., & Stone, L. A. (1991). Counselor certification. In F. Bradley (Ed.), *Credentialing in counseling* (pp. 23–52). Alexandria, VA: American Association for Counseling and Development.

Ginzberg, E. (1971). *Career guidance.* New York: McGraw-Hill.

Glosoff, H. L. (1993). An assessment of the career benefits of state statutory credentials and national board certification as perceived by professional counselors. *Dissertation Abstracts International, 55* (09), 2719. (University Microfilms No. AAC95–03041.

Glosoff, H. L., Benshoff, J. M., Hosie, T. W., & Maki, D. R. (1995). The 1994 ACA model legislation for licensed professional counselors. *Journal of Counseling and Development, 74* (2), 209–220.

Goldenberg, H. (1973). *Contemporary psychology.* Belmont, CA: Wadsworth.

Greenwood, E. (1962). Attributes of a profession. In S. Nosov and W. H. Form (Eds.), *Man, work and society* (pp. 206–218). New York: Basic Books.

Gross, M. L. (1962). *The brain watchers.* New York: Random House.

Hedgeman, B. S. (1985). Rehabilitation counselor certification. *Journal of Counseling and Development, 63*(10), 609–610.

Herr, E. (1985). *Why counseling?* Alexandria, VA: American Association for Counseling and Development.

Hollis, J. W., & Wantz, R. A. (1980). *Counselor preparation: Programs, personnel, trends* (4th ed.). Muncie, IN: Accelerated Development.

Hollis, J. W., & Wantz, R. A. (1993). *Counselor preparation: Programs, personnel, trends* (8th ed.). Muncie, IN: Accelerated Development.

Hosie, T. W. (1991). Historical antecedents and current status of counselor licensure. In F. Bradley (Ed.), *Credentialing in counseling* (pp. 23–52). Alexandria, VA: American Association for Counseling and Development.

Hoyt, K. B. (1974). Professional preparation for professional guidance. In E. Herr (Ed.), *Vocational guidance and human development* (pp. 502–527). Boston: Houghton Mifflin.

Humes, C. W. (1987). *Contemporary counseling: Services, applications, issues.* Muncie, IN: Accelerated Development.

Joint Committee on Testing. (1962). *Testing, testing, testing.* Washington, DC: American Association of School Administrators.

Leahy, M. J., & Holt, E. (1993). Certification in rehabilitation counseling: History and process. *Rehabilitation Counseling Bulletin, 37,* 71–80.

Lewis, J. A., & Hayes, B. A. (1988). Options for counselors in business and industry. In R. Hayes and R. Aubrey, *New directions for counseling and development.* Denver: Love Publishing.

Loesch, L. C. (1984). Professional credentialing in counseling—1984. *Counseling and Human Development, 17*(2), 1–11.

Marino, T. W. (1995a). Battle for testing rights continues. *Counseling Today, 38*(6), 6, 25, 27.

Marino, T. W. (1995b). Facing a challenge to a school counseling program. *Counseling Today, 38*(4), 6, 18.

McDaniels, C. O. (1964). *The history and development of the American Personnel and Guidance Association, 1952–1963.* Unpublished doctoral dissertation. University of Virginia, Charlottesville.

Miller, C. H. (1971). *Foundations of guidance* (2nd ed.). New York: Harper & Row.

Morrissey, M. (1996a). AGLBIC becomes an organizational affiliate. *Counseling Today, 38*(12), 1, 8.

Morrissey, M. (1996b). ASCA postpones disaffiliation vote, AMHCA requests medication. *Counseling Today, 38*(7), 1, 16, 20.

National Board for Certified Counselors (NBCC). (1995a). *Specialty certification.* Greensboro, NC: Author.

National Board for Certified Counselors (NBCC). (1995b). *Wake up to the possibilities. Become a National Certified Counselor, general practice counselor certification information.* Greensboro, NC: Author.

Norris, W. (1954). *The history and development of the National Vocational Guidance Association.* Unpublished doctoral dissertation, George Washington University, Washington, DC.

Ohlsen, M. M. (1983). *Introduction to counseling.* Itasca, IL: Peacock.

Paisley, P. O., & Hubbard, G. T. (1989). School counseling: State officials' perceptions of certification and employment trends. *Counselor Education and Supervision, 29,* 60–70.

Palmo, A. J., & Weikel, W. J. (1986). *Foundations of mental health counseling.* Springfield, IL: Thomas.

Parsons, F. (1894). The philosophy of mutualism. *The Arena, 9,* 738–815.

Parsons, F. (1909). *Choosing a vocation.* Boston: Houghton Mifflin.

Pedersen, P. B. (1991a). Concluding comments to the special issue. Special Issue: Multiculturalism as a fourth force in counseling. *Journal of Counseling and Development, 70*(1), 250.

Pedersen, P. B. (1991b). Multiculturalism as a generic approach to counseling. Special Issue: Multiculturalism as a fourth force in counseling. *Journal of Counseling and Development, 70*(1), 6–12.

Picchioni, A. P., & Bonk, E. C. (1983). *A comprehensive history of guidance in the United States.* Austin: Texas Personnel and Guidance Association.

Psychotherapy Finances. (1995). Survey report: *Managing your practice and your money, Psychotherapy Finances, 21*(1), Whole Issue 249.

Reed, A. Y. (1916). *Vocational guidance report 1913–1916.* Seattle, WA: Board of School Directors.

Reed, A. Y. (1920). *Junior wage earners.* New York: Macmillan.

Reed, A. Y. (1944). *Guidance and personnel services in education.* Ithaca, NY: Cornell University Press.

Remley, T. P. (1991). An argument for credentialing. In F. Bradley (Ed.), *Credentialing in counseling* (pp. 23–52). Alexandria, VA: American Association for Counseling and Development.

Richards, L. S. (1881). *Vocophy*. Marlboro, MA: Pratt Brothers.

Rockwell, P. J., Jr. (1958). *Social concepts in the published writings of some pioneers in guidance*. Unpublished doctoral dissertation, University of Wisconsin, Madison.

Rogers, C. R. (1942). *Counseling and psychotherapy: Newer concepts in practice*. Boston: Houghton Mifflin.

Rogers, C. R. (1951). *Client-centered therapy*. Boston: Houghton Mifflin.

Rudolph, J. (1986). Third-party reimbursement and mental health counselors. In A. J. Palmo and W. J. Weikel, *Foundations of mental health counseling* (pp. 271–284). Springfield, IL: Thomas.

Shertzer, B., & Stone, S. C. (1986). *Fundamentals of counseling*. Boston: Houghton Mifflin.

Shimberg, B. (1982). *Occupational licensing: A public perspective*. Princeton, NJ: Educational Testing Service.

Smith, R. L., Carlson, J., Stevens-Smith, P., & Dennison, M. (1995). Marriage and family counseling. *Journal of Counseling and Development, 74*(2), 154–157.

Stephens, W. R. (1954). *Technical recommendations for psychological tests and diagnostic techniques*. Washington, DC: American Psychology Association.

Stephens, W. R. (1970). *Social reform and the origins of vocational guidance*. New York: Harper & Row.

Stripling, R. O. (1983). Building on the past—A challenge for the future. In G. R. Walls & L. Benjamin (Eds.), *Shaping counselor education programs in the next five years: An experimental prototype for the counselor of tomorrow* (pp. 205–209). Ann Arbor: ERIC/CAPS.

Sue, D. W. (1991). A model for cultural diversity training. Special Issue: Multiculturalism as a fourth force in counseling. *Journal of Counseling and Development, 70*(1), 99–105.

Swanson, C. (1988). Historical perspective on licensure for counselors. In R. L. Dingman (Ed.), *Licensure for mental health counselors* (pp. 1–3). Alexandria, VA: American Mental Health Counselors Association.

Sweeney, T. J. (1991). Counselor credentialing: Purpose and origin. In F. Bradley (Ed.), *Credentialing in counseling* (pp. 23–52). Alexandria, VA: American Association for Counseling and Development.

Throckmorton, E. W. (1992). Mental health counselors and reimbursement decisions: How do third-party payers of mental health benefits decide which mental health providers to pay? Dissertation, Ohio University. *Dissertation Abstracts International 53*(03) (University Microfilms No. AAC 9230310).

Vacc, N., & Loesch, L. (1987). *Counseling as a profession*. Muncie, IN: Accelerated Development.

Vacc, N., & Loesch, L. (1994). *A professional orientation to counseling* (2nd ed.). Muncie, IN: Accelerated Development.

Weikel, W. J. (1985). The American Mental Health Counselors Association. *Journal of Counseling and Development, 63*, 457–460.

Weikel, W. J., & Palmo, A. J. (1989). The evolution and practice of mental health counseling. *Journal of Mental Health Counseling, 11*(1), 7–25.

Weldon v. Virginia State Board of Psychologist Examiners. Corporation Court Opinion (Court Order). Newport News, VA: October 4, 1972.

West, J. D., Hosie, T. W., & Mackey, J. A. (1987). Employment and roles of counselors in mental health agencies. *Journal of Counseling and Development, 66*, 135–138.

Williamson, E. G. (1965). *Vocational counseling: Some historical, philosophical, and theoretical perspectives*. New York: McGraw-Hill.

Zimpfer, D. G. (1992, January). *Insurance experience of licensed counselors*. Paper presented at the 1992 National Conference of the Association for Counselor Education and Supervision, San Antonio, Texas.

Zunker, V. (1994). *Career counseling. Applied concepts of life planning* (4th ed.). Pacific Grove, CA: Brooks/Cole.

Chapter 2

What Does It Mean to Be Psychologically Healthy?

Richard T. Kinnier, Ph. D.

Imagine a psychological health contest between the John Wayne persona of the 1950s' silver screen and the Leo Buscaglia persona of the 1990s' lecture circuit. Which "persona" would win? Among John Wayne's celluloid traits were his stoicism and his readiness to fight. He rarely displayed any weaknesses or "shared his feelings" with anyone. In contrast, Leo Buscaglia's most salient public traits have been his readiness to cry and to share his feelings with everyone. Is "strong and silent" healthier than "vulnerable and expressive?" for males? for females? Does the answer depend entirely on the biases of the judges and the context of a specific time and place?

In this chapter I will seek to identify the main components of psychological health. Since a major goal of most counseling is to reduce psychological distress and increase psychological well-being or health, then it is important to ask, "What does it actually mean to be psychologically healthy?" The question is not an easy one to answer, however. Before I attempt to answer it, let us first consider some of the reasons why it is such a difficult question.

Why Psychological Health Is Difficult to Define

Traditionally, mental health theoreticians and practitioners have avoided trying to establish the criteria of psychological health. Rather, their focus has been more on identifying symptoms of psychological pathology. It has seemed easier for professionals and laypeople alike to agree about the undesirability of certain behaviors and emotions than it has been for them to agree about which behaviors and emotions are most indicative of psychological health. For example, virtually everyone would agree that the self-mutilating behaviors of some autistic children (such as head banging and eye gouging) are pathological behaviors that should be eliminated. In contrast, fewer people would agree that altruistic behavior is indicative of a high level of psychological health. In fact, a popular psychodynamic suspicion about altruistic behavior is that it may often serve as a cover for personal insecurities or feelings of guilt experienced by the altruistic person. Unfortunately, there are no omniscient psychological health judges in this world who can make final authoritative calls on conflicting interpretations.

It may seem tempting, therefore, to define psychological health simply as the absence of agreed-on pathological symptoms and leave it at that. But just because a cigarette smoker has not yet experienced negative consequences from smoking does not mean that the smoker or the behavior of smoking is healthy. And just because a person is not currently observed to be depressed, anxious, or incoherent does not necessarily mean that he or she is psychologically healthy. The state of psychological health must be something more than just being asymptomatic at one point in time. But what?

Unfortunately, the establishment of clear universal criteria for psychological health is impeded by the reality that any conception is inextricably woven into a particular cultural and temporal background (Jahoda, 1958). Imagine the John Wayne and Leo Buscaglia psychological health contest alluded to at the beginning of this chapter. If the contest was held in the America of the 1950s, the John Wayne persona would probably win in a landslide. We might well overhear the judges' approving whispers of "He is a man's man" following John Wayne's presentation. And imagine the 1950s' judges' discomfort as Leo Buscaglia unabashedly and tearfully tried to hug each one of them. Disapproving whispers of "highly emotional" and "quite effeminate" might be overheard during those judges' deliberations. In contrast, in a 1990s' contest Leo would probably be the victor. His same traits might now be labeled as "open" and "sensitive." The John Wayne persona undoubtedly would lose points in the 1990s' contest for his perceived emotional rigidity and sexism. Some of the 1990s' judges might suspect the John Wayne persona of being sexually insecure or even homophobic. The John Wayne persona may well bust the place up after hearing that feedback from the judges. And needless to say, such a violent outburst would not help his ratings at all. We can only guess who would win (and why he would win) in a twenty-first-century contest. Undoubtedly, the outcome would be affected by where the contest was held and who the judges were: John Wayne's fans might be wise to call for the contest to be held within a homophobic culture.

In a more serious vein, there are very real examples of how culture has influenced the presumed criteria of psychological health. Prior to 1973, homosexuality was classified as a psychological disorder or "deviancy" by the American Psychiatric Association. In 1973, the Board of Trustees of the American Psychiatric Association decided to reclassify the orientation of homosexuality as a "preference" (Stoller, Marmor, & Bieber, 1973). In America during the 1970s, assertive behavior came to be viewed by many as indicative of psychological health. During the 1950s, similar behavior would more likely have been regarded as antisocial or selfish, as in Japan both then and now.

Perhaps the biggest change in perceptions about what is considered healthy or "normal" during the past few decades has occurred in the area of "gender appropriate" behavior. A case study is illustrative. Osipow (1983) described a case analysis that occurred during the 1950s in which a woman told her therapist that she wanted to be a mathematician. The therapist interpreted her interest and career plan as an unhealthy rejection of her femininity and an escape from the emotional demands of her life as a woman. The therapist believed that the client had made progress when she finally relinquished her career aspirations and accepted her primary role as a mother. Imagine how a contemporary audience would respond to that case analysis if it were presented today!

That example raises other questions relevant to what it means to be psychologically healthy: Is it healthier for individuals to conform to societal expectations or to rebel against them? Are rebels and heretics who live in "sick" societies extraordinarily healthy? Is any individual or group capable of determining the health of a particular society or individual? Given these perhaps unresolvable issues, it is understandable that few theoreticians have attempted to establish universal criteria of psychological health.

Jahoda (1958) was aware of these issues but nevertheless made the attempt about forty years ago. She developed a list of six criteria for what she called "positive mental health." According to her, the healthy individual (1) has a positive attitude toward him- or herself (self-acceptance), (2) is continually growing or moving toward self-actualization, (3) has a sense of purpose or meaning in his or her life, (4) can function independently or autonomously in the world, (5) perceives reality (without significant distortion), and (6) has attained mastery in the environment (adequate in love and competent in work).

In this chapter I build on and update Jahoda's list of criteria. My goal is to construct a list that is relevant to contemporary North America. Clearly such a list would at least need modification (perhaps even significant revision) for other times and places. Also, the list is not exhaustive, and I expect that some people will disagree with some of my choices. Finally, although it is artificial to dichotomize or separate the mind and the body, I have limited my focus to psychological criteria, as did Jahoda.

The methodology I used to construct the list is fairly informal. Over the course of several years, I have surveyed the relevant psychological literature looking for what various theoreticians and researchers have stated or implied were criteria of psychological health. Also, in counseling courses that I teach I have asked students to create their own lists. As certain themes have emerged repeatedly in the literature, I added them to my list. Criteria that appeared infrequently (such as staying active and living in the present) were not included. I encourage readers to critically evaluate my list. Does each criterion seem reasonable? Is the supporting evidence for its inclusion compelling? From your knowledge and experience, should any of the criteria be modified or deleted? Do you think any other criteria should be added to the list?

1. Self-acceptance (but not self-infatuation)
2. Self-knowledge
3. Self-confidence and self-control
4. A clear (though slightly optimistic) perception of reality
5. Courage and resilience
6. Balance and moderation
7. Love of others
8. Love of life
9. Purpose in life

Figure 2-1   Criteria of Psychological Health

Criteria of Psychological Health

What are the "ingredients" of psychological health? My list consists of nine (see Figure 2-1). Let us consider each.

Self-Acceptance (but not self-infatuation)

Psychologically healthy individuals feel a strong sense of self-acceptance or self-esteem but are not self-obsessed or self-infatuated. There seems to be a consensus among mental health theoreticians that basic self-esteem is an essential component of psychological health (see, for example, Allport, 1961; Baumeister, 1988; Erikson, 1968; Jahoda, 1958; Jung, 1954; Maslow, 1970; Rogers, 1961; Sullivan, 1953). Low self-esteem has been implicated in numerous psychopathologies, such as depression (for example, see Beck, 1991), interpersonal problems (for example, see Sullivan, 1953), and substance abuse (for example, see Newcomb & Bentler, 1989)—to name just a few. Conversely, the variable that correlates highest and most consistently with subjective well-being is self-esteem (see Diener, 1984).

Basic self-acceptance also seems to be a prerequisite for attaining other important criteria of psychological health. As pointed out by Erikson (1968) and Sullivan (1953), individuals must love and respect themselves before they can truly love others. And, according to Maslow (1970), a strong foundation of self-esteem is a prerequisite for becoming self-actualized.

Basic self-esteem should not be confused with unconditional self-esteem, self-infatuation, or extreme self-centeredness, however. Self-infatuation has been identified popularly as the sociopathy of the recent "me decades" (see Smith, 1994). Seligman (cited in Buie, 1988) has observed an increase in the incidence of depression over the past few decades and suggested that the depression may have been caused partly by the "waxing of the individual and waning of the commons" (p. 18). In other words, the glorification or cult of the individual may be hazardous to psychological health. Seligman suggested that this may be so because the self ultimately "is a very small unit" and "is a very poor site for meaning" (p. 18).

The worship of self is not only a rather meaningless endeavor, but it also is usually a lonely one. Extreme self-lovers make poor friends, partners, and parents. Consider the following example of a self-centered therapy junkie I once met. He was the father of two children (ages 7 and 4), but he rarely spent any time with them because of all the "self-growth" workshops he attended. One Saturday morning he got up, quickly fed himself, and was about to leave for yet another group worship of self. His children reminded him of his promise to take them to the park that morning. The father angrily snapped that he was going to his workshop and then responded to their confused and disappointed pleas with the explanation, "I go to these workshops for you—they will help me become a better father." Perhaps this self-infatuated father was actually more interested in his image as a father than in his childrens' needs.

In summary, psychologically healthy individuals are self-accepting. They care about and respect themselves but are not self-infatuated or self-obsessed.

Self-Knowledge

Psychologically healthy individuals know themselves well. They are mostly aware of their true feelings and motives. They are regularly (though not obsessively) introspective.

Of all the goals of psychotherapy and counseling, the goal of self-knowledge is probably the most central and universal. Consistent with Socrates' famous dictum to "Know thyself" and the idea that the "truth will set you free," Freud and his revisionists (such as Adler, Erikson, Fromm, Horney, and Jung) believed that uncovering and understanding one's unconscious needs, fears, and conflicts were prerequisites for psychological health (Hall & Lindzey, 1985). Theoreticians from other major orientations clearly agree about the importance of self-exploration and self-knowledge. For example, Rogers (1961), from the humanistic camp, described the healthy or "congruent" person as one who is clearly aware and accepting of his or her true or organismic feelings. The cognitive behaviorists similarly emphasize the importance of self-knowledge, even though they use different language. For example, Mahoney and Thoresen (1974) entitled a section of their book, which had a cognitive-behavioral orientation, "Know Thy Controlling Variables" (p. 22).

In summary, psychologically healthy individuals are committed to understanding themselves. They regularly (but not obsessively) seek to become aware of and to understand their unconscious motives, true feelings, and/or "controlling variables."

Self-Confidence and Self-Control

Psychologically healthy individuals have confidence in themselves. They can function independently when they need to and be assertive when they want to be assertive. They believe they are basically in control of their lives (that is, have an internal locus of control) and feel efficacious about accomplishing their goals.

The importance of the individual having a basic sense of personal autonomy and competence has been emphasized by numerous theoreticians including Erikson (1963), Fromm (1955), Horney (1950), Jahoda (1958), Maslow (1970), and Rogers (1961). Adler (cited in Hall & Lindzey, 1985) believed that the primary challenge for all individuals is for them to overcome their feelings of inferiority. Failure to do so can result in learned helplessness and an external locus-of-control perspective, both of which are correlates of depression (see Peterson & Seligman, 1984).

Bandura's (1977, 1989, 1995) model of self-efficacy predicts that people who believe that they are capable of attaining a specific goal are more likely to persist in efforts to attain that goal. And although persistence is no guarantee of success, persistence usually increases the chances of success. Successful attainment then reinforces self-efficacy. Thus people who are generally confident or specifically self-efficacious tend to get more of what they want in life than those who are not. Perhaps not surprisingly, the variables of self-efficacy, internal locus of control, and subjective well-being are positively intercorrelated (Diener, 1984).

Assertiveness is generally regarded as healthy behavior. Being assertive allows individuals to get more of what they want and to avoid what they don't want. Assertiveness is an important tool for helping adolescents to resist peer pressure to abuse drugs (see Newcomb & Bentler, 1989). However, extreme assertiveness, like extreme selfishness, can be unhealthy. The behaviors of constantly asserting one's rights, always refusing to yield to others, and never compromising is often seen as obnoxious and selfish. People who exhibit those behaviors risk alienating others and losing friends.

In summary, psychologically healthy individuals are self-confident (although not grandiose). They are able to function autonomously and believe they are largely in control of their own lives. They can be assertive when they need to be, but are not obnoxiously assertive.

A Clear (although slightly optimistic) Perception of Reality

Psychologically healthy individuals basically have a clear perception of reality. Occasional minor distortions of reality are typically on the optimistic side.

Our perceptions of the world obviously are subjective, but fortunately some societal consensus exists about what comprises reality. Significant departures from that consensus (such as glaring hallucinations or illusions) are considered psychotic and clearly unhealthy within mainstream American society. And minor distortions of reality (such as products of the defense mechanisms) have traditionally been considered neurotic (Taylor & Brown, 1988). One traditional goal of psychotherapy for the defense-generated neuroses has been to expose and dismantle individuals' defensive perceptions. Consider an example of rationalization—a person wants a particular job, does not get it, and then tells him- or herself that the job was undesirable anyway. It used to be considered a healthy goal to help such a person to acknowledge his or her repressed feelings of disappointment and hurt from the rejection rather than cover them up.

But recently there has been a subtle shift in attitudes about defense mechanisms and minor illusions among many professional therapists in America (see

Snyder, 1988; Taylor & Brown, 1988, 1994). The new thinking is that the *moderate* and *temporary* use of defense mechanisms and "positive illusions" often can be psychologically beneficial and therefore healthy for many individuals. Adaptive illusions, according to Taylor and Brown (1988), include overly positive self-perceptions and exaggerated perceptions of personal control over situations.

In a way, the intervention of cognitive restructuring can be viewed as training in how to use defense mechanisms and illusions effectively or how to reinterpret events or experiences more positively (for example, see Beck, 1991). In the rationalization example just described, if the person was depressed about the job rejection, a cognitive therapist might likely try to help him or her to reframe the experience so that it was seen as a less disappointing, even a positive one. The chosen reinterpretation may be something like "This rejection may well be due to an error in the employer's judgment. In any case I have learned several things from this experience and am now better prepared for the next job application." Whether this is considered rationalization or adaptive cognitive restructuring, this kind of reinterpretation is generally regarded as healthy these days.

The defense mechanism of denial (as long as it does not take an extreme or long-term form) can also serve as a health-preserving buffer. When many people receive news of a serious medical diagnosis for themselves, their first reaction is often numbness or an inability to fully grasp the implications of the diagnosis. This is a mild form of denial, and it can protect the individual from reacting in an impulsive and possibly, dangerous way (such as committing suicide). Psychologically healthy individuals may first employ this type of mild denial and then drop it as they gradually adapt to the new situation.

An optimistic viewpoint correlates with positive mood and subjective well-being (see Bandura, 1986, 1995; Diener, 1984). From a sociobiological perspective, Tiger (1979) has argued that survival favors the optimist. In primitive times, the optimistic hunter was more likely to continue the hunt than the pessimistic hunter, and long hunts tend to yield more success than short hunts. Thus, optimism, like positive self-efficacy, tends to result in better outcomes for the individual.

In summary, psychologically healthy individuals usually perceive reality clearly, but with a slight bias toward optimism. They view themselves, their potentials, and their futures in a more positive than negative light. Occasionally they employ defense mechanisms in order to cope with acute crisis situations. Their defensive responses are mild and short-term, however.

Courage and Resilience

Psychologically healthy individuals find the courage to confront their own fears, accept responsibility for their behavior, and are prepared to take risks when it is reasonable to do so. They adapt to new situations and "bounce back" after crises and setbacks.

Franklin Roosevelt once said that all we have to fear is fear itself. This idea sums up an underlying principle found within all of the major psychotherapeutic theories about fear and fear reduction—fear is finally overcome only after it is confronted directly. From the psychodynamic perspective, the goal is to uncover and confront the psychic source(s) of one's fears (Hall & Lindzey, 1985). When the sources of the anxieties are revisited and examined with the light of logic, they tend to lose their power to paralyze or imprison the person. This phenomenon might be likened to the child who overcomes his or her fear about what is under the bed by looking under there with a flashlight. The cognitve-behavioral interventions for overcoming fears and phobias (such as systematic desensitization, flooding, and participant modeling) all involve helping the person eventually to confront the feared stimulus. If the feared stimulus is confronted repeatedly and no aversive consequences occur, then the fear is reduced or extinguished. So the key to overcoming fear starts with the person's finding the courage and determination to confront his or her fears and then doing it.

Among the greatest of human fears, according to existentialist and humanistic psychologists (see Hall & Lindzey, 1985), is the fear of responsibility. We are responsible for much of what happens to us—responsible for our successes and failures, and our actions and our choices not to act. Our fear is rooted in the possibility that we may fail to live up to our potential and waste our opportunity. Being healthy may involve accepting that responsiblity. Maslow's paragon of psychological health—the self-actualized person—does accept the personal responsibity and guilt (when it is deserved), admits mistakes, and learns from those mistakes.

Living is a risky business. Psychologically healthy individuals understand and accept that reality. They are also prepared to take additional risks on occasion. Kinnier and Metha (1989) found that the life regret of "I should have taken more risks in my life" was quite common and discriminated between those who were most and least satisfied with how they had lived their lives—more of the least satisfied cited that regret. And 44 percent of the 11,000 women that Kagan (1985) interviewed said that "taking risks" was very important for their own career success.

In a life where danger and risk abound, failures, crises, and setbacks are inevitable. Psychologically healthy individuals accept this reality. They become adept at adapting to new challenging situations and learn how to recover successfully from the inevitable setbacks (Bandura, 1989, 1995). Kobasa, Maddi, and Kahn (1982) identified the constellation trait of "hardiness" that seems to be associated with survival and adaptation. The hardy individual, according to these authors, typically is optimistic, self-confident, purposeful, and tends to reframe crises as new challenges to be met and overcome.

In summary, psychologically healthy individuals bravely confront their fears and accept their responsibility. They are prepared to take risks when appropriate. They accept setbacks and failures as part of life, and as that old popular song says, after a fall they pick themselves up, dust themselves off, and start all over again.

Balance and Moderation

Psychologically healthy individuals live balanced lives—they work *and* play, laugh *and* cry; they are selfish *and* altruistic, logical *and* intuitive. They are not extremists, fanatics, or gluttons. They don't "put all their eggs in one basket," and they rarely do anything in excess (for example, work, eat, or sleep).

This theme of "balance and moderation" emerged within the criteria discussed earlier: the healthy person loves him- or herself, but not too much; is self-knowledgeable, but not self-obsessed; is autonomous, but not a loner; is assertive, but not obnoxious.

The ancient Greek philosophers extolled the virtues of balance and moderation. For example, Aristotle believed that the wisest choice was often located somewhere near the mean of the two opposing options or positions. In this century, Maslow (1971) prescribed that people should seek to integrate their opposing needs (that is, compromise rather than choose an extreme). Aristotle and Maslow implied that the wisest and healthiest among us would, as a rule, seek resolutions or life policies that balance the pull of our opposing values or needs. Kinnier (1984) found some support for this notion—individuals who resolved their conflicts by seeking a middle course were more satisfied with their choices than those who chose one extreme of their "splits."

Balance is a recurring psychological health theme in the literature. Freud (cited in Hall & Lindzey, 1985) recognized that individuals seek a balance between satisfying their instinctual desires and societal demands. He also advocated the reduction, not elimination, of tension within individuals. Jung's writings are replete with the theme of balance. He advocated that the individual seek balance and integration—between the physical and spiritual realms, between the conscious and unconscious levels, and between male and female traits (that is, anima and animus). Gilligan (1982) prescribed that both men and women should attempt to balance their affiliative and achievement needs.

Extremism or immoderation is generally considered a symptom of pathology. Immoderation in activities such as eating, drinking, gambling, or working is often referred to as an unhealthy addiction. Even the behaviors that are normally seen as health promoting (such as physical exercise) can become dangerous activities when done in excess.

In summary, psychologically healthy individuals are not fanatical, extremist, or gluttonous. Instead, they are balanced, grounded, and exercise moderation in most endeavors.

Love of Others

Psychologically healthy individuals love at least one other person (besides themselves). They have the capacity and desire to care deeply about the welfare of another person, persons, and/or humanity in general. Or to paraphrase (liberally) Barbra Streisand, people who need people are the psychologically healthiest people in the world.

It is widely believed by mental health professionals across different theoretical orientations (and apparently by Barbra Streisand also) that the need to belong to a group or family, the capacity to love, and the desire to become close to another person or persons are prerequisites for psychological health (for example, see Adler, 1978; Allport, 1961; Erikson, 1968; Freud, 1930; Fromm, 1955; Jahoda, 1958; Maslow, 1970).

Sullivan (1953) believed that individuals could only be understood as social beings, and Erikson's (1968) psychosocial stages of development similarly emphasize the importance of social relationships for all individuals. Within Erikson's framework, the child first judges whether others can be trusted. As a young adult, the person searches for an intimate relationship. As an older adult, the primary social roles are usually parent, grandparent, and/or mentor. Maslow's (1970) description of the self-actualized person and Adler's (cited in Hall & Lindzey, 1985) construct of "social interest" emphasize that caring about others is one of the most important and fulfilling aspects of life.

One of the greatest fears that people have is the fear of being alone (see Holmes & Rahe, 1967). And in surveys that ask individuals to list the most important things in their lives the constructs of love, romantic relationships, family, and friends consistently are at the top of those lists (for example, see Campbell, 1981; Cantril, 1965; Flanagan, 1978; Klinger, 1977). Intimate relationships are not only considered important, but are also linked to subjective well-being for the individual (see Diener, 1984; Baumeister & Leary, 1995).

In summary, psychologically healthy individuals can and do want to love and care about others. They need others and are intimate with or close to at least one other person throughout their lives.

Love of Life

Psychologically healthy individuals truly appreciate and enjoy various aspects of life. They are generally active, curious, and enthusiastic. They don't take themselves too seriously and appreciate the humorous view of life. They are open to new experiences, are often spontaneous, and do take time to "smell the roses." They tend to view life as an opportunity—an opportunity to learn, to experience new things, and to share with others.

Much of the preceding is a paraphrase of Maslow's (1967, 1970) description of the self-actualized person. Maslow and others (such as Allport, 1961; Fromm, 1955; Jung, 1954) have promoted the psychological benefits of humor, spontaneity, and openness. These traits have also been associated with the more frequent occurence of peak experiences (see Maslow, 1967; Noble, 1987). Peak experiences are often joyful, inspiring, and typically spiritual in nature. Such experiences are not uncommon for those who have been close to death. In interviewing hundreds of people who had experienced "near death" (they were clinically dead for a short period, but then were revived), Ring (1984) discovered recurrent themes: Most of those who had "died" described the experience as exhilarating and clarifying. They became more appreciative of life, more spontaneous, relaxed, and compassionate toward others. Perhaps their dramatic experiences should be instructive to the rest of us about what may matter most in life.

In summary, psychologically healthy individuals are open-minded, somewhat adventurous (though not reckless), and curious. They often feel relaxed and don't take themselves too seriously. They like to laugh. They are continually learning and appreciating others and the mysteries in life.

Purpose in Life

Psychologically healthy individuals have found meaning and purpose in their lives. They are committed to something outside of themselves.

Many writers have emphasized the importance of individuals attaining a sense of meaning and purpose in their lives (for example, see Adler, 1930; Allport, 1961; Erikson, 1959; Frankl, 1959; Fromm, 1955; Klinger, 1977; Maslow, 1959; Rogers, 1961). The humanistic psychologists have paid particular attention to this issue. Although they acknowledge the importance of the individual's basic psychological needs of safety, self-esteem, and connectedness with others, they view the individual's quest for meaning or purpose in life as a universal need and the crowning prerequisite for self-actualization.

A lack of meaning in an individual's life has often been implicated in psychological dysfunction (Maslow, 1959) and even in the tragic act of suicide (Lifton, 1979). Conversely, Frankl's (1959) accounts of concentration camp survivors suggest that human beings can endure the most horrible conditions if they possess a clear sense of meaning or purpose in their lives. Frankl (1959) was fond of paraphrasing Nietzsche's belief that "he who has a *why* to live can bear with almost any *how* (p. xi).

What is meaningful? The humanistic psychologists are quick to stress that each individual must search for and discover that for him- or herself. The humanistic writers also warn that the search for meaning can be frustrating and depressing at times, but as Frankl (1959) consoled—the need to find meaning and the (sometime) agony of the search are not symptoms of illness but of the human condition.

Among the most meaningful aspects of life for many people are work or career, love, family, and a spiritual perspective (Kinnier & Freitag, 1990). Although variation exists between individuals, the important thing, according to Seligman (cited in Buie, 1988), is that individuals find something that is outside of themselves to invest with meaning or purpose—be it a cause, a set of principles, other people, or God. As George Bernard Shaw (1903) so eloquently exclaimed,

> This is the true joy in life, the being used for a purpose, recognized by yourself as a mighty one; the being thoroughly worn out before you are thrown on the scrap heap; the being a force of Nature instead of a feverish selfish little clod of ailments and grievances complaining that the world will not devote itself to making you happy. (p. xxxi)

The Misguided Pursuit of Happiness

Being happy is *not* one of the criteria of psychological health. And, as has been reiterated by countless therapists over the decades—the goal of therapy is health, not happiness. But because the general public tends often to equate psychological health with happiness, in this section I discuss what the literature says about the nature of happiness.

In a review on happiness written over twenty-five years ago, Wilson (1967) formulated a general profile of the "happy" person. Such a person, according to Wilson, is most likely young, physically healthy, self-confident, well educated, well paid, extroverted, worry-free, religious, married, satisfied at work, and has modest aspirations. Diener's updated review (1984) suggests that these variables do correlate (but only moderately) with subjective well-being. For example, on average, wealthy people tend to be slightly happier than poor people, but many wealthy people describe themselves as unhappy, and many poor people consider themselves happy (Campbell, 1981).

In general, much of the research on subjective well-being seems to support the popular idea that happiness is elusive. For example, Diener (1984) pointed out that whereas involuntary unemployment is clearly associated with unhappiness, satisfaction with one's work correlates only moderately. Whereas marital and family satisfaction are strong predictors of subjective well-being, children often have a negative effect on marital satisfaction. And although many couples believe that having children is a prerequisite for fulfillment, voluntarily childless couples do not appear to be less happy than couples with children (see Veevers, 1980). Good health, although a strong predictor of life satisfaction for the elderly (Larson, 1978), is a weak predictor for younger people who tend to take their good health for granted (Diener, 1984).

The empirical research suggests that individuals who believe, "If only I get 'X,' I will be happy," are usually wrong. The great theoreticians of human behavior, including Freud (1930), Frankl (1959), and Maslow (1962) believed that human beings were destined to disappointment if they ever hoped to attain a state of permanent contentment during their lives. According to them, fulfilled needs and accomplishments are inevitably replaced by new needs and goals. In Maslovian terms, human beings are perpetually becoming or striving.

Several theories are useful for explaining how happiness typically eludes those who pursue it. Perhaps the best known is adaptation-level theory (see Brickman, Coates, & Janoff-Bulman, 1978; Helson, 1964). This theory predicts that the effects of positive and negative events and situations such as poverty, wealth, sickness, and health "wear off" over time. As Klinger (1977) described it, "Romantic love notoriously cools if it ripens into a close open relationship. Prestige, power, and fame pall with time. People envied because they lead 'the sweet life' or because they are celebrities nevertheless become bored" (p. 116).

In support of this observation, Brickman and associates (1978) found that state lottery winners were not happier than others after a period of time. Individuals habituate to their changing situations and eventually tend to regress to their previous levels of happiness.

Social comparison also is a dynamic that moderates the individual's perception of being happy or unhappy (see Diener, 1984). Individuals tend to judge their situations regarding wealth, health, prestige, and the like with their peers—and individuals' peer groups change as their environments change. For example, Cantril (1965) found that although disease and premature death are more prevalent in India than America, more Americans expressed concern or worry about their health than Indians. Similarly, relatively wealthier Americans were just as concerned about their economic situations as were Indians. It was in this sense that Tiger (1979) referred to prosperity as meaning not "enough," but "more."

Perhaps a lesson to be derived from the research and theories on subjective well-being or happiness is that the search for happiness "out there" (such as money, career success, the perfect mate, and family) is misguided because expectations tend to exceed reality. The achievement of goals often results in disappointment and subsequent confusion. This is what Oscar Wilde (1908) was referring to when he suggested that there were two tragedies in life—not getting what one wanted and getting it. He felt that getting what one wanted was the real tragedy. Although Oscar Wilde may have overstated the case for poetic impact, the psychological literature suggests that individuals would be wise to have modest expectations and not pursue happiness as a goal in life. As Frankl (1967) warned, " 'pursuit of happiness' amounts to a self contradiction: the more we strive for happiness the less we attain it. Peace of mind also must content itself with being a side effect, for it is self-destroying as an intention" (p. 41).

Summary

In conclusion, psychologically healthy individuals tend not to actively pursue happiness. They know themselves well, love (but are not infatuated with) themselves, and are reasonably self confident. They are autonomous and self-sufficient but also care deeply about others. They confront their fears directly and accept reality as it is (with perhaps a slight bias toward being optimistic). They accept responsibility for their actions, take reasonable risks on occasion, adapt to new situations fairly quickly, and consistently recover after crises or setbacks. They truly appreciate and enjoy various aspects of life and often act spontaneously. They seek balance (some work, some play) and typically maintain a lifestyle of moderation. Finally, they honestly seek and find at least some meaning in their existence that extends beyond self-preservation and self-gratification—they believe in something greater than themselves.

It is clear that these criteria are interdependent. According to Horney (1950), many psychological problems involve vicious circles. An example that Horney (1950) used was that if people are not loved, they often will experience low self-esteem, which often leads to acting out or antisocial behavior. Those who are antisocial are rarely loved by others, which can lead back to more self-loathing (see also Guisinger & Blatt, 1994).

One can think of numerous interdependency dynamics of the criteria described in this chapter. The following are a few: Those who are self-confident and optimistic are more likely to persist in their efforts to achieve their goals. Persistence, more often than the lack of persistence, results in success. The experience of success reinforces self-confidence and optimism, which reinforces persistence. Those who love themselves too little or too much are less likely to establish quality relationships. For those who love themselves too little, the absence of a good relationship can confirm their low self-esteem—"Nobody loves me, therefore I am probably worthless." Those who love themselves too much may need to distort reality significantly in order to explain their social isolation while saving face; for example, they may tell themselves something like "People are intimidated by my incredible intellect." Their distorted (and perhaps repugnant) perceptions of themselves and the world may well further alienate others.

The relationship between the criteria is synergistic. For full psychological health, all must operate in sync. A similar situation appears to exist between the physical and psychological spheres within individuals. The body and the mind (or the physical and psychological) are not separate realms or entities; rather, they function synergistically within the individual. A biological event such as the flu affects the person's emotional state, and a primarily psychosocial event such as being rejected can cause a somatic reaction (such as indigestion). In this chapter I focused exclusively on criteria of psychological health. I did so because of space constraints and do not mean to imply that the mind and body are dichotomous entities. For a discussion on the broader psycho-physio-sociological aspects of health, see Seeman (1989).

As indicated in the introduction, my list of the nine criteria is neither a universal nor a complete list. Basically, this list reflects my inevitably biased review of the literature and informal extraction of criteria that seem relevant to contemporary North American culture. I hope that this chapter may prompt other researchers to undertake a more formal project for identifying the central criteria for psychological/physical health. Such a project should employ more formal research methods, such as using expert judge ratings for selecting, clarifying, and perhaps weighting the criteria. It would be especially useful and interesting if the same project were undertaken within different cultures and repeated over time. That would allow us to discover how relative or universal the various health criteria are.

I would like to conclude by presenting one more rationale for the endeavor of identifying the criteria of psychological health. In contemporary society, the medical and allied professions have established criteria or prescriptions for physical health (as opposed to treatments for illness). For example, the suggestions to exercise regularly and to eat more fiber are commonly heard prescriptions for promoting physical health. Perhaps mental health professionals could make a more powerful impact on problem prevention if they too began publicly advocating specific psychologically healthy attitudes and goals rather than primarily focusing on the elimination of negative attitudes and behaviors.

References

Adler, A. (1930). Individual psychology. In C. Murchison (Ed.), *Psychologies of 1930*. Worcester, MA: Clark University Press.

Adler, A. (1978). Cooperation between the sexes. In H. L. Ansbacher & R. R. Ansbacher (Eds.), *Writings on women, love, and marriage, sexuality and its disorders*. Garden City, NY: Doubleday.

Allport, G. W. (1961). *Pattern and growth in personality*. New York: Holt, Rinehart & Winston.

Bandura, A. (1977). *Social learning theory*. Englewood Cliffs, NJ: Prentice Hall.

Bandura, A. (1986). *Social foundations of thought and action: A social cognitive theory*. Englewood Cliffs, NJ: Prentice Hall.

Bandura, A. (1989). Human agency in social cognitive theory. *American Psychologist, 44,* 1175–1184.

Bandura, A. (1995). Exercise of personal and collective efficacy in changing societies. In A. Bandura (Ed.), *Self-efficacy in changing societies* (pp. 1–45). Cambridge, England: Cambridge University Press.

Baumeister, R. F. (1988, August). *The problem of life's meaning.* Paper presented at the annual convention of the American Psychological Association.

Baumeister, R. F., & Leary, M. R. (1995). The need to belong: Desire for interpersonal attachments as a fundamental human motivation. *Psychological Bulletin, 117,* 497–529.

Beck, A. (1991). Cognitive therapy: A 30-year retrospective. *American Psychologist, 46,* 368–375.

Brickman, P., Coates, D., & Janoff-Bulman, R. (1978). Lottery winners and accident victims: Is happiness relative? *Journal of Personality and Social Psychology, 36,* 917–927.

Buie, J. (1988, October). "Me" decades generate depression. *APA Monitor,* p. 18.

Campbell, A. (1981). *The sense of well-being in America.* New York: McGraw-Hill.

Cantril, H. (1965). *The patterns of human concerns.* New Brunswick, NJ: Rutgers University Press.

Diener, E. (1984). Subjective well-being. *Psychological Bulletin, 95,* 542–575.

Erikson, E. H. (1959). Identity and the life cycle. *Psychological Issues, 1,* 18–164.

Erikson, E. H. (1963). *Childhood and society* (2nd ed.). New York: Norton.

Erikson, E. H. (1968). *Identity; Youth and crisis.* New York: Norton.

Flanagan, J. C. (1978). A research approach for improving our quality of life. *American Psychologist, 33,* 138–147.

Frankl, V. E. (1959). *Man's search for meaning: An introduction to logotherapy.* New York: Simon & Schuster.

Frankl, V. E. (1967). *Psychotherapy and existentialism.* New York: Simon & Schuster.

Freud, S. (1930). *Civilization and its discontents.* (J. Strachey, Trans. & Ed.). New York: Norton.

Fromm, E. (1955). *The sane society.* New York: Rinehart.

Gilligan, C. (1982). *In a different voice.* Cambridge, MA: Harvard University Press.

Guisinger, S., & Blatt, S. J. (1994). Individuality and relatedness. *American Psychologist, 49,* 104–111.

Hall, C. S., & Lindzey, G. (1985). *Introduction to theories of personality.* New York: Wiley.

Helson, H. (1964). *Adaptation-level theory.* New York: Harper & Row.

Holmes, T. H., & Rahe, R. H. (1967). The Social Readjustment Rating Scale. *Journal of Psychosomatic Research, 11,* 213–218.

Horney, K. (1950). *Neurosis and human growth.* New York: Norton.

Jahoda, M. (1958). *Current concepts of positive mental health.* New York: Basic Books.

Jung, C. G. (1954). *The development of personality.* Princeton, NJ: Princeton University Press.

Kagan, J. (1985, October). Who succeeds, who doesn't?: Results of a major survey. *Working Woman,* pp. 113–117, 154–156.

Kinnier, R. T. (1984). Choosing the mean versus an extreme resolution for intrapersonal values conflicts: Is the mean usually more golden? *Counseling and Values, 28,* 207–212.

Kinnier, R. T., & Freitag, E. T. (1990). The best things in life. *Guidance and Counselling, 5,* 11–27.

Kinnier, R. T., & Metha, A. T. (1989). Regrets and priorities at three stages of life. *Counseling and Values, 33,* 182–193.

Klinger, E. (1977). *Meaning and void.* Minneapolis: University of Minnesota Press.

Kobasa, S. C., Maddi, S. R., & Kahn, S. (1982). Hardiness and health: A prospective study. *Journal of Personality and Social Psychology, 42,* 168–177.

Larson, R. (1978). Thirty years of research on the subjective well-being of older Americans. *Journal of Gerontology, 33,* 109–125.

Lifton, R. J. (1979). *The broken connection.* New York: Simon & Schuster.

Mahoney, M. J., & Thoresen, C. E. (1974). *Self-control: Power to the person.* Pacific Grove, CA: Brooks/Cole.

Maslow, A. H. (Ed.). (1959). *New knowledge in human values.* New York: Harper.

Maslow, A. H. (1962). *Toward a psychology of being.* Princeton, NJ: Van Nostrand.

Maslow, A. H. (1967). Neurosis as a failure of personal growth. *Humanitas, 3,* 153–170.

Maslow, A. H. (1970). *Motivation and personality.* (2nd ed.). New York: Harper.

Maslow, A. H. (1971). *The farther reaches of human nature.* New York: Viking Press.

Newcomb, M. D., & Bentler, P. M. (1989). Substance use and abuse among children and teenagers. *American Psychologist, 44,* 242–248.

Noble, K. D. (1987). Psychological health and the experience of transcendence. *Counseling Psychologist, 15,* 601–614.

Osipow, S. H. (1983). *Theories of career development* (3rd ed.). Englewood Cliffs, NJ: Prentice Hall.

Peterson, C., & Seligman, M. E. P. (1984). Causal explanations as a risk factor for depression: Theory and evidence. *Psychological Review, 91,* 347–374.

Ring, K. (1984). *Heading toward Omega: In search of the meaning of the near-death experience.* New York: Quill.

Rogers, C. R. (1961). *On becoming a person.* Boston: Houghton Mifflin.

Seeman, J. (1989). Toward a model of positive mental health. *American Psychologist, 44,* 1099–1109.

Shaw, G. B. (1903). *Man and superman.* London: Constable.

Smith, M. B. (1994). Selfhood at risk. *American Psychologist, 49,* 405–411.

Snyder, C. R. (1988, August). *Self-illusions: When are they adaptive?* Symposium conducted at the 96th annual meeting of the American Psychological Association, Atlanta.

Stoller, R. J., Marmor, J., & Bieber, R. (1973). A symposium: Should homosexuality be in the APA nomenclature? *American Journal of Psychiatry, 130,* 1207–1216.

Sullivan, H. S. (1953). *The interpersonal theory of psychiatry.* New York: Norton.

Taylor, S. E., & Brown, J. D. (1988). Illusion and well-being: A social psychological perspective on mental health. *Psychological Bulletin, 103,* 193–210.

Taylor, S. E., & Brown, J. D. (1994). Positive illusions and well-being revisited: Separating fact from fiction. *Psychological Bulletin, 116,* 21–27.

Tiger, L. (1979). *Optimism: The biology of hope.* New York: Simon & Schuster.

Veevers, J. E. (1980). *Childless by choice.* Toronto: Butterworths.

Wilde, O. (1908). *Lady Windermere's fan.* London: Methuen.

Wilson, W. (1967). Correlates of avowed happiness. *Psychological Bulletin, 67,* 294–306.

Chapter 3

The Helping Relationship

Russell D. Miars, Ph.D   *Carol A Burden, Ed.D.*
Margaret M. Pedersen, M.B.A., M.S.

Most people find themselves engaged in some type of helping relationship nearly every day. Some helping occurs informally, while other helping happens in a more formal way. Friends and family usually help one another in a reciprocal, informal way while helping professionals such as counselors, psychologists, or social workers help their clients within a formal, unidirectional relationship. In a friendship, people share concerns and give each other information, advice, and support. Professional helping, in contrast, places much more responsibility on the helper, who must strive to be objective and helpful in a more directed, purposeful way. The professional helping relationship is unique in that a more independent, mature, fully functioning individual emerges as a result of the helping relationship.

This chapter focuses on the characteristics, knowledge, and skills needed by the counselor to build effective counselor–client helping relationships. The first section describes the helping relationship, and the following sections review what research has shown to be the characteristics of effective counselors and the skills needed to be a good helper or counselor. Throughout the skills sections, you will find examples taken from conversations between a counselor and client; we have

The senior author of this chapter in the first edition was Art Terry, Ph.D., associate professor in the school of education at Portland State University. Dr. Terry died in September of 1993. We wish to acknowledge the contribution he made to the content of the original version of this chapter.

added these examples to demonstrate, more clearly, specific techniques you might use when working with clients. A description of the case from which these excerpts were drawn can be found on page 67. As you read through this chapter, think about yourself and how closely you fit the description of an effective counselor.

What Is the Helping Relationship?

In the helping relationship, individuals work together to resolve a concern or difficulty and/or foster the personal growth and development of one of the two people. Rogers (1961) defined a helping relationship as one "in which at least one of the parties has the intent of promoting the growth, development, maturity, improved functioning and improved coping with life of the other (party)" (p. 39). The goals of any counselor–client relationship, whether in educational, career or personal counseling, can be put into four basic goal areas: changes in behavior and lifestyle, increased awareness or insight and understanding, relief from suffering, and changes in thoughts and self-perceptions (Brammer, 1993).

An important aspect of the helping relationship is that it is a process that enables a person to grow in directions chosen by that person. It is the counselor's job to make the client aware of possible alternatives and encourage client acceptance of responsibility for taking action on one or more of these alternatives.

The helping relationship minimally can be broken down into three phases— that of relationship building, that of challenging the client to find ways to change, and that of facilitating positive client action (Egan, 1994). In the first phase, the goal is to build a foundation of mutual trust and client understanding. Once trust and understanding have been established, the helper, in the second phase, challenges the client to "try on" new ways of thinking, feeling, and behaving. In the final phase, the counselor facilitates client actions that lead toward change and growth in the client's life outside the counseling relationship.

Most helping occurs on a one-to-one basis, and studies of the quality of the counseling relationship have shown that it is more the collaborative attitudes and feelings of the counselor, rather than the specifics of theoretical orientation, that are important for positive outcome (Sexton & Whiston, 1994). Specific procedures and techniques are much less important than the alliance between counselor and client. It is important to understand that it is the way in which the counselor's attitudes and procedures are perceived by the client that makes a difference, and it is the client's positive perception that is crucial to a good helping relationship (Rogers, 1961; Sexton & Whiston, 1994).

The ultimate goal of a professional helping relationship should be to promote the development of more effective and adaptive behavior in the client. The specific goals for a given client are determined collaboratively by the counselor and the client as they interact in the helping relationship. In the next section we examine the characteristics of individuals who serve as effective and competent counselors.

What Are the Characteristics of Effective Counselors?

Effective counselors have specific personal qualities and are able to convey those qualities to the people they help. There is an increasing amount of evidence supporting the concept that helpers are only as effective as they are self-aware and able to use themselves as vehicles of change (Okun, 1992). As you read through this section, you might think about each quality or trait and see how it fits for you.

Combs (1986) summarized thirteen studies that looked at helpers in a variety of settings. These studies supported the view that there are differences in the beliefs of effective and ineffective person-centered helpers. Effective counselors are interested in and committed to an understanding of the specialized knowledge of the field and find it personally meaningful. As such, they are challenged to remain current in their knowledge and skills. They also believe that the people they help are capable, adequate, trustworthy, dependable, and friendly. Effective counselors focus on positive self-beliefs and have confidence in themselves, their abilities, and their worth. They like people and have a feeling of oneness with others. Effective counselors use interventions that focus on the individual's perception of self and expand the individual's view of life rather than narrow it. They are committed to freeing rather than controlling the client and are able to be objectively involved with, rather than alienated from, their clients.

The term "self-actualized" has been used by Patterson (1974) to describe a constellation of characteristics that effective counselors possess. Aware and accepting of self, they are individuals who are likewise aware of their environment and interact with it in a reality-oriented way. In living, they are open to a full range of experiences and feelings, are spontaneous, and have a sense of humor. When interacting with others, they are able to be involved, yet remain somewhat detached (Cormier & Cormier, 1991). They are empathic, compassionate, and believing of the client's world. In the process of dealing with problems and issues, they are able to help clients clearly see their own worlds while adding a fresh perspective to the issues. Respected by others, these individuals are authentic (Pietrofesa, Hoffman, Splete, & Pinto, 1978), perceived as trustworthy (Strong, 1968), and abide by ethical standards of the profession (Gladding, 1996).

Counseling is demanding work, and effective counselors often display high energy levels (Carkhuff, 1986). Intense focusing with another individual, trying to hear clearly, often needing to tolerate ambiguity (Pietrofesa, Hoffman, Splete, & Pinto, 1978), and taking appropriate risks can put heavy demands on the counselor's energy. Therefore, a challenge to individuals pursuing the counseling profession is to have good self-care strategies.

Rogers (1958) identified four conditions that he believed all counselors should provide in the context of a helping relationship. These necessary, but not necessarily sufficient, core conditions were (1) unconditional positive regard for the individual, (2) genuineness, (3) congruence, and (4) empathy. Later, Carkhuff and Berenson (1967) added two additional traits or skills to the list: respect and concreteness. Thirteen years later, Ivey and Simek-Downing (1980) labeled these traits "communications skills," and added warmth, immediacy, and confrontation to the list.

The sections on helping skills that follow the case study are intended to help you gain a better understanding of the traits and skills needed to be an effective counselor.

Case Study

On the intake form, Lisa described herself as 33 and married with three children. She came to counseling because she was feeling desperate and needed to talk her problem over with someone. Concerns about her marriage and her children were at an all-time high. Her husband, Peter, was to come to counseling with her, but backed out at the last minute, hoping that she wouldn't go either.

Peter and Lisa first met when they lived in California; she worked as a waitress in a restaurant where he often came to eat. They started dating, and it wasn't long until they were serious about each other. In Lisa's view, the only obstacle to their marriage was that he was not yet divorced. Peter told her that it would take time, but there was no question he would get a divorce.

They talked about what it would be like to be together. He said she was such a contrast to his wife, whom he described as really crazy. One day he happened to mention that he had two kids—a boy and a girl. They were with his wife, but he'd like to get them before they too became crazy. Soon they were talking about all living together; she would take care of the kids until the divorce was final. This sounded wonderful to Lisa, since she didn't want to be a waitress all her life.

Peter, Lisa, and the children had been living together for three years when they moved to the Chicago area. Peter was tired of his current job and had heard that there were great opportunities there. When they got there, the only work he found that paid a decent wage was that of night watchman at a big plant. He liked the title of "security officer" but really didn't like working nights. This turned out to be a very difficult time for Lisa, because she found out that she was pregnant and she had to keep the kids quiet during the day while Peter slept.

When she came to counseling, Lisa's most immediate concern was that they had just purchased a house, representing themselves as husband and wife. At the time she wasn't worried because she knew that they would soon be married. But several weeks later, she proposed to Peter that they now should legalize their relationship, especially since they had a 2-year-old daughter. Lisa was absolutely appalled when he told her that he had never initiated any divorce action.

As time went on, Lisa became more aware of problems in their relationship. Peter drank too much and became more demanding and threatening. He had hit her only once, but his attitude and the gun he carried made her feel very intimidated and threatened. She didn't want to stay with him, but she had no place else to go.

She was concerned about leaving him because of the children. If she took only their daughter, what might happen to the other two children? She'd grown to love them, but didn't want to be accused of kidnapping. She also wasn't certain that she could support herself, let alone three more!

The intimidation and verbal abuse by her husband escalated, as did the drinking. He forbade her to go to counseling. She knew she must leave him, but didn't know where to go.

Epilogue

With the counselor's help, Lisa explored the alternatives available to her. She called the legal aid service for advice about the children. One evening, he became extremely physically abusive with her and she had to call the police to restrain him. The next day Lisa took the children and moved into a "domestic shelter."

Basic Skills and Concepts

According to Ivey (1994), the aim of counseling is personal and social development. He has described a hierarchy of microcounseling skills that define what the counselor does in an interview to achieve specific results. Ivey's hierarchy rests on a foundation of attending behaviors and basic listening skills. Our list of skills is based on Ivey's model with additional information taken from Cormier and Cormier (1991), Egan (1994), and Ivey (1994).

Attending Skills

Attending behavior, including eye contact, body language, vocal quality, and verbal tracking, is one of the most powerful of the communication skills (Ivey, 1994). In the counseling relationship, counselors communicate through body language and words that their full attention is on the client's nonverbal and verbal behaviors. Eye contact, facial expressions, and body posture are the physical fundamentals that indicate to others that you are either carefully attending or not attending to them.

Eye Contact
Good eye contact is not an unwavering stare, but rather an intermittent yet frequent looking into the eyes of the client. It tells other people that you are interested in them and what they have to say. Effective eye contact occurs more frequently when there is a comfortable distance between counselor and client, when topics being discussed are not too threatening, when neither person is trying to hide something, when there is adequate rapport between counselor and client, and when one is listening rather than talking. Cultural differences abound in what is considered appropriate eye contact (Ivey, 1994). The counselor should first consider cultural differences if eye contact seems strained or awkward in the relationship.

Attentive Body Language
Body orientation can encourage or discourage interpersonal interactions. In our culture, a slight forward body lean and a relaxed, comfortable posture are usually

received favorably and indicate interest in the client. Egan (1994) uses the acronym SOLER to describe this attentive body posture. The letters stand for *Squarely*—face the client, *Open*—body posture, *Lean*—forward slightly, *Eye*—contact, and *Relaxed*—manner.

Distance

The distance between counselor and client also affects communication. There is an optimal "comfort zone" for conversing that is largely controlled by cultural influences. It is about an arm's length in American culture. It is imperative that the counselor be aware of the level of comfort or discomfort that the client is experiencing with the distance and adjust it if necessary.

The distance between counselor and client may become so close that it involves *touch*. Counselors should always be sensitive to the therapeutic value of touch. This involves a consideration of the client issues and sensitivity to the role that touch has played in creating the issue, and what professionals who are considered experts recommend as best practice. For example, it is not recommended that counselors working with individuals traumatized by physical abuse use touch as part of their therapeutic behavior.

Humanistic models suggest that touch that is genuinely felt may help create within the client a willingness to be open and share. Driscoll, Newman, and Seals (1988) found that college students observing videotapes felt that counselors who touched their college-age clients were more caring than counselors who did not. Suiter and Goodyear (1985) found that counselors who used a semiembrace with clients were seen as less trustworthy than counselors who either did not touch, or only touched their clients' hands or shoulders. There was also greater acceptability of touch when it was initiated by female counselors. It must be emphasized, though, that touch without genuine feeling behind it may be more harmful than helpful. The type of touch that is generally considered acceptable is one that is long enough (1–3 seconds) to make contact yet does not create uncomfortable feelings. Most professionals who do touch believe that appropriate touching is contact of the counselor's hand or forearm with the client's hand, arm, shoulder, or upper back, and recognize that gender differences may influence how such contact is interpreted.

Although there are many things counselors can do to convey an interest in their clients, certain mannerisms are distracting. Behaviors such as gum chewing, cigarette smoking, or continual change of body position may seriously affect any interpersonal interaction and convey a sense of counselor disinterest.

Vocal Tone

Another aspect of attending behavior is voice tone. A warm, pleasant, caring voice strongly indicates an interest and willingness to listen to the client. The pitch, volume, and rate of speech can convey much of one's feeling toward another person or situation. Scherer (1986) has shown that specific paralinguistic cues can convey either high or low levels of self-confidence. High levels of confidence are conveyed when you speak in a caring voice that is neither hesitant nor rapid, but that projects inner qualities of warmth, respect, and compassion for the client. These cues of self-confidence can affect client perceptions of counselor expertness, attractiveness, trustworthiness, and associated satisfaction with the counseling relationship (Barak, Shapira, & Fisher, 1988).

Verbal Tracking

Even when the client engages in long, irrelevant discourses, the counselor often needs to remain relaxed and follow the client's topic and logic. The counselor can choose to either attend to or ignore certain portions of the client's statements—this is termed *selective attention*. The portions of the client's statements to which a counselor attends depend on the counselor's theoretical orientation and professional beliefs. It is imperative that counselors be aware of their own patterns of selective attention, for the topics their clients focus on will tend to be partially determined by those topics to which the counselor unconsciously attends.

Silence is another important part of verbal attending behavior. The counselor's ability to remain silent while clients are silent facilitates clients listening to themselves and/or the counselor more carefully. Remaining silent is often an excellent tactic to start a reluctant client talking, because silence is perceived by nearly everyone as a demanding condition that must be filled with a response. The challenge for beginning counselors is learning to be comfortable enough with silence to use it effectively.

The Basic Listening Skills

Active listening is an extremely important dimension of counselors' work (Egan, 1994). Counselors need to be sure that they are hearing the client accurately, and clients must know that the counselor has fully heard them, seen their point of view, and felt the world as they experience it. The basic listening skills that facilitate active listening include client observation; noticing client nonverbal behavior; the use of encouraging, paraphrasing, and summarization statements; the reflection of client feelings; and the use of open and closed questions. The outcome of using these basic listening skills in combination is the establishment of an empathic relationship with the client (Carkhuff, 1969). The overall purpose of empathy is to "understand the situation of another person from that person's perspective" (Berger, McBreen & Rifkin, 1996, p. 210).

Client Observation

Simply observing the client provides the counselor with a rich source of "silent information." Noticing and paying attention to the *physiological cues* expressed in another person's appearance and physique provide a way to identify the internal emotional responses of the other person. Bandler and Grindler (1979) have identified four cues—changes in skin color, lip size, muscle tone, and/or breathing—that can reflect the internal emotional processes and the physiologic changes occurring within the client. These physiologic messages are difficult to hide, because they are generally involuntary reactions of the autonomic nervous system. Observing subtle changes in these areas can silently reveal the moments of emotional change for a client.

The points during the interview at which eye contact is broken, the voice changes, skin color changes, shifts in body posture occur, or when changes in muscle tension or facial expression take place may indicate moments when important information is being revealed. Observations of discrepancies between nonverbal behavior and what is being said should be checked out with the client by the use of such questions as "Are you aware that you are smiling as you talk about the sadness you feel?"

Verbal Behavior

In addition to nonverbal behavior, one can also learn a great deal from the client's verbal behavior. At the most basic level, the counselor should note *topic changes* or *topic exclusions* and any *key words* that appear again and again. For example, when the client continues to use "should" or "ought" statements, that may indicate a lack of control in those areas and should be explored further.

Sentence structure is an important clue to how the client views the world. Is the client the subject or the object of the sentence? (Does the client feel that he or she does the acting, or is acted on?) Are things always in the past, or the present, or the future? Are there key words and descriptions that give a clue to the client's worldview? Hearing certain patterns of words and ideas gives clues to clients' typical thought processes and self-perceptions.

Incongruities, discrepancies, and *double messages* are nearly universal in counseling interviews. They are often at the root of a client's immobility and inability to respond creatively to difficult life situations. The "Freudian slip" is an example of such an incongruity. When counselors notice such incongruities, they may either choose to hold back and say nothing or try to bring the discrepancy into the client's awareness. The emotional state of the client and the impact on the relationship should be the main consideration when making this decision. In time-limited or within certain theoretical frameworks such as Gestalt, immediate confrontation may be the preferred intervention.

Encouraging, Paraphrasing, and Summarizing

The skill of *encouraging* includes the use of both "encouragers" and "restatements," both of which punctuate the interview and provide a smooth flow. Using encouragers such as head nods, an interested facial expression, or verbal utterances such as "umm" or "uh-huh" is an active way to let clients know that they have been heard and understood. Encouragers can be used to influence the direction taken by the client and are part of selective attention as described earlier.

One powerful type of encourager is for the counselor to respond with a restatement of a "key word" or a short phrase from the client's statement, often in a questioning tone of voice. For example,

Lisa: I often feel afraid around him.

Counselor: Afraid of him?

The *paraphrase* always uses some of the same key words from the client's statement, but might add some counselor observations. It is an encapsulated rephrase of the content of the client's message in the counselor's words. The strength of the paraphrase is that the counselor is giving of self, yet is paying primary attention to the client's frame of reference. This skill is frequently very helpful in letting clients clarify issues that may have been cloudy as well as letting them know that they have been heard accurately.

A good paraphrase has four main parts:

1. Noting some aspect of the client's mode of receiving information (visual, auditory, kinesthetic)
2. Key words and constructs used by the client
3. A summary of the essence of what the client has said
4. A checking out of the counselor's accuracy in hearing; such as "Is that right?" or "Is that close?"

To illustrate the elements of a good paraphrase, consider the following example:

Lisa: I'd like to run away and never come back, but what would happen to the kids?

Counselor: It sounds like you're feeling trapped and confused. If you only had yourself to think about, you'd know what to do, but you really care about the children.

Lisa: You're right! I do feel trapped and confused!

Summarizations are similar to paraphrasing, except that they "paraphrase" a longer period of conversation. They gather together a client's verbalizations, facts, feelings, and meanings, and restate them for the client as accurately as possible. This summarization frequently gives the client a feeling of movement as ideas and feelings are explored (Brammer, 1993).

Summarizations may be useful in the beginning of a session to warm up a client or at other times to bring closure to discussion on a theme. They can be used to add direction and coherence to a session that seems to be going nowhere (Egan, 1994). Summarizations are also valuable to counselors as a check on the accuracy of their understanding of the information that has just been gathered.

Here is an example of a summarization in an interview with Lisa:

Counselor: You're feeling overwhelmed because so many things seem wrong— you're feeling the need to be protective of the kids and yourself. You're less certain you'll ever be married or even want to be married to Peter.

Reflection of Feelings

Besides hearing the words of the client accurately, the counselor must uncover and recognize the emotions underlying those words. Reflecting client feelings is very similar to paraphrasing except that the paraphrase is associated with content (such as facts, information), whereas reflection of feelings is associated with the emotions related to the content. This skill is used to discover and sort out positive and negative client feelings and can best be done by using concise statements that connect the client's feelings with the causes of those feelings (Evans, Hearn, Uhlemann, & Ivey, 1993). It is important for the counselor to have learned how to recognize and accurately label emotions such as anger, gladness, sadness, fear, or being scared before trying to reflect these emotions in others.

A reflection of feelings consists of five basic parts:

1. A sentence stem using the client's method of receiving information (auditory, visual, kinesthetic)
2. Use of the pronoun "you"
3. A feeling label or emotion stem
4. A context or setting for the emotion
5. The correct tense of the reflection (frequently it is the present tense; for example, "Right now, you are angry")

You may also want to check to see that the reflection is accurate; for example,

Lisa: I just don't know what to do.

Counselor: It sounds like with all these responsibilities, you're feeling trapped, confused, and immobilized. You're not certain which way to turn. Is that how you feel?

Questions

The use of questions can open communication. In the helping relationship, effective, open communication is especially necessary from the counselor. It facilitates moving the client from self-exploration through increased understanding and finally commitment to appropriate action. By using specific verbal leads, the counselor is able to bring out the major facts, feelings, and self-perceptions that a client brings to the session. Effective use of open and closed questions can encourage the client to talk more freely and openly.

Open questions are considered by some to be the most valuable of the attending skills. Open questions usually begin with "what," "how," "could," or "would" and require the client to provide a longer, more expansive response than simply "yes" or "no." Open questions are used to begin interviews; to encourage clients to express more information; to elicit examples of particular behaviors, thoughts, or feelings; and to increase the client's commitment to communicate. For example,

Counselor: What would you like to discuss today?

(or) *Counselor:* How did that make you feel?

(or) *Counselor:* Could there be other reasons for the way you acted?

Sometimes a client is very talkative and rambles or jumps from topic to topic. In such a case, *closed questions* can be used to gather information, give clarity, gain focus, and narrow the area of discussion. These closed questions usually begin with the word "is," "are," "do," "did." One must use caution, though, because extensive use of closed questions can hinder conversation. A questioning counselor can appear to have all the power in the relationship, and this inequality can destroy the counselor–client relationship, especially during initial encounters.

Clients from some cultures are rapidly turned off by counselor questions, as are those clients who have not developed trust in their counselors. Frequently the same information can be obtained by asking the clients what goals they have, how they feel about those goals, and how they plan to attain them. (Note that asking too many questions at once can confuse clients.) "Why" questions are especially troublesome because they may put clients on the defensive or leave them feeling they must provide a logical explanation for their behavior.

Because questions may cause resistance with some clients, the skills of encouraging, paraphrasing, summarization, and reflection of feeling may be used to obtain similar information yet seem less intrusive to the client.

Self-Attending Skills

Counselors who are aware of their own values, beliefs, and assets are much more likely to find it easier to "be with" clients, help clients explore personal issues, and facilitate client action. Therefore, the self-attending skills are extremely important for each person who wishes to be an effective counselor. There are several components to the self-attending process. Shulman (1979) referred to these counselor components as "tuning-in." The first component in the "tuning-in" process is self-awareness.

Self-Awareness

The personal knowledge and understanding that the counselor has of self and the counseling setting are extremely important to the self-attending process. Practically speaking, the counselor should not consciously rehearse how counselors are "supposed" to be. The effective counselor acts professionally, but does not put on a professional front, play-acting some imaginary expert counselor. Effective counselors know their strengths as well as their weaknesses, and by understanding themselves are able to overcome self-consciousness and devote fuller attention to what the client is trying to disclose.

In the process of learning counseling skills, there may be times when the process seems awkward and uncomfortable. The learning cycle for trainees recognizes that learning counselor skills can sometimes be an unsettling process. Unlearning competing behaviors and relearning new ones in their place take time, a great deal of concentration, and practice. Counselor self-awareness is crucial throughout this process.

Centering and Relaxing

Centering, or getting "in touch" and then "in-tune" with one's person (Brammer, 1993) is an important skill for the counselor to develop. By becoming centered the counselor is able to show more social-emotional presence (Egan, 1994) in the counseling relationship and to give the client his or her undivided attention. With a keener focus than is common in most human interaction, the counselor is better able to empathically understand the client's problems and concerns. Similarly, a significant level of relaxation (both physical and psychological) in the counselor will help clients relax as they face the stress and challenges of the counseling process itself.

Humor

The counselor who can enjoy and use *humor* effectively has an invaluable asset. The healing power of humor has long been valued, but its place in therapy is only slowly gaining respect (Keller, 1984). Although counseling is serious business, there are many truly humorous dimensions to the human condition, and when humor appears as a natural outgrowth of the counselor–client relationship it should be attended to. Humor can provide a means of connecting with clients, and counselors need to affirm any humor presented by their clients. Laughter and joking can release built-up tensions and laughing at one's self can be extremely therapeutic—since it requires seeing one's problems in a whole new perspective.

Nonjudgmental Attitude toward Self

Counselors need to have a broad awareness of their own value positions. They must be able to answer very clearly the questions "Who am I?" "What is important to me?" "Am I nonjudgmental?" (Brammer, 1993).

This awareness aids counselors in being honest with themselves and their clients and in being free from judgments about themselves. In addition, it helps the counselor avoid unwarranted or unethical use of clients to satisfy personal needs. Although counselors may have opinions about traits of people they like and want to associate with, one characteristic of effective counselors is that they try to suspend judgments about their client's lives.

Nonjudgmental Attitude toward Others

This attitude is one of respect for a client's individuality and worth as a person and is very similar to Rogers's (1961) concept of "unconditional positive regard." It allows clients to be open and to be themselves, because they know that the person they are in a relationship with (the counselor) will not be judging them or what they say. The counselor conveys this nonjudgmental attitude by being warm, accepting, and respectful toward the client; this is especially important in the early phases of the relationship.

Respect describes the helping attitude and skill that communicates this acceptance of the client as a person of worth and dignity (Rogers, 1957). In using this skill, the counselor demonstrates a belief in clients' abilities to deal with their own problems in the presence of a facilitative person. Often counselors express this respect by what they do not do, rather than by what they do—such as not giving advice (for example, see Egan, 1994). Respectful counselors use communication skills to actualize the power, ability, and skills already possessed by the client. In other words, the counselor believes in the problem-solving ability of the client. These skills and attitudes are very important in facilitating an effective helping relationship. They communicate a willingness to work with the client and an interest and belief in the client as a person of worth (Cormier & Cormier, 1991).

The way you nonverbally attend to the client is one way you express respect (Egan, 1994). Respectful behavior conveys the message "I'm glad I'm here. I'm glad you're here." Respect is also expressed through appropriate warmth, understanding, and caring.

Communicating respect entails suspending judgment of the client (Cormier & Cormier, 1991; Egan, 1994). Rogers (1967) has effectively described this kind of respect as the ability of the counselor to "communicate to his client a deep and genuine caring for him as a person with potentialities, a caring uncontaminated by evaluations of his thoughts, feelings or behaviors" (p. l02).

Lisa: I am really feeling very helpless. I like staying home and taking care of the kids. Going back to work isn't something I want to do.

Counselor: The dilemma you face is complicated by something that you like to do and something you don't really want to do.

Respect is rarely found alone in communication. It usually occurs in combination with empathy and genuineness.

Genuineness

When counselors relate to clients naturally and openly, they are being genuine. Being a counselor is not just a role played by the individual. Instead, it is the appropriate revelation of one's own feelings, thoughts, and being in the counseling relationship. Egan (1975) cautions "being role free is not license; freedom from role means that the counselor should not use the role or façade of counselor to protect himself, to substitute for effectiveness, or to fool the client" (p. 92).

The effective use of genuineness reduces the emotional distance between the counselor and client (Cormier & Cormier, 1991). It breaks down the role distance and links the counselor and client together, allowing the client to see the counselor as human, and a person similar to him or her. The genuine counselor is spontaneous, nondefensive, and consistent in relationships.

Lisa: Do you think I'm as crazy and mixed up as I feel?

Counselor: Your confusion and indecisiveness make you wonder whether I see you as crazy. I really don't experience you that way.

Concreteness

In the process of exploring problems or issues, a client often presents an incomplete representation of what has happened. The goal of concreteness is to make the information and awareness gained through self-exploration more specific and concrete (Meier & Davis, 1993). It is the task of the counselor to help the client clarify the pieces of the puzzle and fit them together so that the whole makes sense to the client. This clarification increases the likelihood that an organized, specific, workable action plan can be implemented and accepted by the client. When encouraging concreteness, one attempts to focus very specifically on the situation at hand, and tries to make clear all facets of the issue, including the accompanying behaviors and feelings.

There are several ways to help clients become more concrete and focused. When a client makes a vague statement, the counselor can reflect in a more concrete way. At times, a rambling client may need to be focused. The effective use of concreteness in such situations may feel like interrupting, but should lead to increased counselor–client interaction. When counselor invitations to be more concrete or specific are necessary, leads such as "what" and "how" rather than "why" will usually produce more relevant and specific information (Egan, 1994).

Lisa: I'm really confused about what to do.

Counselor: You're feeling stuck, and confused because you always thought you'd be married, and now you're not so certain he wants that to happen.

(or) *Counselor:* What specifically has happened that has led to the confusion?

(or) *Counselor:* Help me to understand what events are most closely related to this confusion you're feeling.

Effective use of concreteness keeps the counseling session productively focused and aims at making vague experiences, behaviors, and feelings more specific. The more specific the information, the better the understanding and the more effective future actions will be.

Advanced Skills and Concepts

The first goal of helping is to help clients tell their story in an understandable way (Egan, 1994). This involves the facilitation of client self-understanding. Such exploration helps both the counselor and client understand the client's problems and concerns. Clients begin to focus and see more clearly the puzzles of their life and are led skillfully to identify the missing pieces and blocks. This exploration involves a look at the real self, and related issues. The process leads to insightful self-understanding that invites the client to change or take action.

Once the beginning counselor is adept at using the basic counseling skills, advanced skills and concepts can be added to the repertoire. These skills and concepts are more action oriented and allow the counselor to facilitate deeper client self-understanding, change, and eventual termination of the helping relationship. The advanced understanding and challenging skills include advanced empathy, self-disclosure, confrontation, and immediacy.

Advanced Understanding and Challenging Skills

Advanced Empathy
Primary empathy forms the foundation and atmospheric core of the helping relationship (Gladding, 1996). It involves listening for basic or surface messages with

frequent, but brief, responses to those messages. The skills of paraphrasing and reflection of feeling serve the counselor well in establishing an empathic base of understanding the client (Carkhuff, 1969). The counselor sees the world from the client's frame of reference and communicates that it has been understood. The goal is to move the client toward identifying and exploring crucial topics and feelings. During this early self-exploration phase, the counselor must be sensitive to signs of client stress or resistance and try to judge whether these arise from lack of accurate response or from being too accurate too quickly. As the counselor moves the client beyond exploration to self-understanding and action, advanced skills become more necessary.

Primary empathy gets at relevant feelings and meanings that are actually stated; the skill of *advanced empathy* gets at feelings and meanings that are hidden or beyond the immediate reach of the client (Egan, 1994). The most basic form of advanced empathy is to give expression and understanding to what the client has only implied. It challenges the client to take a deeper look at self.

Advanced empathy includes the identification of themes presented by the client. Feeling, behavioral, experiential, or combined themes may occur. Once the counselor recognizes the themes, the task is to communicate the relevant ones to the client in a way that will be heard and understood. The themes must be based solidly on an accurate understanding of the client's feelings, experiences, and behaviors and communicated as concretely as possible, using the client's experiences and communication style.

The act of bringing together, in a summarizing way, relevant core material that the client has presented in only a fragmented way is part of advanced empathy. The counselor helps the client fill in the missing links in the information. When it becomes apparent that two aspects of client information are closely linked, this information should be shared, but the counselor must guard against premature speculation or unfounded linkages.

As the counselor explores the deeper, underlying meaning of an experience of the client, the skill of reflecting meaning can be used. It provides a way for the client to develop a new worldview and interpret old situations or information in new ways. Because information is always subject to individual interpretation (Gelatt, 1989), the counselor needs to reframe the situation, belief, or experience to help the client view it from a different perspective and also check out that the interpretation is correct.

Advanced empathy gets at more critical, deeper, and delicate issues and, therefore, puts the client under additional stress. To avoid overwhelming the client and evoking resistances, the counselor's empathetic responses should be tentative and cautious. Leads such as "From what you have said . . . ," "Could it be that . . . ?" or "It seems as if . . . ," may be most helpful.

Counselors may find it helpful to reflect back to clients what they see as the meaning of an experience.

Lisa: Finding out about his kids was somewhat of a surprise.

Counselor: It seems as if finding out about the children didn't matter as long as the two of you were together. Could it be that now the accumulation of surprises and your growing feelings of uneasiness are making you wonder about the relationship?

Self-Disclosure

Hendrick (1988) and Peca-Baker and Friedlander (1987) have found that clients want to have information about their counselors. Sharing oneself can be a powerful intervention for making contact with clients, but it should not be an indiscriminate sharing of personal problems with clients (Egan, 1994).

Self-disclosure is defined as any information counselors convey about themselves to clients (Cormier & Cormier, 1991; Cozby, 1973). It can generate a more open, facilitative counseling atmosphere, encourage client talk and additional trust, and create a more equal relationship. In some instances, a self-disclosing counselor may be perceived as more caring than one who does not disclose. At times, counselor self-disclosure can present a model for clients to increase their own levels of disclosure about events and feelings (McCarthy, 1982).

The use of self-disclosure as a skill involves consideration of timing, goals, genuineness, and appropriateness. Effective self-disclosure does not add another burden to an already burdened client (Egan, 1994), and it should not distract the client from his or her own problems. The counselor must consider how the client will be able to benefit from the information shared.

Perhaps the most important type of self-disclosure is that which focuses on the relationship between you and your client. If you are having a difficult time listening to a client, for example, it could be useful to let them know that it is difficult. However, it helps to only describe your own feelings and reactions and not to judge the client. It may be fairly easy for the counselor to self-disclose, but making the disclosure relevant to the client is the important and more complex task (Ivey, 1994). The counselor's self-disclosure should be genuine and fairly close in mood and content to the client's experience. As a counselor, you must remember that self-disclosure is appropriate only when it is genuine, benefits the client, adds to client movement or understanding, and does not interfere with the counseling process or contribute to raised levels of client anxiety (Cormier & Cormier, 1991). For example,

Lisa: I can't believe I was so dumb and gullible.

Counselor: It seems like you shouldn't have been so trusting. I've found when I get in these situations that it is easy to beat myself up. I've learned instead to think of ways to be nice to myself.

How willing are you to engage in appropriate and relevant self-disclosure? You become vulnerable when you share your own experiences, feelings, and reactions, yet can you expect your clients to become vulnerable in front of you if you rarely show them anything of yourself? Good self-disclosure is a kind of sharing that clients can use to grow, and it lets them know how you're perceiving and experiencing them.

Most evidence indicates that a moderate amount of self-disclosure has more impact than too little or too much. Counselors who disclose very little risk being seen as aloof, weak, and role conscious (Egan, 1994), whereas the counselor who discloses too much may be seen as lacking in discretion, being untrustworthy (Levin & Gergen, 1969), seeming preoccupied (Cozby, 1973), or needing assistance.

Confrontation

Confrontation is a skill that is used when there are discrepancies, conflicts, or mixed messages being sent by the client. The mixed messages may occur between the verbal and nonverbal messages sent by the client or between two contradictory verbal messages. Egan (1975) describes confrontation as "the responsible unmasking of the discrepancies, distortions, games and smoke screens the client uses to hide both from self-understanding and from constructive behavioral change" (p. 158).

When confronting a client, the counselor must always exercise concern for the client's understanding of the challenge so that there will be client progress, not denial and flight. To do this effectively, the counselor must accurately reflect the situations. Using a tentative reflection is important, especially if it is early in the relationship. Consideration should also be given to the state of the client; an already distressed, confused, or disorganized client will not benefit from a confrontation. In fact, confrontation with such clients may add to their distress or confusion.

Lisa: I was really hurt when he told me that he hadn't filed for a divorce at all. All along I thought it had been done three years ago. . . . I just can't leave him.

Counselor: You're feeling really torn. You're not legally married to him, yet something is keeping you in the relationship.

Confrontation should be done with care and may be more effective if done gradually. A gradual confrontation will give the client time to assimilate information. Good counselor practice demands a careful balance between confrontation followed by support in the form of primary empathy, positive regard, and respect (Ivey, Ivey, & Simek-Downing, 1987).

Immediacy

The phenomenon of immediacy involves the counselor's sensitivity to the immediate situation and an understanding of what is occurring at the moment with clients (Pietrofesa, Hoffman, & Splete, 1984). It involves the ability to discuss directly and openly with another person what is happening in the "here and now" of an interpersonal relationship (Egan, 1994). This is sometimes referred to as "you–me" talk.

The use of immediacy combines the skills of confrontation and self-disclosure and requires the counselor to reveal feelings and/or challenge the client to deal more openly with his or her feelings. The purpose of immediacy responses is to help clients understand themselves more clearly, especially what is happening at that moment and how they are relating to the counselor in the session. As interviews move more to the present tense, the counselor's presence in the interview becomes more powerful and important (Ivey, 1994), and the counselor is modeling a kind of behavior that clients can use to become more effective in all their relationships.

Counselors usually know what is happening in a session, but do not always act on it. Acting on what is happening at the moment is part of the phenomenon of immediacy. When either counselor or client has unverbalized thoughts or feelings that seem to be getting in the way of progress, the counselor should bring it up for discussion.

Lisa: I'm not exactly certain how to tell you about all the other messes in my life.

Counselor: It sounds like something is getting in the way of your trusting me to understand everything that's happened in your life.

There are many areas or issues in which the skill of immediacy might be used: trust, differences in style, directionless sessions, dependency, counterdependency, and attraction are areas where "you–me" talk might pay off (Egan, 1994). Other areas might include concern for the client's welfare, lack of follow-through on homework, and the client's questioning of the value of counseling.

Carkhuff (1969) suggests that the counselor ask, during the course of the interview, "What is the client trying to tell me that he or she can't tell me directly?" The answer lies buried in the verbal and nonverbal behavior of the client. The skilled helper can uncover it and make it an "immediacy" topic.

In considering whether to use immediacy, the counselor should decide whether it is appropriate to focus the relationship on here-and-now concerns at this specific time. If so, then counselor-initiated leads will focus on the identification and communication of feelings. The counselor must seriously consider word choice; as in many other cases, a tentative statement may be more inviting of a client response.

Action Skills

The goal of counseling is to have a client come away from the process changed. This growth or change often entails the counselor's and client's working together on an action plan appropriate to the client's stated goals. These action plans should grow out of the counseling work itself and be based in part on the theoretical orientation of the counselor and what is considered the standards for practice in the profession. For instance, a behaviorally oriented counselor will be more inclined to use behavioral contracts and/or systematic desensitization. A transactional analysis therapist, in contrast, will focus on such concepts as ego states, game playing, and life scripts (Gladding, 1996).

It is important for the counselor to remember that the theoretical orientation is secondary to the development of effective core helping skills. These skills seem to be shared by all effective helpers and really address the quality of the interaction between the counselor and the client. With respect to the action phase, for example, Egan (1994) has suggested that the counselor must have skills to help clients choose effective strategies for change and maintain action-based change programs.

Termination Skills

The ending of a helping relationship can be either one of the most gratifying or one of the most difficult and frustrating aspects of the relationship. Termination may occur either by mutual agreement or prematurely. When counselor and client agree that the goals of counseling have been accomplished, they may mutually agree that it is time to terminate. Sadness about parting and some client anxiety may be expected, but by exploring and sharing such feelings, each person is more likely to leave with a sense of growth and accomplishment because goals have been achieved. It is important to leave time to discuss feelings about ending and, for a smooth termination, it is important for both individuals to know when the last session will occur (Meier & Davis, 1993).

Premature termination may be initiated by either the counselor or the client. When counselor-initiated termination occurs, the client needs to be informed as early as possible or reminded that only a limited number of sessions are available. Premature termination occurs most frequently in schools and agencies with session limits. On rare occasions, it may occur because of irreconcilable differences or perceived lack of commitment by the client. When the counselor does terminate the sessions, the reasons must be specified to the client. Most counselors agree that early termination by the counselor violates the premise that clients are in charge of solving their own problems, and early termination may lead to feelings of personal rejection in the client. These feelings should be dealt with before termination is complete. Referring the individual to another agency and/or keeping the door open for future sessions are sometimes helpful.

When the sessions are prematurely terminated by the client, the counselor should try to explore with the client the reasons for termination. Letting clients know that they are in charge of the decision to return in the future can be beneficial, as is the exploration of possible referral resources.

When termination is mutual or initiated by the counselor, several steps can benefit the outcome of the relationship (Ward, 1984). There should be discussion and evaluation of the goals that have already been reached. Closure issues and feelings need to be discussed, and clients need to be prepared for similar happenings in the future. Clients should be prepared for self-reliance and continued self-help. Finally, in the last session discussion is likely to be lighter and more social. Okun (1992), for example, often shares a poster with the client that symbolizes the significance of the client's journey. The termination process should not focus on the generation of new problems or issues but should bring appreciation of the growth that has already occurred.

Summary

The helping relationship consists of three relatively distinct phases: building the relationship, challenging the client to find ways to change, and facilitating positive action. Effective counselors have a number of similar characteristics, including high levels of self-awareness, empathy, genuineness, and respect for others, and an ability to use themselves as vehicles of change.

Effective counselors use attending skills (eye contact, body language, and vocal tone) and basic listening skills (client observation, encouraging, paraphrasing, summarizing, reflection of feeling, and open/closed questions) throughout the helping relationship. Counselor self-attending skills emphasize the importance of the person of the counselor in mediating the communications skills necessary in the helping relationship.

Counselors also need primary and advanced empathy skills as well as the challenging skills of confrontation, self-disclosure, and immediacy. These skills deepen the helping relationship and move the client toward therapeutic change. Counselor action skills facilitate behavioral change around the client's stated goals for counseling. Finally, termination skills are needed to bring closure to, and end, the helping relationship.

References

Bandler, R., & Grindler, J. (1979). Frogs into princes. Moab, UT: Real People Press.

Barak, A., Shapira, G., & Fisher, W. A. (1988). Effects of verbal and vocal cues of counselor self-confidence on clients' perceptions. *Counselor Education and Supervision, 27,* 355–367.

Berger, R. L., McBreen, J. T., & Rifkin, M. J. (1996). *Human behavior: A perspective for the helping professions.* White Plains, NY: Longham.

Brammer, L. M. (1993). *The helping relationship: Process and skills.* Boston: Allyn and Bacon.

Carkhuff, R. (1969). *Helping and human relations* (Vols. 1, 2). New York: Holt, Rinehart & Winston.

Carkhuff, R. R. (1986). *The art of helping* (5th ed.). Amherst, MA: Human Resources Development Press.

Carkhuff, R., & Berenson, B. (1967). *Beyond counseling and therapy.* New York: Holt, Rinehart & Winston.

Combs, A. W. (1986). What makes a good helper? A person-centered approach. *Person-centered Review, 1*(1), 51–61.

Cormier, W. H., & Cormier, L. S. (1991). *Interviewing strategies for helpers: Fundamental skills and cognitive behavioral interventions.* Pacific Grove, CA: Brooks/Cole.

Cozby, P. C. (1973). Self-disclosure: A literature review. *Psychological Bulletin, 79,* 73–91.

Driscoli, M. S., Newman, D. L., & Seals, J. M. (1988). The effects of touch on perception of counselors. *Counselor Education and Supervision, 27,* 344–354.

Egan, G. (1975). *The skilled helper.* Pacific Grove, CA: Brooks/Cole.

Egan, G. (1994). *The skilled helper: A problem-management approach to helping.* Pacific Grove, CA: Brooks/Cole.

Evans, D. R., Hearn, M. T., Uhlemann, M. R., & Ivey, A. E. (1993). *Essential interviewing: A programmed approach to effective communication.* Pacific Grove, CA: Brooks/Cole.

Gelatt, H. B. (1989). Positive uncertainty: A decision-making framework for counseling. *Journal of Counseling Psychology, 36*(2), 252–256.

Gladding, S. T. (1996). *Counseling: A comprehensive profession.* Englewood Cliffs, NJ: Prentice Hall.

Hendrick, S. S. (1988). Counselor self-disclosure. *Journal of Counseling and Development, 66*(9), 419–424.

Ivey, A. E. (1994). *Intentional interviewing and counseling: Facilitating client development in a multicultural society.* Pacific Grove, CA: Brooks/Cole.

Ivey, A. E., Ivey, M. B., & Simek-Downing, L. (1987). *Counseling and psychotherapy: Integrating skills, theory and practice.* Englewood Cliffs, NJ: Prentice Hall.

Ivey, A. E., & Simek-Downing, L. (1980). *Counseling and Psychotherapy*. Englewood Cliffs, NJ: Prentice Hall.

Keller, D. (1984). *Humor as therapy*. Wauwatosa, WI: Med-Psych Publications.

Levin, F. M., & Gergen, K. J. (1969). Revealingness, ingratiation, and the disclosure of self. *Proceedings of the 77th Annual Convention of the American Psychological Association, 4*(1), 447–448.

McCarthy, P. (1982). Differential effects of counselor self-referent responses and counselor status. *Journal of Counseling Psychology, 29,* 125–311.

Meier, S. T., & Davis, S. R. (1993). *The elements of counseling*. Pacific Grove, CA: Brooks/Cole.

Okun, B. F. (1992). *Effective helping* (4th ed.). Pacific Grove, CA: Brooks/Cole.

Patterson, C. H. (1974). *Relationship counseling and psychotherapy*. New York: Harper & Row.

Peca-Baker, T. A., & Friedlander, M. L. (1987). Effects on role expectations on clients' perceptions of disclosing and nondisclosing counselors. *Journal of Counseling and Development, 66*(2), 78–81.

Pietrofesa, J. J., Hoffman, A., & Splete, H. H. (1984). *Counseling: An introduction*. Boston: Houghton Mifflin.

Pietrofesa, J. J., Hoffman, A., Splete, H. H., & Pinto, D. V. (1978). *Counseling: Theory, research & practice*. Chicago: Rand McNally.

Rogers, C. R. (1957). The necessary and sufficient conditions of therapeutic personality change. *Journal of Counseling Psychology, 21,* 95–103.

Rogers, C. R. (1958). The characteristics of a helping relationship. *Personnel and Guidance Journal, 37,* 6–16.

Rogers, C. R. (1961). *On becoming a person*. Boston: Houghton Mifflin.

Rogers, C. R. (1967). *The therapeutic relationship and its impact*. Madison: The University of Wisconsin Press.

Scherer, K. R. (1986). Vocal expression: A review and model for future research. *Psychological Bulletin, 99,* 143–165.

Sexton, T. L., & Whiston, S. C. (1994). The status of the counseling relationship: An empirical review, theoretical implications, and research directions. *Counseling Psychologist, 22*(1), 6–78.

Shulman, L. (1979). *The skills of helping individuals and groups*. Itasca, IL: Peacock.

Strong, S. R. (1968). Counseling: An interpersonal influence process. *Journal of Counseling Psychology, 15,* 215–224.

Suiter, R. L., & Goodyear, R. K. (1985). Male and female counselor and client perceptions of four levels of counselor touch. *Journal of Counseling Psychology, 32*(4), 645–648.

Ward, D. E. (1984). Termination of individual counseling: Concepts and strategies. *Journal of Counseling Psychology, 63*(1), 21–26.

Ethical and Legal Considerations in Counseling

What Beginning Counselors Should Know

Sharon E. Robinson Kurpius, Ph.D.

Here you are, beginning your coursework in counseling as a new master's-degree student. If you are like most of your classmates, you are feeling overwhelmed with all you have to learn. Although excited about your first counseling session, you realize there is much you do not know about making good professional decisions that are both ethical and legal while being helpful to your clients. The purpose of this chapter is to introduce you to the basic ethical concepts and legal guidelines that will influence your behavior as counselors. With that goal in mind, I hope to challenge your preconceived notions regarding right and wrong, moral and immoral, ethical and unethical, and legal and illegal.

First, you need to understand what the word *ethical* means. According to the *Webster's New World Dictionary* (1979), it means "1. having to do with ethics; or of conforming to moral standards, 2. conforming to professional standards of conduct" (p. 210). Notice that these two definitions are distinctly different. The first is a personal phenomenon—that is, what is moral is decided most often by individuals. In contrast, the second encompasses behaviors that are considered ethical by some professional group. In the mental health profession, that group could be the American Counseling Association (ACA), the American Psychological Association (APA), the National Academy of Certified Clinical Mental Health Counselors (NACCMHC), or the National Board of Certified Counselors (NBCC), just to name a few. In this chapter, the discussion of ethics will be based on the guidelines provided by the ACA *Code of Ethics and Standards of Practice* (1995) and by the APA *Ethical Principles of Psychologists and Code of Conduct* (1992).

This chapter is organized into four sections, starting with an exploration of why individuals decide to enter the counseling profession. Then the discussion shifts to counselor competence, client rights, and, finally, the real world.

Choosing to Be a Counselor: An Ethical Beginning

If I asked you, "Why do you want to be a counselor?" what would you tell me? In my experience as an instructor in introductory counseling courses, I have found that there are three primary reasons students want to become counselors. First, they say that, without any concern or benefit for themselves, they want to help others grow and become "healthier." These people see themselves as very altruistic. Second, some need counseling themselves and see this as a very safe way to get help. Of course, they do not realize that students in counseling are expected to do a significant amount of self-examination and introspection regarding who they are and what they can offer clients. This process often causes them stress and discomfort, which may be a manifestation of their denial that they should seek personal counseling. Last, some just want to explore the professional arena of counseling. People who give this last reason are usually very social, outgoing, and like to work with people in a way that is helpful while allowing them to earn a living themselves. This third group causes me little concern; however, I am often concerned about individuals who fit the first two categories.

Throughout your counseling coursework, you will hear and read about the personhood of the counselor and how this is integral to the effectiveness of the counseling process. In 1972, Max Hammer wrote a classic chapter entitled "To Students Interested in Becoming Psychotherapists." According to Hammer, "the kind of person that the therapist is will be the primary determinant of whether or not there will be therapeutic results" (p. 3). He goes on to discuss the most important quality that a prospective counselor should have; that is, the

> capacity to be sensitive enough to clearly and deeply hear and understand in the patient those rejected truths that have become disassociated from himself and have caused his disintegration and which, when heard and understood by the patient, lead to his reintegration, growth and liberation from his conflicts, fears and tensions. (p. 4)

In order to hear and understand the client, the counselor must be psychologically healthy, which Hammer defines as being nondefensive and totally open to the moment-to-moment reality of one's self.

To be fully attuned to a client, the counselor must be in a state of "quiet mind" (Hammer, 1972, p. 7). The quiet mind exists when there is no deliberate thought or mental activity that is attempting to control or evaluate what is occurring in the counseling session, but rather "one just permits thought to come to awareness and watches it without any kind of interference" (p. 7). Hammer refers to this process as a state of creative understanding, during which the "soft whisperings of unconscious thoughts, feelings or impulses" (p. 7) are able to be heard. According to

Hammer, the goal of counseling is for the client to come to his or her own creative understanding, which will result in self-healing.

What prevents a counselor from being able to bring a quiet mind to the counseling session? I agree with Hammer (1972) when he suggested that it is the counselor who gets in his or her own way and that the client "probably cannot grow beyond the level of emotional health and maturity achieved by his [her] therapist" (p. 210). This may be a hard pill for many beginning counselors to swallow. Even more difficult to accept would be Hammer's statement that

> *to be really effective, the therapist needs to know from* personal experience *what the "path" is that leads from internal conflict and contradiction to liberation. If you do not know how to liberate yourself from an internal conflict, fear or pain, then you are not in a position to help others do it either. . . . What right does the therapist have to ask the patient to face his rejected truths and anxiety and to take risks in terms of exposing himself and making himself vulnerable, if the therapist is not willing or able to do so? (p. 12)*

These are the central personal, professional, and ethical issues that all beginning counselors must ponder and answer for themselves. This message is echoed by Corey, Corey, and Callanan (1988) who stated that a willingness to serve as models for clients by *not* asking them to do what you are not willing to do is one of the essential characteristics of effective counselors.

Both Hammer (1972) and Corey et al. (1988) discuss motivations for entering the helping profession. Hammer believed that people often had the wrong reasons, such as the need to be dominant, to be needed and loved, to be a voyeur of others' lives, to be an omnipotent healer, to escape one's own life, and to cure oneself by curing others. Corey et al. indicated that the therapeutic process can be blocked when therapists use the client to fulfill their own needs, to nurture others, to feel powerful or important, or to win acceptance, admiration, respect, or awe. Acknowledging that therapists have their own needs, Corey et al. cautioned that "therapists should be clearly aware of the danger of working primarily to be appreciated by others instead of working toward the best interests of their clients" (p. 31).

In each of these instances, the counselor is primarily meeting his or her own needs, and this is unethical. ACA's (1995) *Code of Ethics* specifically states in section A.5, "Personal Needs and Values," that "In the counseling relationship, counselors are aware of the intimacy and responsibilities inherent in the counseling relationship, maintain respect for clients, and avoid actions that seek to meet their personal needs at the expense of clients." It also states that "counselors refrain from offering or accepting professional services when their physical, mental or emotional problems are likely to harm a client or others." The APA *Ethical Principles* (1992) notes that "Psychologists strive to be aware of their own belief systems, values, needs, and limitations and the effect of these on their work" (Principle B, "Integrity").

An excellent example of the counselor meeting his or her own needs at the expense of a client is the counselor who has a dual relationship with a client (Pope,

1994). Dual relationships occur when there is a professional relationship and a secondary one, which can be of a financial, social, business, friendship, or intimate nature. The most flagrant dual relationship is when the counselor becomes sexually involved with the client. All codes for ethical professional behavior stress that sexual intimacies with clients are unethical:

> *Counselors must not engage in any type of sexual intimacies with current clients and must not engage in sexual intimacies with former clients within a minimum of two years after terminating the counseling relationship. Counselors who engage in such a relationship after two years following termination have the responsibility to thoroughly examine and document that such relations did not have an exploitive nature. (ACA, 1995, section A.7, "Sexual Intimacies with Clients")*

Still, this is the most consistently violated ethical standard among psychologists and the second most frequently claimed violation against counselors (Herlihy & Corey, 1992). When sexual contact becomes part of a therapeutic relationship, the expectation of trust that is essential to the process of therapy is violated (Thoreson, Shaughnessy, Heppner, & Cook, 1993). As Robinson Kurpius (1995) pointed out, regardless of the reason for becoming involved intimately with a client, it is always unethical and often illegal. A counselor who is emotionally healthy does not need to engage in sexual relations with a client nor meet any other personal needs through the counseling relationship.

Based on the writings just discussed and on various ethical guidelines, I would say to all beginning counselor trainees (and to all of us who are already active in the profession), your first ethical responsibility is to be as emotionally healthy as possible, to be continually aware of how your own "unfinished business" could potentially influence your attempts to be helpful to others, and to seek professional help as soon as you are aware that some aspect of your own life may be infringing on your work as a counselor. Your competence is limited by your own self-awareness and psychological health and maturity (Robinson, 1988). If you want to hide anything you are doing in therapy, you probably need to seek immediate supervision or consultation and stop the behaviors that must be hidden (Weiner & Robinson Kurpius, 1995).

Counselor Competence

The above discussion naturally brings us to the topic of counselor competence. The notion that it is unethical to practice beyond the limits of one's competence is widely accepted. According to Robinson Kurpius and Gross (in press), competence can be broken down into five basic aspects:

> *(l) accurate representation of professional qualifications; (2) professional growth through involvement in continuing education; (3) providing only those services for which qualified; (4) maintaining accurate knowledge and expertise in special-*

> *ized areas; and (5) seeking assistance in solving personal issues which could impede effectiveness or lead to inadequate professional services or harm to a client.*

To these I would add your responsibility as counselors-in-training to learn basic skills, to integrate academic study with supervised practice, to develop self-understanding, to seek continual evaluation and feedback, and to become intimately familiar with ethical codes of practice (ACA, 1995, section C, "Professional Responsibility") and relevant laws influencing our profession.

It is your professors' responsibility not only to foster your learning of the preceding but also to be aware of the "academic and personal limitations of students and supervisees that might impede performance" and to "assist students and supervisees in securing remedial assistance when needed, and dismiss from the training program supervisees who are unable to provide competent service due to academic or personal limitations" (ACA, 1995, section F.2, "Counselor Education and Training Programs"). While you are a student, your competence is a shared responsibility between you and your training program. However, after you graduate and enter the professional world, it is your responsibility to remain competent.

One of your primary responsibilities is to recognize your strengths and weaknesses and to offer services only in the areas of your strengths. Defining your areas of competence occurs through both subjective and external evaluation. The subjective component usually involves critical and honest self-examination. Calling this subjective component an internal perspective, Robinson Kurpius and Gross (in press) caution counselors to do everything possible to gain the skills and knowledge basic to the profession. Counselors need to stretch their skills continually by reading and attending to new and developing trends, through attaining postgraduate education, and through attending seminars and workshops aimed at sharpening and increasing both knowledge and skill bases. All counselors must take full responsibility for adhering to professional codes of conduct that address the concepts of proper representation of professional qualifications, for providing only those services for which they have been trained, and for seeking assistance with personal issues that are barriers to providing effective service.

The objective component typically includes completing the appropriate graduate training and taking professional and state credentialing exams in order to solidify your identification with the profession and to verify that you have achieved some level of competence as demonstrated by passing an exam. Some of the exams you may choose to take are the National Board for Certified Counselors (NBCC) exam or the National Academy of Certified Clinical Mental Health Counselors (NACCMHC) exam. The NBCC is the exam most used by states to license counselors. It tests the following content areas: counseling theory, human growth and development, social and cultural foundations, group dynamics, helping relationships, career development, appraisal of individuals, research and evaluation, and professional orientation. Although taking an exam might indicate that you have a minimum knowledge base in the profession, it is not enough. The ACA *Code of Ethics* (1995) clearly states that "Counselors must practice only within the boundaries of their competence, based on their education, training, supervised experience, state and national professional credentials, and appropriate professional experience" (section C.2.a, "Boundaries of Competence"). The APA Ethical Principles (1992) makes a similar statement and adds that

> *Psychologists provide services, teach, or conduct research in new areas or involving new techniques only after first undertaking appropriate study, training, supervision, and/or consultation from persons who are competent in those areas or techniques. (Principle 1.04b, "Boundaries of Competence")*

Although the APA requires training *or* experience, I would prefer to err on the conservative side and stress that both training *and* experience are essential for you to claim competence.

The ethical standards are quite clear regarding what you should do if you are not competent to treat a certain client problem. Your first and best choice is to make an appropriate referral. If there is no one to whom you can refer (which would be an exception rather than a common occurrence), then it is incumbent on you to educate yourself through reading books and journal articles on the presenting problem *and* to seek supervision of your work with the client. You are responsible for the welfare of the client; therefore, it is your professional duty to obtain for that client the best services possible—be it from you or from a professional colleague. Clients are not subjects for your trial-and-error learning but deserve the best professional care possible.

To provide this best possible care, continuing education is a never ending requirement. As one of my doctoral graduates told me, "When I decided that I was really going to be a psychologist and do therapy, I attended every training seminar, conference, and workshop I could so that I could be really good at what I do." Unlike so many graduates, be it from a master's or a doctoral program, he did not perceive himself as a finished product on receipt of his degree. In order to become truly proficient at what he had chosen to do, he had to seek all the advanced didactic and experiential input he could. Only by continually growing himself is he comfortable offering his services to others.

One area of training for which students are often not adequately prepared is diagnosis. Typically, insurance companies will not pay for service unless the client has a DSM-IV diagnosis. The ability to diagnose has been the subject of debate and court proceedings. In Arizona, a social worker diagnosed a client as paranoid, a diagnosis that was confirmed by a consulting psychiatrist (*Cooke v. Berlin,* 1987). When the client later killed a man and was diagnosed as having atypical psychosis, the social worker was sued by the victim's widow. Although the case was eventually settled out of court, it left important questions unanswered. What is the appropriate scope of practice of various mental health professionals? Had there been competent diagnosis, would there have been an assessment of dangerousness resulting in a duty to warn? When can one professional, especially an unlicensed one, provide information to another without the risk of malpractice? These questions all center on knowing the limits of one's competence and behaving within the boundaries of professional training and experience.

A final area of professional competence I would like to discuss is ethically presenting your services and credentials to the public. Most codes of ethics warn professionals against making false claims regarding expertise and qualifications and hold the professional responsible for correcting misrepresentation of their qualifications by others (ACA, 1995, section C.4.a, "Credentials Claimed"). For example, if you are called "doctor" and you do not hold a doctoral degree in counseling or a related field, you must correct this misrepresentation immediately. In advertising services, counselors "may only advertise the highest degree earned which is counseling or a closely related field" (ACA, 1995, section C.3.a, "Accurate Advertising"). One cannot claim that one is a "candidate for" a degree. When trying to build a practice, client testimonials must be avoided, as well as implying unusual or one-of-a-kind abilities (Keith-Spiegel & Koocher, 1985). Although the ACA *Code of Ethics* (1995) does not mention use of media to advertise services, the APA *Principles* (1992) state that paid advertisement must be acknowledged as such (section 3.02e, "Statements by Others").

The Federal Trade Commission has granted considerable freedom for advertising as a result of the *Goldfarb v. Virginia State Bar* (1975) ruling. How and if you advertise your services will require you to weigh carefully what is legally permitted with what is acceptable ethically.

Regardless of the area of service being discussed, you are the first-line judge of your professional competence. Although credentialing bodies, professional organizations, and state legislatures may set standards for practice, you must be the most critical evaluator of your ability to provide service. This often becomes quite a challenge when one's living depends on having clients who will pay for service. Remaining ethical is not always the easy choice.

Client Rights

When clients enter a counseling relationship, they have a right to assume that you are competent. In addition, they have certain rights, known as client rights, as well as responsibilities. These rights have their foundation in the Bill of Rights, particularly the First and Fourth Amendments of the Constitution of the United States, which are freedom of religion, speech, and the press and right of petition and freedom from unreasonable searches and seizures, respectively. The concepts of confidentiality, privileged communication, and informed consent are based on the Fourth Amendment, which guarantees privacy. Privacy has been defined as "the freedom of individuals to choose for themselves the time and the circumstances under which and the extent to which their beliefs, behaviors, and opinions are to be shared or withheld from others" (Siegel, 1979, p. 251, cited in Corey et al., 1988).

Confidentiality and Privileged Communications

The concept of privacy is the foundation for the client's legal right to privileged communication and the counselor's responsibility to hold counseling communications confidential. Confidentiality is a professional concept. It is so important that both the APA (1992) *Ethical Principles* and the ACA (1995) *Code of Ethics* each devote an entire section to confidentiality. However, a client's communications are not confidential in a court of law unless the mental health professional is legally certified or licensed in the state in which he or she practices. Most states grant the clients of state-certified or -licensed mental health professionals (such as psychologists, professional counselors, and marriage and family therapists) the right of privileged communications. This means that clients, not counselors, have control over who has access to what they have said in therapy and protects them from having their communication disclosed in a court of law.

In order for communication to be privileged, four conditions must be met. First, the communication must originate in confidence that it will not be disclosed. Second, confidentiality must be essential to the full and satisfactory maintenance of the relationship. Third, in the opinion of the greater community, the relationship must be one that should be sedulously fostered. Finally, injury to the relationship by disclosure of the communication must be greater than the benefit gained by the correct disposal of litigation regarding the information (Schwitzgebel & Schwitzgebel, 1980). If as a counselor you can claim these four conditions, your clients' communications are not only confidential, but they are also privileged and, therefore, are protected from being disclosed in a court of law. One must remember, however, that there is always a balance between a client's right to privacy and society's need to know.

Despite the importance given to confidentiality and privileged communication, Pope, Tabachnick, and Keith-Spiegel (1987) reported that 62 percent of psychologists in a national survey indicated that they had unintentionally violated a client's confidentiality and 21 percent had intentionally violated a client's confidentiality. These alarming statistics suggest that mental health professionals are at risk for violating this core ethical principle. Therefore, all mental health professionals need to be aware of the professional standards regarding confidentiality and of their state laws governing privileged communication. For example, in most states, if the mental health professional's secretary breaches a client's confidentiality, the professional is guilty of breaching the confidentiality. Secretaries are considered extensions of the certified or licensed mental health professionals to which they are accountable.

There are three global issues that do require one to breach confidentiality. In cases of minors, we have both a legal and ethical responsibility to protect them from "future harm of continued abuse or neglect and to protect children who are insufficiently autonomous to act on their own behalf" (Sattler, 1990, p. 105). Minors are usually considered children under the age of 18; however, some states recognize emancipated minors who are 16 or older. Counselors should know their state laws that apply to minors and breaching confidentiality. Every state has passed a law mandating the reporting of child abuse. Regardless of the counselor's personal feelings about helping a client to overcome his or her abusive behavior, the abuse must be reported. Society has deemed that knowing of and stopping the child abuse outweigh the abuser's right to privacy.

Many states also require that counselors report instances of abuse, neglect, or exploitation of incapacitated adults. In Arizona, incapacitated is defined as "an impairment by reason of mental illness, mental deficiency, mental disorder, physical illness or disability, advanced age, chronic use of drugs, chronic intoxication, other cause to the extent that the person lacks sufficient understanding or capacity to make or communicate responsible decisions" (Arizona Revised Statute 46–451).

Finally, privilege is automatically waived when a client presents a "clear and imminent danger" to self or others (ACA, 1995, section B.1.c, "Exceptions"). A well-known court case that established such mandatory disclosure was *Tarasoff v. Board of Regents of the University of California* (1974, 1976). In this case, a young graduate student, Poddar, from India had been working with a university psychologist regarding his depression and anger resulting from being rejected by a girl, Tatiana Tarasoff. He told the psychologist about his intent to buy a gun. The psychologist notified the campus police both verbally and in writing about his concerns that Poddar was dangerous and should be taken to a community mental health facility. The police interviewed Poddar and released him from custody. The psychologist's supervising psychiatrist decided that the letter to the police and selected case notes should be destroyed. Shortly thereafter, Poddar shot and stabbed Tarasoff to death. The California Supreme Court held that

> *Once a therapist does in fact determine, or under applicable professional standards reasonably should have determined, that a patient poses a serious danger of violence to others, he bears a duty to exercise reasonable care to protect the foreseeable victims of that danger.* (Tarasoff, 1976)

This has been interpreted as the duty to protect or the duty to warn. In these instances, it is the counselor's overriding responsibility to protect an intended, identifiable victim from harm that could result from a client's actions.

Other instances when the privilege is typically lost include when a client introduces his or her mental condition as an element in a court case, when the mental stability of either spouse is introduced in a child custody case, when the counselor is working for the court such as in conducting a court-ordered examination, when the client is suing the counselor, and when the counselor believes that the client is in need of immediate hospitalization for a mental disorder. It is strongly suggested that at the onset of therapy, counselors inform clients about the limits of confidentiality and the specific instances when confidentiality must be breached. Clients can then make informed decisions about what they say in therapy.

Most recently, controversy has arisen over the right of confidentiality of AIDS patients who do not inform their sexual partners of their medical condition. The APA (1991) has taken a leadership role in this area, and at the 1991 annual meeting the Council of Representatives passed the following resolutions:

1. A legal duty to protect third parties from HIV infection should not be imposed.
2. If, however, specific legislation is considered, then it should permit disclosure only when the provider knows of an identifiable third party who the provider has a compelling reason to believe is at significant risk for infection; the provider has a reasonable belief that the third party has no reason to suspect that he or she is at risk; and the client/patient has been urged to inform the third

party and has either refused or is considered unreliable in his or her willingness to notify the third party.

3. If such legislation is adopted, it should include immunity from civil and criminal liability for providers who, in good faith, make decisions to disclose or not to disclose information about HIV infection to third parties.

This resolution provides concrete guidelines for breaching the confidentiality of clients with AIDS. "Unless there is an identifiable victim and the client refuses to behave in a manner that protects this person, the covenant of confidentiality should not be broken" (Robinson Kurpius, 1995, p. 7).

The discussion thus far has focused on confidentiality regarding verbal communications in therapy. Counselors must also be concerned about confidentiality of client records. Snider (1987) makes some very practical and useful suggestions for protecting written material such as case notes and test data. He stresses that the absolute minimum storage is a locked file cabinet—not just a locked office door. If a mistake is made while writing case notes, a single line should be drawn through the written text and initialed and dated by the counselor. Text should never be erased or whited out. Snider also cautions against selling client records to another professional when one retires or leaves his or her practice. Both APA and ACA ethical guidelines indicate that the professional must get consent from a client prior to disclosing or transferring their records. When clients give such consent, they should be informed about what exact information is being released, to whom, for what purpose, and time period for which the signed consent for release is valid (Robinson Kurpius, 1995).

It would be remiss not to discuss subpoenas and how counselors should respond to them in an attempt to protect the client's confidentiality. Regardless of the type of subpoena received—the typical subpoena, which requires your presence at court or a deposition, or a subpoena duces tecum, which requires you to bring your records with you—you should initially claim the privilege for your client (Schwitzgebel & Schwitzgebel, 1980). This forces the court or your client's attorney to require you to breach confidentiality. You then have the option of refusing to testify or to produce your records, in which case you will most likely be ruled in contempt and have to go to jail. In these rare instances, you need to find a personally acceptable balance among what the law requires, what is ethically appropriate, and what you find to be morally correct. Again, this is a personal decision that only you can make since you will be the one experiencing the consequences of your decision.

Informed Consent

This brings us to a discussion of informed consent. According to Everstine et al., (1980), three elements must be present for informed consent to be legal. The first, *competence*, requires that the person granting the consent is able to engage in rational thought to a sufficient degree to make competent decisions about his or her life. Minors cannot give informed consent, and consent must be sought from their parents or legal guardian. Minors give informed assent. The second element, being *informed,* requires that the individual is given the relevant information about the procedures to be performed in a language that he or she can understand. The last element, *voluntariness,* requires that the consent is given freely by the client. All three elements must be present for consent to be informed.

The ACA (1995) *Code of Ethics* is very specific with respect to what should be disclosed to clients in order for them to give informed consent:

> *When counseling is initiated, and throughout the counseling process as necessary, counselors inform clients of the purposes, goals, techniques, procedures, limitations, potential risks and benefits of services to be performed, and other pertinent information. Counselors take steps to ensure that clients understand the implications of diagnosis, the intended use of tests and reports, fees, and billing arrangements. Clients have the right to expect confidentiality and be provided with an explanation of its limitations, including supervision and/or treatment team professionals; to obtain clear information about the case records; to participate in the ongoing counseling plans; and to refuse any recommended services and be advised on the consequences of such refusal. (Section A.3.a, "Disclosure to Clients")*

The APA (1992) *Ethical Principles* requires a fourth element—that the "consent has been appropriately documented" (section 4.02, "Informed Consent to Therapy").

If you are asked by a client to disclose to a third party information revealed in therapy, have the client sign an informed consent form before making any disclosure. You may be surprised to learn that counselors are not even permitted to respond to inquiries about whether they are seeing a person in therapy—even the client's name and status in counseling are confidential, unless the client has granted permission for this information to be released.

One exception is when the client is paying for your services through an insurance company. This automatically grants the insurance company limited access to information regarding the client. The client needs to be made aware of the parameters of the information that will be shared with the insurance company prior to beginning therapy. Again, it is evident how important it is to have potential clients sign an informed consent form before they become clients.

Right to Treatment

Having clients sign informed consent forms implies that they have a right to receive or refuse treatment. Many court cases have been based on the right-to-treatment issue. In the early 1970s, *Wyatt v. Stickney* (1974) was the first case in which the right to treatment was ruled a constitutionally protected right. The case was filed against the state of Alabama on behalf of mentally retarded institutionalized patients who were being kept confined under conditions of psychological and physical deprivation. There was one physician for every 2,000 patients, making adequate care impossible. The court ruled that involuntarily committed patients have a constitutional right to receive "such individual treatment as will give each of them a realistic opportunity to be cured or to improve." In addition, the court required the institution to have individualized treatment plans developed by qualified mental health professionals for each patient. Other rights that committed patients have are the right to their own clothing, to receive minimal pay for labor performed, to receive mail, to exercise several times per week, and to have an appropriate physical environment in which to live.

In *Rogers v. Orkin* (1980) and in *Rennie v. Klein* (1981), courts ruled that clients have the right to refuse treatment. In *Rogers*, the court ruled that the "power to produce ideas was fundamental to our cherished right to communicate." The court indicated that the right to refuse medication and seclusion was a Fourth Amendment right but cited several state interests that can overrule a person's right to this privacy: police power, the right of the state to protect others from harm; *parens patriae*, the duty of the state to prevent the patient's condition from deteriorating; and consideration of the financial costs of operating facilities that may result from extended hospitalization (Levenson, 1989). Rennie held that the right to refuse medication could only be overruled under due process, except in an emergency. All these court cases have provided us with parameters for client rights with respect to treatment issues. Counselors should be constantly alert to the legal issues surrounding this very important client right.

Client Welfare

All the preceding discussion rests on the premise that the counselor's primary obligation is to protect the welfare of the client. The Preamble to the APA (1992) *Ethical Principles* specifically states that it has "as its primary goal the welfare and protection of the individuals and groups with whom psychologists work." A similar statement is made by the ACA (1995) *Code of Ethics:* "The primary responsibility of counselors is to respect the dignity and to promote the welfare of clients" (section A.1.a, "Primary Responsibility"). Dual relationships, counselors' personal needs, and conflicts between employing institutions and client needs all influence client welfare. Dual relationships and counselor needs have already been discussed; attention now needs to be given to the third concern.

Employer conflict and client needs may vary drastically. For instance, suppose you work in a prison setting and an inmate tells you that he or she is using drugs, which is against all prison rules. What are you going to do? Or imagine that you are a school counselor and a 15-year-old tells you that he or she is using drugs. What is in the best interests of each of these clients? How will your behavior affect your relationship with each client, with your future clients, and your position within the institution? Similar conflicts may arise when you are employed by a business or industry and the needs of the employee client may not be in agreement with the goals of the business. To whom do you owe loyalty? To the employer who signs your paycheck, or to the employee client? These questions are not easy to answer, nor is there always one right answer. In cases such as these, you must decide what is ethical based on the most current ethical guidelines and what is right or wrong for you personally.

Thus far, the discussion has focused on individual clients. An additional set of guidelines comes into play when you are doing group work or working with a couple or family. In a group setting, special issues include qualifications of the group leader, informed consent when more than the group leader will be participating in therapy, the limits to confidentiality and to privileged communication when third parties are present in therapy, and understanding how individuals will be protected and their growth nurtured in a group situation. Unlike individual counseling, clients who want to be involved in a group experience need to be screened before being accepted into a group. This screening not only ensures that the client is appropriate for the group but also protects other group members from a potentially dysfunctional group member.

It is evident that client welfare, whether in individual therapy or in group work, rests squarely on the shoulders of the counselor. The counselor must be cognizant of the various aspects of the counseling relationship that can jeopardize the client's welfare and take the steps necessary to alleviate the situation. Robinson Kurpius and Gross (in press) offer several suggestions for safeguarding the welfare of each client:

1. Check to be sure that you are working in harmony with any other mental health professional also seeing your client.
2. Develop clear, written descriptions of what clients may expect with respect to therapeutic regime, testing and reports, recordkeeping, billing, scheduling, and emergencies.
3. Share your professional code of ethics with your clients, and prior to beginning therapy discuss the parameters of a therapeutic relationship.
4. Know your own limitations, and do not hesitate to use appropriate referral sources.
5. Be sure that the approaches and techniques used are appropriate for the client and that you have the necessary expertise for their use.
6. Consider all other possibilities before establishing a counseling relationship that could be considered a dual relationship.
7. Evaluate the client's ability to pay and when the payment of the usual fee would create a hardship. Either accept a reduced fee or assist the client in finding needed services at an affordable cost.
8. Objectively evaluate client progress and the therapeutic relationship to determine if it is consistently in the best interests of the client.

I would be remiss if I ended the discussion of client welfare without mentioning the problems that arise from our technologic society. In this age of computers, client confidentiality is continually at risk, because anyone sophisticated in computer programming can tap into insurance records, university records, and so forth. Testing by computer has become popular, and even the Educational Testing Service now offers college aptitude tests via computer. The question that must be raised, however, is "How secure are individual test results?" We must also ask ourselves whether computer testing and even computer interactive counseling are best for our clients. What about the all-important human element? Again, these questions are not easy to answer. Each of us must struggle with what we are told in the ethical guidelines, our own comfort level with the privacy afforded or not afforded by using computers, and how all this affects client welfare.

Client Rights—Summary

The rights of your clients are many and varied. Perhaps the best statement regarding client rights was prepared by the National Board of Certified Counselors in 1987. The NBCC listed the following client rights and responsibilities:

Consumer Rights

- Be informed of the qualification of your counselor's education experience, and professional counseling certification(s) and state licensure(s).
- Receive an explanation of services offered, your time commitments, and fee scales and billing policies prior to receipt of services.
- Have all that you say treated confidentially and be informed of any state laws placing limitations on confidentiality in the counseling relationship.
- Ask questions about the counseling techniques and strategies and be informed of your progress.
- Participate in setting goals and evaluating progress toward meeting them.
- Be informed of how to contact the counselor in an emergency situation.
- Request referral for a second opinion at any time.
- Request copies of records and reports to be used by other counseling professionals.
- Receive a copy of the code of ethics to which your counselor adheres.
- Contact the appropriate professional organization if you have doubts or complaints relative to the counselor's conduct.
- Terminate the counseling relationship at any time.

Consumer Responsibilities

- Set and keep appointments with your counselor. Let him or her know as soon as possible if you cannot keep an appointment.
- Pay your fees in accordance with the schedule you preestablished with the counselor.
- Help plan your goals.
- Follow through with agreed-on goals.
- Keep your counselor informed of your progress toward meeting your goals.
- Terminate your counseling relationship before entering into arrangements with another counselor.

Notice that the consumer/client responsibilities require the counselor to have provided the client with informed consent at the beginning of therapy. Also note that by the nature of their role, the client cannot behave unethically—only counselors can make that mistake.

Summary

Before you know it, you will be graduating and entering the professional world of counselors, fondly known as the "real world." If you are like most mental health professionals, you will quickly find yourself involved in situations in which you will be uncertain as to what is ethical and what is not. This is not unusual, and the best advice I can give you is to know the ethical guidelines and to consult with colleagues, professional ethics committees, and your ethics professor.

Some situations that typically cause confusion, according to research by Pope et al. (1987), include performing forensic work for a contingency fee; accepting goods (rather than money) as payment; earning a salary that is a percentage of client fees; avoiding certain clients for fear of being sued (very common now with adult survivors of childhood sexual abuse); counseling a close relative or friend of a current client; sending holiday greeting cards to your clients; giving personal advice on the radio or television; engaging in a sexual fantasy about a client; limiting treatment notes to name, date, and fee; inviting clients to an office open house; and allowing a client to run up a large, unpaid bill. From the information provided in this chapter, you should now have some idea about the ethical approach to each of these. But often the ethical answer is not crystal clear, and surrounding circumstances need to be considered.

Robinson and Gross (1989) surveyed 500 members of the American Mental Health Counselor's Association and found that those who had not had a course in ethics had a particularly difficult time recommending ethical behaviors in response to a series of case vignettes. As a result, Robinson and Gross strongly recommended increased graduate-level education focusing on professional ethics. Just knowing the codes is not enough; students also need experience applying the ethical guidelines to case scenarios and need to discuss the moral reasoning behind their decision making.

More and more clients are suing their counselors and psychologists for malpractice. Insurance rates for mental health professionals are soaring, and insurance companies often want to settle out of court rather than bear the costs of fighting to prove your innocence. This may leave you in a vulnerable position. Your best defense is to behave as ethically as possible while doing everything in your power to promote the best interests of your client.

Most of you have entered this profession in order to help others while earning a living for yourself. For me, counseling is a noble profession, especially if you give your best to each of your clients by being aware of when you are burned out, stressed, or just plain tired and by limiting your contact with clients when your personal problems could interfere with the quality of your help. If you keep the ethical codes in mind at all times; strive to be as mentally, emotionally, spiritually, and physically healthy as possible; obtain a thorough graduate education that emphasizes both knowledge and practice; and seek advanced training and supervision when you are in the "real world," then you should be a benefit to your clients and to your profession. With those last tidbits of advice, I welcome you to your journey and evolution as a counselor.

References

American Counseling Association (ACA). (1995). *Code of ethics and standards of practice.* Alexandria, VA: Author.

American Psychological Association (APA). (1991). APA Council of Representatives adopts new AIDS policies. *Psychology and AIDS Exchange, 7,* 1.

American Psychological Association. (APA). (1992). *Ethical principles of psychologists and Code of Conduct.* Washington, DC: Author. Arizona Revised Statute 46–451.

Cooke v. Berlin, ___Ariz.___, 735 P.2d 830 (App. 1987).

Corey, G., Corey, M. S., & Callanan, P. (1988). *Issues and ethics in the helping professions.* Pacific Grove, CA: Brooks/Cole.

Everstine, L., Everstine, D. S., Geymann, G. M., True, R. H., Frey, D. H., Johnson, H. G., & Seiden, R. H. (1980). Privacy and confidentiality in psychotherapy. *American Psychologist, 35,* 828–840.

Goldfarb v. Virginia State Bar. (1975). 421 U.S. 773.

Hammer, M. (1972). To students interested in becoming psychotherapists. In M. Hammer (Ed.), *The theory and practice of psychotherapy with specific disorders.* Springfield, IL: Thomas.

Herlihy, B., & Corey, G. (1992). *Dual relationships in counseling.* Alexandria, VA: American Association for Counseling and Development.

Keith-Spiegel, P., & Koocher, G. P. (1985). *Ethics in psychology: Professional standards and cases.* New York: McGraw-Hill.

Levenson, M. (1989). *Right to accept or refuse treatment: Implications for the mental health profession.* Arizona State University, unpublished manuscript.

National Board for Certified Counselors (NBCC). (1987). *Counseling services: Consumer rights and responsibilities.* Alexandria, VA: Author.

Pope, K. S. (1994). *Sexual involvement with therapists: Patient assessment, subsequent therapy, forensics.* Washington, DC: American Psychological Association.

Pope, K. S., Tabachnick, B. G., & Keith-Spiegel, P. (1987). Ethics of practice: The beliefs and behaviors of psychologists as therapists. *American Psychologist, 42,* 993–1006.

Rennie v. Klein, 476 F. supp. 1294 (D.N.J., 1979, modified, Nos. 79–2576 and 70–2577 3rd Cir., July 9, 1981).

Robinson, S. E. (1988). Counselor competency and malpractice suits: Opposite sides of the same coin. *Counseling and Human Development, 20,* 1–8.

Robinson, S. E., & Gross, D. R. (1989). Applied ethics and the mental health counselor. *Journal of Mental Health Counseling, 11,* 289–299.

Robinson Kurpius, S. E. (1995). Current ethical issues in the practice of psychotherapy. *Ethics in Psychotherapy: Directions in Clinical Psychology, 3,* 2–9.

Robinson Kurpius, S. E., & Gross, D. R. (In press). Professional ethics and the mental health counselor. In W. J. Weikel & A. J. Palmo (Eds.), *Foundations of mental health counseling,* Springfield, IL: Thomas.

Rogers v. Orkin, 634 F. 2nd 650 (1st Cir., 1980).

Sattler, H. A. (1990). Confidentiality. In B. Herlihy & L. Golden (Eds.), *ACD Ethical Standards Casebook* (4th ed). Alexandria, VA: American Association for Counseling and Development.

Schwitzgebel, R. L., & Schwitzgebel, R. K. (1980). *Law and psychological practice.* New York: Wiley.

Snider, P. D. (1987). Client records: Inexpensive liability protection for mental health counselors. *Journal of Mental Health Counseling, 9,* 134–141.

Tarasoff v. Board of Regents of the University of California, 118 Cal. Rptr. 14.551 P2d. 334 (1974).

Tarasoff v. Board of Regents of the University of California, 113 Cal. Rptr. 14.551 P.2d 334 (1976).

Thoreson, R. W., Shaughnessy, P., Heppner, P. P., & Cook, S. (1993). Sexual contact during and after the professional relationship: Attitudes and practices of male counselors. *Journal of Counseling and Development, 71,* 429–434.

Webster's New World Dictionary. (1979). New York: Collins.

Weiner, N. C., & Robinson Kurpius, S. E. (1995). *Shattered: A practical guide for counseling women survivors of childhood sexual abuse.* Washington, DC: Taylor & Francis.

Wyatt v. Stickney, 325 F. Supp. 781 (M.D. Ala. 1971), *sub nom. Wyatt v. Aderholt,* 503 F. 2nd. 1305 (5th Cir. 1974).

Chapter 5

Counseling Theory

Counseling Theory

A Rationale and a Framework for an Eclectic Approach

J. Jeffries McWhirter, Ph.D., ABPP

Benedict T. McWhirter, Ph.D.   *D. Scott Herrmann, M.C.*

Why does a counselor focus on certain events in an interview and ignore others? How does a counselor know what data are important in trying to understand clients? What is involved in the counselor's decision to reflect affect with one client and discuss ideas with another? What method and what criteria does the counselor use to evaluate success or failure as a helper? To answer these questions, one needs to focus on the theoretical foundations that underlie the counselor's behavior. This theoretical foundation is the vehicle by which a person can organize observations into a pattern that will assist in understanding what has been observed. The preceding questions focus on helper behavior that is based on assumptions regarding behavior. Making these assumptions explicit encourages precision in answering the questions.

Unfortunately, practitioners often become frustrated with the amount of literature that focuses on theoretical issues. Underlying this frustration seems to be the belief that theory and practice are dichotomized into two distinct and separate categories. A frequent complaint of practitioners-in-training is directed toward professors and instructors who are too theoretical in their orientations and toward courses that are too theoretical in their content. Students often complain, "All this talk about theory doesn't help me in my situation. Why don't we discuss the practical aspects of helping?" In reality, however, a good theory is highly practical. Theory and practice cannot be dichotomized into two separate camps. Practitioners do operate from a counseling theory. Although they may not have it well defined or be able to verbalize it, some sort of theory is implied by the counselor's beliefs and behaviors.

Individuals who feel they can operate entirely without a theory, even those who assume an anti-theoretical position, are basing their behavior on implicit theory even though vaguely defined. There is no other way they can decide what to do. Intuition, sometimes proposed as a substitute for theory, is itself but a crude type of hypothesizing.

Not infrequently, then, practitioners make only implicit assumptions about their world. They "fly by the seat of their pants." Their decision to behave in a certain way, to focus on certain information, is based on poorly formulated or unconsciously held theoretical formulations. In this situation, therapists' working behaviors are influenced by a tool over which they have little or no control. The explanatory and predictive aspects of theory are greatly limited by its implicitness. The abstractions and inferences derived from observed events have no consistency or pattern.

Human beings, however, abhor isolated events. People must fit events together into a pattern to understand and to control them. Theory is necessary in order to organize the isolated events that confront the counselor. Because the helper's behavior and practice are inextricably intertwined with theory and because the helper's behavior and practice are so crucial to success or failure with the client, counselors have an obligation to develop a systematic theoretical rationale for their work. Counselors do not have the luxury of artists in achieving their aims. The license that artists use in the practice of their art is denied counselors in their practice. Counselors must be precise where artists may be vague, explicit where artists are implicit, use logic and reason where artists may use emotion and connotation. Without a systematic theoretical base, helpers lack the breadth, depth, and consistency that is important to their work. They lack a unifying theme that gives their interactions support and focus. Unexamined and implicit theories contain incongruities that may result in unpredictable and inconsistent counselor behavior. Theories, then, grow out of the need to make sense out of life and provide consistency and unity that allow for greater focus.

Counseling theories are systematic ways of viewing the helping process. Counselors' behavior is influenced by the frame of reference with which they view counseling. Theories are tools, abstractions created by psychologists and counselors to guide them as they explore the intricacies of the client's world. And ultimately theories have a single purpose: to make the organization of information and data more usable, more communicable, and more practical. Essentially, a theory is a hypothetical explanation for observed events. It is a framework that imposes some sort of order on these events and initially is a guess that seems to make sense. Theory is a possible world that can be checked against the real world.

A useful theory goes beyond an explanation of events that have already taken place. It should lead to the prediction of future events that involve the same sort of behaviors. Thus a theory of change must conform to events that have previously been observed and should lead the observer to predict the effects of various elements in the counseling process. If the prediction proves accurate, then the validity of the theory is enhanced and the helper has gained greater control of the problem-solving situation.

To summarize, there are three ways in which counseling theories can help counselors in their quest to help others. First, the theory contributes to a greater understanding of an individual's behavior. It provides a way of organizing relevant, available, and observable data about a client into a framework that allows greater unity and greater predictability. Second, the theory suggests guidelines that provide signs of success or failure of counseling activities. Essentially, the theory becomes a "working model" to explain what clients *may* be like and what *may* be helpful to them. Built into the "working model" is an appreciation of what constitutes success or failure. The end result is twofold: helpers reach a deeper and richer understanding of what their client *is* like, and their theory is enriched in ways that make it more useful in working with future clients. Finally, and perhaps most important for the practitioner, the theory directly influences the strategy of change counselors select to employ with their clients, as well as the counseling procedures that are most applicable with a given client or with a particular presenting problem.

In order to make the theory more useful and more practical, counselors must do two things. First, in so far as they are able, they must make explicit, through conscious evaluation and examination, the informal theory they hold. Second, they must become aware of the more formalized statements of various theoretical positions. These two tasks should not be undertaken in isolation; indeed, they cannot be. Over fifteen years ago, Leona Tyler (1980) suggested that counselors need many different varieties of theoretical concepts with some degree of organization to provide confidence and peace of mind. This sentiment continues to be echoed today by contemporary theorists and clinicians (Hansen, Rossberg, & Cramer, 1994; Lazarus & Beutler, 1993). By examining approaches to counseling that have been expounded by theorists and by increased awareness of the interpersonal hypotheses by which they are operating, counselors can develop a theoretical rationale for their work. The intent of this chapter and the next is to provide the counseling practitioner and the counselor-in-training with working models within major theoretical points of view. Practitioners must develop their own personal theory of change. This can be done by drawing on the appealing ideas of other people who have been particularly adept in developing theoretical formulations of change. It is possible for practitioners to consider a relatively few but central people who have presented systematic and comprehensive theoretical approaches to counseling. Essentially, knowledge of existing theories will help therapists expand on their own perceived theory of change so that their efforts toward helping the client create positive change are enhanced.

"Schools" of Counseling

The existence of a variety of theoretical approaches within counseling and psychology has created problems. One of the striking characteristics of the field has been the prolific growth of "schools" of counseling and therapy. It has recently been estimated that more than 400 separate schools of psychotherapy are currently in existence (Karasu, 1986). Each school has introduced its own innovations in procedures, techniques, and theories, which result in a bewildering diversity of opinion. Much of the problem revolves around the fact that many of the disagreements are statements of opinion and not statements of fact. Most schools were founded by a charismatic leader who attracted loyal disciples. Since there has been very little scientific basis for many approaches, disagreement and hostility based on poorly defined concepts and armchair theories have frequently existed among the various schools. Essentially, schools are the inevitable consequence of theories based on intuition, faith, and tenacity. A partial advantage of the almost semireligious nature of schools is that followers of a particular approach have worked hard to define and elaborate their positions. In attempting to validate the value of their orientation, the writing and research that followed lead many schools to develop a somewhat formal theoretical position.

The existence of these formal theoretical positions is vital to the helping process. They provide counselors with a basis from which to operate with their clients. They provide a way of explaining and predicting client behavior as well as suggesting procedures for altering that behavior. Effective professional counselors must be aware of the basic concepts supporting the major approaches. Counselors who are unaware of formal theories are locked into a world of their own.

Most counseling approaches have reported some success; it seems unlikely that any one current position is entirely correct. The dogmatic schools of counseling and psychotherapy were perhaps necessary for desirable changes of professional and public climate. However, increasing the effectiveness of counselors in dealing with a broad range of client problems will probably demand new integrations of ideas from various approaches (Beutler, Consoli, & Williams, 1995; Howard, Nance, & Myers, 1986; Garfield, 1994). At this point, no single theoretical formulation exists to explain all facets of human behavior. No single approach to counseling—whether it is a theory of personality or a set of techniques for modifying personality—has been found that can completely explain the behavior of all individuals (Goldfried, 1982; Gaw & Beutler, 1995; Ivey, 1980; Tyler, 1980). Consequently, we believe that a major pitfall for counselors is to assume that a single theoretical approach is pertinent to all individuals.

Closely related to the preceding argument is that a single theory may fail to help with a specific client problem. Certain kinds of client problems lend themselves much more directly to certain theoretical explanations and treatments than do other problems (Howard et al., 1986; "Mental health: Does therapy help?" 1995; Seligman, 1994, 1995). In other words, some theoretical approaches are much more pertinent and are more directly applicable to certain presenting problems than are other approaches (Beutler & Clarkin, 1990). In addition, during the course of the helping relationship clients' needs change in terms of the shifting orientation to their problems. New goals emerge as earlier ones are accomplished; new targets present themselves as old ones are influenced to change. Counselors' ability to shift their orientation to meet client needs and goals will potentially improve the chances of effectiveness in positive client outcome (Lazarus, 1990).

One response to limit the preceding problems is to integrate several existing theoretical approaches to counseling in the hope that the helper will be able to apply theory and methods more effectively. In certain areas this integration has taken place (Beutler, 1983; Goldfried, 1995; Howard et al., 1986; Lazarus, 1989). Some thirty years ago, for example, theoretical models in counseling emphasized the difference between the non-directive and the directive stance in the counseling interview. Resulting arguments tended to emphasize a single dimension of the counseling process, and it is not presently adequate to illustrate the various positions now held by many counselors. What was formerly called *nondirective counseling,* frequently seen as passivity on the part of the counselor, engaging in the reflection of feeling, clarification of content, and so forth, is used by most helpers at least a portion of the time. In a similar way, what was formerly called *directive counseling,* often including activity on the part of the counselor, the use of objective data, and even diagnosis of problem behavior is now used by most counselors to some degree in the counseling process. The primary point of this discussion, and the primary proposal here, is that counselors can have greater impact, can become more effective in their work, and can make a greater contribution to their clientele if they purposefully maintain an eclectic position in the selection of a theoretical model and the use of this model in the counseling relationship.

The brand of eclecticism that is proposed here assumes that counselors are highly trained and have some experience in a number of counseling approaches. Indeed, it is negligent for counselors to call themselves eclectic unless they are well versed in a variety of specific theories that support their eclectic position. A thorough knowledge of several counseling theories will broaden helpers' capacity to organize their observations and to plan appropriate interventions. In the working situation, counselors should be at home with a variety of theoretical approaches, and should be able to select an approach to counseling that is most likely to meet the specific needs of clients. Because the concept of eclecticism within counseling is of great importance, it will serve us well to discuss some alternatives to the eclectic approach as well as various aspects of eclecticism.

Eclectic Counseling

Most contemporary surveys of mental health professionals reveal that between 30 and 70 percent of therapists identify themselves as eclectics (Jensen, Bergin, & Greaves, 1990). Eclecticism means to select or to choose methods or doctrines from various sources or systems. Eclectic counseling is based on concepts taken deliberately from a variety of theoretical positions rather than concepts based exclusively on one orientation. The eclectic individual believes that a single viewpoint and theoretical position is limiting and that concepts, procedures, and techniques from many sources must be used to best serve the needs of the person(s) seeking help. When counselors deliberately attempt to incorporate into their practice the terminology, techniques, concepts, and procedures of more than one unified theory, the result is eclecticism. The key word is *deliberately.* True eclectic counselors have a consistent purpose and philosophy in their practice and deliberately use techniques and procedures from various schools that they believe are most appropriate to help each client. From knowledge of cognition, affect, and behavior, and from understanding of environment and systems issues, eclectic helpers develop a repertoire of problem-solving methods. They then select the most appropriate for the particular client and the specific problem.

Eclecticism is frequently misunderstood to mean an indiscriminate and arbitrary collection of theoretical scraps and pieces. When individuals do this and do not make a sincere and serious attempt to understand and include various viewpoints into their counseling practice, they are following a procedure based on the idea that "there's much good to be said on all sides." Eclecticism used in this way is vague, superficial, and non-descriptive, and contributes to the legitimate charge of "fuzzy-headed wishy-washiness." The use of eclecticism in this sense reinforces the belief that eclecticism is popular because it removes the necessity to "take sides" and enables counselors to do what they "want" in counseling.

There are, then, three positions a counselor may adopt in regard to the selection of a theoretical rational. These positions are formalism,[1] syncretism, and eclecticism.

Formalism

Because they have to believe in something, formalist counselors accept an "all or nothing" attitude toward the strongest, most meaningful theory that presents itself to them. If they happen to have selected an adequate theory, they are provided a high degree of consistency and a rational order on which to base their practice. They are able to operate within a circumscribed and formalized theoretical framework. Usually, however, a single theory does not adequately explain or predict the variety of issues, concerns, and client problems that confront counselors. The dilemma that faces the purist counselor is that all aspects of the theory are seen as equally acceptable, useful, and truthful. Figure 5-1 graphically illustrates the formalist position.[2]

Example: Carl Rogers has completely explained the most effective and appropriate ingredients in counseling process and outcome. Consequently, Rogerian person-centered counseling is the all-inclusive, perfect theory of counseling.

Analogy: Prunes are the only kind of fruit worth eating. They taste the best and are the best for you at all times. If you eat prunes, you will need no other fruit.

Problems: The purist approach implies that all parts of the concept are equally strong and defensible. In addition, dogmatic and emotional involvement with the theory are increased and maximized.

---

1. Another term that conveys the same notion is *purism.* The terms *purism* and *formalism* are used interchangeably here.

2. For this section, we have used and paraphrased the schema that Bischof (1964), in his first edition, developed to explain the purist, the synthesist, and the eclecticist positions in theories of personality.

Figure 5-1 Formalist/Purist
The square represents the complete
frame of reference for the counselor.
It is pure, unblemished, and uncontaminated. It includes nothing else.

Syncretism

Helping is an applied science. Counselors are concerned with positive outcomes
and with effectiveness. The majority tend to be pragmatists, discarding that which
does not work and retaining that which does. Not infrequently, a pragmatic attitude leads to the unsystematic and uncritical combination of many threads, scraps,
and pieces of various theories. The origin and intent of many of the ideas are ob-
scured in the general melee of the system. The relationship between the concepts
are loosely formed. The syncretistic position is practical until the time comes for
practitioners to review and challenge one of the threads of their system. As with a
ball of tangled yarn, they cannot do this without pulling apart most of the structure. The unraveling may lead to so much confusion that they become thoroughly
lost within their own system. The syncretist position is summarized in Figure 5-2.

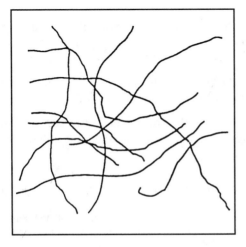

Figure 5-2 Syncretist
The square represents the conceptual
framework of the helper. The interwoven
and interconnected lines are separate ideas
and concepts that overlap and intermingle
with each other into a unified mass.

Example: Rogers, Ellis, Perls, and Wolpe have developed theories that make sense. All of them have been of help to their clients. There is much good to be said about all of them. No one of them provides the best answer about any facet of helping, but taking the best of them will be most useful.

Analogy: The juice from many fruits (prune, orange, bananas, pineapple) are blended and served as one liquid: the perfect drink. It contains a mixture of the best fruit juices combined into one grand and delicious drink.

Problems: The syncretist system does not permit analysis. To examine is to destroy. If one of the components of the approach is called into question, the entire structure is threatened. In addition, there is no rationale or central theme to the mix.

Eclecticism

Eclecticism in counseling is the selection by the helper of an approach that meets the needs of the client and that is particularly adaptable to a problem or situation. Helpers have selected and put into their conceptual framework both theoretical principles and practical procedures that have been examined for their worth. They know where they got a concept; they can locate it in the structure; they can remove it for examination without disordering the system. The pieces of the theory and the practice can receive more, or less, emphasis as seems appropriate. The diagram in Figure 5-3 further explains the eclectic position.

Example: Roger's concepts of accurate empathy, positive regard, and genuineness seem highly important and help form the basic relationship that most counseling approaches use. Wolpe's reciprocal inhibition appears very useful, particularly

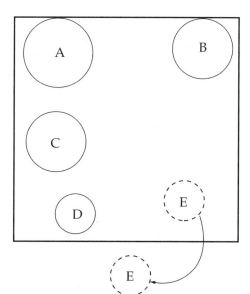

Figure 5-3   Eclecticist
Again, the square represents the helper's frame of reference. The lettered circles represent the various components of the system. The distance between the circles and their varying sizes are important. One component, E, has been removed for examination.

with anxious and fearful clients. Ellis's illogical sentences and their use in the thought process seem particularly suitable for some clients.

Analogy: A fruit salad combining several fruits (prunes, bananas, oranges, pineapples) is served as a single dish with a bonding agent such as a dressing, which serves as a unifying factor.

Problems and Solutions: One needs information, understanding, and exposure to several counseling approaches. The model suggests and allows for continuous evaluation of the distinct components without the destruction of the total structure. Let us assume that component E represents Wolpe's reciprocal inhibition theory and practice. As a counselor continues to see a particular client, he or she becomes aware that the client's need is often related to interpersonal anxiety. The counselor's desire to be an increasingly effective "helper" to the client leads him or her to examine in greater detail the theoretical approaches that may provide the client with additional aid. Having used relaxation training and hierarchy construction to help to test anxiety problems of previous clients, the counselor's further reading, study, and thinking leads him or her to reintroduce reciprocal inhibition theory into his or her eclectic position and to apply that approach to the client's interpersonal anxiety concerns. The theory is evaluated in the context of the client population and in light of a particular client problem.

Figure 5-3 schematically represents several different and important aspects of the eclectic position. The varying size of the circles represents the relative importance that is accorded to the various components. Concepts in A have more weight and carry more value than concepts in B. This is suggested by the difference in size of circles. The distance between A and C and between A and B suggests that there is more similarity between the concepts in A and the concepts in C than there are between A and B.

The figure also demonstrates the allowance for continuous evaluation of the distinct components without the destruction of the total structure. Component E has been pulled out for examination, and the decision to eliminate it or reinsert it may be carried out. The opportunity for continuous evaluation of distinct parts is not possible for the formalist or the syncretist without the destruction of the whole.

Finally, and perhaps most importantly, the model assumes that the eclectic position identifies the sources of the ideas included with the framework. Individuals adopting this position are provided with the ability and security to live with their present theory and return to the original source or to new research findings to compare, evaluate, and extend their ideas.

The bonding agent in the eclectic position is the personness of therapists. Counselors need a variety of theoretical concepts that become understood and organized around and within themselves. Counselors' own personality, philosophy, knowledge, and skills are the principal determinants as to how they choose to interact in a problem-solving situation. Dealing with the client system directly as the change agent or initiating an action system to relieve the problem are strategies determined by the helper. This eclectic model provides an organization that is a dynamic, growing process with a consistent unity that maintains itself in spite of constant modification and extension. The importance of the personality of the helper to eclecticism is crucial and is considered next.

The Personness of the Counselor

Using the eclectic position, individual practitioners must ultimately adopt their own approaches. Not all helpers can be expected to be comfortable with a given problem-solving method. Since counselors differ in value systems, need systems, and personality structure, there must also be differences in the application of the counseling approaches that are used. Just as a counseling technique must be suited to the needs of the client, they must also be suited to the needs of the helper. Counselors draw to themselves approaches that are most congenial. Ideally, these approaches should also provide strong evidence of effectiveness and validity. Counselors integrate these approaches into a conceptualization and a style that they can use effectively. Of course, the helper's selection of various theories is not entirely objective. Counselors' philosophy of life and their own personality influence the data to which they are sensitive. Their philosophy and personality contribute to their counseling repertoire. It is romantic to assume that counselors can accept and internalize that which is foreign and repulsive to their own personal makeup and experience. Counselors cannot operate maturely and professionally in borrowed clothes. Their suit is preferably tailor made, with the cloth and style selected on the basis of their own individual tastes.

Theory follows personality. Therefore, adequate consideration must be given to the personal characteristics of the counselor, and clear self-exploration on the part of the counselor is essential. Indeed, the helper's needs, values, defenses, and perceptions are crucial to the helping process.

Since the "counselor as a person" is a basic element in the counseling relationship, counselors' behavior cannot be contrived, mechanical, and forced if they are to establish an effective working relationship with their client. The theoretical position that counselors choose will ultimately lead them to emphasize certain aspects of their personality in the helping role. The theoretical position should not force the counselor to try to become a radically different person.

An important function of a counselor education program is to provide an opportunity for prospective counselors to learn to develop, test, and modify their own personal theory of counseling. This personal theory is obtained through interpersonal experiences. These experiences are obtained in group and individual counseling sessions in which the student participates as client, in human relations laboratory experiences in group dynamics, and in the counseling practicum. The major objectives of these kinds of experiences are increased awareness of self in interpersonal relationships and increased sensitivity to feedback from others in such relationships. Counselors also develop their personal theory by increased exposure to rich sources of theoretical frames of reference.

Increasing counselor knowledge and understanding, especially *self*-knowledge and *self*-understanding, creates shifts in the counselor's adaptation of theory. Beginning helpers, as they become aware of various approaches, are likely to develop a loose affinity for certain approaches in contrast to other approaches. Indeed, beginning helpers, when they discover a theoretical approach that has high appeal for them, sometimes resemble the proverbial "kid with a new toy." As they learn more about these approaches, as they experience the application of these in simulated, role-played, or "real" situations, they can continue to learn more about themselves and about the components of their eclectic theory. Initially, helpers-in-training should examine the aspects of their personality that create an attraction for a particular theory. Equally important, they should examine the neutral or negative responses toward other theories. This active examination of self and of theories is a continual process whereby counselors increase in both self-knowledge and self-development as well as in an understanding and application of theory. In short, as they continue to develop self-knowledge, the theoretical views tend to become more useful and applicable. Essentially, the various theories become integrated within the context of the individual helper's style.

Consideration must also be given to the influence that personality and helper–client interaction have on counseling process and outcome. The idiosyncratic characteristics and personal qualities of the individual helper must be capitalized on, to promote greater therapeutic benefits for the client. Keeping this consideration in mind, helpers need to develop a conceptual framework that may in part help them to consolidate and define the theories they choose to use.

Psychological Functioning: A Conceptual Framework

One way of conceptualizing how individuals function is in terms of three processes that, on the surface, appear quite distinct and separate: behavior, affect, and cognition. In working with a client, we can usually identify problems, such as deficiencies or excesses of some behaviors, inappropriate or extreme emotions, and faulty, illogical thinking. Often a client's particular problems seems to fall into one of the three categories. The difficulty that a client experiences may manifest itself primarily in one form or another, but in actuality these three processes are always overlapping, interdependent, and mutually reinforcing. Problem behavior may stem from or result in unrealistic thinking and inappropriate emotions, and disturbing feelings may cause or be caused by certain dysfunctional behaviors and unwarranted thoughts. Consequently, a change in one facet will bring about simultaneous modification in the others.

Figure 5-4 illustrates this tripartite model of psychological functioning. The circle represents the total organism, integrating cognitive/thinking, emotional/affective, and behavioral responses and acting as a whole. The divisions between the components delineate the three types of responses, but do not imply static and indivisible processes. The arrows demonstrate the interrelationship, the blending and mingling of the three functions.

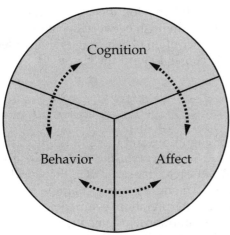

Figure 5-4
A model of psychological functioning

It is important to realize that the interactive relationship depicted in Figure 5-4 exists in *any* problem a person might struggle with. For the purpose of therapeutic intervention, however, it is often useful to separate the problem into its components and examine each aspect individually. This makes it easier to apply specific corrective measures. It also helps clients become aware of the various aspects of their experience and understand better how these aspects influence each other. Since these three components and their interaction are essential to understanding clients and the role of the counselor in the therapeutic process, it is pertinent to discuss each of these components at this time.

Affect

Individuals have an emotional component to their personality. Feelings are extremely important aspects of the inner life of the individual. The terms *feeling, emotion,* and *affect* are all descriptive of a mental state with particular physiological responses and motor expression, and are usually related to some external situation or object.

People do not always distinguish clearly between thoughts and feelings, and our language reflects this confusion. For example, "I feel he doesn't love me anymore" does not express a feeling, but rather a thought. "I feel hurt," in contrast, does express a feeling. When dealing with clients, counselors may have to pay particular attention to eliciting genuine feelings as opposed to cognitive statements couched in "feeling" language.

Behavior

Behavior is viewed as a pattern of responses learned by the person through interaction with the environment. Generally this aspect of individuals refers to their objective, observable behavior that includes motoric responses.

Here again, as part of dealing with behavior, the worker may have to help clients and their significant others to distinguish between behavior and inferences about behavior. "He's lazy" is not a description of behavior—it is an inference. "He does not do his homework and his chores around the house" is a description of behavior.

Cognition

People have an innate capacity for cognition, and thought is one of the most important characteristics of humans. The terms *thinking* and *cognition* refer to the meanings and symbols that people attach to transactions in the world, and the associations they make among events. Among the many cognitive processes that a counselor will be concerned with are interpretation, evaluation, explanation, and inference. We want to examine the assumptions, judgments, and assessments that clients make; the expectations, beliefs, opinions, and convictions they hold; the premises and hypotheses under which they operate; and the conclusions they draw about their experience. All these concepts involve reasoning and thinking and are important contributors to a client's internal and interpersonal dynamics.

Since these processes often occur at a low level of awareness, it is sometimes necessary for counselors to bring the client's thinking out in the open before change can take place. In a similar way, as counselors help the individual identify and clarify affect as well as specify problematic behavior, the stage is set to ameliorate dysfunctional interactions with others. These cognitive processes are especially important in problem solving with families because of the frequency, repetitiveness, and mutual reinforcement of interactions that occurs in families (see Chapter 17).

Most theories of individual counseling tend to focus on a single facet of the client. For example, reality therapy and behavior modification strategies such as operant conditioning and contingency management deal with the person's behavior. Rational-emotive therapy, transactional analysis, cognitive restructuring approaches as well as individual psychology from a framework formed on Adler and Dreikurs tend to highlight the individual's thinking process. Person-centered and Gestalt as well as relationship and techniques to build communication skills tend to affect the feelings of the client. When deciding on specific intervention techniques, it becomes important to select from those approaches that are especially suited to the particular process—behavioral, affective, cognitive—to be changed. In reality, each of the theories, although approaching change from a primary perspective, have also given some acknowledgment to the other areas. To a greater or lesser extent, each expects and obtains change in the other areas.

It is impossible for counselors to deal with all facets of a client in their entirety at the same time. They must focus on only a portion of a client's concerns, and therefore must be concerned with particular feelings, thoughts, and actions only at a particular point in time in the counseling process. The fragments the counselor chooses to focus on are of prime importance, although, again, movement in one area stimulates movement in the others.

Problem-Solving Approaches

As mentioned earlier in this chapter, the present eclectic position does not represent a new theory of counseling, but rather a pragmatic device for applying counseling approaches and techniques. One of the implicit assumptions of this position is that a variety of theoretical approaches have the potential for beneficial application to client problems. More effective helping can be achieved by accepting an eclectic theoretical and technical position. The current eclectic approach offers a frame of reference for the application of counseling theories and approaches and may provide the groundwork for future integration of a variety of theories.

Contemporary research acknowledges the efficacy of specific therapies for specific conditions, including depression, anxiety, panic, and phobias (Kiesler, 1994; "Mental health: Does therapy help?" 1995; Seligman, 1994, 1995). The eclectic helper selects an approach that is most likely to produce client growth and improvement within a particular domain. In order to accomplish this, the practitioner must be thoroughly schooled in various theoretical models; must understand the application of varying approaches that arise out of different theoretical bases, and must have some experience in the practice of that approach.

Philosophical Positions

There are almost as many approaches to the counseling process as there are counselors. However, most counselors owe some allegiance to three major theoretical, philosophical influences—psychodynamic, behavioral (or cognitive-behavioral), and humanistic. Counseling theories have generally emerged from one or the other of these three basic positions. These positions represent a basic philosophical stance that one might take regarding one's perception of the world and of human beings. Historically, these three viewpoints were considered forces that at various points in the development of psychology and counseling became a major focus for the development of personality and counseling theories. The philosophy of these theories provides a backdrop to more specific theories of counseling. In the following chapter, we identify and apply to a client case study three specific counseling theories that have their roots in these three positions. Here we consider the basic philosophy that undergirds the three forces.

Psychoanalytic Theory

Psychoanalytic theory, developed by Sigmund Freud, has the longest history of any of the presently used theories. Freud was the first to discover that human behavior followed certain lawful patterns and thus was the first to bring order out of chaos. In addition to orthodox psychoanalytic therapy, psychoanalytic theory includes the neo-Freudians such as Alfred Adler, Eric Erikson, Eric Fromm, Karen Horney, Carl Jung, Wilhelm Reich, and Harry Stack Sullivan. Similarly, currently popular Eric Berne (transactional analysis), Alexander Lowen (bio-energetics), and even Fritz Perls (Gestalt therapy) all have their roots in traditional Freudian thought. Freud and his colleagues are credited with founding the so-called talking cure (Hansen et al., 1994), upon which most contemporary models of counseling are based.

The basic philosophical underpinnings of psychoanalytic theory suggest that human beings are greatly influenced by unconscious dynamic forces and by early experiences. Unconscious motives and conflicts are central in current, on-going behavior, and irrational forces are quite strong. Individuals are driven by sexual (libido) and aggressive impulses. It is posited that repressed childhood conflicts create current pathology in human interactions.

Traditional psychoanalytic thought holds to a generally negative and deterministic view of humans (Corey, 1991). That is, human beings are selfish, impulsive, and irrational beings whose behavior is predetermined by biological variables. Sexual and aggressive forces dynamically interact to create conflicts for the individual. Individuals repress painful childhood experiences so that some thoughts are more accessible to conscious awareness than others. According to Freud, human beings are determined by irrational forces, biological and instinctual needs and drives, unconscious motivations, and psychosexual events that occurred during the first five years of life.

Behavioral and Cognitive-Behavioral Theory

Behavioral theory was developed out of laboratory research in the 1920s and 1930s principally as a reaction to the inability of scientists to measure and evaluate the outcomes of psychoanalytic approaches to helping. Behavioral therapy placed psychological change and intervention in the context of education (learning) rather than medicine and emphasized the need to predict and measure outcomes based on observable, objective, and measurable variables. Behavioral theory can be separated into two basic approaches. These include the early behaviorism of Watson, Skinner, and others, and the more recent cognitive-behavioral approaches (for example, see Beck, 1995; Ellis, 1994; Lazarus, 1989; Meichenbaum, 1977, 1985). A number of tenets form the basic philosophy of behaviorism. Behavior is learned from situational and environmental factors and not from within the organism. Because all behavior is learned, it can be unlearned. Since people have no control over their behavior from within, there is no self-determinism and human beings are able to be manipulated. Values, feelings, and thoughts are ignored because only concrete observable behavior is considered. In short, situational cues create specific behavior, and that behavior's consequences shape and control it further. Behavior is cued by stimuli that precede it and is shaped and controlled by reinforcing stimuli that follow it. In behaviorism, there is no emphasis on internal factors.

Although behavioral approaches are diverse, some commonalities exist between most. All of them

1. Focus on current influences rather than historical determinants of behavior
2. Emphasize the observation of overt behavioral changes as the main criteria by which treatment is evaluated.

3. Specify treatment goals in concrete, objective terms that aid replication
4. Rely on basic research as a source of hypotheses about treatment and specific therapy techniques
5. Define problems in therapy specifically, so treatment and measurement are possible

A major development in the last several years is the cognitive-behavioral perspective (Mahoney & Lyddon, 1988). Using many of the principles of behaviorism, cognitive behavioral approaches expand and apply behavioral principles to various mediating variables. That is, cognitive-behavioral approaches deal with irrationality and thinking processes as mediators of behavior. Cognitive-behavioral approaches tend to be instructive, directive, and verbally oriented. The individual client's thoughts and feelings are assumed to function in the same way that overt behavior functions. In other words, in the cognitive-behavioral approach thoughts and feelings can be considered either stimuli and/or reinforcement properties (Bandura, 1969, 1977, 1995).

Humanistic Theory

Freudian psychology is concerned with the unconscious and with hidden meanings. Behaviorism provides a polar position with emphasis on observed behavior, stimulus–response patterns, and concrete action. Both approaches have tended to represent mechanistic and predetermined views of human beings, although in more modern forms of these theories an underlying humanism and optimism have developed. This increasingly hopeful and optimistic view of humankind is at least partially due to the major "third force" in psychology—the humanistic tradition.

The humanistic and existential theories of helping focus on the uniqueness of each person's internal perspective, which determines one's reality. This approach emphasizes the here and now, rather than what was or what will be. How people perceive the world and feel about themselves and their environment is emphasized, rather than their adjustment to prevailing societal norms. Humanistic approaches also emphasize affective rather than cognitive or behavioral domains within the individual.

The term "humanistic counseling" does not imply a systematic psychology or a collection of techniques, but rather alludes to a therapeutic attitude based on a philosophy of life and an existence. This humanistic attitude governs the counselor's interactions with the client.

Humanistic counseling evolved both in Europe and the United States as a reaction against the determinism of Freudian psychoanalysis and to the mechanism of the behavioral psychologists. Its major proponents in the United States are Carl Rogers, Rollo May, Victor Frankel, Fritz Perls, Eric Fromm, Abraham Maslow, and Gordon Allport. The humanistic perspective emphasizes the subjective, personal, and experiential aspects of human existence. This approach rejects the idea that objective interpretations and analysis of behavior are more accurate than subjective, personal analyses.

Summary

Theory plays a crucial central role in counseling, as an organizing core for practice. Eclecticism is an appropriate stance for counseling practices when based on a thorough grounding in several theories.The personal characteristics of the helper are of great importance in selecting from theories. Theories also provide a framework to apply selected and combined strategies. The philosophical backdrop for theory development and adaption helps make eclectic choices coherent and effective.

In the next chapter, using a case study methodology, we focus on three specific theories that represent distinct ways in which counselors go about the business of helping clients.

Even though we distinguish separate theories, the principles that we outline in this chapter can be combined to help a specific client. Hopefully, the reader will be able to discern how elements in this chapter are actualized.

References

Bandura, A. (1969). *Principles of behavior modification.* New York: Holt, Rinehart & Winston.

Bandura, A. (1977). Self-efficacy: Toward a unifying theory of behavioral change. *Psychological Review, 84,* 191–215.

Bandura, A. (1995). Excercise of personal and collective efficacy in changing societies. In A. Bandura (Ed.), *Self-efficacy in changing societies.* New York: Cambridge University Press.

Beck, J. S. (1995). *Cognitive therapy: Basics and beyond.* New York: Guilford Press.

Beutler, L. E. (1983). *Eclectic psychotherapy: A systematic approach.* New York: Pergamon Press.

Beutler, L. E., & Clarkin, J. (1990). *Systematic treatment selection: Toward targeted therapeutic interventions.* New York: Brunner/Mazel.

Beutler, L. E., Consoli, A. J., & Williams, R. E. (1995). Integrative and eclectic therapies in practice. In B. Bongar & L. E. Beutler (Eds.), *Comprehensive textbook of psychotherapy: Theory and practice* (pp. 274–292). New York: Oxford University Press.

Bischof, C. J. (1964). *Interpreting personality theories.* New York: Harper & Row.

Corey, G. (1991). *Theory and practice of counseling and psychotherapy* (4th ed.). Pacific Grove, CA: Brooks/Cole.

Ellis, A. (1994). *Reason and emotion in psychotherapy.* New York: Carol Publishing.

Garfield, S. L. (1994). Eclecticism and integration in psychotherapy: Developments and issues. *Clinical Psychology: Science and Practice, 1,* 123–137.

Gaw, K. F., & Beutler, L. E. (1995). Integrating treatment recommendations. In L. E. Beutler & M. Berren (Eds.), *Integrative assessment of adult personality* (pp. 280–319). New York: Guilford.

Goldfried, M. R. (Ed.). (1982). *Converging themes in psychotherapy.* New York: Springer.

Goldfried, M. R. (1995). *From cognitive-behavior therapy to psychotherapy integration.* New York: Springer.

Hansen, J. C., Rossberg, R. H., & Cramer, S. H. (1994). *Counseling theory and process* (5th ed.). Boston: Allyn and Bacon.

Howard, G. S., Nance, D. W., & Myers, P. (1986). Adaptive counseling and therapy: An integrative, eclectic model. *Counseling Psychologist, 14*(3), 363–442.

Ivey, A. E. (1980). Counseling 2000: Time to take charge. *Counseling Psychologist, 8,* 12–16.

Jensen, J. P., Bergin, A. E., & Greaves, D. W. (1990). The meaning of eclecticism: New survey and analysis of components. *Professional Psychology: Research and Practice, 21*(2), 124–130.

Karasu, T. B. (1986). The specificity versus non-specificity dilemma: Toward identifying therapeutic change agents. *American Journal of Psychiatry, 143*(6), 687–695.

Kiesler, D. J. (1994). Standardization of intervention: The tie that binds psychotherapy research and practice. In P. F. Talley, H. H. Strupp, & S. F. Butler (Eds.), *Psychotherapy research and practice: Bridging the gap* (pp. 143–153). New York: Basic Books.

Lazarus, A. A. (1989). *The practice of multimodal therapy.* Baltimore: Johns Hopkins University Press.

Lazarus, A. A. (1990). Can psychotherapists transcend the shackles of their training and superstitions? *Journal of Clinical Psychology, 46*(3), 351–358.

Lazarus, A. A., & Beutler, L. E. (1993). On technical eclecticism. *Journal of Counseling & Development, 71,* 381–385.

Mahoney, M. J., & Lyddon, W. J. (1988). Recent developments in cognitive approaches to counseling and psychotherapy. *Counseling Psychologist, 16*(2), 190–234.

Meichenbaum, D. (1977). *Cognitive-behavior modification: An integrative approach.* New York: Plenum Press.

Meichenbaum, D. (1985). *Stress inoculation training.* New York: Pergamon Press.

Mental health: Does therapy help? (1995, November). *Consumer Reports,* 734–739.

Seligman, M. E. P. (1994). *What you can change & what you can't.* New York: Knopf.

Seligman, M. E. P. (1995). The effectiveness of psychotherapy: The *Consumer Reports* study. *American Psychologist, 50*(12), 965–974.

Tyler, L. E. (1980). The next twenty years. In J. M. Whiteley & B. R. Fretz (Eds.), *The present and future of counseling psychology.* Pacific Grove, CA: Brooks/Cole.

P a r t **2**

Counseling Skills

The responsibilities of counselors, regardless of the setting in which they implement their roles, require that they be competent to provide clients with a variety of services. These services cannot be implemented unless counselors have mastered a number of core knowledge and skills areas. This section of the text provides the reader with an overview and introduction to the counseling skills, and associated knowledge base, that become the focus of much of the counselor education and supervision experience.

Chapter 6, "Individual Counseling: Traditional Approaches," provides information on approaches to working therapeutically with individual clients, including more in-depth descriptions of differing approaches such as Freudian, cognitive-emotional therapy, and Rogers's client-centered approach. Mechanisms of change within the individual are discussed, as well as rationales for understanding how individual problems develop. Chapter 7, "Individual Counseling: Brief Approaches," describes and discusses models for brief therapies. This topic is an important one to the role of the counselor given the impact of managed care and emphasis on cost containment.

Chapter 8, "Group Counseling," presents the basic components of group counseling, including a discussion of the history of group counseling, types of group work, qualities of the effective group leader, stages of group life, and common myths that beginning counselors and therapists often hold about the nature of group work.

Counseling as a profession had its roots in the vocational guidance movement of the early part of this century, and working with career and vocational issues remains a significant part of many counselors' roles today. Chapter 9, "Career Counseling: Counseling for Life," provides an introduction to the different theories and styles of career counseling. It also outlines the stages of career exploration and tools and interventions that the career counselor can use to assist the client in such a search. The author describes the major vocational tests that a counselor might use to gain more information about a client's career and vocational needs.

The role of testing and use of assessment instruments within the counseling profession are described in more depth in Chapter 10, "Counseling Uses of Tests." The authors present a number of key terms and concepts and describe various categories of tests that a counselor might have occasion to use with a client.

Chapter 11, "Diagnosis in Counseling," provides a comprehensive outline of the major categories currently used by the therapeutic community in providing accurate diagnosis and assessment. The importance of diagnosis to the overall counseling process is described, as well as the benefits and risks inherent in the process of diagnosis.

Counselors need to remain open to new innovative methods and theories that may increase their professional effectiveness. Part 2 concludes with Chapter 12, "Specialized Approaches to Counseling," which describes a number of alternative approaches to working with clients. Many of these approaches are becoming more well known as their effectiveness is demonstrated. Such alternative therapies include music and art therapy, movement therapy, and the creative use of guided imagery. Such interventions are exciting in the possibilities they present for the counselor wishing to assist his or her client in self-expression and personal growth; such approaches are becoming more and more widely used.

Individual Counseling

Traditional Approaches

Benedict T. McWhirter, Ph.D.

J. Jeffries McWhirter, Ph.D., ABPP   *Gary J. Loya, M.S.*

In the last chapter we identified three philosophical positions that counselors might adopt as they go about the business of developing an approach to counseling that is most appropriate for them. In this chapter we present a specific counseling theory approach for each of the philosophical positions that illustrates that theoretical framework. The three theories that we focus on are psychoanalysis and the psychodynamic approach (Freud, 1915–1917, 1949); rational-emotive therapy (Ellis, 1962), representing a cognitive-behavioral approach; and person-centered therapy (Rogers, 1951), reflecting the humanistic tradition. For each of the theories, we discuss the theoretical rationale underlying problem development, case conceptualization, and the mechanisms of change proposed by the theory that facilitates client growth. In addressing the behavioral change component of the theory, we include the techniques and processes of interventions that are used in counseling.

We apply each of the theoretical approaches to a single case study to illustrate the counseling process. Our intent is to provide the reader with an understanding of the underlying assumptions and specific intervention strategies that each theory has developed to help clients deal with their concerns. The following case study, the story of "Sally," is based on the case records of one of the authors, modified to ensure anonymity.

Since this chapter is designed to present an overview of the three traditional approaches to counseling, the reader needs to be aware that our discussion is restricted to these three approaches. Consequently, at the end of this chapter we have provided a Suggested Reading list for those who wish to pursue an in-depth study of these approaches to counseling. To aid the reader in putting these three selected approaches in perspective within the broad field of theory, the following information is provided. The three approaches selected for presentation in this chapter are listed after the general theories.

Psychodynamic
Psychoanalysis (Freud)
Analytic theory (Jung)
Contemporary psychoanalytic theory (Erikson)
Individual psychology (Adler, Dreikurs)
Interpersonal theory of psychiatry (Sullivan)
Neurosis and aggression (Horney)
Social psychology (Fromm)
Personology (Murray)
Organismic theory (Goldstein)

Behavioral/Cognitive-Behavioral
Rational-Emotive Therapy (Ellis)
Transactional analysis (Berne)
Reality therapy (Glasser)
Operant conditioning (Skinner)
Social modeling (Bandura)
Reciprocal inhibition (Wolpe)
Cognitive behavior modification (Meichenbaum, Beck)

Humanistic
Person-Centered (Rogers)
Gestalt therapy (Perls)
Logotherapy (Frankl)
Psychology of being (Maslow)
Existential (May, Binswanger, Yalom, Jourard)

The Story of Sally

Sally is a 36-year-old European-American woman who entered counseling hoping to deal with a variety of issues and concerns that had been bothering her and getting in the way of her leading a fulfilling life. She expressed the desire to improve her interactions with significant others, co-workers, and acquaintances. She reported being troubled by intense feelings of depression and loneliness, as well as feelings of anger and resentment that she harbors toward people in her past and present. Sally hoped to decrease what she referred to as her "bitchy" behavior, to stop interpreting messages and situations in a consistently self-critical way, and to put closure on a two-year dating relationship.

Sally described a very difficult childhood in which her father's family continuously criticized and ridiculed her. She pointed out that her parents never defended her and even restricted her from protesting against her relatives' verbal abuse. She felt that from a very early age she experienced rejection and loneliness. Sally reported that her intimate relationships as an adult have mirrored her relationships with her relatives as a child. In other words, Sally believed that she has consistently involved herself with people who are similar to those family members who have caused her so much emotional pain in the past. She was married and divorced three times, and described each of these relationships as being very destructive: her first husband beat her, her second husband was a drug addict, and her last husband "wanted a mother." She explained that her marriage relationships reflected her need to win people over and gain their approval, especially people who remind her of past relatives who never approved of her and were so "emotionally abusive" toward her.

Sally expressed concern that she now gives herself the same negative messages that she has heard all her life. She reported that she does not understand why she continues to "kick herself" in spite of the fact that she now lives a thousand miles away from her family. She stated that at times she really hates herself. She expressed strong fears of being mistreated and rejected in the future, as she has been in the past. She expressed frustration with her behavior, but tended to avoid an in-depth disclosure of her feelings, which were very intense and difficult for her to manage. Sally began counseling with an expressed desire to change or better manage these complex emotions and issues in her life.

Let us turn now to our counseling theories to discover how each would identify the development of Sally's problems and intervene to modify her affect, cognition, and behavior so that she would be able to lead a more productive and satisfying life.

A Psychodynamic Approach

The purpose of this section is to present an overview of Freudian psychology and theoretical constructs that may be useful to beginning therapists. The psychodynamic approach discussed here is not pure Freudian psychotherapy. Although based on traditional psychoanalytic theory, this presentation is influenced by contemporary trends in psychodynamic thought; see Kohut (1985) and Robbins (1989) for excellent discussions on more recent directions in the use of psychoanalytic theory in counseling.

Rationale: How Problems Evolve

The psychodynamic orientation stresses the influence of genetic impulses or *instincts*, the concept of life energy or *libido*, the influence of the client's life history—*psychosexual* and *psychosocial* development—on personality formation and the irrational, unconscious sources of human behavior (Robbins, 1989). Freud (1949) viewed people as inherently instinctual creatures, driven by their striving for infantile gratification. Throughout life, the individual is strongly motivated to seek out satisfaction of one of two primitive instinctual drives: sex and aggression. Therefore, a conflict is engendered between instinctual desires and the control of these emotions that must be maintained in the social world of "reality." To cope with this conflict, *defense mechanisms*, some conscious and others unconscious, are used that deny, falsify, and/or distort reality. As a consequence, the ego is protected from intrusive thoughts and instinctual energy or *psychic energy* is rechanneled into socially approved outlets. However, one's emotional awareness and perceptions of self and others are often inhibited by the defense mechanisms used.

Freud's (1915–1917) conceptualization of the unconscious and different levels of awareness is probably the most significant contribution of psychoanalysis to the field of psychology. Freud held that three different levels of consciousness influence personality development and functioning: the conscious, the preconscious, and the unconscious. The *conscious* level consists of those thoughts of which the individual is aware at the moment. The *preconscious* includes information that can be brought to the conscious level with relative ease. In traditional psychoanalytic theory, the third level of awareness, the *unconscious*, is the most important component of the mind because it largely determines human behavior.

Some unconscious information cannot readily be brought to the conscious level because it is too anxiety provoking to one's ego. Indeed, resistance to acknowledging its existence is blocked by employing ego defense mechanisms. For example, a person may truly hate his or her father, yet be unaware that these feelings exist and/or unable to accept that they do. In psychoanalytic theory, the importance of these unconscious feelings is that they constantly strive to become conscious, and the individual then expends considerable psychic energy to keep them in the unconscious. Thus people are in a perpetual state of internal conflict, often unaware of the cause of this struggle to prevent unacceptable, anxiety-provoking feelings and emotions from entering their consciousness.

The conflict at the unconscious level is postulated as being an ongoing battle for control of psychic energy among the three structural components of the personality. These are known as the id, the ego, and the superego. The *id* is the original system of personality, present at birth, that is characterized as the primary source of psychic energy (libido) and is the place where instincts reside; it is driven by the pleasure principle—an infantile need for immediate gratification. The second structural component of the personality is the *ego*, which functions to maintain an individual's contact with the external world or reality; it is governed by the reality principle—realistic and logical thinking designed to satisfy needs in a socially acceptable manner. The ego serves as a mediator between the superego and the id. In traditional Freudian theory, the ego is sometimes seen as being at the mercy of the other two competing forces. In more modern theory, however, the task of the therapist is seen as helping the ego decide and balance id and superego (Kohut, 1985). The third component of the personality is the *superego*, which serves as the person's moral code of conduct. Analogous to the popular concept of "conscience," the superego results from the social mores and parental moral attitudes that are internalized by the child during development.

Anxiety is a state of tension that serves as the motivating force within the person, and frequently results from the constant conflict among the id, ego, and superego. For example, negative emotions develop from unconscious memories of past childhood experiences, from frightening impulses driven by the id (such as aggressive desires that may be forbidden), from guilt derived from an overly self-critical superego, or from the inadequacy of the ego to resolve these internal conflicts. Anxiety serves as a warning to the ego that it is in danger of being overwhelmed, and therefore anxiety may be repressed by the ego defense mechanisms. However, ego defense mechanisms also tend to deny, falsify, or otherwise distort reality (Freud, 1936). Consequently, the individual's personality development is impeded, and realistic problem-solving strategies can also remain underdeveloped.

The complex task of the counselor is to help the client uncover the structure of anxiety so that personality reconstruction can begin. In the case of Sally, the psychodynamically oriented counselor believes that the origin and solution to her problems lie deep within her unconscious. For example, her excessive anxiety and depression might well be explained by the conflict between her angry, hostile feelings toward her parents and her superego, which continues to insist that parents are to be loved. Her ego defense mechanism of turning against self and identification with the aggressor, force her to expend considerable energy hiding the conflicts from herself and contribute to her self-defeating behavior.

A primary therapeutic task is to help Sally become more aware of her style of handling her anxiety and the underlying causes of her depression. Subsequently, more personally satisfying and socially approved ways of resolving these tensions and conflicts are discovered, helping Sally to develop more mature ways to use her psychic energy and to become more aware of problematic behaviors that result from unconscious impulses.

Mechanisms of Change

The goal of psychodynamic counseling with Sally is to make her conscious of unconscious material. The two means by which this is done is through *transference* and a *working alliance*. Gelso and Carter (1985, 1994) provide an in-depth discussion of these components of the counselor–client relationship. The scope of this chapter only allows us to explore briefly here the dynamics and importance of these change processes in psychodynamic theory.

Transference

Transference occurs when the client reexperiences in therapy emotions and attitudes originally present in earlier relationships, often the parent–child relationship (but others as well), and focuses these past feelings and emotional and behavioral reactions on the counselor. In the case of Sally, transference expressed itself in Sally's negativistic attitude about the perceived lack of help she was receiving from the counselor. In discussions with her about her early childhood psychosocial development (see Erikson, 1968), it became clear that this aspect of her personality was developed in her relationship with her cousins. Eventually she was able to work through her unresolved conflicts with her cousins by means of the transference relationship.

The counselor interpreted the transference relationship in order to help Sally understand how she was misperceiving, misinterpreting, and misresponding to the counselor, and to other people outside the counseling relationship, as a consequence of experiences in her earlier relationships with her cousins. The transference relationship helped her achieve a corrective emotional experience by means of *abreaction,* or "reliving" the original tension-evoking emotional experience. This "new" emotional experience provided a *catharsis* or release of tension and anxiety resulting from the process of bringing repressed ideas, feelings, wishes, and memories of the past into consciousness.

Working Alliance

The interpretation of the transference experience and Sally's acceptance of it were based on the *therapeutic alliance* developed between the counselor and Sally. Conceptually, the working alliance construct has its foundation in Freud's emphasis on the client–therapist collaboration in treatment (Connor-Greene, 1993). The primary focus of early writings emphasized the "therapeutic alliance" detailing the client's identification with the therapist, focusing on the more affective aspects of the client's collaboration in therapy. It was not until Greenson's (1967) writings that the therapeutic alliance was more comprehensively described as a *working alliance,* suggesting that the client's motivation and ability to work in the treatment situation were crucial for treatment success. A more contemporary conceptualization of the working alliance identifies both the client–therapist relationship and the client's collaborating in the tasks of treatment as central to positive therapeutic outcome (Gaston, 1990; Lambert & Bergin, 1994).

Bordin (1976) took the working alliance concept out of its psychoanalytic context and reframed it from a more pantheoretical viewpoint. He built on Greenson's (1967) earlier work but separated the working alliance from its attachment to the process of transference. His focus was on the conscious partnership of the client and the therapist working together to bring about change. Although Bordin perceived the working alliance as an integrated relationship, he defined three constituent components that in combination define the quality and strength of the working alliance. These three elements were tasks (in-counseling behaviors and cognitions), goals (outcomes), and bonds (the complex network of positive personal attachments between the client and the counselor).

Horvath and Greenberg (1989) stated that the significant departure for Bordin (1976) from previous theorists was to conceptualize the client–therapist interdependence along the dimension of mutuality. Bordin's concepts of task, goal, and bond involve collaboration and depend on the degree of concordance and joint purpose between the counselor and client. In other words, the client is much more a problem solver and the counselor becomes more directive in the approach to therapy (Bergin & Garfield, 1994). The counselor and the client agree on which in-therapy and outside-therapy tasks will be helpful in obtaining the goals of counseling. In the case of Sally, the working alliance was carefully nourished by the counselor to facilitate positive counseling outcomes.

Summary of the Psychodynamic Approach

In order to be effective with their clients, counselors using a psychodynamic approach need to recognize that there are intrapsychic forces motivating people that are not entirely conscious. They must understand the significance of childhood experiences and use the concept of transference in the counseling relationship. They need to know how people defend themselves from external and internal threats with ego defense mechanisms and other methods of resistance. Finally, a counselor using this approach needs to effectively create a working alliance that facilitates the counseling process. In so doing, transference dynamics can be interpreted for clients so that they can experience an abreactive catharsis of their debilitating past history.

A Cognitive-Behavioral Approach

The history of cognitive-behavior therapy has evolved through various theoretical positions. Some of the important stages of that evolution include behavior modification (Skinner, 1938, 1953) and its expansion into applied behavioral analysis (Michael, 1991; Morris, 1992), and imaginal systematic desensitization (Wolpe, 1982). Each of these approaches represents traditional reinforcement theories whose primary focus, although not exclusively, is to modify observable behaviors, without addressing intervening variables.

With the advent of cognitive-behavioral therapies such as rational-emotive therapy (Ellis, 1962), social learning theory (Bandura, 1977) and social cognitive theory (Bandura, 1991, 1993), cognitive therapy (Beck, 1976), and cognitive-behavior therapy (Meichenbaum, 1977), internal self-regulatory variables became pivotal determinants of behavior. The reader must keep in mind that the list of cognitive-behavioral therapeutic approaches given here is only representative and not exhaustive. The emphasis on the cognitive mediated aspects of behavior has facilitated a focus in therapy on client attributions, appraisals, expectations, and belief systems. These intrapsychic variables are viewed as integral cognitive processes in their effects on emotions and behaviors.

Albert Ellis is considered one of the most influential theorists in the field of cognitive-behavioral approaches to counseling. We will use his system of rational-emotive therapy, or RET (Ellis, 1962, 1993a) to illustrate one cognitive-behavioral approach and will apply RET in conceptualizing therapeutic interventions for Sally.

Rationale: How Problems Evolve

Rational-emotive therapy (RET), the fundamentals of which were developed by Albert Ellis in 1955, is based on the premise that emotional disturbance has several important cognitive, emotive, and behavioral sources. Although emotional disturbance or "neurosis" does not develop entirely from cognition or thinking, the etiology of unhealthy behaviors is heavily influenced by the process of an internal dialogue that is negatively affected by the individual's *irrational beliefs*. According to Ellis, human beings develop strong *preferences* for achievement, approval, comfort, and health, which are life goals. Due to a human innate propensity to construct absolutist demands, preferences can easily be transformed into irrational beliefs, which are dogmatic musts, shoulds, and oughts that become the standard by which social situations are measured. The interaction between irrational beliefs and social stimuli creates debilitating emotional reactions for the individual. In short, an underlying principle of RET is that a person feels what he or she thinks (Ellis, 1993a).

Rational-emotive therapy is based on a humanist and constructivist approach to conceptualizing the human agency (Ellis, 1993c). RET is concerned with the individual's systemic, phenomenological field and suggests that people strive to achieve life goals that are usually centered on remaining alive and being reasonably happy, such as attaining success, love, and comfort. The path to achieving these goals, however, is regularly blocked by interpersonal or environmental adversities that Ellis calls *activating events*. Ellis has proposed the ABC model of emotional disturbance (1993a) to describe this process.

During the process of maturation, the individual develops characteristic *beliefs* (B's) that are used to interpret and take action in response to these adversities or activating events (A's). An individual's belief system consists of *rational beliefs*, which are *preferences* that create appropriate emotional and behavioral consequences, and *irrational beliefs*, which are dogmatic musts and absolutist demands that create inappropriate and dysfunctional consequences. Therefore, cognitive, emotive, and behavioral *consequences* (C's) are created by the imposition of the individual's belief system on the activating events. Thus, when a preponderance of irrational beliefs compared to rational beliefs comprises the individual's belief system, emotional disturbance and unhealthy behaviors will result (Ellis, 1993a).

When RET was first practiced an emphasis was placed on ego disturbance—that is, self-induced emotional disturbance created by self-denigrating irrational or illogical thinking. However, it was soon recognized that people also had *discomfort disturbance* or *low frustration tolerance* (LFT), again caused by irrational beliefs, that are especially characterized by the individual's belief that other people and external conditions absolutely *must* be a certain way (Ellis, 1993b). As a consequence, Ellis added to the idea of ego disturbance the idea of discomfort disturbance, or LFT. Throughout his writings, Ellis (1993a) has maintained that ego and discomfort disturbance often occur simultaneously and significantly interact to cause severe neurotic problems.

In short, Ellis (1993a) maintains that emotional disturbance is the result of irrational and illogical thinking that occurs in the form of internalized sentences or verbal symbols that are generated from an irrational system of beliefs. Thus, according to RET, people are largely responsible for their emotional disturbances resulting from their irrational thinking. Ellis recognizes that emotion reflects a complex mode of behavior that is intricately tied to a variety of sensing and response processes and states. Nevertheless, the process of behavior change is built on the premise that people need to change their way of thinking (cognitive restructuring) in order to correct their irrational belief systems. Therefore, RET takes an active-directive approach in *disputing* a client's antiempirical and overgeneralized self-statements—the client's irrational beliefs. The objective is "to persuade and teach clients to vigorously, powerfully, and persistently think, feel, and act against their demandingness and to return to their preferences" (Ellis, 1993c, p. 199). Next we consider each of these components of RET—A, B, and C—separately and how they might relate to Sally's concerns and behaviors.

Activating Event

Usually a precipitating activating event or adversity is what motivates a person to enter counseling. In the case of Sally, her recent volatile breakup with a man she had been dating for two years brought on a great deal of stress and depression. The relationship, and the manner in which it ended, led Sally to begin to recognize her pattern of entering into destructive relationships, and the need to seek help to alter her typical interpersonal patterns of behavior.

Beliefs

The events that brought Sally to counseling were partially a realization that her emotional reactions within the relationship were not successful in eliciting either the desired responses from her partner or permitting Sally to maintain an emotional equilibrium. She became aware that her own emotions, thoughts, and behaviors within the relationship contributed to its termination, as well as to other problems in her life. Her system of irrational beliefs about relationships and her negative beliefs about herself led her to feel depressed. Her beliefs were characterized by self-statements such as "I absolutely need to be loved by this person in order to be happy and whole" and "Since I made mistakes in the relationship, I am to blame for its failure." Sally's failure to understand the causes of her dysfunctional life, and the impact of her belief system, are what prompted her to begin counseling.

Consequences

For many clients, the negative emotions of guilt, anger, depression, and anxiety are emotional consequences that appear to be directly caused by the activating event. RET posits that these emotional consequences are actually caused by clients' beliefs about the activating event. In Sally's case, she strongly believed that her feelings of rejection, sadness, and depression were directly related to the emotional turmoil in her relationship with her father and his family and not simply in her current relationship. Sally felt that she was repeatedly rejected and indirectly told that she was a terrible person. She communicated these feelings by disclosing in counseling that her parents would not allow her to "fight back" when her relatives criticized and "verbally abused" her. These past events, augmented by similar current events in her life, appear to be at the root of her own belief system about herself and the world around her. But in RET it is precisely this belief system that mediates the link between the activating event and the emotional consequence and not just the event itself, such as the ending of her two-year relationship, that creates turmoil. Therefore, RET focuses on changing a client's system of irrational and illogical beliefs.

Mechanisms of Change

Belief System

Identifying the client's belief system is a major focus of RET and is a key mechanism of change (Ellis, 1993a). The belief system is the *mediating variable* between the activating event and inappropriate consequences or emotional disturbance. Since most people draw a direct connection between activating events (A's) and consequences (C's), the main goal of the RET counselor is to help clients identify their irrational beliefs (B's) and thinking that underlie the emotional disturbance. Ellis (1962) originally identified ten irrational beliefs that all humans have that inevitably lead to pervasive dysfunctional behavior. Although he later added to the original list of irrational beliefs (Ellis & Whiteley, 1979), Ellis (1993a) has recently concluded that all these beliefs can be synthesized into three general categories of irrational beliefs, each including a rigidly prescribed must, should, or demand:

1. "I *(ego) absolutely* must *perform well and win significant others' approval or else I am an* inadequate, worthless person."
2. "You *(other people)* must *under all conditions and at all times be nice and fair to me or else* you *are a* rotten, horrible person!"
3. "Conditions *under which I live absolutely* must *be comfortable, safe, and advantageous or else the world is a* rotten place, I can't stand it, *and life is hardly worth living."* (p. 7)

Two main tenets of RET counseling are to (1) demonstrate to the client that his or her self-talk is a primary source of emotional disturbance, and (2) help the client to restructure his or her internal sentences in order to eliminate the underlying irrational beliefs. Sally felt that she had always been the object of abusive jokes, criticized incessantly, and told in a variety of ways that she was a worthless, unlikable person. She also made self-deprecating statements during her counseling sessions, such as "I need to prove to myself that I'm acceptable"; "The most I could hope for is to be stuck with losers and to be victimized"; and "I guess I need to be lectured to; I don't like yelling at myself, but that's what I end up doing." Following the two main tenets of RET, the counselor helped Sally clarify how she perceived events and interpreted messages from others as well as from herself, and helped her dispute her beliefs. As a consequence of this process, Sally was able to acknowledge her irrational beliefs concerning her need to be accepted and approved by others in all situations or feel that she was worthless as a person. Furthermore, she recognized that she was not able to perform perfectly in all situations, but nevertheless remained a "good" person.

Dispute

The real work of rational-emotive counseling involves the disputing of the client's irrational beliefs. The counselor actively challenges the client's existing belief system with the intent of eliminating the irrational beliefs and helping the client to develop and internalize a set of more positive and rational beliefs. Therefore, the process of uncovering the illogical, irrational nature of Sally's internal messages was the primary focus of counseling. As noted, the counselor provided new, supportive and logical self-statements such as "I can be disliked by certain people and still be a good and worthwhile person."

In counseling sessions, the illogical need to be loved by everyone at all times was consistently disputed. This strategy had a very positive effect as Sally began to realize that her self-critical, irrational belief system intensified her depression and anger, contributing to other problems in her relationships. By changing her belief system, she began to recognize more effective and positive ways of seeing herself and of relating with others. Homework was assigned with the intent of practicing her newly acquired rational beliefs. Whenever she felt that she was being disliked or rejected by someone, she was instructed to repeat three times to herself the following sentence: "I am still a good and worthwhile person, even if this person does not appreciate me." Again, the objective was to develop both socially and personally appropriate *preferences*, supported by rational beliefs, and to eliminate *absolutist demands*.

Changing the client's irrational belief system is not a straightforward process. The focus on disputing irrational beliefs typically produces changes in behavior and diminishes discomfort disturbance, but does so over time and as the client is able to integrate new information. Nevertheless, the client is encouraged to notice these changes and to celebrate their emergence. Thus, in working with Sally the RET counselor would proceed through the process of evaluating and explaining the ABCs of Sally's behaviors in order to have her thoroughly incorporate a new rational belief system.

Summary of Rational-Emotive Therapy

The basic assumption of the RET approach to counseling is that most people in our society develop many irrational ways of thinking. These irrational thoughts lead to inappropriate behavior and disturbing emotional reactions that create ego and discomfort disturbance. RET counseling is structured to facilitate clients' recognition of their irrational beliefs and alter their interpersonal patterns of behavior so that they are based on more functional, logical beliefs. The accomplishment of this goal requires an active/directive counselor who is at once supportive and at the same time has the capacity to actively engage and challenge the client (Ellis, 1993c).

A Person-Centered Approach

In this section we discuss person-centered therapy, one of the major theories in the humanistic framework. This theory, developed by Carl Rogers (1951, 1957), has been known during its evolution as *nondirective, client-centered, Rogerian,* and *person-centered* therapy. The present use of the term *person-centered therapy* reflects Roger's expanding scope of influence, including his interest in how people obtain, possess, share, or surrender *power* and *control* over others and themselves (Corey, 1991).

Rationale: How Problems Evolve

A central issue in person-centered therapy is how the individual perceives the world. What the individual perceives in his or her *phenomenological field* is more important than the "actual" reality. In other words, what the individual *perceives* to be occurring *is* the reality. Thus, a consistent effort to understand and experience as far as possible the unique qualities of each client's subjective world is fundamental to person-centered therapy. The focus is not primarily with past causes of behavior; rather, person-centered therapy focuses on current experiences, feelings, and the interpersonal relationships of the individual.

Person-centered therapy is based on a belief that people act in accordance with their self-concept. One's self-concept is heavily influenced by experiences interacting with others and the environment. In order for a healthy self-concept to emerge, a person requires unconditional positive regard, such as love, support, respect, acceptance, and nurturing.

Often in childhood, as well as later in life, a child is given conditional positive regard by parents and significant others in his or her life. In other words, parents and others communicate to the child, either directly or indirectly, exactly what the child must be or how the child must act in order to receive positive regard. Feelings of self-worth develop if the person behaves in accordance with these prescribed emotional and behavioral patterns because acceptance and approval are thereby achieved. Sometimes, however, children may have to deny or distort their perception of a given situation when their personal needs conflict with the expectancies of someone that they depend on for approval.

The individual is thus caught in a dilemma because of the incongruence between personal growth needs and needs for positive regard. On the one hand, if a person does not do as others wish, he or she is not valued and accepted. On the other hand, if a person conforms, he or she disregards personal needs to evolve a self-concept predicated on internally derived goals. In this case, the ideal self that the person is striving to become is thwarted. The larger the discrepancy between the *real self* and the *ideal self*, the more incongruence a person experiences. In other words, conflict arises when individuals must choose between personal needs for *self-actualization* and the approval that significant others provide that is conditional to certain behaviors, thoughts, or feelings.

One's self-concept is a learned attribute, starting from birth and progressively developing through childhood, adolescence, and adulthood. In Sally's case, she experienced a conflict between the conditions of receiving positive regard, or validation, that were placed on her as a child and the experience of evolving as a person who had unique needs and goals. For example, she received messages from her parents that she should not "fight back" or confront her cousins and other relatives for being verbally abusive toward her. Her parents communicated to her, "You're better than they are, you don't need to fight back." Much of Sally's present negative interpersonal interactions with others reflect a self-concept that has attempted to incorporate messages such as this example. But this message is contradictory to her need to feel safe, assertive, and protected. Therefore, Sally harbors a great deal of anger and resentment toward her family and toward others who remind her of her family that consistently frustrated her self-actualizing potential. She frequently uses inappropriate anger, lashing out at people in current relationships because they "remind" her of family members against whom she was never able to "fight back."

Sally's poor self-concept resulted in part from a long history of negative and/or mixed messages from others that have been internalized. In addition, the conflict between how she should be and act in order to be a "good," acceptable person, and how she, in fact, behaves toward and thinks about others exacerbates the incongruence between her real self and her ideal self. For a long time Sally has given herself the message that she is an undesirable, unacceptable person. Unfortunately, Sally's self-concept was formed on this premise, and she now finds it difficult to respond to others and to herself in a caring and accepting way. Her marriage relationships validated her negative self-image because they have "proven" to her that she is a "failure," a "victim," and will "always be stuck with losers."

Mechanisms of Change

Self-Actualization
Within the humanistic framework, the self-actualizing tendency is the primary motivating force of the human organism. *Self-actualization* is an inherent tendency in people to move in directions described by words such as *growth, adjustment, socialization, independence, self-realization,* and *fully functioning.* Thus, in the humanistic philosophy that underlies the person-centered approach, humans have an innate capacity to interact with their environment in ways designed to maintain and enhance their self-concept. Rogers (1951) emphasized that the client's natural capacity for growth and development is an important human characteristic on which counseling should focus. For example, in spite of the negative experiences that Sally has had in her life and her subsequent emotional pain, anger, and self-defeating behaviors, she has an innate predisposition to be self-actualized. This predisposition can be nourished and drawn out, given a facilitative psychological climate.

Core Conditions for Constructive Personality Change
In his classic article, Rogers (1957) identified the core conditions that must exist in order for constructive personality change to occur:

1. *The two persons are in psychological contact.*
2. *The first, whom we shall term the client, is in a state of incongruence, being vulnerable or anxious.*
3. *The second, whom we shall term the therapist, is congruent and integrated in the relationship.*
4. *The therapist experiences unconditional positive regard for the client.*

5. *The therapist experiences an empathic understanding of the client's internal frame of reference and endeavors to communicate this experience to the client.*

6. *The communication to the client of the therapist's empathic understanding and unconditional positive regard is to a minimal degree achieved. (p. 96)*

Rogers identified three personal characteristics, or attitudes, of the therapist that are essential before a therapeutic relationship can be established: (1) genuineness, or congruence, (2) unconditional positive regard, and (3) empathy. These characteristics offered by the counselor to the client result in a therapeutic climate that allows the client's self-actualizing tendency to flourish. Due to the centrality of their importance to person-centered therapy, we will describe each of these characteristics.

Genuineness.   Genuineness or congruence, is the counselor's capacity to be "real" in the relationship. Thus, *genuineness* is used to denote honesty, directness, and sincerity, and an absence of a professional façade. Rogers (1961) defines genuineness as follows: "By this we mean that the feelings that the counselor is experiencing are available to his awareness, that he is able to live with these feelings, be them in the relationship, and able to communicate them if appropriate. . . . It means that he is being himself, not denying himself" (p. 417). Genuineness, then, is the counselor's ability to be psychologically open and *present* with the client in therapy. The counselor is "real" in the relationship, demonstrating a consistency between his or her own feeling/experiencing at the moment and his or her verbal and nonverbal communications to the client.

In Sally's case, the counselor's willingness to be genuine in the relationship with her provides Sally with a psychological climate that can be trusted, thereby facilitating her self-disclosure. The counselor's genuineness and openness to being present with Sally is a crucial element contributing to her change process. It allows her to be real and to come into psychological contact with her counselor, expressing her feelings with the knowledge that she is and will be supported.

Unconditional Positive Regard.   This counselor characteristic has also been referred to as "nonpossessive warmth," and "regard" and is equivalent to respect, appreciation, and acceptance of another person. It can be described as the counselor's ability to experience an acceptance of every aspect of the client's personality. "Nonpossessive" or "unconditional" implies that the counselor does not qualify his or her acceptance of the client, but accepts the client fully as a separate person with a right to his or her own thoughts, words, actions, and feelings.

Unconditional positive regard is a crucial component of the counseling relationship with Sally, especially in light of the fact that Sally's self-worth has previously been validated only when she has responded and behaved in an explicitly defined and prescribed manner. The counselor offers positive regard with no conditional stipulations. This caring, accepting attitude of Sally's individuality emerges from the belief that she can discover within herself the necessary resources for her own growth. Eventually, Sally will come to understand that she is capable of taking charge of her own life.

Empathy.   Empathic understanding, or empathy, may be defined as an active, immediate, continuous process of *living* another's feelings, their intensity, and their meaning instead of simply observing them. The accuracy of a counselor's empathic understanding and sensitivity to the client's feelings and experiences as they are revealed during the moment-to-moment interaction of the counseling session conveys the counselor's interest in appreciating the client's phenomenological world. The counselor strives to sense fully and accurately the inner world of the client's subjective experience. The concept of *accurate empathy*, like the other counselor attributes, has evolved over the years in the direction of freeing the counselor to be a more active participant in the therapeutic encounter. High levels of accurate empathy go beyond recognition of obvious feelings to an exploration of and communication about perceptions of underlying client messages.

In one interview, Sally said that her depression and feelings of resentment typically drove her to do things to others that pushed them away or kept them from getting close to her. Sally expressed how she behaved, but failed to indicate her feelings about the consequences of her behavior. The counselor focused on these unspoken feelings, assisting Sally's process of making contact with them and, ultimately, with the more intimate aspects of her inner self. When the counselor asked Sally to describe her loneliness, she began to cry. Since loneliness was the result of her behaviors toward others, but a feeling she had never previously identified, helping her to recognize and deal with her loneliness was a major factor in her continuing growth.

Summary of the Person-Centered Approach

A major assumption of person-centered therapy is the belief in the individual's innate motivation toward self-actualization and in the individual's potential to become a *fully functioning* person. A person will generally seek help in therapy when a significant incongruence between his or her real self and ideal self develops. The main intent in counseling is to develop a relationship between the counselor and the client that will facilitate the client's capacity for understanding his or her unhappiness and moving on to constructive personal growth. Crucial to the creation of this relationship are the counselor's characteristics of genuineness, unconditional positive regard, and accurate empathy. Therefore, creating and maintaining a nonthreatening, anxiety-free relationship in which client growth can take place is an essential component of person-centered therapy.

Summary

Three counseling theories within the psychodynamic, cognitive-behavioral, and humanistic traditions in psychology are Freudian psychoanalytic and general psychodynamic theory, Ellis's rational-emotive therapy, and Rogers's person-centered therapy. Individual therapy from the psychodynamic perspective focuses on unconscious intrapsychic forces, childhood experiences, ego defense mechanisms, and the notion of transference in the therapeutic relationship. Building a working alliance in therapy in order to interpret and confront transference dynamics and defense mechanisms is critical to successful counseling. Individual counseling from Ellis's approach focuses on the role of irrational thinking that people maintain about the world and self that leads to inappropriate behavior and to disturbing emotional reactions. Confronting irrational beliefs and learning more functional, logical beliefs about interpersonal patterns is central to the therapy process. Person-centered therapy is based on the belief that people have an innate motivation toward self-actualization, have the capacity for understanding their unhappiness, and can become fully functioning. Therapy focuses on developing the relationship between the client and counselor, marked by counselor genuineness, unconditional positive regard, and accurate empathy. Maintaining this nonthreatening, anxiety-free relationship is an essential component of successful person-centered therapy. Each of these theories has made enormous contributions to the process of counseling individuals toward achieving positive change, growth, and self-understanding. The case of Sally illustrates these contributions.

References

Bandura, A. (1977). *Social learning theory*. Englewood Cliffs, NJ: Prentice Hall.

Bandura, A. (1991). Social cognitive theory of self-regulation. *Organizational Behavior and Human Decision Processes, 50,* 248–287.

Bandura A. (1993). Perceived self-efficacy in cognitive development and functioning. *Educational Psychologist, 28*(2), 117–148.

Beck, A. T. (1976). *Cognitive therapy and the emotional disorders*. New York: International Universities Press.

Bergin, A. E., & Garfield, S. L. (1994). Overview, trends, and future issues. In A. E. Bergin & S. L. Garfield (Eds.), *Handbook of psychotherapy and behavior change* (4th ed., pp. 821–830). New York: Wiley.

Bordin, E. S. (1976). The generalizability of the psychoanalytic concept of the working alliance. *Psychotherapy: Theory, Research and Practice, 16,* 252–260.

Connor-Greene, P. A. (1993). The therapeutic context: Preconditions for change in psychotherapy. *Psychotherapy, 30,* 375–382.

Corey, G. (1991). Person-centered therapy. In *Theory and practice of counseling and psychotherapy* (4th ed., pp. 203–229). Pacific Grove, CA: Brooks/Cole.

Ellis, A. (1962). *Reason and emotion in psychotherapy*. New York: Stuart.

Ellis, A. (1993a). Fundamentals of rational-emotive therapy for the 1990s. In W. Dryden & L. K. Hill (Eds.), *Innovations in rational-emotive therapy* (pp. 1–32). Newbury Park, CA: Sage.

Ellis, A. (1993b). *The intelligent woman's guide to dating and mating*. New York: Stuart.

Ellis, A. (1993c). Reflections on rational-emotive therapy. *Journal of Consulting and Clinical Psychology, 61*(2), 199–201.

Ellis, A., & Whiteley, J. M. (1979). *Theoretical and empirical foundations of rational-emotive therapy*. Monterey, CA: Brooks/Cole.

Erikson, E. H. (1968). *Identity: Youth and crisis*. New York: Norton.

Freud, A. (1936). *The writings of Anna Freud, Vol. 2: The ego and the mechanisms of defense*. New York: International Universities Press.

Freud, S. (1915–1917). *Introductory lectures on psychoanalysis*. London: Hogarth Press.

Freud, S. (1949). *An outline of psychoanalysis*. New York: Norton.

Gaston, L. (1990). The concept of the alliance and its role in psychotherapy: Theoretical and empirical considerations. *Psychotherapy, 27,* 143–153.

Gelso, C. J., & Carter, J. A. (1985). The relationship in counseling and psychotherapy: Components, consequences, and theoretical antecedents. *Counseling Psychologist, 13,* 155–243.

Gelso, C. J., & Carter, J. A. (1994). Components of the psychotherapy relationship: Their interaction and unfolding during treatment. *Counseling Psychologist, 41*(3), 296–306.

Greenson, R. R. (1967). *Technique and practice of psychoanalysis.* New York: International Universities Press.

Horvath, A. O., & Greenberg, L. S. (1989). Development and validation of the working alliance inventory. *Journal of Counseling Psychology, 36*(2), 223–233.

Kohut, H. (1985). *Self psychology and the humanities: Reflections on a new psychoanalytic approach.* New York: Norton.

Lambert, M. J., & Bergin, A. E. (1994). The effectiveness of psychotherapy. In A. E. Bergin & S. L. Garfield (Eds.), *Handbook of psychotherapy and behavior change* (4th ed., pp. 143–189). New York: Wiley.

Meichenbaum, D. (1977). *Cognitive-behavior modification.* New York: Plenum Press.

Michael, J. (1991). Historical antecedents of behavior analysis. *Applied Behavior Analysis Newsletter, 14*(2), 7–12.

Morris, E. K. (1992). The aim, progress, and evolution of behavior analysis. *Behavior Analyst, 15,* 3–29.

Robbins, S. B. (1989). Role of contemporary psychoanalysis in counseling psychology. *Journal of Counseling Psychology, 36*(3), 267–278.

Rogers, C. R. (1951). *Client-centered therapy.* Boston: Houghton Mifflin.

Rogers, C. R. (1957). The necessary and sufficient conditions of therapeutic personality change. *Journal of Consulting Psychology, 21,* 95–103.

Rogers, C. R. (1961). *On becoming a person.* Boston: Houghton Mifflin.

Skinner, B. F. (1938). *The behavior of organisms.* New York: Appleton-Century-Crofts.

Skinner, B. F. (1953). *Science and human behavior.* New York: Macmillan.

Wolpe, J. (1982). *The practice of behavior therapy* (3rd ed.). Elmsford, NY: Pergamon Press.

Suggested Reading

Psychodynamic Theory

Brenner, C. (1974). *An elementary textbook of psychoanalysis* (rev. ed.). Garden City, NY: Doubleday (Anchor).

Freud, A. (1946). *The ego and the mechanisms of defense.* New York: International Universities Press.

Freud, S. (1949). *An outline of psychoanalysis.* New York: Norton.

Gelso, C. J., & Carter, J. A. (1994). Components of the psychotherapy relationship: Their interaction and unfolding during treatment. *Counseling Psychologist, 41*(3), 296–306.

Kohut, H. (1985). *Self psychology and the humanities: Reflections on a new psychoanalytic approach.* New York: Norton.

Robbins, S. B. (1989). Role of contemporary psychoanalysis in counseling psychology. *Journal of Counseling Psychology, 36*(3), 267–278.

Teyber, E. (1992). *Interpersonal process in psychotherapy: A guide for clinical training* (2nd ed.). Pacific Grove, CA: Brooks/Cole.

Cognitive-Behavioral Theory

Bandura, A. (1986). *Social foundations of thought and action: A social cognitive theory.* Englewood Cliffs, NJ: Prentice Hall.

Bandura A. (1993). Perceived self-efficacy in cognitive development and functioning. *Educational Psychologist, 28*(2), 117–148.

Beck, A. T. (1976). *Cognitive therapy and the emotional disorders.* New York: International Universities Press.

Dryden, W. (1994). Reason and emotion in psychotherapy: Thirty years on. *Journal of Rational-Emotive and Cognitive-Behavior Therapy, 12*(2), 83–99.

Dryden, W., & Hill, L. K. (1993). *Innovations in rational-emotive therapy*. Newbury Park, CA: Sage.

Ellis, A. (1993). Fundamentals of rational-emotive therapy for the 1990s. In W. Dryden & L. K. Hill (Eds.), *Innovations in rational-emotive therapy* (pp. 1–32). Newbury Park, CA: Sage.

Heward, E. L., & Cooper, J. O. (1992). Radical behaviorism: A productive and needed philosophy for education. *Journal of Behavioral Education, 2*(4), 345–365.

Michael, J. (1991). Historical antecedents of behavior analysis. *Applied Behavior Analysis Newsletter, 14*(2), 7–12.

Morris, E. K. (1992). The aim, progress, and evolution of behavior analysis. *Behavior Analyst, 15,* 3–29.

Person-Centered Therapy

Ford, J. G. (1991). Rogers's theory of personality: Review and perspectives. *Journal of Social Behavior and Personality, 6*(5), 19–44.

Graf, C. (1994). On genuineness and the person-centered approach: A reply to Quinn. *Journal of Humanistic Psychology, 34*(2), 90–96.

Orlov, A. B. (1992). Carl Rogers and contemporary humanism. *Journal of Russian and East European Psychology, 30*(1), 36–41.

Rogers, C. R. (1951). *Client-centered therapy*. Boston: Houghton Mifflin.

Rogers, C. R. (1961). *On becoming a person*. Boston: Houghton Mifflin.

Rogers, C. R. (1980). *A way of being*. Boston: Houghton Mifflin.

Rogers, C. R., & Sanford, R. C. (1985). Client-centered psychotherapy. In H. I. Kaplan, B. J. Sadock, & A. M. Friedman (Eds.), *Comprehensive textbook of psychiatry* (4th ed., pp. 1374–1388). Baltimore: Williams & Wilkins.

Tobin, S. A. (1991). A comparison of psychoanalytic self psychology and Carl Rogers's person-centered therapy. *Journal of Humanistic Psychology, 31*(1), 9–33.

Individual Counseling

Brief Approaches

Rolla E. Lewis, Ed.D.   Conrad Sieber, Ph. D.

There are numerous brief approaches to counseling (Koss & Butcher, 1986). Because surveying all the literature regarding brief therapy is beyond the scope of this chapter, our goal is to help counselors appreciate the richness found in brief approaches by revealing both the variety and depth available to counselors. In selecting for variety, we may cut short or even leave out brief approaches others consider worthy of note. In selecting for depth, we may choose brief approaches other counselors would exclude from such a chapter.

Although this chapter does not explore Adlerian, rational-emotive behavior therapy, or reality therapy's approaches to brief therapy, each of these schools has developed effective brief approaches. For example, Shulman (1989) finds similarities between Adlerian psychotherapy and some forms of brief therapy by pointing out that rapid assessment, flexibility, and active interpretation of emotions and goals are part of the Adlerian approach, whereas, in his usual understatement, Ellis (1989, 1990, 1996) proposes rational-emotive behavior therapy as a briefer and better form of therapy. Ellis states the ABC method is probably the most effective brief method for changing fundamental "disturbance-creating attitudes." In a similar vein, Palmatier (1990) submits an approach using reality therapy and brief strategic therapy. Palmatier offers linkages for counselors interested in applying both approaches.

Because ours is a brief chapter on brief therapies, we have referred to a number of sources for students to pursue further study (Cooper, 1995; Friedman, 1993; Koss & Shiang, 1994; Walter & Peller, 1992; Wells & Giannetti, 1990; Zeig & Gilligan, 1990). Theoretically, brief therapy ranges from psychodynamic to behavioral perspectives. Temporally, brief therapy ranges from one to twenty-five sessions. Twenty-five is considered the maximum number of sessions for brief therapy, and single-session therapy is considered an effective brief approach (Koss & Butcher, 1986; Rosenbaum, Hoyt, & Talmon, 1990). Yet overemphasis on length of treatment may be somewhat misleading, because brief therapists argue that the short duration of therapy results from using effective and efficient therapies (Cade & O'Hanlon, 1993; Zeig & Gilligan, 1990).

Cooper (1995) offers eight technical features common to the various forms of brief therapy:

1. *Maintenance of a clear, specific treatment focus;*
2. *A conscious and conscientious use of time;*
3. *Limited goals with clearly defined outcomes;*
4. *An emphasis on intervening in the present;*
5. *Rapid assessment and integration of assessment within treatment;*
6. *Frequent review of progress and discarding of ineffective interventions;*
7. *A high level of therapist–client activity;*
8. *Pragmatic and flexible use of techniques (p. 14)*

Coupled with the technical features they have in common, certain values are shared by brief therapists (Cooper, 1995; Koss & Butcher, 1986; Koss & Shiang, 1994). Brief therapists embrace pragmatism and parsimony in their therapeutic approach. They see human change as the inevitable and build on client resources and competence. Brief therapists use homework, recognize that significant change occurs outside of therapy, and believe that life outside of therapy is more important than therapy itself. In addition, brief-therapy advocates recognize that there are times when therapy does not help, and therapy is best when it is focused on specific contexts and problems (Cade & O'Hanlon, 1993; Cooper, 1995; Durrant & Kowalski, 1993; Wells & Giannetti, 1990).

This chapter focuses on short-term dynamic therapies that are firmly rooted in Freud's psychoanalytical perspective and the interactional therapies that find their roots in the work of Gregory Bateson and Milton Erickson.

Brief Psychodynamic Approaches

There are several brief psychodynamic approaches. This section focuses on the common elements found within brief psychodynamic therapy, specific forms of brief dynamic therapies with additional emphasis on James Mann's time-limited therapy.

Common Elements of Brief Psychodynamic Therapy

The elements shared in the therapeutic process by the brief dynamic therapies include client selection, therapeutic goals, and techniques.

Client Selection.   One way to improve outcomes in short-term dynamic psychotherapy has been through client selection. Koss and Butcher (1986) and Koss and Shiang (1994) establish four main criteria for selecting clients. These include clients with behavioral problems of acute onset, good previous adjustment, good relationship skills, and high motivation. Clients with strong ego resources—that is, those who are emotionally mature, autonomous, adaptive to life's challenges, and able to work collaboratively with a therapist—are the best candidates for short-term dynamic therapy (Strupp, 1981). Strupp (1981) reports that clients' suitability for short-term dynamic therapy can usually be determined within the first three sessions. In contrast to these fairly limiting criteria, Malan (1976b, as cited in Strupp, 1981) reported that people with major character disorders may also benefit from brief dynamic approaches.

Clients who are not good candidates include those with major dependency needs, problems with impulse control, self-centeredness, masochism, and self-destructiveness (Koss & Butcher, 1986). As Strupp (1981) points out, the exclusion criteria are not dissimilar from those of psychoanalysis in general. It should be noted that these selection criteria lack connection to diagnostic categories found in the *Diagnostic Statistical Manual of Mental Disorders* or *DSM-IV* (American Psychiatric Association, 1994) where the focus is on symptomatology. Instead, the criteria focus on personality organization, which is the fundamental structure of a patient's personality as developed in childhood.

Goals and Techniques.   The goals of time-limited psychodynamic therapy are limited. They often include helping clients understand dynamic (internalized) conflicts from the past in the context of their current lives. Rather than restructuring clients' personalities, the goal is to work through these conflicts in the present. As with all time-limited psychotherapy, technical flexibility is very important.

Refinements in technique as a means of achieving desired outcomes have also been a concern. Strupp (1981) describes two important techniques: the use of interpretation and the focus on a dynamic conflict. Interpretation as a primary technique has been emphasized by many short-term dynamic therapies. Examples include interpretations focusing on oedipal conflicts, linking client–therapist conflicts to clients' parental figures, and separation issues. Thus, there is an attempt to identify a core conflictual theme in a client's current dilemma that has led to the present distress. Strupp (1981) suggests that to be effective, time-limited dynamic therapists must bring the conflict alive in the transference, enabling clients to struggle in the present with a painful conflict from the past. The timing of interpretation is important and must come at the crucial moment during their transference struggles when clients are ready to hear the interpretation. Strupp (1981) states that interpretations may be highly effective if they are of the kind that appeal and make sense to clients and to which they can respond positively. The interpretation then provides an important "missing piece" in clients' understanding of their difficulties. Essentially, the message must have personal meaning to clients.

Major emphasis in the literature on time-limited dynamic therapy techniques has also been on the management of transference (clients' responding to the therapist in ways connected to important people in their past, such as parents). When working with transference, there is a need for flexibility of approach, empathy, and ability to form a constructive therapeutic alliance. Furthermore, therapists must minimize clients' negative transference reactions, while capitalizing on positive transference. Negative transference, for example, could involve clients responding to a therapist as if he or she were a critical parent, while an example of positive transference might involve clients responding to a therapist as if he or she were an admired, supportive person from their past. Negotiating the interpersonal process in these therapies means therapists must have patience with the pace and limited scope of time-limited dynamic therapy.

Forms of Brief Dynamic Therapies

Limiting the Duration of Psychoanalytic Therapy—Franz Alexander
Alexander (1946, as cited in Worchel, 1990) attempted to shorten the duration of psychoanalytic therapy by advocating flexibility in selecting techniques for specific clients' psychopathology. Significantly, he recognized the need to select appropriate clients for such treatment. Accordingly, important client characteristics for short-term dynamic therapy included ego strength and flexibility, capacity to be actively involved in the therapeutic process, high motivation for change, and responding positively to interpretation.

Tavistock System—David Malan
The Tavistock system was first developed by Balint's group at the Tavistock Clinic in London, England. Malan (1976a, 1979, as cited in Worchel, 1990), a member of this group, reported on the outcomes of this brief dynamic approach. Client selection focused on highly motivated and highly responsible individuals. Several criteria were deemed important, including motivation for insight and change, psychological-mindedness, ability to find a therapeutic focus (oedipal or loss), and good relationships outside therapy. Clients found inappropriate for such treatment included those with histories of long-term hospitalization, drug addiction, serious suicide attempts, incapacitating chronic phobic symptoms, or chronic obsessional symptoms. Important techniques included early interpretation of transference reactions, thorough interpretation of negative transference reactions, and attempts to link the transference relationship to clients' relationships with their parents. During the process of termination, grief and anger are worked through as thoroughly as possible.

Short-Term Anxiety Provoking Psychotherapy—Peter Sifneos
Sifneos's (1972, 1979, as cited in Worchel, 1990) short-term anxiety-provoking therapy is regarded as most appropriate for highly motivated and highly responsive clients with neurotic disturbances. Client selection emphasizes a circumscribed chief complaint, meaningful relationships in early childhood, ability to interact

flexibly with the therapist and to express feelings appropriately, psychological mindedness, and good motivation to change. Therapists must develop a specific psychodynamic formulation with a focus that is oedipal in nature, highlighting internal conflicts within clients that grew out of their childhood desire to unite with the opposite-sex parent in opposition or rivalry with the same-sex parent. In adulthood, oedipal conflicts may be experienced as anger toward people in positions of authority. Short-term anxiety provoking techniques involve rapid establishment of rapport and a therapeutic alliance, using open-ended and forced-choice questions, early clarification of transference feelings for the therapist, repeated use of anxiety-provoking questions, and confrontation. In addition, therapists repeatedly demonstrate to clients their neurotic pattern of behavior, emphasize the creation of a corrective emotional experience that leads to new problem-solving skills, and look for tangible signs of behavior change outside the therapeutic relationship, with the goal being early termination.

Intensive Short-Term Dynamic Therapy—Habib Davanloo

The previous therapies deal with the problem of major client resistance through client selection, whereas Davanloo (1978, as cited in Worchel, 1990) has developed a treatment appropriate for the whole spectrum of structural neuroses, except for those clients with highly fragile egos (limited internal coping resources and vulnerability to regression and decompensation). Davanloo describes a typology of neuroses consisting of four main types.

First are the highly motivated and responsive clients with relatively limited problems and essentially healthy personalities suffering from phobic, obsessional, or depressive symptoms. Relationship problems may also be part of these clients' difficulties. The single focus here is typically an oedipal conflict or loss.

The second group consists of moderately resistant clients with more complex problems. These clients have diffuse neurotic disturbances and characterological problems and often experience difficulty being assertive and realizing their potential. Here there are many foci, usually involving oedipal conflicts, sibling rivalry, and loss. These difficulties are often related to clients' defenses or phobic and obsessional symptoms.

Third are the very resistant, poorly motivated clients who have diffuse symptoms and character pathology (a well-established pattern of behavior that is dysfunctional and believed to have become an integral part of clients' personalities). Often their lives and relationships are interfered with by chronic phobic, obsessional, depressive, and other neurotic difficulties. This group includes clients with panic disorder, depressive disorder, functional, and somatization disorder. They often have interpersonal difficulties focused on conflicts over intimacy and closeness. These clients often have a history of traumatic experiences in early childhood, multiple losses, and so on.

Davanloo (1978, as cited in Worchel, 1990) describes a fourth group of clients who are very resistant, and poorly motivated, with major ego syntonic character pathology (their pathology is experienced as an accepted, congruent part of their personalities). Thus motivation for change may be limited, because ego syntonic character pathology leaves clients with little dissonance concerning their behavior and oblivious to its negative impact on others.

Davanloo (1978, as cited in Worchel, 1990) uses a system of trial therapy for selecting clients who would be inappropriate for the other short-term dynamic therapies because they are not highly motivated and responsive. These trial therapies are a few sessions in duration and designed to test clients' potential response to treatment. They are used as a diagnostic tool, a method for client selection, intervention, teaching, and research. This process involves developing a plan for evaluation, clinical diagnosis, a psychodynamic formulation of the clients' difficulties, a biopsychosocial assessment, and a treatment plan.

The technique of "unlocking the unconscious" developed for use with highly resistant clients is designed to identify unconscious conflicts that are interfering with clients' lives. This technique involves a high degree of activity by therapists to manage clients' resistance and extensive use of the transference to explore clients' unconscious conflicts. In working through the transference, therapists focus on two basic triangles. The first involves internal conflicts consisting of three dimensions: impulse/feeling (I/F), anxiety (A), and defense (D). The second, the "triangle of the person," consists of the transference relationship (T), current significant people (C), and past significant people (P). The second triangle includes those significant people in the past with whom clients have unresolved conflicts and those with whom clients currently have conflicts. It also contains the transference relationship with the therapist. The trial therapy has two major phases: the preinterpretive phase, in which therapists handle resistance, and the interpretive phase, which starts after the first breakthrough into the unconscious takes place (Davanloo, 1978; as cited in Worchel, 1990).

Time-Limited Therapy—James Mann

The remainder of this section explores in more detail the time-limited dynamic therapy, developed by James Mann at Boston University. Mann (1981) states that the crucial principles of his treatment are the conscious and unconscious meaning and influence of time and a method developed to elicit the central issue. The central issue is defined as understanding the underlying meaning of the problems clients bring into treatment and using this knowledge to guide the therapy throughout its course. Mann's model employs a specific structural framework with a precise, predetermined goal and a predetermined time limit that stays the same for each client. Mann's specific focus on time itself becomes a bridge to formulating the central issue. The explicit focus on and use of time proves illuminating in the context of understanding time-limited dynamic therapy.

Mann's Therapeutic Process

Time.   According to Mann, one way to view time is as a means of integrating in our minds and feelings "what was, what is and what will be." Although consciously we may be thinking about current events in our lives, on an unconscious level our thoughts and/or feelings are not restricted to that particular moment. Significant events from the past trigger memories that are often unconscious because we are motivated not to remember and our defenses protect us from these memories. Memories involving people of importance to us cannot be separated from time and its meaning to us. As themes from the past, present and future are identified, the clients' awareness of time is expanded. Thus, the goal of treatment is to help clients confront their past, improve their ability to cope with the present, and become empowered to shape the future.

None of us can escape the limitations of time. Yet there are many ways to attempt to do so through the use of alcohol and drugs, antianxiety medication, and so on. People by nature are affected by their memories, which are linked to significant people from the past. Memories and feelings about past important relationships affect reactions to people in the present. Transference reactions repeatedly display thoughts, feelings, and behaviors that at various moments are connected. Every moment of time includes past, present, and future. From this viewpoint, time not only progresses from past to present to future, but also has a reciprocal relationship in which one period of time cannot be experienced without the other. Thus past, present, and future are bound together.

Awareness of time and the ongoing relationship between it and memories reflect the connection between time and early object relations (that is, important relationships, such as those with parents). Thus the experience of time is invariably connected to affect. The greater the pain associated with a conflictual memory, the more the person will defend against and repress the affect connected to it. Typically, time is experienced as a background presence. We are aware of it, but it does not interfere with our ongoing experience. The more time enters into awareness, the more likely the presence of psychopathology. For instance, in depressed clients there is an experience of everything being past, such that there is no present and the future seems impossible. Anxiety raises fears about the uncertainty of the future, a fear of what may happen. Although the essence of the fear is unconscious, it is experienced consciously, with a distinctly future orientation.

Mann (1981) points out that in contrast to other medical specialties, therapists are explicit about the issue of selling time to clients. They know how much time they will have to work with during any one session. Therapists have tended to ignore the conscious and unconscious meaning and experience of time in their clients as well as themselves. In long-term therapy, clients and therapists experience treatment as timeless, and each tends not to pay much attention to the issue of time. Usually time becomes most important only as treatment moves toward termination, although short-term therapies by definition imply a time limit. Unless clients know explicitly the duration of their treatment, however, they may have the fantasy that it will be timeless. The more uncertainty about the length of treatment, the more clients are influenced by regressive, infantile, and dependent wishes.

As these wishes continue and are fostered by the sense of timelessness of treatment, they can lead to the hope that the therapist will turn back time. Therefore, according to Mann (1981), the more clearly the duration of treatment is articulated, the more rapidly the infantile fantasies are confronted with the realities of the adult, of real time, and of the work that must be done. That is, at the time clients begin to establish a working alliance with therapists, they experience on an unconscious level feelings associated with important childhood parental figures. The separation anxiety produced by this experience is temporarily relieved by connection with the therapist. Mann (1981) notes that psychotherapy, whether brief or long term, becomes an attempt at reunion and a battle against separation. Therapists must then use their assessment skills to determine the degree of ego functioning and, therefore, the resources available to clients in coming to terms with moving from union to accepting separation.

When clients are happy and content with their lives, time's passage may hardly be noticed. For clients who come to therapy, time may be felt quite acutely and is perceived as moving quite slowly. Clients seek treatment when they perceive and focus on some internal or external challenge to their reality. From a dynamic point of view, this is a challenge that recurs and is not new in its unconscious meaning to clients. The clients' orientation and evaluation of the present (time) is found in their perception of adequacy to face the recurrent challenge. The ego becomes aware of needing to cope with a threat in order to maintain psychological equilibrium and to maintain individuals' needs and aspirations. Individuals ask themselves whether they can cope with the current threat, judging their capabilities on past experience. When the answer involves fear about adequacy, anxiety and depression may be experienced, and these are related to the issue of time. That is, in assessing personal adequacy anxiety is mobilized to overcome the threat, whereas feeling inadequate leads to depression. Usually clients are uncertain of their coping abilities and thus experience both anxiety and depression. Thus Mann (1981) states that when they come to a therapist for help, clients are saying that they are uncertain as to whether or not they have a future. In addition, feelings connected to the past, present, and future are searching for some form of resolution. The connection between time and emotion then becomes the link between time and the central issue, which is established from the client's history and which is attended to throughout therapy.

Defining the Central Issue.   In Mann's time-limited psychotherapy, the goal in establishing a central issue or focus is to "bypass defenses, control anxiety, and at the same time, stimulate a rapid working alliance and positive transference" (Mann, 1981, p. 33). Mann recommends history taking over one to three sessions to determine the scope of clients' problems and to identify the central issue. Specifically, therapists listen for recurrent events that have triggered pain in clients' lives. Similarities may not be found in the details of the events themselves, but rather symbolically and in the reactions of clients. Mann (1981) states that single painful events in clients' past are not deemed important unless they are of an overwhelming, traumatic nature. Instead, Mann focuses on clients' present and "chronically" endured pain. The pain itself provides a message to clients concerning their feelings about themselves. This pain may from time to time enter awareness but usually is suppressed, denied, or defended against. In formulating the central issue, a distinction is typically made between the material clients share with therapists and what therapists select as the focus for counseling. Thus, according to Mann (1981), the central issue includes time, affect, and self-image. Mann believes that clients come for counseling because of this "time bound image of the self," which lies beneath their complaints, symptoms, character traits, and way of behaving. Evaluation ends once the central issue has been formulated and presented to clients.

Goals and Techniques.   In this therapy, the goal is for clients to experience the painfully hidden parts of themselves, a source of great pain, to which the counselor responds with empathy and understanding. Therapists are advised to communicate their understanding of the extensive efforts clients have made to overcome their pain and that it is this pain that underlies their symptoms. Identifying the central issue can create a sense of hope that they can be helped and promotes a rapid working alliance and positive transference. In this way the defense mechanisms typically triggered by exploring the clients' conflictual relationships are circumvented. Mann (1981) suggests that once a positive transference has been developed, the nature of clients' difficult relationships will emerge later in treatment. The statement of the central issue aligns therapists with clients instead of creating a sense of being victimized by others. This approach, which focuses on developing optimism and connection with the therapist, triggers the unconscious experience of reunion with early parental figures. According to Mann (1981), the primary goal of time-limited dynamic therapy is the resolution of present and chronically endured pain created by a persistent negative self-image. Thus, alleviating symptoms is not a goal but occurs as a result of the therapeutic process, which addresses clients' negative self-image.

Mann (1981) believes that clients who come for treatment are fundamentally motivated to change and want therapists' help in this process. In order to nurture this motivation, therapists recognize the high degree of anxiety at the first meeting and use their skills to help manage clients' anxiety, which is connected to the threat of the unknown. Coming to the point of stating the central issue involves therapists' recognition of clients' intense anxiety. Clients who realize therapists know what they are struggling with gain a sense of relief and hope. Anxiety is further relieved when therapists communicate that they will work together with the client to understand how these negative feelings about themselves came to be.

Thus the central issue in Mann's (1981) model involves time, affects, and image of the self. This formulation of clients' conflicts leads to memories and the objects attached to these memories. As Mann (1981) points out, defining the central issue in this manner determines how the transference manifests itself during the course of treatment. Usually clients acknowledge the accuracy of the central issue and communicate this to therapists. Once the central issue has been presented to clients and is accepted, twelve sessions are offered, with the present session being the first and the date of the final session being clearly announced. Clients are informed that the work of the twelve sessions will be to understand how they came to feel this way about themselves.

The Case of the Young Man Who Stayed at Home

The following case vignette demonstrates identifying a central issue and coming to an agreement to work together over a twelve-session period.

Therapist: What brings you in today?

Client: I'm feeling down, my friends have all gone off to college and I'm still living at home.

Therapist: Tell me more about your situation and what you're doing while living at home.

Client: I'm living with my dad and working at his business. When I decided to do this, I thought it was the right decision to learn the family business, but now I'm not sure.

Therapist: It sounds like you are feeling stuck.

Client: Yeah, I get angry at my dad and myself, because when I made the decision I thought it would be the best thing, and I didn't want him to be alone because my mom had left him six years ago.

Therapist: Tell me more about your parents' divorce.

Client: My mom left six years ago, and I happened to walk in when they were having their last argument and I remember my mom yelling at him that he was no longer going to be controlling her and making her decisions.

Therapist: It sounds like there are two issues here: loyalty to your father and making your own choices.

Client: Yeah, I thought it was right but now I'm angry with my father and wondering who has control, sometimes I feel it was his decision 'cause when I see my friends come back from college I'm real jealous.

Therapist: Earlier you said you were also angry with yourself. Tell me more about that.

Client: Because I don't know if I'm making my own decisions or just going along with my dad.

Therapist: Although you've made every effort to make your own choices, something seems to get in the way, making it difficult for you to do what's in your own best interest.

Client: I don't know what my own best interest is.

Therapist: I wonder if your difficulty choosing has something to do with feelings you have about yourself.

Client: Yes, I was an idiot, I made the wrong decision.

Therapist: Tell me more about feeling like an idiot.

Client: I'm an idiot, I feel like I'm wasting my life by staying at home, that I'm just living out my dad's dream of who I am, not my own.

Therapist: How long have you felt this way?

Client: Longer than I thought about till now, I think my dad always defined me, and now I don't know who I am.

Therapist: So, despite your efforts to become your own person, something has made it difficult for you to really know who you are and what you need to do for yourself.

Client: Yeah, but maybe it's my dad, maybe it's me. . . .

Therapist: My suggestion is that over the twelve weeks we have together we focus on the issue of your knowing yourself better and understanding what has made it difficult for you to make decisions that are best for you.

Interactional Brief Approaches

Focus on Problem Solving

The model of brief therapy developed at the Mental Research Institute (MRI) is referred to as the MRI brief therapy approach, brief problem-solving therapy, and brief problem-focused therapy (Cooper, 1995; Fisch, 1990; O'Hanlon & Weiner-Davis, 1989). MRI was founded in Palo Alto, California, by Don Jackson in 1958. The innovative experimental attitude at MRI was influenced by a separate research group from Menlo Park, California, lead by Gregory Bateson from 1952 to 1962, which included John Weakland, Jay Haley, Don Jackson, and William Fry, Jr. Haley notes of Bateson's group, "Data of various types were used in the research: Hypnosis, ventriloquism, animal training, popular moving pictures, the nature of play, humor, schizophrenia, neurotic communication, psychotherapy, family systems and family therapy" (quoted in Cade & O'Hanlon, 1993, p. 2). During the ten-year project, Bateson's group investigated a variety of topics such as cybernetics, communication, paradox, and logical types. Throughout the project's history, the Bateson group members consulted with the psychiatrist Milton Erickson, who used hypnosis, indirect suggestion, stories, metaphors, and riddles to help his clients change (Cooper, 1995; Haley, 1973; O'Hanlon, 1987, 1990; Zeig & Gilligan, 1990). The Bateson group's open and experimental approach toward learning about people and behavior clearly influenced the members at the Mental Research Institute, which included Don Jackson, John Weakland, Jay Haley, Jules Ruskin, Virginia Satir, and Paul Watzlawick.

In 1966, Richard Fisch opened the Brief Therapy Center at MRI to see what therapeutic results could occur in a strictly limited period of a maximum of 10 one-hour sessions that focused on the main presenting complaint, using active techniques to promote change, and searching for the minimum change required to resolve the presenting problem (Fisch, Weakland, & Segal, 1982). There were no attempts to develop insight, because problems were considered interactional in nature. For the brief problem-solving approach, the therapeutic goal was to resolve the presenting problem as it occurs between people. The emphasis was on change and outcomes, not knowledge. It was assumed that change would be easier if people did something differently or if they looked at the situation differently.

Fisch et al. (1982) cite four reasons for clients' coming to therapy: (1) the clients have concern about behavior, actions, thoughts, or feelings of themselves or someone with whom they are significantly involved; (2) the problem or concern is described as deviant in the sense of being unusual or inappropriate and "distressing or harmful, immediately or potentially, either to the behaver . . . or to others" (p. 11); (3) the clients reported their efforts or those of others about stopping or changing the behavior have been unsuccessful; and (4) clients or those concerned about them seek professional help in changing the situation because they have not been able to make the change on their own.

Clients enter therapy because they want change. In MRI's problem-focused brief therapy, problem formation and problem maintenance are seen as parts of a vicious circle process where clients' attempts to change the problem have been mishandled, leaving clients stuck (Watzlawick, Weakland, & Fisch, 1974). Because people create problems by misinterpreting ordinary life difficulties, clients' attempts to change the problems sometimes aggravate the problem. Clients (and for that matter, therapists with clients) get stuck because of the way they view and behave around the problem. "We are talking only of views, not of reality or of truth, because we believe that views are all we have, or ever will have" (Fisch et al., 1982, p. 10). Thus the therapeutic goal is to interrupt the vicious circle and initiate resolution of the problem. Therapists assess where clients are stuck, what they are doing to get unstuck, and how to influence them to stop doing what they regard as logical or necessary (Fisch, 1990).

Helping clients get unstuck sometimes involves reframing the problem. "To reframe . . . means to change the conceptual and/or emotional setting or view point in relation to which a situation is experienced and to place it in another frame which fits the 'facts' of the same concrete situation equally well or even better, and thereby changes its entire meaning" (Watzlawick et al., 1974, p. 95). The technique, drawn in large measure from the work of Milton Erickson, seeks to infuse new meaning into a situation (O'Hanlon, 1987). Watzlawick et al. (1974) cite the example of Tom Sawyer's reframing the drudgery of whitewashing the fence into something fun and attractive, and then having his friends accept the "reality" that whitewashing can be pleasurable.

The Therapeutic Process

Assessment.   During the initial stages of treatment, the brief problem-solving therapist must gather adequate information seen as basic to every case. The assessment should include:

1. A clear understanding of the essential complaint. Who does the problem belong to? "'Who is doing what that presents a problem, to whom, and how does such behavior constitute a problem?'" (Fisch et al., 1982, p. 70). The questioning is persistent, firm, and polite.
2. A complete and precise understanding of just what "solutions" have been attempted, especially any efforts being made currently. The basic thrust and details regarding these "solutions" should be identified.
3. Determination of the client's minimal goals and the criteria for evaluating the achievement of those goals.
4. Use of the client's position, language, and values in the assessment. "However questionable or undesirable an aspect of the client's life may seem, we are disinclined to intervene unless the client has some complaint about it" (Fisch et al., 1982, p. 122).
5. Determination of who is most invested in change. Who is the customer? Who is the complainant? Fisch et al. (1982) state, "Get the 'window shopper' down to business" (p. 43).

Therapist Maneuverability.   It is one thing to know how best to proceed; it is quite another to have the freedom to move in the direction one thinks is best. Since clients are viewed as often hindering therapeutic efforts out of desperation or fear that things will get worse, it is crucial for therapists to keep their options open. Several tactics suggested by Fisch et al. (1982) include:

1. Avoid taking definite positions prematurely. Taking firm positions may be aversive to the clients' sensibilities and values.
2. Take time. Defer implicit pressure to perform as therapists.
3. Help clients commit to a position. This limits clients' maneuverability. Therapists should use qualifying language to avoid making a commitment to a position. At the same time, therapists should get clients to be specific.
4. Take a one-down position and ask the client for help. The one-down position puts clients at ease and allows therapy to proceed like two people having a conversation.
5. Work with the complainant(s). Determine who is discomfited by the problem. Is it the client or another person?

Intervention.   Since clients' "attempted solutions" are viewed as maintaining and perpetuating the problem, the interventions planned by the therapist will be directed toward helping clients depart from their solutions. This may be accomplished by either interdicting the problem-maintaining behavior or by altering clients' view of the problem so that it is no longer viewed as a problem. Problem-solving brief therapists view problems as arising from five basic attempted solutions clients maintain. Interventions arise from therapists' responses to problems being maintained by these five basic solutions:

1. *Attempting to force something that can only occur spontaneously.* Clients' concerns with bodily functioning, personal and sexual performance, and so forth fall into this category. Clients become "enmeshed in the painful solution of trying to coerce a performance that can only occur spontaneously" (Fisch et al., 1982, p. 130). In one example of a client complaining of obsessive ruminations, the therapist suggests that the client begin controlling the obsessive thoughts by setting a time for them to begin. Instead of resisting the ruminations, the client is given the opportunity to control them by bringing the thoughts forth at a prescribed time of day when the thoughts were normally not occurring.

2. *Attempting to master a feared event by postponing it.* These are usually self-referential complaints regarding shyness, creative blocks, performance blocks (stage fright), and so on. Clients basically attempt to prepare for the feared event in such a way that the event will be mastered in advance, and avoid the actual doing. The intervention involves exposing the client to the task while requiring nonmastery. One shy male client was directed to go to a public place, like a bar or skating rink, and approach the most desirable-looking woman with the introduction "'I would like to get to know you better but I am very shy talking with women'" (Fisch et al., 1982, p. 139). The client was directed further to expect possible rejection and not to go out with the woman, because the assignment was designed to deal with rejection, not to meet women. The essential strategy involves exposing the client to the feared task while restraining the client from successfully completing it.

3. *Attempting to reach accord through opposition.* These problems involve conflict in an interpersonal relationship that centers on issues requiring mutual cooperation. These problems include marital disputes, employee disputes, and other conflicts commonly referred to as power struggles. "Complainants with these problems engage in the attempted solution of haranguing the other party to comply with their demands . . . and . . . demand that the other party treat them with respect, care, or deference" (Fisch et al., 1982, p. 140). The brief problem-solving solution in this case is to get the complainant to take a "one-down" position.

4. *Attempting to attain compliance through volunteerism.* These problems result from the perceived inability or abhorrence to asking something of another. "The common thread involves one person attempting to gain compliance from another while denying that compliance is being asked for" (Fisch et al., 1982, p. 154). The overall strategy here is to get the person with the problem to ask directly for what he or she wants.

5. *Confirming the accuser's suspicions by defending oneself.* These problems result from one person suspecting another of an act both parties view as wrong. Usually one accuses the other of infidelity, excessive drinking, dishonesty, delinquency, and the other, by the act of denying the accusation, actually confirms the accuser's suspicions. It places both in an accuser/defender role. One technique for breaking up this interaction is to agree with the accuser. Fisch et al. (1982) share the story of an elderly couple who had been playing the game for over thirty years. The wife accused the husband that "he was no fun," and the husband denied it. After he began agreeing with her, she stopped accusing him and the game ended.

Additional General Interventions.   Coupled with the five approaches just listed are four other general interventions. One, "Go slow," is an intervention that is used with clients whose main attempted solution is trying too hard. The authors recommend against any overt optimism or assuming a worried expression if there is any acknowledgment of good news. Two, dangers of improvement might be considered an extension of "Go slow" because the client is asked to recognize the possible dangers in resolving the problem. If clients lose weight, they may have to buy a new wardrobe, or if they improve their sexual performance, their partner may not be able to keep up with them. Three, "making a U-turn" is a shift to an opposite direction because the directive or strategy is not working. This tactic is especially effective when the therapist has inadvertently taken the wrong position with a client. Four, how to worsen the problem is used when advising clients to continue the ineffective approach they are using. It is generally used with clients who are having difficulty changing what they are doing (Fisch et al., 1982).

Termination is done without fanfare. Generally, goals are assessed and the client is given a simple goodbye. In fact, according to Fisch et al. (1982) it may be important to terminate with a "doubtful and cautionary note" (p. 179).

Focus on Solutions

Solution-focused therapy is the model of brief therapy developed at the Brief Family Therapy Center (BFTC) in Milwaukee, Wisconsin, by Steve de Shazer. Similar to the MRI approach, the solution-focused approach looks closely at the pattern of interaction around the complaint, approaches for changing the pattern, and creating outcomes. Like MRI, the BFTC draws on Gregory Bateson's theoretical ideas and Milton Erickson's clinical work.

The shift de Shazer offers involves directing attention away from problems and toward solutions. For solution-focused therapists, the solution-finding process holds therapeutic promise, and the therapeutic task entails helping clients to develop expectations of change and solutions. Solution-focused therapists pay relatively little attention to the details of the complaint, and instead highlight how the client will know when the problem is solved. For BFTC therapists, the key to brief therapy is using what clients bring to meet their needs in such a way that clients will be able to make a satisfactory life for themselves (de Shazer, 1985, 1990, 1991; Walter & Peller, 1992).

More than assessing how problems are maintained or how to solve them, solution-focused therapy argues that helping people involved in troublesome situations requires getting them to do something different, even if it seems irrational, irrelevant, bizarre, or humorous (de Shazer, 1985). No problem occurs all the time, and using clients' strengths and resources for bringing about change is crucial. One goal involves getting clients to envision their future without the presenting problem. When clients are able to do that, the problem is diminished (de Shazer, 1990).

The Therapeutic Process

Assessment. The BFTC group assumes clients want to change. "Resistance" is not an issue for solution-focused therapists because they attempt to connect the clients' present with the future, complimenting clients on what they are already doing that is useful, and suggesting something for them to do that might be good for them. De Shazer (1985) offered twelve building blocks of complaint and six basic assumptions for viewing and changing clients' complaints.

The twelve complaints usually include

1. *A bit or sequence of behavior*
2. *The meanings ascribed to the situation*
3. *The frequency with which the complaint happens*
4. *The physical location in which the complaint happens*
5. *The degree to which the complaint is involuntary*
6. *Significant others involved in the complaint directly or indirectly*
7. *The question of who or what is to blame*
8. *Environmental factors such as jobs, economic status, living space, etc.*
9. *The physiological or feeling state involved*
10. *The past*
11. *Dire predictions of the future*
12. *Utopian expectations. (de Shazer, 1985, p. 27)*

The six basic assumptions that de Shazer (1985) offers to help therapists draw maps of client complaints and construct solutions are:

1. Constructing complaints to involve behavior that is brought on by the client's world view.
2. Recognizing that complaints are maintained by clients thinking the decision they made about the original problem was the only thing to do, and thus getting trapped into doing more of the same.
3. Understanding that minimal changes are necessary when initiating change. There can be a "ripple effect." Once change is initiated, additional changes will be generated by the client to solve the complaint.
4. Using the clients' view of what reality would look like without the complaint, solution-focused therapists generate ideas for what to change.
5. Suggesting a new frame or new frames of reference and new behavior based on this new view, resolution of the problem can be promoted.

6. Viewing change holistically, a change in one part of the system will likely effect changes in other parts of the system.

Intervention.   Solutions, not problems, are the primary focus in solution-focused therapy. Emphasis placed on problems moves the client in the wrong direction and is based on a faulty assumption. Solution-focused brief therapy is cooperative, and oriented toward change, solutions, the present, and the future.

Because solution-focused therapy assumes that therapists and clients coconstruct perspectives on the problem, establishing rapport and promoting cooperation are crucial initial moves in therapy. Change is an interactional process, and it is essential that therapists "fit" into the world view of clients in order to jointly construct a problem that can be solved. If done effectively, therapists shape and change the process so clients can solve their own problems in therapy.

The presession change question technique involves seeking exceptions to the problem or exploring the solutions clients have been attempting. The goal is to create an expectation for change, emphasize the active role and responsibility of clients, and demonstrate that change happens outside of therapists' offices. Therapists simply ask, "Since the last time we met, have you been noticing some changes in yourself or discovering a new way of looking at the problem?"

Another technique involves searching for exceptions. Finding exceptions to when clients feel stuck helps clarify the conditions for change by reorienting clients to the hope of finding a solution, implying clients have strengths and ability to solve problems, providing tangible evidence of resolution, and helping clients discover forgotten personal resources. Exceptions might include therapists' questions such as:

"When did you manage this problem in the past? What did you do differently?

"Tell me when things were just a little better."

De Shazer (1985) describes working with a couple who were complaining about arguing. He asked them to describe what life would be like after they quit arguing. After the couple described what life would be like after these arguments, they no longer had an investment in arguing. Life would be better when they stopped fighting.

The miracle question is another technique that helps clarify goals and highlight exceptions to the problem by stimulating the client to imagine a solution and remove constraints to solving the problem, and by building hope for change. With this technique clients are asked, "Suppose that one night, while you were asleep, there was a miracle and this problem was solved. How would you know? What would be different?" (de Shazer, 1991, p. 113). Such questions allow clients to envision their lives without the problem.

Scaling questions is another technique designed to make the abstract concrete by quantifying intangibles, placing power with clients, and demonstrating change. Clients are asked, "On a scale of 1 to 10, where 1 means you have no influence over your problem, and 10 means you have total influence, where would you place yourself today?" To support the initial question, therapists add further questions such as "Where would others place you on this scale?" and "What do you need to move a fraction of a point up the scale?"

These brief examples show how each technique attempts to induce doubt regarding the severity and dominance of the problem by helping clients find exceptions to the occurrence of the problem. Finding that the problem is not always occurring now or in the future allows clients to define a goal of not interacting with the problem. As the name suggests, solution-focused therapy concentrates on creating the expectation of solutions.

Focus on Solutions and Narrative

Solution-oriented brief therapy is the approach developed by William H. O'Hanlon and Michele Weiner-Davis based on the work at both MRI and BFTC, as well as Milton Erickson's clinical work. It is an approach that focuses on people's competence, with therapists cocreating solvable problems with clients. The approach has a future goal orientation concerned with bringing about positive outcomes for clients. Emerging from the MRI and BFTC approaches, solution-oriented therapists attempt three actions:

1. *Changing what clients are doing in regards to their actions and interactions around the situation perceived as problematic.*
2. *Changing the clients' frames of reference and their view of the situation viewed as problematic.*
3. *Evoking resources, solutions, and strengths to bring to the situation perceived as problematic. (O'Hanlon & Weiner-Davis, 1989)*

Solution-focused and solution-oriented therapy both use self-reinforcing patterns of thought and behavior; the intention in separating them is to show the continuing drift toward constructivism and narrative in brief therapy (Cade & O'Hanlon, 1993; Cooper, 1995; Friedman, 1993; Neimeyer & Mahoney, 1995; Walter & Peller, 1992). O'Hanlon and Weiner-Davis (1989) point out, "If the client walks into a behaviorist's office, he will leave with a behavioral problem. If clients choose psychoanalysts' offices, they will leave with unresolved issues from childhood as the focus of the problem" (p. 54). O'Hanlon and Weiner-Davis (1989) explain that clients' complaints are negotiated and "cocreated" with therapists, and the solution-oriented approach begins the therapeutic process by looking for clients' strengths, solutions, and competence.

The Therapeutic Process

Assessment and Interventions

Assessment is viewed as directly tied to therapists' metaphors and assumptions. "We have never had a client with an unresolved oedipal conflict or an overactive superego. Just lucky, we suppose!" (O'Hanlon & Weiner-Davis, 1989, p. 54). Furthermore, solution-oriented therapists look at problems not as pathological manifestations but as ordinary difficulties encountered in life.

Assessment and intervention are not separated into distinct steps. In fact, the initial interviewing process is viewed as an intervention. Because interviewing uses solution-oriented techniques, "clients can experience significant shifts in their thinking about their situations during the course of the [first] session" (O'Hanlon & Weiner-Davis, 1989, p. 77). Solution-oriented therapists use presuppositional questioning, such as "What were the good things about the dinner?" rather than "Did anything good happen at the dinner?" Such approaches begin with the way clients perceive and talk about their problems. By looking for exceptions to the problem, solution-oriented therapists attempt to normalize or depathologize problems, making problems simply a natural response to life events.

O'Hanlon and Weiner-Davis (1989) offer eight techniques for changing patterns of doing or viewing problems:

1. The frequency or rate of the performance of the complaint could be changed. Have the client who goes on candy binges slowly eat candy when not on a binge.
2. The timing of complaint performance could be changed. Have depressed clients schedule their depression for a specific time of the day.
3. The duration of the performance of the complaint could be changed. Have the compulsive handwasher wash the left hand five minutes and the right hand thirty seconds.
4. The location of the performance of the complaint could be changed. The authors describe a situation where a wife and husband were directed to move their arguments into the bathroom with the husband getting undressed and laying down in the bathtub and the wife sitting fully clothed on the toilet. The couple's subsequent actions and laughter broke their pattern of chronic arguments.
5. The complaint pattern could have one or more elements added to it. Clients are told to put on their favorite shoes or dress before bingeing.
6. The sequence of components or events in the complaint pattern could be changed. A teen was directed to tape-record her father's lectures. Then, at the appropriate time when her father was about to lecture her again, the teen was told to play the lecture back and thereby beat her father to the punch.
7. The complaint pattern could be broken into smaller pieces or elements. Spouses were told to conduct their arguments on paper with each person taking turns to write five minutes, then to exchange their papers.
8. The complaint performance could be linked to the performance of some burdensome exercise. In this case, people who are chronically late may have to do something they hate to do for the same duration of time they are late. For instance, if they hate cleaning the bathroom, they must spend one minute cleaning the bathroom for each minute they arrive late.

In each instance, solution-oriented interventions are negotiated with the clients within a collaborative relationship where change is expected. The interventions are designed to help clients change their "doing" or "viewing" of problems, and the goal is to help clients look toward possibilities rather than problems.

The approach involves using what is going right rather than focusing on what is going wrong.

Solution-oriented therapy may be augmented by the narrative approach and constructivist theory that views humans as actively engaged in a process of making meanings and creating stories (de Shazer, 1991; Neimeyer & Mahoney, 1995). For example, the brief solution-oriented approach encourages counselors to use stories, anecdotes, parables, and humor to help clients change. Cade and O'Hanlon (1993) regard "therapy as . . . akin to reediting: going through a person's story and helping them rewrite parts of it" (p. 172). In a similar vein, the narrative therapists White and Epston (1990) attempt to help clients move from problem-saturated stories to more hope-filled alternative stories. Like solution-oriented therapists, Epston and White (1995) believe clients have "personal solution knowledges" that help them move beyond "expert knowledges" and toward authoring the story of their own lives.

White and Epston's (1990) techniques for helping clients achieve victory over their own lives range from techniques designed to help clients view problems differently to giving parties, certificates, ribbons, and therapy-ending rituals. One technique, "externalization of the problem," is very innovative because the problem is redefined in such a way as being outside of clients. For example, if clients' presenting problems involve depression, therapists might ask, "How long has the depression been pushing you around?" Thus, the depression becomes a controllable object *outside* of clients, rather than an internalized enduring condition *within* clients.

An Intervention with an Adolescent

The separate works of Amatea (1989), Durrant (1995), Metcalf (1995), and Selekman (1993a, b) reveal the practical applications that problem-focused, solution-focused, solution-oriented, and narrative approaches have for adolescent and school-age populations. The styles range from Amatea's (1989) interpretation of problem-focused therapy for school behavior problems to Selekman's (1993a, b) improvisational melding of all these approaches to address adolescent difficulties. Durrant (1995) and Metcalf (1995) both advocate changing the way professional helpers think about difficulties by encouraging helpers to focus energy on solutions and competencies rather than problems. Change comes from helping people (adults and adolescents) think and act differently about problematic situations.

The Case of the Girl Who Knew She Was Stupid

Barbara, a 16-year-old female student, met with the school counselor regarding her class selection for the upcoming school year. Barbara was enrolled in a college prep program, and she had a 3.6 GPA on a four-point scale. Neither parent had completed college, but both encouraged Barbara to go to college in order to "get a good job" that would pay "good money." During an earlier session in the later part of the school year with the school counselor, Barbara expressed a sense of feeling stupid and a desire to drop a class needed to meet the college entrance requirements.

Barbara: I'm stupid. I want to drop German.

Counselor: Drop German. That's a big decision. Umm. When did stupidness start standing in your way?

Barbara: A long time ago.

Counselor: By looking at your GPA, I see that stupidness certainly hasn't blocked your way to good grades.

Barbara: You just don't know.

Counselor: Right, I might not know how hard you've worked. Here's what I do know. By looking at my computer screen, I see a college prep student with a 3.6 GPA. That shows me you've outwitted stupidness and that you have a pretty full Smart Bank. It also shows me you have not let stupidness push you around or make you quit. You've pushed stupidness around.

Barbara: Maybe. I still want to drop German next year.

Counselor: Is it stupidness or German that's pushing you around?

Barbara: German. My teacher doesn't help me at all. She just passes us all along, and I'm not prepared for next year. I don't know a thing.

Counselor: Not a thing? On a scale of 1 to 10, how would you rate what you know now in German compared to what you knew before you took German?

Barbara: About a 5.

Counselor: We're half-way there. It's not a 10, but it's a solid start. As I see it, you have a pretty full Smart Account. Your 3.6 GPA is just numbers on my screen, but it indicates your hard work, resources, and wealth. I think you have other accounts elsewhere, like a Knowing What to Do Account. What made you come in here to see me?

Barbara: I don't know. I just wanted to figure things out.

Counselor: And here we are. It will take some planning and effort but together we'll make German work.

Barbara: Okay.

This case shows the use of externalizing the problem, scaling questions, and metaphor. The first step in this intervention was externalizing stupidness to become an object that was standing in Barbara's way. Barbara then shifted the external problem to German and the German teacher. Obviously, the teacher may be part of the problem, but using scaling questions helped establish that Barbara was "half-way there" in her knowledge of German. The counselor pointed out the fact that Barbara made the appointment, revealing her own solution-finding skills. Two subsequent sessions focused on strategies for dealing with her German teacher and developing a plan for being successful in meeting the requirements necessary to get into college.

Ethical Concerns

There are a number of ethical concerns raised about brief therapy, such as issues of therapist influence, client welfare, not addressing the underlying problem, and abandonment. Koss and Shiang (1994) state, "no evidence exists to suggest that brief psychotherapy produces any greater negative effects than long-term psychotherapy" (p. 689). Most people do not enter therapy to receive "overhauls." Surprisingly, given that the median therapeutic duration is six to eight sessions, it might be said that operationally therapy *is* short term. Besides the pressure of third-party payments to reduce the cost of psychotherapy, most people want to be helped as quickly as possible without spending a great deal of time or money (Bergin & Garfield, 1994).

Traditional psychodynamic therapies have been directed toward helping clients achieve insight or awareness, whereas most brief therapies have been concerned with getting clients to do things. This active relationship raises questions for some. The problem-focused approach used at MRI is frequently described as manipulative and questioned on ethical grounds. Fisch (1990) argues that manipulation is unavoidable in therapy, and the real issue is facing up to how therapists acknowledge their manipulation and assessing the therapeutic outcome. Fisch states, *"Ethical and responsible therapy involves working with the client's reality (frame of reference, world view, etc.) rather than requiring clients to accept the therapist's reality"* (1990, p. 430). Indeed, brief therapy may be more ethical than long-term care if we are evaluating treatment on the basis of effective and efficient outcomes. In brief therapy, treatment is collaborative, clients' presenting complaints are taken seriously by therapists, clients determine the success of treatment, and it is consumer oriented (Cooper, 1995). Maybe brief therapists should question the ethics around prolonged long-term care. Counselors are faced with the demands of third-party payers, research regarding the effectiveness of brief approaches, and clients who "do not seem to want to spend a great deal of time and money on their personal psychotherapy but prefer to be helped as quickly as possible" (Bergin & Garfield, 1994, p. 9). Other models that focus on effectiveness and efficiency may be necessary to address both long-term and brief approaches. Using brief, intermittent psychotherapy throughout a person's life cycle is a valid approach to helping clients (Cummings & Sayama, 1995), as is the Active Living Model being developed by Joan Avis at the University of San Francisco, which focuses on specific stages in life (personal communication, December 7, 1995).

The concern is not simply with duration and timing in therapy. Longer and briefer therapeutic approaches are still based primarily on the spoken medium, and, to some extent, both long-term and short-term therapies exclude nonverbal and written interventions. Psychotherapy that integrates work with the body has been pushed to the edge of the profession, whereas issues of embodiment are crucial to the therapeutic process (Neimeyer & Mahoney, 1995). In addition, L'Abate (1992, 1994) proposes the use of writing as an intervention that could be used separately or with verbal and nonverbal therapies. L'Abate's (1992, 1994) concern is not a dualistic long-term versus short-term debate, but with drawing on theories and practices that help people live more effective lives. Counseling is moving beyond metaphors of infectious disease and ideas of permanent "cures" and toward helping people find solutions to some natural problems that are part of living. Ethically, it is time to open our eyes to verbal, nonverbal, and written interventions that help bring about effective and efficient change in clients.

Summary

Common assumptions found in brief psychodynamic and interactional approaches to short-term therapy include pragmatism and parsimony, a view that human change is inevitable, the desire to build on client resources and competence, and the recognition that significant change occurs outside of therapy and that life outside of therapy is more important than therapy itself.

Central concerns in brief psychodynamic therapy include client selection, defining achievable therapeutic goals, and improving therapeutic techniques. Focus is usually placed on selecting clients with good ego strength who are highly motivated to change and who have good relationship skills and a circumscribed problem. The exception is Davanloo's intensive short-term dynamic therapy, which does not exclude less motivated clients who have fewer ego resources. Techniques most often focus on identifying a dynamic conflict and the use of interpretation to bring this conflict into conscious awareness. Therapeutic goals involve working through this dynamic conflict from the past, in the present. Finally, the two hallmark characteristics of Mann's time-limited therapy model are explicit focus on time and identification of a central issue.

The interactional brief approaches explored in this chapter are not concerned with insight, but rather with helping people see and respond to problems differently. For interactional brief therapists, problems are maintained by ineffective strategies for solving them. In fact, de Shazer's approach directs clients away from problems and toward solutions. Solution-focused therapy is concerned with getting people to do things differently, whereas solution-oriented therapy is concerned with cocreating solvable problems with clients. Cade and O'Hanlon (1993) have likened brief therapy to editing a person's story, and narrative therapists have added to effective approaches by introducing techniques such as externalizing the problem (White & Epston, 1990).

Brief therapies challenge the counseling profession to change. Third-party payers, research regarding the effectiveness of brief approaches, and clients who prefer to be helped as quickly as possible support professional change. Brief approaches have become "acceptable," but at least four questions must be asked: Will counselors see brief approaches as integral to the growth and development of a profession where one size or approach does not fit all people? Moreover, are we ready to appreciate the variety of approaches in our profession, ranging from brief approaches to psycho-spiritual approaches? Are we ready to investigate verbal, nonverbal, and written interventions in our attempts to find effective and efficient strategies to help people change? Finally, are we ready to look at what works and come to grips with who pays for it? After all, this profession has defined time as money.

References

Alexander, F. & French, T. M. (1946). *Psychoanalytic therapy.* New York: Ronald Press.

Amatea, E. S. (1989). *Brief strategic intervention for school behavior problems.* San Francisco: Jossey-Bass.

American Psychiatric Association. (1994). *Diagnostic and statistical manual of mental disorders* (4th ed.). Washington, D C: Author.

Bergin, A. E., & Garfield, S. L. (Eds.). (1994). *Handbook of psychotherapy and behavior change* (4th ed.). New York: Wiley.

Cade, B., & O'Hanlon, W. H. (1993). *A brief guide to brief therapy.* New York: Norton.

Cooper, J. F. (1995). *A primer of brief psychotherapy.* New York: Norton.

Cummings, N., & Sayama, M. (1995). *Focused therapy: A casebook of brief intermittent psychotherapy throughout the life cycle.* New York: Brunner/Mazel.

Davanloo, H. (Ed.). (1978). *Basic principles and techniques in short-term dynamic psychotherapy.* New York: Spectrum Press.

de Shazer, S. (1985). *Keys to solution in brief therapy.* New York: Norton.

de Shazer, S. (1990). What is it about brief therapy that works? In J. K. Zeig & S. G. Gilligan (Eds.), *Brief therapy: Myths, methods, and metaphors* (pp. 90–99). New York: Brunner/Mazel.

de Shazer, S. (1991). *Putting difference to work.* New York: Norton.

Durrant, M. (1995). *Creative strategies for school problems: Solutions for psychologists and teachers.* New York: Norton.

Durrant, M., & Kowalski, K. (1993). Enhancing views of competence. In S. Friedman (Ed.), *The new language of change: Constructive collab-oration in psychotherapy* (pp. 107–137). New York: Guilford Press.

Ellis, A. (1989). Rational-emotive therapy. In R. J. Corsini & D. Wedding (Eds.), *Current psychotherapies* (4th ed., pp. 197–238). Itasca, IL: Peacock.

Ellis, A. (1990). How can psychological treatment aim to be briefer and better?—The rational-emotive approach to brief therapy. In J. K. Zeig & S. G. Gilligan (Eds.), *Brief therapy: Myths, methods, and metaphors* (pp. 291–302). New York: Brunner/Mazel.

Ellis, A. (1996). *Better, deeper, and more enduring brief therapy: The rational emotive behavior therapy approach.* New York: Brunner/Mazel.

Epston, D., & White, M. (1995). Termination as a rite of passage: Questioning strategies for a therapy of inclusion. In R. A. Neimeyer & M. J. Mahoney (Eds.), *Constructivism in psychotherapy* (pp. 339–354). Washington, DC: American Psychological Association.

Fisch, R. (1990). Problem-solving psychotherapy. In J. K. Zeig & W. M. Munion (Eds.), *What is psychotherapy?: Contemporary perspectives* (pp. 269–273). San Francisco: Jossey-Bass.

Fisch, R., Weakland, J. H., & Segal, L. (1982). *Tactics of change: Doing therapy briefly.* San Francisco: Jossey-Bass.

Friedman, S. (Ed.) (1993). *The new language of change: Constructive collaboration in psychotherapy.* New York: Guilford Press.

Haley, J. (1973). *Uncommon therapy: The psychiatric techniques of Milton H. Erickson.* New York: Norton.

Koss, M. P., & Butcher, J. N. (1986). Research on brief psychotherapy. In S. L. Garfield & A. E.

Bergin (Eds.), *Handbook of psychotherapy and behavior change* (3rd ed., pp. 627–670). New York: Wiley.

Koss, M. P., & Shiang, J. (1994). Research on brief psychotherapy. In A. E. Bergin & S. L. Garfield (Eds.), *Handbook of psychotherapy and behavior change* (4th ed., pp. 664–700). New York: Wiley.

L'Abate, L. (1992). *Programmed writing: A self-administered approach for interventions with individuals, couples and families.* Pacific Grove, CA: Brooks/Cole.

L'Abate, L. (1994). *A theory of personality development.* New York: Wiley.

Malan, D. H. (1976a). *The frontier of brief psychotherapy.* New York: Plenum Press.

Malan, D. H. (1976b). *Toward the validation of dynamic psychotherapy.* New York: Plenum Press.

Malan, D. H. (1979). *Individual psychotherapy and the science of psychodynamics.* Woburn, MA: Butterworths.

Mann, J. (1981). The core of time-limited psychotherapy: Time and the central issue. In S. H. Budman (Ed.), *Forms of brief therapy* (pp. 25–43). New York: Guilford Press.

Metcalf, L. (1995). *Counseling toward solutions: A practical solution-focused program for working with students, teachers, and parents.* West Nyack, NY: Center for Applied Research in Education.

Neimeyer, R. A., & Mahoney, M. J. (Eds.). (1995). *Constructivism in psychotherapy.* Washington, D C: American Psychological Association.

O'Hanlon, W. H. (1987). *Taproots: Underlying principles of Milton Erickson's therapy and hypnosis.* New York: Norton.

O'Hanlon, W. H. (1990). A grand unified theory for brief therapy: Putting problems in context. In J. K. Zeig & S. G. Gilligan (Eds.), *Brief therapy: Myths, methods, and metaphors* (pp. 78–89). New York: Brunner/Mazel.

O'Hanlon, W. H., & Weiner-Davis, M. (1989). *In search of solutions: A new direction in psychotherapy.* New York: Norton.

Palmatier, L. L. (1990). Reality therapy and brief strategic interactional therapy. *Journal of Reality Therapy, 9,* 3–17.

Rosenbaum, R., Hoyt, M. F., & Talmon, M. (1990). In R. A. Wells & V. J. Giannetti (Eds.), *Handbook of the brief psychotherapies* (pp. 165–189). New York: Plenum Press.

Selekman, M. D. (1993a). *Pathways to change: Brief therapy solutions with difficult adolescents.* New York: Guilford Press.

Selekman, M. D. (1993b). Solution-oriented brief therapy with difficult adolescents. In S. Friedman (Ed.), *The new language of change: Constructive collaboration in psychotherapy* (pp. 138–157). New York: Guilford Press.

Shulman, B. H. (1989). Some remarks on brief therapy. Special issue: Varieties of brief therapy. *Individual Psychology: Journal of Adlerian Theory, Research, and Practice, 45* (1–2), 34–37.

Sifneos, P. E. (1972). *Stort term psychotherapy and emotional crisis.* Cambridge, MA: Harvard University Press.

Sifneos, P. E. (1979). *Short term psychotherapy: Evolution and technique.* New York: Plenum Press.

Strupp, H. H. (1981). Toward the refinement of time-limited dynamic psychotherapy. In S. H. Budman (Ed.), *Forms of brief therapy* (pp. 219–242). New York: Guilford Press.

Walter, J. L., & Peller, J. E. (1992). *Becoming solution-focused in brief therapy.* New York: Brunner/Mazel.

Watzlawick, P., Weakland, J., & Fisch, R. (1974). *Change: Principles of problem formation and problem resolution.* New York: Norton.

Wells, R. A., & Giannetti, V. J. (Eds.). (1990). *Handbook of brief psychotherapies.* New York: Plenum Press.

White, M., & Epston, D. (1990). *Narrative means to therapeutic ends.* New York: Norton.

Worchel, J. (1990). Short-term dynamic psychotherapy. In R. A. Wells & V. J. Giannetti (Eds.), *Handbook of the brief psychotherapies* (pp. 193–216). New York: Plenum Press.

Zeig, J. K., & Gilligan, S. G. (Eds.). (1990). *Brief therapy: Myths, methods, and metaphors.* New York: Brunner/Mazel.

$$C \ h \ a \ p \ t \ e \ r \quad \mathit{8}$$

Group Counseling

David Capuzzi, Ph.D.   *Douglas R. Gross, Ph.D.*

The twenty-first century poses problems and possibilities that should be of high interest to the beginning counselor enrolled in a counselor education program and considering becoming a group work specialist. If we believe that the 1950s may have symbolized "the individual in society," the 1960s "the individual against society," the 1970s "the individual's conflict with self," and the 1980s "the individual's integration into the family," the society of the 1990s and beyond may clearly be characterized as "the individual's integration with the machine" (Shapiro & Bernadett-Shapiro, 1985). Much of the work in educational, employment, and day-to-day living situations will be done by computers; connections among colleagues, friends, and family members will be maintained by telephone lines, word processors, and modems. The replacement of consistent social contact with friends and co-workers by the video display terminal will create a much greater need for interpersonal communication on a person-to-person basis. Groups will provide an antidote to human isolation, and more and more counselors and other human development specialists will be called on to serve as group facilitators. The beginning counseling and human development specialist will experience an explosion of opportunities and escalating concomitant responsibilities as a group work specialist.

There are a number of reasons why the responsibilities of a group work specialist are so important to address. A facilitator must be skilled in catalyzing a therapeutic climate in a group and in monitoring therapeutic factors inherent in the group (Ohlsen & Ferreira, 1994). Facilitators must also be able to assess which clients they can assist given the facilitators' level of skills, to describe their services and aspects of the group experience, to engender trust and confidence, and to answer questions about client rights and responsibilities, confidentiality, and expectations for change.

The purpose of this chapter is to provide an introduction to group work for those interested in pursuing follow-up education and experience in the context of master's and doctoral graduate preparation. The history of group work, types of groups, stages of group life, characteristics of group facilitators, responsibilities and interventions in groups, myths connected with group work and issues and ethics of group work will be overviewed.

The History of Group Work

Beginnings

As noted by Vriend (1985), the first half of the twentieth century was characterized by lively interest, experimentation, and research in the promising new field of group dynamics. Behavior in small groups, leadership styles, membership roles, communication variables, and so on were all examined and studied for their application to groups in a variety of settings (Hare, Borgatta, & Bales, 1967).

In 1947, a history-making conference in Bethel, Maine, was attended by a multidisciplinary group of researchers and practitioners from university and community settings throughout North America. The National Training Laboratory (NTL) in Group Development of the National Education Association held its first "laboratory session," at which T-groups (the "T" is for training) and the laboratory method were born (Bradford, Gibb, & Benne, 1964). First, using themselves as experimental subjects, participants at the conference created a laboratory situation in which the behavior of the participants was more important than any effort or technique employed. The situation created a safe place for group members to explore their own behavior, feelings, and the responses of others to them as people separate from social, work, and family roles. Under the direction of the NTL, such conferences continued each summer and the T-group movement grew and achieved national visibility.

As time passed, T-groups appeared on university campuses and in other settings. The T-group provided a fresh concept with tremendous appeal as opportunity was provided for group members to become more "sensitive," to "grow emotionally," and to "realize their human potential." The country began hearing about the "human potential movement" and of exciting developments in California, particularly at the Esalen Institute at Big Sur and at the Center for the Studies of the Person founded by Carl R. Rogers and his colleagues. Soon there were a variety of marathon and encounter groups; it was an era of openness, self-awareness, and getting in touch with feelings.

The 1960s and 1970s

The 1960s were a time of social upheaval and questioning. There were riots on campuses and in cities as civil rights groups struggled to raise the consciousness of the nation about unfair discrimination and prejudice. Leaders such as John F. Kennedy and Martin Luther King, Jr., became the idolized champions and international symbols of a people's determination to change a society and to promote social responsibility. The nation united in grief-stricken disbelief as its heroes were martyred, and determination to counter the human rights violations of the decades escalated.

As the 1960s ended, the encounter groups movement, emphasizing personal consciousness and connection with others, reached its zenith, then gradually waned as events such as the Charles Manson killings, the Watergate scandal, the first presidential resignation in the history of the United States, the group killings en route to the Munich Olympics, and the rise of fanatic cults made people in all parts of the country question the extent to which permissiveness and "human potential" should be allowed to develop (Janis, 1972; Rowe & Winborn, 1973).

For professionals in education and mental health, however, the 1960s and 1970s were decades of maintained interest in group work despite the highs and lows of societal fervor and dismay. Mental health centers conducted more and more group sessions for clients, and counselor education, counseling psychology, psychology, and social work departments on university campuses instituted more and more coursework and supervised experiences in aspects of group work. In 1973, the Association for Specialists in Group Work (ASGW) was formed, and by 1974 it had become a division of the American Counseling Association (at that time named the American Personnel and Guidance Association). Similar developments took place in the context of other large professional groups such as the American Psychological Association and the National Association of Social Workers.

The 1980s

The 1980s witnessed increasing interest in group work and in working with special populations. Groups were started for alcoholics, adult children of alcoholics, incest victims, adults molested as children, people who are overweight, underassertive people, and those who have been victims of violent crimes. Other groups were begun for the elderly, for those dealing with death and other losses, for people with eating disorders, smokers, and victims of the Holocaust (Shapiro & Bernadett-Shapiro, 1985). This increasing specialization brought with it an increasing need for higher standards for preparation of the group work specialist, as evidenced by the development of training standards for group work specialists (ASGW, 1983) and the inclusion in the standards of the Council for Accreditation of Counseling and Related Educational Programs (CACREP, 1988) of specific group work specialist preparation guidelines for the graduate-level university educator to follow. At the same time, this increasing specialization brought with it a reliance on self-help groups composed of individuals who share a specific affliction. Usually such groups are not facilitated by a professional, and this circumstance can conflict with the values and standards of professional group work.

The 1990s and Beyond

The escalating interest in group work and in working with special populations so evident in the decade of the 1980s, has continued into the last decade of the century. The 1983 ASGW standards for training of group counselors was revised, and a new set of standards was adopted in 1991 (ASGW, 1991). Although the 1991 standards built on the 1983 standards emphasizing the knowledge, skills, and supervised experience necessary for the preparation of group workers, the newer standard broadened the conception of group work, clarified the difference between core competencies and specialization requirements, defined the four prominent varieties of group work, and eliminated the previously made distinctions among different kinds of supervised field experience (Conyne, Wilson, Kline, Morran, & Ward, 1993). In addition, CACREP, in its 1994 revision of accreditation standards, reemphasized the importance of group work by identifying principles of group dynamics, group leadership styles, theories of group counseling, group counseling methods, approaches used for other types of group work, and ethical considerations as essential curricular elements for all counselor education programs (CACREP, 1994).

Although the issues and ethics of group work are overviewed at the end of this chapter, it should be noted that the practice of the group work professional will require increasing levels of expertise and an enhanced ability to participate in and apply the results of needed research. The history-making national conference for group work specialists, conceptualized and sponsored by ASGW in early 1990 in Florida and repeated during subsequent years in other parts of the country, symbolizes the importance of group work to the clients served by the counseling and human development professional.

Types of Groups

Most textbooks for introduction-to-counseling courses begin the discussion of group work by attempting to make distinctions among group therapy, group counseling, and group guidance. In general, *group therapy* is described as being longer term, more remedially and therapeutically focused, and more likely to be facilitated by a facilitator with doctoral-level preparation and a more "clinical" orientation. *Group counseling* may be differentiated from group therapy by its focus on conscious problems, by the fact that it is not aimed at major personality changes, by an orientation toward short-term issues, and by the fact that it is not as concerned with the treatment of the more severe psychological and behavioral disorders (Corey, 1995). The term *group guidance* usually is descriptive of a classroom group in a K-through-12 setting in which the leader presents information or conducts mental health education. In contrast to a group therapy or group counseling situation involving no more than eight to ten group participants, a group guidance experience could involve twenty to forty group participants, lessening opportunities for individual participation, and facilitator observation and intervention.

For the purposes of this chapter, ASGW's definitions of the four group work specialty types are presented next as a point of departure for classifying groups (Conyne et.al.,1993). The reader may wish to do additional reading relative to group "types" from sources such as Corey (1995), Dinkmeyer and Muro (1979), Gazda (1984), and Ohlsen (1977).

Task/Work Groups

The group worker who specializes in promoting the development and functioning of task and work groups seeks to support such groups in the process of improving their function and performance. Task and work group specialists employ principles of group dynamics, organizational development, and team building to enhance group members' skills in group task accomplishment and group maintenance. The scope of practice for these group work specialists includes normally functioning individuals who are members of naturally occurring task or work groups operating within a specific organizational context.

It is important to note that graduate coursework for specialists in task and work groups should include at least one specialization course in organizational management and development. Ideally, coursework should be taken in the broad area of organizational psychology, management, and development to develop an awareness of organizational life and how task and work groups function within the organization. In addition, a task/work group specialist might also develop skill in organizational assessment, training, program development, consultation, and program evaluation.

Clinical instruction for training in working with task/work groups should include a minimum of thirty clock hours (forty-five clock hours are recommended) of supervised practice in leading or coleading a task/work group appropriate to the age and clientele of the group leader's specialty area(s) (such as school counseling, community counseling, and mental health counseling).

Guidance/Psychoeducational Groups

The psychoeducational group specialist educates group participants. Such participants may be informationally deficient in some area (such as how to cope with external threats, developmental transitions, or personal and interpersonal crises). The scope of practice of psychoeducational group leaders includes essentially normally functioning individuals who are "at risk" for, but currently unaffected by, an environmental threat (such as AIDS), who are approaching a developmental transition point (such as new parents) or who are in the midst of coping with a life crisis (such as suicide of a loved one). The primary goal in psychoeducational group work is to prevent the future development of dysfunctional behaviors.

Coursework for specialization in psychoeducational groups should include at least one specialization course that provides information about community psychology, health and wellness promotion, and program development and evaluation. Ideally, psychoeducational group specialists would also take coursework in curriculum design, group training methods, and instructional techniques. Psychoeducational group specialists should also acquire knowledge about the topic areas in which they intend to work (such as AIDS, substance abuse prevention, grief and loss, coping with transition and change, and parent effectiveness training).

Clinical instruction for preparing to facilitate psychoeducational groups should include a minimum of thirty clock hours (forty-five clock hours are recommended) of supervised practice in leading or coleading a psychoeducational group appropriate to the age and clientele of the group leader's specialty area(s) (such as school counseling, community counseling, and mental health counseling).

Counseling Groups

The group worker who specializes in group counseling focuses on assisting group participants to resolve the usual, yet often difficult, problems of living by stimulating interpersonal support and group problem solving. Group counselors support participants in developing their existing interpersonal problem-solving competencies so that they may become more able to handle future problems of a similar nature. The scope of practice for their group work includes nonsevere career, educational, personal, interpersonal, social, and developmental concerns of essentially normally functioning individuals.

Graduate coursework for specialists in group counseling should include multiple courses in human development, health promotion, and group counseling. Group counseling specialists should have in-depth knowledge in the broad areas of normal human development, problem identification, and treatment of normal personal and interpersonal problems of living.

Clinical instruction for counseling groups should include a minimum of forty-five clock hours (sixty clock hours are recommended) of supervised practice in leading or coleading a counseling group appropriate to the age and clientele of the group leader's specialty area(s) (such as community counseling, mental health counseling, and school counseling).

Psychotherapy Groups

The specialist in group psychotherapy helps individual group members remediate in-depth psychological problems or reconstruct major personality dimensions. The group psychotherapist differs from specialists in task/work groups, psychoeducational groups or counseling groups in that the group psychotherapist's scope of practice is focused on people with acute or chronic mental or emotional disorders characterized by marked distress, impairment in functioning, or both.

Graduate coursework for training in group psychotherapy should include multiple courses in the development, assessment, and treatment of serious or chronic personal and interpersonal dysfunction. The group psychotherapist must develop in-depth knowledge in the broad areas of normal and abnormal human development, diagnosis, treatment of psychopathology, and group psychotherapy. Clinical instruction for working with psychotherapy groups should include a minimum forty-five clock hours (sixty clock hours recommended) of supervised practice in leading or coleading a psychotherapy group appropriate to the age and clientele of the group leader's specialty area(s) (such as mental health counseling or community counseling).

Stages of Group Life

In an outstanding article, David G. Zimpfer (1986) pointed out that since the 1940s much has been written about the developmental phases or stages through which a small group progresses over time (Braaten, 1975; Bales, 1950; Hare, 1973; Golembiewski, 1962; Hill & Gruner, 1973; Thelen & Dickerman, 1949; Tuckman, 1965). He also noted that recent contributions to this topic range from descriptive, classificatory schemes (such as the initial, transitional, working, and final stages presented by Corey in 1985) to detailed analyses of a single phase of group development (such as the 1965 exploration of authority relations in T-groups presented by Reid). Zimpfer's recommendation to the group work specialist is to select the theory or model of small-group development that applies to the kind of group to be conducted. After studying a variety of models and conceptualizations of the developmental stages of groups and calling on our own collective experience, we propose a composite conceptualization (Capuzzi & Gross, 1992) of the stages of group life. In our view, the developmental process consists of four stages: (1) the definitive stage, (2) the personal involvement stage, (3) the group involvement stage, and (4) the enhancement and closure stage.

Definitive Stage

The length of time associated with this stage in group development varies with the group and is best explained in terms of the individual group member's definition of the purpose of the group, commitment and involvement in it and the degree of self-disclosure he or she is willing to do. Characterizing this stage of development are questions such as Whom can I trust? Where will I find support? Will I be hurt by others' knowing about me? How much of myself am I willing to share? These questions, and the lack of immediate answers, typify members in the definitive stage as anxiety, excitement, nervousness, and self-protective dialogue increase. The dialogue during this stage tends to be of a social nature (small talk) as the members test the waters of group involvement. To help group members deal effectively with the definitive stage, the group leader needs skills in dealing with issues such as trust, support, safety, self-disclosure, and confidentiality.

In the definitive stage in group development, individuals define, demonstrate, and experiment with their own role definitions; they "test" the temperament, personality, and behaviors of other group members; and they arrive at conclusions about how personally involved they are willing to become. The individual's movement through this stage can be enhanced or impeded by the group's makeup (age, gender, number, values, attitudes, socioeconomic status, and so on), the leadership style (active, passive, autocratic, democratic), the group's setting (formal, informal, uncomfortable, relaxed), the personal dynamics the individual brings to the group (shy, aggressive, verbal, nonverbal), and the individual's perceptions of trust and acceptance from other group members and from the group leader.

The definitive stage is crucial in group development because this stage can determine for the individual (and therefore for the group) future involvement, commitment, and individual and group success or failure as the group progresses.

Personal Involvement Stage

Once individuals have drawn conclusions about their commitment and role in the group, they move into the personal involvement stage of group development. This stage is best described in terms of member-to-member interactions—the sharing of personal information, confrontation with other group members, power struggles, and the individual's growing identity as a group member. Statements such as "I am," "I fear," "I need," and "I care" are characteristic of this stage of group involvement. Through speech and behaviors, the individual member demonstrates the degree of personal sharing he or she is willing to invest and confirms the commitment made during the definitive stage.

The personal involvement stage is one of action, reaction, and interaction. Both fight and flight are represented in this stage as individuals strive to create a role within the group. This creating process often involves intense member-to-member interactions followed by a retreat to regroup and become involved again. The interactions that ensue not only enhance the member's place within the group, but also aid in firmly establishing the group as an entity in its own right.

The personal involvement stage offers the individual the opportunity to try out various behaviors, affirm or deny perceptions of self and others, receive feedback in the form of words or behaviors, and begin the difficult process of self-evaluation. Individual involvement in this stage of group development is crucial to the eventual outcome of the group.

Group Involvement Stage

As a result of the information about self gained in the personal involvement stage, group members move into the group involvement stage, characterized by self-evaluation and self-assessment of behavior, attitudes, values, and methods used in relating to others and also by members' channeling their energies to better meet group goals and purposes. During this stage, the term *member* and the term *group* become somewhat more synonymous.

Degrees of cooperation and cohesiveness replace conflict and confrontation as members, now more confident in their role in the group, direct more of their attention to what is best for the group and all its members. This stage reveals increasing role clarification, intimacy, problem exploration, group solidarity, compromise, conflict resolution, and risk taking.

The group, with its purposes and goals, is now merging with the individual purposes and goals of its members. Individual agendas are being replaced by group agendas, and the members are identifying more with the group. Bonding is taking place between members as they join forces to enhance the group and, in turn, enhance self in relation to the group. References to "insider" and "outsider" differentiate the group and the member's life outside the group. Members grow protective of other group members and also of the group itself. The group and its membership take on special significance unique to those who are part of the process. This melding of member and group purposes and goals is necessary to the group's ongoing success.

Enhancement and Closure Stage

The final stage in a group's life is often described as the most exhilarating but also the saddest aspect of group work. The exhilaration stems from the evaluation and reevaluation that are so much a part of the final stage. The evaluative aspect consists of reevaluation of the group process and individual and group assessment of change, in conjunction with individual and group reinforcement of individual member change, and a commitment to continue self-analysis and growth. Members have an opportunity to share significant growth experiences during the group tenure, and they receive feedback, generally positive, from other group members and the leader. Members are encouraged to review the process of the group and to measure changes that have taken place since their first entering the group to this period just before closure. Member statements at this stage of group development tend to be along the lines of "I was . . . now I am," "I felt . . . now I feel," "I didn't . . . now I do," and "I couldn't . . . now I can."

The sadness in this final stage centers on leaving an environment that provided safety, security, and support, and individuals who offered encouragement, friendship, and positive feedback. A major concern seems to be whether the individual will ever be able to replace what he or she found in the group and be able to take what was learned in the group and apply it elsewhere. The answer to both questions is generally yes, but the individual is too close to the experience to have this self-assurance. Our experience indicates that this stage often ends with members' unwritten agreement to continue group involvement and, more specifically, to continue contact with members of the present group. Most group members find, after distancing themselves from the group, that neither of these activities is essential. The gains they made from the group experience will serve them well as they move into other facets of their lives.

The movement from group initiation to group termination varies. Groups differ in this movement process for a myriad of reasons, and no one conceptualization has all the answers or addresses all the issues inherent in the group process. This framework can provide, however, guidelines for working with groups.

Characteristics of Group Facilitators

Many writers who are expert in group counseling have described the personal traits and characteristics of effective group counselors (Corey, 1995; Dinkmeyer & Muro, 1979; Kottler, 1983). As expressed by Gerald Corey in 1995,

> *Group leaders can acquire extensive theoretical and practical knowledge of group dynamics and be skilled in diagnostic and technical procedures yet be ineffective in stimulating growth and change in the members of their groups. Leaders bring to every group their personal qualities, values, and life experiences. In order to promote growth in the members' lives, leaders need to live growth-oriented lives themselves. In order to foster honest self-investigation in others, leaders need to have the courage to engage in self-appraisal. If they hope to inspire others to break*

away from deadening ways of being, they need to be willing to seek new experiences themselves. In short, the most effective group direction is found in the kind of life the group members see the leader demonstrating and not in the words they hear the leader saying. (p. 53)

We believe that there are characteristics that the effective group leader must possess in order to do an effective job of facilitating group process. The reader is directed to sources such as Arbuckle (1975), Carkhuff and Berenson (1977), Jourard (1971), Truax and Carkhuff (1967), and Yalom (1975) for earlier readings on this topic. Corey's 1995 presentation is summarized next as a constructive point of departure for the beginning counselor.

Presence. The leader's ability to be emotionally present as group members share their experience is important. Leaders who are in touch with their own life experiences and associated emotions are usually better able to communicate empathy and understanding because of being able to relate to similar circumstances or emotions.

Personal Power. Personal power comes from a sense of self-confidence and a realization of the influence the leader has on a group. Personal power that is channeled in a way that enhances the ability of each group member to identify and build on strengths, overcome problems, and cope more effectively with stressors is both essential and "curative."

Courage. Group facilitators must be courageous. They must take risks by expressing their reactions to aspects of group process, confronting, sharing a few life experiences, acting on a combination of intuition and observation, and directing the appropriate portion of the group movement and discussion.

Willingness to Confront Oneself. It takes courage to deal with group members; it is not easy to role model, confront, convey empathy, and achieve a good balance between catalyzing interaction and allowing the group to "unfold." It also takes courage on the part of the group leader to confront oneself. As Corey (1995) so aptly stated,

> *Self-confrontation can take the form of posing and answering questions such as the following:*
>
> - *Why am I leading groups? What am I getting from this activity?*
> - *Why do I behave as I do in a group? What impact do my attitudes, values, biases, feelings, and behaviors have on the people in the group?*
> - *What needs of mine are served by being a group leader?*
> - *Do I ever use the groups I lead to satisfy my personal needs at the expense of the members' needs? (p. 55)*

Self-confrontation must be an ongoing process for the leader, since the leader facilitates the capacity of members in a group to ask related questions about themselves.

Sincerity and Authenticity. Sincerity on the part of a group counselor is usually considered to be related to the leader's genuine interest in the welfare of the group and the individual group member. Sincerity also relates to the leader's ability to be direct and to encourage each member to explore aspects of self that could easily be distorted or denied completely. Effective leaders are able to be real, congruent, honest, and open as they respond to the interactions in a group. Authenticity means that the leader knows who he or she really is and has a sense of comfort and acceptance about self. Authenticity results in an ability to be honest about feelings and reactions to the group in a way that is constructive to individuals as well as the group as a whole.

Sense of Identity. Group leaders often assist members of a group in the process of clarifying values and becoming "inner" rather than "outer" directed. If the leader of a group has not clarified personal values, meanings, goals, and expectations, it may be difficult to help others with the same process.

Belief in Group Process and Enthusiasm. Leaders must be positive and enthusiastic about the healing capacity of groups and their belief in the benefits of a group experience. If they are unsure, tentative, or unenthusiastic, the same "tenor" will develop among members of the group. As will be noted in a subsequent discussion of myths, the outcome of a group experience is not totally dependent on the leader; however, the leader does convey messages, nonverbally as well as verbally, that do have an impact on the overall benefit of the experience.

Inventiveness and Creativity. Leaders who can be spontaneous in their approach to a group can often facilitate better communication, insight, and personal growth than those who become dependent on structured interventions and techniques. Creative facilitators are usually accepting of members who are different from themselves and flexible about approaching members and groups in ways that seem congruent with the particular group. In addition, a certain amount of creativity and spontaneity is necessary to cope with the "unexpected"; in a group situation, the leader will continuously be presented with comments, problems, and reactions that could not have been anticipated prior to a given session.

Group Facilitation: Responsibilities and Interventions

Responsibilities

One of the most important responsibilities of counselors interested in becoming group work specialists is to gain a thorough understanding of what elements or factors are important in making groups effective in helping those who participate. Even though the group approach is a well-established mode of "treatment," anyone interested in facilitating a group must ask and understand the question of what about groups makes them effective. One difficulty in answering such a question is that the therapeutic change that results from group participation is a result of a complex set of variables, including leadership style, membership roles, and aspects of group process.

In a fascinating discussion of this topic, George and Dustin (1988) promote Bloch's (1986) definition of a therapeutic factor as "an element occurring in group therapy that contributes to improvement in a patient's condition and is a function of the actions of the group therapist, the patient, or fellow group members" (p. 679). Although this definition sounds somewhat "clinical," its application to all types of groups is apparent because it helps distinguish among therapeutic elements, conditions for change, and techniques. Conditions for change are necessary for the operation of therapeutic elements but do not, in and of themselves, have therapeutic force. For example, a sense of belonging and acceptance—a therapeutic element that enhances personal growth in groups—cannot emerge unless the "condition" of the actual presence of several good listeners in the group exists. Likewise, a technique, such as asking members to talk about a self-esteem inventory they have filled out, does not have a direct therapeutic effect but may be used to enhance a sense of belonging and acceptance (George & Dustin, 1988).

Group work specialists have a responsibility to understand the research that has been done on therapeutic elements of groups so they can develop the skills to create a group climate that enhances personal growth. Corsini and Rosenberg (1955) published one of the earlier efforts to produce a classification of therapeutic elements in groups. They abstracted therapeutic factors published in 300 pre-1955 articles on group counseling and clustered them into nine major categories:

1. *Acceptance:* a sense of belonging
2. *Altruism:* a sense of being helpful to others
3. *Universalization:* the realization that group members are not alone in the experiencing of their problems
4. *Intellectualization:* the process of acquiring self-knowledge
5. *Reality testing:* recognition of the reality of issues such as defenses and family conflicts
6. *Transference:* strong attachment to either the therapist or other group members
7. *Interaction:* the process of relating to other group members that results in personal growth
8. *Spectator therapy:* growth that occurs through listening to other group members
9. *Ventilation:* the release of feelings that had previously been repressed

In 1957, in an attempt to take the classification of therapeutic elements in groups further, Hill interviewed nineteen group therapists. He proposed the six elements of catharsis, feelings of belongingness, spectator therapy, insights, peer agency (universality), and socialization. Berzon, Pious, and Farson (1963) used group members rather than leaders as the source of information about therapeutic elements. Their classification included the following:

1. Increased awareness of emotional dynamics
2. Recognizing similarity to others
3. Feeling positive regard, acceptance, and sympathy for others

4. Seeing self as seen by others
5. Expressing self congruently, articulately, or assertively in the group
6. Witnessing honesty, courage, openness, or expressions of emotionality in others
7. Feeling warmth and closeness in the group
8. Feeling responded to by others
9. Feeling warmth and closeness generally in the group
10. Ventilating emotions

A very different set of therapeutic elements connected with group experience was proposed by Ohlsen in 1977. His list differs from earlier proposals in that it emphasizes client attitudes about the group experience. Ohlsen's paradigm included fourteen elements that he labeled as "therapeutic forces":

1. Attractiveness of the group
2. Acceptance by the group
3. Expectations
4. Belonging
5. Security within the group
6. Client readiness
7. Client commitment
8. Client participation
9. Client acceptance of responsibility
10. Congruence
11. Feedback
12. Openness
13. Therapeutic tension
14. Therapeutic norms

In what is now considered a landmark classification of "curative factors," Yalom (1970, 1975) proposed a list of therapeutic elements based on research he and his colleagues conducted:

1. Installation of hope
2. Universality
3. Imparting of information
4. Altruism
5. The corrective recapitulation of the primary family group
6. Development of socializing techniques
7. Imitative behavior
8. Interpersonal learning
9. Group cohesiveness
10. Catharsis
11. Existential factors

It is not possible to present all the possibilities for viewing the therapeutic elements of a positive group experience. It is possible, however, to encourage the beginning counselor to study the research relating to these elements prior to facilitating or cofacilitating groups under close supervision.

In an interesting discussion of facilitator responsibilities, Ohlsen and Ferreira (1994) discuss the topic from a very practical perspective. Understanding which clients can be helped through participation in a group, being able to describe a potential group experience to a client, understanding how to conduct an intake or pregroup screening interview, teaching group members how to be good clients and good helpers, mastering skills for structuring, norm setting and feedback, and recognizing when to terminate a group and assist members to continue their growth after the group terminates are among the responsibilities Ohlsen and Ferreira (1994) address. We recommend further reading on this topic as the reader pursues information on the role of the group work specialist.

Just as the importance of understanding the responsibilities of a group facilitator cannot be stressed enough, the topic of interventions or techniques used by facilitators is important to consider.

Interventions

Numerous approaches to the topic of intervention strategies for groups can be found in the literature on groups. Corey (1995) approached the topic by discussing active listening, restating, clarifying, summarizing, questioning, interpreting, confronting, reflecting feelings, supporting, empathizing, facilitating, initiating, setting goals, evaluating, giving feedback, suggesting, protecting, disclosing oneself, modeling, linking, blocking, and terminating. Dinkmeyer and Muro (1971) discussed the topic by focusing on promoting cohesiveness, summarizing, promoting interaction, resolving conflicts, tone setting, structuring and limit setting, blocking, linking, providing support, reflecting, protecting, questioning, and regulating. Bates, Johnson, and Blaker (1982) emphasized confrontation, attending behavior, feedback, use of questions, levels of interaction, and opening and closing a session. They also presented the four major functions of group leaders as traffic director, model, interaction catalyst, and communication facilitator.

Individuals new to the profession of counseling may better relate to the topic of intervention strategies by becoming familiar with circumstances during which the group leader must take responsibility for intervening in the group's "process." A helpful model (and a favorite of ours) is that presented by Dyer and Vriend in 1973 in terms of ten occasions when intervention is required:

1. *A group member speaks for everyone.* It is not unusual for a member of a group to say something like "We think we should . . . ," "This is how we all feel," or "We were wondering why . . ." This happens when an individual does not feel comfortable making a statement such as "I think we should . . ." or "I am wondering why . . ." or when an individual group member is hoping to engender support for a point of view. The problem with allowing the "we" syndrome to operate in a group is that it inhibits individual members from expressing individual feelings and thoughts. Appropriate interventions on the part of the group leader might be

"You mentioned 'we' a number of times. Are you speaking for yourself or for everyone?" Or "What do each of you think about the statement that was just made?"

2. *An individual speaks for another individual in the group.* "I think I know what he means" or "She is not really saying how she feels; I can explain it for her" are statements that one group member may make for another. When one person in the group speaks for another, it often means that a judgment has been made about the capacity of the other person to communicate or that the other person is about to self-disclose "uncomfortable" information. Regardless of the motivation behind such a circumstance, the person who is allowing another group member to do the "talking" needs to evaluate why this is happening and whether the same thing occurs outside the group. In addition, the "talker" needs to evaluate the inclination to make decisions and/or rescue others.

Appropriate interventions include saying, "Did Jim state your feelings more clearly than you can?" or "How does it feel to have someone rescue you?" Possible interventions for the "talker" are statements such as "Did you feel that June needed your assistance?" and "Do you find it difficult to hold back when you think you know what someone else is going to say?"

3. *A group member focuses on persons, conditions, or events outside the group.* Often group counseling sessions can turn into "gripe sessions." Complaining about a colleague, friend, or a partner can be enjoyable for group members if they are allowed to reinforce each other. The problem with allowing such emphasis to occur is that such a process erroneously substantiates that others are at fault and that group members do not have to take responsibility for aspects of their behavior.

Possible interventions for the group leader include saying, "You keep talking about your wife as the cause of your unhappiness. Isn't it more important to ask yourself what contributions you can make to improve your relationship?" Or "Does complaining about someone else really mean you think you would be happier if he or she could change?"

4. *Someone seeks the approval of the leader or a group member before or after speaking.* Some group members seek nonverbal acceptance from the leader or another group member (a nod, a glance, a smile). Such individuals may be intimidated by authority figures or personal strength or may have low self-esteem and seek sources of support and acceptance outside themselves. One possible intervention is for the leader to look at another member, forcing the speaker to change the direction of his or her delivery. Another possibility is to say something like "You always look at me as you speak, almost as if you are asking permission."

5. *Someone says, "I don't want to hurt her feelings, so I won't say what I'd like to say."* It is not unusual for such a sentiment to be expressed in a group, particularly in the early stages. Sometimes this happens when a member thinks another member of the group is too fragile for feedback; at other times such reluctance arises because the provider of the potential feedback is concerned about being "liked" by other group members. The group leader should explore reasons for apprehension about providing feedback, which can include asking the group member to check with the person to whom feedback may be directed, to determine whether such fears are totally valid.

6. *A group member suggests that his or her problems are due to someone else.* Although this item overlaps with item 3, this situation represents a problem different from a "group gripe" session. A single group member may periodically attribute difficulties and unhappiness to someone else. Interventions such as "Who is really the only person who can be in charge of you?" Or "How can other people determine your mood so much of the time?" are called for in such a case. We are not suggesting a stance that would be perceived as lacking empathy and acceptance. It is, however, important to facilitate responsibility for self on the part of each group member.

7. *An individual suggests that "I've always been that way."* Such a suggestion indicates irrational thinking and lack of motivation to change. Believing that the past determines all one's future is something that a group member can believe to such an extent that his or her future growth is inhibited. The group leader must assist such a member to identify thinking errors that lead to lack of effectiveness in specific areas. Such a member needs to learn that he or she is not doomed to repeat the mistakes of the past. Possible statements that will stimulate examination of faulty thinking and assumptions are "You're suggesting that your past has such a hold over you that you will never be any different" and "Do you feel that everyone has certain parts of his or her life over which he or she has no control?"

8. *Someone in the group suggests, "I'll wait, and it will change."* Often group members are willing to talk about their self-defeating behavior during a group session but aren't willing to make an effort outside the group to behave differently. At times they take the position that they can postpone action and things will correct themselves. A competent group leader will help members develop strategies for doing something about their problems outside the group and will develop a method of "tracking" or "checking in" with members to evaluate progress.

9. *Discrepant behavior appears.* Group leader intervention is essential when discrepancies occur in a member's behavior in the group. Examples of such discrepancies include a difference in what a member is currently saying and what he or she said earlier, a lack of congruence between what a member is saying and what he or she is doing in the group, a difference between how a member sees himself or herself and how others in the group see him or her, or a difference between how a member reports feelings and how nonverbal cues communicate what is going on inside. Interventions used to identify discrepancies may be confrontational in nature, because the leader usually needs to describe the discrepancies noted so the group member can begin to identify, evaluate, and change aspects of such behavior.

10. *A member bores the group by rambling.* Sometimes members use talking as a way of seeking approval. At times such talking becomes "overtalk." The leader can ask other members to react to the "intellectualizer" and let such a person know how such rambling affects others. If such behavior is not addressed, other members may develop a sense of anger and hostility toward the "offender."

In addition to the interventions described in this list, the reader should be alerted to the necessity to be prepared to resolve resistance in groups. Clark (1992), Higgs (1992), Ohlsen and Ferreira (1994), and Ormont (1993) provide some excellent guidelines on this aspect of the group leader's role.

Myths Connected with Group Work

Counselors who are group work specialists are usually quite enthusiastic about the benefits for clients of participation in a small group. Indeed, the outcomes of a competently facilitated group experience can be such that personal growth occurs. Often the memory of such an experience has an impact on clients well into the future. However, group work, as with other forms of therapeutic assistance (such as individual or family), can be for better or for worse (Carkhuff, 1969). Many group workers follow a belief system that can be challenged by empirical facts.

Beginning counselors are well advised to be aware of a number of myths connected with group work so they don't base their "practices" on a belief system not supported by research (Anderson, 1985).

Myth 1: "Everyone Benefits from Group Experience"

Groups do provide benefits. The research on the psychosocial outcomes demonstrate that groups are a powerful modality for learning that can then be used outside the group experience (Bednar & Lawlis, 1971; Gazda & Peters, 1975; Parloff & Dies, 1978). There are times, however, when membership in a group can be harmful. Some research shows that one of every ten group members can be hurt (Lieberman, Yalom, & Miles, 1973). The research findings that seem to relate most to individuals who get injured in groups suggest some important principles for the beginning counselor to understand: (1) those who join groups and who have the potential to be hurt by the experience have unrealistic expectations, and (2) these expectations seem to be reinforced by the facilitator who coerces the member to meet them (De Julio, Bentley, & Cockayne, 1979; Lieberman et al., 1973; Stava & Bednar, 1979). Prevention of harm requires that the expectations members have for the group are realistic and that the facilitator maintains a reasonable perspective.

Myth 2: "Groups Can Be Composed to Ensure Effective Outcomes"

The fact is that we do not know enough about how to compose groups using the pregroup screening interview. In general, objective criteria (such as age, sex, socioeconomic status, and presenting problem) can be used to keep groups homogeneous in some respects, but behavioral characteristics should be selected for on a heterogeneous basis (Bertcher & Maple, 1977). The most consistent finding is that it is a good idea to compose a group in such a manner that each member is compatible with at least one other member (Stava & Bednar, 1979). This practice seems to prevent the evolution of neglected isolates or scapegoats in a group.

The essence of group process in terms of benefit to members and effective outcomes is perceived mutual aid, such as helping others, a feeling of belonging, interpersonal learning, and instillation of hope (Butler & Fuhriman, 1980; Long & Cope, 1980; Yalom, 1975).

Myth 3: "The Group Revolves around the Charisma of the Leader"

It is true that leaders influence groups tremendously, but there are two general findings in the research on groups that should be noted. First, the group, independent of the leader, has an impact on outcomes. Second, the most effective group leaders are those who help the group develop so that members are primary sources of help to one another (Ashkenas & Tandon, 1979; Lungren, 1971).

As noted by Anderson (1985), research on leadership styles has identified four particular leader functions that facilitate the group's functioning:

1. Providing: *This is the provider role of relationships and climate-setting through such skills as support, affection, praise, protection, warmth, acceptance, genuineness, and concern.*
2. Processing: *This is the processor role of illuminating the meaning of the process through such skills as explaining, clarifying, interpreting, and providing a cognitive framework for change or translating feelings and experiences into ideas.*
3. Catalyzing: *This is the catalyst role of stimulating interaction and emotional expression through such skills as reaching for feelings, challenging, confronting, and suggesting; using program activities such as structured experiences; and modeling.*
4. Directing: *This is the director role through such skills as setting limits, roles, norms, and goals; managing time; pacing; stopping; interceding; and suggesting procedures. (p. 272)*

Providing and processing seem to have a linear relationship to outcomes: the higher the providing (or caring) and the higher the processing (or clarifying), the higher the positive outcomes. Catalyzing and directing have a curvilinear relationship to outcomes. Too much or too little catalyzing or directing results in lower positive outcomes (Lieberman et al., 1973).

Myth 4: "Leaders Can Direct through the Use of Structured Exercises or Experiences"

Structured exercises create early cohesion (Levin & Kurtz, 1974; Lieberman, et al., 1973); they help create early expression of positive and negative feelings. However, they restrict members from dealing with such group themes as affection, closeness, distance, trust, mistrust, genuineness, and lack of genuineness. All these areas form the very basis for group process and should be dealt with in a way that is not hampered by a large amount of structure. The best principle around which to plan and use structured exercises to get groups started and to keep them going can best be stated as "to overplan and to underuse."

Myth 5: "Therapeutic Change in Groups Comes About through a Focus on Here-and-Now Experiences"

Much of the research on groups indicates that corrective emotional experiences in the here-and-now of the group increase the intensity of the experience for members (Levine, 1971; Lieberman et al., 1973; Snortum & Myers, 1971; Zimpfer, 1967). The intensity of emotional experiences does not, however, appear to be related to outcomes. Higher-level outcomes in groups are achieved by members who develop "insight" or cognitive understanding of emotional experiences in the group and can transfer that understanding into their lives outside the group. The Gestaltists' influence on groups in the 1960s and 1970s (Perls, 1969) suggested that members should "Lose your mind and come to your senses" and "Stay with the here-and-now." Research suggests that members "use your mind and your senses" and "focus on the there-and-then as well as on the here-and-now."

Myth 6: "Major Member Learning in Groups Is Derived from Self-Disclosure and Feedback"

There is an assumption that most of the learning of members in a group comes from self-disclosure in exchange for feedback (Jacobs, 1974). To a large extent, this statement is a myth. Self-disclosure and feedback per se make little difference in terms of outcomes (Anchor, 1979; Bean & Houston, 1978). It is how self-disclosure and feedback are used that appears to make the difference (Martin & Jacobs, 1980). Self-disclosure and feedback appear useful only when deeply personal sharing is understood and appreciated and the feedback is accurate (Berzon, Pious, & Farson, 1963; Frank & Ascher, 1951; Goldstein, Bednar, & Yanell, 1979). The actual benefit of self-disclosure and feedback is connected with how these processes facilitate empathy among members. It is empathy, or the actual experience of being understood by other members, that catalyzes personal growth and understanding in the context of a group.

Myth 7: "The Group Facilitator Can Work Effectively with a Group without Understanding Group Process and Group Dynamics"

Groups experience a natural evolution and unfolding of processes and dynamics. Anderson (1979) labeled these stages as those of trust, autonomy, closeness, interdependence, and termination (TACIT). Tuckman (1965) suggested a more dramatic labeling of forming, storming, norming, performing, and adjourning. We suggested a four-stage paradigm earlier in this chapter. Two reviews, which include over 200 studies of group dynamics and group process (Cohen & Smith, 1976; La Coursiere, 1980), revealed remarkably similar patterns (despite differences in the labels chosen as descriptors) in the evolution of group processes as a group evolves through stages. It is extremely important for group facilitators to understand group processes and dynamics to do a competent job of enhancing membership benefits derived from participation.

Myth 8: "Change Experienced by Group Participation Is Not Maintained over Time"

Groups are powerful! Changes can be maintained by group members as much as six months to a year later even when groups meet for only three or four months (Lieberman et al., 1973).

Myth 9: "A Group Is a Place to Get Emotionally High"

Feeling good after a group session is a positive outcome but is not the main reason for being in a group in the first place. Some group members have periods of depression after group participation because they don't find elsewhere, on a daily basis, the kind of support they receive from other members of the group. Group members should be prepared for this possibility and assisted in their ability to obtain support, when appropriate, from those around them.

Myth 10: "A Group's Purpose Is to Make Members Close to Every Other Member"

Although genuine feelings of intimacy and cohesiveness develop in effective groups, intimacy is the by-product and not the central purpose of the group. Intimacy develops as individual members risk self-disclosure and problem solving and other group members reach out in constructive ways.

Myth 11: "Group Participation Results in Brainwashing"

Professional groups do not indoctrinate members with a particular philosophy of life or a set of rules about how each member "should be." If this does occur in a group, it is truly a breach of professional ethics and an abuse of the group. Group participation encourages members to look within themselves for answers and to become as self-directed as possible.

Myth 12: "To Benefit from a Group, a Member Must Be Dysfunctional"

Group counseling is as appropriate for individuals who are functioning relatively well and who want to enhance their capabilities as it is for those who are having difficulty with certain aspects of their lives. Groups are not only for dysfunctional people.

Issues and Ethics: Some Concluding Remarks

Although a thorough discussion of issues and ethics in group counseling is beyond the scope of this chapter, it is important for the beginning counselor to be introduced to this topic. The guidelines in *Professional Standards for Training of Group Counselors* (ASGW, 1991) are excellent points of departure for the counselor interested in groups, as are the *Ethical Guidelines for Group Leaders,* published in 1980 by the Association for Specialists in Group Work (ASGW). In addition, both sets of guidelines serve as useful adjuncts to the *Code of Ethics and Standards of Practice* of the American Counseling Association (1995).

ASGW (1991) recommends that the group work specialist acquire *knowledge competencies* (for example, understanding principles of group dynamics, the roles of members in groups, and the contributions of research in group work), *skill competencies* (for example, diagnosing self-defeating behavior in groups, intervening at crucial times in group process, and using assessment procedures to evaluate the outcomes of a group), and *supervised clinical experience* (such as observing group counseling, coleading groups with supervision, and participating as a member in a group). Interestingly, these very training standards have become an issue with some counselor preparation programs as they struggle to obtain a balance between the didactic and clinical components of the set of educational and supervisory experiences required to prepare an individual to do a competent job of group counseling. The clinical supervisory aspects of preparing the group work specialist are costly for universities, and often counselor educators are encouraged to abandon such efforts in favor of classroom didactics.

Another example of some of the issues connected with group counseling has to do with continuing education after the completion of master's and/or doctoral-degree programs. Although the National Board for Certified Counselors (NBCC) requires those who achieve the National Certified Counselor (NCC) credential to obtain 100 contact hours of continuing education every five years, there is no specification of how much this professional enhancement activity should be focused on aspects of group work if group work is the declared area of specialization of an NCC. In time, there may be a specific continuing education requirement for the group work specialist.

The *Ethical Guidelines for Group Leaders* (ASGW, 1991) help clarify the nature of ethical responsibilities of the counselor in a group setting. These guidelines present standards in three areas: (1) the leader's responsibility for providing information about group work to clients, (2) the leader's responsibility for providing group counseling services to clients, and (3) the leader's responsibility for safeguarding the standards of ethical practice. One of the greatest single sources of ethical dilemma in group counseling situations has to do with confidentiality. Counselors have an obligation not to disclose information about the client without the client's consent unless the client is dangerous to self or others. Yet the very nature of a group counseling situation makes it difficult to ensure that each member of a group will respect the others' right to privacy.

Other issues such as recruitment and informed consent, screening and selection of group members, voluntary and involuntary participation, psychological risks, uses and abuses of group techniques, therapist competence, interpersonal relationships in groups, and follow-up all form the basis for considerable discussion and evaluation. In addition, these issues emphasize the necessity of adequate education, supervision, and advance time to consider the ramifications and responsibilities connected with becoming a group specialist.

Group experiences can be powerful growth-enhancing opportunities for clients, or they can be pressured, stifling encounters to be avoided. Each of us has a professional obligation to assess our readiness to facilitate or cofacilitate a group. Our clients deserve the best experience we can provide.

Summary

The use of groups of all types is increasingly important to the role of the counselor in a variety of settings. As the decades have passed, emphasis has shifted from T-groups to encounter groups to working with special populations. Self-help groups of all types are flourishing. The ASGW standards for the training of group counselors have received widespread acceptance.

ASGW's definitions of the four group work specialty types (task/work, guidance/psychoeducational, counseling, and psychotherapy groups), information about stages of group life, and research on the characteristics of group facilitators have also enhanced the ability of the group work specialist to function in the best interests of clients in groups. In addition, the more group work specialists know about their responsibilities and the interventions they need to master, myths connected with group work, and issues and ethics associated with group practicum, the more competent they will be as facilitators of group experiences. The importance of broad-based education and carefully supervised group practicum and other clinical experiences for group work specialists cannot be overemphasized.

References

American Counseling Association. (1995). *Code of ethics and standards of practice*. Alexandria, VA: Author.

Anchor, K. N. (1979). High-and-low-risk self-disclosure in group psychotherapy. *Small Group Behavior, 10*, 279–283.

Anderson, J. D. (1979). Social work with groups in the generic base of social work practice. *Social Work with Groups, 2*, 281–293.

Anderson, J. D. (1985). Working with groups: Little-known facts that challenge well-known myths. *Small Group Behavior, 16*(3), 267–283.

Arbuckle, D. (1975). *Counseling and psychotherapy: An existential-humanistic view*. Boston: Allyn and Bacon.

Ashkenas, R., & Tandon, R. (1979). Eclectic approach to small group facilitation. *Small Group Behavior, 10*, 224–241.

Association for Specialists in Group Work (ASGW). (1980). *Ethical guidelines for group leaders.* Alexandria, VA: Author.

Association for Specialists in Group Work (ASGW). (1983). *Professional standards for training of group counselors.* Alexandria, VA: Author.

Association for Specialists in Group Work. (1991). Professional standards for training of group workers. *Together, 20,* 9–14.

Bales, R. F. (1950). *Interaction process analysis: A method for study of small groups.* Reading, MA: Addison-Wesley.

Bates, M., Johnson, C. D., & Blaker, K. E. (1982*). Group leadership: A manual for group counseling leaders* (2nd ed.). Denver: Love Publishing.

Bean, B. W., & Houston, B. K. (1978*). Self-concept and self-disclosure in encounter groups. *Small Group Behavior, 9,* 549–554.

Bednar, R., & Lawlis, G. (1971). Empirical research in group psychotherapy. In S. L. Garfield and A. E. Bergin (Eds.), *Handbook of psychotherapy and behavior change* (2nd ed., pp. 420–439). New York: Wiley.

Bertcher, H. J., & Maple, F. F. (1977). *Creating groups.* Newbury Park, CA: Sage.

Berzon, B., Pious, C., & Farson, R. (1963). The therapeutic event in group psychotherapy: A study of subjective reports by group members. *Journal of Individual Psychology, 19,* 204–212.

Bloch, S. (1986). Therapeutic factors in group psychotherapy. In A. J. Frances & R. E. Hales (Eds.), *Annual Review* (Vol. 5, pp. 678–698). Washington, DC: American Psychiatric Press.

Braaten, L. J. (1975). Developmental phases of encounter groups and related intensive groups. *Interpersonal Development, 5,* 112–129.

Bradford, L. P., Gibb, J. R., & Benne, K. D. (Eds.). (1964). *T-group theory and laboratory method: Innovation in re-education.* New York: Wiley.

Butler, T., & Fuhriman, A. (1980). Patient perspective on the curative process: A comparison of day treatment and outpatient psychotherapy groups. *Small Group Behavior, 11,* 371–388.

Capuzzi, D., & Gross, D. R. (1992). *Introduction to group counseling.* Denver: Love Publishing.

Carkhuff, R. R. (1969). *Helping and human relations: A primer for lay and professional helpers,* Vol. 2, *Practice and research.* New York: Holt, Rinehart & Winston.

Carkhuff, R. R., & Berenson, B. G. (1977). *Beyond counseling and therapy* (2nd ed.). New York: Holt, Rinehart & Winston.

Clark, A. J. (1992). Defense mechanisms in group counseling. *Journal for Specialists in Group Work, 17*(3), 151–160.

Cohen, A. M., & Smith, D. R. (1976). *The critical incident in growth groups: Theory and techniques.* La Jolla, CA: University Associates.

Conyne, R. K., Wilson, F. R., Kline, W. B., Morran, D. K., & Ward, D. E. (1993). Training group workers: Implications of the new ASGW training standards for training and practice. *Journal for Specialists in Group Work, 18*(1), 11–23.

Corey, G. (1985). *Theory and practice of group counseling* (2nd ed.). Padific Grove, CA: Brooks/Cole.

Corey, G. (1995). *Theory and practice of group counseling* (4th ed.). Pacific Grove, CA: Brooks/Cole.

Corsini, R., & Rosenberg, B. (1955). Mechanisms of group psychotherapy: Processes and dynamics. *Journal of Abnormal and Social Psychology, 51,* 406–411.

Council for Accreditation of Counseling and Related Educational Programs (CACREP). (1988). *Accreditation procedures manual and application.* Alexandria, VA: CACREP.

Council for Accreditation of Counseling and Related Educational Programs (CACREP). (1994). *CACREP accreditation standards and procedures manual* (January 1994). Alexandria, VA: Author.

De Julio, S. J. , Bentley, J., & Cockayne, T. (1979). Pregroup norm setting: Effects on encounter group interaction. *Small Group Behavior, 10,* 368–388.

Dinkmeyer, D. C., & Muro, J. J. (1971). *Group counseling: Theory and practice.* Itasca, IL: Peacock.

Dinkmeyer, D. C., & Muro, J. J. (1979). *Group counseling: Theory and practice.* (2nd ed.). Itasca, IL: Peacock.

Dyer, W. W., & Vriend, J. (1973). Effective group counseling process interventions. *Educational Technology, 13*(1), 61–67.

Frank, J., & Ascher, E. (1951). The corrective emotional experience in group therapy. *American Journal of Psychiatry, 108,* 126–131.

Gazda, G. (1984). *Group counseling* (3rd ed.). Dubuque, IA: Brown.

Gazda, G. M., & Peters, R. W. (1975). An analysis of human research in group psychotherapy, group counseling and human relations training. In G. M. Gazda (Ed.), *Basic approaches to group psychotherapy and group counseling* (pp. 38–54). Springfield, IL: Thomas.

George, R. L., & Dustin, D. (1988). *Group counseling: Theory and practice.* Englewood Cliffs, NJ: Prentice Hall.

Goldstein, M. J., Bednar, R. L., & Yanell, B. (1979). Personal risk associated with self-disclosure, interpersonal feedback, and group confrontation in group psychotherapy. *Small Group Behavior, 9,* 579–587.

Golembiewski, R. T. (1962). *The small group: An analysis of research concepts and operations.* Chicago: University of Chicago Press.

Hare, A. P. (1973). Theories of group development and categories for interaction analysis. *Small Group Behavior, 4,* 259–304.

Hare, A. P., Borgatta, E. F., & Bales, R. F. (Eds.). (1967). *Small groups: Studies in social interaction* (Rev ed.). New York: Knopf.

Higgs, J. S. (1992). Dealing with resistance: Strategies for effective group. *Journal for Specialists in Group Work, 17*(2), 67–73.

Hill, W. F. (1957). Analysis of interviews of group therapists' papers. *Provo Papers, 1,* 1.

Hill, W. F., & Gruner, L. (1973). A study of development in open and closed groups. *Small Group Behavior, 4,* 355–381.

Jacobs, A. (1974). The use of feedback in groups. In A. Jacobs & W. W. Spradline (Eds.), *The group as an agent of change* (pp. 31–49). New York: Behavioral Publications.

Janis, I. L. (1972). *Victims of groupthink: A psychological study of foreign-policy decisions and fiascos.* Boston: Houghton Mifflin.

Jourard, S. (1971). *The transparent self* (Rev ed.). New York: Van Nostrand Reinhold.

Kottler, J. A. (1983). *Pragmatic group leadership.* Pacific Grove, CA: Brooks/Cole.

La Coursiere, R. (1980). *The life-cycle of groups: Group development stage theory.* New York: Human Sciences.

Levin, E. M., & Kurtz, R. P. (1974). Participant perceptions following structured and nonstructured human relations training. *Journal of Counseling Psychology, 21,* 514–532.

Levine, N. (1971). Emotional factors in group development. *Human Relations, 24,* 65–89.

Lieberman, M. A., Yalom, I. D., & Miles, M. B. (1973). *Encounter groups: First facts.* New York: Basic Books.

Long, L. D., & Cope, C. S. (1980). Curative factors in a male felony offender group. *Small Group Behavior, 11,* 389–398.

Lungren, D. C. (1971). Trainer style and patterns of group development. *Journal of Applied Behavioral Science,* 689–709.

Martin, L., & Jacobs, M. (1980). Structured feedback delivered in small groups. *Small Group Behavior, 1,* 88–107.

Ohlsen, M. M. (1977). *Group counseling* (2nd ed.). New York: Holt, Rinehart & Winston.

Ohlsen, M. M., & Ferreira, L. O. (1994). The basics of group counseling. *Counseling and Human Development, 26*(5), 1–20.

Ormont, L. R. (1993). Resolving resistances to immediacy in the group setting. *International Journal of Group Psychotherapy, 43*(4), 399–418.

Parloff, M. B., & Dies, R. R. (1978). Group therapy outcome instrument: Guidelines for conducting research. *Small Group Behavior, 9,* 243–286.

Perls, F. (1969). *Gestalt therapy verbatim.* New York: Bantam.

Reid, C. H. (1965). The authority cycle in small group development. *Adult Leadership, 1,* 308–310.

Rowe, W., & Winborn, B. B. (1973). What people fear about group work: An analysis of 36 selected critical articles. *Educational Technology, 13*(1), 53–57.

Shapiro, J. L., & Bernadett-Shapiro, S. (1985). Group work to 2001: Hal or haven (from isolation)? *Journal for Specialists in Group Work, 10*(2), 83–87.

Snortum, J. R., & Myers, H. F. (1971). Intensity of T-group relations as function of interaction.

International Journal of Group Psychotherapy, 21, 190–201.

Stava, L. J., & Bednar, R. L. (1979). Process and outcome in encounter groups: The effect of group composition. *Small Group Behavior, 10,* 200–213.

Thelen, H., & Dickerman, W. (1949). Stereotypes and the growth of groups. *Educational Leadership, 6,* 309–316.

Truax, C. B., & Carkhuff, R. R. (1967). *Toward effective counseling and psychotherapy: Training and practice.* Chicago: Aldine.

Tuckman, B. W. (1965). Developmental sequences in small groups. *Psychological Bulletin, 63,* 384–389.

Vriend, J. (1985). We've come a long way, group. *Journal for Specialists in Group Work, 10*(2), 63–67.

Yalom, I. D. (1970). *The theory and practice of group psychotherapy.* New York: Basic Books.

Yalom, I. D. (1975). *The theory and practice of group psychotherapy* (2nd ed.). New York: Basic Books.

Zimpfer, D. G. (1967). Expression of feelings in group counseling. *Personnel and Guidance Journal, 45,* 703–708.

Zimpfer, D. G. (1986). Planning for groups based on their developmental phases. *Journal for Specialists in Group Work, 11*(3), 180–187.

Career Counseling
Counseling for Life

Ellen Hawley McWhirter, Ph.D.

> *Trying to eliminate her nervous fidgeting by clasping her hands under the table, the novice counselor watches as the cards are handed out. Who will this first client be? Am I going to know what to say?*
>
> *The anticipation builds as each member of the practicum group is provided with demographics and a single phrase describing the client's main concern. She releases a hand to reach for the blue index card and quickly skims its contents. Female, OK; age 23, great; concern. . . . The counselor stifles a sigh of disappointment. No thrill, no challenge here: "Seeking career counseling."*
>
> —Ellen H. McWhirter

A study by Pinkney and Jacobs (1985) suggests that beginning counselors may have negative attitudes about career counseling and are disinterested in spending time in career counseling activities. Similar findings have been reported among counseling psychology graduate students (Heppner, O'Brien, Hinkelman, & Flores, 1996). Some of these negative attitudes may be based on the impression that career counseling is no more than a process of going through endless inventories and reference material to find the right job for a rather dull, helpless person. Contrary to these impressions, however, career counseling is an intriguing and complex area of counseling that requires an in-depth knowledge of human nature and involves an active, collaborative relationship between the counselor and the client. Although there may be some distinctions between personal and career counseling, most authors agree that there is considerable overlap between the two (for example, see Betz & Corning, 1993; Croteau & Thiel, 1993). I hope that the information provided in this chapter will diminish any unfounded negative impressions the reader may have and illustrate the variety and challenge inherent in the tasks of career counselors.

Condensing the theory and practice of contemporary career counseling into a single chapter is a formidable task and requires the elimination or scant coverage of many important aspects of career counseling. The purpose of this chapter is to introduce the beginning counselor to a developmental perspective of career counseling and to introduce the basic components and activities that are considered the territory of the career counselor. To accommodate this purpose within space limitations, I will minimize evaluation and critique of current theories and interventions. I will emphasize description and provide references for more detailed analysis of the history, theory, and research related to career counseling. The beginning counselor is urged to consult contemporary career textbooks such as those by Isaacson and Brown (1993), Osipow (1983), Seligman (1994), and Sharf (1992) and journals such as the *Journal of Vocational Behavior*, the *Career Development Quarterly*, the *Journal of Career Assessment*, the *Journal of Counseling and Development*, and the *Journal of Counseling Psychology*.

Before proceeding with a discussion of career development theories, three definitions are in order. Recognition of the pervasive nature of work in human lives has led to broader and more developmental definitions of career than existed early in this century. Drawing from the National Vocational Guidance Association (1973), *career* is defined in this chapter as "a time-extended working out of a purposeful life pattern through work undertaken by the individual." The term *career development* refers to "the total constellation of psychological, sociological, educational, physical, economic, and chance factors that combine to shape the career of any given individual" (NVGA, 1973). Finally, *career counseling* may be described as:

> *a series of general and specific interventions throughout the life span, dealing with such concerns as self-understanding; broadening one's horizons; work selection, challenge, satisfaction, and other intrapersonal matters; work site behavior, communication, and other interpersonal phenomena; and lifestyle issues, such as balancing work, family, and leisure. Thus career counseling primarily involves career planning and decision making while encompassing many other matters, such as integrating life, work, family and social roles, discrimination, stress, sexual harassment, bias, stereotyping, pay inequities, and "tokenism" (Engels, Minor, Sampson, & Splete, 1995, p. 134)*

Thus presenting problems in career counseling might include difficulty responding to a homophobic workplace, marital dissatisfaction related to a dual-career situation, poor decision-making skills, lack of knowledge about wheelchair-accessible leisure options, role conflicts and poor stress management skills, or any of the more traditional issues brought to career counseling such as fear of interviews, lack of occupational information, need to develop a résumé, or desire to choose or change a career.

The knowledge and skills required for competent career counseling have been specified in the context of preparation standards (Council for Accreditation of Counseling and Related Educational Programs, or CACREP, 1994) and career counselor certification requirements (National Board for Certified Counselors, or NBCC, 1993). Engels et al. (1995) note that in order to pursue certification as a career counselor, people must first pass the National Counselor Examination and obtain National Counselor Certification. Hence competence in personal counseling is fundamental to career counselors. Although beyond the scope of this chapter, the reader is encouraged to learn how the field of career counseling has developed in the twentieth century.

Theories of Career Counseling

Krumboltz (1989) argues that although the purpose, emphasis, and vocabulary of the major theories of career counseling may differ, there are no fundamental disagreements among them. Comparing theories to maps, Krumboltz points out how they are similar: both represent an oversimplification of reality; both distort certain features; both employ symbols to depict reality and are intended to provide a big picture; and, finally, the usefulness of both maps and theories depends on the purpose for which they are used. The various career counseling theories represent different aspects of the same territory; no one theory covers the entire area, and the theories overlap. Although further development is needed in career theory, the ultimate goal is not to develop a "perfect" theory but theories that are "perfect" for given purposes.

Among the implications that might be drawn from Krumboltz' analogy is one very pertinent to the beginning career counselor. Theoretical viewpoints cannot be adopted or rejected on the basis of their "goodness" or "badness" without specifically considering their intended scope, emphasis, and purpose. A theory useful for understanding one aspect of the career development process may shed little light on another. Rigid adherence to one particular theory may, therefore, be detrimental to understanding the career process in its entirety. This means, not that one should carry about a hodgepodge of unrelated concepts and explanations, but rather that theories should be used according to their intended purposes.

Some of the major theories of career development are briefly described next. Although only the most central concepts of each have been presented, more detailed reviews of each theory and critiques of the related research are available in the texts just mentioned.

Trait-and-Factor Theory

Frank Parsons
The trait-and-factor approach to career counseling was established in the work of Parsons (1909), and most authors credit the origin of vocational counseling to Frank Parsons. Although the turn of the century witnessed a variety of innovative

guidance programs, Parsons conceptualized a model for career guidance that is still viable in contemporary formulations of career counseling. Parsons was concerned about the difficult social problems experienced by immigrants new to the United States and viewed assistance with vocational selection as one means of alleviating their impoverished status. Hawks and Muha (1991) argue that recommitment to the social change orientation characterized by Parsons is crucial to optimizing the educational and occupational attainment of young people, and especially ethnic minority youth, in our still-stratified society.

Parsons proposed a three-step model for helping individuals choose a vocation, summarized as follows: (1) develop knowledge about self, including aptitudes, interests, and resources; (2) develop knowledge about the world of work, including the advantages, disadvantages, opportunities, and requirements associated with different occupations; and (3) find a suitable match between the individual and the world of work (Parsons, 1909). His work stimulated increased interest in vocational guidance nationwide (Zunker, 1994), and elements of trait-and-factor theory inform most contemporary theories of career development (Isaacson & Brown, 1993).

A career counselor subscribing to the trait-and-factor approach would structure the counseling experience according to the three steps outlined by Parsons (1909). First, the counselor would generate information about the client's aptitudes, interests, goals, resources, and so on. Next, the counselor would use his or her knowledge of occupations to assist the client's exploration of possible career alternatives. After the client has accrued a sufficient amount of self- and occupational knowledge, the counselor would facilitate the client's choice of an occupation consistent with the identified personal qualities and interests.

John Holland

The work of John Holland has been classified under both trait approaches to career development (Osipow, 1983) and personality-based theories of career development (Isaacson, 1985). Holland (1973, 1985) assumes that people develop relatively permanent sets of behaviors or personalities that they seek to express through occupational choices. In addition, he asserts that people project their views of themselves and of the work world onto occupational titles. Assessment of these projections serves to identify information about the occupational areas that might be most satisfying for an individual, as well as to illuminate relevant aspects of the individual's personality.

Holland (1973) proposes that there are six basic types of work environments in U.S. society, and six corresponding modal personal orientations. Modal personal orientations are the way the person typically responds to environmental demands. People achieve the most work satisfaction when their work environment matches their modal personal orientation. For example, positions in education or social welfare are considered "social" occupational environments and would be most suited to "social" personal orientations, that is, people who perceive themselves to be sociable, skilled at dealing with others, and concerned with helping others and solving human problems. Some people are dominant in one particular orientation, whereas others exhibit a combination of orientations in their interactions with the environment.

The five orientations in addition to the "social" orientation are "realistic," "investigative," "conventional," "enterprising," and "artistic." "Realistic" people are described as practical, concrete, and rugged, as interested in activities requiring physical strength, and as less likely to be sensitive and socially skilled. Corresponding work environments are found in the skilled trades such as plumbing or machine operation, and in the technical trades such as mechanics and photography.

"Investigative" people are described as preferring to think rather than act, as intellectual, abstract, and analytical. Work environments most suited to the investigative orientation are scientific, such as those of the chemist or mathematician, as well as the technical environments of the computer programmer and the electronics worker.

"Conventional" people are practical, well-controlled, conservative, and prefer structure and conformity to the abstract and the unique. Conventional environments are typified in those of the office worker, the bookkeeper, and the credit manager.

An "enterprising" individual is likely to prefer leadership roles, and to be aggressive, extroverted, persuasive, and dominant. Managerial positions in personnel and production, and positions in real estate, life insurance, and other sales areas correspond most closely to the "enterprising" work environment.

Holland's final personality orientation, "artistic," corresponds to people who are imaginative, independent, expressive, and introspective; their preferred work environments include those of the artist, the musician, and the writer. Holland (1973) provides a much more detailed description of the modal orientations, which may be helpful for the counselor interested in further exploration of these concepts.

Counselors grounded in Holland's approach will generally attempt to determine the client's modal personal orientation and then explore corresponding work orientations. In this sense, the trait-and-factor approach is represented. Several instruments are available for assessing modal orientations, the most common of which are probably the *Strong Interest Inventory: Applications and Technical Guide* (1994) and Holland's *Self-Directed Search* (1985). Lofquist and Dawis's (1969, 1984) work adjustment theory is another extension of trait-and-factor approaches to career counseling.

Social Learning Theory

Perhaps the foremost proponent of the social learning approach to career counseling is Krumboltz (Krumboltz, Mitchell, & Jones, 1976; Kinnier & Krumboltz, 1984; Mitchell & Krumboltz, 1990). Mitchell & Krumboltz (1990) identify four types of factors that influence career decision making: (1) genetic endowment and special abilities, (2) environmental conditions and events, (3) learning experiences, and (4) task approach skills. They define task approach skills as the skills an individual applies to new tasks and problems, including cognitive processes, work habits, and values. Every individual is born into specific environmental conditions with certain genetic characteristics; these interact to influence the life experiences, opportunities, and learning of the individual. Learning experiences are followed by rewards or punishments that also influence the individual's development. According to Mitchell & Krumboltz, career choice is influenced by individuals' unique learning experiences in the course of their lifetimes.

Task approach skills, self-observation generalizations, and actions are the result of an individual's learning experiences. Self-observation generalizations are the self-statements people make after assessing their performance or potential performance against learned standards. They are expressed in the form of interests. Actions are decision-related behaviors that emerge from the individual's task-approach skills and self-observation generalizations.

A counselor approaching career clients from a social learning perspective would be interested in the learning experiences that have influenced the client's career development. Often a client's inaccurate self-observations, maladaptive beliefs (Mitchell & Krumboltz, 1990; Lent & Brown, 1996), or deficient task approach skills are a barrier to exploration of potential career choices. The counselor's role is to assess each of these possibilities and others in the process of facilitating the client's career choices. Kinnier and Krumboltz (1984) present a helpful discussion of major obstacles in career counseling and techniques for overcoming them consistent with a social learning perspective.

Social Cognitive Theory

Lent, Brown, and Hackett (1994) proposed a theoretical model of career choice and implementation grounded in Bandura's general social cognitive theory. Their model emphasizes the importance of personal agency in the career decision-making process and attempts to explain the manner in which both internal and external factors serve to enhance or constrain this agency. Lent et al. (1994) claim that career interests directly influence career choice goals (career aspirations), which increases the likelihood of certain career choice actions (such as declaring an academic major). Contextual and social cognitive factors are hypothesized to directly influence the development of career interests, goals, and actions. Contextual factors include discrimination, socioeconomic status, job availability, educational access, perceived and real barriers, and other influential environmental factors. Lent et al. (1994) argue that the particular effect that contextual factors have on an individual's career choice often depends on her or his personal appraisal of and response to that factor. The social cognitive factors include self-appraisals such as self-efficacy expectations, or beliefs about one's performance abilities in relation to specific tasks, (Bandura, 1982) as well as outcome expectations, or beliefs about the likely consequences of given behaviors. Lent et al. (1994) propose that contextual and social cognitive factors are responsible for shaping the experiences that lead to the development of interests and choices, as well as the relationship between interests and choices and between career choices and attainments. Even if an individual possesses high levels of career self-efficacy, high outcome expectations, and interests that are congruent with those expectations, she or he may still avoid selection of a particular career if she or he perceives insurmountable barriers to career entry or career goal attainment. This model represents an important contribution to understanding career interests, choices, and implementation, because it integrates the social forces of racism, sexism, and classism that shape the career development process of all individuals, as well as related contextual/environmental factors such as role models, socialization, and perceived opportunities and barriers. The growing body of literature on the career development of people of color (for example, see Arbona, 1990; Bingham & Ward, 1992; Fouad & Bingham, 1995; Martin & Farris, 1994; McWhirter, 1996) as well as the broader literature on counseling people of color (for example, see Atkinson, Morten, & Sue, 1983; Comas-Diaz & Greene, 1994; Sue & Sue, 1990) consistently stresses the influences of these contextual factors. Career counseling implications include acknowledging and clarifying the mutual influences of context and cognitions in the career development process and providing opportunities to test and enhance self-efficacy and outcome expectations.

Developmental Theories

Developmental career theories view the selection and implementation of careers as part of a long-term developmental process that begins early in life and ends with death. Developmental theorists recognize the contributions of early experiences, life events and opportunities, and the maturation process on the development of interests, the exploration process, and career outcomes. Most contemporary theories of career choice incorporate elements of the developmental perspective. In this chapter, "career" has been defined from a developmental perspective in recognition of the widespread acceptance of career as an ongoing, lifelong process.

Ginzberg, Ginsburg, Axelrad, and Herma (1951) were among the first theorists to link the developmental theory with occupational choice. Their work, along with the work of Teideman and O'Hara (1963) and others, has been valuable in shaping developmental theories. Two developmental approaches are briefly discussed in this section. First, major components of the work of Donald Super are presented. Readers may wish to consult a special issue of the *Career Development Quarterly* (1994, vol. 43, no. 1) devoted to Super's tremendous contributions to career development theory. Next Linda Gottfredson's (1981) theory of circumscription and compromise is presented.

Donald Super

Super (1957, 1963, 1990) contended that individuals select occupations consistent with their self-concept. He argued that the manner in which people implement their self-concepts into occupational choices is a function of their developmental life stage. It therefore follows that vocational behaviors should be examined in the context of the particular demands of a person's developmental life stage. The vocational developmental stages formulated by Super are as follows: (1) growth (ages

0–14) is characterized by the development of interests, aptitudes, and needs in conjunction with the self-concept; (2) exploration (ages 15–24) consists of a tentative phase of narrowing down options; (3) establishment (ages 25–44) is characterized by choosing and implementing a career and stabilization within that career; (4) maintenance (ages 45–64) involves the continued efforts to improve work position; and (5) disengagement (ages 65 and above) is characterized by preparation for retirement and retirement itself. While providing age ranges, Super recognized individual variation in passage through the stages; he also noted that recycling of the stages often occurs during reconsideration of career plans or career changes. Each stage has a corresponding set of developmental vocational tasks.

Throughout the life span, individuals are called on to fulfill the demands of a variety of roles, such as child, student, leisure participant, citizen, worker, and homemaker. The life career rainbow (Super & Neville, 1986b) provides a physical representation of how these roles may overlap with and influence vocational development and behaviors. Career maturity is another important concept proposed by Super (1974), and concerns to the readiness of individuals to make good vocational choices. Assessment of the client's career maturity often helps to set the stage for appropriate interventions (Sharf, 1992). Fouad and Arbona (1994) review the research on the applicability of Super's model to people of color.

Linda Gottfredson

Gottfredson's (1981) theory of circumscription and compromise incorporates elements of a social systems approach into a developmental perspective, and focuses on the influence of gender, social class, and intelligence on career aspirations and choices. According to her theory, all people have a unique "zone of acceptable alternatives," consisting of the range of occupations acceptable for consideration and reflecting their view of where they fit in society. This zone is bounded by the greatest and least amount of effort individuals are willing to expend in order to attain that career, as well as by their willingness to pursue careers nontraditional for their gender. For example, an individual might consider a range of occupations perceived to be more prestigious than secretarial work, such as nursing or management, but not as demanding as becoming a physician or a lawyer. If the individual is male, he might automatically rule out nursing because it is a traditionally female profession and inconsistent with his perceived gender role.

Gottfredson (1981) postulates that as the self-concept develops, people become oriented to the implications of size and power (ages 3–5), sex roles (ages 6–8), social evaluation (ages 9–13), and finally, as their interests emerge, they become oriented to or aware of their internal unique self (ages 14 and older). The zone of acceptable alternatives is narrowed or circumscribed as age increases; occupations perceived as incongruent with sex roles are the first occupations to be eliminated, followed by occupations perceived as too low in prestige for peoples' respective social classes, and finally, those requiring too much effort are eliminated. When compromise in occupational choices is required, Gottfredson argues that people will first sacrifice their interests related to work—that is, their internal unique self—followed by prestige. Only as a last resort will people compromise on their perception of gender roles and choose an occupation that they believe is suited for the opposite sex. Sharf (1992) summarizes research findings related to Gottfredson's theory.

Assumptions and Diversity

The majority of career counseling theories were developed based on the behaviors of able-bodied, heterosexual, middle- to upper-class white males. This is true of most traditional counseling theories. Hence, there are numerous, unspoken assumptions embedded in many contemporary approaches to career counseling. Our ability to work effectively as career counselors is contingent on our awareness of these assumptions and willingness to critically reflect on the appropriateness of any theory, technique, or strategy with a given individual. Career interventions suited for white middle-class males will not necessarily be appropriate for or meet the needs of other individuals. Theoretical developments such as the social cognitive model (Lent et al., 1994) are crucially important because they integrate central factors shaping the reality of women, ethnic minorities, gay and lesbian individuals, and people with disabilities such as the influence of discrimination, perceived barriers, self-efficacy and outcome expectations, and environmental support. A small number of resources are offered next; this is by no means an exhaustive list, and the reader is encouraged to explore far beyond these resources in developing competencies consistent with the needs of our diverse society.

Contemporary researchers have increased emphasis on women's career development in the last several decades. "Acceptable" career options for women have grown from teacher or homemaker to limitless possibilities, although considerable gender role stereotyping of occupations and gender stratification continue. Career counselors must be prepared to deal with child care concerns, sexual harassment, dual career related stress, and other issues that were not previously considered relevant to career counseling. The steadily rising number of employed middle-class white women over the past several decades has brought attention to these and other issues that women of color and women of lower socioeconomic status—who have historically been strongly represented in the workforce—confronted without recognition or assistance for a much longer time period. Considerations and recommendations for working with female career clients are provided in special issues of the *Journal of Career Development* (1988, vol. 14, no. 4), and *Applied Psychology: An International Review* (1988, vol. 37, no. 2). Chapters by Fitzgerald and Weitzman (1992) and Osipow (1983) may also prove very helpful in identifying and addressing issues pertinent to female career clients. Finally, texts such as Betz and Fitzgerald's (1987) *The Career Psychology of Women* and Walsh and Osipow's (1993) *Career Counseling for Women* are excellent resources.

Resources for career counseling with ethnic minority clients have accumulated much more slowly. Texts by Isaacson (1985), Osipow (1983), Yost and Corbishley (1987), and Zunker (1994) address this topic with varying amounts of detail; Sharf (1992) addresses career counseling issues related to women and people of color in every chapter of his text. Sample articles addressing cultural issues in the context of career counseling include Fouad and Arbona (1994), Fouad & Bingham (1995), Ibrahim, Ohnishi, and Wilson (1994), Pine and Innis (1987), as well as a special issue of the *Career Development Quarterly* (1993, vol. 42, no. 1). Probably the most comprehensive source of information to date is Leong's (1995) *Career Development and Vocational Behavior of Racial and Ethnic Minorities.*

The Americans with Disabilities Act (ADA) of 1990 has raised consciousness among employers, counselors, and to some extent, the general public about the rights of people with disabilities. The implications of this act for career counselors are numerous; Crist and Stoffel (1992) offer an excellent analysis of the ADA with respect to employees with mental impairments. Nagler's (1993) *Perspectives on Disability* is a helpful and comprehensive resource that includes a focus on the multidimensional impact of the ADA. To properly serve their clients, career counselors must be familiar with the ADA.

Only quite recently has the literature addressed career counseling with gay, lesbian, and bisexual people. Issues related to coming out, workplace outing, fear of AIDS, job discrimination based on sexual orientation, workplace homophobia, as well as dual-career and parenting versus career issues, illustrate the intersection between sexual orientation and career counseling. Gelberg and Chojnacki's (1995) article on their process of becoming gay, lesbian, and bisexual affirmative career counselors offers a realistic perspective of the challenges this endeavor represents. Gay/lesbian career development is the focus of a special issue of the *Career Development Quarterly* (1995, vol. 44, no. 2).

Is it possible to be knowledgeable about all cultures and all types of disability? to fully understand the complexities of gender and sexual orientation as they interact with career development? The answer to these questions is no; however, it is certainly possible to develop an approach to all clients that explores and honors their individual differences. Such an approach requires ongoing self-education through reading, consultation with colleagues, attending workshops, and so on, as well as ongoing critical self-reflection on biases and assumptions (McWhirter, 1994).

A Framework for Career Counseling

The remainder of this chapter is devoted to presenting a simple schema for conceptualizing the career counseling process, with specific recommendations for counselors identified along the way. Horan (1979) describes counseling in terms of three phases: assessment, intervention, and evaluation. This model provides a simple organizational framework for incorporating the wide range of activities that constitute career counseling (Kinnier & Krumboltz, 1984). In addition, Salomone (1988) contends that many career counselors operate under the assumption that there are three stages to career counseling: self-exploration, exploration of the world of work, and creating a satisfying match between self and work. Recall that these steps are rooted in the work of Parsons. What is missing from this model, argues Salomone, are two additional stages: implementing educational and vocational decisions, and assisting clients to adjust to the new environment resulting from their career decision. It is often assumed that once a career choice has been made and steps toward achieving this goal identified, the counseling process is finished. However, for many clients implementing these steps represents a barrier equal to the original problem of making a career decision. In addition, beginning a new job or an educational program may involve a variety of income, relationship, and general lifestyle adjustments. Consideration of these factors enables counselors to be responsive to the various developmental needs of their clients during different points in the counseling process. Each of Salomone's (1988) five stages can be incorporated into the intervention or second phase of counseling.

Assessment

The assessment phase of career counseling begins when the client walks through the door. As with personal counseling, the counselor should immediately begin gathering information via both nonverbal and verbal behaviors. The client's eye contact, posture, self-presentation, and manner of dress may all provide pieces of information that enhance the counseling process. For example, feedback about a client's tendency to mumble and avoid eye contact may prove extremely useful to the client with a string of unsuccessful interviews. Well-developed and acute powers of observation lead to feedback that is more concrete and potentially useful to the client.

Verbal assessment procedures must incorporate the basic listening skills described in Chapter 3 of this text. Consistent use of these listening skills will facilitate an atmosphere in which the client feels safe, understood, and accepted. The counselor should identify early in the session what the client is seeking in career counseling. As we have defined career from a developmental perspective, a wide array of problems and concerns fall under the rubric of "career," and an even wider range of goals may unfold in the assessment process. Counselors should view client goals as a function of the client's developmental stage and tailor interventions accordingly. By carefully establishing what the client hopes to get out of career counseling, the counselor can address misconceptions and unrealistic expectations right from the start. Direct and open-ended questioning, paraphrasing, and perception checking facilitate this process.

Another component of the assessment phase is clarification of the counselor's style and approach to counseling and of the client's role. Unfortunately, many clients perceive counseling as a set of dictates or answers to be passively swallowed without any effort on their part. Allowing clients to participate in this fashion not only puts a great burden on the counselor but also is a great disservice to the client. An active and collaborative role in which clients are responsible for their actions and choices facilitates the empowerment of clients and leaves them better prepared to deal with future problems and concerns (McWhirter, 1991, 1994). Throughout the process of assessment, the counselor actively lays the groundwork for establishing a positive working relationship with the client.

Before moving to the intervention phase of counseling, it is important to establish the results of the client's previous efforts to resolve his or her vocational dilemma, or to estimate a baseline of the behavior the client wishes to change or develop. For example, if the client is interested in developing job search skills, the counselor should establish which skills the client possesses at the outset of counseling. Knowing the client's initial state is an extremely important, and often neglected, prerequisite to evaluation of counseling interventions. Readers will note that many of the interventions discussed next could also be considered components of the assessment phase.

Intervention

Once the nature of counseling has been clarified and a specific goal or goals have been established, the intervention phase of career counseling may begin. Interventions vary depending on the specific needs of the client, the theoretical framework of the counselor, and the counselor's knowledge of available resources. The number of assessment instruments, references, and resources related to career development has expanded so rapidly in the past two decades (Rounds & Tinsley, 1984) that the beginning counselor may find the prospect of intervention a bit overwhelming. In this section, some of the most common intervention approaches and instruments are presented.

Because most career interventions are useful across several theoretical frameworks, they are not discussed in reference to specific theoretical orientations. This section is divided according to Salomone's five stages. This arrangement is more applicable to clients interested in career exploration and selection than those with concerns related to dual careers and other issues; however, it provides an efficient way to present, in a limited space, information central to career counseling. Readers should note that interventions discussed with respect to one stage are not always associated with that stage of counseling in actual practice; individual client needs, rather than adherence to a formula, should influence the type and order of the interventions employed.

Stage 1: Gaining Knowledge about the Client's Self Interests

Because of the important relationship between interests and occupations, many career interventions incorporate a process of identifying and exploring the client's interests. A variety of approaches to interest measurement exist; Isaacson and Brown (1993) categorize these approaches as qualitative and objective. Several qualitative approaches are presented first, followed by descriptions of several popular objective interest inventories. More detailed information about inventories and the other tests discussed in this chapter is available in the Buros's *Mental Measurements Yearbook* series; in Kapes, Mastie, and Whitfield's *A Counselor's Guide to Career Assessment Instruments* (1995); and in the *Journal of Career Assessment*. Finally, several microcomputer programs with an interest assessment component are described.

Qualitative approaches to interest assessment include structured interviews, such as the life career assessment, or the LCA, discussed in detail by Gysbers and

Moore (1987). Career genograms—the detailed analysis of a family's work-related history—may help the client to identify concrete areas of interest and how they developed (Brown & Brooks, 1991; Gysbers & Moore, 1987; Okiishi, 1987). As there may be differences between the interests assessed by objective inventories and those verbally expressed by the client, measures such as the self-administered Vocational Card Sort (Slaney, 1978) have been recommended to identify career interests (Slaney & Slaney, 1986). Review of the client's previous jobs, activities, and accomplishments may provide another starting point for discussion of interests. The counselor must be sure to break down each experience into its component parts to avoid erroneous conclusions. For example, the client who volunteers at a nursing home may enjoy interacting with the elderly; in contrast, attractive features of the job could be related to autonomy, being in charge of other volunteers, working in the kitchen, or a host of other possibilities. The counselor and client should attempt to draw up a highly specific list of interests, as this will facilitate the task of identifying potential options. Martin and Farris (1994) offer an excellent framework for qualitative, culturally appropriate career assessment with Native Americans. Goldman (1990) notes that the advantages of qualitative assessment include a greater degree of adaptability with respect to individual characteristics such as gender and ethnicity.

Qualitative approaches may be used alone or in conjunction with objective assessment instruments. The counselor should provide the client with information concerning the use of assessment instruments so that they can determine together whether this is a desirable option. The decision to use objective assessment instruments should be carefully considered, for although they often save time, objective instruments typically require less activity on the part of the client, and may indirectly communicate to clients that they are not capable of identifying their own interests. In addition, indiscriminate reliance on instruments can lead to a "gas station" style of counseling: drive in, take test, explain, drive out, "thank you for shopping at the counseling center." Finally, objective assessment instruments have been plagued by gender and racial bias, and evidence of reliability and validity should be prerequisite for using such instruments with women and people of color. Career assessment with people of color is the focus of a special issue of the *Journal of Career Assessment* (1994, vol. 2, no. 3); Walsh and Osipow (1993) include a chapter on gender bias in career assessment. The counselor should employ a system of self-checks to assess continuously whether the client is receiving optimal service with the use of an objective instrument.

The Strong Interest Inventory. The Strong Interest Inventory (SII) is among the most widely used interest inventories. It was created by Strong in 1927, and most recently revised by Harmon, Hansen, Borgen, and Hammer (1994). The results of the 317-item SII permit clients to contrast their interests with those of people in over 100 different occupations. Separate scales exist for males and females, to reduce bias related to gender differences. Contrary to many a client's hopes, the SII does not provide information concerning how successful a person might be in a chosen field, nor does it indicate areas that a client should or should not pursue.

What it does provide is a launching point for exploring career options that have never been considered, and a point of departure for discussing why certain career interests are congruent or incongruent with those of people employed in that field. The SII is organized according to Holland's (1973) typology of modal orientations, so the client can easily determine the orientations with which his or her interests most closely coincide. This may help the client to focus in on a particular group of careers to explore more thoroughly. Research investigating the validity of the SII with Latinos, African Americans, Native Americans, and Asian Americans has produced mixed findings; several reviews of this research are available in the special issue of the *Journal of Career Assessment* noted earlier, as well as in the new 1994 Strong manual (Harmon et al., 1994).

Self-Directed Search.   The Self-Directed Search (SDS) was developed by John Holland and published in 1985 by Psychological Assessment Resources. The SDS is a self-administered inventory that assesses an individual's activities, competencies, and career interests, and translates this information into matching career options. The results of the inventory correspond with Holland's occupational typology and are also cross-referenced with the *Dictionary of Occupational Titles* (DOT). The SDS is thorough and relatively easy to administer.

Kuder Occupational Interest Survey.   The Kuder Occupational Interest Survey (KOIS) was developed by G. Frederick Kuder in 1966 and most recently revised by Zytowski (1985). The KOIS is published by Science Research Associates. Form DD provides interest comparisons to people in a variety of occupations and college majors, making the inventory useful for high school and college students and out-of-school adults (Isaacson, 1985). Fewer data are available on the validity and reliability of this instrument because it is relatively new. Form E focuses on the initial stages of self- and occupational exploration, and is most useful to students in grades 8 through 10.

Microcomputing Programs.   There are several interactive microcomputer programs designed to facilitate a client's self-exploration of interests. Each program also contains other components, such as values assessment, occupational information, and skills assessment. A brief review of three such programs follows. Before using microcomputer systems, the counselor may wish to consult Krumboltz's (1985) discussion of the presuppositions underlying computer use in career counseling.

SIGI+ is an extension of SIGI, the System of Interactive Guidance and Information, which is described in a later section of this chapter. SIGI+ contains nine components, beginning with a system overview followed by a self-assessment section. In this section, users are guided through an inventory of their interests, values, and skills. Other sections of SIGI+ allow users to learn about careers that correspond to the results of their inventory, as well as providing advice on financial assistance, suggestions for decision making, training requirements for specific occupations, and a large quantity of additional occupational information.

The Discover program, like SIGI+, contains interest, ability, and values inventories to facilitate the user's self-assessment. Strategies for identifying occupations, occupational information, and information about educational institutions are available with the Discover program. In addition, Discover contains a section that incorporates Holland's Self-Directed Search. A newer version of Discover, called Discover for Adult Learners, was developed for unemployed adults or those in the process of school or job market reentry or career changes. Among other developments, Discover for Adult Learners contains a skills inventory that incorporates the user's previous work experiences. Finally, Eureka's Micro Skills (Maze & Mayall, 1983) is a computer program that begins with a skills inventory similar to the process described in Bolles's *What Color Is Your Parachute?* (1985). This inventory is especially useful for adults reentering the workforce or changing careers, owing to its focus on experience as well as interests.

Aptitudes

Gathering knowledge about the self should also include assessment of the client's aptitudes and skills. Knowing what the client does well facilitates the identification of career-related skills or careers at which the client may succeed. One common informal way to assess aptitudes is by reviewing grades in various subject areas. However, this presents only a limited amount of information. Clients should be encouraged to identify the specific types of class activities in which they were successful: oral presentations, group projects, detailed notetaking, debates, and so on. Work-related successes should also be noted: was the client ever complimented for achievements in productivity, facility cleanliness, or recordkeeping? Clients might be encouraged to interview others for additional information about their special talents or skills. Be wary of the client who claims a general lack of proficiency; such a claim is usually more reflective of a low self-concept or low self-efficacy expectations than of actual performance. The counselor should be prepared to dig deeply and specifically to obtain information about aptitudes, because obvious signs of success such as grades and awards are often the only signs to which people attend. In addition to the informal information gathering, some circumstances may warrant the use of an aptitude test.

Differential Aptitude Test.   The Differential Aptitude Test (DAT) was developed by Bennet, Seashore, and Westman. The DAT manual was most recently updated in 1981 and is published by the Psychological Corporation. Several forms have been developed and revised. The DAT is widely used across the country by schools and counseling services and has proven extremely useful to high school students trying to determine how they might fare in future educational endeavors. Counselors should be aware that although this instrument is useful in predicting general academic success, it is not useful for predicting success in specific academic areas, nor does prediction extend to the area of occupational success.

General Aptitude Test Battery.   The General Aptitude Test Battery (GATB) was developed and published by the U.S. Employment Service in 1947, with periodic revisions since that time. A unique advantage of the GATB is that this test allows clients to compare themselves with actual workers in specific occupations. The GATB has often been used to assist in job placement, and can be used in conjunction with the new Employment Service Interest Inventory to facilitate the exploration of job possibilities in the DOT and the *Occupational Outlook Handbook,* or OOH (Isaacson, 1985). Additional aptitude tests are reviewed in the Buros's Mental Measurement Yearbook series. Lent et al. (1994) note that self-perceptions of aptitude, or self-efficacy expectations, may be as important if not more important than aptitude in guiding vocation-related choices. Thus self-efficacy expectations should be assessed in conjunction with aptitudes.

Values

Values clarification is an important component of the career counseling process (Kinnier & Krumboltz, 1984). In order to make realistic decisions about future occupational pursuits, an individual should have a good idea about the relative importance of values such as family time, income, prestige, autonomy, and a wide variety of other values that are affected by the nature of an occupation. For example, an individual who highly values family time is not likely to be satisfied with a traveling sales position, nor would someone valuing autonomy fare well in a job that involves constant scrutiny by a supervisor. Mael (1991) offers an excellent discussion of the factors influencing career-related behaviors of observant Jews, illustrating the interaction of specific values and religious practices with the world of work.

Often clients begin career counseling without ever having considered the relationship between occupational choices and value satisfaction. The counselor must be prepared to initiate and accompany the client's exploration of values, as well as anticipate the potential value conflicts and means of satisfaction in the occupations under consideration. Leong and Gim (1995) provide a discussion of career-relevant personality characteristics and values among Asian Americans; exploration of such resources is especially important when working with an individual of a sociocultural background distinct from that of the counselor.

Changing values are not infrequently the impetus of a decision to seek career counseling. Loss due to death, divorce, or changes in health status may necessitate a reprioritization of values. In such a case, income may replace helping others, or job security may supersede autonomy in an individual's values hierarchy. Counselors should be sensitive to the changing nature of values over an individual's life span and the implications of value changes for career choices.

Kinnier and Krumboltz (1984) have summarized the basic processes involved in many values clarification exercises. They find that most such exercises include one or a combination of the following: identification and analysis of the values issue; examination of past experiences, preferences, behaviors, and decisions that are related to the present issues; investigation of how others view the issue (by direct questioning or imagining what respected others would do in a similar situation); testing or self-confrontation about tentative choices, positions, or resolutions; finding personal environments that are conducive to clear thought about, or temporary escape from, the issue ("sleeping on it" or quiet meditation); and making the "best" tentative resolution and living in accordance with it, revising if needed. Counselors can use widely available strategies devised and published by others, or create their own variations of values clarification techniques.

Some clarification exercises involve consideration of values in light of one's mortality. The "lifeline" exercise requires the client to imagine having a terminal illness and to review priorities from this mind set; "epitaph" and "obituary" exercises require clients to write down their own version of how they want to be remembered after they have died (Kinnier & Krumboltz, 1984).

The Work Values Inventory developed by Super (1970) is one example of an objective instrument for assessing work-related values. Other available instruments include The Minnesota Importance Questionnaire (Weiss, Dawis & Lofquist, 1981) and the Values Scale (Super & Neville, 1986b). The latter two instruments are designed to explore both work-related and personal values.

The System of Interactive Guidance and Information (SIGI) is a microcomputer program primarily geared toward helping users clarify their most important values and providing information about careers consistent with the values identified. There are ten values that the user must evaluate in terms of importance: income, prestige, independence, helping others, security, variety, leadership, interest field, leisure, and early entry. In a review of research on computer-assisted counseling systems, Cairo (1983) reports that SIGI users better understood their values and career goals, had better knowledge about sources of job satisfaction, had more definite overall career plans, and felt more confident about their decision-making abilities after using the SIGI program.

Stage 2: Gaining Knowledge about the World of Work

Career counselors are responsible for introducing clients to resources for occupational information. More specifically, part of the counselor's job is to ensure that clients are able to obtain career-related information independently in the future. Occupational information is vast and constantly changing, and keeping up to date can be a staggering task. Fortunately, many resources are available that significantly reduce the amount of time and research required of both the counselor and the client. In this section, informal, formal, and microcomputer sources of career information are presented.

Informal processes of obtaining career information can be interesting and rewarding for the client. The most direct way to find out about a career of interest is to talk to someone already doing it! The client can locate potential interviewees from a variety of sources including friends, relatives, and classmates; local alumni associations, service and professional organizations; and even the local phone directory. The counselor may help the client formulate a set of questions that will maximize the amount and value of the information yielded by the subsequent interview. "Shadowing," or following individuals on the job, is an option that provides an even more concrete idea of what a particular career involves.

College and university campuses provide another rich source of occupational information. Clients may wish to seek out instructors in their field of interest for insights into the nature of specific occupations. Libraries offer journals and magazines serving professional audiences; these resources provide information on current developments and the cutting edge of research in the field. In addition, libraries contain reference materials such as labor market statistics, occupational forecasts, and descriptive information.

Three excellent reference materials that may be found in counseling centers, career development centers, and libraries are the *Dictionary of Occupational Titles* (DOT), the *Occupational Outlook Handbook* (OOH), and the *Guide for Occupational Exploration* (GOE). These periodically updated manuals provide detailed information in everyday language about hundreds of specific occupations. The GOE is useful in linking interest inventory results with the occupations listed in the DOT, and provides information such as the nature of specific jobs, the skills and abilities required, how to prepare for entry into the field, and how to determine whether such work might be of interest to an individual. Occupations discussed in the DOT and the GOE are classified according to a nine-digit coding system. Counselors should be familiar with the particular classification system in use before introducing references to clients, in order to maximize utility and minimize client confusion. Beale (1987) discusses ways to use the DOT with students that may be applied to the counseling setting.

Computerized guidance programs are another source of occupational information. The Guidance Information System (GIS) allows the user to access information in any of six files: occupations, four-year colleges, two-year colleges, graduate schools, financial aid information, and armed services occupations (Isaacson, 1985). The user simply enters the characteristics of interest into the computer and is provided with a listing of corresponding schools, programs, or occupations. For example, a client may be interested in pursuing a liberal arts degree at a private institution in the East or the Midwest. Using GIS, the client can enter these characteristics and receive a list of private eastern and midwestern schools that provide degrees in liberal arts. SIGI and Discover also have large amounts of occupational information. The relative ease with which computer files can be updated and accessed makes computers an invaluable source of current occupational information.

Stage 3: Creating a Match

The third stage of career counseling involves the process of deciding which occupations are consistent with the client's skills, interests, and values. Eventually the client must pick one or a group of closely related occupations to pursue. The counselor can facilitate this process by assisting in the decision-making process.

Decision making is a part of life, but unfortunately many people lack the skills important for making effective decisions. Decision making within career counseling has been conceptualized in terms of four components: (1) conceptualizing the problem as one of choice, (2) enlarging the response repertoire, (3) identifying discriminative stimuli, and (4) selecting a response (Olson, McWhirter, & Horan,

1989). Enlarging the response repertoire involves generating a large number of alternative actions. Identifying discriminative stimuli involves weighing the advantages and disadvantages of each potential course of action, as well as assessing the probable results of each. For example, although the advantages of writing a Pulitzer Prize–winning book are many, the probability of doing so is quite slim. Teaching clients this or other decision-making models provides them with a skill generalizable to a multitude of situations and helps ensure subsequent satisfaction with the decisions they make. It is important to integrate cultural values into the decision-making process. For example, the involvement of parents and other family members in career decision making varies quite a bit across cultures, and counselors should not assume that mainstream middle-class Western values such as " 'independent' decisions" and "whatever makes me happy" are salient for a given client (for example, see Yang, 1991).

Stage 4: Implementing a Decision

Salomone (1988) raises the issue that once a decision has been made, the task of the career counselor is not over. The client may lack specific skills, support, or information necessary for successful implementation of the decision. The counselor should be prepared to assist the client in developing these skills, locating sources of support, or obtaining the information in areas such as résumé writing, interviewing, assertiveness, or communication. If part of the client's decision involves actions such as changing a behavior, developing a hobby, or participating in a new organization, the counselor can be a valuable source of support and encouragement. Often the simple scheduling of tasks is enough motivation for the hesitant client to follow through on decisions.

Anxiety may interfere with the client's motivation to carry out a plan of action. Anxiety is often founded on irrational beliefs or expectations. According to Kinnier and Krumboltz (1984), maladaptive or irrational beliefs are a common obstacle to career development, and they recommend cognitive restructuring as one means to address this problem. Cognitive restructuring involves identifying irrational beliefs and replacing them with rational and realistic thoughts. Nevo (1987) has identified a set of common irrational beliefs with respect to careers; for example, "There's only one perfect job for me." The counselor's familiarity with the job world and with the client's skills and personality can be used to reduce anxiety and encourage action.

Stage 5: Adjusting to the New Setting

Sometimes the goals established in career counseling will result in the client's moving into a new environment. This may be the result of a job promotion, the start of a new job, enrollment in an academic program, a change of residence, or a combination of these and other changes. The client may be challenged to cope with a new set of demands and expectations, as well as to interact with unfamiliar groups and individuals. Issues often perceived as the sole territory of personal counseling are commonly encountered in career counseling. Often clients are dealing with career concerns as a result of or in conjunction with developmental issues such as divorce, changes in ethnic identity status, children leaving home, coming out as gay or lesbian, changing financial circumstances, or changes in health.

Communication and human relations skills training may help the client interact in a healthy and productive way with new co-workers, supervisors, and acquaintances. Assertiveness training may help clients secure what they need from the environment and safeguard their rights without infringing on the rights of others. Stress inoculation and relaxation training may assist clients to deal with the anxiety associated with these new situations. Strategies for dealing with loneliness, frustration, and feelings of inadequacy may also serve an important function at this time of transition.

At the close of this section, it is important to emphasize again that the arrangement of specific interventions with specific stages in career counseling is by no means set in stone. For example, cognitive restructuring may be called for as the client begins the self-assessment process and at a variety of other points in the career counseling process. In addition, career counseling interventions need not follow each and every one of the five steps identified by Salomone (1988). Rather, the process should be dictated by the nature of the client's concern and the plan that the counselor and client establish together.

Evaluation

The third phase of Horan's (1979) counseling model is evaluation. As indicated earlier, evaluation is a sorely neglected aspect of career counseling. Although many career counselors are aware of the immediate effects of counseling, such as the choice of a college major, in general practice there is very little formal follow-up. It is good practice for counselors to end every counseling relationship with an evaluation of the process. Such an evaluation may be incorporated into one of the final sessions and is of benefit to both the counselor and the client (McWhirter, 1994). Potential closing topics to cover are similar to those of personal counseling: the relative helpfulness of the counselor's suggestions and interventions; the degree of comfort experienced by the client throughout the process; the extent to which the client felt respected and understood; the extent to which the client felt him- or herself to be an active participant and collaborator; topics on which the client might have wanted to spend more or less time; and what the client might like to have done differently. Feedback for clients might include the counselor's perceptions of their relevant strengths and weaknesses, changes and progress noted by the counselor, and suggestions for future directions.

There is also a need in career counseling for more formal evaluations of the relative effectiveness of various interventions. Surprisingly little is known about how various career interventions affect the vocational development process. The vocational journals mentioned earlier in this chapter provide an excellent source of research findings related to career interventions.

Summary

In this chapter I have provided a definition of career counseling that is consistent with current developmental notions of career, as well as an overview of several major theories of career counseling. Assumptions embedded in traditional career counseling theories have been noted, with suggestions for additional reading that focus on the career development and career counseling needs of women, people of color, people with disabilities, and gay/lesbian/bisexual people. A framework is offered that provides a general, though flexible, organizer for viewing the roles and activities of the career counselor, and is applicable to working with a variety of clients and client concerns. The framework includes descriptions of resources for gathering information about the client and about the world of work, as well as issues relevant to each step in the career counseling process.

It should be evident by now that career counseling is closely related to personal counseling and requires the same competencies in relationship formation, listening skills, multicultural and diversity skills, and knowledge of theory required by personal counseling. In addition, career counselors must become familiar with an ever growing literature on career resources, assessment instruments, effective interventions, and theoretical developments. The importance of work in people's lives makes career counseling a central emphasis and invaluable speciality area both now and in the future.

References

Arbona, C. (1990). Career counseling research and Hispanics: A review of the literature. *Counseling Psychologist, 18*(2), 300–323.

Atkinson, D. R., Morten, G., & Sue, D. W. (1983). *Counseling American minorities: A cross-cultural perspective* (2nd ed.). Dubuque, IA: Brown.

Bandura, A. (1982). Self-efficacy mechanism in human agency. *American Psychologist, 37*(2), 122–147.

Beale, A. V. (1987). Discovering the treasures of the D.O.T.: Activities that work. *School Counselor, 34*(4), 308–311.

Betz, N. E., & Corning, A. F. (1993). The inseparability of "career" and "personal" counseling. *Career Development Quarterly, 42*(2), 137–142.

Betz, N. E., & Fitzgerald, L. (1987). *Career psychology of women.* Orlando, FL: Academic Press.

Bingham, R. P., & Ward, C. M. (1992, August). *Career counseling with ethnic minorities.* Paper presented at the Annual Meeting of the American Psychological Association, Washington, DC.

Bolles, R. N. (1985). *What color is your parachute?* Berkeley, CA: Ten Speed Press.

Brown, D., & Brooks, L. (1991). *Career counseling techniques.* Boston: Allyn and Bacon.

Cairo, P. C. (1983). Evaluating the effects of computer-assisted counseling systems: A selective review. *Counseling Psychologist, 11*(4), 55–59.

Career assessment with racial and ethnic minorities. (1994). Special feature of *Journal of Career Assessment, 2*(3).

Comas-Diaz, L., & Greene, B. (Eds.). (1994). *Women of color: Integrating ethnic and gender identities in psychotherapy.* New York: Guilford Press.

Council for Accreditation of Counseling and Related Educational Programs (CACREP). (1994). *The practice of professional counseling: Specialized curricular experiences in career counseling.* Alexandria, VA: Author.

Crist, P. A. H., & Stoffel, V. C. (1992). The Americans with Disabilities Act of 1990 and employees with mental impairments: Personal efficacy and the environment. *American Journal of Occupational Therapy, 46*(5), 434–443.

Croteau, J. M. & Thiel, M. J. (1993). Integrating sexual orientation in career counseling: Acting to end a form of the personal-career dichotomy. *Career Development Quarterly, 42*(2), 174–179.

Engels, D. W., Minor, C. W., Sampson, Jr., J. P., & Splete, H. H. (1995). Career counseling specialty: History, development and prospect. *Journal of Counseling and Development, 74*(2), 134–138.

Fitzgerald, L. F., & Weitzman, L. M. (1992). Women's career development: Theory and practice from a feminist perspective. In H. Daniel Lea & Zandy B. Leibowitz, *Adult career development: Concepts, issues, and practices* (2nd ed., pp. 124–160). Alexandria, VA: National Career Development Association.

Fouad, N. A., & Arbona, C. (1994). Careers in a cultural context. *Career Development Quarterly, 43*(1), 96–104.

Fouad, N. A., & Bingham, R. P. (1995). Career counseling with racial and ethnic minorities. In W. Bruce Walsh and S. H. Osipow (Eds.), *Handbook of vocational psychology: Theory, research, and practice* (2nd ed., pp. 331–366). Mahwah, NJ: Erlbaum.

Gelberg, S., & Chojnacki, J. T. (1995). Developmental transitions of gay/lesbian/bisexual-affirmative, heterosexual career counselors. *Career Development Quarterly, 43*(3), 267–273.

Ginzberg, E., Ginsburg, S. W., Axelrad, S., & Herma, J. L. (1951). *Occupational choice: An approach to a general theory.* New York: Columbia University Press.

Goldman, L. (1990). Qualitative assessment. *Counseling Psychologist, 18,* 205–213.

Gottfredson, L. S. (1981). Circumscription and compromise: A developmental theory of occupational aspirations. *Journal of Counseling Psychology, 28*(6), 545–579.

Gysbers, N. C., & Moore, E. J. (1987). *Career counseling: Skills and techniques for practitioners.* Englewood Cliffs, NJ: Prentice Hall.

Harmon, L. W., Hansen, J. I., Borgen, F. H., & Hammer, A. L. (1994). *Strong Interest Inventory: Applications and technical guide.* Palo Alto, CA: Consulting Psychologists Press.

Hawks, B. K., & Muha, D. (1991). Facilitating the career development of minorities: Doing it differently this time. *Career Development Quarterly, 39,* 251–260.

Heppner, M. J., O'Brien, K. M., Hinkelman, J. M., & Flores, L. Y. (1996). Training counseling psychologists in career development: Are we our own worst enemies? *Counseling Psychologist, 24*(1), 105–125.

Holland, J. L. (1973). *Making vocational choices: A theory of careers.* Englewood Cliffs, NJ: Prentice Hall.

Holland, J. L. (1985). *The self-directed search: Professional manual 1935 edition.* Odessa, FL: Psychological Assessment Resources.

Horan, J. J. (1979). *Counseling for effective decision making: A cognitive behavioral perspective.* Belmont, CA: Wadsworth.

Ibrahim, F. A., Ohnishi, H., & Wilson, R. P. (1994). Career assessment in a culturally diverse society. *Journal of Career Assessment, 2*(3), 276–288.

Isaacson, L. E. (1985). *Basics of career counseling.* Boston: Allyn and Bacon.

Isaacson, L. E., & Brown, D. (1993). *Career information, career counseling, and career development* (5th ed.). Boston: Allyn and Bacon.

Kapes, J. T., Mastie, M. M., & Whitfield, E. A. (1995). *A counselor's guide to career assessment instruments* (3rd ed.). Alexandria, VA: National Career Development Association.

Kinnier, R. T., & Krumboltz, J. D. (1984). Procedures for successful career counseling. In N. Gysbers (Ed.), *Designing careers: Counseling to enhance education, work and leisure.* San Francisco: Jossey-Bass.

Krumboltz, J. D. (1985). Presuppositions underlying computer use in career counseling. *Journal of Career Development, 12*(2), 165–170.

Krumboltz, J. D. (1989, August). *The social learning theory of career decision making.* Paper presented at the annual convention of the American Psychological Association, New Orleans.

Krumboltz, J. D., Mitchell, A. M., & Jones, G. B. (1976). A social learning theory of career selection. *Counseling Psychologist, 6*(1), 71–81.

Lent, R. W., & Brown, S. D. (1996). Applying social cognitive theory to career counseling: An overview. *Career Development Quarterly, 44*(4), 310–321.

Lent, R. W., Brown, S. D., & Hackett, G. (1994). Toward a unifying social cognitive theory of career and academic interest, choice, and performance. *Journal of Vocational Behavior, 45,* 79–122.

Leong, F. T. L. (Ed.). (1995). *Career development and vocational behavior of racial and ethnic minorities.* Hillsdale, NJ: Erlbaum.

Leong, F. T. L., & Gim, R. H. C. (1995). Career assessment and intervention with Asian-Americans. In F. T. L. Leong (Ed.), *Career development and vocational behavior of racial and ethnic minorities.* Hillsdale, NJ: Erlbaum.

Lofquist, L. H., & Dawis, R. V. (1969). *Adjustment to work.* Englewood Cliffs, NJ: Prentice Hall.

Lofquist, L. H., & Dawis, R. V. (1984). Research on work adjustment and satisfaction: Implications for career counseling. In S. Brown & R. Lent (Eds.), *Handbook of counseling psychology.* New York: Wiley.

Mael, F. A. (1991). Career constraints of observant Jews. *Career Development Quarterly, 39*(3), 341–349.

Martin, W. E., Jr., & Farris, K. K. (1994). A cultural and contextual decision path approach to career assessment with Native Americans: A psychological perspective. *Journal of Career Assessment, 2*(3), 258–275.

Maze, M., & Mayall, D. (1983). *Eureka Skills Inventory counselor's manual.* Richmond, CA: Eureka Corporation.

McWhirter, E. H. (1991). Empowerment in counseling. *Journal of Counseling and Development, 69*(3), 222–227.

McWhirter, E. H. (1994). *Counseling for Empowerment.* Alexandria, VA: American Counseling Association Press.

McWhirter, E. H. (1996). Perceived barriers to education and career: Ethnic and gender differences. *Journal of Vocational Behavior, 49.*

Mitchell, L. K, & Krumboltz, J. D. (1990). Social learning approach to career decision making: Krumboltz's theory. In D. Brown & L. Brooks (Eds.), *Career choice and development.* San Francisco: Jossey-Bass.

Nagler, M. (1993). *Perspectives on disability.* Palo Alto, CA: Health Markets Research.

National Board for Certified Counselors (NBCC). (1993). *Specialty certification 1994.* Greensboro, NC: Author.

National Vocational Guidance Association (NVGA), American Vocational Association (AVA). (1973). *Position paper on career development.* Washington, DC: Authors.

Nevo, O. (1987). Irrational expectations in career counseling and their confronting arguments. *Career Development Quarterly, 35*(3), 239–250.

Okiishi, R. W. (1987). The genogram as a tool in career counseling. *Journal of Counseling and Development, 66*(3), 139–143.

Olson, C., McWhirter, E. H., & Horan, J. J. (1989). A decision-making model applied to career counseling. *Journal of Career Development, 16*(2), 19–23.

Osipow, S. H. (1983). *Theories of career development* (3rd ed.). Englewood Cliffs, NJ: Prentice Hall.

Parsons, F. (1909). *Choosing a vocation.* Boston: Houghton Mifflin.

Pine, G. J., & Innis, G. (1987). Cultural and individual work values. *Career Development Quarterly, 35*(4), 279–287.

Pinkney, J. W., & Jacobs, D. (1985). New counselors and personal interest in the task of career counseling. *Journal of Counseling Psychology, 32*(3), 454–457.

Rounds, J. B., Jr., & Tinsley, H. E. A. (1984). Diagnosis and treatment of vocational problems. In S. Brown & R. Lent (Eds.), *Handbook of counseling psychology.* New York: Wiley.

Salomone, P. R. (1988). Career counseling: Steps and stages beyond Parsons. *Career Development Quarterly, 36,* 218–221.

Savickas, M. L. (1993). Special section: A symposium on multicultural career counseling. *Career Development Quarterly, 42*(1), 3–55.

Savickas, M. L. (1994). Festschrift issue: From vocational guidance to career counseling: Essays to honor Donald E. Super. *Career Development Quarterly, 43*(1), 3–112.

Savickas, M. L. (1995). Special section: Gay/lesbian career development. *Career Development Quarterly, 44*(2), 146–203.

Seligman, L. (1994). *Developmental career counseling and assessment* (2nd ed.). Thousand Oaks, CA: Sage.

Sharf, R. S. (1992). *Applying Career Development Theory to Career Counseling.* Pacific Grove, CA: Brooks/Cole.

Slaney, R. B. (1978). Expressed and inventoried vocational interests: A comparison of instruments. *Journal of Counseling Psychology, 25,* 520–529.

Slaney, R. B., & Slaney, F. M. (1986). Relationship of expressed and inventoried vocational interests of female career counseling clients. *Career Development Quarterly, 35,* 24–33.

Sue, D. W., & Sue, D. (1990). *Counseling the culturally different:* Theory and Process. New York: Wiley.

Super, D. E. (1957). *The psychology of careers.* New York: Harper.

Super, D. E. (1963). Self-concepts in vocational development. In D. E. Super et al. (Eds.), *Career development: Self-concept theory.* CEEB Research Monograph No. 4. New York: College Entrance Examination Board.

Super, D. E. (1970). *Work Values Inventory.* Boston: Houghton-Mifflin.

Super, D. E. (1974). *Measuring vocational maturity for counseling and evaluation.* Washington, DC: National Vocational Guidance Association.

Super, D. E. (1990). A life span, life-space approach to career development. In D. Brown, L. Brooks, & Associates (Eds.), *Career choice and development: Applying contemporary theories to practice* (2nd ed., pp. 197–261). San Francisco: Jossey-Bass.

Super, D. E., & Neville, D. D. (1986a). *The Salience Inventory.* Palo Alto, CA: Consulting Psychologists Press.

Super, D. E. & Neville, D. D. (1986b). *The Values Scale.* Palo Alto, CA: Consulting Psychologists Press.

Teideman, D. V., & O'Hara, R. P. (1963). *Career development: Choice and adjustment.* Princeton, NJ: College Entrance Examination Board.

United States Employment and Training Administration. (1979). U.S. Department of Labor.

Walsh, W. B., & Osipow, S. H. (1993). *Career counseling for women.* Hillsdale, NJ: Erlbaum.

Weiss, D. J., Dawis, R. V., & Lofquist, L. H. (1981). *The Minnesota Importance Questionnaire users manual.* Minneapolis: Vocational Psychology Research, University of Minnesota.

Women's occupational plans and decisions. (1988). Special issue of *Applied Psychology: An International Review, 37*(2).

Yang, J. (1991). Career counseling of Chinese American women: Are they in limbo? *Career Development Quarterly, 39*(4), 350–359.

Yost, E. B., & Corbishley, M. A. (1987). *Career counseling.* San Francisco: Jossey-Bass.

Zunker, V. G. (1994). *Career counseling: Applied concepts of life planning* (4th ed.). Pacific Grove, CA: Brooks/Cole.

Zytowski, D. G. (1985). *Kuder DD Occupational Interest Survey manual supplement.* Chicago: Science Research Associates.

Counseling Uses of Tests

Larry C. Loesch, Ph.D., NCC   *Nicholas A. Vacc, Ed.D., NCC*

In view of counselors' ever-increasing needs for valid information about their clients, the importance of the relationship between counseling and testing continues to increase. In the introduction of his historically significant text *Using Tests in Counseling*, Goldman (1971) proposed that testing and counseling are inextricably linked. He wrote, "The types of tests used, and the ways in which testing is conducted, differ to some extent, but all have in common a relationship between counselor and counselee in which the latter's well-being, adjustment, and choices are paramount" (p. 1).

Unfortunately, some counselors have been reluctant to accept the proposal that testing is an integral part of counseling. Instead, they view testing as an "adjunct" to their counseling activities. This perspective ignores the reality that counselors quite routinely, but subjectively, gather and interpret information from and about their counselees. More effective counselors acknowledge that subjective information gathering and interpretation are important parts of counseling processes. They also recognize that more systematic appraisal (testing) procedures can facilitate and enhance achievement of counseling goals and the efficiency of their counseling efforts.

Some counselors' attitudes toward testing, in part, reflect confusion about semantics. *Measurement* may be considered the assignment of numeric or categorical values to human attributes according to rules (Cronbach, 1990). *Assessment* subsumes measurement and can be considered the data-gathering process or method (Drummond, 1992). *Evaluation* subsumes assessment and can be considered the interpretation and application of measurement data according to rules (Vacc & Loesch, 1994). *Appraisal* is sometimes considered synonymous with assessment

(Vacc & Loesch, 1994), but more frequently with evaluation. Unfortunately, *testing* has been used as a synonym for each and all of these terms!

Testing (particularly as a synonym to appraisal/evaluation) can involve value judgments being made about measurement results, and therefore about people. For this reason, testing has become equated with "labeling" people. Most counselors do not want to be viewed as "labeling" people, because labeling connotes being "nonhumanistic" or "uncaring." Thus counselors often decry testing based on mis-applied connotations. It is not the act of making judgments that must be avoided, for counseling processes are fraught with counselors' value judgments. Rather, it is making unfounded and/or invalid value judgments that must be avoided. Given the substantial evidence that clinicians' subjective judgments correlate poorly with more objective indices of human attributes (Groth-Marnat, 1990), counselors are well advised to seek the best assessment procedures available. Thus, testing, when properly understood and used, is a significant aid, not a hindrance, to the counseling process.

Uses of Tests in Counseling

Anastasi (1988) and Cronbach (1990) have listed general uses for testing, while others (such as Drummond, 1992; Hood & Johnson, 1991; and Vacc & Loesch, 1994) have identified more specific counseling applications. The following is a summary of primary counseling-related uses of testing.

Preliminary (Problem) Exploration and/or Diagnosis

For counseling processes to be efficient, counselors must gain accurate information about clients as rapidly as possible. One means of gaining accurate information to improve counselors' efficiency is testing. Substantive information about clients' characteristics, behaviors, or problems can be gained expeditiously when testing is an integral part of initial counseling activities.

Testing in this context has several distinct advantages to counselors' interactions with clients. First, it enhances comprehensive and systematic inquiry. Second, testing enables (in most cases) normative comparison of a client's personal data with that of other, similar people. Third, it typically results in a relatively concise summary of client characteristics. Finally, testing may "uncover" client characteristics about which the client is unaware. Overall, testing facilitates counselors in obtaining essential information faster.

Selection or Screening

Testing in this context usually involves evaluation of applicant attributes (such as level of aptitude or capability) for use in educational, admission, or business/industry employment decision making. Test results often are used to supplement more subjectively obtained information (personal judgments) so that decision making is better and more efficient, thereby benefiting both applicants and employers.

Testing for selection or screening purposes has advantages similar to those for preliminary exploration or diagnosis. Comprehensive information can be obtained systematically and rapidly. For example, it is common in employment screening situations for applicants to complete a "test battery" as part of the application process. The ability to make normative comparisons of test results is particularly important in selection or screening processes. Admissions officers and employment personnel often establish "statistical decision-making rules," based on numeric test result criteria, to supplement personal judgment criteria in decision-making processes.

Placement and/or Planning

Test results are often used by counselors to help determine the most appropriate situations (for example, educational programs or occupational categories) in which to place people. This use of testing is akin to the selection or screening use, except the focus of placement is typically narrower than that for a selection process. For example, determining assignment to a particular program of studies within an institution of higher education is usually a narrower focus than determining eligibility for admission to the institution. Similarly, determining an applicant's appropriate job classification may be narrower in scope than determining the applicant's suitability for employment.

Testing for placement usually involves obtaining data about level of aptitude or competence. Tests used for such purposes may assess general attributes (for example, when intelligence test scores are used as one of the criteria for placement in an academically gifted student program) or relatively specific abilities (for example, when work sample tests are used to determine the speed with which a person can perform a job-specific task).

Planning for the uses of tests usually involves assessing level of an ability or competency. Often the processes are indistinguishable. In some instances, tests are used specifically to determine areas of functioning where increased competence is needed. Planning involves identifying the best ways to facilitate the necessary improvement.

Facilitation of Self-Understanding

A primary reason clients seek counseling services is to facilitate self-understanding. Counselors' effectiveness in facilitating clients' self-understanding is largely contingent on clients' trust in the counselor. Clients must strongly "believe in" counselors before they will accept exploration into areas of self-understanding. This trust is difficult to achieve in early stages of the counseling process. Testing is one means by which counselors can obtain information that enhances feedback to clients. Use of "objective" test information may then serve to increase counselors' "credibility" with their clients.

The normative aspects of test results may also be useful in facilitating clients' self-understanding. Clients often wish to know how their characteristics, attributes, abilities, or behaviors compare with those of other people. Test results provided in normative contexts can be a basis for comparison. One possible use for clients would be to identify specific aspects of themselves they may wish to change. Testing in the capacity of facilitating self-understanding serves to help clients identify counseling goals.

The testing process, when focusing on characteristic behaviors, also facilitates clients' self-understanding. Many tests incorporate logical, systematic, and relatively "transparent" approaches to analysis of human behavior. Thus actually engaging in the testing process may enable clients to learn new ways of evaluating themselves.

Assessment of Individual Progress

Effective counseling is synonymous with client change, which is presumably perceived by clients as positive. However, demonstration of client change is often difficult, particularly if left to subjective interpretations by clients or counselors. Testing can be a more objective way of obtaining client change information. For example, pre- and postcounseling assessments of client attitudes, attributes, and/or behaviors can provide data for evaluating the degree of change.

One of the more difficult aspects of counseling is maintaining a high level of client motivation throughout the counseling process. This difficulty increases as the length of the counseling process increases. The counselor's provision of "encouraging" feedback, as well as client's self-monitoring, helps maintain client motivation. However, these are subjective processes. Periodic use of tests that yield "objective" indications of client change can be a powerful reinforcer of client motivation.

Licensure or Certification

Testing has recently become a significant factor in many professional counselors' personal careers. A greatly increased emphasis on counselor credentialing in the past decade has resulted in the development of several major, national counselor certifications as well as state-level counselor licensure procedures. With these procedures, counselors have to exceed a minimum criterion score on an examination in order to become certified or licensed. Thus the counseling profession has embraced testing as an effective and efficient method for obtaining useful information.

Basic Concepts in Testing

Tests used for counseling and related purposes are usually evaluated by three major attributes: validity, reliability, and appropriateness.

Validity

Validity is commonly defined as the extent to which a test measures what it purports to measure (Drummond, 1992; Hood & Johnson, 1991). Messick (1989) clarified that common definition when he wrote, "Validity is an integrated evaluative judgment of the degree to which empirical evidence and theoretical rationales support the *adequacy* and *appropriateness* of *inferences* and *actions* based on test scores or other modes of assessment" (p. 13). Messick's definition emphasizes that, ultimately, validity is based on judgment and is the most important criterion in considering how test results are used. Validity is the primary criterion on which any test should be evaluated (Gregory, 1992).

Three major types of validity are discussed in the professional literature. The term *content validity* refers to the extent to which a test is an accurate representative sample of the domain to which inferences will be made (Friedenberg, 1995). Domains of interest to counselors include human attributes, characteristics, behaviors, attitudes, and abilities. Content validity evaluation is usually associated with measures of cognitive abilities. *Construct validity* is the accuracy with which test scores reflect levels or degrees of psychological constructs (Friedenberg, 1995). Construct validity is particularly important for evaluating measures of personality dynamics, attitudes, or interests. The term *criterion-related validity* refers to the extent to which test scores are predictably associated with other, often behavioral, criteria (Friedenberg, 1995). Performance and competence measures in particular must have criterion-related validity.

Reliability

The consistency of measurement results yielded by a test is known as *reliability* (Anastasi, 1988; Cronbach, 1990). Similar to validity, three types of reliability are usually described in the literature. *Stability,* sometimes called *test–retest reliability,* indicates the likelihood of a person achieving the same or a similar test score if the test is administered on two or more different occasions. *Equivalence,* sometimes called *parallel forms reliability,* indicates the extent to which two versions of a measure yield the same or essentially similar results. *Internal consistency reliability* indicates the extent to which items within a test (or subscale) correlate with one another (are internally consistent). The type of reliability deemed most important depends on the nature of the testing situation.

Appropriateness

A test is appropriate if factors extraneous to the purpose and nature of the test itself (for example, size of print type used, testing conditions, or reading level of test content) have no influence on performance or response to the test.

Validity, reliability, and appropriateness are interrelated but not necessarily interdependent. A valid test is necessarily reliable and appropriate. However, a test can produce reliable (consistent) but invalid results. Similarly, an inappropriate test (for example, one for which the content reading level is too high for respondents) can produce reliable but not valid results.

Two terms commonly used to describe tests are *norm referenced* and *criterion referenced*. The distinction between the two types of tests is usually made in regard to the interpretation of the results from each type (Gregory, 1992). In norm-referenced testing, a respondent's test score is reported in comparison to performance on the same test by other people. Percentiles, or other "standardized," scores are commonly used to indicate *relative* performance. For example, a person whose score is at the eighty-fifth percentile is interpreted to have performed on the test at a level equal to or surpassing 85 percent of the people in the "norm" group for the test. These persons presumably are similar to the respondent in important ways. Norm-referenced testing necessitates establishment of normative data but not of specific behavioral criteria.

In criterion-referenced testing, a respondent's test score is interpreted in comparison to some specified behavioral domain or criterion of proficiency. A respondent's score indicates how many criterion-specific tasks (items) the respondent completed successfully. Criterion-referenced testing involves the development of specific behavioral criteria and the relationships of test items to those criteria.

Test Types

Tests have been characterized and/or differentiated through the use of a wide variety of other terms. The following are brief descriptions of terms commonly used in the testing literature.

Standardized Tests

Mehrens and Lehmann (1991) indicated that *standardized tests* usually are commercially prepared by measurement experts and incorporate uniform sets of items, administration procedures, and scoring procedures. They also emphasized that "standardized" does *not* mean that the test *necessarily* accurately measures what it is intended to measure. Conversely, so-called nonstandardized tests frequently are user prepared, and administration procedures may vary depending on the situation.

Individual and Group Tests

Individual tests are designed to be administered to one person by a single administrator. These tests usually involve the administrator "tailoring" the testing procedure, such as determining the time allowed for responding, to a specific respondent and/or testing situation. A group test is one that can be administered to more than one person at a time.

Power and Speed Tests

In most types of testing, interest is in maximum and/or thorough respondent performance. Therefore, testing time allotments exceed time needed by most respondents to complete the test. Such tests are called *power tests*. Intellectual ability, aptitude, and achievement tests are common examples of power tests. In contrast, *speed tests* involve speed of performance as a dynamic in the assessment process. Task completion tests (such as typing or other manual dexterity skills tests) are common examples of speed tests.

Vertical and Horizontal Tests

Tests that have different but conceptually and structurally related forms based on some hierarchy (such as age category, developmental level, or grade) are known as *vertical tests*. Tests conceptually and structurally related that assess within a number of different domains simultaneously within a defined category (such as classroom or gender group) are known as horizontal tests. Aptitude or achievement "test batteries," such as those commonly used in schools, are both vertical and horizontal tests.

Structured and Unstructured Tests

These tests differ by the response task. In a structured test, the respondent is presented with a clear stimulus (such as an item stem) and instructed to select the appropriate response from those presented (such as response choices). In an unstructured test, the respondent is presented with a clear or an ambiguous stimulus and instructed to construct a response. This differentiation is evident in different types of personality inventories.

Computerized Tests

Rapid technologic advancements are being made in the uses of computers, particularly microcomputers, for testing. In computerized testing, the respondent "interacts" with a computer by providing responses, usually through keyboard input, to stimuli (such as questions) presented on a computer monitor. Both the number and type of tests being transformed to computer application is increasing at an exponential rate.

The major advantages of computerized testing are that responses are made easily, respondents have considerable control over the rate of interaction (responding), test scoring and data analyses are rapidly completed, and local "data sets" (such as local normative data) are easily established. The major limitations of computerized testing concern the "security" of the tests and testing procedures (APA, 1986). Significant recent improvements in computerized testing have helped to minimize these concerns, however. Computerized testing holds promise to become the "method of choice" in the near future.

Paper-and-Pencil Tests

A majority of tests are "paper-and-pencil" tests, where respondents provide responses directly on tests, test booklets, or accompanying answer or response sheets. However, the connotation of the term "paper-and-pencil tests" has been broadened beyond the restrictive (literal) definition to encompass almost all structured tests, including computerized versions of those tests.

Performance Tests

Tests that require respondents to complete physical tasks to allow evaluation of skill or competence levels are known as *performance tests*. They also are sometimes referred to as "work sample" tests. Performance or work sample tests are used most frequently in the context of vocational or vocational rehabilitation counseling.

Additional Assessment Methods

The following are methods that may be thought of as tests because they yield data for evaluation purposes. However, they differ from the preceding tests in that data are not necessarily provided by the person to whom the data applies.

Structured and Open-Response Interviews

In a structured interview, the interviewer asks the interviewee a predetermined set of questions. Responses from the interviewee are classified (or coded) into predetermined potential response categories. Questions posed in an open-response interview are also predetermined, but categories of potential responses are not. Rather, post hoc analyses are made in the attempt to "sort out" respondent information.

Rating Scales

The use of rating scales involves a rater providing an indication of another person's *level or degree* of an attribute, attitude, or characteristic in terms of predetermined stimuli (such as items or criteria). Rating scales may be used to assess "live" behavior or through media (such as audio tape, videotape, or photographs) that record the behavior.

Behavior Observations

In making behavior observations, an observer views (sometimes on videotape) a person in a situation and records *frequencies* with which predetermined behaviors occur. Behavior observation and rating techniques are often used in the same contexts. For example, counselor trainees' verbal responses in counseling sessions are typically counted by type and rated for level of effectiveness by supervisors.

Checklists

When used as assessment techniques, checklists contain either sets of behaviors or attributes. For behaviors, responses usually reflect *perceived* frequencies of occurrence. For attributes, responses usually reflect *perceived* presence or absence. Checklist responses can be self-reported, provided by another person (such as a counselor), or both.

Documents Pertinent to Testing

There are at least four types of documents pertinent to testing with which counselors should be familiar. In *ethical standards documents*, which are covered in Chapter 4 in this book, counselors should be familiar with the sections pertaining to testing. *Guidelines for uses of tests* are covered later in this chapter. The third type is *test manuals*. A good test manual contains the theoretical bases of the test; evidence of validity, reliability, and appropriateness; normative or criterion data; and other information necessary for proper use of the test. Good tests have good test manuals, and good counselors make use of those manuals. Indeed, maximum benefit cannot be derived from a test unless the user is familiar with the material presented in the test manual.

The fourth type of testing documents is the single document *Standards for Educational and Psychological Testing* (APA, AERA, & NCME, 1985). These standards were developed through collaborative effort of the American Psychological Association (APA), American Educational Research Association (AERA), and National Council on Measurement in Education (NCME), and are published by APA. The standards are the recognized criteria against which tests, testing procedures, test manuals, and other test information should be evaluated. Counselors should become thoroughly familiar with these standards in order to critique, select, and use tests effectively for counseling purposes. A revised set of these standards is soon to be released, and counselors should always refer to the most recent version.

Recent Trends in Testing

A relatively recent but highly significant trend in testing is application of item response theory (IRT) in test development practices. McKinley (1989) wrote:

> The attractiveness of IRT as both a research and measurement tool is derived primarily from its parameter invariance *properties. The property of invariance* means that the item statistics that are obtained from the application of the IRT model are independent of the sample of examinees to which a test (or other instrument) is administered. Likewise, the personal statistics obtained for examinees are independent of the items included in the test. This is in marked contrast to more traditional statistics, such as item and examinee proportion-correct or number-correct scores. (p. 37)

In "traditional" item analyses, resultant statistics are, technically, applicable only to the norm (usually a group) from which the response data were derived; other groups would have other item statistics. Relatedly, item statistical data in traditional analyses are unique to the set of items included. Use of IRT models yields data that are, theoretically, invariant with regard to both the sample of examinees and the sample of items.

Thorough discussion of IRT models is beyond the scope of this chapter. However, interested readers are referred to McKinley (1989) for a good overview of IRT or to Hambleton (1989) for a complete discussion. The advent of IRT models has resulted in the development of far better tests, particularly in testing for achievement, aptitude, and licensure or certification.

Another recent trend in testing is the use of more theoretically sound and legally defensible methods for establishing minimum criterion scores. A minimum criterion score is the "cutoff point" in a test's score range. Persons who achieve a score above the minimum criterion score set for the test are distinguished from those who do not. For example, counselor licensure or certification examinations have minimum criterion scores. Counselors who obtain a score exceeding the minimum criterion score have fulfilled one of the licensure or certification ability criteria. Similarly, minimum criterion scores have been established for examinations used for academic admissions or for employment screening.

Minimum criterion scores have long been used, but traditionally they have been set capriciously. More recently, methods such as those conceived by Nedelsky, Ebel, and Anghoff have been used in a variety of circumstances (Jaeger, 1989). These methods result in more equitable decision making and thereby greatly improve the validity of test results for decision-making purposes. Counselors who are involved in using tests for decision-making (such as selection) purposes should become familiar with various "accepted" methods for establishing minimum criterion scores.

Test Bias

No discussion of basic concepts in testing would be complete without a discussion of test bias. Anastasi (1988) wrote that "The principal questions that have been raised regarding test bias pertain to validity coefficients . . . and to the relationship between the group means on the test and on the criterion" (p. 194). Test bias becomes evident when at least two distinctly identifiable groups achieve different results on a test. These differences can be attributed to factors (such as gender or race) that, theoretically, should not be bases for the differences. It is important to note that although test bias is usually thought of as a characteristic of test items, its most significant (and usually detrimental) impact concerns interpretations of test data and the actions taken on the basis of these interpretations.

A variety of methods have been developed to alleviate test bias, including empirical means. Test developers are conscientiously striving to produce nonbiased tests. Nonetheless, there remains a considerable number of biased tests. Therefore, counselors must be sensitive to test results that may be biased. They should strive to ensure that their interpretations of test results are not flawed from being based on biased data.

Major Types of Tests

Specific tests are usually described according to their respective individual characteristics, such as those described in the previous section. More commonly, tests are grouped according to the general human dynamic being assessed. Therefore, counselors typically use five major types of standardized tests: achievement, aptitude, intelligence, interest, and personality.

Achievement Tests

Achievement tests are developed to measure the effects of relatively specific programs of instruction or training (Mehrens & Lehmann, 1991). Accordingly, achievement tests are used widely in educational systems and institutions. However, achievement tests are also used in business and industry settings to determine the need for or effects of "on the job" or other specialized training. In either case, achievement tests are designed to provide information about how much has been learned up to the date of assessment as a result of educational experiences.

Structured or guided learning activities, such as school curricula, are intended to enable participants to learn the content of specific knowledge and skill domains. Achievement tests are developed to be related to those domains. Thus, content validity considerations are particularly important in evaluating achievement tests. As achievement tests are generally administered one time at the end of a course of study, internal consistency reliability is a primary consideration in their evaluation.

Achievement tests typically are subdivided into three types: single subject matter, survey batteries, and diagnostic. The purpose of *single subject matter* achievement tests is to assess level of knowledge retention for a specifically defined content domain. This type of test is most commonly used in schools. However, they are sometimes used in other specialized training programs such as construction or trade apprenticeship programs. *Survey battery* achievement tests are collections of single subject matter tests. Achievement test batteries contain subtests, each of which is designed to measure achievement in a specific area. Achievement test batteries have several advantages over a collection of single subject matter tests. Administration procedures are simplified by the similarity in each subsection. Testing costs often are less for achievement test batteries, because printing, test booklet binding, and answer sheet printing and processing costs are usually minimized. The greatest advantage of achievement test batteries, however, is that all subtests in the battery have the same norm group. This commonality facilitates comparisons among a respondent's relative levels of achievement across areas tested.

Diagnostic achievement tests are primarily concerned with measuring skills or abilities. For example, diagnostic tests can be used to determine which reading, writing, or mathematical skills students are able to perform. Diagnostic achievement tests are sometimes referred to as "deficit measurement" tests because they reveal skills that have not yet been mastered. Subsequent instruction can be focused specifically on the development of these skills. It should be noted that although diagnostic tests identify skills that have not yet been achieved, they do not reveal *why* the skills have not been achieved. Achievement tests yield descriptive but not causal relationship results.

Clearly there is a trend toward the development of criterion-referenced achievement tests paralleling the trend toward development of curricular competency objectives in schools. This latter trend should help clarify the objectives schools are trying to accomplish. However, it may result in greater tendencies to "teach to the test," particularly when curricular and test objectives and competencies are highly similar. Therefore, counselors using achievement tests should consider the instruction underlying results.

Aptitude Tests

Traditionally, aptitude tests have been defined as tests intended for the prediction of an individual's future behavior. For example, aptitude tests have been used to predict future performance in an academic curriculum area or in a specialized vocational activity such as computer programming. The traditionally used definition has the advantage of implying how the tests are to be used (that is, for prediction). However, the definition does not clarify why aptitude tests have greater predictive power than other types of tests, or how they differ from other types of tests.

The nature and purposes of aptitude testing are best conceived within the global context of evaluation of human abilities. Within that context, intelligence testing is considered to be the measurement and evaluation of potentially generalized human functioning. Aptitude testing within that context is conceived as measurement and evaluation of potential functioning within more specific domains of human behavior. In general, the narrower the domain of human functioning into which prediction is to be made, the easier it is to develop effective predictive tests. Thus, aptitude tests have greater predictive power because they usually focus on specific areas of human functioning.

The physical formats of most aptitude tests are similar to other measures of cognitive functioning (such as intelligence or achievement tests). They frequently contain multiple-choice items, with a few tests containing manual or other dexterity tasks. The difference between aptitude and achievement tests lies in the criteria to which the items are theoretically related. Items in achievement tests are presumed to be related to academic and other learning experiences to which respondents have been *previously* exposed. Items in aptitude tests are presumed to be related to learning or occupational tasks that respondents will be *expected* to master or accomplish in the future.

Although theoretical distinctions can be made between aptitude and achievement tests, practical distinctions are difficult to operationalize. All human performance on tests is contingent on respondents' previous learning and life experiences. For example, there is considerable debate as to whether the Scholastic Assessment Test (SAT; formerly called the Scholastic Aptitude Test) is an achievement or an aptitude test. Ostensibly, it is an aptitude test because it is used primarily to predict secondary school students' performance in college curricula. Presumably, individual items are closely related to the types of mental functioning tasks that college students are required to master. However, SAT scores have high positive correlations with students' high school grade point averages (GPAs), which have high positive correlations with secondary school level achievement tests. Further, most students who complete the SAT have been enrolled in "college prep" curricula that focused on mastery of academic skills (skills necessary for successful performance in college). School systems publicize increases in the average SAT scores for graduates (as if the SAT were an achievement test), whereas colleges extol the positive correlations between SAT scores and GPAs (as if the SAT were an aptitude test). The debate will not likely end soon.

Aptitude tests are usually categorized into either single-domain or multifactor batteries. The differentiation is the same as that for achievement tests. Single-domain aptitude tests focus on a specific aspect of human performance such as a particular type of academic performance or job behavior. Aptitude (multifactor) test batteries are assemblies of single-domain tests, having a common format, administration procedure, and norm group. Regardless of type, criterion-related validity (specifically *predictive* validity) is most important for aptitude tests. Similar to achievement tests, internal consistency reliability is the most important type for aptitude tests. For large-scale testing programs, equivalent forms reliability also is important.

Counselors use aptitude test results primarily in academic and/or vocational counseling contexts. Because of the "faith" many people place in aptitude test results, it is imperative that counselors establish that aptitude tests have validity for the respective contexts in which predictions are made. Erroneous "predictions" of performance can have long-term detrimental effects for clients.

Intelligence Tests

No area in testing has attracted more heated debate than the nature and effective measurement of intelligence (Anastasi, 1988). Considerable interest exists among professionals in being able to evaluate an individual's "level of mental ability" because of the many significant implications that can be derived from such knowledge. However, although many of these implications serve the benefit of humankind, some can be construed as highly unethical. Therefore, it may be best that neither a definitive explanation nor a fully valid measurement of intelligence has yet been conceived.

The voluminous literature on intelligence testing prohibits more than cursory coverage of the topic. Therefore, only a few of the major concepts are addressed here. At the core of intelligence testing is how intelligence is defined. Some, following the lead of Binet, conceive of intelligence as a *unitary* (also called unifactor) construct. In brief, they believe that intelligence is a single, generalized human abil-ity that underlies all human functioning. The most well-known example of such a test is the Stanford–Binet Intelligence Test (S-BIT). In contrast, others, following the lead of Wechsler, believe that intelligence is the sum total of a large and diverse set of more specific mental abilities. That is, they believe that intelligence is a *multifac-tor* construct. A variety of intelligence tests have been developed based on these de-finitions, such as the Wechsler Adult Intelligence Scale–Revised (WAIS-R) and the Kaufman Assessment Battery for Children (K-ABC). The result is that different in-telligence tests yield from one to twenty or more (subscale) scores depending on the definition used as the basis for the respective tests.

Intelligence tests are also classified as *group* or *individual* tests. Group intelli-gence tests are usually of the "paper-and-pencil" variety. They are heavily depen-dent on facility in use of language, and are designed to be administered to large groups of people during a single administration. As the name implies, individual intelligence tests are designed to be administered to one person at a time. Individ-ual intelligence tests place emphasis on the use of language (through inclusion of "paper-and-pencil" components), but also include "performance" tasks to be com-pleted by respondents. The significant advantage of individual intelligence tests over group intelligence tests is that competent administrators can learn much about *how* a person responds to a testing task (method of problem solving and/or affective reactions) by careful observation during the testing session. The signifi-cant disadvantage of individual intelligence testing is the cost of administering tests on an individual basis.

Intelligence tests (or subsections of them) are also described as verbal or non-verbal. A "verbal" intelligence test necessitates competent use of language, such as providing definitions of words in a "vocabulary" subtest. In a "nonverbal" intelli-gence test, people can respond without having to interpret written or spoken lan-guage. Traditionally, such tests have been composed of a variety of tasks involving figures, diagrams, symbols, or drawings. However, the term has come to include "performance" tests (or subtests) in which the respondent physically manipulates objects. Most well-accepted individual intelligence tests include both verbal and nonverbal subtests. Most group intelligence tests are verbal, although a few non-verbal ("culture-fair") group intelligence tests have been developed.

The immense general interest in intelligence assessment has subjected intelli-gence testing to intense scrutiny, which has resulted in substantial criticism being aimed at intelligence tests. A common criticism is that intelligence tests are really "academic aptitude" tests; items in them seem closely related to the types of abili-ties needed to be successful in academic systems. Another criticism is that intelli-gence tests are biased; they favor people from upper socioeconomic classifications because of the types of values reflected in the tests. However, the most significant criticism for counselors is that intelligence tests are culturally and/or racially bi-ased. Arguments and counterarguments have emerged as to whether, how, or why intelligence tests are racially or culturally biased. At the very least, there is a basis for questioning possible bias in intelligence tests. Therefore, counselors who intend to use intelligence tests should spend considerable time studying available expository and empirical information about intelligence testing.

Interest Inventories

Interest inventories were developed as a means to assess a person's relative preferences for (feelings about) engaging in a variety of conceptually related activities (Anastasi, 1988; Cronbach, 1990; Drummond, 1992; Hood & Johnson, 1991). Among the most well-known interest inventories are the Strong Interest Inventory and the Kuder Occupational Interest Survey. Although the vast majority of interest inventories focus on assessment of vocational interests, avocational (or leisure) interest inventories are sometimes useful to counselors. However, the following discussion relates only to vocational interest inventories because of their predominance.

Vocational interest inventories are intended to provide information on a person's interests in various vocations or occupations. To achieve this goal, respondents indicate their degree of preference on a scale with incremental values for each of a large set of activities. The activities that respondents prefer are obtained and related to types of work activities that are characteristic of various occupations. Noteworthy is that activities for which preference information is obtained may not be obviously related to particular occupations. That is, respondents typically do not know which activities are conceptually and/or empirically related to particular occupations.

Associations between activities and occupations are established by having people who report being "satisfied" in an occupation indicate their preferences for a variety of activities. Activities that are most frequently preferred by "satisfied" workers become associated with the respective occupations. Thus vocational interest assessment is a comparison of a respondent's pattern of activity preferences with those of people reporting satisfaction in various occupations. Vocational interest assessment has reached a degree of sophistication such that interest levels in a wide variety of occupations are achieved through responses to a small number of items (activities).

For counseling purposes, the basic assumption underlying interest assessment is that people are prone to engage in activities they prefer. Thus, a *very* simplistic view of "vocational" counseling is that of pairing people's interests with activities inherent in occupations, with interest assessment as a major component of the process. However, such a simplistic view belies the limitations of vocational interest assessment.

Chief among the limitations of interest assessment is that "high interest in" an occupation is not necessarily synonymous with "aptitude for" an occupation. Unfortunately, clients who are poorly counseled often erroneously assume that interest and aptitude are equivalent, and may subsequently make misinformed decisions. Another limitation of interest assessment is susceptibility to response sets. For example, some people report high levels of interest in particular activities because they believe it is socially acceptable to do so. Perhaps this explains why many young people "overselect" the "higher" professions as occupational goals although they do not have the requisite aptitudes for those professions. A third limitation is reliability. Interests often fluctuate because of the influences of life experience, maturation, social context, and/or economic need. Thus, even the best of vocational interest inventories have low stability reliability coefficients. Finally, there is the potential for gender bias in interest assessment. Gender roles and situations in the workplace are clearly changing. These changes result in gender-specific or non–gender-specific normative data for interest inventories. Development costs restrict frequencies of instrument and/or normative refinements. Therefore, the continuing possibility exists that vocational interest inventory results can be misinterpreted because of gender bias.

These limitations notwithstanding, assessment of vocational interests is used frequently by counselors. Several reasons underlie this trend. One is that clients seek the most expedient means of finding satisfying and rewarding work. A second reason is that interest assessment is not threatening to clients; it is acceptable to have a lack of interest in an area. A third is that clients view interest assessment as a way to understand themselves without fear of disclosing their "deficiencies." In summary, counselors and clients favor interest assessment because it provides information that is easily obtained in counseling processes.

Personality Inventories

A definition of personality assessment is difficult because of its multifaceted nature. However, personality inventories are designed to yield information about a person's characteristics, traits, behaviors, attitudes, opinions, and/or emotions (Anastasi, 1988; Cronbach, 1990; Gregory, 1992; Hood & Johnson, 1991). Personality assessment is particularly germane to the work of counselors, but it is the most complex type of assessment. Counselors should be knowledgeable in psychometric principles and personality theory. In addition, they should have substantive supervised practice before using personality assessment instruments.

Personality inventories are classified as *structured* or *unstructured*. Structured personality inventories contain a set of items that are interpreted in the same way by all examinees. These inventories contain a set of potential item responses from among which a respondent selects one as most appropriate (pertinent to or characteristic of self). Structured personality inventories are sometimes referred to as *self-report inventories* (Anastasi, 1988). Responses are selected by respondents, not from the interpretations of administrators. Structured personality inventories yield quantitative scores based on predetermined scoring criteria. They are intended to be interpreted in comparison to normative data. The Minnesota Multiphasic Personality Inventory–2, Sixteen Personality Factor Questionnaire, and California Psychological Inventory are among the more well-known self-report personality inventories.

Unstructured personality inventories contain stimuli that can be interpreted in different ways by different respondents. Unstructured personality inventories are sometimes referred to as "projective" tests, because in many of them respondents are required to "project" thoughts or feelings onto the stimuli presented. The Rorschach Inkblot Test, Thematic Apperception Test, and the House–Tree–Person test are the best known examples of projective personality inventories. Although "scoring" procedures have been developed for some unstructured personality inventories, results are more commonly "clinical interpretations" of responses made.

Personality inventories have a number of limitations, many of which are similar to those for interest inventories. For example, personality inventories are susceptible to "faking." In these instances, clients subvert the validity of the assessment by providing responses they believe will make them "look good" or "look bad." Personality inventories also are susceptible to invalidity through contextual bias. What is a "perfectly normal" response in one context may be evaluated as an exceptionally deviant response in another. Clients may also perceive the use of personality inventories as threatening. Although clients may be intrigued about the nature of their personalities, fear of "negative" attributes often outweighs curiosity-based motivation to respond openly and honestly.

The use of personality inventories can be beneficial in helping clients gain insights into their functioning. However, most counselors do not receive extensive training in personality assessment. Therefore, they should restrict the use of personality inventories to clients who are functioning normally but who have areas of concern they want to remediate. In general, counselors will derive most benefit from use of structured or self-report inventories.

Responsibilities of Test Users

Counselors' effective use of tests is directly related to the degree of responsibility they assume. Historically, guidelines for responsible uses of tests had to be extrapolated from statements of ethical standards. A vast majority of counselors have attempted to use tests ethically and, therefore, responsibly. However, their effort was limited by lack of specificity in ethical standards statements. In response to this situation, the American Counseling Association (ACA, formerly the American Association for Counseling and Development, AACD), through its Association for Assessment in Counseling (AAC, formerly the Association for Measurement and Evaluation in Counseling and Development, AMECD), developed the guidelines entitled *Responsibilities of Users of Standardized Tests (RUST)* (ACA/AAC/AMECD, 1989). The following are comments on major sections of those guidelines.

With regard to test decisions, counselors (as test users) are responsible for determining information assessment needs and clarifying the objectives for and limitations of testing for each circumstance. Thus counselors (not clients or others) have the final authority for decisions about test use in their profession. Qualifications of test users also are an important factor in the testing process. They should be considered with regard to the purposes of testing, characteristics of the tests, conditions of test use, and the roles of other professionals.

The test selection guidelines emphasize that careful consideration should be given to each test's validity, reliability, appropriateness, and other technical characteristics. Also, respondent participation in the test selection process is desirable, if appropriate and/or possible. Test administration procedures should be conducted by qualified administrators who give proper test orientation and directions in appropriate testing conditions. To ensure accurate results, test scoring should be conducted only by fully qualified people.

Provided within the guidelines are test interpretations in the contexts of uses for placement, prediction, description, assessment of growth, and program evaluation. The importance of appropriate norms, technical factors, and the effects of variations in administration and scoring are emphasized. Guidelines for communicating test results in individual or group contexts also are presented.

Unfortunately, only these brief comments on the RUST statement can be provided here. Counselors who use tests should carefully read the entire statement.

Testing in Program Evaluation

Counselors should be familiar with the "program evaluation literature." However, many counselors erroneously believe that generating and reporting test results is synonymous with program evaluation. Testing is an aspect of program evaluation, but a "testing program" does not replace program evaluation. Effective program evaluation involves gathering a wide variety of both objective (empirical) and subjective information about program impacts. Test results are just one part of this process.

Formative and *summative* are the two major types of program evaluation processes. In formative program evaluation, data are gathered while the program is in progress so that process adjustments and modifications can be made to maximize the program's effectiveness. Summative program evaluation involves gathering data at the conclusion of a program in order to determine the extent of the program's impact. Carefully and effectively designed program evaluation processes usually encompass both types.

Testing and test results can be used in either type of program evaluation process. For example, test data derived while counseling and/or other programmatic activities are being conducted can be used to identify needed changes in those activities. Test data obtained after a program has been concluded can be used for analysis and evaluation of which activities were effective. In either case, if tests are used within appropriate guidelines they can be invaluable resources in program evaluation processes.

Just as program evaluation is not synonymous with testing, neither is it synonymous with research. However, research designs and principles often are incorporated into program evaluation processes. Specifically, summative program evaluation processes typically involve "pre–post" testing, which includes administering tests before a program begins and administering the same (or equivalent) forms at the program's end. In addition to the concern about test validity, this type of procedure requires concern for the appropriateness and reliability of tests used. Thus the major concerns regarding test use for counseling purposes are at least equally important for program evaluation purposes.

The need for counselors to be accountable for their activities has been widely publicized. Program evaluation processes should be a part of counselors' accountability efforts because these processes reflect the full scope of services rendered by counselors. However, counselors need to be involved in program evaluation activities because competent counselors know about tests and testing, and therefore should serve as resources for development of program evaluation procedures.

Summary

Testing is an integral and legitimate part of a counselor's professional functioning. However, counselors have a choice about the attitudes they adopt toward testing. They can view it as a "necessary evil" and employ minimal effort toward testing functions, or they can take the time and effort to gain understanding of psychometric principles, tests, and testing processes. Such efforts will reap the many benefits of the fully effective uses of tests in counseling. Counselors who adopt this latter perspective will find that testing is a valuable resource, and one that enhances many of their professional activities.

References

American Counseling Association/Association for Assessment in Counseling (ACA/AAC). (1989). *Responsibilities of users of standardized tests (RUST)*. Alexandria, VA: Author.

American Psychological Association (APA). (1986). *Guidelines for computer-based tests and interpretations*. Washington, DC: Author.

American Psychological Association (APA), American Educational Research Association (AERA), & National Council on Measurement in Education (NCME). (1985). *Standards for educational and psychological testing*. Washington, DC: APA.

Anastasi, A. (1988). *Psychological testing* (6th ed.). New York: Macmillan.

Cronbach, L. J. (1990). *Essentials of psychological testing* (6th ed.). New York: Harper & Row.

Drummond, R. J. (1992). *Appraisal procedures for counselors and helping professionals* (2nd ed.). New York: Macmillan.

Friedenberg, L. (1995). *Psychological testing: Design, analysis, and use*. Boston: Allyn and Bacon.

Goldman, L. (1971). Using tests in counseling (2nd ed.). New York: Appleton-Century-Crofts.

Gregory, R. J. (1992). *Psychological testing: History, principles, and applications*. Boston: Allyn and Bacon.

Groth-Marnat, G. (1990). *Handbook of psychological assessment* (2nd ed.). New York: Wiley.

Hambleton, R. K. (1989). Principles and selected applications of item response theory. In R. L. Linn (Ed.), *Educational measurement* (3rd ed., pp. 147–200). New York: American Council on Education & Macmillan.

Hood, A. B., & Johnson, R. W. (1991). *Assessment in counseling: A guide to the use of psychological assessment procedures*. Alexandria, VA: American Counseling Association.

Jaeger, R. M. (1989). Certification of student competence. In R. L. Linn (Ed.), *Educational measurement* (3rd ed., pp. 485–514). New York: American Council on Education & Macmillan.

McKinley, R. L. (1989). An introduction to item response theory. *Measurement and Evaluation in Counseling and Development, 22,* 37–57.

Mehrens, W. A., & Lehmann, I. J. (1991). *Measurement and evaluation in psychology and education* (4th ed.). Fort Worth, TX: Holt, Rinehart, & Winston.

Messick, S. (1989). Validity. In R. L. Linn (Ed.), *Educational measurement* (3rd ed., pp. 13–104). New York: American Council on Education & Macmillan.

Vacc, N. A., & Loesch, L. C. (1994). *A professional orientation to counseling* (2nd ed.). Muncie, IN: Accelerated Development.

Chapter *11*

Diagnosis in Counseling

Linda Seligman, Ph.D., LPC

Alice, age 20, consulted a counselor at her college because of feelings of depression. She told the counselor that she had barely been able to get out of bed for the past month. She had been eating little, had strong feelings of unexplained guilt, had not attended most of her classes, and had thought about cutting her wrists to end it all. She could offer no explanation for her mood change and said she had never felt like this before.

Michael, age 28, sought help for depression from a community mental health center. Although he had been going to work and fulfilling his family obligations, he had felt very hopeless for over a month. Michael reported a ten-year history of unstable moods with long periods of depression as well as episodes of hyperactivity and high elation.

Susan, age 11, was brought to her pediatrician by her mother, who stated that Susan had been depressed and crying for the past month, since her parents separated. Although she does become much more cheerful when her father visits and had been going to school regularly, she was moody and irritable much of the time.

Robert, age 45, sought help from a psychiatrist for long-standing depression. He had a history of alcohol and drug abuse, of multiple physical complaints, and of several alcohol-related accidents. He had begun several treatment programs but had not been able to remain drug or alcohol free for more than a few weeks.

Cheryl, too, sought counseling for depression. At 35, she had achieved a great deal. Married with two children, she was a successful writer and photographer. However, she had been troubled by feelings of sadness of at least several years' duration that she had been unable to ward off on her own. Although she had been

Appreciation is extended to Stephanie Hardenburg, doctoral student at George Mason University, who assisted with the preparation of this manuscript.

able to function well and conceal those feelings from others, she had finally decided to seek help.

All five of these people sought help for depression. However, their depressions differ in several respects: presence of an apparent precipitant, duration, frequency, severity, and accompanying symptoms. Similarly, the diagnoses, the treatments, and the prognosis for each person's disorder differ.

Alice is probably experiencing a Major Depressive Disorder, Single Episode, with Melancholic Features. This form of depression tends to respond fairly quickly to several forms of counseling (such as cognitive or brief psychodynamic counseling), often in combination with antidepressant medication. Michael is suffering from a Bipolar I Disorder, Most Recent Episode Depressed. This disorder is frequently chronic without treatment but is very amenable to treatment through a combination of counseling and medication. Susan has experienced a recent loss and is reacting to that loss with an Adjustment Disorder with Depressed Mood. Family counseling seems most likely to alleviate Susan's sadness. Robert may well be suffering from a Substance-Induced Mental Disorder, caused by his long-standing substance use. Prognosis here is far less favorable, and treatment may entail hospitalization. Cheryl has probably been troubled by a form of depression called Dysthymic Disorder. Medication and hospitalization are usually not needed for treatment of this disorder but its response to counseling varies and is difficult to predict.

The importance of diagnosis can be seen from these examples. Without an accurate diagnosis, counselors are likely to have difficulty determining the proper treatment for a disorder, assessing whether counseling is likely to be helpful, and deciding whether a medical referral is indicated. In the preceding examples, Susan, and probably Cheryl, are good candidates for counseling. Alice and Michael are also likely to benefit from counseling, but as part of a team effort, with counselors and psychiatrists working together to ameliorate the depression. Robert's case is too complicated by physiological concerns for counseling to be a primary focus of treatment at present. Perhaps once he has been medically evaluated and detoxified, counseling can facilitate his adjustment to a healthier lifestyle and complement other forms of treatment.

Benefits of Diagnosis

Estimates indicate that 40–50 million Americans have mental or addictive disorders (Maxmen & Ward, 1995). According to Hinkle (1994, p. 174), "At the foundation of effective mental health care is the establishment of a valid psychodiagnosis." An accurate diagnosis is essential in determining the appropriate treatment for a mental disorder and in indicating when counseling is likely to be effective and when a referral is necessary. However, there are many other reasons why diagnosis is a fundamental skill in the counselor's repertoire (Hershenson, Power, & Seligman, 1989; Seligman, 1996).

1. A diagnostic system provides a consistent framework as well as a set of criteria for naming and describing mental disorders.

2. Knowing the diagnosis for a client's concerns can help counselors anticipate the typical course of the disorder and develop a clearer understanding of the client's symptoms.

3. Using a diagnostic system promotes accountability; it enables counselors to make use of the growing body of literature on treatment effectiveness (for example, what types of interventions are most likely to ameliorate a given disorder), and to assess and improve the quality of their counseling.

4. The process of counseling employs a common language, used by all other mental health disciplines, thereby facilitating parity, credibility, communication, and collaboration.

5. Diagnoses are linked to several standardized inventories (for example, the Minnesota Multiphasic Personality Inventory and the Millon Clinical Multiaxial Inventory), enabling counselors to understand these inventories and use them as a source of information on their clients.

6. Counselors are on safer legal ground and are less vulnerable to malpractice suits if they make diagnoses and treatment plans according to an accepted system.

7. Using a standardized system of diagnosis facilitates counselors' eligibility for third-party payments for their services, thereby making counseling affordable to many people who would not otherwise be able to receive help.

8. The use of standard diagnostic terminology helps counselors to research the nature and effectiveness of their practice and demonstrate accountability.

9. Sharing diagnoses with clients, when appropriate, can help them to understand what is happening to them and to experience less guilt and self-blame related to the problems they are presenting and their need for help. Knowing that others have experienced similar symptoms and that information is available about their conditions can also reassure clients.

10. Explaining to clients that they have a diagnosable mental disorder can unbalance their previously established views of their difficulties and can help them to take a fresh look at their issues and perhaps increase their openness to treatment.

11. Clients' awareness that they have a diagnosable mental disorder can reduce the likelihood that they will blame others for their problems and that they will erroneously externalize their concerns.

12. The use of diagnoses helps counselors determine which clients they have the skills and training to help as well as which clients would benefit from a referral.

Risks of Diagnosis

Although many benefits come from the use of a standard diagnostic system, some risks also are inherent in the use of such a system:

1. Attaching a diagnostic label to someone can be stigmatizing if misused and can lead to negative perceptions of that person at school, at work, or in the family if the diagnosis becomes known.

2. In some cases, knowing the diagnostic term for a person's symptoms can be more discouraging and threatening than viewing the problem in lay terms. For example, parents may be more comfortable dealing with a child they view as behaving badly than with one who has a Conduct Disorder.
3. Diagnosis can lead to overgeneralizing, to viewing clients as their mental disorders (for example, a Borderline, a Depressive) rather than as a person with a particular set of concerns, and can promote a focus on pathology rather than on health.
4. Although the linear process of diagnosis can facilitate information gathering and treatment planning, it also can make it more difficult to think about people in developmental and systemic terms and to take a holistic view of clients and their environments.
5. Similarly, attaching a diagnostic label to one person puts the focus of treatment on the individual rather than on a family or social system. This can reinforce the family's perception of that person as its only problem and can make it more difficult for a family to work together on shared issues and concerns.
6. The diagnosis of some mental disorders can have a negative impact on people's ability to obtain health or disability insurance and can affect their employment if they are in high-risk or security-related positions.
7. In addition, the widely accepted systems of diagnosis have all grown out of a Western concept of mental illness and may have limited relevance to people from other cultures.

Although some risks clearly are inherent in the process of diagnosis, most of the risks can be avoided by skillful counseling, judicious presentation of diagnostic information to avoid misunderstanding by clients and their families, and maintenance of the clients' confidentiality whenever possible. Counselors, then, can maximize the benefits and minimize the risks of diagnosis.

Growing Importance of Diagnosis

Some counselors and students in counseling, particularly those who are primarily interested in counseling in school or business settings, may feel uncomfortable with the idea of making diagnoses. They may view their role as emphasizing support, crisis intervention, and information giving and may refer people who have mental disorders to other mental health practitioners. Consequently, they may feel little need to learn about diagnosis. Other counselors may have a strongly humanistic, multicultural, or family systems emphasis in their counseling and may believe that the process of labeling clients is antithetical to their idea of the counselor's role.

However, changes in the field of counseling make it important for all counselors to be familiar with the process of diagnosis. Until the 1970s, "counselor" usually meant school counselor. In the past twenty years, however, the counselor's role has expanded greatly, with particular growth in mental health counseling. The

American Mental Health Counselors Association, with over 12,000 members, is one of the two largest divisions of the American Counseling Association. By 1995, forty-three states had licensure or certification for counselors and ten states had passed Freedom-of-Choice legislation that requires insurance companies to provide third-party payments for the services of all credentialed mental health professionals in that state. Mastery of diagnosis not only improves the effectiveness of mental health counselors but also is required by many places of employment where diagnoses are needed for accountability, determination of treatment effectiveness, recordkeeping, and third-party payments.

Counselors in schools and businesses should also be familiar with the process of diagnosis, although for somewhat different reasons. Being able to make a diagnosis of a person's concerns enables those counselors to determine whether they can provide services that will help the client or whether a referral is needed; it can help them to select the most appropriate referral, and it can help them anticipate the client's probable response to treatment. Making a diagnosis also can help counselors in schools and businesses to assess whether clients should remain in the school or business, possibly with some extra help, or whether the client needs an environment providing more support and assistance. Diagnosis, therefore, is an important skill for both mental health counselors and those working in other settings.

The DSM-IV and Other Diagnostic Systems

The most widely used diagnostic system in the United States is the *Diagnostic and Statistical Manual of Mental Disorders* (DSM). The most recent edition of this volume, the DSM-IV, was issued in 1994 by the American Psychiatric Association (1994a). The first edition of the DSM, containing 108 categories of mental disorder, was published in 1952 (Hohenshil, 1993). Developed primarily by and for psychiatrists, it presented a psychobiological view of the nature of emotional disorders. It was replaced in 1968 by the DSM-II, a landmark publication in the field of mental health that looked at mental disorders primarily in terms of psychoses, neuroses, and personality disorders.

The DSM-III was introduced in 1980. Field tests involving over 500 clinicians were used to maximize the validity of that volume. In addition, psychologists, as well as a small number of social workers and counselors, worked along with psychiatrists to develop this revision of the DSM. The DSM-III was more comprehensive and detailed than its predecessor and was designed to be more precise and less stigmatizing in its language. The DSM-III made some major changes in definition and terminology used for mental disorders. For example, the term *neurosis,* which had become a pejorative and common term in the language, was no longer recommended; Depressive Neurosis, for example, was renamed Dysthymia. Schizophrenia was defined more narrowly and was used to describe only severe disorders involving evident loss of contact with reality.

A revised version of the DSM-III, the DSM-III-R, was published in 1987. The DSM-III-R reflected changes arising from increased knowledge of mental disorders as well as from changes in attitudes and perceptions. For example, the diagnosis of Homosexuality was excluded from this edition, reflecting greater understanding as well as increased acceptance of homosexuality.

The task force and work group of the latest edition, the DSM-IV, began its efforts in 1988 and was a large, diverse group of mental health professionals, with many practicing clinicians. The primary justification for a change from the DSM-III-R to the DSM-IV was compelling empirical support. Three criteria were used to determine revisions: extensive literature reviews, to be published in the five-volume *DSM-IV Sourcebook* (American Psychiatric Association, 1994b and future years); clinical trials; and two drafts of the DSM-IV that invited feedback to determine whether support was available for a suggested change. The DSM-IV, like the DSM-III and DSM-III-R, is deliberately atheoretical. The DSM-IV includes over 300 categories of mental disorders, as well as extensive descriptive information, much of which focuses on gender, ethnicity, and cultural patterns in mental disorders. This reflects great progress in making the DSM- IV sensitive to differences related to group membership.

The frequent revisions of the DSM demonstrate that knowledge of mental disorders is a vital and changing body of information. New material is constantly being discovered about biochemistry, the emotions, and their interaction and impact. In many ways, we are still novices in our understanding of the psychology of people. As a result, our current information is often inadequate and imprecise. Although the DSM makes an important contribution to clarifying and organizing mental disorders, it is a complex publication whose skillful use requires sound clinical judgment as well as experience. A subsequent section of this chapter provides an introduction to the major types of mental disorders and provides readers some familiarity with the DSM-IV. Browsing through the volume, reading about diagnoses of interest, and making diagnoses of case studies will increase comfort and familiarity with that sometimes intimidating volume. However, using the DSM with true ease rarely comes without considerable clinical experience.

Although the DSM-IV seems to be the standard for diagnostic nomenclature in the United States, another system of diagnosis is also used, particularly in medically oriented settings. The *ICD-10 Classification of Mental and Behavioural Disorders* (World Health Organization, 1992), known in the United States as the ICD-10, is an international publication of the World Health Organization. The code numbers of the ICD-10 are coordinated with the DSM-IV, and clinicians may refer to Appendix H of the DSM-IV to determine the appropriate ICD-10 diagnosis if necessary.

Definition of a Mental Disorder

The DSM-IV defines a mental disorder as "a clinically significant behavioral or psychological syndrome or pattern that occurs in an individual" (American Psychiatric Association, 1994a, p. xxi). Responses that are expectable or culturally sanctioned are not considered mental disorders. According to the DSM-IV, at least one of three features, distress, impairment, and/or significant risk, must be present in order for a client to be diagnosed as having a mental disorder. Although these features are often present in combination, illustrations are provided of the features in isolation, to clarify their nature.

Beth sought counseling after her fiancé broke their engagement for the third time. She was a successful lawyer who continued to perform well at her job despite her personal turmoil. A very private person, Beth continued to see her friends and family and go to work every day, showing little or no evidence of her distress. However, every night she cried herself to sleep and even had some fleeting suicidal thoughts. Although Beth manifested no impairment nor was she really at risk, she was certainly experiencing considerable distress and had a diagnosable mental disorder, Adjustment Disorder With Depressed Mood.

In contrast, Frank, a 14-year-old who was brought to counseling by his parents, reported that life was great; he saw his parents' nagging as his only problem. For the past year, Frank had cut classes frequently and spent several days each week hanging out at the neighborhood shopping center with his friends, he disobeyed his parents' rules, had frequent arguments with family and teachers, and usually seemed angry and annoyed. Frank had little distress about his situation and was not yet in danger. Frank's diagnosis, Oppositional Defiant Disorder, was characterized primarily by impairment. Although Frank did not perceive himself as having any impairment, his problem in social and academic functioning met the criteria for this disorder.

Hilda reported neither distress nor impairment when she consulted a counselor at the suggestion of her family physician. At 5 feet, 6 inches, tall, Hilda weighed 100 lbs. and was quite pleased with her figure, estimating that she had only another 5 to 10 pounds to lose. Hilda had the diagnosis of Anorexia Nervosa, Restricting Type, and had dieted herself into a life-threatening physical condition, putting her at risk.

Some symptoms that do not cause significant distress, impairment, or risk and are expectable responses are not viewed as mental disorders. For example, Jessica consulted a counselor after the birth of her third child within the past five years. Although she was a caring and knowledgeable parent, she felt overwhelmed and had difficulty asking for help and managing her time. Counseling could certainly help Jessica handle the many demands on her and the stress she and her husband were feeling, but Jessica did not have a mental disorder. Her reactions caused no risk to herself or the children, did not reflect impairment, and were characterized by appropriate, understandable, and manageable distress. Jessica would be described as experiencing a Phase of Life Problem rather than a mental disorder.

Multiaxial Assessment

Whether or not people who present for counseling have mental disorders, a multiaxial diagnosis offers counselors a way to organize the information they have on clients' symptoms, their physical conditions, their levels of coping, and the stressors they are experiencing. A full multiaxial assessment involves viewing a person according to five axes. Axis I includes what the DSM calls Clinical Disorders and Other Conditions That May Be a Focus of Clinical Attention. All disorders and conditions in the DSM-IV are included in Axis I with the exception of the Personality Disorders and both Mental Retardation and Borderline Intellectual Functioning, listed on Axis II. These Axis II listings may involve less severe symptoms than some of those on Axis I but they have a pervasive and enduring impact on a person's life.

People may have one or more diagnoses or conditions on Axis I or Axis II, or one or both of these axes may have no diagnosis or condition listed. Each diagnosis has a code number provided in the DSM. When a diagnosis is listed, both the name and the code number are specified (for example, "307.51 Bulimia Nervosa"). In addition, clinicians generally specify the severity of a mental disorder, using the terms *Mild*, *Moderate*, and *Severe*. The phrase In Partial Remission describes symptoms that for an individual once met the criteria for a mental disorder but now are manifested in more limited ways. The phrase In Full Remission describes disorders whose symptoms no longer are evident in the individual but that remain clinically relevant, perhaps because the person still receives medication for the disorder. A new descriptor in the DSM-IV, Prior History, allows disorders to be listed that may have been absent for years but remain noteworthy, perhaps because they have a tendency to recur under stress. The DSM also provides terminology to be used when no diagnoses are listed on Axis I or on Axis II (for example, "V71.09 No Mental Disorder on Axis II"). When more than one diagnosis is listed on an axis, they are listed in order of treatment priority. The Principal Diagnosis is assumed to be the first diagnosis on Axis I unless otherwise specified. The DSM-IV also offers the optional use of the descriptor Reason for Visit, to be used if the presenting concern is not viewed by the clinician as the principal diagnosis.

Axis III includes General Medical Conditions. On this axis, clinicians list physical disorders that may be relevant to a person's emotional condition. This would include such conditions as migraine headaches that might be related to stress as well as conditions such as cancer or diabetes that might have an impact on a person's emotional adjustment. Although clinicians may informally list signs and symptoms on Axis III in their own notes, an official multiaxial assessment should include only medically verified physical conditions on Axis III.

On Axis IV, clinicians list Psychosocial and Environmental Problems that may be having an impact on a client. Clinicians may use their own labels for these stressors and also can organize them according to the DSM categories of stressors. These include problems with one's primary support group; problems related to the social environment; problems related to educational, occupational, or housing concerns; economic problems; and problems related to the access to health care services or to interaction with the legal system. Counselors should cite only stressors that have occurred within the past year, unless an earlier stressor is especially relevant to the current diagnosis; for example, combat experiences that are related to a diagnosis of Posttraumatic Stress Disorder.

Axis V includes a Global Assessment of Functioning rating, a scale ranging from 1 to 100, on which the counselor rates the client's current functioning. (Highest level of functioning also can be rated if the clinician chooses.) Ratings below 50 indicate people with severe symptoms who need close monitoring and probably medication and perhaps hospitalization. Ratings above 50 indicate higher levels of functioning. Most people who are seen for counseling in outpatient settings seem to have ratings between 50 and 70.

Axes IV and V are particularly useful in treatment planning. Clients with many stressors listed on Axis IV and low ratings on Axis V are experiencing considerable stress and have poor levels of functioning. They may require a multifaceted treatment plan, including counseling, medication, and possibly hospitalization. Clients with an opposite profile—few stressors on Axis IV and high ratings on Axis V—are experiencing more manageable stress and have good coping mechanisms. Such clients are likely to make good use of brief counseling.

The following example of a multiaxial assessment illustrates how such a diagnosis can quickly provide a broad and rich picture of a client:

Axis I:	V71.01 Adult Antisocial Behavior
	315.2 Disorder of Written Expression, Mild
Axis II:	301.20 Schizoid Personality Disorder
Axis III:	346.20 Headaches, cluster
Axis IV:	Psychosocial stressors: Arrest
Axis V:	Current global assessment of functioning (GAF), 45; highest GAF in the past year, 60

The preceding multiaxial assessment was made on a 37-year-old Latino man, Dennis Ruiz, who had been arrested and charged with assault and battery. Ruiz lived alone and earned a living by raising dogs. One of his dogs had escaped to a neighbor's yard where the dog damaged some plants and frightened the neighbor's son. The neighbor dealt with this by shooting and killing the dog. When Ruiz discovered this, he smashed the window of his neighbor's car and physically attacked the neighbor.

Prior to this, Ruiz had no legal problems and was viewed by his neighbors as a loner but as someone who was always available to help when cars or other machinery broke down. Ruiz had left high school when he was 16, reporting poor grades and discouragement. He had lived on a small farm, raising dogs, since that time. He had little contact with others, except that necessitated by his business, but reported being contented with his life.

The multiaxial assessment provides insight into the dynamics of this client's attack on his neighbor. His primary source of success and gratification was his dogs. His dogs were the focus of his life. Consequently, his strong response to the shooting of his dog reflected the impact this event had on his life. He had no history of criminal or violent behavior and was unlikely to present a danger to others in the future.

Axis I reflects the current incident (Adult Antisocial Behavior) and this client's long-standing learning disorder, which limited his success in school as well as his career opportunities. Axis II lists his Schizoid Personality Disorder, reflected in his lack of interest in interpersonal relationships, his preference for solitary activities, and his usual detached state. Ruiz's medically diagnosed headaches are listed on Axis III, contributing to his constricted lifestyle. The primary stressor was his arrest and the threat of incarceration, which would prevent him from caring for his dogs. Axis V indicates that his highest—and usual—level of functioning is moderately impaired, particularly in terms of relationships. The current GAF of 45 reflected his aggressive behavior toward his neighbor and his continued rage. This multiaxial assessment was instrumental in obtaining probation for Ruiz, with the condition that he obtain counseling to help him with impulse control and communication skills.

Review of the DSM-IV

The mental disorders and conditions contained in the DSM-IV are divided into seventeen broad categories. Although this chapter is not designed to teach or interpret the DSM, a brief review of the seventeen sections is provided here to give readers some general familiarity with the major types of mental disorders. Many specific mental disorders and conditions included in each broad category will not be cited here. Readers planning to use the DSM with their clients will need to study that book and probably take coursework or training in the use of the DSM. The American Counseling Association offers many professional development workshops on the DSM as well as a home study program (Seligman, 1995). In addition, study guides are available to facilitate mastery of the DSM. These include *Study Guide to DSM-IV* (Fauman, 1994) and *DSM-IV Made Easy* (Morrison, 1995). Also helpful is the *DSM-IV Casebook* (Spitzer, Gibbon, Skodol, Williams, & First, 1994).

Disorders Usually First Diagnosed in Infancy, Childhood, or Adolescence

The largest and most comprehensive category in the DSM is "Disorders Usually First Diagnosed in Infancy, Childhood, or Adolescence," which includes disorders that typically begin during the early years, although some may persist into adulthood. Many of the other diagnoses in the DSM can be applied to children and adolescents, but most of the disorders they experience will be included in this first category. Types of disorders in this group include Mental Retardation, Learning Disorders, Motor Skills Disorder, Pervasive Developmental Disorders such as Autism, Attention-Deficit/Hyperactivity Disorder and Disruptive Behavior Disorders (for example, Conduct Disorder and Oppositional Defiant Disorder), and Communication Disorders (for example, Stuttering, Phonological Disorder). Also included in this category are the Feeding and Eating Disorders of Infancy or Early Childhood such as Pica, Tic Disorders including Tourette's Disorder, and the Elimination Disorders (Encopresis and Enuresis). Other disorders in this section include Separation Anxiety Disorder, Selective Mutism, Reactive Attachment Disorder, and Stereotypic Movement Disorder.

Of the disorders in this section, Learning Disorders, Attention-Deficit/Hyperactivity Disorder, Conduct Disorder, Oppositional Defiant Disorder, and Separation Anxiety Disorder are particularly important to school counselors and others working with children of elementary school age. Children with Learning Disorders typically have both social and academic impairment. Although they are usually of normal intelligence, they have inordinate difficulty mastering a particular area of learning such as reading or mathematics and consequently may experience teasing, criticism, and frustration. They usually need both counseling and academic help. Children diagnosed with Attention-Deficit/Hyperactivity Disorder also tend to have academic, social, and, often, family problems as a result of their high level of motor activity, distractibility, and impulsivity, making it difficult for them to concentrate and engage in rewarding activities with family and friends. Conduct Disorder, involving repeated violations of laws and rules (for example, stealing, vandalism, and truancy) is sometimes the precursor of adult antisocial or criminal behavior. Consequently, rapid treatment of this disorder is important although client resistance and mistrust may be high. Separation Anxiety Disorder has been known as school phobia and typically involves difficulty separating from parents, accompanied by an avoidance of school. Early intervention is crucial here, too, because the longer this disorder persists, the more difficult it is for the child to return to school. Oppositional Defiant Disorder involves angry, defiant, and argumentative behavior and sometimes accompanies Attention-Deficit/Hyperactivity Disorder and Conduct Disorder. Family counseling is especially important in treatment of Oppositional Defiant Disorder.

Delirium, Dementia, and Amnestic and Other Cognitive Disorders

Delirium, Dementia, and other cognitive disorders all involve some type of transient or permanent damage to the brain. Causes can include an injury, drug or alcohol use, exposure to a toxic chemical or other substance, disease such as HIV or Parkinson's disease, or an abnormal aging process as in Alzheimer's disease.

Counselors are rarely qualified to diagnose or treat either the cognitive disorders just listed or the disorders due to general medical conditions described next. However, they should be familiar with the nature and typical symptoms of these disorders so that they may refer clients whom they suspect of having such disorders to a psychiatrist or neurologist for a conclusive diagnosis. Counselors may work with clients with these disorders as part of a treatment team; the counselor may provide therapy to the family of the affected person or may counsel the client to facilitate social and occupational adjustment in light of any limitations that may be imposed by the disorder. Primary treatment, however, will come from a physician.

Mental Disorders Due to a General Medical Condition

The section entitled Medical Disorders Due to a General Medical Condition is a new section in the DSM. It includes Personality Change Due to a General Medical Condition, such as that caused by temporal lobe epilepsy, and Catatonic Disorder Due to a General Medical Condition, such as that caused by encephalitis.

Substance-Related Disorders

The DSM-IV section on Substance-Related Disorders includes psychological and behavioral disorders associated with substance use (Substance Abuse and Substance Dependence), as well as induced or physiological disorders resulting from drug or alcohol use, such as Intoxication, Tolerance, and Substance Induced Mood Disorder. Counselors should specify whether a person with Substance Abuse or Dependence is experiencing Physiological Dependence, is in remission, is on agonist therapy such as methadone, or is in a controlled environment such as a halfway house. The Substance Use Disorders are divided into Substance Abuse and Substance Dependence (usually the more severe and pervasive of the two). These diagnoses describe people who use alcohol or any other substances (for example, amphetamines, cannabis, cocaine, hallucinogens, inhalants, nicotine, opioids or sedatives) in a self-damaging way, usually with the knowledge that they are being harmed by their substance use. Although these people may continue to maintain employment and may present a positive façade to friends and family, their performance and relationships are usually adversely affected by their substance use, and they may be endangering their lives by their dysfunctional behavior. Counselors in nearly all settings should be familiar with the diagnosis and treatment of these prevalent disorders, particularly counselors working in employee assistance programs (EAPs). Treatment for substance use disorders typically involves a multifaceted approach, including group, individual, and family counseling; education; and participation in a peer support group (such as Alcoholics Anonymous or Rational Recovery).

Schizophrenia and Other Psychotic Disorders

The disorders included in this section, Schizophrenia and Other Psychotic Disorders all are characterized by symptoms of loss of contact with reality. Schizophrenia involves a severe, pervasive loss of contact with reality, often including auditory hallucinations, and lasting at least six months. Types of Schizophrenia include Paranoid, Disorganized, Catatonic, Undifferentiated, and Residual Types. Schizophreniform Disorder has the same criteria as Schizophrenia but the symptoms are less than six months in duration. Delusional Disorders are characterized by nonbizarre delusions lasting at least one month. An example is a man who became convinced without reason that his wife was having a series of affairs. Delusional Disorders typically are circumscribed and are more likely than Schizophrenia to have an apparent precipitant and to begin abruptly. Brief Psychotic Disorder is characterized by symptoms of Schizophrenia or Delusional Disorder that are less than one month in duration. When psychotic symptoms have a precipitant—for example, the loss of one's family in an accident—and when the symptoms begin suddenly rather than gradually, the prognosis for recovery is generally good. This usually is the case with Brief Psychotic Disorder. Schizoaffective Disorder includes criteria for both the diagnosis of Schizophrenia and a Mood Disorder (Major Depressive Disorder or Bipolar Disorder). Shared Psychotic Disorder involves two people, usually in a close relationship, who have a shared delusional belief. Psychotic Disorders Due to a General Medical Condition are included in this section, such as psychosis resulting from lupus.

Mood Disorders

The Mood Disorders section of the DSM includes disorders characterized primarily by manic or depressive features. Manic features are less commonly presented by clients than are depressive ones. Manic features are typified by elevated, expansive, or irritable mood; grandiosity; distractibility and agitation; and excessive pleasure seeking. One client, a man in his mid-twenties, employed as a teacher and planning to get married, reported during a manic episode that he had decided he was destined to be a Hollywood movie star. He resigned from his job, bought an expensive sports car, enrolled in three acting classes, and prepared to move to California. Clearly, manic features can be very disruptive and self-destructive. Their treatment usually involves both medication and counseling.

Clients experiencing depression present quite different symptoms. They may feel helpless, discouraged, and even suicidal; experience excessive guilt and self-blame; and have little interest or pleasure in anything. Sleeping and eating problems as well as fatigue are also common. Cognitive-behavioral and brief psychodynamic approaches to treatment are often used to treat depression, frequently in combination with medication.

Diagnoses in this category include Major Depressive Disorder (severe depression of at least two weeks' duration), Dysthymic Disorder (long-standing moderate depression), and Bipolar I and II Disorders and Cyclothymic Disorder, which combine depressive and manic or hypomanic symptoms. Each diagnosis is described by specifiers indicating the patterns and features of the disturbance such as Seasonal Pattern, Postpartum Onset, or Melancholic Features. This section is an important one for counselors because of the prevalence of Major Depressive Disorder in both inpatient and outpatient settings.

Anxiety Disorders

Anxiety is another symptom that is frequently presented in counseling. Several of the anxiety disorders involve a phobia, a persistent and exaggerated fear of an object or situation, leading to impairment through avoidance of the feared stimulus. Examples of these disorders include Social Phobia (fear of social embarrassment), Agoraphobia (fear of places from which escape is difficult or help might not be readily available, such as crowds or public transportation), and Specific Phobia (fear of a specific object or situation such as heights or snakes). Panic Disorder, characterized by unexpected feelings of physical and emotional panic; Obsessive-Compulsive Disorder, characterized by recurrent unwanted thoughts or impulses; Posttraumatic Stress Disorder and Acute Stress Disorder, triggered by exposure to traumatic experiences such as rape and natural disasters; and Generalized Anxiety Disorder (pervasive and excessive anxiety and worry lasting at least six months) also are included in this section. Acute and/or Posttraumatic Stress Disorder are frequently encountered by counselors on hot lines or in crisis centers; they involve a cluster of symptoms (such as withdrawal, reexperiencing the trauma, and anxiety) following a traumatic event (such as rape or accident). Anxiety symptoms sometimes mimic those of physical conditions, and thorough diagnostic evaluation is important. Properly diagnosed, most anxiety symptoms respond well to a multifaceted treatment plan, including improving coping mechanisms, desensitization, relaxation, and, in some cases, medication (Seligman, 1990).

Somatoform Disorders

People with Somatoform Disorders are commonly referred for counseling by their physicians. These clients strongly believe they are experiencing some physical ailment; however, medical examinations fail to find any physical cause for their complaints. People with these disorders typically have difficulty managing stress and expressing themselves verbally; their physical complaints characteristically are a way of expressing their negative feelings. Types of Somatoform Disorders include Somatization Disorder, characterized by many unverified physical complaints; Conversion Disorder, involving impairment in motor or sensory function such as paralysis or blindness without medical cause; Pain Disorder; Hypochondriasis (preoccupation with the idea of having a serious illness); and Body Dysmorphic Disorder, characterized by an imagined flaw in one's appearance.

Factitious Disorders

People with Factitious Disorders rarely present themselves for counseling in a straightforward fashion (Seligman, 1990). These people enjoy the role of patient and deliberately feign physical or psychological symptoms so that they can assume a sick role. What has been called Factitious Disorder by Proxy involves causing another person to feign or experience medical complaints. The histories of people with Factitious Disorders often involve experiencing illness as rewarding, and they learn this dysfunctional way of getting attention. Little is known about treatment for this disorder, because it is not often treated successfully in counseling.

Dissociative Disorders

The best known of the Dissociative Disorders is Dissociative Identity Disorder (DID), formerly called Multiple Personality Disorder. This disorder was exemplified on television and film through the cases of Eve and Sybil. Dissociative Amnesia, Dissociative Fugue, and Depersonalization Disorder are also included in this section. All these disorders involve an alteration in consciousness (such as memory loss or alternate personality states) that is neither organic nor psychotic. Until recently, these disorders were believed to be rare. However, new information on their prevalence is providing a different picture, although DID remains a controversial diagnosis.

Sexual and Gender Identity Disorders

The DSM-IV divides the Sexual and Gender Identity Disorders into three groups: Sexual Dysfunctions, Paraphilias, and Gender Identity Disorders. The three are very different in terms of their nature and treatment. Paraphilias involve sexual urges or behaviors that interfere with social adjustment and relationships. Examples are Exhibitionism, Fetishism, Sexual Sadism, Voyeurism, and Pedophilia (sexual activity with children). People with these disorders are often resistant to change but may seek treatment because of a court mandate or at the insistence of an unhappy partner. In contrast, people with Sexual Dysfunctions such as a Sexual Desire Disorder, an Arousal Disorder, Orgasmic Disorder, Premature Ejaculation, or a Sexual Pain Disorder are usually eager for help, although they, too, may have been urged into treatment by an unhappy partner. Gender Identity Disorders are characterized by strong and persistent cross-gender identification, accompanied by discomfort with one's assigned sex. Prognosis for treatment of Sexual Disorders seems strongly related to motivation.

Eating Disorders

Eating Disorders are especially prevalent among adolescent females and, if left untreated, can be severely self-damaging and even fatal. Anorexia Nervosa (Restricting, Binge Eating, or Purging Type) is primarily characterized by a body weight that is 85 percent or less than expected, as well as by an intense fear of weight gain. Bulimia Nervosa (Purging or Nonpurging Types) entails frequent consumption of large quantities of food, often accompanied by self-induced vomiting or excessive use of laxatives or diuretics to avoid weight gain. Treatment usually is conducted in a group setting and involves both cognitive-behavioral and psychodynamic interventions.

Sleep Disorders

Sleep Disorders may be described as Primary (not related to other medical or mental disorders) or as related to other specific diagnoses. Emotions, environment, lifestyle, and physiology may all be causative factors in these disorders. They include Insomnia; Hypersomnia, characterized by excessive sleeping or fatigue; Narcolepsy, in which a person suffers from irresistible attacks of sleep; Breathing-Related Sleep Disorder; Circadian Rhythm Sleep Disorder, usually caused by an irregular or unusual sleep schedule; and Nightmare, Sleep Terror, and Sleepwalking Disorders. Sleep disorder clinics are available that can facilitate diagnosis of these disorders by tracing the client's brain wave activity and monitoring sleep patterns.

Impulse-Control Disorders Not Elsewhere Classified

Disorders in the DSM-IV section titled Impulse-Control Disorders Not Elsewhere Classified typically involve a repetitive cycle in which people have a buildup of tension and anxiety. They release the tension in some dysfunctional and destructive way, then may be apologetic and promise change, only to repeat the cycle. Disorders described in this section of the DSM include Intermittent Explosive Disorder (repeatedly engaging in impulsive, aggressive, or destructive behaviors such as spouse abuse), Kleptomania (stealing objects that are not needed), Pathological Gambling, Pyromania, and Trichotillomania, a disorder that involves pulling out the hairs on one's head or body. Treatment for these disorders typically involves behavioral counseling as well as help with stress management and interpersonal relationships.

Adjustment Disorders

People who respond to a stressor (or multiple stressors) with mild to moderate (but clinically significant) impairment within three months of the stressor are described as having an Adjustment Disorder. The type of Adjustment Disorder (such as With Depressed Mood, With Anxiety, or With Disturbance of Conduct) should be specified when the diagnosis is made. This diagnosis can be maintained for a maximum of six months following the termination of the stressor. If symptoms persist beyond that time, the diagnosis must be changed. These disorders, among the mildest mental disorders found in the DSM-IV, are common in people going through negative life changes (such as a divorce, a bereavement, or being fired from a job) but also can be found in people experiencing usually positive life changes (such as marriage, the birth of a child, or graduation). These disorders generally respond well to crisis intervention or solution-focused counseling.

Personality Disorders

Personality Disorders, listed on Axis II of a multiaxial assessment, are long-standing, deeply ingrained disorders, typically evident by adolescence or early adulthood. Although these disorders usually are less severe than such disorders as Schizophrenia and Bipolar I Disorder in terms of the impairment they cause, they are among the most treatment resistant of the disorders. Personality Disorders typically are manifested by pervasive patterns of dysfunction that show up in all areas of a person's life. Although people with these disorders may experience considerable unhappiness and seek help, they usually do not have a clear and positive self-image, a set of effective coping mechanisms, or an array of healthy peer relationships to draw on. Consequently, counseling for people experiencing Personality Disorders is often either a lengthy and challenging process or is terminated prematurely.

Personality Disorders take many forms. They can be characterized by patterns of suspiciousness, isolation, antisocial behavior, mood instability, grandiosity, dependence, or perfectionism. For example, many people with histories of criminal and irresponsible behavior, dating back to childhood, are diagnosed as having Antisocial Personality Disorder, often seen by counselors working in corrections or substance abuse settings. Other Personality Disorders frequently seen in counseling include Dependent, Borderline, Histrionic, and Narcissistic Personality Disorders. Less often seen in counseling are people with Paranoid, Schizoid, Schizotypal, Avoidant, and Obsessive-Compulsive Personality Disorders. For more information on personality disorders, readers are referred to Millon (1995).

Other Conditions That May Be a Focus of Clinical Attention

The conditions that the DSM-IV discusses under the heading Other Conditions That May Be a Focus of Clinical Attention are not viewed as mental disorders, but may be a focus of attention in counseling. These descriptors may be used alone to describe a person who does not have a mental disorder, or they may be used along with one or more mental disorders on a multiaxial assessment to indicate important areas to be addressed in treatment. Included among the Other Conditions are Psychological Factors Affecting Medical Condition, in which emotional or behavioral patterns are adversely affecting a medical disorder: Medication-Induced Movement Disorders such as Neuroleptic-Induced Tardive Dyskinesia: Relational Problems including Partner, Parent-Child, Sibling, and other interpersonal difficulties; and Problems Related to Abuse or Neglect. Additional conditions listed in this section include Acculturation Problem, Age-Related Cognitive Decline, Identity Problem, Religious or Spiritual Problem, Occupational Problem, Phase of Life Problem, and Borderline Intellectual Functioning (listed on Axis II) among others. Although people who present with these conditions and who do not have accompanying mental disorders may seek counseling and may derive considerable benefit from that process, they typically are emotionally healthy people with good resources who have encountered a difficult period in their lives. Often people with these disorders, like people with Adjustment Disorders, learn and grow considerably from the counseling process.

Diagnosis in Context

This chapter has focused primarily on diagnosis. However, diagnosis is only one of three steps counselors should take before counseling a person. The other two steps, intake interviews and treatment planning, are briefly discussed next.

Intake Interviews

Intake interviews precede diagnosis and provide the information on which a diagnosis is made. Some agencies have a formal intake process that may include a prospective client being asked a series of predetermined questions, completing some forms and inventories, and possibly even meeting with more than one clinician (for example, a counselor and a psychiatrist). In other settings, such as private practices and college counseling settings, the first counseling session usually serves as an intake interview. In a less structured way, the counselor gathers sufficient information about the client to enable the counselor to assess the urgency of the client's situation, to orient the client to the counseling process, to determine the client's suitability for counseling in that setting (or to make a referral), to formulate a diagnosis, and to develop a treatment plan.

Intake interviews vary widely in terms of their duration and thoroughness. They may be as brief as fifteen minutes, focusing on presenting concerns and their development, or they may extend over several sessions of an hour or more in length, seeking to elicit a comprehensive and in-depth picture of the client. Topics typically included in an intake interview include identifying information (such as client's age, occupation, and marital status), presenting concerns, previous emotional difficulties, treatment history, present life situation, information on family of origin and present family, developmental history, leisure activities, relationships, education, and career and medical history (Seligman, 1996). While conducting an intake interview, counselors should gather information not only from the clients' words but also from their appearance, their behavior during the interview, their interaction with the counselor, their mood and display of emotion, their contact with reality, and their thinking process. That information can be summarized in a mental status evaluation and is important in helping the counselor make an accurate diagnosis.

Treatment Planning

Treatment planning is the third step in the process that begins with the intake interview, continues with a multiaxial assessment according to the DSM-IV, and culminates in the treatment plan. This three-step process has been compared to the shape of an hourglass (Hershenson et al., 1989). The information collected during the intake interview provides breadth to the counselor's picture of the client. This information is processed and condensed into a diagnosis, analogous to the narrow part of the hourglass. The focus is then expanded once again with treatment planning. Beginning with the establishment of mutually agreed-on objectives, the treatment plan provides counselors with a map to guide their work with their clients.

Many models have been developed for treatment plans. One that I developed, the "DO A CLIENT MAP," is presented here (Seligman, 1990, 1996). The title of the model is a mnemonic device, with each letter in the name reflecting one of the important areas to be addressed in treatment planning:

1. Diagnosis according to the DSM-IV
2. Objectives of treatment
3. Assessment procedures
4. Clinician
5. Location of treatment
6. Interventions
7. Emphasis of treatment (such as supportive or confrontational)

8. Numbers (individual, group, or family counseling)
9. Timing (duration and scheduling of sessions)
10. Medication
11. Adjunct services
12. Prognosis

By responding to each item in the outline of a treatment plan, counselors can develop a comprehensive and useful guide for working with a client.

Illustration of the Three-Step Process

The following case provides an abbreviated version of the three-step process of intake interview, multiaxial assessment or diagnosis, and treatment plan. The case begins with a short summary of information obtained from the intake interview with the client, continues with a multiaxial assessment, and finishes with a brief treatment plan.

Intake Information

Amber, a 15-year-old African American female, requested some help from her school counselor, who referred her and her family to a community mental health center. Amber was living with her mother, her 12-year-old brother, and her stepfather of two months. Amber's father had died three years ago in an automobile accident. Amber stated that she was very angry at her mother for remarrying and could not understand what attracted her to her new husband, Jeff. Amber reported that her mother expected her to call Jeff "Dad" and to participate in family outings. Amber spent as much time away from home as she could and reported sadness and loss of interest in academic and social activities since her mother's marriage.

Before that event, Amber had been a quiet and capable student, earning satisfactory grades and participating in several school clubs. She had a small circle of girlfriends and had recently begun to date. Other than some grief and withdrawal around the time of her father's death, Amber had been well adjusted, and no history of problem behavior was reported. She seemed to be in good health and rarely missed school. She was of above-average intelligence and was well oriented to reality.

Diagnosis

Axis I:	309.0 Adjustment Disorder with Depressed Mood, Acute
Axis II:	V71.09 No diagnosis or condition on Axis II
Axis III:	No physical disorders or conditions
Axis IV:	Psychosocial stressors: Problems with primary support group (death of father, mother's remarriage)
Axis V:	Current GAF: 65

Treatment plan

Objectives:
1. Reduce Amber's level of sadness
2. Improve her relationships with her mother and stepfather
3. Increase her interest in academic and social activities

Assessments: Beck Depression Inventory, Family Functioning Scale

Clinician: No specific counselor variables are indicated here; arguments could be made for assigning Amber to either a male or a female counselor. Her preference for counselor's gender and ethnicity will be considered.

Location: Outpatient: private practice, or community mental health center.

Interventions: A cognitive orientation will be emphasized; Amber is telling herself that she must not allow anyone to usurp her father's position in the family, and this is causing dysfunction. However, affect (sadness, anger) and behavior (avoidance of family, destructive patterns of communication) also need to be addressed. Such techniques as cognitive restructuring, practicing improved communicating skills, monitoring mood levels, and planning activities would be used in individual counseling. Family counseling will follow a communications approach such as that of Virginia Satir, helping Amber's parents to allow a more gradual development of the stepfather–stepdaughter relationship, helping Amber to reestablish her close tie to her mother and understand her mother's decision to remarry.

Emphasis: Counseling will initially be supportive and accepting but will rapidly encourage Amber to deal with her grief and build on her own coping skills.

Numbers: Individual counseling will be combined with family counseling with the whole family as well as with Amber and her mother, Amber and her stepfather, and Amber and both parents.

Timing: Weekly 50-minute counseling sessions will be scheduled for approximately three to four months.

Medication: A referral for medication is not indicated.

Adjunct services: Involvement in a rewarding and ongoing peer activity will be encouraged. Tutoring might be needed in any school subjects in which Amber has fallen behind.

Prognosis: The prognosis is excellent, in light of the diagnosis and Amber's previously high level of functioning as well as her family support.

The Future of Counseling and Diagnosis

Diagnosis has become an essential skill of the counselor. According to the American Counseling Association's "Code of Ethics and Standards of Practice" (1995, p. 36), "Counselors take special care to provide proper diagnosis of mental disorders." As of 1990, nearly 80 percent of students in counseling were taught to make diagnoses (Ritchie, Piazza, & Lewton, 1991).

The 1990s has witnessed the growth of private practice and managed care, increasing emphasis on accountability for counselors, the expansion of the counselor's role to include both relatively well-functioning people and those with severe mental disorders, and the growth of most master's degree programs in counseling to forty-eight or more credits. All these trends indicate that more and more counselors will be taught to make accurate diagnoses and to formulate effective treatment plans and that these skills will be essential to successful counseling.

Summary

This chapter has reviewed the important benefits that knowledge of diagnosis and the DSM can bring to counselors. It also cites some possible pitfalls of the diagnostic process that counselors should try to avoid. An overview was presented of the process of multiaxial assessment according to the 4th edition of the *Diagnostic and Statistical Manual of Mental Disorders* (American Psychiatric Association, 1994a). The seventeen categories of mental disorder and conditions were discussed.

Diagnosis is one piece of a three-step process that facilitates effective counseling. An intake interview and review of any records precedes the diagnosis and yields the information that is needed for a diagnosis. A treatment plan then can be developed, based on the diagnosis or multiaxial assessment and reflecting knowledge of the appropriate use of approaches to counseling. The DO A CLIENT MAP format is a helpful method of treatment planning.

References

American Counseling Association. (1995, June). Code of ethics and standards of practice. *Counseling Today*, 33–40.

American Psychiatric Association. (1994a). *Diagnostic and statistical manual of mental disorders* (4th ed.) (DSM-IV). Washington, DC: Author.

American Psychiatric Association. (1994b). *DSM-IV sourcebook*. Washington, DC: Author.

Fauman, M. A. (1994). *Study guide to DSM-IV*. Washington, DC: American Psychiatric Association.

Hershenson, D. B., Power, P. W., & Seligman, L. (1989). Mental health counseling theory: Present status and future prospects. *Journal of Mental Health Counseling, 11*(1), 44–69.

Hinkle, J. S. (1994). The *DSM-IV*: Prognosis and implications for mental health counselors. *Journal of Mental Health Counseling, 16*(2), 174–183.

Hohenshil, T. H. (1993). Teaching the *DSM-III-R* in counselor education. *Counselor Education and Supervision, 32*(4), 267–275.

Maxmen, J. S., & Ward, N. G. (1995). *Essential psychopathology and its treatment*. New York: Norton.

Millon, T. (1995). *Disorders of personality*. New York: Wiley.

Morrison, J. (1995). *DSM-IV made easy*. New York: Guilford Press.

Ritchie, M. H., Piazza, N. J., & Lewton, J. C. (1991). Current use of the *DSM-III-R* in counselor education. *Counselor Education and Supervision, 30*(3), 205–211.

Seligman, L. (1990). *Selecting effective treatments*. San Francisco: Jossey-Bass.

Seligman, L. (1995). *DSM-IV: Diagnosis and treatment planning home stu dy*. Alexandria, VA: American Counseling Association.

Seligman, L. (1996). *Diagnosis and treatment planning in counseling* (2nd ed.). New York: Plenum Press.

Spitzer, R. L., Gibbon, M., Skodol, A. E., Williams, J. B. W., & First, M. B. (1994). *DSM-IV casebook*. Washington, DC: American Psychiatric Association.

World Health Organization. (1992). *ICD-10 classification of mental and behavioural disorders*. Geneva: Author.

Chapter 12

Special Approaches to Counseling

Ann Vernon, Ph.D.

Effective counseling establishes a therapeutic relationship to help clients think, feel, and behave in more self-enhancing ways. As Caple (1985) noted, "Clients come to counseling seeking a different potentiality, a way to find something better than they presently know" (p. 173). In effect, the counselor makes a commitment to help clients become more aware, to conceptualize their experiences differently, and to see themselves and their ways of being more constructively. According to Hutchins and Cole (1986), in this process the client actively helps resolve specific personal issues. This implies that the counselor won't "fix it" so that the client will feel and act better, but rather that a mutual "working together" process can help the client overcome the dysfunctional aspects that interfere with her or his life.

Counseling has basically been a mental arena, characterized by a predominately verbal orientation, according to Nickerson and O'Laughlin (1982). In their opinion, this verbal orientation is very limiting. These authors advocate action therapies that use nonverbal relationship modes as an alternative to the traditional verbal approaches. They stress the importance of developing "a more relevant and effective means of helping people cope with psychological problems and life stresses" (p. 5). Allan and Clark (1984) concurred with this viewpoint, stating that verbal techniques alone are not sufficient for reluctant or nonverbal clients. Gladding (1995) echoed Allan and Clark's position, noting that if counselors are too rigid and mechanical in applying theory and techniques, they will encounter resistance.

For many clients who seem relatively unaffected by the counseling process, standard techniques alone are inadequate (Lawson, 1987). These clients may benefit more from approaches that combine theory and practice in more flexible, creative ways, while at the same time focusing on the unique as well as universal qualities of clients (Gladding, 1995).

In the 1980s, information about counseling for individual learning styles began to appear in the literature and seems to support Nickerson and O'Laughlin's (1982) contention that verbal approaches to counseling are often ineffective (Griggs, 1983, 1985; Griggs, Price, Kopel, & Swaine, 1984). The term *learning style* refers to the way a person perceives and responds to the learning environment. Griggs (1983) cited the following learning style elements: environmental stimuli such as light, sound, and temperature; emotional stimuli such as structure, persistence, motivation, and responsibility; sociologic stimuli such as peers, adults, self, and group; physical stimuli such as auditory, visual, tactual, kinesthetic, and time of day; and psychological stimuli such as cerebral dominance and global, analytic, impulsive, and reflective stimuli.

The learning style approach assumes that individuals have unique learning patterns that should be accommodated in the counseling process. If this is not done, the client may resist (Griggs, 1985). Griggs identified counseling techniques in addition to verbal interaction that are compatible with different learning styles: art therapy, imagery, bibliotherapy, psychodrama, and mime. Nickerson and O'Laughlin (1982) cited all of these as effective, action-oriented, creative therapies. Gladding (1992) identified the visual arts, writing, music, play, and literature as creative approaches that can be adapted to fit a variety of client needs and populations.

This chapter describes a variety of creative, specialized counseling approaches that may be used either as a complement to a predominately verbal orientation with a client, or as the primary therapeutic method. These approaches may be used with clients of all ages and in a variety of settings such as schools, hospitals, or mental health centers. As Nickerson and O'Laughlin (1982) noted, these therapies are relevant for nonverbal clients, and for anyone who "needs to explore and to integrate their behavior in a comprehensive and effective fashion" (p. 7). Gladding (1995) agreed with Nickerson and O'Laughlin, noting that creative approaches help clients as well as counselors see things from a different, more positive, perspective. According to Gladding, "Clients from all backgrounds can benefit from using a creativity approach regardless of whether the form is fixed, such as with some creative exercises, or spontaneous" (p. 4).

Art

In the past two decades, the use of art therapy appears to be increasing, particularly in work with children (Allan & Clark, 1984; Allan & Crandall, 1986; Dufrene, 1994; Pinholster, 1983). Vondracek and Corneal (1995) defined art therapy as "the use of art in a therapeutic setting to foster an individual's psychological growth and well-being" (p. 294). These authors referred to art within the therapeutic context as a means of bringing subconscious material into awareness, which in turn leads to perception and interpretation. Howe, Burgess, and McCormack (1987) stated that "Expressing one's thoughts through art is one way to externalize a distressing event and to prepare for healing and recovery" (p. 35). Riley (1987) emphasized that art is especially effective with children because it is usually perceived as nonthreatening.

Although the majority of research on art therapy has focused on making the unconscious material explicit, art therapy can also be used to increase understanding of conscious material. For example, a client can be encouraged to express his or her anger resulting from a loss in a drawing, and the client and therapist can discuss what the drawing symbolizes and the feelings it evoked.

Rubin (1988) noted that "art, like talk, is simply a way of getting to know each other, another mode of communication" (p. 181). Cited as being particularly effective with reluctant, nonverbal clients, Allan and Clark (1984) stated that painting and drawing can facilitate growth and change as the counselor helps the client focus on symbolic areas of pain and growth in an accepting, understanding manner. Eydenberg (1986) indicated that art provides an emotional outlet for people who have difficulty communicating their needs, feelings, and desires and is an effective way to help them begin to understand their confusion.

According to Vondracek and Corneal (1995), counselors use art therapy with children, adolescents, adults, and the elderly. It is used in a variety of settings, such as schools, prisons, rehabilitation centers, hospitals, and clinics. Art therapy is now not only being used to work with people who have problems, but also it is more prevalent in helping "normal" clients, where the emphasis is on growth and self-development (Wadeson, 1982).

The Process

Many art forms can be used to help clients gain self-awareness and work through emotional conflicts: painting, sculpting, modeling with clay, photography, drawing, printing/designing, or graphic art. Gladding (1992) identified using already existing artwork as a means of introducing images that facilitate communication and understanding. In addition, Gladding (1992) discussed the use of body outlines and serial drawing as visual art forms that can be used with clients to help uncover troublesome issues.

According to Kenny (1987), the goal is communication between the helper and the client rather than mastery of art form or content. In the process, the client is encouraged to express feelings symbolically through an art form. As Allan (1982) noted, the counselor's role is basically that of a listener who responds to the client and allows him or her time and space to initiate interaction. After a given interval, the counselor might invite the client to share by issuing a simple invitation such as "Would you like to tell me what's happening in your picture?" If working with a more seriously disturbed client with whom art media is used in each session, Allan indicated that the counselor's role may change. After several sessions, the counselor might become more active by relating the art to what is occurring in real life as well as emphasizing positive aspects that indicate growth.

Art media is an effective means of initiating contact with a client, as illustrated in the following example. Amanda, a third-grader, was referred by her teacher because she seemed preoccupied and unhappy. In the initial meeting, the counselor noted that Amanda seemed quite anxious and hesitant. To establish rapport and facilitate expression, the counselor put some modeling clay on the table and invited Amanda to play with it. At first Amanda just rolled the clay around without molding it. The counselor made no comment, but simply communicated an attitude of acceptance. Presently Amanda began to shape the clay into a bridge. Next she made a car and attached small clay dots to the car. As she placed the car on the bridge, the bridge collapsed. At this point the counselor asked Amanda if she would like to tell her about what was happening. Amanda explained that the dots were people—her family. The counselor reflected that something must have happened to the family in the car, and Amanda began to talk about how her family had had an accident because her Dad and Mom were drunk. She shared her feelings of fright and how she took care of her brothers and sister after the accident. As she talked, she began to roll the clay and pound it, tears streaming down her cheeks. As the counselor supported her, it became apparent that the feelings Amanda needed to express would be more readily verbalized in future sessions as the counselor began to help Amanda deal with her painful situation.

Art media can be used in the manner previously illustrated, or in a more directed manner to facilitate a process. For example, clients could be instructed to draw their family, paint their life story or their dreams, or illustrate a book that describes a situation with which they are dealing. They could be asked to sketch and color themselves in moods that they experienced recently, or be invited to draw a picture representing something that they need in their life. Designing a T-shirt, a banner, or a bumper sticker with a motto they feel describes them are good ways to encourage personal growth and sharing, particularly with resistant adolescent clients.

Photography can also be used effectively to elicit feelings and create awareness. Amerikaner, Schauble, and Ziller (1982) outlined a method of using twelve client-created photographs describing how the client sees self to stimulate self-awareness. Gladding (1992) described using old photographs to help the elderly participate in a life review process. Photographs can also help clients assess what is blocking their personal effectiveness, as in the case of Tim.

Tim, a 35-year-old male, referred himself for counseling because he felt overwhelmed at work and under extreme stress. In the initial session, Tim described feeling overwhelmed by his obligations and commitments at work, home, and in the community. In the next session, the counselor handed Tim a Polaroid camera and asked him to take pictures of things, people, and places that were important to him and that he, perhaps at one time, had enjoyed. She also asked him to take pictures of things, places, or people that he thought were contributing to the stress and the feeling of being overwhelmed. He was instructed to put these pictures into two separate envelopes—one for the things that were important to him, and the other for the factors that he thought were contributing to the stress.

The following week, Tim returned with his pictures, which served as a springboard for a discussion about the events in his life that were taking precedence over the things that were important to him, and about his feelings of "have to" versus "want to." Tim was asked to go through his envelope of pictures that created stress and select some that he could eliminate from his life. By actually being able to "see" what his stressors were, Tim found it easier to identify what he could more readily eliminate. Then he and the counselor worked on strategies for dealing with the other sources of stress.

Implementation Considerations

In employing art, Rubin (1988) cautioned that experience and skill are necessary if working at a sophisticated level, but that specific training in art is not essential with simple expressive work and minimal interpretation.

Rubin (1988) also noted that therapeutic work through art may be one way for clients to feel in charge when other parts of their life are overwhelming. As a trusting relationship is established, the counselor invites the client to share the meaning from his or her perspective. In essence, the counselor observes the client's work as it develops, attends to the nonverbal and verbal communication offered, and responds to clarify.

Kenny (1987) and Protinsky (1978) identified the following factors that may help the counselor understand clients' artwork by considering the larger context of their world:

1. In Western culture, dark colors or heavy shading generally indicate sadness, depression, or anger; excessive use of white may indicate emotional rigidity.
2. Small figures, particularly of self, may indicate insecurity, anxiety, or low self-esteem.
3. Sadness, violence, aggression, or other emotional disturbance are often represented with dark images, storms, accidents, fighting, or murder.
4. Texture of materials can provide insight: aggressive, angry clients might select bold or tough materials, whereas a nonassertive client might choose watercolors or something softer.
5. Clients with emotional disturbances tend to depict figures more grotesquely, stiff and rigid, or unintegrated, with some body parts being exaggerated. Excessive shading may indicate high anxiety.

The basic function of art therapy is to facilitate emotional expression from clients who do not communicate well verbally and to execute the counseling process more effectively through visual representation. Art therapy can be used to put the client at ease during an initial session, can be used strategically in later sessions to help the client clarify and gain awareness, or can be used over a period of several sessions as the main vehicle to work through painful issues. As Kenny (1987) noted, "Although art itself does not resolve conflict or eliminate sources of anxiety, it does provide space in which awareness, acceptance, and growth can occur" (p. 33). Gladding (1992) emphasized that art helps awaken clients to "a new sense of self and deeper understanding of their intra- and interpersonal relationships" (p. 66).

Approaches to Art Therapy (Rubin, 1987), *The Art of Art Therapy* (Rubin, 1984), and *Windows to Our Children* (Oaklander, 1978) are excellent resources for the professional interested in learning more about using art in a counseling relationship.

Imagery

The use of imagery, which Gladding (1992) described as visualization or seeing with the mind's eye, has increased in recent years, especially in career counseling, life planning, and personal counseling—see Skouolt, Morgan, and Negron-Cunningham (1989). According to Skouolt et al. imagery "allows the client and counselor to bring into awareness unconscious material that is already influencing choices . . . and allows the client to try on alternative roles" (p. 287). Witmer and Young (1987) noted that imagery facilitates awareness of personal values, emotions, goals, conflicts, and spiritual desires. Gladding (1992) emphasized that imagery is a "universal and natural modality for helping people engender change" (p. 42).

There is good rationale for using imagery in counseling. First of all, many clients already use imagery to help them learn new material or remember things (Gladding, 1992). Secondly, imagery can help people change behavior. Siegel (1986) noted that because the body cannot distinguish between a vivid mental experience and an actual physical experience, clients who use imagery may actually perform better. The use of imagery also teaches clients how to stimulate creativity and develop cognitive flexibility. In addition, because many client problems are connected to images of self and others, using imagery to change perspectives is helpful. Finally, imagery promotes a holistic approach (Gladding, 1992).

Although free daydreams are often cited as one form of imagery, this section describes the use of guided imagery and concrete images to help a client reconceptualize events and change behavior.

Guided Imagery

Guided imagery is a structured, directed activity designed to increase artistic expression, personal awareness, and concentration (Myrick & Myrick, 1993). In guided imagery, the counselor orchestrates a scenario for the client that consists of stimulus words or sounds to serve as a catalyst for creating a mental picture (Myrick & Myrick, 1993). Sometimes called *guided fantasy,* the process involves inducing relaxation, the actual fantasy, and processing the fantasy (Skouolt et al., 1989). The use of relaxation is important because it helps bridge the gap between prior activities and the imagery experience to move the client's focus from external to internal.

Myrick and Myrick (1993) identified the following guidelines when using guided imagery:

1. Create a scripted story. This is particularly helpful because it allows the counselor to select words that connote vivid textures and other senses.
2. Introduce the concept of guided imagery, and instruct the client to sit or lie in a relaxed position, focusing on breathing.
3. Read the script slowly, using a quiet and soothing voice to help create vivid images.
4. Bring closure to the experience by stopping at a pleasant place accompanied by positive feelings. Inform the client that you are getting ready to stop, and as you count to three slowly, have the client open her or his eyes and stretch.
5. Invite the client to discuss the experience, focusing on positive aspects of the activity as well as his or her experiences with obstacles and how he or she overcame them.

The following script was used with a middle-aged woman who suffered from anxiety and procrastinated about completing housework and other chores. After being instructed to relax, Jana was invited to involve herself in this imagery experience.

Setting: Imagine that it is next Monday. *(pause).* You are waking up in the morning. What time is it? *(pause)* You get up and eat breakfast. Who is there? *(pause)* You finish breakfast. You don't have to leave for work until noon. What needs to be done? What do you do first? *(pause)* How do you see yourself doing this task, and how long does it take? Is anyone helping you? If not, how are you feeling about that? *(pause)* You finish this activity. What do you do now? *(pause)* It is now time to get ready to leave for work. *(pause)*

Work: You are now at work. Are you working alone, or are you interacting with others? What tasks are you doing? Are you enjoying them? *(pause)*

Home: You have left work and are home again. Are you alone? *(pause)* If not, who is there? Do you interact with them? *(pause)* It is time to get dinner. Do you do this alone, or does anyone help you? *(pause)* Now it is after dinner. What do you do? Who is with you? *(pause)* Now it is time for bed. Tomorrow you will not work and will be at home all day. What will you do? *(pause)*

End: You may open your eyes, and we will discuss your experience.

In processing the imagery exercise, Jana said that it was not difficult to see what needed to be done, but it was hard to visualize what she would do first. Once she did select a task, it wasn't too difficult to see herself taking the necessary steps to complete it. She saw herself alone in doing the housework and resented that. She described the work portion of her day, where she had no trouble completing necessary tasks, as basically enjoyable.

In reflecting on the exercise, it seemed helpful for Jana to list the chores that needed to be done each day so she wouldn't become anxious about deciding what to do. It was also appropriate to begin teaching her some assertiveness skills so that she could negotiate for equity with the housework. The guided imagery effectively helped the counselor and client clarify issues and pinpoint target areas for goal setting and skill development.

Guided imagery has also been used successfully in career counseling where clients are asked to image "A Day in the Future"; "The Opposite Sex," growing up as the opposite sex and holding a job usually held by the opposite sex; or "Mid-Career Change or Retirement," focusing on shifting from the present career focus (Skouolt et al., 1989). Myrick and Myrick (1993) also emphasized the importance of this approach in helping children increase school success and improve working relationships in school.

Use of Concrete Images

Images can also be used therapeutically in isolation to help stimulate thinking that can lead to more productive behavior. When using images this way, the counselor tries to relate the image to something familiar to the client or something that conveys a type of metaphor, as in the following example.

Eighteen-year-old Nat was in counseling for depression. Irrational beliefs in the form of exaggerations, overgeneralizations, and awfulizations contributed to his depression. In the session when the image was introduced, Nat was discussing an incident with his girlfriend. He assumed that because she didn't call him every day, she didn't care about him. He said he couldn't stand it if she found someone else.

In previous sessions, the counselor had helped Nat dispute these irrational beliefs, but they continued to be quite prevalent. As Nat and the counselor were working on these irrational beliefs in the present session, the counselor glanced out the window and noticed a bug zapper. She called it to Nat's attention and asked him to watch the zapper and describe how it operated. The counselor explained to Nat that he could image that his head was a zapper, too—when he started to think irrationally, he should visualize these irrational thoughts being deflected, just like the bugs were when they hit the zapper. Although this may seem simplistic, it helped Nat stop the irrational thinking more effectively because he could quickly recall the bug zapper image and use this to trigger his disputations before he felt the negative effects of the irrational beliefs.

In listening carefully to the client's problem, it is not difficult to think of helpful images. Children who have difficulty controlling impulsive behavior might be asked, when they start to feel out of control, to visualize a stop sign. Pairing the visualization with self-statements such as "I don't have to hit—I can walk away" increases the effectiveness of the image. A child who is reluctant to go to bed because she or he is afraid of monsters can visualize herself or himself in a scary Halloween costume, frightening away any monsters that might come into the room.

Thorne (1985) pointed out these benefits of imagery: it can be performed anywhere, it is nonthreatening and safe, and it strengthens problem-solving abilities, encourages creative thinking, helps in integrating internal and external data, and helps clients learn about themselves. Although imagery might not work for everyone, for many clients it is an extremely effective method to access information and resolve problems.

Hypnotherapy

In hypnotherapy, hypnosis is used in conjunction with various forms of psychotherapy (Vondracek & Corneal, 1995). Wright and Wright (1987) stressed that in everyday life, everyone has experiences that resemble hypnosis. They asserted that hypnosis is an effective way to help clients become more aware of their inner experiences, to reexperience past events, and to envision new possibilities.

Winsor (1993) cited three styles of hypnosis: *directive,* which is based on simple commands; *Ericksonian,* which relies on indirect methods such as stories, confusion techniques, and metaphors; and *permissive,* in which the client and hypnotherapist contract to help the client gain access to an altered state of consciousness.

Hypnosis is generally induced as part of therapy, or in conjunction with pain reduction. In either case, Wright and Wright (1987) outlined some general conditions that assist in effective implementation of hypnosis, including having a reasonable degree of trust in the therapist as well as experiencing a reduction of sensory input and fixation of attention that increases awareness of one's inner life. Implicit in these conditions is that the client experience a general state of relaxation that promotes induction.

Because hypnosis is used in conjunction with therapy, the specific procedures used in hypnotherapy depend on the theoretical framework of the therapist. Hypnotherapy is often used in conjunction with behavior therapy, eclectic therapy, and supportive therapies (Weitzenhoffer, 1989), as well as psychoanalysis (Vondracek & Corneal, 1995).

Procedures generally employed in hypnotherapy include posthypnotic suggestions, affect enhancement, time reorientation, and symptom substitution (Brown & Fromm, 1986). Posthypnotic suggestions usually address something the client has been wanting, such as to stop binging and purging. The therapist delivers the suggestion, assuming that it will be long lasting and have a powerful impact on the client's behavior. Affect enhancement is used with emotionally constricted clients who want to be more aware of their affective experiences. The therapist makes statements to help the client recognize and describe feelings; for example, "You will now become aware of a feeling . . . you will be able to recognize it and describe it to me. . . ."

In time reorientation, the client may be regressed to an earlier period of time in her or his life to gain new perspectives about early events, or may participate in time distortion, where the client imagines a rapid series of scenes in order to discover new ways of coping (Wright & Wright, 1987). Symptom substitution is used to help clients give up a debilitating symptom and substitute a less serious symptom. For example, the therapist may suggest to a hypnotized client who has been practicing self-mutilation by cutting her arms with glass, that she instead scratch her arms with her nails.

Critics have raised questions about the use of posthypnotic suggestions and other hypnotic practices because they represent undue influence over the client's behavior or encourage antisocial behavior. Weitzenhoffer (1989) noted that under hypnosis, a client's defenses may be reduced before he or she is ready to deal with the repressed material. This author stressed the importance of proper training for practitioners who use hypnotherapy. When used appropriately, hypnotherapy has been used successfully with weight control, phobias, sexual dysfunction, and smoking cessation (Fromm, 1987). Winsor (1993) stated that hypnosis has regained scientific credibility in the past fifty years and is used to treat a growing number of medical as well as psychological problems.

Music

Music, which has played an important role in healing and nurturing, is another effective counseling approach to use with a variety of populations (Maas, 1982; Michel, 1985; Newcomb, 1994). Gladding (1992) described music as a "therapeutic ally to the verbal approaches to counseling" (p. 14) and noted that music is a creative experience that can be used to initiate other counseling processes. Because most clients enjoy singing, dancing, or listening to music, this can be an ideal approach for clients who have difficulty expressing themselves verbally (Newcomb, 1994).

Music has been used to increase self-esteem and assertiveness, as well as to develop interpersonal relationship skills and a sense of purpose (Maas, 1982). Music has also been used successfully with the mentally challenged, institutionalized elderly, emotionally disturbed, and sensory impaired clients (Maas, 1982) and with depressed clients in a hospital setting (Wadeson, 1982). Maranto (1993) recommended using music with the elderly and in treating stress disorders. Michel (1985) stressed the importance of music therapy in treating individuals with behavioral or psychological disorders, delinquent behavior, or drug addiction. Gladding (1992) discussed the effectiveness of music with children, adolescents, families and couples, and clients with chronic illnesses.

Music is a catalyst for self-expression and can result in a number of therapeutic changes, including heightened attention and concentration; stimulation and expression of feelings; and insight into one's thinking, feeling, and behavior (Thaut, 1990). Bowman (1987) noted that music is a versatile tool that can reduce anxiety, elicit memories, communicate feelings, develop rapport, and intensify or create moods. Music is energizing and also has a calming effect.

Although music can be used as the primary method of treatment, it can also be incorporated into the therapy experience to facilitate the process more effectively. Or music may be used to introduce or convey messages in classroom guidance sessions and to clarify issues as a "homework" assignment. Song lyrics or CDs are perhaps the most accessible form of music, but for improvisation purposes, a guitar, drum, shakers, xylophone, or keyboard are useful.

Applications

Music can effectively establish rapport, particularly with teenagers, who are often not self-referred. Having the radio softly tuned into a popular rock station when the client walks into the office can help facilitate communication and relaxation. Generally, it is best left to the client to initiate conversation about the music, but if she or he doesn't, the counselor might comment on the song, inquire whether or not the client likes to listen to music, and then ease into the traditional get-acquainted phase of the session. After a first session, one teenager commented to me that he was surprised to hear the music and that it didn't make it seem like he was "going to a shrink." This helped establish trust by communicating to the client that the counselor had some understanding of where he was coming from.

To help clients get more in touch with what they are thinking and feeling, music can be a useful homework assignment. The client is invited to bring in CDs or record songs that illustrate how she or he is thinking or feeling that week. Clients can also find songs that express who they are, their conflicts, or their hopes. This is effective especially for teenagers, since music is such an important part of their life experience.

This approach was used with 14-year-old Annette, a depressed, nonverbal client who asked to see a counselor because of home conflicts. Despite the fact that she had initiated the counseling, it was difficult for Annette to express what was happening at home and why she was so upset. Annette was very willing to do the music assignment and came back the following week with several tapes. The counselor invited her to play the tapes, briefly reflected on what she thought was expressed through the music, and then encouraged Annette to share how the songs related to her experiences. Annette opened up some, which facilitated verbal exchange about the problems.

After several sessions of discussing and working through some of her difficulties, Annette was again asked to bring in songs that told more about her current feelings. This time the songs were less conflictual and more hopeful. The use of music homework had helped the counselor understand Annette's pain and confusion so they could begin dealing with it. The music also provided a useful way to determine therapy progress.

Newcomb (1994) described using songwriting to promote increased self-awareness and facilitate emotional release. She also noted that song lyrics can be used to teach children about positive interpersonal relationships and suggested pairing children up and having them draw to music as a way to increase communication and cooperation.

Songs can also be used with children in classroom guidance lessons (Bowman, 1987). Depending on the particular theme of the lesson, the songs selected could be hard rock lyrics that communicate useful messages, or songs from albums that contain guidance-oriented material, such as *Free to Be . . . You and Me* by Marlo Thomas (1979) or *Imagination and Me* by Joe Wayman (1974). For example, with primary children the song "It's All Right to Cry" from the Marlo Thomas album can introduce a lesson on how everyone feels sad from time to time and that crying is a natural way to help deal with sad feelings. After playing the recording, children can be invited to sing the song. A discussion can follow about the main points in the song. Follow-up activities include making paper plate faces to portray feelings such as happy, sad, mad, or disappointed, and inviting children to describe situations in which they have felt these emotions.

Advantages

Because music is a popular medium and readily available, counselors are only limited by their creativity to specific applications. Music can easily be integrated into counseling sessions to help clients clarify issues, communicate problems, or monitor progress. It can also be used improvisationally to encourage risk taking, spontaneity, and creative expression. Clients might be invited to experiment with various musical instruments to create a piece of music that is meaningful to them. Putting words to the music adds yet another dimension. Improvisations can also be applied effectively in a group setting to encourage cooperation and cohesiveness.

If clients respond to the use of music, it provides a pleasurable way to connect with them to stimulate personal awareness and growth.

Writing

Writing offers a powerful way for clients to clarify feelings and events and gain a perspective on their problems. Brand (1987) noted that writing contributes to personal integration and provides a cathartic experience. For many clients, seeing something in writing has more impact than hearing it.

Writing as a therapeutic experience can take numerous forms, and the reader is encouraged to experiment with the variations later described to meet a client's needs most effectively. Obviously, for very young children writing must be more simplistic, or the counselor may choose to serve as the recorder. In addition, some clients don't find certain forms of writing helpful, and therefore it is important to gear the assignment to what the counselor deems will be most useful for achieving the therapeutic goals.

Therapeutic writing approaches range from structured to more open-ended. Examples of each are described in the following sections.

Autobiographies

Autobiographies are generally written one of two ways—describing a particular segment or aspect of one's life, or writing a chronicle that covers all of one's life history (Hutchins & Cole, 1986). How the autobiography is used depends on which approach most effectively assists the client to clarify concerns, express feelings, and work toward resolution. In either case, once the client provides the written material, the counselor helps the client clarify the issues by asking questions, probing for feelings, confronting discrepancies in the writing, identifying specific concerns, and setting goals for change.

In one case in which this approach was used, the counselor determined that because the client was struggling with a relationship with her spouse, it would help her to chronicle all past significant relationships and indicate how these relationships were established, what was meaningful about them, how they were terminated, and how the client felt. Having done this assignment, the client and counselor identified some patterns in the way that the client reacted to significant others.

In other instances, it might benefit the client to write a more detailed account of her or his life to see how perceptions and values change over time and to develop some perspective about the future.

Correspondence

We typically think of correspondence as appropriate when face-to-face contact isn't possible. However, correspondence can also help clarify concerns and expression in other ways. For example, clients can be encouraged to write letters to themselves to give themselves positive feedback about an accomplishment or some advice about how to handle a particular problem.

Clients may also find it useful to write a letter (probably unsent) to a person with whom they are in conflict to help them express thoughts and clarify issues. This approach was used with an elderly client who was angry with his sister. To help him diffuse the anger and develop some perspective about the problem, he first put his thoughts on paper and then discussed his feelings with the counselor. The counselor helped him identify the behaviors that upset him and speculate on alternative viewpoints. As a homework assignment, the client rewrote the letter. When he brought it in the following week, the concerns were more succinctly expressed and the anger was more focused. The counselor showed the client ways to express the anger more assertively and how to dispute overgeneralizations and exaggerated thinking.

In this example, the client sent his letter, and it did not affect the relationship negatively, as the first letter might have. Instead, the first letter served as a valuable catharsis and a tool for the counselor to help the client clarify the problem and develop skills to address it more effectively.

In other cases, clients may not use the counselor as an editor, but may simply write a letter as a way of dealing with feelings. After they have written the letter, they may keep it, give it to the person with whom they are in conflict, or tear it up. It is important for clients to realize that an unedited letter that generally contains a lot of anger may create more problems when received. On the other hand, such a letter can serve as a springboard for getting problems out in the open.

Journaling

Journaling is another form of expressive writing that some clients find useful. When unstructured journaling is used, the client is invited to write down thoughts and feelings about events each day. The journal can then be used as catharsis. During each session, the counselor can invite clients to share anything from the journal that they felt was significant, anything they would like help with, or items they want to talk more about. With clients who are not very verbal, the journal can illuminate issues to encourage discussion. Journaling allows for self-expression and the acceptance of feelings, relieves emotional pain, and allows clients to start dealing with emotions on a cognitive and objective manner (Mercer, 1993). By recording thoughts and feelings, both client and counselor are better able to understand the dimensions of the problem and monitor behavior.

Journaling can also be more structured, however; for example, the counselor can present the client with a list of suggestions to guide the writing. These suggestions may include identifying events that were pleasurable or upsetting, goals that were accomplished, people whom they did or did not enjoy being with, and feelings about each of these topics. Often clients initially need these guidelines but don't generally rely on the structure for long.

Structured Writing

Structured writing can be open-ended sentences, questionnaires, or writing in session. Hutchins and Cole (1986) cautioned that writing does not replace counselor–client interaction, but rather serves as a starting point for discussion as well as a way to help the client generate and synthesize data.

Open-ended Sentences

Open-ended sentences may be used to establish rapport to determine areas of concern to address during the counseling sessions. Children or adolescents, who are often more nonverbal, may readily respond to open-ended sentences. These can provide a valuable source of information and set the client at ease with a structure to which she or he can respond. With very young children, the counselor can serve as the recorder so the child doesn't have to labor over writing.

Open-ended sentences can be general starters such as these:

"I get upset when . . ."

"If I could change something about me, it would be . . ."

"I am happy when . . ."

"In my free time I like to . . ."

Or the starters may be geared more specifically to an area of concern the client previously expressed such as

"I wish my friends would . . ."

"Three things I consider important in a friend are . . ."

"I think friends should . . ."

Both of these strategies effectively collect information about thoughts and feelings that can be used as the counselor helps the client sort through concerns. In employing open-ended sentences, it is important to gear the starters to the client's age level. It is not necessary to have a long list of starters—the real purpose is to elicit information that can be used in the counseling session, not simply to collect data.

Questionnaires

Questionnaires generally elicit more information than open-ended sentences, but the counselor is cautioned not to overwhelm the client with excessive amounts of paper-and-pencil data collection. This approach can stimulate the client to reflect on aspects of her or his life, but is not intended to completely replace spoken exchanges between counselor and client.

Questionnaires can elicit information on specific events, activities, or feelings, such as

"What three major decisions have had the most impact on your life?"

"What aspects of your relationship with your parents have had the most impact on your life?"

"How do you feel about the relationship you had with your siblings as you were growing up?"

Writing in Session

For many clients, seeing things in print has more impact than hearing them. For this reason, clients might be encouraged to take notes during the counseling session and refer to these notes during the interim to work on aspects of the problem. In working with young children or clients who labor over writing, the counselor may opt to record key ideas that might be useful to the client.

Poetry

Woytowich (1994) noted that "writing can help relieve pressure and help us to 'get on with life'" (p. 78). This author described the effective use of poetry to help school-aged clients deal with depression and feeling suicidal. For clients who are unsure about writing poetry, Woytowich suggested asking specific questions about the event. As clients tell their story, the counselor writes down what is shared and gives it back to them in the form of verses.

Gladding (1995) discussed the idea of prescribing a specific poem related to a client's problem. Reading the poem helps the client understand she or he is not alone in experiencing this emotion. After reading the poem, the client is encouraged to do her or his own writing for further self-expression.

Poetry can be a form of catharsis and can also provide a liberating, therapeutic effect that increases understanding and contributes to more accurate self-perceptions (Bates, 1993). In addition, poetry enables clients to use words to reconstruct reality. Bates described poetry as "a way of seeing and ultimately, a way of knowing" (p. 155).

Poetry can be used by therapists to help prevent their own burnout and promote self-renewal (Gladding, 1987). It can also be used as a catalyst for growth and healing in hospitals, nursing homes, prisons, adult education centers, and chemical dependency units (Hynes, 1990).

The following poem was written by a 16-year-old girl. Allison presented herself to the public as having it "together." Although she was very reluctant to express her feelings and let anyone know how vulnerable she was, Allison accepted the invitation to write about her feelings through poetry, and this became the vehicle for discussing the dichotomy between the public and the private personas, as well as the hurt, anger, and confusion she was experiencing.

Why?

I didn't ask for much—
Only an answer.
Is that too much to ask for?
Why?
Why me?
Why am I the one who gets almost everyone I've cared for taken away or changed
*   so I don't know the same person any more?*
Why me?
What have I done to have my family and friends expect extraordinary things out
*   of me?*
Why me?
Why do all these people treat me with disregard and disrespect?
I know how our society is, yet they seem to be going beyond that in my case.
They all say, "You're strong—you'll pull through" if "you just believe in
*   yourself."*
Don't they realize that people can only take so much before they feel like taking
*   action?*
Sometimes I think ending it all would just be easier, but if I did that, they would
*   be winning.*
That is something I can't allow—my hatred of them and their belief that I am
*   worth nothing is what drives me.*
Just wait—I'll prove them all wrong.
Then they will be the ones to suffer.
When I succeed they'll try to kiss up to me, but I'll just tell them to go to hell.
That's all they deserve.
The way they think they're superior, you'd think they were some version of a
*   "superior race."*
Why are they considered to be important when their parents are apparently
*   influential—that doesn't make them better.*
I shouldn't hold grudges, but after how they've treated me, I can't do
*   anything but.*
If someone else was in my shoes—they'd see. They all think they know me—they
*   are wrong.*
They don't even have a clue.
Maybe some day if they get more mature they might understand.
Understand why I am forced to act the way I do.

As they say, "It's lonely at the top."
More lonely than they'll ever know.
Why me?

Bibliotherapy

The term *bibliotherapy* refers to a process designed to help individuals solve problems or better understand themselves through their response to literature or media (Pardeck, 1994). According to Pardeck (1994), the goals of bibliotherapy include (1) providing information and insight about problems, (2) communicating new values and attitudes, (3) creating an awareness of how others have dealt with similar problems, (4) stimulating discussion about problems, and (5) providing solutions.

Bibliotherapy has been used to increase academic and emotional development with children with serious emotional disturbances (Bauer & Balius, 1995, Pardeck & Pardeck, 1993), to enhance self-esteem in learning disabled children (Brooks, 1987), and to help clients cope with stress and change (Pardeck, 1994). Berger (1988) discussed using bibliotherapy as a way of helping clients work through grief, and Gold (1988) described ways in which bibliotherapy increased socialization and self-actualization.

According to Gladding (1992), bibliotherapy can be practiced with disturbed clients, with clients who have moderate emotional and behavioral problems, and with a normal population to enhance development. Borders and Paisley (1992) also discussed the developmental approach, stressing the importance of using bibliotherapy in classroom guidance sessions with children.

Bibliotherapy is especially effective for clients who process things visually as opposed to auditorily. The author recalls working with a couple experiencing relationship difficulties. She was attempting to stop the cycle of blame and increase this couple's understanding of their communication differences and ways of perceiving the world. Since verbal efforts had not been successful, she suggested they read a book as a homework assignment. When the couple arrived for the next session, they were eager to share their insights. The information they had learned provided them with new perspectives and information they needed to move to the next level of problem solving regarding their relationship issues.

In addition to literature in print, movies can be used as a bibliotherapy tool. This approach is particularly effective with adolescents who spend a great deal of time watching movies, but who may not pick up a book. Movies that depict events or emotions similar to those of the client can facilitate insight and emotional catharsis in addition to identification of coping strategies.

The Process

Gladding (1992) noted that in the bibliotherapy process, "a triadic connection" (p. 73) is fostered. This triad includes the piece of literature, the client, and the facilitator who helps the client process an insight and apply it to his or her own life.

Before using bibliotherapy, it is important to have a relationship built on trust and rapport. Also, the client and the counselor should agree on the presenting problem and complete some preliminary problem exploration (Pardeck & Pardeck, 1993).

In selecting books for treatment, it is important to consider the presenting problem. Also, the practitioner should select books that contain believable characters and situations that offer realistic hope. Reading level is also an important consideration.

Pardeck (1994) noted that it is often more effective to suggest rather than prescribe books. This author also emphasized that discussion, counseling, and follow-up activities are an essential part of the bibliotherapy process.

Play

"The natural medium of communication for children is play and activity" (Landreth, 1987, p. 253). Landreth (1993) noted that toys are the words children use to express emotions. Because children's experiences are often communicated through play, it becomes an important vehicle to help them know and accept themselves. Through play, children are able to act out confusing or conflicting situations. Play therapy is increasingly being used by school counselors, family therapists, and practitioners in private practice and agencies (Ariel, Carel, & Tyano, 1985; Campbell, 1993).

Play Therapy Approaches

Schaefer (1985) described three major approaches to play therapy: psychoanalytic, structured, and relationship. In the psychoanalytic approach, an interpretation of the child's action and words, as well as an analysis of the transference relationship, provides the child with insight into unconscious conflicts. A wide variety of toys is available for this play therapy, and the child is free to select toys as she or he wishes.

In the structured, more controlled approach, the counselor selects the appropriate toys that facilitate working on a particular problem. By structuring the play so that the child experiences the stressful situation, the counselor can reflect feelings to help release the emotional problem. If, for example, a child was having night terrors, the counselor might provide toy monsters who talked to each other during the play. This helps to release the fears. The counselor may also play with the child to elicit other emotions (Schaefer, 1985).

The relationship approach is nondirective and stresses the importance of the counselor–child relationship. The counselor creates an atmosphere where the child feels accepted and understood so that the child can experience inner conflicts and work toward resolution. The assumption is that the child has the ability to solve problems and grow once she or he experiences this accepting relationship. The therapist allows the child to move at a pace commensurate with her or his emotional and developmental abilities and remains sensitive to the child's feelings at all times. In this approach, the child is free to select toys from a wide variety of materials provided. The counselor actively observes and reflects the child's thoughts and feelings.

Uses of Play

Ginott (1982) noted that "the child's play is his talk and the toys are his words" (p. 145). Play can be used in several different ways to meet the developmental needs of all children. Amster (1982) identified the following uses of play:

1. *For diagnostic understanding.* The counselor notes the child's interactions, inhibitions, preoccupations, perceptions, and expressions of feelings and ideas.

2. *To establish a working relationship.* For children who may be fearful, nonverbal, or resistant, the use of play can help establish an accepting relationship, as in the case of Ryan.

Ryan, age 6, was referred for inability to relate effectively to others. In the initial interview he sat as far away from the counselor as possible and only shook his head in response to questions. Instead of continuing to talk, the counselor got out a can of shaving cream and squirted some onto a large tray. Then she started playing with it, shaping it into different forms. Ryan watched for a few minutes and then hesitantly approached the table and began to play. The counselor added more shaving cream and some food coloring. Ryan's eyes widened, and he began making pictures out of the cream and chatting about what he was creating. By initiating the play that stimulated Ryan to interact, the counselor was able to establish a working relationship.

3. *To facilitate verbalization.* Frequently children will not or are not able to verbalize feelings about events. Play can be used to facilitate verbalization as well as provide a means of dealing with the issue. In the following situation, the counselor used a dart game to elicit angry feelings.

Dan was a behaviorally disordered third-grader who was hostile and aggressive with other children and adults. After an angry confrontation with the principal, the teacher requested that the counselor work with Dan. Knowing that he would be defensive, the counselor set up a dart board equipped with rubber-tipped darts. When Dan entered the office, the counselor simply invited him to play darts. After several minutes of play, the counselor commented to Dan that he was really throwing the darts as if he were angry. Dan didn't comment, but simply continued to play. After a while he stopped and sat down. The counselor asked if there was anything he'd like to talk about, and he began to share situations in which other kids picked on him, he'd call them names and then got in trouble for name calling. After discussing this for a while, the counselor asked Dan if he'd like to come back again to talk more about his anger and what he could do about it. He agreed to come, but expressed a desire to play darts again. Using the dart board initiated verbalization and let Dan express his hostile, angry feelings.

4. *To teach new ways of playing and behaving in daily life.* Many children simply lack social skills or are anxious about their performance. Play is a good vehicle for teaching alternative behaviors.

For example, 6-year-old Amy was the youngest in her family. The teacher reported that several children had complained that every time Amy played a game, she had to win. If she wasn't winning, she changed the rules. The counselor invited Amy to play a board game, and when she tried to change the rules, the counselor commented on this. They discussed Amy's need to win and what it said about her if she didn't win. After several sessions of this nature, the counselor invited several of Amy's friends in to play. Amy played the game without changing the rules. This experience seemed to successfully teach her alternative behaviors to help her interact more appropriately.

5. *To help a child act out unconscious issues and relieve tension.* Play is used as a catharsis and a way to act out fear and anxiety.

Regardless of how play is used, the therapeutic relationship is extremely important. Showing interest in what the child chooses to do and being patient and understanding are crucial.

Selection of Materials

Landreth (1993) discussed the importance of selecting play materials that facilitate (1) exploration of real-life experiences, (2) expression of a wide range of feelings, (3) testing of limits, (4) expressive and exploratory play, (5) exploration and expression without verbalization, and (6) success without prescribed structure. This author warned against using mechanical or complex toys or materials that required the counselor's assistance to manipulate. In an earlier article, Landreth (1987) listed examples of toys to facilitate exploration of real-life experiences, including dolls, doll houses and furniture, play dishes, toy trucks, and cars. Crayons, clay, paints, puppets, Nerf balls, pipe cleaners, chalk, and newsprint were cited as examples of materials to facilitate creative expression. Dart guns, rubber knives, toy soldiers, and a pounding board or Bobo clown were identified as toys that allowed children to act out and test the limits.

Toys selected should be in good condition. It is also important not to have so many toys that the room is cluttered and junky. The specific use of the toys depends on whether the approach is structured, where the counselor selects the toys to fit the child's problem, or nondirective, in which the child has more freedom to choose materials.

Games

Board games provide another way to establish rapport, facilitate verbalization, release feelings, and teach new behaviors. For preadolescents and adolescents in particular, board games can make counseling more enjoyable and thus more productive.

Games such as checkers or chess generally work well in establishing rapport, as do other commercial board games. Once rapport has been established, the counselor may want to develop some games that specifically address the concerns with which the child is working. The case of Stephanie illustrates this point.

Stephanie, a fourth-grader, was frequently upset because she overgeneralized about what her peers were thinking and therefore assumed that they didn't like her, were upset with her, or didn't ever want to be her friend. To help her recognize how she upset herself by mistaking what she thought for factual information, the counselor and Stephanie played a game called "Facts and Beliefs" (Vernon, 1989). They took turns drawing statements, identifying whether they were facts or beliefs, and putting an F or B on the game board. Examples of statements included "Girls are smarter than boys," "Kickball is a game," and "Kids who go to this school are wonderful."

After the game was completed, the counselor asked Stephanie to identify the difference between a fact and a belief, and then had her make up some of her own fact and belief cards based on her encounters with friends. They were able to discuss Stephanie's tendency to mistake a fact ("My friend didn't sit by me in the lunchroom") from a belief ("Because she didn't sit by me, there must be something wrong with me and she must not like me anymore"). The game was a concrete way of helping this fourth-grader work through her problem.

The actual process of play therapy is complex and needs more explanation than this brief overview. The value of play therapy is undisputed, and the reader is encouraged to read *Play Therapy: The Art of the Relationship* (Landreth, 1991), *The Play Therapy Primer* (O'Connor, 1991), or the *Handbook of Play Therapy* (Schaefer & O'Conner, 1983).

More Creative Approaches

The number of creative approaches used in a counseling session is endless. The only limiting factors are the counselor's own creative abilities to develop effective methods of helping the client resolve issues. I have found the following approaches helpful in the process of working with clients.

Props

Using props during a session can stimulate thinking or elicit emotion about a problem. Props are a way, other than words, to reach the client. For example, a woman who was constantly pessimistic was given a set of old eyeglasses and four round circles of paper—two black and two pink. She was instructed to tape the black paper on the glasses and talk about her day from a "doom and gloom" perspective. Next she was asked to substitute the pink paper and describe her day as if she were looking through "rose-colored glasses." She and the counselor then discussed the difference in the two perspectives and set some goals for developing a more optimistic perception of events.

In working with a 5-year-old on her anxieties about entering first grade, the counselor brought in a shoe box and some construction paper. Together they decorated it and labeled it the "worry box." Next the counselor served as a recorder and wrote down each of Leslie's concerns about first grade on a separate card. After Leslie identified all of her concerns—and all of them had to do with school—the counselor suggested that the worries could stay in the box since school didn't start for two months. She suggested they put the box on a shelf in the closet and concentrate instead on ways to be happy during the summer. Leslie liked this idea. When school was ready to start in the fall, she had forgotten all about the problems.

With another young client, using a tape recorder helped him become less dependent on the counselor and more skilled at solving his own problems. Adam had lots of worries, such as what he should do if someone teased him, what he should do if his mother wasn't home after school, and what he should do if he didn't understand how to do his schoolwork.

Because Adam's father was concerned that Adam might be "inventing" some problems because he really liked coming to counseling, the counselor decided to teach Adam how to be his own counselor. When he arrived for his session, she asked Adam what was bothering him that week. He shared a situation about his friend teasing him, and the counselor helped Adam develop some tease tolerance techniques. Adam was to ask himself if he was what his friend said he was, if names could hurt him, and how he could handle the situation if he couldn't control what came out of the other person's mouth. Next the counselor said that she would pretend to be Adam and that Adam could be the counselor. As the counselor, Adam was asked to help solve a problem similar to his real one. After role-playing this, Adam was given a tape recorder and a blank tape. During the week, whenever he had a problem, he could use the tape recorder and first be the person who has the problem and then switch roles and pretend to be the counselor who helps him solve the problem.

When Adam returned for his next session, he played the tape for the counselor. He had recorded several problems and had done a good job of helping himself deal with his problems.

Props were useful in a marriage counseling session when a rope helped a couple see the "tug of war" state of their marriage and to understand how they each felt controlled. Each person held one end of the rope, pulled on it, and verbalized one of the ways she or he felt controlled by the partner. The counselor wrote down each of the statements so the couple could also see what each other said. This simple activity was a good stimulus for mobilizing some energy and illuminating some of the issues that needed to be solved.

Homework Suggestions

To facilitate self-reliance, homework assignments can effectively extend the concepts dealt with during the counseling session. The following ideas can be adapted and expanded on, depending on the clients' age:

1. Have clients make a "mad pillow," which they decorate with pictures of things or people with whom they feel angry. When they experience anger, they can pound the pillow rather than act aggressively toward another person.
2. Suggest that when clients worry excessively about minor, as opposed to major problems, they can buy a bubble pipe. As they use it, they can visualize the minor problems "blowing away."
3. Have people who are dealing with a lot of anger write down on separate pieces of paper situations in which they have been angry. They should then collect as many rocks as they have slips of paper and go to a river or open field. As they throw the rock away with force, they can yell out the name of the anger-provoking situation.
4. If clients have difficulty accomplishing tasks because they're overwhelmed with the amount of work to be done, invite them to buy a timer, set it for a given amount of time to work and a given amount of time to relax.
5. Recommend that clients make books of written text and/or illustrations to express their perceptions about a problem and their methods of solving it.

Group Applications

The specialized individual counseling approaches previously described can usually be applied in a group context. Each of the approaches is discussed with a brief explanation of group applicability.

Art

To facilitate group cohesiveness, participants can make a collage to represent their group, using finger paint and scraps from fabric and paper. In a self-awareness group, members could tear a shape out of construction paper that tells something about themselves as a way to introduce themselves to the group. To teach cooperation, group participants could be given paper, tape, and magazines and instructions to design an object of beauty. Roles that members play in developing this project could then be discussed. In a group setting, members might take turns drawing symbols that they feel represent other group members as a way to provide feedback on how they come across to others.

Imagery

Guided imagery can be readily applied to a group setting. In a classroom or small group, students could be led in a guided imagery relative to test taking, task completion, stress management, or cooperative behavior with classmates.

Guided imagery has also been used extensively in career development (Skouolt et al., 1989). Sarnoff and Remer's (1982) use of guided imagery in a group setting effectively helped participants generate career alternatives.

Music

Musical activities facilitate self-awareness and interpersonal relationships. In a classroom setting, students can compose and perform their own compositions related to guidance topics: feelings, self-concept, decision making, friendship, or values. Newcomb (1994) noted that music can be used in classroom guidance as an energizer, to set the mood, to develop group cohesiveness, or as a way of emphasizing the theme of a lesson.

Bowman (1987) described the "feelings ensemble." A group is divided into smaller groups of five or six, and each group is given a feeling word that becomes the title of their composition. They are instructed to make up and perform a song in front of the large group that describes their feeling word. They may use sound makers such as pencils or rulers, or the counselor can provide them with whistles, horns, harmonicas, or kazoos. After several minutes of planning, each group performs while other members attempt to guess what feeling they are expressing.

Music is also a good way to build group identity and cohesiveness. Group members can compose a song or select a recording that expresses who they are. An alternative activity is the musical collage. Each individual group member selects short segments of songs that have meaning, and tapes each of these segments to create a collage. After listening to each person's collage, group members discuss how the music represents that individual (Bowman, 1987).

Writing

Various forms of writing can be adapted for group use. Open-ended sentences can become a get-acquainted activity or prompt discussion and sharing. Questionnaires are also used this way, or they can be adapted to the specific focus of the group. For example, members of a stress management group might be given a questionnaire about ways they deal with stress. As responses are shared, members will benefit from hearing others' ideas.

In a classroom setting, students can be given journal topics related to self-awareness, clarification of values, or feelings about various issues. Examples of topics include

"Something I like best about myself is . . ."

"Something I feel strongly about is . . ."

"Something I'm good at doing is . . ."

"Something that I value highly is . . ."

Topics of this nature encourage self-exploration. Journal writing can be further shared in student dyads or triads to clarify responses. In such a situation, participants must feel comfortable with the sharing and have the option to pass if they wish.

Bibliotherapy

Borders and Paisley (1992) suggested that bibliotherapy be used not only in problem-centered interventions in individual or small-group counseling, but also with children in classroom guidance, to promote developmental growth.

Their research indicated that the use of stories is an effective approach to help children solve problems and enhance personal growth.

Play

For younger children, particularly in a school setting, play can be highly effective in a small group of four or five children to improve socialization skills. One or two children in the group are selected as good models; the targeted individuals may need to develop cooperative versus competitive behavior, learn to control aggression, become more comfortable with group interaction, or learn to share.

In the group setting, the play is generally more structured and the toys used are selected to help children work on the desirable behaviors. For instance, if two of the children in the group have difficulty sharing, the counselor may have only one can of blocks for all group members to use. As the children play with the blocks, the counselor reflects on the interaction and involves the children in discussing how it feels when friends share or don't share, thus seeking to develop behaviors that will transfer to other situations.

Board games can also be developed for group use. For an activity on feelings, for example, a game called "Feel Wheel" (Vernon, 1989) helps children develop a feeling vocabulary. Tic-tac-toe can be adapted to teach positive and negative behaviors in interpersonal relationships (Vernon, 1989).

Conclusion

Specialized approaches to counseling offer creative ways to supplement or give an alternative to the traditional verbal approaches. For counseling to be meaningful and effective, it is necessary to engage the client, and specialized approaches can do this in an enjoyable, self-motivating way. Gladding (1992) noted that approaches of this nature are "process-oriented, emotionally sensitive, socially directed, and awareness-focused" (preface) and can help clients from diverse backgrounds enhance their development.

The specialized approaches are not limited to the descriptions in this chapter. Movement, dance, drama, humor, and puppetry are other approaches that can meet client needs. No "universal" format exists for application; the creativity of the counselor and assessment of what would most effectively engage the client guide the implementation. The training needed to use these specialized approaches depends on whether they are used to supplement a verbal approach or constitute the major aspect of the counseling. As Nickerson and O'Laughlin (1982) note, the issue is perhaps one of degree. In other words, a counselor does not have to be an artist to use some art with clients who are not able to express themselves verbally, but if art were the primary modality, further training would be needed.

Specialized approaches have been used successfully with children and adolescents (Gladding, 1992; Pardeck, 1994; Rubin, 1988), the mentally retarded (Roth & Barrett, 1982), chronic hospital populations (Lieff, 1982), learning disabled clients (Landreth, Jacquot, & Allen, 1982), clients with eating disorders (Brown, 1991), and child abuse victims (In & McDermott, 1982). They can be used to treat specific problems or can be applied preventively, particularly in school settings.

The diversity of specialized counseling approaches can help effectively address a wide range of client needs. These methods move counseling beyond the mental arena, which relies on verbal techniques, to a more comprehensive orientation using a multitude of approaches.

Summary

Although counseling has traditionally been characterized by a verbal orientation, practitioners are now encouraged to explore other methods to help people cope with psychological problems. In this chapter, a variety of specialized approaches to counseling were described. These approaches have been found to be effective for a variety of problems presented by both children and adults.

As discussed in this chapter, specialized approaches to counseling are often creative and can be adapted to fit the client's learning style. Art, imagery and writing were identified as appropriate strategies for clients of all ages. Specific ways to use music, bibliotherapy, and play were also described. Implementing approaches of this nature can enhance the counseling process because they combine theory and practice in flexible ways to focus on the unique aspects of the client and the problem.

References

Allan, J. (1982). Social drawing: A therapeutic approach with young children. In E. T. Nickerson & K. O'Laughlin (Eds.), *Helping through action: Action-oriented therapies* (pp. 25–32). Amherst, MA: Human Resource Development Press.

Allan, J., & Clark, M. (1984). Directed art counseling. *Elementary School Guidance and Counseling, 19,* 116–124.

Allan, J., & Crandall, J. (1986). The rosebush: A visualization strategy. *Elementary School Guidance and Counseling, 21,* 44–51.

Amerikaner, M., Schauble, P., & Ziller, R. (1982). Images: The use of photographs in personal counseling. In E. T. Nickerson and K. O'Laughlin (Eds.), *Helping through action: Action-oriented therapies* (pp. 33–41). Amherst, MA: Human Resource Development Press.

Amster, F. (1982). Differential uses of play in treatment of young children. In G. L. Landreth (Ed.), *Play therapy: Dynamics of the process of counseling with children* (pp. 33–42). Springfield, IL: Thomas.

Ariel, S., Carel, C. A., & Tyano, S. (1985). Uses of children's make-believe play in family therapy: Theory and clinical examples. *Journal of Marital and Family Therapy, 11,* 47–60.

Bates, M. (1993). Poetic responses to art: Summoning the adolescent voice. *Journal of Poetry Therapy, 3*, 149–156.

Bauer, M. S., & Balius, F. A. (1995). Storytelling: Integrating therapy and curriculum for students with serious emotional disturbances. *Teaching Exceptional Children, 27*, 24–29.

Berger, A. (1988). Working through grief by writing poetry. *Journal of Poetry Therapy, 1*, 11–19.

Borders, S., & Paisley, P. O. (1992). Children's literature as a source for classroom guidance. *Elementary School Guidance and Counseling, 27*, 131–139.

Bowman, R. P. (1987). Approaches for counseling children through music. *Elementary School Guidance and Counseling, 21*, 284–291.

Brand, A. G. (1987). Writing as counseling. *Elementary School Guidance and Counseling, 21*, 266–275.

Brooks, R. (1987). Storytelling and the therapeutic process for children with learning disabilities. *Journal of Learning Disabilities, 20*, 546–550.

Brown, D., & Fromm, E. (1986). *Hypnotherapy and hypnoanalysis.* Hillside, NJ: Erlbaum.

Brown, M. H. (1991). Innovations in the treatment of bulimia: Transpersonal psychology, relaxation, imagination, hypnosis, myth, and ritual. *Journal of Humanistic Education and Development, 30*, 50–60.

Campbell, C. A. (1993). Play, the fabric of elementary school counseling programs. *Elementary School Guidance and Counseling Journal, 28*, 10–16.

Caple, R. (1985). Counseling and the self-organization paradigm. *Journal of Counseling and Development, 64*, 173–178.

Dufrene, P. (1994). Art therapy and the sexually abused child. *Art Education, 47*, 6–11.

Eydenberg, M. G. (1986). Art therapy for the severe and profound. *Child and Family Behavior Therapy, 8*, 1–3.

Fromm, E. (1987). Significant developments in medical hypnosis during the past 25 years. *International Journal of Clinical and Experimental Hypnosis, 35*, 231–245.

Ginott, H. G. (1982). A rationale for selecting toys in play therapy. In G. L. Landreth (Ed.), *Play therapy: Dynamics of the process of counseling with children* (pp. 145–152). Springfield, IL: Thomas.

Gladding, S. T. (1987). The poetics of a "check out" place: Preventing burnout and promoting self-renewal. *Journal of Poetry Therapy, 1*, 95–102.

Gladding, S. T. (1992). *Counseling as an art: The creative arts in counseling.* Alexandria, VA: American Counseling Association.

Gladding, S. T. (1995). Creativity in counseling. *Counseling and Human Development, 28, 1*, 1–12.

Gold, J. (1988). The value of fiction as therapeutic recreation and developmental mediator: A theoretical framework. *Journal of Poetry Therapy, 1*, 135–148.

Griggs, S. A. (1983). Counseling high school students for their individual learning styles. *Clearing House, 56*, 293–296.

Griggs, S. A. (1985). Counseling for individual learning styles. *Journal of Counseling and Development, 64*, 202–205.

Griggs, S. A., Price, G. E., Kopel, S., & Swaine, W. (1984). The effects of group counseling on sixth-grade students with different learning styles. *California Journal of Counseling and Development, 5*, 28–35.

Howe, J. W., Burgess, A. W., & McCormack, A. (1987). Adolescent runaways and their drawings. *Art in Psychotherapy, 14*, 35–40.

Hutchins, D. E., & Cole, C. G. (1986). *Helping relationships and strategies.* Pacific Grove, CA: Brooks/Cole.

Hynes, A. (1990). Poetry: An avenue into the spirit. *Journal of Poetry Therapy, 4*, 71–81.

In, P. A., & McDermott, J. F. (1982). Play therapy in the treatment of child abuse. In G. L. Landreth (Ed.), *Play therapy: Dynamics of the process of counseling with children* (pp. 284–293). Springfield, IL: Thomas.

Kenny, A. (1987). An art activities approach: Counseling the gifted, creative and talented. *Gifted Child Today, 10*, 33–37.

Landreth, G. L. (1987). Play therapy: Facilitative use of child's play in elementary school counseling. *Elementary School Guidance and Counseling, 21*, 253–261.

Landreth, G. L. (1991). *Play therapy: The art of the relationship.* Muncie, IN: Accelerated Development.

Landreth, G. L. (1993). Child-centered play therapy. *Elementary School Guidance and Counseling
Journal, 28*, 17–29.

Landreth, G. L., Jacquot, W. S., & Allen, L. (1982).
Using play therapy in a team approach to
learning disabilities. In G. L. Landreth (Ed.),
*Play therapy: Dynamics of the process of counsel-
ing with children* (pp. 284–293). Springfield, IL:
Thomas.

Lawson, D. M. (1987). Using therapeutic stories in
the counseling process. *Elementary School
Guidance and Counseling, 22*, 134–142.

Lieff, J. (1982). Music as healer: Therapy with a
chronic hospital population. In E. T. Nickerson & K. O'Laughlin (Eds.), *Helping through
action: Action-oriented therapies* (pp. 258–261).
Amherst, MA: Human Resource Develop-
ment Press.

Maas, J. (1982). Introduction to music therapy. In
E. T. Nickerson & K. O'Laughlin (Eds.), *Helping through action: Action-oriented therapies* (pp.
87–100). Amherst, MA: Human Resource Development Press.

Maranto, C. D. (1993). Music therapy and stress
management. In P. M. Lehrer & R. L. Woolfolk
(Eds.), *Principles and practice of stress management* (2nd ed., pp. 407–422). New York: Guilford Press.

Mercer, L. E. (1993). Self-healing through poetry
writing. *Journal of Poetry Therapy, 6*, 161–168.

Michel, D. (1985). *Music therapy: An introduction*
(2nd ed.). Springfield, IL: Thomas.

Myrick, R. D., & Myrick, L. S. (1993). Guided imagery: From mystical to practical. *Elementary
School Guidance and Counseling, 28*, 62–70.

Newcomb, N. S. (1994). Music: A powerful resource for the elementary school counselor.
Elementary School Guidance and Counseling, 29,
150–155.

Nickerson, E. T., & O'Laughlin, K. (Eds.). (1982).
*Helping through action: Action-oriented thera-
pies*. Amherst, MA: Human Resource Development Press.

Oaklander, V. (1978). *Windows to our children*.
Moab, UT: Real People Press.

O'Connor, K. J. (1991). *The play therapy primer*.
New York: Wiley.

Pardeck, J. T. (1994). Using literature to help adolescents cope with problems. *Adolescence, 29*,
421–427.

Pardeck, J. T., & Pardeck, J. A. (1993). *Bibliotherapy:
A clinical approach for helping children*. New
York: Gordon and Breach.

Pinholster, R. (1983). From dark to light: The use of
drawing to counsel nonverbal children. *Elementary School Guidance and Counseling, 17*,
268–273.

Protinsky, H. (1978). Children's drawings as emotional indicators. *Elementary School Guidance
and Counseling, 13*, 249–255.

Riley, S. (1987). The advantages of art therapy in
an outpatient clinic. *American Journal of Art
Therapy, 26*, 21–29.

Roth, E. A., & Barrett, R. P. (1982). Parallels in art
and play therapy with a disturbed retarded
child. In E. T. Nickerson and K. O'Laughlin
(Eds.), *Helping through action: Action-oriented
therapies* (pp. 180–188). Amherst, MA: Human
Resource Development Press.

Rubin, J. A. (1984). *The art of art therapy*. New York:
Brunner/Mazel.

Rubin, J. A. (1987). *Approaches to art therapy*. New
York: Brunner/Mazel.

Rubin, J. A. (1988). Art counseling: An alternative.
Elementary School Guidance and Counseling, 22,
180–185.

Sarnoff, D., & Remer, P. (1982). The effects of guidance imagery on the generation of career alternatives. *Journal of Vocational Behavior, 21*,
299–308.

Schaefer, C. E. (1985). Play therapy. *Early Child Development and Care, 19*, 95–108.

Schaefer, C. E., & O'Conner, K. L. (1983). *Handbook
of play therapy*. New York: Wiley.

Siegel, B. S. (1986). *Love, medicine, and miracles*.
New York: Harper & Row.

Skooult, T. M., Morgan, J. I., & Negron-Cunningham, H. (1989). Mental imagery in career
counseling and life planning: A review of research and intervention methods. *Journal of
Counseling and Development, 67*, 287–292.

Thaut, M. H. (1990). Neuropsychological processes in music relevance in music therapy. In
R. F. Unkefer (Ed.), *Music therapy in treatment*

of adults with mental disorders: Theoretical bases and clinical interventions (pp. 3–32). New York: Macmillan.

Thomas, M. (recording artist). (1979). *Free to be . . . You and me* (record album). Carthage, IL: Good Apple.

Thorne, C. R. (1985). *Guided imagery and fantasy in career counseling.* Unpublished master's thesis, New Mexico State University, Las Cruces.

Vernon, A. (1989). *Thinking, feeling, behaving: An emotional education curriculum for children.* Champaign, IL: Research Press.

Vondracek, F. W., & Corneal, S. (1995). *Strategies for resolving individual and family problems.* Pacific Grove, CA: Brooks/Cole.

Wadeson, H. (1982). *History and application of art therapy.* In E. T. Nickerson and K. O'Laughlin (Eds.), *Helping through action: Action-oriented therapies* (pp. 180–188). Amherst, MA: Human Resource Development Press.

Wayman, J. (composer). (1974). *Imagination and me.* Carthage, IL: Good Apple.

Weitzenhoffer, A. M. (1989). *The practice of hypnotism, Vol. 2: Applications of traditional and semi-traditional hypnotism—Nontraditional hypnotism.* New York: Wiley.

Winsor, R. M. (1993). Hypnosis—A neglected tool for client empowerment. *Social Work, 38,* 603–608.

Witmer, J. M., & Young, M. E. (1987). Imagery in counseling. *Elementary School Guidance and Counseling, 22,* 5–15.

Woytowich, J. M. (1994). The power of a poem in the counseling office. *School Counselor, 42,* 78–80.

Wright, M. E., & Wright, B. A. (1987). *Clinical practice of hypnotherapy.* New York: Guilford Press.

Counseling in Specific Settings

This section describes the basic environments in which counselors today are most likely to work. Chapter 13, "School Counseling," provides a comprehensive overview of the many roles and professional activities that school counseling today may involve. The repertoire of skills that a school counselor may be required to draw on are outlined: personal, individual, or group counseling; consultation; group guidance; and testing and other appraisal activities. The range of settings for educational counseling, from elementary through university and community college counseling, are outlined, with attention to the special responsibilities and talents required for each particular environment. The authors point out how important it is for school counselors to act as generalists, being able to perform a number of services and roles and to refer students to other specialized services when necessary.

Chapter 14, "Counseling in Mental Health and Private Practice Settings," describes the other major settings in which the counselor may practice. The authors outline the history of mental health counseling and describe the process of how counseling expanded from its early vocational focus to encompass therapeutic, mental health activities. They present major events that have influenced this process, such as the Community Mental Health Act of 1963, which provided federal funding for community mental health agencies and programs, and consider the possibilities for the future of mental health counseling in the 1990s. Mental health counselors have been engaged in a continuing process to earn recognition as mental health professionals similar to social workers, psychologists, and psychiatrists, and this process has supported the movement toward counselor licensure. As more and more states have passed legislation enabling counselors, both in mental health and other specializations, to be recognized as practicing professionals, more and more counselors have chosen to go into private practice, either as a full-time career option or as an adjunct to their other work. Both the positive aspects and the negative aspects of starting a private practice are outlined for the counselor.

As these chapters indicate, the role of counselors has continuously expanded and will inevitably continue to do so. As the opportunities for therapeutic mental health professions increase in our society, so will the settings and environments in which counselors may choose to practice.

Chapter *13*

School Counseling

Claire Cole Vaught, Ed.D.

Trivia Quiz

1. Which professional group must understand developmental stages of clients from infancy through geriatric years?
2. Which person on the school's instructional staff generally has the highest professional training requirement?
3. Which person in the school was likely successful in a different career requiring different training before changing career paths?
4. Which is the only professional group in the American Counseling Association (ACA) to produce two different journals, as well as other publications for its members?
5. Which professional group in the school has little organizational power, but often greatest influence, over what happens in students' lives?

Answers to Trivia Quiz

1. *School counselors.* Counselors in educational settings span the range from preschool programs for infants with disabilities to community college programs for senior citizens. Counselors in schools work with arguably the most diverse population in the mental health field.
2. *School counselors.* The school counseling license usually requires at least master's-level training; at the university counseling level, often a doctorate.
3. *School counselors.* In many states, school counselors are credentialed only after they have been teachers, requiring a different preparation.
4. *School counselors.* The American School Counselor Association (ASCA) is the only ACA division to publish two journals: *The School Counselor* and *Elementary*

School Guidance and Counseling. ASCA also publishes books, monographs, and other materials on topics of interest to school counselors.

5. *School counselors.* Although having little authority through position—counselors rarely supervise anyone else or have authority over other professionals in a school—counselors often play a key role in the school through their ability to persuade others to act in the best interests of students. Counselors also receive more information about the school than anyone else other than the principal—from parents, students, teachers, and community members—and, therefore, may have more knowledge than just about anyone else about what is really going on in the school. Lacking the formal authority of the administrators and the professional numbers of the teachers, counselors rely on their communication skills to influence a school to be a healthy place for students.

The counseling profession in school settings is alive and thriving in most places. As the educational mission of the schools has expanded to include previously unserved student populations, so has the role of the school counselor, requiring a multiculturally competent counselor. Student clients include infants with developmental disabilities served in their homes and in schools; children in primary and elementary schools; early adolescents in middle and junior high schools; adolescents in high schools; and adults from young to elderly in community college, college, university, and other postsecondary schools. Students represent every race, creed, cultural, and ethnic group, requiring a multiculturally competent counselor (Coleman, 1995); economic levels from homeless, abject poverty to affluent and rich; intellectual and physical conditions from disabled to gifted; mental health from suicidal to stable; and personal outlooks from surly to sunny, from despondent to hopeful. School counseling has become virtually a cradle-to-grave profession serving almost everybody, in almost every condition of life, at some time in their lives.

Overview of School Counseling

From the inception of counseling in schools as a narrow vocational focus for a small number of secondary students, the current menu of services offered in educational settings has changed. Indeed, the settings themselves have changed. Counselors are found working in homes of students; in public elementary, middle, and high schools; in community and junior colleges; in proprietary schools ranging from elite schools for children to vocational and professional training centers; and in colleges and universities, where services may more closely resemble mental health counseling in a private clinic.

A menu of services is offered by counselors in educational settings (Baker, 1992). These services include:

- Educational and career information and counseling from preschool through retirement
- Parent and family counseling from infancy through college years

- Personal counseling from learning to get along with others in kindergarten through marital counseling at university counseling centers
- Work with social issues from child abuse and neglect of tots through alcohol, date rape, or AIDS counseling at the university setting, often requiring consultation with other helping professionals
- Coordination of services for clients from feeding and clothing neglected children to financial aid and job placement for postsecondary students

Professionals involved in counseling students in educational settings may have different educational backgrounds and perspectives:

- School counselors, with training in individual and group techniques of counseling, information needed by students, and family counseling
- School psychologists and social workers, with additional training in testing and appraisal, clinical techniques, and abnormal behavior
- Clinical psychologists, counseling psychologists, licensed professional counselors, and psychiatrists (often on a consultation basis) with more training than school counselors, often in a specialized area such as family systems, eating disorders, or other pathology
- Substance abuse counselors, with extensive background in treatment and prevention of substance abuse
- Family planning counselors, often nurses or nurse practitioners with a medical orientation
- Teachers, administrators, and others in teacher advisory or home-based guidance programs, with basic training in listening and responding skills and referral procedures

These professionals are supported by other people including clerical and data-processing assistants, peer helpers, interns or graduate assistants, parent volunteers, residence hall advisers, and paraprofessionals who may assist in such places as career centers.

Services

Most school counselors, whether they are in public, private, or postsecondary settings, approach their work from a developmental point of view, such as the life career development perspective suggested by Gysbers and Henderson (1988). These authors believe that certain characteristics are common to students at different times in their lives and that much of the counseling program can be planned around those developmental events. A child in primary school is developmentally experiencing separation from parents and home. The elementary counselor plans classroom guidance activities that emphasize independence, learning to be a part of a group, and understanding community helpers. The preadolescent in middle school is entering puberty; the middle school counselor plans ways to help students understand emotional and physical changes related to puberty. Group counseling for middle school students may help them to explore new social opportunities and responsibilities, as boys and girls notice each other in more mature ways. The high school counselor recognizes that developmentally adolescents plan for future education and careers. Much work at the high school level centers around educational and career information and decision making. University counselors recognize independence issues of young adults and emphasize responsible behavior in social settings as young people live away from home for the first time.

All the counselor's time cannot, however, be directed toward developmental concerns. For individual students, problems arise that assume crisis proportions: divorce or death of a parent, pregnancy, substance abuse, criminal or violent behavior, and many other occurrences call for crisis intervention, which may be followed up later by developmentally appropriate counseling. For example, a pregnant teen may first have to decide issues relating to abortion, marriage, or being a solo parent. Once the crisis is managed, developmental counseling about her life options regarding further education and career planning can commence. However, until the crisis is mitigated developmental issues will probably go on hold as a first priority of both the student and the counselor.

Many events in the elementary counseling office differ from events in the university counseling center, but school counselors at all levels provide some basic services. These include counseling, consultation with other professionals, coordination of services, evaluation and testing, and classroom or group guidance and information giving (Hutchins & Vaught, 1997).

Counseling

Counseling is the common denominator of services offered at virtually all educational settings. Counseling can be developmental in nature, discussing concerns and milestones that most students encounter during a particular period of their lives. Or it may be crisis intervention, with the counselor helping a student with an immediate acute problem that needs immediate resolution or relief. Counseling, or the helping process, can be defined as "a one-on-one relationship between a helper and client (or group) . . . [where] the goal is to assist the client in taking steps to work through concerns and achieve realistic goals" (Hutchins & Cole, 1992, p. 4). The counselor helps students to

1. *Define a concern* or problem. Usually this concern comes from the student, but sometimes someone else—a teacher, parent, another student—originates the contact with the counselor.
2. *Set realistic goals* to change behavior related to that concern. Occasionally the institution sets the goals: to avoid missing any more days from school, for instance, or to plan a program leading to graduation.
3. *Design strategies* to meet those goals. These are things that a student can realistically do to meet the goal: maintain a high enough grade average to get into college and meet standards to play a sport, for instance.
4. *Evaluate progress* toward meeting the goals, redefining procedures as necessary. A student might need periodic assistance of a peer helper to learn to resolve conflict without fist fighting, for example.

In most programs, counseling is the basic service and consumes the greatest amount of the counselor's time. In some school settings, counselors may be required to spend a designated portion of their day in direct counseling, such as in Virginia, where public school counselors must, by state regulation, document at least 60 percent of their time in counseling students or their parents.

Both group and individual counseling are important techniques in schools. Much individual counseling must be done, but group counseling is a much underused technique. Group counseling may be developmental in nature, such as helping middle school children learn ways to resolve conflict without violence. It may be used for acute problems presented by only a few students, such as a grief-and-loss group for students who have lost a family member through death or divorce.

Most school counselors understand the value of group counseling, but many do not believe themselves skilled in this area. Others run into institutional hurdles as they try to schedule students to meet together as a group. Groups vary in size and topic from level to level, with very small groups of children on the elementary level doing structured activities with the counselors, and larger, more "rap session"–type groups in high school or university residence halls.

The concerns presented to the counselor will vary greatly: from the preschooler's fear of leaving Mommy, to the sixth-grade boy's worry about why he is so much shorter than everyone else, to the high school girl's panic over pregnancy, to the community college student's debating employment versus further schooling, requests for help will be very different at different levels of schooling. The school counselor will decide who is best served in individual counseling, who best in a group, and who best with some of both.

Consultation

Consultation with other professions is an indirect relationship in which the counselor works with someone else who then works directly with the client (Brown & Srebalus, 1988). A school counselor may consult with parents and teachers, helping them to learn strategies that will then enable them to work more effectively with the child and student (McGee & Fauble-Erickson, 1995). A counselor in a school also typically works with other helping professionals in the community for the benefit of the student (Hobbs & Collison, 1995). If the parents of a third-grader believe they need counseling as an entire family, it is likely that the school counselor will refer them to a family therapist outside the school setting. The school counselor, with permission of the parents, typically consults with the therapist to give a view of the child during school hours. The therapist will probably make suggestions to the school counselor about how school personnel can work more effectively with the third-grader. The relationship between the school counselor and the family therapist is one of consultation. Consultation also occurs within a university. If a university student is suicidal, a counseling center professional will likely make contact with student health services, requesting evaluation, perhaps medication, or in-patient admission. A school counselor consults with teachers regularly for the benefit of their mutual student.

Consultation may be developmental in nature, such as when a dietitian works with a school counseling staff to plan how to present information on how to help adolescent girls to have healthy attitudes toward their weight and body image. A consultant may assist with crisis counseling or planning, such as may occur when a natural disaster such as a hurricane or earthquake traumatizes a group of students.

Coordination of Services

Coordination of services for a particular student is sometimes the result of consultation. The counselor is often the contact person for helping professionals both within and outside the school, coordinating those professionals' efforts on behalf of the student. Often the school counselor is the contact person for educational specialists not within the school building, such as the speech therapist, occupational therapist, school psychologist, school social worker, and other itinerant specialists provided by the school system. If a helping service is not provided by the school or university, chances are the counselor knows where to refer a client for that service. For example, a community college counselor can refer a military veteran for services available through government channels. One extension of service often coordinated by the school counselor is the teacher advisory program often found in a middle school, where teachers and others in the building extend a quasi-counseling program through periodic contact with small groups of students (Cole, 1993; Killin & Williams, 1995).

Evaluation, Testing, and Other Forms of Appraisal

Evaluation, testing, and other forms of appraisal are often the domain of the school counselor (Muro & Kottman, 1995). Often the counselor is responsible for the standardized testing program for the general school population, sometimes coordinating administration of the tests and usually interpreting and analyzing the results. The counselor also assists with other kinds of appraisal, such as classroom observation of students with disabilities. Rarely does a school counselor do individual testing; the school psychologist has that role. School counselors receive training in testing and other forms of evaluation as a part of their professional preparation. Results of tests are very helpful to school counselors in advising students of their educational options and in helping them plan career paths. Results on an entrance examination for law or medical school, for example, weigh heavily in career counseling for upper-level university students.

Appraisal is a part of a developmental counseling program, such as helping all students assess their academic achievement and career interests. It may be used for acute or crisis situations for individual students, such as a depression inventory for a student exhibiting signs of distress.

Classsroom or Group Guidance and Other Information Services

Classroom or group guidance and other information services, what Baker (1992) refers to as *pedagogical services*, are typically offered in schools. The content of the sessions varies greatly from one level of schooling to the next, but in almost all educational settings, counselors have an instructional role to impart information to students. Most of these programs are developmental and are offered to all or most students at a particular grade level. Some classroom guidance may, however, relate to problem situations and be crisis oriented, such as an AIDS or alcohol awareness program designed to prevent problems, perhaps targeted at a high-risk group.

Information giving varies greatly for counselors working in different kinds of schools. First-graders learn about community helpers, whereas high school and college students attend seminars on how to prepare a résumé. Fifth-graders learn what to expect in middle school, and community college students learn how to transfer to a university. Almost all counselors offer career and educational information, as well as other topics, through direct teaching either in small groups in seminar-type settings or in classroom groups, such as elementary classroom guidance programs.

Settings

Counseling occurs in many different educational settings, distinguished by the organization of the school. Elementary, middle, high, and postsecondary counselors are usually seen as separate and distinct branches of school counseling, with different training appropriate to the age and developmental level of the student clients. There is much crossover: a middle school counselor may seek employment as an elementary or a high school professional, or a school counselor may enter the realm of the community college. Occasionally a student personnel worker in higher education will decide to become a public school counselor and apply first-hand knowledge about college to high school students' counseling interests. Each level can be clearly characterized, and people develop skills and knowledge for a specific level of educational setting. Increasingly, each level is seen as a distinct specialty, with credentialing defined by the level of school in which the counselor works. Tryneski's (1993) *Requirements for Certification of Teachers, Counselors, Librarians, and Administrators for Elementary and Secondary Schools* lists certification requirements for the fifty states as of 1993–1994.

Elementary School Counseling

Elementary school counseling is the latest area of growth for school counseling. School counselors have been in high schools for many years but are only recently found in many elementary schools. In recent years, many states have mandated or encouraged counseling for all elementary students, creating the fastest-growing population of new school counselors. Many states require a specific endorsement in elementary counseling, including coursework in child development and elementary counseling techniques, as well as practicum experience and perhaps prior teaching experience at the elementary level. Typically, higher ratios of counselors to students—perhaps one counselor to 500 students or more—exist in elementary schools than at secondary levels. Often the peripatetic elementary counselor serves students in more than one elementary school on an itinerant basis.

Individual and small-group counseling combine with a classroom guidance program to enable an elementary counselor to meet with such a large student clientele. Elementary counselors spend much time in consultation with teachers and with parents, who are often very involved with their children's education at the elementary level. Elementary counselors usually use puppets, songs, and games as a part of their classroom guidance presentations. As more attention is drawn toward early intervention with students who are potential school dropouts, the elementary counselor may assume a much more prominent position in early intervention with at-risk students.

A typical day for an elementary school counselor might look like this:

8:00 A.M.   Meet with new student and mother; check completion of registration forms, immunizations, and so forth; review records from previous school, noting former special education placement, and confer with principal about which teacher should receive the student.

8:30   Introduce student to teacher and to peer helper; confer with mother, answering her questions about eligibility for free breakfast and lunch.

8:40   Check in with Cindy, who is overcoming school phobia; chat briefly and give her a pat on the back.

8:45   Greet Antonio in his fourth-grade classroom and give him much praise for bringing his homework, a problem discussed in his counseling group last week.

8:50   Organize calendar for the day, noting phone calls to make and letters to be written.

8:55   Make telephone calls to five parents, concerning Rodney's low achievement in reading, Arthur's teacher's recommendation that he be tested for the gifted program, Cindy's success so far in school today, Letitia's interest in geology and an upcoming Saturday program, and a request for a conference with Robin's teacher and the principal.

9:20   Conduct classroom group guidance for kindergarten.

9:50   Same lesson, another classroom.

10:15   Counsel four individuals referred by their teachers for about twenty minutes per student, including collecting them from and returning them to their classrooms: David about his parents' divorce, Jennifer about her black eye (child abuse?), Mikey about having a Big Brother, Melendez about an after-school tutorial program.

11:35   Eat lunch, chatting with other teachers eating lunch; travel to other school.

12:30	Confer with principal about upcoming registration and orientation for next year's kindergarten students.
1:00	Conduct classroom group guidance, third-grade class.
1:30	Conduct same lesson, another third-grade class.
2:00	Counsel group of five boys who get in fights.
2:45	Confer with Sampson's teacher about his belligerent attitude toward authority.
3:00	Meet with Susan's parents, teacher, and the principal about her chronic health problems and homebound instruction.
3:30	Attend committee meeting in central office to work on county-wide guidance curriculum.

Middle or Junior High School Counseling

Middle or junior high school counseling is less well defined than either elementary or high school counseling. Although almost one-fourth of public school students are in middle grades, generally described as grades 5 through 8, less literature is available to describe what the counselor does at this level. Some states, encouraged by organizations such as the National Middle School Association, have defined certification requirements and training programs for those working in middle-level schools, including counselors. Where a counselor-to-student ratio exists in regulations, it is likely to be lower than elementary, but higher than the numbers of students assigned to a high school counselor—perhaps one counselor for 400 students. Many middle-level counselors are former high school counselors who chose to move to the middle grades, desiring an earlier intervention or a work setting where more counseling and less recordkeeping and counting of credits occurs. Others, unfortunately, were relegated to the middle school because they were unsuccessful in high schools.

Although few counselors in middle schools today have been trained specifically for that level, middle school counselors are continually seeking additional coursework, conference presentations, state department assistance, publications, and resource materials designed specifically for that level. The National Middle School Association offers several publications dedicated to middle-level counseling and both *The School Counselor* and *Elementary School Guidance and Counseling* journals publish articles on middle grades counseling. The *NASSP Bulletin,* primarily an administrators' journal, also publishes articles on middle-level counseling; see several referenced at the end of this chapter.

Counselors in middle schools work with interdisciplinary teams of teachers, sometimes assigned as a member of the team. Parents seek the assistance of middle school counselors as their children move into adolescence. Group counseling is probably the most effective strategy for working with middle-level students, because their peer affiliations are so strong at this age. Career and educational counseling take on new interest and meaning for students as they make course choices that affect their future educational and occupational options. Feeling the conflicts and uncertainties of changing from children to adolescents, middle-level students want to know how to get along better with everyone: their peers, boyfriend/girlfriend, parents, siblings, teachers, and others (Vaught, 1995).

One organizational feature of many middle schools is the teacher advisory program, in which teachers become first-line advisers to a small group of students. The intent of such a program is for each student to be known well by at least one adult in the building. Group guidance activities often happen as a part of the teacher advisory program in middle schools. The role of the counselor in such a program may be to plan the guidance portion of the program; to provide training for teachers and others who will serve as advisers; and to function as an adviser for a small group. Where there is a teacher-advisory program, there will likely be more referrals to the counselor because teachers know their students well and refer them to counselors for more assistance than the teacher-adviser can provide.

A typical day for a middle school counselor might look like this:

8:00 A.M.   Chat briefly with three seventh-grade girls before teacher advisory (TA) session starts—no special topic.

8:05   Attend parent conference with George, his parents, and the sixth-grade Hero (student-named) team about his unwillingness to do homework.

8:30   Meet with Mrs. Gray's TA group, since her substitute feels uncomfortable carrying out the listening activity.

9:00   Organize day, check with secretary to see whether letters of invitation to next week's guidance advisory committee have generated RSVP's, make space arrangements for that meeting, discuss refreshments with secretary.

9:15   Return parent phone calls.

9:30   Counsel individually with five students, one drop-in and four previously scheduled, concerning Carmen's dislike of participating in PE class, Vincent's application for the summer gifted program, Tony's fear of being beaten up in the bathroom, David's getting assigned to in-school suspension (again!), Sara's possible participation in the group for students whose parents are divorcing.

10:30   Participate in weekly team meeting with seventh-grade Power Rangers (student-named) team to discuss several students' progress.

11:30   Conduct Lunch Bunch in guidance office—counseling group for overweight students.

12:15   Conduct Lunch Bunch—study skills group.

1:00   Counsel group of students having trouble getting along with peers.

2:00	Meet with high school counselors to discuss changes in course offerings.
3:00	Return parent phone calls.
3:30	Attend parent conference with eighth-grade Top Bananas (student-named) team and Serona's mother about remedial summer school.
7:00	Host parent group, and present information on "Understanding the Early Adolescent."

High School Counseling

High school counseling is the historically established area of school counseling. Some people still in high school counseling were trained through the 1958 National Defense Education Act (NDEA), which funded institutes in the late 1950s and early 1960s. About 13,000 counselors received training in the first five years of that program (Borow & Humes, 1987). With the service usually mandated through state and regional accrediting standards, high school counselors enjoy the lowest—although far too high—counselor-to-student ratios in the public schools, perhaps 350:1 or lower. High school counselors are also more likely to have clerical assistance, owing to the high volume of paper with which they must contend, especially college transcripts for students. Often they specialize in one or two grade levels: the senior counselor might, for example, work with seniors year after year, becoming an expert on college admissions, opportunities in the military, and other such topics. Sometimes a counselor begins work with a group of students entering as ninth- or tenth-graders and continues with that group through their senior year.

Educational and career counseling are important aspects of a high school counselor's job, since students must attain credits in a prescribed manner to graduate. Traditionally, the counselor is responsible for maintaining student records and helping young people make logical course selections for future education and work. Computer skills are important for a counselor when, as is usually the case today, a computerized data system is used for school records.

Counseling becomes crucial as students make decisions about choosing colleges or applying for jobs; entering the military or evading registration for the draft; whether or not they will "just say no" or get involved with drugs, alcohol, sex, and a host of other adult decisions foisted on many young adolescents. Whereas counselors at elementary and middle-level grades have earlier opportunities for intervention when perhaps the consequences for their students are not so grave, high school counselors are presented problems demanding immediate solutions that have long-range implications, such as whether or not to drop out of school or to continue a pregnancy. One recent survey (Libsch & Freedman-Doan, 1995) showed that students not planning to attend college were generally less satisfied with the amount of counselor intervention they received in the areas of educational and career counseling than were students planning to attend college.

Many counselors find themselves deeply involved in their students' personal problems that demand solutions before career and educational planning can be relevant. High school counselors must be aware of the society in which their students live, so that students believe their counselors understand the dimensions of young people's problems. Some high school students see their counselors as hopelessly out of sync with the times, unable to intervene or even to understand the pressures faced by today's teenagers. Some counseling programs use peer counselors to establish credibility and to help keep the counselors current about young people's concerns. The role of the high school counselor has been under study for the last several years, due to criticism such as that mentioned earlier: working too much with college bound students and not enough with others. In recent years, however, high school counselors seem to enjoy more confidence from their publics.

A typical day for a high school counselor might look like this:

8:00 A.M.	Meet with teachers of advanced placement classes to discuss screening procedures for class entrance.
8:30	Confer with secretary to check on progress of sending out transcripts and recommendations to colleges; write three recommendations.
9:15	Counsel individuals by appointment: Bobbi's Armed Services Vocational Aptitude Battery (ASVAB) scores and military options; Alfred's college options; Sid's decision about dropping out of school; Thalia's worry about pregnancy; Neala's concern that she cannot afford graduation announcements and senior pictures; Chick's fear that he doesn't have the right credits to graduate; Jimmy's lack of a place to spend the night since his dad kicked him out.
11:00	Meet with department heads to revise course selection guide.
12:30	Lunchtime counseling group: non-English-speaking students' adjustment to school.
1:30	Attend meeting about alternative school placement for Leonard, who brought a weapon to school.
2:30	Meet with homebound program teacher to arrange instruction for Allen, who was injured in a car wreck.
2:45	Return phone calls; make notes on day.
3:00	Meet with college representative about being included in College Night.
3:30	Make presentation to faculty meeting on symptoms of depression in students and beginning a crisis intervention team.
7:30	Meeting with parents about financial aid for post-secondary schools.

College/University Counseling

College/university counseling is often more specialized than is public school counseling. Although coordinated under the umbrella of student services, often one group does admissions counseling; another, career counseling and job placement; another, residence hall advising; and yet another, personal counseling in a counseling center. In a smaller institution, one counselor may work in more than one of these areas. Counseling in some schools is limited to academic advising and perhaps job placement assistance.

Admissions officers recruit various populations: minority students, outstanding high school students, athletes and musicians, transfers from community colleges, and other special groups. They also shepherd students through the application and manage the admissions process. They have a great deal of contact with high school counselors and often talk to students at high school college night programs with recruiters from other higher education institutions. Often admissions personnel also help students garner financial aid. They give campus tours and orient students and their parents to the campus and the programs available.

Career counselors and placement officers offer career counseling, sometimes helping students choose majors or showing them what careers extend from majors already selected. They show students how to prepare résumés and placement files; how to dress and prepare for interviews; and sometimes actually arrange interviews for students. They often sponsor career days, where prospective employers visit campus to explain future job options to students. They recruit the recruiters who hire their students and arrange for these potential employers to visit campus and have access to students. Sometimes placement services extend to alumni, as well as to currently enrolled students.

Those responsible for student life on campus usually belong to the student personnel team on a college or a university campus. Their job duties range from arranging social activities at the beginning of the year where new students meet others, to promoting alcohol awareness programs, to monitoring the activity of sororities, fraternities, and other organizations, to supervising student life in the residence halls. Often they plan preventive programs such as AIDS awareness or other such topics of concern to college-age students. Much of their work may be done in conjunction with the student health services, as well as with the counseling center professionals.

Professionals employed in a university counseling center are likely to be doctoral-level clinical or counseling psychologists or licensed professional counselors, often working in consultation with a psychiatrist. They work much as they would at any other mental health center, on an appointment basis, seeing people with a wide variety of mental health concerns: depression, sexuality, substance abuse, independence from parents, marital/relationship issues, poor self-concept, and other such topics. They provide group and individual counseling and may offer study skills or other such courses.

Some undergraduate colleges are primarily preprofessional schools, where a majority of those receiving a baccalaureate degree go on to law, medical, dental, business, or some other professional graduate school. In these colleges, the job of the counselors and placement officers revolves around helping students take the right tests, pursue scholarships and fellowships, and do the other things necessary to get into the next level of schooling.

Community College Counseling

Community college counseling follows much the same model as does university counseling, except for the absence of residence halls. A lot of community college students are part-time students, many of whom return to the workforce or to education after a gap of many years. Thus community college counselors typically work with a wider age span than do university or college student personnel workers. In a larger community college, one counselor may work with veterans' affairs, another with dropouts seeking further education, and another with women returning to the workplace after several years' absence. Community college counselors must know about work placement opportunities for their students, but also must be very familiar with transfer requirements for four-year colleges and universities. Often a community counselor closely resembles a high school counselor in the effort to help a student think through future plans for work and education.

In many states, the cost of community college courses makes an education available to many who could not afford to attend other schools. Frequently a community college counselor works with first-generation college students who do not have a family tradition of education beyond high school. An important part of a community college counselor's job, as with any counselor, is to ensure that students see all possible options. Community college counselors often help students successfully bridge the gap between high school and college.

There is probably no typical day for a college or university counselor because of the diversity of the job of the counselor at that level. The counselor in a postsecondary institution is likely to be more specialized than is the public school counselor.

Other School Settings

Counselors also work in other school settings that have educational missions. A counselor in a very competitive private school, for example, may have as a prime task getting as many students as possible into prestigious colleges and universities. A counselor in a parochial school may add young people's spiritual welfare to the tasks already listed. Young people who are schooled in a detention home or prison system may have counselors who try to correct their antisocial behavior and help them understand the norms and requirements of society. Young people hospitalized for long-term conditions, residents of children's homes, and other such children and young adults outside the usual public school system likely have one benefit of some educational counseling. School counselors may be asked by home-schooling parents to respond to some of the counseling needs of their children. Whatever the setting, the process of counseling remains the same.

Differences from Nonschool Settings

Counseling in an educational setting differs somewhat from similar work in an agency, private practice, or other noneducational setting.

1. The counselor in an educational setting has a clearly defined mission: to help the student learn. Many factors impinge on learning, including family and peer influences, personal motivation, ability, degree of mental health of the student, and many more. The school counselor's role is to help the student arrange the components of life so that learning can occur. Although the counselor may do family counseling or intense personal counseling, the school counselor's client is the student, and the counselor's efforts are directed toward helping that student achieve well in school.

2. *Students in an educational setting are usually readily available to the counselor.* In an agency or private practice, a client may or may not keep an appointment. In a public school, generally the counselor can readily find the student. In fact, the counselor has the authority to command a student to come to the counseling office—not done very often, and not conducive to counselor–client trust—which is absent in most other professional settings.

3. *School counselors do not work in isolation.* There are many other people in the building also interested in the same student: teachers, administrators, school psychologist, peers, and others. The counselor works in the school as a social system, whereas a private practitioner may see the client only as an individual or as a part of a small family unit. The school counselor thus must understand how to "work the system" for the benefit of the student and must be able to work in collaborative fashion with others surrounding the student.

4. *School counselors work with adults as well as students.* In an agency or private practice setting, a counselor may be able to limit practice to one age group, with only minimal contact with clients of another age group. Not so in a school, where the counselor must be able to build rapport and trusting relationships with both students and adults.

5. *School counselors work with a normal population.* Most young people in schools are mentally healthy most of the time. Most of the school counselor's efforts are directed toward a normal, healthy, reasonably well-adjusted clientele.

6. *The school counselor is accountable to someone, probably a school administrator, and ultimately to the public.* There is likely to be more monitoring of the school counselor's work than the work of a counselor in other settings.

7. *Conversely, there is probably less clinical supervision for school counselors than for other counseling professionals.* Typically the only other comparably trained person (or persons) in the building is another school counselor. Those making decisions about the work of the counselor are probably not counselors. Sometimes there is a person in the district office who is responsible for the overall school counseling program, but usually only in larger systems does this person provide clinical supervision.

8. *The job of the school counselor is relatively protected.* Mostly its continuation does not depend on someone's whim or the economy, although in some states hard budget times have led to decline or elimination of school counseling programs. In many states, school counseling positions are mandated by state education regulations. University and college counselors do not enjoy this degree of protection, however.

9. *School counselors work with large numbers of people, including some whom they would not choose as clients.* They rarely have the option of transferring a student client to another counselor or of refusing to enter into a counseling relationship. They are pretty much stuck with who is assigned to them.

10. *Often school counselors see involuntary clients.* Someone else—a teacher, parent, administrator, or special education committee—decides that the student needs counseling, placing the student and counselor in a relationship that neither of them chose. An old joke says, "How many counselors does it take to change a light bulb?" with the punch line "Only one, but the light bulb has to want to be changed." It is difficult to work with clients who do not see the need for change, especially in the direction desirable to the school or to parents.

11. *Much of the school counselor's work can be developmental and not focused on crisis.* The role can be primarily working with students to enhance their career and educational development, with the lesser part of the program devoted to crisis counseling. Certainly elementary and middle grades counselors attempt to focus on developmental counseling.

12. *There can be a lot of paperwork associated with the school counselor's job.* Although many high school counselors have clerical assistance, many, probably most, elementary and middle school counselors do not. Student records, transcripts, college application forms, observation forms for special education students, reports associated with testing, and on and on, can consume a counselor's time. Adequate clerical assistance can be invaluable to free a counselor to use skills and training. Sometimes a trusted volunteer can assist with some clerical duties.

13. *The school counselor is a generalist.* Counselors in schools work with careers, educational options, social problems, testing, families, substance abuse, and a whole host of other areas. Counselors in agencies or private practice might specialize in any one of these areas. Rarely is a school counselor able to specialize, although counselors may have particular knowledge for the students they work with, such as college admissions procedures.

14. *School counseling is a recognized branch of the profession.* Although the public may not be really clear about what a licensed professional counselor does, most people have at least a hazy—although too often negative—notion about what school counselors do. School counselors must work hard to make their publics view them in a positive manner, but they do not have to break new ground to identify themselves to people.

15. *School counselors have trouble agreeing on what their role should be.* When they explain it to others, they tend to speak in jargon that does not delineate exactly what they do. They have been writing role statements and debating the role and function of the school counselor since the job appeared in public schools. But there is not yet clear agreement, especially in the minds of the public, legislators, and school boards, about just what the job is. Fortunately, most agree it is important, even if they are not sure just why.

Trends and Future Directions

Some issues are in the forefront of the counseling profession today. Many of these were identified by John Krumboltz, David Capuzzi, Norman Gysbers, and myself (Clair Cole Vaught) in a symposium called the "20/20 Conference" jointly sponsored by ACA (then American Association for Counseling and Development, or AACD) and ERIC/CAPS in 1987 in Washington, DC. This conference attempted to look backward twenty years and forward twenty years in the counseling profession and was chronicled in *Building Strong School Counseling Programs* (Walz, 1988).

Issues and areas of concern facing school counselors today include these:

1. Most school counselors work in a multicultural setting. How do counselors work with multicultural populations, many of whom come from very different cultures from most school counselors? What do counselors need to know about Asian Americans, African Americans, Native Americans, Hispanic Americans, and other American ethnic groups, not to mention non-English-speaking immigrants and political refugees? How does the counselor learn about the cultural values of those individuals and families? Are there techniques more or less appropriate for individuals from different backgrounds?
2. Counselors must learn to work with other special populations who may be very far from the counselor's personal experience: the economically disadvantaged, including the homeless; students seeking to know more about sexual orientation; substance abusers; those with eating disorders; pregnant teenagers; the chronically ill; and others. How do counselors learn all they need to know about resources for working with these special groups?
3. Schools represent an ever-more-diverse population. How do school counselors prepare themselves to work with this population? How does a university counselor help the learning disabled or severely orthopedically impaired student? How will AIDS affect the schools of our nation?
4. Violence in schools is a chief worry of professionals, parents, and students. What is the counselor's role in helping young people learn to solve conflicts peaceably? How does a counselor help calm a school where children have witnessed violent death?
5. School counselors often find their days consumed by crisis counseling when they believe they should be working with developmental, noncrisis issues. As more societal issues intrude into the lives of children and young people, school counselors see more and deeper crisis situations than in previous years, squeezing out the time allocated for developmental counseling programs.

6. School counselors believe more and more that they cannot work with the student without attempting to help the family as well. What is the school counselor's responsibility to the family? Who is the client: the student, or the troubled family that is impairing the educational capacity of the student? Should school counselors be trained as family therapists? Should schools employ licensed professional counselors or clinical/counseling psychologists to do family therapy, as an adjunct to school counseling?

7. The day of the school counselor is often consumed with paperwork and other noncounseling duties, especially at the secondary level. How does the school counselor clearly define an appropriate role, in order to pass along routine clerical tasks, administrative duties, and other noncounseling roles to other, more appropriate people?

8. High school counselors have received more criticism than other kinds of school counselors the past several years. What does the public want from high school counselors, and what job conditions (such as smaller caseloads and more secretarial assistance) are necessary for that to be accomplished?

9. Elementary school counselors have recently been under attack in some states from the conservative right. What is the actual objection raised by these vocal parents (and nonparents)? How can elementary counselors present themselves in the best light and rally support? How can they convince others they do not use mind-altering techniques nor invade the privacy of the individual or the family, unless something criminal occurs? How can DUSO the Dolphin (Dinkmeyer & Dinkmeyer, *Developing Understanding of Self and Others*, 1982) be vindicated?

10. Clinical supervision is a need expressed by many school counselors. How can school counselors receive the kind of supervision they need to continue to hone their skills? Is a peer supervision model feasible? If so, how can it be instituted?

11. School counselors often wonder whether what they do actually makes a difference in the lives of their students. What studies should be undertaken to determine what methods, strategies, and program components work the best, for which students, under which conditions?

12. There appear to be no national data, gathered state by state, on likely numbers of vacancies in school counseling. Will we need more or fewer school counselors in the coming years? What kind of data collection method do we need to be able to tell people about the future in school counseling?

13. For many youth today, the future appears hopeless. How can counselors instill hope, offer options, circumvent suicide, reduce dropout rates, increase the numbers of youth in schools instead of prisons?

14. Many university programs in the United States prepare school counselors. What do students need to learn before they go to work in schools? What courses, field experiences, computer skills, and other methods best fit them to become effective school counselors? What is the university's role in getting new ideas and practices to those already trained and in school counseling jobs?

15. Often the public seems unaware of what school counselors do. How can the public's often negative image of the school counselor be improved? How can

school and university counselors demonstrate their worth to the students they serve and to those who make budgetary decisions?

16. Legal and ethical issues often rear their heads in counselors' offices. With whom may the counselor share information, about what? What safeguards exist to protect the counselor who intends to intervene on behalf of a client? How does the counselor keep up to date on legal issues and ethical practice?

Summary

School counseling is alive and well in the elementary, middle or junior high, and high schools, and in the community and junior colleges, colleges, and universities of this country. A well-trained cadre of school and postsecondary counselors serve students, from prekindergarten through graduate school and senior citizens returning to school late in life.

School counselors provide educational, career, and personal counseling to students. They plan developmental counseling programs, but their time is often consumed with crisis interventions for acute problems. They coordinate and consult with other professionals on behalf of their students. They use tests and other means to appraise their students' ability and achievement. They provide counseling to families, as well as to their students. School counselors find joy in the success of their students, and frustration in what they perceive to be failures. They look for new ways to help their students to be successful in school and later in life.

References

Baker, S. (1992). *School counseling for the twenty-first century*. New York: Merrill.

Borow, H., & Humes, C. (1987). Origins and growth of counseling. In C. Humes (Ed.), *Contemporary counseling*. Muncie, IN: Accelerated Development.

Brown, D., & Srebalus, D. (1988). *An introduction to the counseling profession*. Englewood Cliffs, NJ: Prentice Hall.

Cole, C. (1993). *Nurturing a teacher advisory program*. Columbus, OH: National Middle School Association.

Coleman, H. (1995). Cultural factors and the counseling process: Implications for school counselors. *School Counselor, 42*(3), 180–186.

Dinkmeyer, D., and Dinkmeyer, D., Jr. (1982). *DUSO I*. Circle Pines, MN: American Guidance Service.

Gysbers, N., & Henderson, P. (1988). *Developing and managing your school guidance program*. Alexandria, VA: AACD Press.

Hobbs, B., & Collison, B. (1995). School community agency collaboration: Implications for the school counselor. *School Counselor, 43*(1), 58–65.

Hutchins, D., & Cole, C. (1992). *Helping relationships and strategies* (2nd ed.). Pacific Grove, CA: Brooks/Cole.

Hutchins, D., & Vaught, C. (1997). *Helping relationships and strategies* (3rd ed.). Pacific Grove, CA: Brooks/Cole.

Killin, T., & Williams, R. (1995). Making a difference in school climate, counseling services, and student success. NASSP Bulletin, 79(570), 44–50.

Libsch, M., & Freedman-Doan, P. (1995). Perceptions of high school counseling activities: Response differences according to college plans. *NASSP Bulletin, 79*(570), 51–59.

McGee, L., & Fauble-Erickson, T. (1995). The multifaceted role of guidance and counseling in the middle level school. *NASSP Bulletin, 79*(570), 16–19.

Muro, J., & Kottman, T. (1995). *Guidance and counseling in the elementary and middle school.* Madison, WI: Brown and Benchmark.

Tryneski, J. (1993). *Requirements for certification of teachers, counselors, librarians, and administrators for elementary and secondary schools* (58th ed.). Chicago: University of Chicago Press.

Vaught, C. (1995). A letter from a middle school counselor to her principal. *NASSP Bulletin, 79*(570), 20–23.

Walz, G. (Ed.). (1988). *Building strong school counseling programs.* Alexandria, VA: AACD Press.

Chapter *14*

Counseling in Mental Health and Private Practice Settings

David K. Brooks, Jr., Ph.D.

During the late 1960s counselors began to diverge from the path that led from graduate school directly to more or less traditional positions in educational settings. The following three decades witnessed such an acceleration of this divergence that by the midpoint of the 1990s the profession of counseling finds itself in a brave new world that bears little resemblance to the environments in which its practitioners applied their craft nearly thirty years ago.

In 1965, certification had only one meaning. Now it has nearly half a dozen. Counselor education curricula thirty years ago were focused on the preparation of practitioners for secondary schools, graduating students after 30 semester hours, often without a practicum. Today professionally accredited programs at the master's degree level range in length from 48 to more than 60 semester hours and prepare students to practice as specialists in more than half a dozen different program tracks. In 1965 any talk of diagnosis and treatment of mental and emotional disorders would have been viewed as heresy in counseling circles. In 1995 such issues are not only incorporated into the curricula of most counselor education programs, but also they are written into state law and federal regulations as competencies expected of professional counselors.

The diversification of counseling from its roots in educational and vocational guidance to the multiplicity of health care and community service settings in which the majority of its members now work is a fascinating story. It would be much less interesting if the leaders of the profession and its organizations had planned it this way. Fortunately for the telling of the story, they did not.

Counselors: Out of School and Out of Work

For most of the decade of the 1960s, the job market for graduates of counselor education programs was a near cornucopia. Until late in the decade, funding and programmatic support for school guidance positions were strong in virtually all areas of the United States. Beginning with the National Defense Education Act of 1958 and continuing with the Elementary and Secondary Education Act of 1965, federal funding for school guidance and counseling programs and parallel support at the state level set the kinds of expectations that counselor education programs took as a green light to produce as many graduates as possible.

Supply, Demand, and New Job Market Realities

As the decade of the 1960s neared an end, however, the budgetary demands of the war in Vietnam exerted a squeeze on federal dollars that was felt in many human services programs, including school counseling program funding. The reduction in federal support was soon followed by a corresponding decrease in state funding. School counseling positions were not on the endangered list, but they were not nearly as numerous as formerly. As often happens in such situations, there was a lag time during which the supply of graduates substantially outpaced the demand for positions. Before counselor education programs responded with enrollment policies that were more in keeping with the new realities of the school counseling market, several classes of graduates had experienced real hardship in finding the kinds of positions for which they had been prepared.

A similarly adverse situation began to manifest itself for counselors trained at the doctoral level. Because counselor education programs were shrinking in size, university positions for counselor educators were decreasing correspondingly. The other major career path for doctoral counselor education graduates—that of becoming licensed psychologists and pursuing positions either in university counseling centers or in the Veterans Administration—was increasingly blocked by new regulatory barriers erected by state psychology licensing boards.

For newly graduated counselors at both master's and doctoral levels, therefore, the 1970s dawned with new realities and new uncertainties. Listings for practitioner positions in traditional educational and vocational settings were flooded with applicants. A de facto freeze was in effect for new hires in counselor education positions. It was clear that new options and new settings would have to be explored, or a generation of counselor education graduates would be lost to the profession.

Mental Health, Agency, and Private Practice: Applying Counseling Skills in Different Settings

The Community Mental Health Centers Act of 1963 provided federal funding to establish community-based treatment centers as alternatives to the state hospital system that had been the cornerstone of public mental health services since the nineteenth century. Several significant federal studies (Brooks & Weikel, 1986) had suggested community mental health centers (CMHCs) were both more humane and more effective than the mental health "warehouses" that many state hospitals had become.

The legislation anticipated that the CMHCs would be staffed by multidisciplinary treatment teams that included both the four "core provider" professions of psychiatry, psychology, social work, and nursing as well as paraprofessionals whose training background was unspecified. As the centers opened and as staffing patterns began to emerge, the "paraprofessional" positions were often filled by master's-level counselor education graduates.

Counselors trained at the doctoral level also found CMHCs to be receptive to their skills. Denied licensure as psychologists by state boards, they were often classified as psychologists by the centers, whose employees were frequently exempt from licensure requirements.

Community mental health centers were not the only noneducational settings in which counselor education graduates found employment in the late 1960s and early 1970s. Youth services bureaus, women's health centers, programs for displaced homemakers, cooperative employment training programs, parole programs, drug and alcohol rehabilitation programs, and community-based veterans' centers were but a few of the nontraditional settings in which counselors worked.

Mental Health Counseling: The Identity Emerges

These kinds of postgraduate experiences had several effects on the profession. First of all, counselors discovered that they could be effective with client populations and issues very different from those for which many of them had been trained. In-service education programs, clinical supervision, and daily on-the-job training in CMHCs and other community-based settings, combined with their graduate training in individual and group counseling, appraisal, career development, and other basics of counselor education programs, fitted counselors to function in these environments with special combinations of skills and perspectives that were valued by supervisors, peers, and clients alike.

Another effect of the increasing numbers of counselors working in community settings, one that took a little longer to become apparent, was the reciprocal influence on graduate counselor education programs. In response to the needs of graduates in these different settings, institutions began to incorporate coursework in psychopathology and diagnosis and treatment planning. Perhaps more important was the changing nature of practicum and internship experiences. Once limited to school settings or to on-campus laboratories, practicum and internship opportunities were increasingly available in the kinds of agency settings in which students were most likely to work after graduation. And some of the on-site supervision was beginning to be provided by the counselor education graduates who had broken the ground for counselors in these settings several years earlier.

A third effect of the emergence of counselors in CMHCs and other agency settings was the continuing awareness on the part of these professionals that they were different. They filled positions sometimes labeled as "psychologist" or "social worker," but more often were classified as "psychiatric aide" or "mental health worker II." Despite the fact that they were rarely accorded identity in their work settings as counselors, they did not seek to attach themselves to their "core provider" colleagues. Reinforcing the sense of "differentness" was the reality of a status differential defined, among other criteria, by often significant differences in compensation between counselors and members of the core provider disciplines. Regardless of the level of clinical skill attained, counselors in CMHCs usually found it difficult to escape the most apparent vestiges of the "paraprofessional" stigma under which many of them were hired.

Closely related to these status and salary dimensions of identity was the lack of credentialing mechanisms that defined who counselors were, what their training was, and what their areas of clinical competence were. Prior to the late 1970s, the only credentialing affecting counselors was the special case of teacher certification that endorsed counselors for practice in public schools. Not only was there substantial variability from state to state in the requirements for school counselor certification, but also the credential was in no way viewed as transferable to mental health or community agency settings. For all intents, therefore, counselors in these settings had no credentialing, either statutory or professional.

The other major shortcoming that such counselors experienced was the lack of a professional organization that represented their interests and responded to their needs. What was then the American Personnel and Guidance Association (APGA) had no division for counselors who worked in mental health agencies. Existing divisions for counselors in employment service, rehabilitation, and public offender settings met the needs of only a few. What was needed was a new association or a new division of APGA that was specifically aimed at counselors in mental health and other community agency settings.

In the mid-1970s, forces were set in motion that were to address the difficulties that counselors were experiencing both in credentialing and in professional identity. Because these forces were soon to overlap and interact with each other, the formation and development of a new professional organization will be dealt with first, even though its inception was chronologically somewhat later than the beginnings of counselor licensure.

The American Mental Health Counselors Association

The incorporation of the American Mental Health Counselors Association (AMHCA) in Florida in November 1976, was the result of correspondence, organizational spadework, and, most important, an optimistic and idealistic vision of what the future of the mental health services delivery system ought to be about.

According to Weikel (1985), letters to the editor of the *APGA Guidepost* began appearing in 1975 that solicited interest in forming a new professional organization for counselors in mental health and other community agencies. After about a year of nonresponse, these petitions found a receptive audience in Nancy Spisso and James J. Messina of the Escambia County Mental Health Center in Pensacola, Florida. They responded to a letter from a group of counselors in Janesville, Wisconsin, and at the same time began to stir up interest among friends and colleagues from the counselor education program at the University of Florida in Gainesville, of which Spisso was a recent graduate and where Messina had been an NIMH postdoctoral fellow. The so-called Gainesville–Janesville axis was forged, which turned out to be only the beginning of a nationwide response to Spisso and Messina's idea.

Within weeks, several hundred people had signed on and plans were in the works to petition APGA for division status. Unfortunately for this initial effort at affiliation, the APGA board of directors had just passed a moratorium on the establishment of new divisions. The core leadership of AMHCA decided to found an independent organization that would maintain close communication with APGA and perhaps seek division affiliation at a later time.

It was soon evident that "mental health counselor" was a professional identity with broad appeal and that there was a potentially sizable membership for the fledgling organization that was just waiting to be tapped. Growing to nearly 1,500 members in less than a year and a half, AMHCA held its first national conference in March 1978 (Weikel, 1985). The leadership decided to approach APGA once again about becoming a division. This time the APGA board was receptive, but the AMHCA membership on the ratification ballot nearly rejected affiliation. Even though some members resigned and some rather heated rhetoric was exchanged at this time, AMHCA became APGA's thirteenth division, effective July 1, 1978. Membership continued to grow, and soon the disaffected former members' negative effect on membership statistics was overcome.

AMHCA and APGA: An Uneasy Marriage

Almost from the beginning of its status as an APGA division, AMHCA challenged the parent organization on its priorities, its stewardship of fiscal resources, and on its record of effective advocacy for counselors' interests.

Founded in 1952 as the result of a merger between four existing organizations, APGA was almost totally focused on educational issues in its legislative agenda at the state and federal levels because the majority of its members worked in educational settings, both in K–12 public schools and in higher education. Most of the individuals involved in APGA governance were practitioners in such settings or were considered educators who trained school counselors and student personnel specialists. When AMHCA leaders began talking about mental health issues as association legislative priorities, their arguments did not always fall on deaf ears, but often fell on ears belonging to fellow counselors in need of time and reorientation to more fully understand what the arguments were about.

The AMHCA leaders even questioned the name of the parent organization, insisting that APGA should change its name so that the word "counseling" was included. At first, no one outside the AMHCA leadership took this argument seriously, but after several years of agitation and alliance building, mental health counselors were successful in accomplishing their objective. A coalition led by AMHCA and by the American College Personnel Association (ACPA), one of APGA's founding divisions, persuaded the APGA senate in March 1983, to adopt American Association for Counseling and Development (AACD) as the parent organization's new name, effective July 1 of that year. The AMHCA leadership's first choice for a new name had been American Counseling Association, but the consensus necessary for so dramatic a change would take nearly a decade more to build.

The AMHCA continued to grow, passing the American School Counselor Association (ASCA) as AACD's largest division in 1985 and reaching the 10,000-member milestone early in 1986. The division's leaders found that legislative and organization priorities based on support for credentialing, on high standards for training, and on "bread-and-butter" issues such as third-party insurance reimbursement and advocacy for the right to practice had not only a sustained appeal for attracting new members, but also that such priorities, if argued long and persuasively enough, tended to become AACD issues as well, within the limits that the following examples demonstrate.

In July 1987, the AACD governing council committed itself to a new task force on third-party reimbursement. This action was taken only after it was pointed out that private practitioners were the largest single group within the AACD membership; that there were more private practitioners within AACD than school counselors at the elementary, middle, and secondary levels; and that insurance reimbursement was not just an AMHCA issues, because the numbers of private practitioners within AACD exceeded AMHCA's total membership.

Similarily, the governing council in the following spring adopted criteria equivalent to those long advocated by AMHCA as the standard that the association would recognize in its efforts aimed at reimbursement in both public and private sectors. This was probably a more radical step than the council otherwise would have taken, had AMHCA not been previously successful in achieving CHAMPUS (Civilian Health and Medical Program of the Uniformed Services) recognition for mental health counselors (see the section on recognition and reimbursement, later).

The AMHCA leadership thus found that the governing council was always more willing to embrace issues for which the statistics were unarguable or those that the federal government had already endorsed. Making AMHCA's case in the context of the logic of the situation, the social desirability of taking a proactive stance, and the wisdom of setting standards that did not regress toward the mean were always more difficult.

Fiscal Management and Frustration

Among its other continuing issues with AACD leadership and management, AMHCA insisted from the very beginning on getting its money's worth out of AACD affiliation. The AACD fiscal policies governing the ways in which division funds are handled, interest charges, investment options, and simple reporting of accounts were among the practices AMHCA challenged. In most instances, AMHCA was successful in arguing for policy changes so that divisions' fiscal resources were used to best advantage.

Even with these successes there remained a strong feeling, particularly among AMHCA's council of past presidents, that the relationship with AACD had outlived its usefulness. The division's "dinosaurs" had no direct voice in policy, but their influence was considerable during the decade of the 1980s primarily because of the strong personal bonds among the past presidents and because they actively sought to mentor new leaders.

Each presidency from 1980 on had ended with a certain amount of frustration that AACD's responsiveness to mental health counseling issues was always limited by the attitude of "We can only give you so much attention and support because we have to be attentive to the issues of the smaller divisions." This, when compared with the legislative success of sibling organizations such as the American Association for Marriage and Family Therapy, who benefit from a more single-minded agenda, has caused AMHCA's past leaders to seriously weigh the advantages of going it alone.

Stepping Up to the Brink

In late 1993 and early 1994, the AMHCA board of directors took steps to disaffiliate from the American Counseling Association (ACA; the name had been changed from AACD in 1991). The ACA was in serious financial difficulty, and several divisions were concerned that they might lose their own resources to bail out the parent body. All but a few of the AMHCA council of past presidents, however, saw this as a time to stand with ACA and called on the membership to vote against disaffiliation in an every-member referendum held in March 1994. By a majority approaching 75 percent, the membership rejected disaffiliation and, in effect, repudiated their elected leaders. As this book goes to press, yet another disaffiliation move is being initiated by the AMHCA board of directors. The outcome of such efforts cannot be predicted at this time.

The irony of these efforts to separate from ACA is that AMHCA, after years of unsuccessful attempts, finally managed to elect two of its past presidents, back to back, as ACA president. A goal of nearly twenty years' standing, to use the ACA presidency as a vehicle for accomplishing the mental health counseling agenda, was achieved at the same time that AMHCA's elected leaders were seeking to disaffiliate from ACA.

Recognition, Reimbursement, and Managed Care

Among AMHCA's goals from its founding had been the notion that mental health counselors should be recognized as service providers on an equal footing with the other nonmedical mental health disciplines: clinical psychology, social work, psychiatric nursing, and marriage and family therapy. Its professional certification standards (see the following section) had been designed with this goal in mind, the somewhat radical position being advanced that demonstrated competence rather than academic degree should be the criterion by which providers were recognized.

As early as 1981, AMHCA leaders were seeking recognition for mental health counselors as eligible providers under Social Security programs. The first breakthrough at the federal level came as the result not of a legislative success, but of a bureaucratic one. CHAMPUS, after three years of lobbying by AMHCA, in 1987 recognized certified or licensed mental health counselors as providers eligible for reimbursement under its programs with physician referral. Building on that victory, AMHCA next sought inclusion for mental health counselors as recognized providers under the Federal Employees Health Benefits Program (FEHBP). This legislative effort was unsuccessful as a single initiative, becoming less desirable as a goal as concern grew about inclusion of mental health counselors as eligible providers in a comprehensive national health care program.

Concurrent with these public sector initiatives has been substantial activity to achieve recognition by private insurance programs. The most direct route to such recognition is amendment of state insurance codes to permit "freedom of choice" statutes to extend to counselors as eligible providers. Such efforts were successful early on in Virginia, Texas, Montana, and Vermont, with de facto recognition in numerous other states.

The movement toward managed care, such as offered by health maintenance and preferred provider organizations (HMOs and PPOs), among others, has complicated mental health counselors' efforts in the recognition and reimbursement arena. Apparently operating beyond the reach of most freedom-of-choice statutes, managed care plans have as their primary objective the reduction of health care costs. All providers, in both physical and mental health domains, tend to be viewed by the managed care sector in the context of cost-effectiveness rather than in terms of clinical effectiveness as caregivers. Although mental health counselors can definitely undercut other provider groups in the fees they charge, such action would probably be counterproductive in the long run. Navigating these tricky and potentially treacherous waters is one of the major challenges currently facing the AMHCA leadership.

Mental Health Counselors and Credentialing

A couple of years before AMHCA was organized, attention within the counseling community began to be focused on the issue of credentialing. Initial concern surrounded the disenfranchisement of doctoral-level counselor education graduates by state psychology licensing boards. The focus was soon broadened, however, to encompass master's-level counselors as well. Mental health counselors were not involved in these early efforts because AMHCA had not yet been founded and because when it was, the new organization directed its energies toward different credentialing objectives for the first several years.

Professional Certification

The clinical element in AMHCA's strategy to achieve parity with the other non-medical mental health providers was the structure it established in 1979 to administer a professional certification process for mental health counselors. The National Academy of Certified Clinical Mental Health Counselors administered its first examination to fifty "pioneer" certificants in February 1979 and was formally chartered as an independent, free-standing certification body in July of that year. It was closely allied to AMHCA, but in order to meet the standards recommended by a series of federal studies and embodied by the National Commission of Health Certifying Agencies (NCHCA), it was necessary for the academy to be legally separate from the professional organization (Brooks and Weikel, 1986).

The academy's certification process required applicants to submit an appliction form and nonrefundable fee, together with transcripts of graduate coursework, documentation of supervised experience, and recommendations from clinical supervisors. If those had been the only requirements for admission to the examination, thousands of counselors doubtless would have flocked to the academy banner. Two additional requirements caused the expected flood of applicants to more nearly resemble a trickle. The first of these was the requirement that applicants submit a taped sample of clinical work accompanied by a critique. The second requirement, since dropped, was that recommendations from three present or former clients be submitted. Although these criteria were not unreasonable by themselves, the combined effect presented a very discouraging prospect for large numbers of potential applicants, who were perhaps as influenced by the "hassle factor" of these latter requirements as they were by the sheer terror of peer review.

The NCHCA was founded with the intent that voluntary national certification would eventually replace state licensure as the credential of choice. The NCHCA standards were designed to become, for all health-related professions, the criteria by which eligibility for insurance reimbursement was determined. Thus the academy's certification procedures, while setting what were viewed as extremely high professional standards, were also grounded in bread-and-butter pragmatism.

The CCMHC: A Rigorous Credential with Little Acceptance

Unfortunately for the academy's founders, the rest of the health care community did not wholeheartedly buy into the NCHCA approach of voluntary national certifications replacing state licensure as the predominant modality of professional credentialing. The mental health provider disciplines, especially psychology and social work, had been successful in their legislative efforts at achieving passage of state licensure laws and were not about to abandon the fruits of their labors. Furthermore, the insurance community showed itself in the 1970s and 1980s to be less than enthusiastic about national voluntary certification. Although individual certified clinical mental health counselors (CCMHCs) were reimbursed by health insurance plans in most states, the pattern of such recognition was far from uniform.

Confounding the acceptance of the CCMHC credential within the counseling profession was the establishment in 1982 of the National Board for Certified Counselors (NBCC). Created to develop a national generic certification, NBCC was funded at a much higher level than the academy and, following an extensive publicity campaign, attracted within the profession broad interest for its embryonic credential. The resulting widespread awareness coupled with an extremely liberal "grandfathering" policy led to numbers of applicants that exceeded even the most optimistic predictions. Nearly 14,000 individuals had been certified by NBCC by the time the "grandfathering" period expired.

With so few of their own demonstrating interest in the rigorous academy certification process and with such widespread acceptance of a generic, nonclinical credential, AMHCA leaders found themselves literally in a situation of being all dressed up with no place to go—no place, that is, except to the counselor licensure movement that was experiencing such difficulty in the early 1980s.

Mental Health Counselors and Licensure

Because the AMHCA leadership was so committed to national certification as represented by the CCMHC, relatively little interest was devoted to the counselor licensure effort that had been underway since 1974 under the aegis of the APGA (later AACD) licensure committee. After nearly a decade's work, by 1983 counselor licensure laws had been passed in only seven states. Six of these states were in the South (Virginia, Arkansas, Alabama, Texas, Florida, and North Carolina) and the only one outside the region (Idaho) wasn't exactly a major population center. Clearly this was an area of professional endeavor that could benefit from the energy and commitment of mental health counselors.

At the time the first AMHCA licensure committee was appointed in 1979, the APGA licensure committee had been in operation for five years. Active licensure committees had been functioning for some time in ASCA and in the Association for Counselor Education and Supervision (ACES). As might be expected, the ASCA licensure committee was principally involved in educating school counselors about licensure and in encouraging them to become active in their state efforts. The ACES licensure committee had undertaken several research efforts, primarily membership surveys to determine the impact of exclusion by state psychology boards on ACES members' professional interests and to ascertain how important the growing counselor licensure movement was to ACES members.

The War Chest Grant Program

The AMHCA licensure committee set a somewhat different group of priorities for itself. Membership education was a small piece of the agenda, because whereas most mental health counselors knew the importance of licensure for their professional survival, not everyone was aware of the connections between licensure and academy certification.

Making resources available to state licensure committees that had direct applicability to the legislative process was AMHCA's top priority. The "War Chest" grant was the vehicle developed for this purpose. Ignoring AACD's advice about making funds directly available for lobbying purposes, even to the point of grants being available to pay lobbyists, the AMHCA committee literally put its money where its mouth was. The grants program gave mental health counselors instant entrée and status in the operations of state licensure committees because the AMHCA committee demanded evidence of mental health counselor involvement before it released grant funds.

In 1981 Florida became the fifth state to pass a counselor licensure law and the first to use "licensed mental health counselor" rather than "licensed professional counselor" as the title protected by law. There was not substantive difference between the Florida law and the previous licensure statutes whose terminology sounded more "generic," in terms of definitions, academic and experience requirements, or examination requirements. Several of the states that followed Florida in using this title included somewhat more clinical emphases in their legislative language or in their regulations. Some also specified that the academy examination be used (a practice abandoned in the late 1980s), but regardless of the protected title most counselor licensure laws, passed since mental health counselors began assuming leadership roles in state-level political activity have tended not to be overly specialized either in language or intent.

Unfinished Business

As successful as the counselor licensure effort has been during the last twenty years, there are still several pieces of unfinished business as far as mental health counselors are concerned. First, recognition by both third-party (traditional health insurance) policies and managed care plans remains to be accomplished. It seems desirable to attack both of these issues simultaneously, because if third-party payers are targeted by themselves, the managed care segment of the industry may continue to grow so rapidly that it overtakes its more traditional cousin, rendering the "freedom of choice" issue moot.

The second piece of unfinished business has to do with translating the recognition resulting from successful licensure efforts to positions and descriptions in state personnel classification systems. No state, following the passage of a licensure law, has moved directly to ensure that mental health counselors are subsequently included by title in the personnel systems that dictate staffing patterns in community mental health centers and other wholly or partially publicly funded agencies. The effect is that although many mental health counselors enjoy the benefits of licensure in private practice, their colleagues in public agencies may still suffer from many of the same status and salary inferiorities that existed before the licensure laws were passed.

A third area in need of being resolved has to do with training standards and accreditation. The AMHCA had become a founding member of the Council for Accreditation of Counseling and Related Educational Programs (CACREP) when that body was established as the counseling profession's accreditation agency in 1981. Through the first three versions of training standards, mental health counseling was not recognized as a program track on the same footing as school counseling and student affairs practice. The designation preferred by CACREP was "counseling in community and other agency settings." Finally, in the standards revision that became effective in 1988 mental health counseling was recognized as a separate program area for accreditation, but "community counseling" was retained as a category without specific content.

Mental health counseling apparently faced the same struggle for identity within the counseling profession as it did among peer professions outside of counseling. The issue was somewhat resolved in the next round of standards revision, which became effective in 1994. Mental health counseling was again described as a specialization, but community counseling was retained with curriculum content very similar to mental health counseling, with the exception of diagnosis and treatment of mental and emotional disorders. In the 1994 standards, community counseling also became an "umbrella" under which emphases in career counseling and gerontological counseling, among others, were clustered.

Dealing with the CCMHC

In the early 1990s, mental health counselors needed to decide what to do about the CCMHC. The academy's certificants numbered less than 10 percent of those certified by NBCC. Was this elite credential, which seemed so unattainable to so many mental health counselors, worth preserving, promoting, and financially supporting? Should the NBCC develop a speciality in clinical counseling, comparable to the speciality it administered in career counseling? Should the CCMHC standard be maintained in future government relations efforts and in determining which providers should be included in managed care panels? These issues were so controversial within AMHCA leadership circles that to mention them in public, let alone take a position on them, required a high level of both personal confidence and professional identity.

Finally, in 1993, after several years of intermittent discussions, the academy board of directors decided to bring its certification process under the NBCC umbrella. It appeared that such a move would resolve the academy's chronic financial difficulties and ensure the survival of the credential. What it lost in autonomy, the academy gained in the promise of stability. Whether the credential will become more attractive to practitioners in the future than it has been in the past remains to be seen.

Mental Health Counseling: Identity, Definitions, and Training

A young, dynamic profession can be expected to undergo changes over time, especially in the way it sees itself. Mental health counseling has certainly exemplified this phenomenon. Although there is no discernible movement toward orthodoxy in

---

Mental health counseling is . . .

the process of assisting individuals or groups, through a helping relationship, to achieve optimal mental health through personal and social development and adjustment to prevent the debilitating effects of certain somatic, emotional, and intra- and/or interpersonal disorders.

Source: AMHCA, 1978, p. 19

the provision of professional counseling services, involving the principles of psychotherapy, human development, learning theory, group dynamics, and the etiology of mental illness and dysfunctional behavior to individuals, couples, families, and groups, for the purpose of treating psychopathology and promoting optimal mental health.

Source: NACCMHC, 1985

Figure 14-1   Two Definitions of Mental Health Counseling

terms of identity or definition, it is interesting to compare two definitions that were formulated about seven years apart. This comparison is framed in Figure 14-1.

Clearly, mental health counseling, at least in terms of the way its leaders saw it, became more clinically oriented during the period of time from shortly after its founding to the mid-1980s. It is not too difficult to see that each definition was shaped to some extent by a political agenda. In 1978 the principal purpose was to define differences between mental health counseling and other specializations *within* professional counseling. By 1985, the aim had shifted toward defining mental health counseling so that it resembled the other mental health disciplines, especially those that were already receiving insurance reimbursement for their services.

Differences within the Counseling Profession

What are the differences that these definitions reflect? How does mental health counseling differ from school counseling, from career counseling, or from student affairs practice?

First, mental health counseling differs from its sibling counseling specializations in the age of its clientele and in the probable type of presenting problem. Mental health counselors are more likely to deal with an adult client population, although some practitioners specialize in working with children and adolescents. Unlike school counselors and student affairs practitioners, therefore, mental health counselors deal with clients across the life span, even though most of the clients they see are likely to be adults past traditional college age.

Most mental health counselors espouse a developmental perspective in terms of the way in which they view their clients. In this respect they are similar to school counselors and to student affairs practitioners. They are much more likely, however, to work with clients whose presenting problems extend beyond what would Figure 14-1 indicates, mental health counselors deal with the diagnosis and treatment of mental and emotional disorders. Even so, most practitioners do not view their clients in the context of a medical or illness model. Rather, the treatment planning tends to focus on assessing client strengths and on psychoeducational approaches to helping clients overcome deficits.

Mental health counselors also differ from other counseling practitioners in the extent to which they work with couples and families. To be sure, school counselors are involved in parent conferences and work with children from dysfunctional families and student affairs practitioners deal with couples issues in collegiate settings, but neither are as likely to be involved in treating couples or families over time as are mental health counselors.

Another difference between mental health counselors and other practitioners within the counseling "family" relates to the type and extent of interprofessional and interdisciplinary collaboration and consultation. Mental health counselors are much more likely to receive referrals from physicians and other health care providers than are counselors in educational settings. Similarly, physician consultation may also be necessary because the clients of mental health counselors sometimes need medication or even hospitalization in order for treatment gains to be maximized.

Finally, mental health counselors are more likely than their counseling colleagues to be in work settings where entrepreneurship is necessary for economic survival. School counselors and student affairs practitioners must promote their services, to be sure, but their survival in a position is not usually tied to the number of clients who come through the office door. With mental health counselors, the situation is different, especially if they are in private practice. Accordingly, mental health counselors must constantly cultivate referral sources among fellow professionals as well as perform community service activities such as free speeches and workshops that keep their visibility high.

Similarities and Differences with Other Mental Health Professions

Mental health counseling is similar to all the other mental health provider disciplines in that all of them offer psychotherapy as a service to clients. From this point of commonality differences begin to emerge among the professions. Only psychiatrists, for example, can prescribe medication for their clients, but practitioners of each of the other disciplines must be knowledgeable about psychotropic medication because all of them, sooner or later, will have to refer a client to a psychiatrist for medication as an adjunct to psychotherapy.

Mental health counselors are like psychologists in that both professions tend to focus on individuals in their environments, both are skilled in psychometric instrumentation and its interpretation, and both are trained in individual, group, and often family-intervention modalities. The professions differ in that psychology considers the doctorate to be the academic minimum for independent practice, whereas counseling takes the position that the master's degree with appropriate supervised experience is both the entry level and the terminal degree for practice. Another difference is that mental health counselors are trained in career development, while most psychologists (unless they are counseling psychologists) are not. Psychologists are, however, more likely to be trained in and to use projective measures of personality.

Counselors share with social workers their view of the master's degree as the standard for independent practice. In terms of their perspective on clients, social workers tend to see individuals in the context of communities and view community resources as important adjuncts to psychotherapy. Counselors, in contrast, although not denying the importance of such resources, tend to put less emphasis on them as elements in a treatment plan. Social work training includes less training in psychological testing and in research than does that received by most counselors and even with the relatively new specialization of occupational social work, career development is not a curricular element in most social work training programs. Social workers usually have a broader range of opportunities for supervised field experience than do counselors, especially in hospital and other health care settings.

Mental health counselors and marriage and family therapists also share the terminal master's degree in common as the standard for independent practice. An important difference emerges in the area of theoretical orientation. Whereas mental health counselors typically represent a wide range of theoretical perspectives and most describe themselves as eclectic in both theory and practice, marriage and family therapists, with few exceptions, tend to embrace some variation of a family systems approach as the basis for interventions. Marriage and family therapy training requires extensive clinical experience working with couples and families under supervision, but as with social work, little emphasis is placed on psychological assessment and career development.

Each of the nonmedical provider disciplines draws on important historical, theoretical, research, and practice backgrounds to form its identity and to shape the interventions and perspectives of its practitioners. It should not be construed, however, that each profession's members are vastly different in performance from those of the other professions once the door to the therapy or consultation room is closed. Client experiences are likely to be very similar if they are working with practitioners, regardless of discipline, of more or less equivalent levels of expertise.

Professional Preparation of Mental Health Counselors

As has already been mentioned, mental health counseling was recognized by CACREP in both its 1988 and 1994 standards revisions as a separate program track for accreditation purposes. Mental health counseling had previously been lumped into an amorphous entity known as "community" or "agency" counseling. As of February 1996, ten programs have been approved for accreditation under the 1988 and 1994 standards as mental health counseling programs. This compares with eighty-four programs accredited under various versions of community counseling standards (D. Jacobs, personal communication, February 28, 1996).

Most mental health counselors have master's degrees in counseling, academic credits well past the master's degree, extensive conference, seminar, and workshop training, independent reading and study, and several years of clinical experience under supervision. Some also have advanced institute training in particular approaches such as psychoanalysis, Gestalt, or rational-emotive therapy. Most mental health counselors who have been in practice for a considerable period of time have learned what they know largely as the result of on-the-job training, usually with a hefty dose of supervision.

The CACREP standards for mental health counselor preparation are, therefore, an investment in the future of the profession. They do not reflect even remotely the level of formal graduate training received by most mental health counselors. This is not to imply that because formal graduate training may have been less than present training standards require, most mental health counselors are less than competent. On the contrary, the success and acceptance mental health counselors have experienced in those states in which licensure has been a reality for eight to ten years argue rather convincingly that these most recent arrivals on the mental health practice scene are very competent, indeed.

The Practice of Mental Health Counseling

When AMHCA was founded in 1976, it was expected that the majority of its members would work in community mental health centers. That may have been the pattern in the very early days, but by 1983 the largest single group within the membership (22 percent) was reported as private practitioners. Members reporting employment in community mental health centers represented only 11 percent, the fourth largest group within the association (AACD, 1983). By 1989, the private practice contingent had more than doubled in size, accounting for more than 46 percent of the AMHCA membership. This number has continued to grow, but more slowly because of the impact of managed care. Mental health counselors working in community mental health centers continued to decline proportionately, representing only 8 percent of AMHCA's membership by 1989, whereas counselors working in other types of community agencies accounted for less than 8 percent of the total. In terms of the overall AACD membership, in 1989 only 4.5 percent of the members reported working in community agencies, while 3.2 percent indicated employment in a community mental health center. By contrast nearly 25 percent of AACD members reported their primary work setting as being private practice (AACD, 1989).

What does all this mean? Recent conversations with some of the founding members of AMHCA yielded two factors that could not have been foreseen at the time the association was organized that, in their eyes, account for the rapid growth of the private practitioner contingent and the steep decline in the numbers of counselors working in community mental health centers and other community agencies.

The first of these factors was the phenomenal success of the counselor licensure movement during the decade of the 1980s. When AMHCA was founded, only Virginia had passed a counselor licensure law and by the beginning of the new decade only Arkansas and Alabama had joined the ranks. The early AMHCA leadership can certainly be forgiven for all the energy it put into voluntary professional certification as a desirable alternative to licensure. By early 1996, forty-two states and the District of Columbia had counselor licensure laws on the books—an incredible record of legislative accomplishment.

The other major element accounting for differences in the AMHCA membership profile can best be described in two words—Ronald Reagan. There is no evidence to support the contention that the budget cuts suffered by community mental health centers were any more draconian than those borne by any other community agency, but the effect of the fiscal axe was more than sufficient to get the job done. Counselors in community mental health centers suffered a double blow. First, the CMHCs themselves were not nearly as bureaucratically entrenched as many agencies with longer histories and more stable sources of funding. Second, counselors had entered the CMHCs as paraprofessionals, and regardless of their level of clinical expertise, they did not hold the "power" positions enjoyed by members of more established professions. As has been noted, part of the unfinished business of the counselor licensure movement is to effect change in the state personnel classification systems that, in most instances, determine the status hierarchy in CMHCs.

The Lure of Private Practice

With counselor licensure laws passing at the rate of two or three each year and with the bleak prospects in agency settings showing no signs of alleviating, it is not surprising that during the decade of the 1980s mental health counselors saw opportunities for themselves in an entrepreneurial environment fostered by the Reagan administration. Some entered the private sector on a part-time basis, while others formed group practices to share the risk of setting up a new business. Regardless of how they got started, the important thing to note is that they *did* get started—and in significant numbers. The 10,000+ ACA members who report themselves as being in private practice are probably only a fraction of the total number, especially when one considers that there are approximately that many licensed professional counselors in the state of Texas alone!

Many counselors who have worked in agencies or schools have fantasies about private practice that collide with the realities of this new arena almost as soon as it is entered. The first fantasy usually has to do with being one's own boss. In retrospect, most private practitioners view this as a tradeoff for a regular salary check and regular working hours. The reality is that if one doesn't work, one doesn't earn any money, and to have work, one frequently has to see clients at their convenience rather than one's own. Being one's own boss seems of minor importance to most private practitioners most of the time.

Another fantasy is the expectation of being able to put paperwork aside and really deal with clients—really *be* a counselor. The reality here is that while the total impact of paperwork may be of lesser magnitude, there are limits to one's effectiveness with clients past a certain point. Most mental health counselors in private practice limit themselves to around two dozen individual clients per week, at the most. Many practitioners find that the energy they have to give to the individual therapeutic relationship simply does not extend beyond this number. More than twenty-five individual client hours per week creates a real stressor and constitutes a block to therapeutic effectiveness.

The paperwork of private practice consists of such items as billing, filing insurance claims, promoting workshops, maintaining records of ongoing professional development for renewal of credentials, and keeping appropriate client records. Counseling, regardless of setting or specialization, is not a profession that can be practiced without paperwork of some kind. It's a matter of what kind of paper one prefers.

One of the private practice fantasies that for many practitioners has some reality base is that there is a great deal of variety—or at least there is the potential for variety. If approximately half of one's work hours (most private practitioners spend less) are spent in individual therapy, what does one do with the rest? Group counseling and psychotherapy are certainly options, but most private practitioners engage in consultation, training, supervision, and sometimes part-time teaching to round out their schedules. Such activities not only provide variety, but also many of them nourish the referral base for the psychotherapy part of their practice. Remember, there is no such thing as a stable practice—it is either growing or declining. To be in a growing practice means constantly working on professional contacts and referral sources.

A hazard of private practice that receives little attention is the dimension of loneliness. This is particularly true if one is in solo practice. The most damaging result of such isolation is, of course, burnout. Private practitioners must attend to their needs for both personal and professional support systems if they are to continue to maintain their effectiveness as therapists and avoid the tragedy of burnout.

Summary

Mental health counseling has a colorful and somewhat turbulent professional history. Beginning in the 1960s with the passage of the Community Mental Health Centers Act of 1963, a need was established for trained personnel to meet the demands of the new legislation. Such personnel did not exist, and through the efforts of mental health practitioners steps were taken to bring a solution to the problem. The declining employment possibilities for counselors in educational institutions further added to this problem.

Although professional associations for counseling existed, no one professional group addressed the specific issues and needs of the developing mental health professional. The American Mental Health Counselors Association (AMHCA), incorporated in Florida in 1976, filled this void and through its efforts forever changed the professional direction of not only mental health counseling but also the national professional association then known as the American Personnel and Guidance Association (APGA).

Mental health counseling, regardless of the setting, is a challenging, growing dynamic professional specialization. Deciding to become a mental health counselor requires self-awareness, self-discipline, flexibility, creativity, and mental toughness to survive the hard times. It also requires compassion, sensitivity, and therapeutic competence. In all these respects mental health counseling resembles counseling in other settings. What makes it different? Basically, the differences boil down to this: a clientele that extends across the life span, with particular attention to the adult years; dealing with client problems that are more debilitating than those usually encountered by school counselors or student affairs practitioners; a greater likelihood of dealing with couples and families than counselors of other specializations; diagnosis and treatment of mental and emotional disorders from a developmental perspective using psychoeducational interventions; collaboration and consultation with physicians and other health care providers; and the probability that supporting one's practice will require an entrepreneurial bent.

References

American Association for Counseling and Development (AACD). (1983). *AACD and division membership report.* Alexandria, VA: Author.

American Association for Counseling and Development (AACD). (1989). *AACD and division membership report.* Alexandria, VA: Author.

American Mental Health Counselors Association (AMHCA). (1978). *Report of AMHCA Certification Committee.* Unpublished report, AACD, Washington, DC.

Brooks, D. K., Jr., & Weikel, W. J. (1986). History and development of the mental health counseling movement. In A. J. Palmo & W. J. Weikel (Eds.), *Foundations of mental health counseling* (pp. 5–28). Springfield, IL: Thomas.

National Academy of Certified Clinical Mental Health Counselors (NACCMHC). (1985). *Definition of mental health counseling.* Alexandria, VA: Author.

Weikel, W. J. (1985). The American Mental Health Counselors Association. *Journal of Counseling and Development, 63,* 457–460.

P a r t 4

Counseling Special Populations

In the previous parts of this book, the basic skills and theoretical bases for counseling were described. In Part 4, "Counseling Special Populations," these skills are applied to a number of specific groups with whom a counselor may work. Each of these special populations demands different combinations of skill, knowledge, and experience from the counselor.

Chapter 15, "Counseling Children and Adolescents," provides a comprehensive overview of the current therapies and interventions that counselors are finding effective in working both with children and with adolescents and summarizes the developmental and psychological concerns children and adolescents face. The authors describe a number of the major approaches used with such clients, including play therapy, individual counseling, family therapy, group work, and behavior modification. A case study is presented to examine a specific application of these interventions and programs.

Demographic statistics predict that the percentage of individuals over the age of 55 will be increasing in the coming decades. A knowledge of the specific counseling needs of older individuals will become increasingly more important as our society moves into the twenty-first century and beyond. Chapter 16, "Counseling the Older Adult," presents a detailed description of the field of gerontological counseling. The specialized needs and social realities of elderly individuals are presented. The importance of viewing older clients as individuals, and not from the basis of cultural stereotypes about aging and the elderly, is stressed. Specific developmental challenges that older individuals must cope with are outlined. The current therapeutic approaches most widely used with older clients, such as reality orientation, reminiscing groups, and remotivation therapy, are described.

Family therapy assumes a systems approach to counseling and stresses the overall interpersonal context in which the client's problems are occurring. Chapter 17, "Counseling Couples and Families," provides a historical framework for viewing the development of marriage and family counseling and outlines the central concepts of family systems theory. The author presents an overview of the different schools of family therapy and stresses the importance of maintaining an integrative and eclectic approach to understanding and learning from these approaches. Core issues that often emerge in family counseling, such as boundary problems, low self-esteem, and inappropriate family hierarchies, are described. Stages in marriage and family counseling are outlined, with descriptions of appropriate interventions for each particular level.

Chapter 18, "Counseling Gay, Lesbian, and Bisexual Clients," surveys a field of growing importance to counselors. Issues involving gay individuals are becoming more visible in our society. Although clients who happen to be gay should be viewed as individuals first and as gay people second, the authors stress the importance for the counselor to maintain a sensitivity to the special concerns of gay clients. Self-identity, self-esteem, and relationship concerns may take on an enhanced intensity with gay clients, owing to the significant social, psychological, and interpersonal stresses they may experience. The authors also provide an appendix of resources and organizations for gay individuals and for counselors wishing more information on related issues.

Most counselors, regardless of their particular work setting or client population, will need to confront the issue of effective multicultural counseling. Chapter 19, "Counseling Ethnic Minority Clients," addresses these concerns and provides a framework for understanding the economic and social environments in which many multicultural issues arise. Barriers to effective multicultural counseling are discussed within their historical context, and the current state of multicultural counseling within the United States is surveyed. The authors stress the importance of appropriate models of counselor education that provide training free from cultural stereotypes and biases. Guidelines for developing effective multicultural counseling skills are presented, including the necessity of each professional counselor's examining his or her own prejudices and assumptions about multicultural clients and about the counseling process itself.

Finally, this section concludes with Chapter 20, "Counseling Clients with Disabilities," in which overviews of both the goals and of the major interventions for working with disabled clients are discussed. Physical, cognitive, and emotional factors in understanding disabilities are reviewed, with emphasis on helping clients to improve their overall quality of life and to come to terms with the conditions of their particular disability. The professional qualifications and necessary training for counselors wishing to pursue rehabilitation as a career choice are described.

Chapter 15

Counseling Children and Adolescents

Larry B. Golden, Ph.D.   *Ardis Sherwood-Hawes, M.S.*

Counseling interventions for children and adolescents have historically been grounded in research findings that were developed with adult populations (Sherwood-Hawes, 1993). These "adult" counseling theories and techniques were subsequently shaped to address childhood and adolescent mental health issues. Support for research on childhood dysfunction and the influence of developmental stages on the experience of childhood has been neglected.

Why should the treatment of children and adolescents be regarded as unique? Distinctive issues associated with childhood and adolescent mental health require specialized counseling strategies: (1) children have less verbal ability than adults, (2) children have a more immediate sense of time than adults, (3) children are usually not in a position to refer themselves for counseling, (4) children are less likely to accept personal responsibility for a problem than adults, and (5) adolescents especially resent being the "identified patient" (Vernon, 1993). These issues fly in the face of assumptions drawn from the field of adult counseling and psychotherapy!

Childhood and Adolescent Counseling Considerations

Developmental Concerns for Counselors

There is a fundamental difference between counseling strategies that are suitable for children and adolescents and those for the adult population. The developmental processes of memory, language, conditional thinking, categorization abilities, and perception of rules have a significant impact on the effectiveness of any counseling strategy. An understanding of these developmental processes will facilitate anticipatory interventions and help the counselor predict the success of an intervention at a particular developmental stage.

Children are unique individuals who manifest a diverse range of dissimilar behavioral histories, temperamental traits, cognitive skills, and social and emotional capacities. The counselor should be aware of the child's developmental history, personal capacity for development, the probability of future developmental events, and the child's cultural background.

Children process experiences differently at various points of their development because of changes involved in physical, cognitive, social, and emotional processes. For example, children in the preoperational stages of cognitive development will probably not be capable of using abstract rules for self-control (Berk, 1996). Young children who have not yet mastered language skills are poorly served by traditional counseling and psychotherapy, which are highly dependent on verbal communication.

Personality differentiation is, of course, less advanced in childhood than it is in adolescence and adulthood. Younger children have not yet developed an autonomous concept of self and lack an adequate frame of reference regarding reality, possibility, and value. They do not have the benefit of tempering the impact of current events with the moderating influence of past experiences and tend to exaggerate the importance of occurrences. Therefore, children can have considerably more difficulty coping with stressful events than adolescents and adults. In addition, children's dependency on adults make them highly vulnerable to experiences of rejection, disappointment, and failure (Carson, Butcher, & Mineka, 1996).

Illustrative of appropriate therapeutic approaches for young children are family therapy, play therapy used alone or in combination with talking therapy, rewarding desirable behaviors, modeling, painting, drawing, therapeutic games, and rehearsing activities with children. Special therapeutic aids include dolls, puppets, stories, and fairytales.

Identification of Problems and Referral to Counseling

The problem behaviors of childhood emerge as part of the normal development process (for example, the "terrible twos" or the "identity crisis" of adolescence). Children commonly manifest disturbing behaviors such as lying, destructiveness, excessive fears, hyperactivity, and fighting. On occasion, adults will regard these developmentally normal problem behaviors as indicative of pathology and refer for treatment. Left alone, problems associated with a developmental stage are likely to disappear with the passage of time.

Children are referred to counseling for many reasons. They may be manifesting dysfunctional reactions to stressful events in the home such as divorce and maladaptive parenting practices, they may be victims of sexual or physical abuse, or they may be misbehaving or underachieving in school. Counselors should be aware that it is difficult to gauge childhood reactivity in response to stress. For example, a child may act out in similar ways in response to the death of a pet gold-fish and to a divorce!

Because children are generally referred to counseling by other people (such as parents and teachers), they usually do not see themselves as having a problem. Children and young adolescents tend to perceive their problems as externally de-rived, and not until late adolescence do young people begin to understand that their behavior might be a result of internal factors, such as their own thoughts and emotions (Rice, 1995).

Adolescents may balk at the idea of counseling because they may not see any value or reason for it. The teenager's struggle for autonomy and ubiquitous "off my back" messages to adults have direct ramifications for counselors. Counselors (with the exception of peer helpers) may be seen by adolescents as their parents' "hired guns." Furthermore, adolescents tend to be action oriented, and they may not readily respond to a "talking cure" (Golden, 1994). Teens *are* responsive to in-terventions that recognize their overriding desire for autonomy. Counselors of ado-lescents are advised to establish "preparing for leaving home" as a goal of therapy. The task then becomes one of assisting teens and their parents in planning for a successful "launch"!

Focus of Treatment

Parent, family, and school all contribute to the day-to-day functioning of children and adolescents. It is difficult, if not impossible, to isolate childhood misbehavior from "systemic" dysfunction. A fundamental question involves the focus of diag-nosis, assessment, and treatment. Should that focus be the individual child, family, peers, or school? Should the focus be "wide angle" and incorporate all domains? This chapter discusses individual counseling strategies that are especially useful with childhood and adolescent populations, considerations for adolescent group counseling, and a systems approach to counseling.

Counseling Strategies for Children and Adolescents

Counseling Approaches with Children

Younger children are fundamentally dependent on adults and often undergo a sense of powerlessness when they are faced with new, unpredictable events (such as going to the hospital, starting school, or the birth of a sibling) and real or imagi-nary frightening experiences (such as the fear of becoming lost or being abandoned by their parents, parental fights, divorce, or abuse). Children struggle to make sense of a world over which they exercise little personal control.

Play therapy and behavior modification techniques are generally the best ap-proaches for young children. Small children are "naturals" as clients. They tend to be more amenable to adult influences. Children have an abiding faith that adults want to help them, and consequently they do not offer major resistance to counseling. Because of this intrinsic dependency of children on adults, the counselor should strive to develop a respectful counselor-to-child relationship. Counselors can convey respect and acceptance of children by attentively listening, attributing importance to the child's viewpoint, and encouraging the child's efforts (Sherwood-Hawes, 1993).

Play Therapy

The healing power of play therapy resides in the relationship between child and counselor. According to Moustakas (1959), "The alive relationship between the therapist and the child is the essential dimension, perhaps the only significant reality, in the therapeutic process and in all interhuman growth" (p. xiii). Play therapy helps children express feelings; it provides a language that serves as a springboard for communication.

Virginia Axline, a "founder mother" of play therapy, readily acknowledged Carl Rogers's contributions. Axline's philosophy and methodology represent a translation of person-centered counseling into the language of childhood. For Axline (1993), the play therapy room is a "growing ground" where the child is the center of the universe. There is no adult direction, nagging, or intrusion. In Axline's playroom, the child is permitted complete freedom of expression. Imagine a world without competition, without hurry, in which the child is accepted completely! Under these ideal conditions, children can try on new ideas, and perhaps new personalities, for size.

Procedures.   Virginia Axline (1993) outlined the following basic principles of play therapy. The therapist

1. Develops a warm relationship with the child.
2. Unconditionally accepts the child.
3. Establishes an atmosphere of permissiveness in which the child is completely free to express feelings.
4. Reflects the feelings the child is expressing.
5. Maintains respect for the child's ability to solve his or her own problems. The child is responsible for change.
6. Does not direct the child's actions or conversation. The child leads; the therapist follows.
7. Does not hurry the child. Therapy is a gradual process.
8. Initiates only those limits that are needed to anchor the therapy to reality. Limits help the child feel safe. The child realizes that if behavior or feelings get out of hand, the therapist will help the child reestablish control.

The playroom should be equipped with a variety of expressive materials: modeling clay and finger paints encourage creativity, dolls and puppets allow the child to set the stage for family interactions, and toy guns and knives enable the child to act out aggressive feelings. The child's play may emerge from actual situations or represent a fantasy.

Indications and Limitations.   Play therapy is especially useful with withdrawn children who turn negative affect inward (as opposed to acting out). These children's unexpressed and unresolved feelings may be manifested as dysfunctional symptoms (such as bed-wetting, nightmares, and school failure).

Play therapy is not without its blind spots. In some cases, through a process called "triangulation," children misbehave in order to preserve a conflicted parental relationship. The child's symptoms enable the parents to avoid painful communication with each other. With its intense focus on the therapist–child relationship, such family dynamics may be ignored. Therefore, the play therapist must be alert to the signs of a troubled marriage. Counselors are advised to use play therapy in tandem with family interventions and consultation with school personnel.

Behavior Modification

The basic assumptions that support behavior modification are simple.

1. The behavioral counselor treats the behavioral manifestations of a psychological disorder. This is not to say that internal motives do not exist. Rather, the core of the psyche is a difficult, and in some cases forbidden, terrain, which may or may not yield, even after years of psychoanalysis. Behavioral counseling is more efficient.
2. "Here and now" behavior and situations that maintain problematic behaviors are the domain of the behavioral counselor. Historical information is useful only as it relates to current problem behaviors. Furthermore, changes in internal psychological states do not necessarily result in improved functioning.
3. Maladaptive behaviors are acquired through the same principles of learning as are normal behaviors. For example, aggressive behaviors can be learned through observation of an adult model (Berk, 1994). Similarly, we know that more appropriate social behaviors (for example, social skills) are also learned through modeling.
4. The goal of therapy is the achievement of measurable target behaviors (Sharf, 1996). This permits an ongoing assessment of progress.
5. Behavior that is rewarded will be repeated. Therefore, it is important to find out what the child experiences as rewarding and whether the reward is readily available.

Procedures.   Control of environmental contingencies is essential. It is not surprising, therefore, that behavior modification works best with "captive" populations (such as prison inmates, patients committed to psychiatric wards, and children in public schools). For example, a third-grader could be rewarded with a piece of sugarless candy for staying in his or her seat during a thirty-minute reading group. This intervention would fail if the child (1) were free to quit coming to school, (2) were satiated with sugarless candy, and/or (3) did not like sugarless candy. The ultimate goal, after gradually withdrawing the reward, is for the targeted or desired behavior to become habitual and environmentally reinforced.

Indications and Limitations.   Behavior modification is especially effective with younger children and can even be used with infants. Behavioral techniques are commonly used to reduce tantrums, to toilet train very young children, and to improve school performance. Behavior modification is more difficult with adolescents, because reinforcers can get expensive. A 6-year-old will behave to earn a "happy face" sticker; a 16-year-old may insist on a pickup truck with four-wheel drive! Moreover, teenagers are developmentally ready to benefit from a combination of cognitive and behavioral interventions.

Many people object to behavior modification because they view reinforcement of desirable behavior as nothing more than bribery. Parents do not want to "pay" their children to do their homework, brush their teeth, or use common courtesy. They want their children to be motivated by a sense of altruism, consideration, and responsibility. In reality, parents are almost always engaged in behavior modification. When parents yell at children or spank them, they are trying to convince them that a particular unwanted behavior has a high price. When parents ignore an "obnoxious" behavior, they are attempting to extinguish the recurrence of that activity. When parents praise, they are telling their children that they want them to maintain a certain behavior. Unfortunately, much of this behavior modification is unplanned and is not successful because the interventions are inconsistent. Worse yet, these haphazard attempts can rely heavily on punishment strategies. Punishment is highly effective in changing behavior, but it has an unfortunate side effect. Punishment generates anger. Behavior modification is most appropriate when it is used to systematically teach good habits to children who are not yet cognitively ready for internal forms of motivation.

Because it is so powerful, issue has also been taken with the ethics of using behavior modification. What if the laws that govern human behavior were to fall into the hands of unscrupulous political leaders who would use them for social control? For what comfort it may be, human beings have proven themselves to be very, very difficult to control, and George Orwell's *1984* has come and gone.

Counseling Approaches with Adolescents

Whereas play therapy and behavioral modification are ideally suited for children, other approaches are "on target" for adolescents. Interventions for adolescents must recognize the unique features of adolescent development. Adolescents experience profound physical changes, rapid growth in cognitive ability, a hunger for peer approval, a bruising struggle for autonomy, and an onslaught of psychosocial stress. Teenagers must cope with conflict with parents and peers, rejection by same-sex or opposite-sex friends, and worries about the future. At a deeper level they must confront attachment- and autonomy-related issues, such as separation from family, leaving home, and getting a job (Rice, 1995). Each generation of teenagers faces new and unprecedented issues, such as family instability and the threat of AIDS. Today's teens must make choices that often transcend their experiential capabilities. Contemporary adolescents must make decisions about sexual intercourse, contraception, abortion, family planning, and alcohol and drug use.

Adolescents are subject to biological drives that have a powerful impact on emotional, cognitive, and behavioral development (Berk, 1996). For example, girls who begin puberty early are more likely to become sexually active, and early maturing adolescents of either sex are more likely to seek out older friends than themselves who encourage them in delinquent behavior (Berk, 1994).

Most teenagers are convinced that adults (especially parents) cannot comprehend their experience. This cognitive generalization encourages the adolescent tendency to be secretive and rebellious in responding to parental guidelines. Another cognitive fault is the "imaginary audience," the tendency of teens to regard themselves as actors who are constantly on stage (Elkind, 1979). This belief that they are the focus of everyone's attention generates a painful self-consciousness. Teens deal with this by going to great lengths to conform and avoid embarrassment. Showing up at school wearing the "wrong" clothes can be a traumatic episode!

Freud (1917) saw the struggle to establish independence from parents as central to the development of a strong ego. It was expected that in separating themselves, adolescents would resort to rebellion and outright hostility. Although teenagers may actively seek autonomy, they are ambivalent about leaving the safety of the nest, and alternately express conflicting messages: "Let me go!" and "Don't push me out!" Small wonder that parent eagles destroy the nest immediately after their fledglings take flight!

There is some good news. During adolescence, cognitive thinking processes become more flexible and abstract. Adolescents have the capacity to consider logically all the possibilities of a situation in order to solve a problem. They can deal with "what if": "What if I have sex? What happens if I get pregnant?" This new capacity for thinking opens the door to cognitive counseling.

Cognitive Counseling

Albert Ellis is due credit for his ardent promotion of the cognitive approach that he dubbed rational-emotive therapy (RET). Counselors today have come to see the advantages of working with the conscious human mind, and cognitive psychology is a fertile field of scientific investigation.

The cognitive counselor assumes that feelings and behavior are mediated by thoughts (Corey, 1996). Unless an individual is actively psychotic (for example, schizophrenic), conscious thoughts are accessible and malleable. Conversely, emotions may be buried and difficult to surface, and observable behaviors may be subject to forces in the environment that are beyond the control of the individual.

The cognitive counselor regards emotional disturbance and disordered behavior as the consequence of disturbed thinking. People who are psychologically disturbed introduce a bias into the way they process information. According to Beck and Weishaar (1995), these cognitive distortions may take many forms.

1. *Arbitrary inference.* This distortion results when an individual adheres to a belief even when pragmatic data contradicts the belief. Arbitrary inference is illustrated by the athlete who has previously experienced success in competition, places last in a single event, and concludes, "I am washed up! I'm a loser."

2. *Selective abstraction.* A person uses a detail taken out of context to conceptualize an entire situation. For example, after hearing a story about how her sister had been picked on when she started a new school, a new student feels fearful and refuses to come to school.

3. *Overgeneralization.* A person uses an isolated incident to develop a rule and then applies the rule to unrelated situations. An example is a youngster who enjoys a cigarette without ill effects and then starts smoking heavily.

4. *Magnification and minimization.* The individual exaggerates the significance of an event or experience. An illustration of this phenomenon is a teenager who "catastrophizes," "I'll die if I don't get a date for the prom."

5. *Personalization.* Individuals attribute external events to themselves without evidence that logically supports a causal connection. For example, a student raises her hand to ask a question, but the teacher responds to another student instead. The student concludes, "I must have done something to make the teacher angry with me."

6. *Dichotomous thinking.* A person polarizes experiences at one of two extreme positions. It's all or nothing! An example is a high school student who says, "If I don't get accepted at an Ivy League school, I would just as soon not go to college at all."

Procedures.   The cognitive counselor is interested in an attitude shift that changes the way the client thinks about a problem. As youngsters move from the "concrete egocentrism" of middle childhood into adolescence, they are no longer restricted by the world of things (Rice, 1995). They can reflect on possibilities not yet experienced and project themselves into the future, and into the experience of other people. Behavior and emotion can be anticipated and controlled.

The counselor's task is to change the way the disturbed adolescent client thinks about the world; to transform a self-defeating egocentric view to a sociocentric or other-oriented viewpoint. Beck and Weishaar (1995) describe the therapeutic interventions that make this "attitude shift" possible.

1. *Collaborative empiricism.* The counselor and the client work as a team. They are "detectives," examining the evidence behind any assumption. For example, they might test the logic behind the assumption that, no matter how hard he or she tries, the client will not be able to improve his or her grades in algebra.

2. *Socratic dialogue.* This term refers to a mode of inquiry. The counselor asks questions to help the adolescent define the problems, explore the meaning of events, and consider the consequences of maintaining maladaptive thoughts and behaviors. The following are examples of "Socratic" questions: "How would you account for your father's anger with you?" "Describe exactly what happens when you ask a girl to go out with you." "Is your strategy for making friends working for you?"

3. *Guided discovery.* The counselor helps the client design new experiences or behavioral experiments that lead to new perspectives. The counselor might sug-

gest that a student stay after class to ask the algebra teacher for help and report back on what happens. The student might also be asked to visualize this same situation and to imagine what the teacher might feel when asked for help.

There are other strategies that engage adolescents at a cognitive level. For example, the adolescent's home and school environments should provide opportunities to make choices in real-life situations. Many adolescents haven't had much experience in decision making. Counselors can use psychodrama, storytelling, bibliotherapy, and videotaped scenarios to help youngsters to project themselves into the experience of others.

Jay Haley describes a powerful cognitive-behavioral strategy in his book *Leaving Home: The Therapy of Disturbed Young People* (1980). Haley prompts teenage clients and their parents to redefine cognitively their perceptions of adolescent rebellion and come to understand that the teenager is trying to become independent. Then Haley questions his teenage clients about their practical plans for leaving home, pointing out that many young people fail in the attempt because they are inadequately prepared. For example, 15-year-old Cindy has tried to run away from home only to "crawl" back, unable to support herself. Note that this process of preparation for a crucial life task can be ego enhancing for both parent and teenager.

Counselor: (to Cindy) "Cindy, the most important job you have to do is to make realistic plans for leaving home. What will you need to succeed? How can your parents help you get ready?"

Indications and Limitations.   It is important to consider the child's level of cognitive development in order to select an appropriate intervention along a continuum from *behavioral* to *cognitive* approaches. Although there are exceptional cases in which cognitive counseling has been effective with small children, most young clients benefit from behavioral or affective approaches.

Adolescents, in contrast, simultaneously think and behave in a synthesized process, and cognitive and behavioral interventions are most effective when they are used at the same time. However, the cognitive organizational abilities of the adolescent client will quite likely determine how, if at all, new behavior will generalize beyond a specific treatment setting. As for affect, if teenagers can learn to think through a problem and then solve it successfully, they will begin to feel better, as well.

Group Counseling

Group counseling is particularly suited for adolescents because it coincides with their need for group belonging. A group approach provides a setting in which teens can discover that their paradoxical involvements, emotions, and problems are not unique. The group experience provides a safe environment for adolescents to express their conflicting feelings, practice communication skills, test limits, become more accepting of others, and combat feelings of loneliness and isolation (Corey & Corey, 1992).

As the reader might imagine, there are a wide variety of topics that teenagers might wish to discuss. However, there are certain themes that are of concern to most young people. Some general themes for discussion are (1) coping with feelings of depression, guilt, anxiety, anger, rejection, loneliness, and so on; (2) managing conflicts with teachers, parents, and friends; (3) sex roles; (4) love, sex, and intimacy; (5) developing a strong self-identity; and (6) the struggle toward autonomy. Group members may choose which subjects are most meaningful to them. The format, however, should remain flexible because members may spontaneously introduce crucial personal problems that are not related to the scheduled theme (such as suicide of a friend).

Group counseling works best in an atmosphere of trust and acceptance (Posthuma, 1996). Such a milieu encourages the risk taking that leads to growth.

Corey and Corey (1992) introduce teenagers to the group experience in such a way that they will have realistic expectations of what to expect right from the start. Group members are invited to express themselves honestly without censoring or rehearsing. Group members are encouraged to talk about fears they have about being in the group. The group leader is responsible for creating an accepting climate; nevertheless, Corey and Corey (1992) want group members to know that each individual is responsible for what they get from the group. Teenagers in small groups benefit by a great deal of freedom, yet it is also true that limits and boundaries are essential and must be clear (Bergin, 1993). Corey and Corey (1992) suggest specific ground rules for adolescent groups, including the following:

- Attendance is required, and participation is expected.
- Everyone is responsible for protecting confidentiality.
- No one can come to group meetings under the influence of drugs or alcohol.
- Smoking is not allowed during the sessions.

Group counseling is a specialized field that is fraught with unique legal and ethical problems. Counselors who do group work with adolescents are advised to consult the standards for knowledge, skill competencies, and supervised experience that are recommended by the Association for Specialists in Group Work (1990).

A Systems Strategy

Experienced counselors are aware of the importance of working closely with the family when a child exhibits behavior problems. The family is in a powerful position to support or sabotage the best efforts of counselors and teachers. Family therapy is a method that focuses on the family in an attempt to help solve a child's behavior problems. (The reader is referred to Chapter 17 in this book, which is devoted to couples and family therapy.) Brief family consultation is still another way to incorporate the home and school milieu in an effort to help solve a child's behavior problems. Brief family consultation is a short-term strategy that is ideally suited to a school or agency setting where there are limitations on time. The skills involved draw on those that are taught in most counselor education programs: active listening, behavior modification, and interpersonal communication.

Brief Family Consultation

Brief family consultation, together with family therapy, are based on systems theory. Systems theorists assume that the presenting problem of the client is an interactive concern for all family members. Individual problems are seen as relationship problems. If a child is referred for counseling, it is assumed that he or she is the family symptom bearer, that all members of the family share some responsibility for maintaining psychopathology, and that the family should be the focus of treatment. Families, like most systems, are organized along hierarchical lines and function according to definite rules (Goldenberg & Goldenberg, 1996). If one member of the family receives counseling, and changes, the delicate balance of roles and rules of the family may be upset. Other family members may become anxious and attempt to undermine counseling. Thus it is important to include the family in all therapy sessions.

Procedures.   A functional family can make rapid gains in counseling, but a dysfunctional family may bog down in rigidly fixed patterns of communication and may resist the counselor's attempts at change. Therefore, a quick method of assessing the family is important to the success of a short-term strategy.

When evaluating the capacity of a particular family to respond to a brief intervention, the counselor can expect the functional family to achieve high scores on each of the following criteria: parental resources, absence of chronicity, communication between family members, parental authority, and rapport with professional helpers (Golden, 1994).

1. *Parental resources.* Do these parents have the capability to provide for their child's basic need for food, shelter, and care? A stable marriage, an extended family, and gainful employment are resources that work in favor of the counselor's attempt to bring a child's misbehavior under control. In contrast, immature single parents have fewer resources at their disposal, and families that have a history of extreme poverty or alcoholism bring very limited resources to the task of managing childhood behavior problems.

2. *Absence of chronicity.* An acute problem with an identifiable psychosocial stresser presents an opportunity for behavior management, but a chronic problem indicates that the family may need long-term therapy. A parent's response such as "She's always been a difficult child" suggests a less favorable prognosis than "His grades have gone downhill since October. That's when I lost my job."

3. *Communication between family members.* Can family members communicate well enough to solve problems? According to Satir (1972), there is a normal tendency to close down communication during periods of distress. In dysfunctional families, closed communication is the rule, not the exception. This closed system is maintained by yelling, blaming, sarcasm, or, more ominously, silence.

The following interaction illustrates a closed, defensive posture:

Counselor: (to Kristi) Tell your parents how much spelling homework you will be willing to do next week to earn television privileges.

Father: (angrily interrupts) She would have to change her entire attitude, to say nothing of her personality.

Mother: It seems to me that the teacher is the one who needs a change of attitude. It is ridiculous to expect a child to do hours of homework after being in school all day.

With his sarcastic outburst, Father ensures that a meaningful dialogue with Kristi will be avoided. Mother reinforces her daughter's dependency by speaking on her behalf against the teacher. Her intervention also serves to deflect a discussion of Kristi's problems.

4. *Parental authority.* Are parents effective in asserting authority? Parents in functional families hold an "executive" position within the family organization. In dysfunctional families, parents surrender authority in the hope that conflict with a child can be avoided. Children from such families are often out of control.

5. *Rapport with professional helpers.* Can parents and professionals work together as a team? Are the child's teachers responsive to parents? Do parents return phone calls? Are they punctual for conferences? Central to the issue is a commitment to be persistent in the attempt to accomplish the goals of the treatment plan. The functional family does its "homework."

An accurate assessment of family functioning helps the counselor decide whether a short-term or a long-term intervention strategy is appropriate for a given family. A brief family consultation may be appropriate for a misbehaving child in a functional family, whereas a child from a dysfunctional family may benefit from a more family-oriented therapeutic approach. A family that exhibits seriously disordered behavior, such as alcoholism, child abuse, psychosis, or suicide, may require a crisis intervention and perhaps residential treatment for the disturbed family member.

Brief family consultation with a functional family is an intervention that is especially appropriate for the school counselor. The consultation process requires three to five face-to-face, 30- to 45-minute family conferences. This process is best described by an example of what the counselor might say to the parents in the initial interview. In this case, the child presents a problem of failing to complete homework assignments.

Counselor: I am interested in working with you for a short period of time to help you get Mike to complete his homework every day. I think you can manage this situation with only a little help from me. There is cause for optimism. With the exception of homework, Mike earns average grades and is well behaved. As parents, you have shown that you want to cooperate with Mike's teachers to get this problem solved. For my part, I'll coordinate a team effort to include you, Mike's teachers, and Mike himself, if he is willing. If he is not, we are still going to try to change his behavior.

If the child's problems are school related, teachers are included in the behavioral plan. Typically, the task of the teacher is to provide the parent with a daily report of the child's behavior.

The family (and perhaps the teacher) will want to know about time commitment. When a brief consultation exceeds five family conferences without a resolution of the problem, another option, such as referral for family therapy, is necessary. Note that the contacts with the family are called "conferences," not "sessions," because of the therapeutic associations of the latter term. Likewise, the term "consultation" serves to emphasize that the family does not need, nor will it receive, "therapy."

According to Haley (1980), parents must agree on three issues if they are to manage their child's behavior: (1) the specific behaviors that are desired from the child, (2) the mechanism by which the parents will know whether their child has behaved in the desired way, and (3) the consequences for behavior or misbehavior. If marital discord surfaces, parents should be encouraged to work toward agreement for the good of the child and deal with their marital problems at some later time.

Haley (1980) emphasizes the importance of putting parents in charge of managing the child's behavior problem. The distressed child is making a plea, albeit indirect, for parental control. The counselor should encourage the parents to take control of the resources that could serve as reinforcers. For example, an adolescent who is "independently wealthy," sporting a big allowance and a room full of electronic gear, is in a position to ignore his or her parents' demand for behavior change. In this case, the child's allowance should be reduced to zero. He or she can earn money by behaving responsibly.

Family members may shut down communications in response to stressers, such as those caused by a child's misbehavior. Unfortunately, it is precisely during a stressful episode that open communication is most important. A gentle and respectful application of basic, active listening skills (such as paraphrasing and reflection) usually facilitates communication among family members.

Many of the best-laid behavioral plans are defeated by ambivalence. In any brief strategy, the motto must be "Go for it!" Continuation of problematic behavior, even in an otherwise competent child, may result in a negative and habitually dysfunctional style of coping with stress.

Indications and Limitations.   A systems intervention can have great advantages over individual counseling. After all, children live with their families, not with their counselors. However, there are circumstances when an individual approach would be desirable. If the family system is highly maladaptive or destructive, the counselor may need to help the child develop sufficient self-worth and enough self-reliant behavior to function independently.

A weakness of the systems approach is that the process is crippled if a key family member refuses to participate. Another limitation is that an exclusive focus on family relationships may result in the neglect of the psychodynamics of individual family members.

The Case of Andrew

Andrew K., a third-grader, was referred to the Parent Consultation Center by his school guidance counselor.[1] The center offers consultations on childhood behavior problems. Families are seen for a maximum of five conferences.

Andrew and his mother, a single parent, attended the first conference. The presenting problem was that Andrew was "hyper." His teachers complained that he would not remain seated in class; he poked, tripped, and teased the other children; and he failed to complete assigned work. Mrs. K. also reported behavior problems at home. For example, Andrew had to be constantly "nagged" to finish the morning routine of getting dressed, brushing his teeth, eating breakfast, and so on. If his mother pushed him too hard, Andrew would "throw a fit." Andrew spent every third weekend with his father, and Mrs. K. said that Andrew's behavioral problems were more extreme after these visitations. She also reported that Andrew wet the bed following his weekends with his father. Prior to the divorce, which was finalized the summer before Andrew started third grade, there had only been occasional teacher complaints about behavior problems.

The consultant asked if there were any activities that held Andrew's attention for longer than thirty minutes. Mrs. K. said that Andrew could stay riveted on computer games for hours, he was an alert soccer player, and he could concentrate for extended periods of time when he drew pictures of dinosaurs. Apparently Andrew's hyperactivity was selective.

It was agreed that on-task, in-seat behavior during language arts would be targeted. By the second conference, Mrs. K. had asked for and was getting daily written reports from Andrew's language arts teacher. For each fifteen-minute period that Andrew stayed in his seat and remained on task, the teacher affixed a star to a chart that Andrew kept at his desk. At home, the stars were redeemed for a variety of prizes chosen by Andrew—a trip to the zoo, pizza, Nintendo playing time, and so forth.

By the third conference, there had been a dramatic improvement. The fourth conference followed a weekend visitation with Mr. K., and the "hyper" behavior returned full force. Within a day, however, Andrew was back on track. At the fifth and final conference, Mrs. K. and Andrew proudly displayed a string of star-laden charts from the language arts teacher.

The bed-wetting, however, was getting worse. Mrs. K. was convinced that the tension caused by Andrew's visitations with Mr. K. was to blame. She said that

[1] The Parent Consultation Center is a collaborative project of the Northside Independent School District in San Antonio, Texas, and the University of Texas at San Antonio. The pilot project was funded by a grant from the Counseling and Human Development Foundation.

Andrew's father wanted to punish her, and that he used Andrew as a tool for his revenge. She felt that Andrew might be better off if he didn't see his father at all.

In an individual interview, Andrew said that he felt that both parents said "mean" things about the other, and he felt "torn in two pieces." The consultant explained to Mrs. K. that her son was paying a very high price for this ongoing conflict and made a referral for family counseling. The family therapist saw the parents, both separately and together, for a total of twenty sessions. Occasionally Andrew was included. The goals of family therapy were to (1) convince both parents that Andrew would suffer if they were unable to manage their mutual animosity; (2) create a path for direct communication, thereby preventing messages being sent through Andrew; and (3) encourage Andrew to accept the premise that he could love both his parents without being disloyal to either. As the parents were able to mediate their hostile impulses toward each other, the frequency of Andrew's bed-wetting subsided.

The success of the brief consultation demonstrates the efficiency of behavioral techniques and a team approach. Parental sniping, however, threatened to sabotage the behavioral gains. The family therapist brought rationality to an otherwise chaotic family system, and the parents responded with alacrity to brief consultation and family therapy. Andrew was the direct beneficiary of this intervention, because children require order and predictability in their lives.

With the benefit of hindsight, the K. family was evaluated on a scale of "1" (very weak) to "5" (very strong), using the criteria described in this chapter.

1. *Parental resources.* Although the parents were divorced, Mrs. K., the custodial parent, was financially secure. Mr. K.'s visitation rights were respected, and he made regular child support payments. However, the power of this family to resolve problems was diminished by the recent divorce. (Score = 3)
2. *Chronicity.* "Hyper" behavior and bed-wetting were reported as only occasional problems prior to the third grade. (Score = 5)
3. *Communication among family members.* Andrew and his mother talked directly and honestly. Communication between the parents was "nonexistent." (Score = 2)
4. *Parental authority.* Mrs. K. was a decisive disciplinarian. Her fear that Andrew would someday choose his father over her, however, served to undermine her authority. (Score = 2)
5. *Rapport with professional helpers.* Mrs. K. was conscientious in follow-through on reports from Andrew's language arts teacher. Both parents were willing participants in family therapy. (Score = 5)

Summary

It is easier to list the problems that children do not have than it is to identify the myriad of emotional and behavioral maladies to which they are so vulnerable. Small children can be the victims of genetic and/or environmental deficits and can learn to adapt to distressful experiences with dysfunctional behaviors.

Unfortunately, the majority of emotionally and behaviorally disturbed children who need counseling interventions are unable to obtain assistance for themselves. Societal and parental attitudes and economic factors can, too often, determine which disturbed children receive help. When early problematic behaviors are untreated, the conduct that is difficult to tolerate in a child can become dangerous and uncontrollable in a teenager. The adolescent propensity for risk taking, inability to delay gratification, hunger for and fear of autonomy, and need for peer approval can magnify and aggravate disordered behaviors.

A major concern for researchers and professionals who work with children is the identification of, and early intervention for, children who are at risk. Studies and counseling efforts are being directed toward identifying conditions in children's lives that elicit and/or maintain problem behaviors and intervening before these children develop chronic and debilitating psychological problems.

Many of the potential dilemmas faced by modern young people are so serious that certain situations demand much more than personal counseling. For example, to prevent substance abuse or adolescent pregnancy we must initiate massive educational programs. The counseling professional's role in these preventive approaches is to convey our knowledge about childhood and adolescent developmental processes and strategies for behavioral change to the educational effort.

In the final analysis, the counselor's major contribution, the *raison d'être* for the profession, is to enable personal growth in the context of a special relationship. It is a privilege to counsel with young people. Even when they are suffering from profound and dispiriting problems, they are often more amenable to change than are adults.

References

Association for Specialists in Group Work. (1990). *Professional standards for the training of group workers* (Working document). Alexandria, VA: Author.

Axline, V. (1993). *Play therapy.* New York: Ballantine.

Beck, A. T., & Weishaar, M. E. (1995). Cognitive therapy. In R. J. Corsini & D. Wedding (Eds.), *Current psychotherapies* (5th ed., pp. 229–261). Itasca, IL: Peacock.

Bergin, J. J. (1993). Small-group counseling. In A. Vernon (Ed.), *Counseling children and adolescents.* Denver: Love Publishing.

Berk, L. E. (1994). *Child development* (3rd ed.). Boston: Allyn and Bacon.

Berk, L. E. (1996). *Infants, children, and adolescents* (2nd ed.). Boston: Allyn and Bacon.

Carson, R. C., Butcher, J. N., & Mineka, S. (1996). *Abnormal psychology and modern life* (10th ed.). New York: HarperCollins.

Corey, G. (1996). *Theory and practice of counseling and psychotherapy* (5th ed.). Pacific Grove, CA: Brooks/Cole.

Corey, M. S., & Corey, G. (1992). *Groups: Process and practice* (4th ed.). Pacific Grove, CA: Brooks/Cole.

Elkind, D. (1979). Imaginary audience behavior in children and adolescents. *Developmental Psychology, 15,* 38–44.

Freud, S. (1917). Introductory lectures on psychoanalysis. In J. Strachey (Ed.), *The standard edition of the complete psychological works of Sigmund Freud* (Vol. 16). London: Hogarth Press.

Golden, L. (1994). Brief strategies in counseling with families. *Family Counseling and Therapy, 4,* 1–10.

Goldenberg, I., & Goldenberg, H. (1996). *Family therapy: An overview* (4th ed.). Pacific Grove, CA: Brooks/Cole.

Haley, J. (1980). *Leaving home: The therapy of disturbed young people.* New York: McGraw-Hill.

Moustakas, C. (1959). *Psychotherapy with children.* New York: Harper Colophon.

Posthuma, B. W. (1996). *Small groups in counseling and therapy: Process and leadership* (2nd ed.). Boston: Allyn and Bacon.

Rice, F. P. (1995). Human development across the life span (2nd ed.). Englewood Cliffs, NJ: Prentice Hall.

Satir, V. (1972). *Peoplemaking.* Palo Alto, CA: Science and Behavior Books.

Sharf, R. S. (1996). *Theories of psychotherapy and counseling: Concepts and cases.* Pacific Grove, CA: Brooks/Cole.

Sherwood-Hawes, A. (1993). Individual counseling: Process. In A. Vernon (Ed.), Counseling children and adolescents (pp. 19–49). Denver: Love Publishing.

Vernon, A. (Ed.). (1993), *Counseling children and adolescents.* Denver: Love Publishing.

Chapter *16*

Counseling the Older Adult

Douglas R. Gross, Ph.D.   *David Capuzzi, Ph.D.*

Paul was in the final semester of his master of counseling program and was just beginning his internship. With the advice of his program chairperson, Paul had purposely selected a clinic setting that served people 65 years of age and older. He had been interested in working with older adults and had taken several courses designed to provide him with information and experience in working with this population. His orientation to the setting had been completed two days ago; today he was to see his first client.

As he prepared for the session, Paul reviewed many of the things he had learned in his university coursework. His office had been arranged so that the client, a 72-year-old widow, would have both easy access and a comfortable chair. The time scheduled for the appointment had been arranged to accommodate both the client's concerns regarding transportation and an appointment with a physician in the same complex. He knew that she was somewhat resistant to seeking help and that he would need to reassure her of the benefits of counseling. He was also aware that their age difference—he was 29 and she was 72—might be a barrier to communication, and he would need to take this into consideration.

An initial interview and an orientation meeting had been conducted by the intake person in the clinic, and the schedule of fees had been explained to the client, who agreed to it. Paul had reviewed the material collected during the intake interview and knew that she was contemplating moving from her home into a residential setting. The case material revealed that she did not accept this move. Paul's role was to explore with the client her feelings regarding the move and alternatives she might consider.

The client arrived at the clinic a few minutes prior to the scheduled time. She was accompanied by her son and asked that he be allowed to join her in her counseling session with Paul. Paul had not anticipated this but, wishing to make the client feel more comfortable, agreed. Paul's office was quickly rearranged to accommodate the son, and the session began.

During the session, the son told Paul that his mother's health no longer allowed her to live alone. Based upon his mother's physician's recommendation and with his mother's agreement, arrangements had been made to move her to a full care facility. In the past two weeks, however, his mother had become very disturbed about this move. She now felt that with more assistance from her son and his family she could remain in her home. Based upon her physical condition, however, this would not be possible. Her son stated that his mother was aware of this and was denying the reality of the situation. Tears were obvious as the client discussed how much she loved her home and its memories and how she needed to remain independent as long as possible. The session had reached a stalemate with both parties holding to their positions. Paul decided to talk with each person separately, and the son said that he would wait outside.

In the sessions that followed, Paul explored the fear and anger that the client was feeling. She was afraid of losing her independence and angry that her son was not willing to take care of her as she had always taken care of him. She felt that she was being placed in the facility to die. She knew that she needed a good deal of special care but she felt that with her son's help she could remain in her own home. Paul understood her strong need for independence rather than dependence, and he wanted to do what he could to make this a possibility.

During his session, the son explained that the move had been discussed at length, and he felt that his mother was accepting the fact that she could no longer remain alone. He was surprised by her current reaction and was at a loss as to what could be done to make the transition as positive as possible. He stated that he loved his mother and would do nothing to hurt her. The move was both supported and encouraged by her physician.

Paul brought the client and her son together and shared with them his perceptions of the situation. He encouraged them to talk with each other, as each had talked with him, and asked if they would be willing to return to the clinic to continue to discuss the situation. The client seemed somewhat hesitant, but did agree to return the following Tuesday.

Paul sat for a short time after the client and her son left his office reviewing what had taken place. He decided that he needed to talk with his supervisor regarding the session and what he had done. Perhaps he should have done more to resolve the situation. He could see both sides of the issue, but his feelings were more strongly on the side of the client. He wanted her to be able to remain independent and felt that he needed to develop more of an advocacy role in assisting the client and her son to bring a more positive solution to the situation.

This scenario is one that is occurring more and more in various mental health settings. Counselors and mental health workers are being called on to work with a clientele for which many are ill prepared. The clientele are older adults who, owing to the lengthening of the life span, are increasing in numbers and will continue to have a profound impact on all areas of counseling and therapy. Today there are more than 33 million people 65 years of age or older. Based on the projections of the American Association of Retired Persons (AARP, 1994), this figure will climb to more than 40 million by the year 2010. The impact of this growing population has been addressed by numerous authors (Birren & Birren, 1990; Brody & Semel, 1993; Coleman & Bond 1990; Gross, 1987, 1988; Myers, 1995). According to Gross (1988), "The growing body of literature in the area of counseling and intervention strategies for the elderly addresses the emerging recognition that this population will continue to present itself in growing numbers to the counseling professional" (p. 3).

The purpose of this chapter is to present information relative to counseling the older adult. This information will enable the reader to develop an understanding of the demographics, the general and unique nature of the problems presented, research into counseling approaches that have proven to be effective, and recommendations that should aid the counseling/mental health professional to serve this population more effectively. In this chapter, the term "older adult" refers to people 65 years and older.

Demography of Aging

To understand the demographics of the aging population in the United States, it is important that the reader understand this numerical increase and its growing diversity in relation to age, sex, and marital status; geographic distribution; race and ethnicity; retirement, employment, and income; and physical and mental health status. It is not the purpose of this chapter to present an in-depth analysis of these diverse factors. Each is presented to provide the reader with an overview, which should aid counselors and other mental health professionals to better understand this growing population that is and will continue to become an ongoing part of their caseloads.

The growing number of older adults within the United States constitutes an escalating portion of our total population. According to Toseland (1990), "The population of older persons in the United States is growing in the 1990s at a more rapid rate than other segments of society. This growth is expected to continue well into the twenty-first century" (p. 3). Projecting these figures into the twenty-first century, Butler, Lewis, and Sunderland (1991) see this population reaching 50 million by the year 2030. This number would represent approximately 17.0 percent of the total population and reflects a 5.0 percent increase over the 12.1 percent this population currently constitutes. In discussing these trends, Myers (1989) states, "The proportion of older persons in the population was 1:25 in 1900, 1:9 in 1986, and is projected to be 1:5 in 2030" (p. 2).

A Composite Picture

Older adults are too often viewed as a fairly homogeneous group of individuals. A closer look at variations in this grouping will prove this view to be far from the truth. This population is quite diverse and parallels the diversity found in other segments of our population. The following discussion of these demographic variations highlights this diversity.

Age, Sex, and Marital Status

The older adult population itself is aging. According to AARP (1994), one of the most rapidly growing age categories is that of people 85 years and older (the old-old). This population has increased twenty-seven times between 1900 and the present and is expected to continue to be its fastest growing segment. In comparison, people 75 to 84 (the middle-old) have increased 14 percent, and people 65 to 74 (the young-old) have increased 10 percent. According to Brody and Semel (1993),

> *with an increase in the number of people surviving into the upper age range, the elderly population itself is growing older. In 1980 the young-old (age 65 to 74) outnumbered the oldest-old (age 75 and older) by 3 to 2. By the turn of this century half of the elderly population is expected to be 65 to 74 and half will be age 75 and older. (p. 141)*

Variation is also noted in the percentage of males to females. Of the approximately 33 million people 65 years of age and older, 19.5 million are older women, and 13.3 million are older men: a sex ratio of 147 women for every 100 men (AARP, 1994). Approximately 50 percent of these older women are widows, whereas only 24 percent of older men are widowers. Only 18 percent of older men live alone or with nonrelatives, compared with 43 percent of older women.

These figues are probably not too surprising, given the data related to the greater life expectancy of women. What is surprising, however, is the fact that older men tend to remarry if they lose a spouse and women do not. The figures (AARP, 1994) indicate that 77 percent of older men tend to live in newly constructed family environments as compared with 42 percent of the older women. Because women tend to marry older men and also to live longer, the American female can expect to be a widow for approximately twenty-five years.

Geographic Distribution

There is a degree of similarity between the distribution of older adults and the distribution of the general population. States with the largest populations tend to have the largest number of older adults. According to the 1994 AARP report, the following nine states have the highest population of older adults: California, Florida, New York, Pennsylvania, Texas, Illinois, Ohio, Michigan, and New Jersey. Placing this in a different perspective, the states with the highest proportion of older adults, based on their total population, are as follows: Florida (18.6 percent), Pennsylvania (15.8 percent), Iowa and Rhode Island (15.5 percent each), West Virginia (15.3 percent), Arkansas (15.0 percent), North Dakota (14.8 percent), South Dakota (14.7 percent), Nebraska and Missouri (14.2 percent each), Connecticut (14.1 percent), and Massachusetts (14.0 percent).

The belief that a majority of older adults uproot themselves and move is not true. The majority of older adults continue to live in the same location. Of those who do move, approximately half move within the same community and the other half have tended to move to the following states: Nevada (22 percent); Alaska (19 percent); Arizona (11 percent); Hawaii, Utah, and New Mexico (10 percent each); and Wyoming and Colorado (9 percent each) (AARP, 1994).

Race and Ethnicity

Racial and ethnic differences provide yet another variation within this population. AARP (1994) reported that in 1993 approximately 85 percent of people 65 years of age and older were white, with the remaining 15 percent composed of blacks (8 percent), Hispanics (4 percent), Asians or Pacific Islanders (2 percent), and American Indian or Native Alaskan (1 percent). Comparing this to the total population within the United States, these percentages contrast to the general population breakdown, in which 80 percent are white and 20 percent are nonwhite. Due to birth rates, increased life expectancy, and immigration figures, it would seem safe to predict that by the twenty-first century racial and ethnic minorities will account for increasing percentages of the older adult population in the United States.

Retirement, Employment, and Income

Retirement, which at one point in our history was considered a luxury, is today the norm. According to the Special Committee on Aging (SCOA, 1983), 66 percent of older males were employed in the labor force in 1900. Today less than 17 percent of this population is employed, and the projections are that this percentage will continue to decline as we move into the twenty-first century. The percentages for females for this same period show a much more stable pattern: 10 percent in the labor force in 1900, and a projection of 7 percent in the early part of the next century (AARP, 1994). The people who tend to remain in the labor force after the age of 70 are those classified as professionals and those who are craftspeople. Both these categories are descriptive of the self-employed.

Retirement brings with it a set of unique circumstances surrounding the older adult and is related to employment and income. According to Butler et al. (1991), a majority of those who retire do so with incomes stemming from pensions (16 percent), Social Security (38 percent), savings (26 percent), employment (17 percent), and assistance from relatives (3 percent). For the most part, this income is "fixed" and generally represents approximately 40 percent of the income the individual was receiving prior to retirement. With inflation generally on the rise in this country, the reductions, coupled with the "fixed" nature of the income, place the individual in a position of having to manage more carefully his or her income to meet not only the basic costs of living, but also the added costs, specifically those that deal with increasing taxes and expenses associated with health care, that come with retirement. AARP (1994), in discussing income related to the older adult, indicated the following:

The median income of older persons in 1993 was $14,963 for males and $8,499 for females. After adjusting for a 1992–1993 inflation rate of 3%, these figures represented no significant change in "real" income from 1992 for both women and men. (p. 9)

Physical and Mental Health

One of the stereotypical pictures of older adults is the view of individuals as frail, weak, and suffering from a myriad of chronic disorders. As with all stereotypes, nothing could be further from the truth. According to Lemme (1995), "Most adults are in good health and experience few limitations or disabilities. Nearly 71% of adults over age 65 living in the community (that is not in institutions) report their health as excellent, very good, or good" (p. 374). Based on findings such as these, 80 percent of older adults are able to maintain the activities of daily living without the necessity of medical assistance. According to Myers (1989), "Health status and independent daily functioning are not significantly reduced until at least age 75, but more likely reduced by age 85 or older" (p. 6).

Older adults accounted for nearly 35 percent of all hospital stays and 46 percent of all days of care in hospitals in 1992. The average length of this hospital stay was 8.2 days for older people, compared to only 5.1 days for people under 65 (AARP, 1994). Even though older adults are seen by physicans nearly twice as often as their younger counterparts, the overall health status of the majority of older people is seen as excellent or good.

The mental health picture for older adults indicates that even though 27 percent of all admissions to public mental hospitals are over 65, only 2 to 4 percent are represented in out-patient mental health treatment facilities (Butler et al., 1991). These percentages may reflect a variety of factors. It could be that, based on values and attitudes, they do not see the benefit in seeking such treatment. They may not understand the concepts that underlie counseling and therapy. It could be that the mental health facility, based on personnel and facilities, is not prepared to work with this population. Regardless of the reasons, older adults, like their younger counterparts, can benefit from such assistance and need to receive information and encouragement from the mental health professional.

Problems and Concerns of Older Adults

From a psychological viewpoint, the emotional and psychological problems of older adults differ slightly from the emotional and psychological problems of their younger counterparts (Burlingame, 1995; Gross, 1988). For example, feelings of anxiety, frustration, guilt, loneliness, despair, worthlessness, and fear are prevalent across all age levels. The young, as well as the old, must learn to cope daily with a multitude of life situations that test their emotional stability. The process of aging, however, brings with it a set of circumstances not only unique, but also telescoped into a brief period of years. These circumstances—physiologic, situational, and psychological in nature—force older adults into changing patterns of behavior and lifestyles that have been developed and ingrained over long periods of time. The following are examples of the changing life circumstances older adults are forced to confront.

Example 1: Loss of Work Role Identity, Increased Amount of Leisure Time, and Decreased Financial Support

For older adults, the onset of retirement, either by choice or law, removes them from activities that for many years have been the focus of their self-identity. This work/career identity shaped not only their family life and their interactions with family members, but also their social life outside the family. What they did for a living was so much a part of who they were and how they were valued both by self and by others that this loss often creates an identity crisis. The degree of severity that surrounds this issue is related to the older adult's ability to create a new identity.

With retirement comes increased amounts of leisure time—time for which many older adults are ill prepared. Leisure time, the dream of the full-time employee, often becomes the nightmare of retirees. What will they do with this time? What will be done to replace the daily routines so much a part of their working years? How will they relate to significant others now that they are together for extended periods of time? These and other questions need to be addressed, and education and planning are necessary if older adults are to make a positive transition from work to leisure.

Retirement also brings a significant reduction in income. The majority of older adults enter this period of life on fixed incomes representing approximately 40 percent of their incomes prior to retirement. With increasing inflation, added expenses for health care, and rising taxes, they often move from a financially independent state to a financially dependent state, needing greater support from family, friends, and state and federal agencies. They may also find their lifestyles restricted so that they may better conserve their fixed resources today to meet the continually escalating financial world of tomorrow.

Example 2: Loss of Significant Person(s) and Increased Loneliness and Separation

The aging process brings with it the reality of the terminal nature of relationships. Loss of significant people, due to geographical relocation or death, occurs often during this life period. Marital and social relationships on which much of the significance of life centered end, and older adults are called on to cope and to find meaning in other aspects of their life. Sometimes this can be done with the support of family and friends. Sometimes it requires the intervention of helping professionals trained to work with this aspect of the aging process. In either case, the loss and its accompanying separation from the secure and familiar are issues that aging people must confront.

Example 3: Geographic Relocation and Peer and Family Group Restructuring

Although the majority of older adults do not relocate during this life period, those who do by choice or by extenuating circumstances find themselves adjusting both to new environments and to the building of new family and social relationships. The reasons for such relocations vary with the individual. Often they represent movements to areas that are more conducive to leisure lifestyles, areas that are less demanding based on physical and physiologic disabilities, or areas that are closer to significant family members. Even when the relocation is by choice, the reconstruction process that follows is never easy and often brings with it stress, frustration, loneliness, separation, and regret.

Example 4: Increased Physiologic Disorders and Increasing Amounts of Dependence

Health often becomes a major issue for older adults. Even though, as reported earlier, the majority report their health as good to excellent, it is a period marked by physiological decline. The body, like any complex machine, is beginning to wear down. The stress, anxiety, and frustration of this process takes a heavy toll. Older people are often called on to cope with health-related situations, both their own and those of loved ones, that demand both personal stamina and financial resources. Either or both of these may not be in great abundance during this period of life.

To compensate, older adults are often forced to depend on others both for support and financial resources. Such dependence, following a life characterized by productivity and independence, is often difficult for them to accept. The resulting anger, depression, and loss of self-esteem need to be addressed if the individual is to cope effectively with the situation.

When these major life changes are viewed in terms of the rapidity of their onset, the lack of preparation for their encounter, and society's negative attitudes regarding older adults, the prevalence of emotional and psychological problems is brought into clear focus. Any one of these changing life situations can produce emotional and psychological difficulties for the individual. In combination, they place the individual in a situation where he or she must develop coping strategies.

In seeking to deal with the myriad of physiological, situational, and psychological changes that are part of the aging process, older adults turn for assistance to family, friends, the church, physicians, counselors, and state and federal agencies. In doing so, they encounter both personal and societal barriers. These barriers include but are not limited to the following:

1. Lack of recognition of the need for help
2. Personal values and fears regarding seeking assistance

3. Ageism on the part of the helping professional
4. Society's negative attitudes regarding older adults
5. Practical problems such as transportation and financial limitations
6. Lack of awareness of existing support services
7. Family pressure to keep problems within the family
8. Separation from family members who could provide assistance

These factors place older adults "at risk"—at risk from both personal attitudes and values that keep them from seeking needed assistance and from lack of attention by the many professionals who could serve them. Counselors and mental health professionals are part of this professional service group. Given demographic projections, they will see older adults as clients in increasing numbers. It is therefore imperative that they become aware of what techniques and interventions are most appropriate and how to expand on their existing skills to better serve this population. Furthermore, counselors working with this group must explore their feelings regarding the aging process, examine personal and social values and attitudes about aging, and acquire a solid foundation of information regarding the physiological, psychological, and sociological aspects of aging.

Counseling Principles

A basic premise of this chapter is that there is a common core of counseling approaches that are applicable across the life span. Skills in rapport building, active listening, ability to demonstrate caring, support, respect, and acceptance are as applicable to the client age 80 as the client age 8 (Warnick, (1995). According to Waters (1984),

> Regardless of the age of your client, you as a counselor need to communicate clearly, respond both to thoughts and feelings, ask effective questions, and confront when appropriate. It also is important to help people clarify their values and their goals in order to make decisions and develop action plans to implement these decisions. (p. 63)

The basic goal and approach of counseling are not age related. The goal of all counseling is to assist the individual in problem resolution and behavior change, regardless of age. When working with older adults, counselors need not put aside their basic skills and techniques and adopt a new set. What they need to do is to develop an awareness of the aging process and the factors within it that may necessitate adapting existing skills and techniques to more effectively meet the needs of this population.

Such adaptations are best understood in terms of a set of general counseling recommendations that are more applicable to the older adult than, perhaps, to the younger client. Such recommendations are directed at compensating for some of the "changing life situations" and "barriers" discussed earlier. The following recommendations have general applicability to both individual and group counseling.

1. *Counselors should expend more effort in enhancing the dignity and worth of the older adult.* Given ageist attitudes within society and often within the helping professions, these clients are often led to believe that they are less valuable than younger people. Counselors need to devote time and energy in restoring self-esteem and encouraging clients to review their successes, accomplishments, and positive aspects of their changing lifestyles. Further support for this recommendation can be found in McWhirter (1994), Waters & Goodman (1990), and Warnick (1995).

2. *Counselors need to expend more effort in "selling" the client on the positive benefits to be derived from counseling.* Given long-established values and attitudes, the client may well view counseling and the seeking of such assistance as a sign of weakness and place little value on the positive results of such a process. The counselor needs to reinforce the client's seeking assistance and to demonstrate, through actions, the positive results that are possible through counseling. Further support for this recommendation can be found in Burlingame (1995), Hoyt (1993), and Sherman (1993).

3. *Counselors must attend more to the "physical environment" of counseling than might be necessary with a younger client.* Because of decreasing physical competencies, attention needs to center on factors such as noise distractions and counselor voice levels due to hearing loss, adequate lighting for those with visual impairments, furniture that will enhance the physical comfort of the client, thermostatic control to protect against extremes in temperatures, office accessibility, and the removal of items that impair ease of movement. Shorter sessions may also be appropriate, because older adults may experience difficulty sitting in one position for a long time. Further support for this recommendation can be found in Gross (1991).

4. *Counselors should address counselor–client involvement and the role of the counselor as advocate.* The counselor in this situation needs to take a much more active/doing role to better serve the client. This active/doing role may involve contacting agencies, family, attorneys, and other support personnel for the client. It may also entail serving as advocate for the client, to represent effectively the needs and grievances of the older adult. It might also entail transporting the client or taking the counseling services to the client, as would be the case with "shut-ins" or those who are incapacitated. Further support for this recommendation can be found in Gladding (1995).

5. *Counselors need to think in terms of short-term goals that are clear-cut and emphasize the present life situation for the client.* Many of the problems the client presents deal with day-to-day living situations. The counselor, in helping the client find solutions to these problems, not only reinforces the positive aspects of the counseling process, but also encourages the client to continue seeking assistance. Further support for this recommendation can be found in Burlingame (1995) and Myers (1989).

6. *Counselors should pay attention to the dependence/independence issue characteristic of work with older adults.* Changing life circumstances often force them into a more dependent lifestyle. The reasons vary from client to client but may be centered around health, finances, and family. The counselor needs to realize that a certain degree of dependence may well benefit the client and needs to be encouraged until the client is ready once again to assume an independent role. The majority have functioned somewhat independently most of their adult lives. They often need assistance in seeing that it is still possible. Further support for this recommendation can be found in Brody and Semel (1993).

7. *Counselors must be sensitive to the possible age differential between themselves and clients and to the differing cultural, environmental, and value orientations that this difference in age may denote.* With the exception of peer counseling, the counselor generally is much younger than the client. This age difference can generate client resistance, anger, or resentment. It is important that the counselor be aware of this and learn to deal with it in an appropriate manner. The counselor, depending on his or her attitudes regarding aging, may experience some of the same feelings as the client. Dealing with this at the beginning should enhance the probability of success. Further support for this recommendation can be found in Gross (1991).

8. *Counselors need to have some perspective on the client's "place in history" and the significance this place holds in determining values and attitudes.* People whose significant developmental period took place during the Depression years of the 1930s or the war years of the 1940s may well be espousing values characteristic of that era. The counselor needs to accept this and not expect this person to easily incorporate values and attitudes descriptive of the 1990s. Further support for this recommendation can be found in Gross (1991).

9. *Counselors should be cautious in the use of diagnostic tools (tests) with this population.* Unlike their younger counterparts, older adults have limited recent experience with such instruments, and tests may create undue anxiety. It is also important to keep in mind that many diagnostic instruments used in mental health do not have norm groups for this population, and therefore the results obtained have questionable degrees of reliability and validity. It is important that the counselor, prior to using such tools, determine whether tests are the best means of gaining the types of data needed. Discussions of the numerous problems associated with this recommendation can be found in Birren and Schaie (1990) and Gintner (1995).

Counseling Procedures

Because the basic goal and approach of counseling are not age related, all theoretical systems, techniques, and intervention styles are applicable to this older adult population and are currently being used. One of the most comprehensive reviews of outcome research in counseling older people in the past twelve years was conducted by Wellman and McCormack (1984). They reported the results of more than ninety studies. In this report, a myriad of approaches, including psychoanalytic (Brink, 1979), developmental (Kastenbaum, 1968), brief task-centered therapy (Saferstein, 1972), behavior management (Nigl & Jackson, 1981), peer counseling (Hayes & Burk, 1987), and cognitive behavioral (Meichenbaum, 1974) were cited. The results varied, but all approaches appear to support the use of psychological intervention with this population. According to the authors, much of the research reviewed suffered from methodological weaknesses centering on controls, sampling, and sound theoretical rationales. They indicate, however, that procedures such as (1) regular continued contact, (2) brief psychotherapy approaches, (3) task-oriented and structured activities, (4) high levels of client involvement, (5) multidisciplinary team and peer counseling, and (6) group work all seem to hold promise in working with older adults. The authors further indicated that given their review the following goals for counseling older adults appear often:

1. *To decrease anxiety and depression*
2. *To reduce confusion and loss of contact with reality*
3. *To increase socialization and improve interpersonal relationships*
4. *To improve behavior within institutions*
5. *To cope with crisis and transitional stress*
6. *To become more accepting of self and the aging process (p. 82)*

Authors such as Birren and Schaie (1990); Butler et al. (1991); Burlingame (1995); and Warnick (1995) also address the issues of counseling and differing theoretical approaches to working with older adults. According to Butler et al. (1991),

> *All forms of psychotherapy—from "uncovering" to "supportive" to "reeducative" and from Freudian to Jungian to Rogerian—can contribute to both a better understanding of the psychology and psychotherapy of old age. Further integration and eclectic utilization of all contemporary personality theories and practices, including the life-cycle perspective of human life along with the use of medication, when appropriate, are needed. (p. 407)*

Both individual and group approaches to working with older adults are supported in the literature (Brody & Semel, 1993; Capuzzi & Gross, 1991; Gladding, 1995; MacLennan, Saul, & Weiner, 1988; Toseland, 1990). Which is the most appropriate depends on the client, the nature of the presenting problem, the resources available to both the client and the counselor, and the setting in which the counseling takes place. Along with the life circumstances identified earlier, it is important to keep in mind that treatment for older adults presents the same variety of problems presented by younger clients. Issues dealing with alcohol and drug usage, abuse, loss, family, marriage, divorce, suicide, crime victimization, and career and avocational areas are often found to be continuing concerns. Both individual and group approaches to this population are applicable.

Individual Approaches

In providing individual counseling or therapy to older adults, counselors have a variety of techniques, intervention strategies, and theoretical systems available to them. The only limitations seem to be those related to the skills and expertise of the counselor. Keeping in mind the eight principles mentioned previously, the following counseling skills are highly applicable to this population. Further support for these skills can be found in Burlingame (1995).

Active Listening Skills

Older adults, as with their younger counterparts, need to be heard. Use of such techniques as visual contact, encouragers, reflection of both content and feeling, paraphrasing, clarifying, questioning, and summarizing are all appropriate. Such techniques, when used appropriately, serve as encouragers, demonstrate caring, concern, and interest, and provide the client with an opportunity to share, vent feelings, be understood, and gain self-respect.

Nonverbal Skills

Counseling older adults will be enhanced if the counselor is aware of and able to use effectively his or her knowledge of nonverbal communication patterns. Attention paid to body posture, eye contact, tone level, and rate of speech, although not the "royal road" to a person's inner self, is one road that aids the counselor in better understanding the client's communication more completely.

Relationship Variables

Relationship building with older adults may demand more effort on the part of the counselor. The skills mentioned in this section should aid in facilitating this process, but it is important to keep in mind that establishing trust with a much older person may require the counselor to give consideration to his or her language, appearance, solicitous attitude, and values and attitudes related to aging.

A second factor related to relationship building centers on the client's need for both support and challenge. Counselors working with this population need to understand that their view of older adults as fragile may temper their ability to provide the challenge. If challenge is not part of the counseling process, the client may be denied the opportunity for change and growth.

Counseling Strategies

The following strategies are not presented in any priority listing. Each needs to be given careful consideration in working individually with this population.

1. Take into consideration the longevity of the client's life. In doing so, stress the positive accomplishments and encourage the client to use the many coping skills that he or she has demonstrated in reaching this stage of life.
2. Stress the benefits that counseling can provide. Often older adults view such assistance as a weakness on their part and believe counseling carries with it a

stigma. Perhaps the words used to describe the service will need to be changed to attract this population. It might be more acceptable for the person to attend a discussion group rather than a therapy group.

3. Give attention to the physiologic needs of the client as these relate to mobility, hearing loss, visual acuity, and physical condition (for example, sessions may need to be of shorter duration owing to the clients' inability to sit for extended periods of time).

4. Depending on the various professionals who may be working with the client (for example, physician, social worker, and agency personnel), counselors may need to establish more collaborative relationships than might be the case with the younger client.

5. Do not rule out problem areas that you believe are applicable only to a younger population. Drugs, alcohol, and relationships are all viable issues in dealing with older adults. Also, keep in mind that loss, and its impact, are more often experienced by this population.

6. In the selection of intervention techniques, use what is workable based on the special needs and attitudinal set of the client. Certain techniques, owing to their physical nature or affective emphasis, may not be appropriate for this population.

Group Approaches

Counselors who decide to use a group approach with the older adult can gain a great deal of information and direction from reviewing such authors as Capuzzi and Gross (1991); MacLennan et al. (1988); and Toseland (1990). These authors not only offer special considerations that need to be made for working with older adults in groups such as time parameters, member selection, and group size, but also specify the types of groups that have proven to be particularly helpful with this population. Some of the advantages of the group approach mentioned by these authors include (1) discovering common bonds, (2) teaching social skills, (3) aiding in feelings of loneliness, (4) giving mutual assistance, (5) sharing feelings, and (6) providing shared purposes.

Whether selecting an individual or group modality for working with older adults, it is important to keep in mind that certain approaches to both individual and group work have been designed specifically to deal with this population from a rehabilitative perspective. The needs of the individual in a life care facility may be quite different from the individual who maintains an independent lifestyle. In working with the individual in the life care facility, the following selected approaches have proven to be helpful.

Reality Orientation Therapy

Reality orientation therapy, which combines both individual and group work, is directed at the individual who has experienced memory loss, confusion, and time–place–person disorientation. The thrust of reality orientation therapy is the repetition and learning of basic personal information such as the individual's name, the place, the time of day, day of the week and date, the next meal, time of bath, and so on. If done on an informal basis within the care facility, it should be done on a twenty-four-hour basis, and it should be used by all people who have contact with the elderly person. On a formal basis, this is done in a class setting.

Milieu Therapy

Milieu therapy, which may make use of both individual and group work, is based on the concept that the social milieu of the care facility itself can be the instrument for treatment. The environment is organized to provide a more homelike atmosphere, with the individual taking more responsibility, trying new skills, and being involved in decision making in a somewhat safe environment. Levels of activity, self-care, and self-worth have increased.

Reminiscence Groups

These groups are designed to encourage the sharing of memories with groups of six to eight members and are conducted in both institutional and noninstitutional settings. This approach is similar to the "life review" process and in a group setting enhances a cohort effect, helping members identify and share accomplishments, tribulations, and viewpoints, while at the same time increasing opportunities for socialization. Music, visual aids, and memorabilia are often used to aid in stimulating group discussion.

Remotivation Therapy

Remotivation therapy, which can be done in either a group or individual setting, seeks to encourage the moderately confused patient to take a renewed interest in his or her surroundings by focusing attention on the simple, objective features of everyday life. Common topics are selected such as pets, gardening, and cooking, and people are encouraged to relate to these topics by drawing on their own life experiences.

In working with the greater percentage of older adults who continue to live independent lives, self-help groups, assertiveness training groups, growth groups, support groups, and the variety of special topic groups find equal applicability in work with this population as they do with a younger client population. Is counseling with older adults different from work with younger clients? The answer seems to be one of selective emphasis. In both individual and group work, all counseling interventions have applicability. The counselor needs to adapt his or her approach to accommodate the unique factors that parallel the aging process.

Summary

As older adults increase in number, more will be seen in counseling. Counselors whose preparation has primarily focused on working with a younger population need to adapt this preparation to work more effectively with these clients. Counselor educators need to revise existing preparation programs to provide a curriculum that incorporates both didactic and experiential programming related to this population.

The counseling needs of older adults are very similar to those of the younger client. When differences exist, they are best described in terms of a set of circumstances that are characteristic of the aging process. The following recommendations can help the beginning counselor better understand what he or she needs to do to prepare for this clientele:

1. Counselors need to secure information regarding the aging process and physiological, sociological, and psychological factors that have an impact on this process.
2. Counselors need to clarify their values regarding aging from both self and other person perspectives. These values and attitudes will either enhance or impede their success with the older adults.
3. Counselors need to be aware of the client's "place in history" and the significance this place holds in formulating values and attitudes that impact the client's view of the counseling process.
4. Counselors need to emphasize short-term goals with older adult clients. These goals need to be clearly understood and accepted by the client and should place emphasis on the present life situation of the client.
5. Counselors need to be aware of some of the drawbacks to using various diagnostic tools with an older adult population. Counselors may need to seek out more creative ways of data gathering.
6. Counselors need to pay more attention to the physical setting in which counseling takes place. This environment needs to encourage, not discourage, the older adult's participation.
7. Counselors need to view their role with the client more from an advocacy perspective. They need to be more actively involved with the day-to-day life of the client. As with any "at risk" population, efforts to reduce this risk call for more active participation.
8. Counselors need to be willing to go to the client and not always expect the client to come to them. It may be necessary to take counseling to the client's home or to other settings due to the physical limitations of the older adult.
9. Counselors need not fear or be apprehensive about involvement with older adults. They differ from their younger counterparts generally in increased life experiences and the rapidity of change descriptive of the aging process.
10. Counselors need to use the longevity and the developed coping strategies that accompany the aging process to enhance the clients' present life situation. These clients have an advantage inasmuch as they have proven qualities of survival, that the counselor can use to improve self-esteem, interpersonal relations, family problems, loneliness, dependence versus independence, and a myriad of other concerns representative of this population.

The common theme of these recommendations is that counselors must pay more attention to and show more concern for the older adult. They must recognize their unique needs and, more importantly, treat them as fully deserving of the care counselors provide younger people.

References

American Association of Retired Persons (AARP). (1994). *A profile of older Americans*. Washington, DC: Author.

Birren, J. E., & Birren, B. A. (1990). The concepts, models, and history of the psychology of aging. In J. E. Birren & K. W. Schaie (eds.), *Handbook of the psychology of aging* (3rd ed., pp. 3–20). San Diego: Academic Press.

Birren, J. E., & Schaie, K. W. (1990). *Handbook of the psychology of aging* (3rd. ed.). San Diego: Academic Press.

Brink, T. L. (1979). *Geriatric psychotherapy*. New York: Human Sciences.

Brody, C. M., & Semel, V. G. (1993). *Strategies for therapy with the Elderly*. New York: Springer.

Burlingame, V. S. (1995). *Gerocounseling: Counseling elders and their families*. New York: Springer.

Butler, R. N., Lewis, M., & Sunderland, T. (1991). *Aging and mental health: Positive psychosocial and biomedical approaches* (4th ed.). New York: Macmillan.

Capuzzi, D., & Gross, D. R. (Eds.). (1991). *Introduction to counseling: Perspectives for the 1990s*. Boston: Allyn and Bacon.

Coleman, P., & Bond, J. (1990). Aging in the twentieth century. In J. Bond & P. Coleman (Eds.), *Aging in society* (pp. l–16) London: Sage.

Gintner, G. G. (1995). Differential diagnosis in older adults: dementia, depression, and delirium. *Journal of Counseling and Development, 73*(3), 346–351.

Gladding, S. T. (1995). *Counseling: A comprehensive profession* (3rd ed.). Englewood Cliffs, NJ: Merrill/Prentice Hall.

Gross, D. R. (1987). Aging and addiction: Perspective and recommendations. *Arizona Counseling Journal, 12*(1), 29–35.

Gross, D. R. (1988). Counseling and the elderly: Strategies, procedures and recommendations. *Ccounseling and Human Development*. Denver: Love Publishing.

Gross, D. R. (1991). Counseling the elderly. In J. Carlson and J. Lewis (Eds.), *Family counseling: Strategies and issues* (pp. 209–223). Denver: Love Publishing.

Hayes, R. L., & Burk, M. J. (1987). Community-based prevention for elderly victims of crime and violence. *Journal of Mental Health Counseling, 9*(4), 210–219.

Hoyt, M. (1993, Fall). Brief therapy can be the best therapy. *The Provider, MCC Behavioral Care*, pp. 1–3.

Kastenbaum, R. (1968). Perspectives on the development and modification of behavior in the aged: A developmental field perspective. *Gerontologist, 8*, 280–283.

Lemme, B. H. (1995). *Development in adulthood*. Boston: Allyn and Bacon.

MacLennan, B. W., Saul, S., & Weiner, M. B. (Eds.). (1988). *Group psychotherapies for the elderly*. Madison, CT: International University Press.

McWhirter, E. H. (1994). *Counseling for empowerment*. Alexandria, VA: American Counseling Association.

Meichenbaum, D. (1974). Self-instructional strategy training: A cognitive prosthesis for the aged. *Human Development, 17*, 273–280.

Myers, J. (1989). *Adult children with aging parents*. Alexandria, VA: American Association for Counseling and Development.

Myers, J. (1995). From "forgotten and ignored" to standards and certification: Gerontological counseling comes of age. *Journal of Counseling and Development, 74*(2), 143–149.

Nigl, A. J., & Jackson, B. (1981). A behavior management program to increase social responses in psychogeriatric patients. *Journal of the Geriatrics Society, 29*, 92–95.

Saferstein, S. (1972). Psychotherapy for geriatric patients. *New York State Journal of Medicine, 72*, 2743–2748.

Sherman, E. (1993). Mental health and successful adaptation in later life. *Generations, 17*(1), 43–46.

Special Committee on Aging (SCOA). (1983). *Developments in aging: 1983* (Vol. 1). Washington, DC: U.S. Government Printing Office.

Toseland, R. W. (1990). *Group work with older adults.* New York: New York University Press.

Warnick, J. (1995). *Listening with different ears: Counseling people over 60.* Fort Bragg, CA: QED Press.

Waters, E. (1984). Building on what you know: Techniques for individual and group counseling with older people. *Counseling Psychologist, 12*(2), 63–74.

Waters, E., & Goodman, J. (1990). *Empowering older adults.* San Francisco: Jossey-Bass.

Wellman, R., & McCormack, J. (1984). Counseling with older persons: A review of outcome research. *Counseling Psychologist, 12*(2), 81–96.

Counseling Couples and Families

Cass Dykeman, Ph.D.   *Frank C. Noble, Ed.D.*

The placement of this chapter in a section called "Counseling Special Populations" confirms Duncan Stanton's (1988) contention that "Non-family therapists often view family therapy as (a) a modality, that (b) usually involves the nuclear family" (p. 8). He goes on to point out the inaccuracy of this conception, explaining that family therapy is based on a point of view that emphasizes the contextual nature of psychological problems:

> *More fundamentally, it (family therapy) is a way of construing human problems that dictates certain actions for their alleviation. Its conceptual and data bases differ from most other (especially individually oriented) therapies in that the interpersonal context of a problem and the interplay between this context and the symptoms are of primary interest. An index patient is seen as responding to his or her social situation; those around the patient are noted to react to this response; the patient then reacts "back," and so on, in an on-going, give and take process. Interventions designed to alter this process derive from such interactional formulations. (p. 8)*

It is, of course, possible for a counselor who is oriented to the treatment of individuals to interview the members of a client's family in the course of treatment. How-

The author of this chapter in the first edition was Frank Noble, Ed.D., professor emeritus of Arizona State University. Dr. Noble died in October 1994. In his memory and because the chapter retains some of the original content and structure as he designed it, we retain his name as second author.

TABLE 17-1   Two Contrasting Views of Therapy: Psychodynamic and Family Systems

	Psychodynamic	Family Systems
Causality	Linear	Recursive
Time Focus	Past	Present
Pathology	Intrapsychic	Interpersonal
Assessment	Individual	Systemic
Therapy	Long term Catharsis Transference Abreaction Insight	Brief Reframing Restructuring Problem solving Behavior change
Therapist	Passive	Active

ever, this rarely occurs, because the individual orientation places the source of dysfunction within the client rather than focusing on the context in which the symptoms occur. Table 17-1 illustrates some of the other differences in perspective between a psychodynamic and a family therapy point of view. The psychodynamic approach is based in Freudian theory, and emphasizes internal constructs such as the id, ego, and superego; in contrast, family therapy is primarily based in systems theory and emphasizes interpersonal behavior. To further illuminate this paradigm shift, several concepts from systems theory (adapted from Sieburg, 1985) are illustrated here within a human behavioral context:

Fundamental Unity. The universe is one system with infinite levels of subsystems; analysis at any level needs to consider the levels above and below. To understand the individual, it is essential to analyze both the interindividual context and the intraindividual subsystems. A person's strange behavior may be caused by dysfunctional family interactions or by chemical imbalance in the individual's blood.

System Change. Change in any part of a system affects the whole system. If therapy with an individual is successful, the system of which the client is a part is affected. Unfortunately, we know of those changes only through the selective filter of our client, and we know our chances of success are diminished by the homeostatic drag of the system.

Recursive Causality. Inherent in the first two concepts is a nonlinear epistemology. Thus our observation that A causes B is due only to our punctuation of a behavioral sequence that fails to see what follows from B or what preceded A. Every act (or nonaction) provokes feedback, which alters the nature of the next act. In a family, "Does he drink because she nags?" (his punctuation) or "Does she nag because he drinks?" (her punctuation).

Homeostasis. Systems use negative feedback to maintain a steady state; positive feedback creates change in the system. If one member of a family begins to change, perhaps as the result of individual therapy, the usual routine interactions of the family are disrupted, and the family will send messages designed to bring the person in therapy back into line.

Viability. The viability of a system is based on order and structure; entropy is disorder. In addition to structure, which is a static quality, the system must also be open to new input if it is to be capable of accommodating to its changing environment. A family with young children needs a generational hierarchy, but the hierarchy must also be open to modification as the children mature.

With this brief description of systems concepts, perhaps the following definition of family therapy, as stated by Wynne (1988), can be presented:

> *Family therapy is a psychotherapeutic approach that focuses on altering interactions between a couple, within a nuclear family or extended family, or between a family and other interpersonal systems, with the goal of alleviating problems initially presented by individual family members, family subsystems, the family as a whole, or other referral sources. (pp. 250–251)*

The History of Family Therapy

The history of family therapy is relatively brief. It begins in the 1950s, with the seminal contributions of Nathan Ackerman, Theodore Lidz, Lyman Wynne, Murray Bowen, and Carl Whitaker. All these psychiatrists, originally trained in the prevailing psychodynamic model, broke away from its restrictive influence and began to see that dysfunctional behavior was rooted in the individual's past and present family life. Each of these pioneers arrived at this insight relatively independently: Ackerman through his research on the mental health problems of the unemployed in Pennsylvania; Lidz at Yale studying the families of schizophrenics; Wynne in Massachusetts treating patients with psychosis and ulcerative colitis, and later doing research, at the National Institute of Mental Health (NIMH), on the families of schizophrenics; Bowen through his work with families at the Menninger Foundation and later with Wynne at NIMH; Whitaker through seeing families at Oak Ridge (Tennessee) and his later work at Emory University with families that had a schizophrenic member. In his preface to *The Psychodynamics of Family Life* (1958), the first book-length treatment of this point of view, Ackerman said,

> *This approach attempts to correlate the dynamic psychological processes of individual behavior with family behavior in order to be able to place individual clinical diagnosis and therapy within the broader frame of family diagnosis and therapy. It has been necessary, therefore, to explore a series of interrelated themes: the interdependence of individual and family stability at every stage of growth from infancy to old age; the role of family in the emotional development of the child; the family as stabilizer of the mental health of the adult; the family as con-*

veyor belt for anxiety and conflict and as a carrier of the contagion of mental ill-
ness; the interplay of conflict between family and community, conflict in family
relationships, and conflict within individual family members; and breakdown in
adaptation and illness as symptoms of the group pathology of the family. (p. viii)

With this statement, he did much to set the agenda for the next three decades.

During this same period, an unusual group of people assembled in Palo Alto to study the communication processes of schizophrenics. The project was headed by Gregory Bateson, an anthropologist, who hired Jay Haley, a recent graduate in communications theory, Don Jackson, a psychiatrist, and John Weakland, whose initial training was in chemical engineering. Early in the project, Haley began consulting with Milton Erickson, who was known at that time primarily as a hypnotherapist. From this rich melange emerged the beginnings of strategic family therapy. In 1959, Jackson founded the Mental Research Institute (MRI) in Palo Alto and invited Virginia Satir to join him. When the Bateson project ended in 1961, Haley and Weakland also joined the staff at MRI.

Satir diverged from the pragmatic approach of strategic therapy when she left MRI to join the human potential movement at the Esalen Institute. With the publication of her book *Conjoint Family Therapy* in 1964, she established her own approach to family treatment, which incorporated elements of the thinking of the group at MRI within a framework of Gestalt and experiential therapy.

Structural family therapy emerged on the East Coast in the work of Salvador Minuchin and his colleagues at Wyltwick School and later the Philadelphia Child Guidance Clinic (PCGC). At Wyltwick, Minuchin worked with the families of delinquent boys, and at PCGC he did research on families with a member who was psychosomatic. Each of these projects resulted in a book that enriched our understanding of family functioning (Minuchin, Montalvo, Gurney, Rosman, & Schumer, 1967; Minuchin, Rosman, & Baker, 1978). He was joined by Haley in 1967, and they worked together for ten years. As might be expected, the concepts of strategic and structural therapy have much in common. Haley, who met his second wife, Cloe Madanes, at the PCGC, left with her in 1977 to found the Family Therapy Institute of Washington, DC.

Murray Bowen began his career at the Menninger Foundation and focused his research on families with a schizophrenic member. He continued this at the NIMH, where, in 1954, he had the families of schizophrenic youngsters actually live in the hospital so that he could observe their interactions. In 1959, he moved to Georgetown University Medical Center, where he worked for the rest of his career.

Last, but not least, is Carl Whitaker. Whitaker began his career as a gynecologist, but soon switched to psychiatry. He was chief psychiatrist at Oak Ridge, Tennessee, where he first began bringing the family into treatment with his patients. He moved from Oak Ridge to the chair of the department of psychiatry at Emory University in 1946. The publication of his first book, *The Roots of Psychotherapy* (Whitaker & Malone, 1953) led to his dismissal, and he went into private practice for ten years. The book, which he coauthored with his colleague, Thomas Malone, challenged much of traditional psychodynamic thinking and was resoundingly condemned by the psychiatric establishment. In 1965, Whitaker began teaching at the

University of Wisconsin. He would remain at this institution through the rest of his professional life. He referred to his work as "symbolic-experiential family therapy."

For a more complete treatment of the history of family therapy, see the *Handbook of Family Therapy* (Gurman & Kniskern, 1991).

Preview

Although it would be possible to follow this brief historical introduction with a detailed description of each of the major therapeutic approaches, I have elected to take a different approach. I contend that family therapy has moved beyond the "schools of therapy" orientation and that a systematic eclecticism is now possible. For the reader who is interested in a comparison of the various approaches, Table 17-2 presents a comparative assessment of some of the relevant aspects of family therapy.

The present attempt to reduce the emphasis on the differences between various approaches to family therapy has the support of at least one of the major figures in the field. Salvador Minuchin, writing as early as 1982, also decried the tendency to fragment the field into schools of therapy:

> *In early explorations of family therapy, the field increased its sophistication and expanded its territory. Naturally, the early explorers staked the unmarked corners with their trade names: strategic, systemic, structural Bowenian, experiential, and so on. The old-timers knew that their private truths were only partial, and when they met around a cup of coffee, they gossiped about the beginnings and shared their uncertainties and hopes. But, lo and behold, their institutions grew, and they needed large buildings to accommodate all their students. Slowly, before anybody realized it, the buildings became castles, with turrets and drawbridges, and even watchmen in the towers. The castles were very expensive and they needed to justify their existence. Therefore, they demanded ownership of the total truth. . . . But the generation of elders is becoming older. The castles are becoming very expensive to run and, like the English aristocracy, the lords of the manor will soon be opening them only on Sunday for the new generation of tourists. Those who come to my castle will not find me there. (p. 662)*

In what follows I have attempted to synthesize what I regard as some of the most useful of the ideas of the several therapists just referred to. I will begin first with a family systems perspective on the diagnosis of family dysfunction. This will be followed by sections on how to conduct the initial interview, family therapy techniques, legal and ethical questions, and research.

Diagnosis of Family Dysfunction

Tolstoy said in the opening line of *Anna Karenina*, "All happy families resemble one another, but each unhappy family is unhappy in its own way." Family therapists tend to reverse this position, believing that good family functioning is based in

TABLE 17-2   A Comparison of Family Therapy Approaches

	Strategic (Haley)	Structural (Minuchin)	Transgenerational (Bowen)	Experiential (Whitaker)	Conjoint (Satir)
Who is included in therapy?	Everyone involved in the problem	Whoever is involved and accessible	The most motivated family member(s)	Who he or she decides should come	The pattern is flexible
What is the theory of dysfunction?	Confused hierarchy, communication, rigid behavioral sequences	Boundaries (enmeshed or disengaged), stable coalitions; power	Fusion (emotions control, symbiosis with family of origin), anxiety, triangulation	Rigidity of thought and behavior	Low self-esteem, poor communication, triangulation
What are the goals of therapy?	Solve the problem, restore hierarchy, introduce flexibility	Solve the problem, change the structure, increase flexibility	Greater differentiation of self, reduced anxiety	Increase family creativity, greater sense of belonging and individuation	Improved communication, personal growth
What is the method of assessment?	Structured initial interview, intervene and observe the reaction, focus on the present	Joining the family to experience its process, chart the family structure, focus on the present	Detailed family history over several generations using the genogram, focus on the past	Informal, not separated from treatment, focus on both past and present	Family life chronology is used to take history and assess present functioning
What are the intervention procedures?	Directives are used to change behavior; they may be straightforward, paradoxical, or ordeals	Reframing is used to change the perception of the problem; structure is changed by unbalancing and increasing stress	Reducing anxiety by providing rational, untriangulated third party; coaching to aid in differentiation from family of origin	Increasing stress to force change, reframing symptoms as efforts at growth, affective confrontation	Modeling and coaching clear communication, family sculpting, guided interaction
What is the stance of the therapist?	Active, directive, but not self-revealing; planful, not spontaneous	Active, directive, personally involved; spontaneous; humorous	Interested but detached; reinforces calmness and rationality	Active, personally involved; encourages and models "craziness," cotherapy	Active, directive,1 matter-of-fact, nonjudgmental; models open communication

diversity, while family dysfunction is due to narrowness and rigidity. Haley (1987) goes so far as to argue that therapies that have a picture of "ideal" functioning are in fact limiting, in that they impose "a narrow ideology, thus preventing the diversity that human beings naturally display. To put the matter simply, if the goal of therapy is to introduce more complexity, then imposing on clients a psychological explanation of their own and other people's behavior is antitherapeutic" (p. 233).

When a systems orientation is applied to psychological problems, the diagnosis of the difficulty is very different from that presented in the DSM-IV, the *Diagnostic and Statistical Manual of Mental Disorders*, 4th ed. (American Psychiatric Association, 1994). Rather than focusing on the internal state of the individual, the family systems approach looks for pathology in the interactions that occur between people who have significance for each other.

Rather than adopting a linear model of causality, the family systems approach perceives causality as circular or recursive. It's not that a child is rebellious because his or her father is too authoritarian, or that the father is authoritarian because the child is rebellious, but that both are caught up in a chronic, repetitive sequence of behavior: the "game without end."

Rather than focusing on the way people think or feel, the family systems therapist tends to focus on what they do. The purpose of family therapy is not insight, but behavior change.

Within the broad commonality of the systems orientation, each of the major family therapists has emphasized different aspects of human functioning as the source of symptomatic behavior. The following sections provide a compilation of the thinking of a number of family therapists regarding symptomatic behavior.

Family Life Cycle

Family dysfunction is often the result of a failure to accomplish the developmental tasks demanded by the family life cycle (Table 17-3). The fullest conceptualization of a stage approach to family development is generally attributed to Carter and McGoldrick (1989), although the concept dates back to the 1950s (Gerson, 1995). Since Carter and McGoldrick, most of the major family therapists have acknowledged the significance of family life cycle changes as a major source of stress and disequilibrium for the family. Inherent in the life cycle concept is the idea that certain developmental tasks must be accomplished during periods of transition from one stage to another. Successful movement to the next development stage requires changes in the roles and structure of the family. If the family is unable to accommodate to the need for change, stress and symptomatology will occur.

The demand for change is a normal part of family development. It is not these normal difficulties that create the problem, but rather the chronic mishandling of them. It is the attempted solution that is the problem. Denying the need for change, treating a normal developmental change as if it were a problem, and striving for perfection are all likely to result in family distress. In general, the reaction of a dysfunctional family to a demand for change is met by doing "more of the same." For

TABLE 17-3   Stages of the Family Life Cycle

Family Life Cycle Stage	Emotional Process of Transition: Key Principles	Second-Order Changes in Family Status Required to Proceed Developmentally
1. Between Families: The Unattached Young Adult	Accepting parent–offspring separation	• Differentiation of self in relation to family of origin • Development of intimate peer relationships • Establishment of self in work
2. The Joining Of Families Through Marriage: The Newly Married Couple	Commitment to new system	• Formation of marital system • Realignment of relationships with extended families and friends to include spouse
3. The Family with Young Children	Accepting new members into the system	• Adjusting marital system to make space for child(ren) • Taking on parenting roles • Realignment of relationships with extended family to include parenting and grand-parenting roles
4. The Family with Adolescents	Increasing flexibility of family boundaries to include children's independence	• Shifting of parent–child relationship to permit adolescent to move in and out of system • Refocus on mid-life marital and career issues • Beginning shift toward concerns for older generation
5. Launching Children and Moving On	Accepting a multitude of exits from and entries into the family system	• Renegotiation of marital system as a dyad • Development of adult to adult relationships between grown children and their parents • Realignment of relationships to include in-laws and grandchildren • Dealing with disabilities and death of parents (grandparents)
6. The Family in Later Life	Accepting the shifting of generational roles	• Maintaining own and/or couple functioning and interests in face of physiological decline; exploration of new familial and social role options • Support for a more central role for middle generation • Making room in the system for the wisdom and experience of the elderly; supporting the older generation without overfunctioning for them • Dealing with loss of spouse, siblings, and other peers and preparation for own death; Life review and integration

Source: The Changing Family Life Cycle: A Framework for Family Therapy (2nd ed., p. 15) by B. Carter and M. McGoldrick, 1989. Boston: Allyn and Bacon. Copyright © 1989 by Allyn and Bacon. Reprinted by permission.

example, a girl becomes a teenager and exerts more autonomy, parents become concerned for her safety and morality, they introduce or increase their control over her behavior, the girl resents their attempt to control her autonomy and rebels, the parents increase their control, and so on. (Gerson, 1995). In a family with young children, a problem might arise when the grandparents have difficulty in giving up their parental role with their own children, thus interfering with the discipline of their new grandchildren.

The problems associated with family life cycle changes are exacerbated in remarried families. This exacerbation occurs because an individual's development is out of synchronization with the developmental stage of his or her family. For example, a newly remarried family is focused on issues of inclusion and forming a viable entity; if that family contains an adolescent, he or she is focused on issues of separation and individuation.

Fusion in the Nuclear Family and/or the Family of Origin

Bowen (1994) conceived a scale of differentiation of self from 0 to 100. At the low end of the scale, people are fused or enmeshed with their families to the extent that they are unable to think or act independently. Their lives are ruled by emotional reactivity. According to Bowen, people diagnosed as schizophrenic would be extremely fused.

At the upper end of the scale, people have achieved emotional separation from their families, are able to act autonomously, and can choose to be rational in emotionally charged situations. The individual's level of differentiation is closely related to the differentiation of his or her parents, and the process is transgenerational in nature. People with low levels of differentiation (fusion) are particularly reactive to environmental stressors, and when under stress are likely to resolve it by (1) withdrawal, (2) conflict, (3) dysfunction of one spouse, or (4) triangulation of a child that results in dysfunction. When the last occurs, that child, who is caught in the tug of war between the parents, will be even less differentiated than the parents. This is the basis of the intergenerational transmission of dysfunction (Bowen, 1991, 1994).

Boundary Problems

According to Minuchin (Minuchin & Fishman, 1981), family boundaries are created by implicit rules that govern who talks to whom about what. When no rules exist, everyone is privy to everyone else's thoughts and feelings. Thus family boundaries become diffuse and individuals become enmeshed (fused). When the rules are too strict and communication breaks down, the boundary is said to be rigid and the individuals disengaged. The preferred state is to have clear rules that allow both for individuation and togetherness. The similarity of this concept to Bowen's idea of differentiation of self is obvious, but Minuchin has developed it to refer to both extrafamilial boundaries and intrafamilial boundaries that separate subsystems (holons).

Family dysfunction can occur because the family is either disengaged from or enmeshed with the external environment. This is frequently a problem with re-married families where rules regarding contact with ex-spouses either may be rigid or lacking. Dysfunction can also occur when internal subsystems of the family are enmeshed or disengaged. The classic dysfunction in our culture is the mother who is enmeshed with a child (cross-generational coalition) and the father who is disengaged from both.

Dysfunctional Sequences

Haley (1987) believes family dysfunction is often caused by behavioral sequences that are rigid, repetitive, and functionally autonomous. He describes such a sequence as follows:

> 1. *One parent, usually the mother, is in an intense relationship with the child. By* intense *is meant a relationship that is both positive and negative and where the responses of each person are exaggeratedly important. The mother attempts to deal with the child with a mixture of affection and exasperation.*
> 2. *The child's symptomatic behavior becomes more extreme.*
> 3. *The mother, or the child, calls on the father for assistance in resolving their difficulty.*
> 4. *The father steps in to take charge and deal with the child.*
> 5. *Mother reacts against father, insisting that he is not dealing with the situation properly. Mother can react with an attack or with a threat to break off the relationship with father.*
> 6. *Father withdraws, giving up the attempt to disengage mother and child.*
> 7. *Mother and child deal with each other in a mixture of affection and exasperation until they reach a point where they are at an impasse. (pp. 121–122)*

Such patterns can repeat ad infinitum unless some new behavior is introduced into the sequence. It perhaps needs to be pointed out that the dysfunctional behavior should not be "blamed" on any of the individuals; all are equally involved and each could change the sequence by introducing a new incompatible element. Unfortunately, the family members are not usually aware of the complete sequence and in any case punctuate the sequence in such a way as to hold themselves blameless.

Hierarchy Problems

Haley (1987) and Minuchin (Minuchin & Nichols, 1993) both stress the importance of hierarchy problems in family dysfunction. Problems can occur when the hierarchy is either absent, ambiguous, or culturally inappropriate; that is, when no one is in charge, when it is unclear who is in charge, or when the person wielding the power is not sanctioned by cultural mores. Dysfunction may also be due to coalitions that cut across generational boundaries. An example of the latter would be when a father and child collude to avoid what they feel are the mother's overly rigid rules. Another common example would be in a family where there is marital conflict, and both parents try to enlist the children on their side of the argument.

Communication Problems

Virginia Satir (1983) placed special emphasis on the ways that people in a family communicate as a source of dysfunction. Communication may be inadequate owing to lack of clarity; for example, information is deleted: "People get me down." (Which people? How do they do that?) Communication can also be confusing because of a lack of topic continuity. This occurs when people are not really listening and their responses to the other become non sequiturs. When people are unwilling to reveal themselves or commit themselves to a statement or request, communication falters (for example, "I don't suppose you would like to go to my mother's with me?" rather than "I would like you to go with me to my mother's").

Sometimes communication is problematic because it is incongruent; either the nonverbal behavior or vocal tone communicates a message that contradicts the verbal content. Such incongruency is often the basis for irony and humor, but when it is unintentional and the message is not clarified, the receiver does not know how to respond. In the extreme case, this is the classic "double bind" described by Bateson, Jackson, Haley, and Weakland (1956). Satir (1983) describes this bind and the effect that such incongruent communication can have on a child:

> *How do mates unconsciously induce a child to behave in such a way that he eventually gets identified as a "patient?". . . . What conditions must be present for a child to experience the pressures associated with a double bind?*
>
> a. *First, the child must be exposed to double-level messages repeatedly and over a long period of time.*
> b. *Second, these must come from persons who have survival significance for him. . . .*
> c. *Third, perhaps most important of all, he must be conditioned . . . from an early age not to ask, "Did you mean that or that?" but must accept his parents' conflicting messages in all their impossibility. He must be faced with the hopeless task of translating them into a single way of behaving. (pp. 45–46)*

Low Self-Esteem

Satir (1983) also posits low self-esteem as the basis of much family difficulty. She describes a process similar to Bowen's (1994) intergenerational transmission process to reveal how low self-esteem not only affects the individuals and couples, but also is "inherited" by their children. Description of the entire process is beyond the scope of this chapter. The essential elements include low self-esteem in both marital partners, intolerance of each other's differences, and seeking to improve their sense of self-esteem through their children. If the parents don't agree on how the children should behave, the children are confronted with the impossible task of pleasing both parents (another type of double bind). Because they cannot please both parents, the children develop low self-esteem and may also become symptomatic.

Conflict over Which Family of Origin to Model

Whitaker says, "We assume that dysfunction is related to the struggle over whose family of origin this new family is going to model itself after. One way to view etiology asserts there is no such thing as a marriage; it is merely two scapegoats sent out by families to perpetrate themselves" (Whitaker & Keith, 1981, p. 196). Young people who come from a common cultural background may be less likely to experience this problem, but in our polyglot society the appropriate behaviors for "wife" or "husband" are often unclear, or represent role conflicts. When a child enters the picture before these roles are synchronized, the new roles of "mother" and "father" further complicate the picture. Often the young couple find themselves acting just like their parents, although they are reluctant to admit it.

Narrow Rigid Beliefs and Self-Perceptions

In a sense this brings us full circle. To the extent that one's beliefs are narrow and unchanging, adaptation to the demands of a changing environment or the developmental demands of the family life cycle will be difficult. Milton Erickson held "that individuals with a symptom were constricted by their own certainties, their own rules, whether these rules guided their belief system, their perceptions of self, their patterns of physiological response or relational habits, or their own ideas of contingency (i.e., if A, then B)" (Ritterman, 1986, p. 37). The symptom, per se, is not the problem, but instead is "a metaphorical expression of a problem and attempt at resolution . . . the underlying problem is understood to be inflexibly patterned behavior resulting from internal and/or interactional rules that proscribe available choices and prevent the resolution of developmentally routine or unusual life dilemmas" (Ritterman, 1986, p. 36).

When an individual or a family is unable to resolve a difficulty, it is assumed that the conscious mind is imposing a narrow, restrictive mind set that does not allow the creative recovery of the resources necessary to solve the problem. From this point of view, the conscious, rational mind must be diverted to allow the creative potential of the unconscious to function. This is done through hypnosis or the use of indirect methods such as metaphor.

The Initial Interview

In order to gain a better understanding of how family therapists work, let us take a look at how the initial interview is conducted. The following description owes a great deal to Jay Haley (1987), but also incorporates ideas from other therapists.

Presession Planning

Whenever possible, the therapist should determine in advance who will attend the session and have at least a general idea of the nature of the presenting problems. Whitaker and Bumberry (1988) call this the "battle for structure" and place great emphasis on the importance of the therapist determining who will attend the first session. They believe that if the therapist does not have control at this stage, therapeutic leverage is lost and the family is less likely to be helped. Taking control may entail a presession telephone call or the use of an intake form. On the basis of the data derived from this initial contact, a presession plan should be developed that will include the counselor's hypotheses about the underlying basis of the presenting problem, areas of inquiry that must be addressed to reject or confirm the hypotheses, and a general plan for the session.

The Joining Stage

The most important task of the initial interview is to join with the family, accommodating to their affective tone, tempo, language, and family structure. This is done through mimesis (Walsh & McGraw, 1996). Mimesis is a therapeutic skill "used by the therapist to join with the family and become like family members in the manner or content of their communications" (Sauber, L'Abate, Weeks, & Buchanan, 1993, p. 255). Foreman and Cava (1993) advocate matching the family's style even to the extent of matching breathing, body movements, and representational system predicates (visual, auditory, kinesthetic). Care needs to be taken, however, that this does not become an offensive burlesque.

Tracking is another joining technique and consists of little more than Rogers-like "uh-huh's," reflection of content, and asking for clarification. During this time, the therapist should avoid comment or interpretation (Haley, 1987).

A third aspect of joining is maintenance. This aspect of joining involves the therapist's sensing the family's structure and acting in such a way as to be included within it (Minuchin & Nichols, 1993). If Dad acts as the "central switchboard" in this family, the therapist accommodates to that and contacts other members through him.

During the joining stage, the therapist should not allow the introduction of material related to the family problem. Only after some social contact has been made with every family member should the next stage begin (Haley, 1987). Joining, of course, is not finished at the end of this stage, but must be of concern throughout the therapy.

More structured approaches to joining include the use of family chronologies and genograms (Weber & Levine, 1995). A genogram is a family tree drawing that records information about family members and their relationships over at least three generations (McGoldrick & Gerson, 1985). Both of these techniques, however, go beyond the joining stage and also gather data relevant to the problem.

The Problem Statement Stage

When significant contact has been made with all family members in the social or joining stage, the therapist introduces the problem stage. During the joining stage, the therapist has learned something of the family structure and hierarchy and uses this information to decide to whom the first question should be directed. Haley (1987) recommends that "the adult who seems less involved with the problem be spoken to first, and the person with the most power to bring the family back be treated with the most concern and respect" (p. 22). He also says that, in general, it is unwise to begin with the identified patient (IP).

Don't attempt to force a mute member to speak. This will often be the IP, who has lots of practice in resisting adult coercion. Instead, ask another family member, "What would Johnny say if he chose to talk?" This can be repeated in a round robin if necessary, and in most instances the mute member will feel the need to defend himself or clarify his real feelings.

The second decision the therapist must make is how the problem question should be framed. The question can be as vague as "What brings you here today?" or as specific as "What is the problem for which you are seeking help?" It can also be framed to elicit etiologic information or be future-focused on the kinds of changes that are desired. I generally prefer ambiguity and a focus on the future: "When this therapy is successful, how will your family be different?"

When everyone has had an opportunity to express what they see as the "pain in the family" (Satir, 1983), the therapist can begin to flesh out the details that will help to clarify the function that the problem serves in the family. The following series of questions may prove helpful.

1. Who has the problem?
2. Where else have you sought help, and how did it work for you? What has been tried, by whom, and for how long? Is there anything you have tried that you feel could have been done more?
3. Why is the symptom a problem? Does anyone in the family not consider the symptom a problem? Who in the family is most upset by the problem?
4. How often does it occur? when? where? Who reacts to it? in what way? What happens just before it occurs? What happens next?
5. When did the symptom begin? Why did you come in now?
6. How do you account for the problem?
7. Do the parents agree or disagree about the problem, its cause, and the best solution?
8. What would happen if the symptom got better or worse?
9. What do you hope will happen as the result of coming here? What is your ideal goal? What would you settle for? How optimistic are you about improvement? What do you want to see the identified patient doing two weeks from now that would show progress? (adapted from Bergman, 1985)

The Interaction Stage

When the problem has been reasonably clarified or when it has become clear that the family is not in agreement regarding the nature of the problem, it is time for the therapist to introduce the interaction stage. During the earlier two stages, the therapist has maintained his or her centrality in the communication network, speaking in turn to each of the family members and blocking interruptions and attempts at dialogue between family members. This procedure tends to reduce tension and provide order and relatively clear communication and also establishes the therapist's power and leadership in the therapeutic process. The focus in the problem phase has been on clarifying how the family views the problem. In the interaction stage, the therapist's focus will be on determining the patterns of interaction that sustain the problem. In order to get this information the therapist asks the family to "dance" in his or her presence (Kershaw, 1992).

This occurs most easily and naturally when the family is not in agreement regarding the problem. When this is true, the therapist can encourage them to discuss their differences and try to reach agreement. During this phase it is crucial that the therapist abdicate the center of the communication network. All attempts to communicate with the therapist should be referred back to a family member. The therapist does not, however, completely abandon the leadership position; instead, the role changes to being the director of the family drama, introducing a third party when two seem to reach an impasse, or asking family members to change their seating patterns to facilitate new encounters (Grove & Haley, 1993; Minuchin & Nichols, 1993).

If family members are in agreement regarding the problem that brings them to therapy (usually focusing on one person as the cause of the difficulty), they can be asked to perform the problem. "When Johnny doesn't take out the garbage, what happens? Who is first to notice? Show me how it works." In order to get the family to act, rather than talk about the problem, it will be necessary for the therapist to get to his or her feet, help the family to build an appropriate stage set (in fantasy), and set the scene into action.

Interactions that are developed from the idiosyncratic information presented by the family are most likely to reveal the information needed to understand the problem. Unfortunately, some families are so uncommunicative that the therapist is unable to elicit enough information to stage an appropriate interaction. When this occurs, it is well to have a few preplanned interaction situations available. One that is often useful, particularly in families with young children, is to ask the family to enact a day in their lives. Establish who sleeps where, move them into the appropriate places, and then have the alarm go off. If it is to be successful, the therapist will need to coach this interaction, slowing it down and focusing on the most simple, concrete details of family life. In a large family, who has access to the bathroom at what time is often a major source of conflict. Care must also be taken to ensure that all family members become involved. Other generic interactions might be to plan a family vacation together, or decide how to spend a free Saturday. Or, using building blocks or crayon and paper, have the family draw their living quarters and discuss who spends the most time with whom in what part of the house.

The purpose of the interaction stage is to determine the family hierarchy, to reveal any stable coalitions, to locate diffuse or rigid boundaries between family subsystems, and hopefully to reveal the chronically repeating interactional sequence that sustains the problem behavior. When this information has been obtained, the therapist is in a position to develop the interventions that will lead to beneficial change.

In-Session Conference

When the therapist is working with an observing team, or even when working alone, it is useful at this point to leave the family and take a few minutes to think about what has been observed in order to abstract from the concrete interactions the patterns that need correction. When working with an observing team, it is often true that the observers are more able to perceive these patterns than the therapist, who is immersed in the hypnotic pull of the family dance. Moran et al. (1995) give an excellent description of the use of such a team. The purpose of the in-session conference is to assess the accuracy of the presession hypotheses and to reformulate them in light of the new data gathered during the session. When this has been done, it is possible to design directives (homework) that will begin to change the family's dysfunctional interactions. In some instances the appropriate homework is not clear, but some homework should still be assigned. Family therapy, or any kind of therapy for that matter, is unlikely to be successful if the therapy is encapsulated in the therapeutic hour. The therapist needs to make an assignment that will establish an ongoing process to keep the therapy salient throughout the week. When the therapist makes a homework assignment without being sure of its relevance, it is comforting to keep Jeff Zeig's dictum in mind. Zeig, who is an Ericksonian hypnotherapist, says his approach to therapy is "ready–shoot–aim" (personal communication, 1988). In other words, if you wait until you are absolutely sure of your interventions, therapy will be a long, drawn-out process. If you go with your hunches, and learn from the results, you will probably hit the bull's-eye much sooner.

Goal-Setting Stage

As Haley (1987) has said, "If therapy is to end properly, it must begin properly—by negotiating a solvable problem and discovering the social situation that makes the problem necessary" (p. 8). The purpose of the goal-setting stage is to reach agreement with the family on a solvable problem and to initiate a process that will alter the social situation in such a way that the problem is no longer necessary. It is essential that the problem to be solved be stated in behavioral terms, so that one will know when it has been solved. It is equally essential that the problem be one that the therapist believes is capable of solution. Often the process of operationalizing the complaint is sufficient to produce a solvable problem. When a "rebellious child" problem is operationalized to "staying out after curfew," we have a target on which one can draw a bead. However, some problems, and this would include most of the categories of the DSM-IV (1994), are not capable of solution. With ambiguous problems, the therapist must reframe the problem in such a way that it can be solved and in such a way that the family will accept it. This is not an easy task and sometimes taxes the therapist's creative resources. A notable example would be a case in which Haley reframed a case of schizophrenia as "pseudoschizophrenia" and then went on to help the family specify how the IP's behavior might be improved. It cannot be emphasized enough that the problem to be solved must be stated in behavioral terms; that is, never negotiate to "improve communication," "raise self-esteem," or "make our family more cohesive."

When agreement has been reached regarding the problem, the therapist should assign homework that will have face validity with regard to the problem, but will also address the underlying structural or sequential changes that are necessary. In the case of "pseudoschizophrenia" just mentioned, we might assume that the family is obsessively monitoring the patient, watching for abnormal behavior. An assignment that would use the obsessive nature of the family (pacing) and still institute a change would be to ask the family to keep an elaborate baseline measure of the "normal" behavior of the patient and bring it to the next session.

In a family with a daughter who is not keeping an assigned curfew, it might appear that the rebelliousness is being secretly (and perhaps unconsciously) reinforced by the father. An intervention might be to put Dad in charge of the daughter's behavior for a week, asking him during the session to negotiate with his daughter the expectations and consequences of noncompliance.

Initial sessions, particularly with large families, often cannot be conducted within the usual fifty-minute hour. If it is not possible to schedule a longer session, it is likely that it will take more than one session to establish the therapeutic contract. When this is true, one should still attempt to give some kind of homework assignment that will increase the power of the therapy. When in doubt, a good first step is asking family members to each keep a baseline of the behavior that they see as problematic.

Ending Stage

The therapist should end the session by setting a second appointment and specifying who should be present. The family should not be asked whether they want to return; this should be assumed unless someone indicates otherwise.

Postsession

When working with a team, there should be a postsession debriefing to give an opportunity to share various perceptions of the family and the response to the interventions. When working alone, it is essential to record your impressions of the presenting problem, the family structure, hypotheses regarding needed changes, and, most importantly, the homework that was assigned. The latter should be recorded verbatim, if possible, in order to check on the family compliance.

Family Therapy Techniques

In the preceding section the focus was on the process of conducting the initial interview. In this section, I focus on the techniques used by the therapist throughout the therapy. The techniques offered here are derived from several therapeutic points of view.

Circular Questioning

Following Bateson's dictum that "information is a difference; difference is a relationship (or a change in the relationship)," the Milan group developed a technique they refer to as "circular questioning" (Benson, Schindler, & Martin, 1991; Walsh & McGraw, 1996). The circularity referred to here is epistemological; their questions are intended to uncover the complementarity of family relationships that make the presenting symptom necessary for family homeostasis. Every member of the family is invited to tell how he or she sees the relationship between two other family members, or between two different periods of time, or any other difference likely to be significant to the family. For example,

1. In terms of family relationships: "Tell us how you see the relationship between your sister and your mother."
2. In terms of specific interactive behaviors: "When your father gets mad at Bill, what does your mother do?"
3. In terms of differences in behavior: "Who gets most upset when Jimmy wets the bed, your father or your mother?"
4. In terms of ranking by various members of the family of a behavior or interaction: "Who is closest to your grandmother? Who is next, and next?"
5. In terms of change in the relationship before and after a precise event: "Did you and your sister fight more or less before your mother remarried?"
6. In terms of differences in respect to hypothetical circumstances: "If one of you kids should have to stay home, not get married, who would be best for your mother? your father?" (adapted from Fleuridas, Nelson, & Rosenthal, 1986)

Perhaps it should be mentioned here, parenthetically, that this procedure would be anathema to some other therapists, including Virginia Satir, who specifically proscribes "gossiping" and "mind reading." However, the Milan group has demonstrated that often more can be obtained by asking a person what he or she thinks about others than by asking more personal questions. When this is done in the family context, where all can hear and respond, the result is quite different from results of an interview with an individual.

Reframing

Haley (1987) says, "It cannot be emphasized enough that the problem the therapist settles on must be a problem which the family wants changed but which is put in a form that makes it solvable" (p. 38). Although some problems presented by families lend themselves readily to therapeutic intervention, frequently it is necessary for the therapist to reframe the problem. Reframing may include the following:

1. *Operationalizing*—casting the problem in observable, behavioral terms. The problem of "a child who is driving us crazy" is reframed by specifying the specific behaviors that are problematic and asking the parents to keep a record of their frequency of occurrence.
2. *Emphasizing complementarity*—describing the problem in an interactional context, rather than as the property of one member of the family. A father who is depressed is asked, "Who makes you depressed?"
3. *Denominalizing*—removing a reified diagnostic label and replacing it with a behavior that can be consciously controlled. Anorexia might be reframed as "a girl who refuses to eat."
4. *Positive connotation*—describing the symptomatic behavior as positively motivated in the service of the family system. A defiant, delinquent boy is described as particularly sensitive to family conflict and his behavior as a sacrificial act designed to keep the parents from divorce.

Giving Directives

Giving directives involves creating or selecting an intervention that will attack the hypothesized basis of the presenting problem. According to Haley (1987), giving directives has several purposes:

> *the main goal of therapy is to get people to behave differently and so to have different subjective experiences. Directives are a way of making those changes happen. . . . directives are used to intensify the relationship with the therapist. By telling people what to do the therapist gets involved in the action . . . directives are used to gather information. When a therapist tells people what to do, the ways they respond give information about them and about how they will respond to the changes wanted. Whether they do what the therapist asks, do not do it, forget to do it, or try and fail, the therapist has information she would not otherwise have.* (p. 56)

Directives can be categorized as oriented toward either compliance or defiance. Compliance-oriented directives are offered to families who may be expected to carry out the assignment as given. When the therapist wants the family to carry out the directive, the following should be considered:

1. The directive should be framed in such a way as to use the language and imagery of the family and be focused on solving the problem presented by the family.

2. Avoid asking the family not to do something; ask them to do something different.
3. Ask everyone to do something.
4. Be extremely concrete and repetitive (unless you have reason to be otherwise).
5. Arrange for concrete, specific feedback.
6. Practice the homework during the session, or at least ask the family to tell you in their own words what the assignment includes.
7. Use antisabotage techniques: brainstorm reasons why they might not be able to comply; suggest probable problems that might interfere with compliance; discuss how they can overcome the problems.

Compliance-oriented directives can be either straightforward or paradoxical; the main idea is that you want them to be carried out. An example of a straightforward directive would be to ask Dad to be in charge of the discipline and to ask Mom to keep a record of problem behaviors and report them for his consideration. An example of a compliance-oriented paradoxical directive would be to prescribe the symptom to occur at a special time and place.

The following are some examples of compliance-oriented directives:

1. *Caring days:* Ask a hostile couple to act as if they care for each other by daily performing five minor behaviors requested by his or her spouse (LeCroy, Carrol, Nelson-Becker, & Sturlaugson, 1989).
2. *Role reversal:* Ask a disengaged husband to give his enmeshed wife a vacation from responsibility for the children. He is to be totally responsible for the meting out of discipline; she may consult with him, but is not to be in charge.
3. *Safe practice:* Ask a man who is afraid of job interviews to apply for jobs that he would not take if they were offered.
4. *Surprise:* Ask a couple who are hostile and out of touch with each other to plan a surprise that will please the other, but would be so out of character that the other could never guess what it would be. Each should attempt to guess what the other will do, making a written record of his or her guesses.
5. *Symptom prescription:* Ask a single mother with two boys who are disrespectful to their mother and constantly fighting to hold a daily wrestling match where she is the referee and will enforce fair fighting; boys are to agree to reserve their fighting to these bouts. Mother is to insist on "the bouts" even if the boys are unwilling.

Defiance-oriented directives are offered to families whom one assumes to be resistant. The intention is to have the family defy the therapist in such a way as to eliminate the problem behavior. Defiance-oriented directives are always paradoxical. When the therapist wants the family to defy the directives, the following should be considered:

1. Do this only with families that have demonstrated their resistance.
2. Use this only after you have joined the family sufficiently to make noncompliance a significant issue. Your relationship to the family should be clearly defined as one of bringing about change.

3. The problem to be solved should be clearly defined and agreed on.
4. The rationale for the directive must use the family language and imagery and provide an acceptable rationale for the directive. Haley (1987) says that designing paradoxical directives is easy; you simply observe how the family members are behaving and ask them to continue. How you make the directive appear reasonable and how you react to changes that occur are the hard parts.
5. Give the directive and ask for a report.
6. When the family reports that they did not carry out the homework, condemn the noncompliance and be puzzled and surprised by the symptom reduction. Don't take credit for the change!
7. Repeat the directive and warn against relapse.

The following are some examples of defiance-oriented directives:

1. *Positive connotation.* Reframe the problem behavior in positive terms and indicate that it would be dangerous for the family to change.
2. *Symptom increase.* Recommend that the problem behavior be increased in order to get a better understanding of it.
3. *Restraining.* Recommend that the family slow down in its attempts to solve the problem.
4. *Symptom retention.* Advise the family to retain a certain percentage of the problem in order to remember how awful it was.
5. *Predict relapse* of a symptom that has been brought under control.

Ordeals

Ordeals are offered to families who are highly motivated to change but can't seem to accomplish their purpose. An ordeal is a behavior that is more obnoxious, frustrating, and time consuming than the symptomatic behavior. The family must agree to perform the ordeal whenever the symptom occurs. Haley (1993b) noted that in order to be successful, the ordeal should contain the following elements:

1. The problem must be clearly defined.
2. The person must be committed to getting over the problem.
3. An ordeal must be selected with the client's collaboration: "the ordeal should be voluntary by the person and good for the person experiencing it, but not necessarily for the person imposing it . . . to inadvertently cause a person to suffer is one thing; to arrange it deliberately is quite another" (Haley, 1984, p. 13).
4. The directive must be given with a rationale.
5. The ordeal must continue until the problem is solved.
6. The ordeal is in a social context. The therapist must be prepared to assist in the systemic reorganization that the elimination of the symptom will require.

An example of an ordeal might be a bulimic woman with a stingy husband. The woman has been bingeing and forcing herself to vomit for years. Her husband becomes aware of the symptom and they come to therapy. After establishing a relationship with them and ensuring the couple's commitment to solving both problems, the therapist might offer the following ordeal. When the wife feels she can no longer avoid a binge, she and her husband should go to the store and buy all the foods that the wife prefers to binge on, spending at least $25. They are then to return home, and together they are to unwrap all the food and stuff it down the garbage disposal. This is to continue until the wife no longer feels the need to binge.

Jay Haley developed the concept of ordeal therapy as the result of his experience with Milton Erickson. He presents some of Erickson's cases that use the ordeal in *Uncommon Therapy: The Psychiatric Techniques of Milton H. Erickson, M.D.* (Haley, 1993c); his further development of the concept is presented in his book *Jay Haley on Milton H. Erickson* (Haley, 1993b).

Rituals

Rituals can be used in therapy to help an individual or family move from one status or state to another. Rituals are particularly helpful in closing off past anger and guilt. The following examples illustrate their use:

> *Closing Off the Past.* A couple who couldn't resist fighting over wrongs done by the other in the past were asked to write down all their complaints, put them in a box, wrap them carefully, and bury them outside the therapist's window. They were told that the past was buried there and if they wanted to fight over it, they would have to come to the therapist's office. (Coppersmith, 1985)

> *"Rites of Passage."* A Christian couple were having difficulty dealing with their 13-year-old son. They were overinvolved and too restrictive; he was increasingly rebellious. They were asked to plan a "Christian bar mitzvah" to symbolize his coming of age.

Ambiguous Assignments

Assignments that are mysterious and apparently unrelated to the presenting problem can be helpful in encouraging a family to find its own solution to its problems. Although what is to be done should be absolutely clear, the purpose for doing it should be completely obscure at least to the clients. The purpose of the assignment is to depotentiate conscious, linear thinking about the problem and allow creativity in reframing to take place. Milton Erickson often asked people to climb Squaw Peak. The peak, located in north Phoenix near his home, offered a considerable, but not unreasonable, challenge and provided plenty of time to think about why the task was assigned (Lankton, 1988).

Another example is a task that a therapist assigned to a 30-year-old son who was having trouble leaving home: "I'd like you to go to the store and buy a goldfish and everything you will need to take care of it." Interestingly, he defied the directive and instead bought a Christmas cactus because "it will be easier to take with me when I leave after the holidays."

Assigning Directives

When a directive has been determined, the therapist must also decide how to present it to the family members in a way that they will accept it (or in the case of paradox, reject it). It is important to allow plenty of time to seed the intervention, assign it, clarify it, and practice it. It is also important to couch the task in the family's language and to tie task completion to the presenting problem. Whenever possible, dramatize the assignment by delaying the actual presentation as you ruminate on whether the family is really ready for it. The extreme of this dramatization is the "devil's pact" where the assignment is delayed for several sessions and offered only after the family has agreed to comply without knowing what the assignment will be.

Haley (1993a) decries the fact that most clinical training does not include the development of skill in the area of assigning directives and hence that most clinicians must learn it on their own. He indicates most of his own skill in this area was learned from Milton Erickson (Haley, 1993b).

Collecting the Homework

A cardinal rule of this sort of therapy is to be sure to collect the homework and to take either compliance or noncompliance very seriously. If the homework is ignored or not given sufficient attention, that signals very clearly to the family that compliance is not necessary. The reaction (or nonreaction) of the family to the assignment allows us to aim more carefully on our second attempt.

When the family has carried out the task, congratulate them and encourage them to process the experience. Do not explain why the assignment was given or interpret the outcome.

When the family has only partially complied or did not carry out the task, it is often best for the therapist to take the blame for the noncompliance. This assumption of blame indicates to the family that either (1) the assignment was not sufficiently concrete and specific enough for this family to understand or (2) the therapist has miscalculated and the family was really not ready for such a task at this time. In either case, in order to demonstrate their capacity for understanding or their readiness for change, the family will be motivated to complete the next task that is assigned (Haley, 1987).

The techniques offered in this section are, of course, only a brief introduction to the procedures used by various family therapists. Unfortunately, space does not allow a more complete discussion. I am particularly conscious of having omitted the in-session techniques of Virginia Satir (1983) and Carl Whitaker (Connell, Whitaker, Garfield, & Connell, 1990) and the coaching techniques associated with the transgenerational work of Murray Bowen (Kerr & Bowen, 1988). Two very useful sources for family therapy techniques are the *Clinical Handbook of Couple Therapy* (Jacobson & Gurman, 1995) and *101 Interventions in Family Therapy* (Nelson & Trepper, 1993).

Professional Issues

Specialization or Profession?

At the present time there exists a strong debate as to whether family therapy is a professional specialization or a distinct profession (Huber, 1994). Members of a number of different professions (psychiatry, nursing, psychology, counseling, and social work) practice family therapy as a professional specialization. In addition, there are mental health practitioners who practice family therapy exclusively and view this work as distinct from the activity of other professions. These practitioners go by the title of marriage and family therapists (MFTs). Who is going to win the debate? Huber (1994) suggested that this debate most likely will be resolved as a "both–and." That is, *both* MFTs and other mental health professionals will practice family therapy *and* marriage and family therapy will be viewed as a distinct profession.

Professional Associations

A number of professional associations serve mental health practitioners who work with families. The professional association for MFTs is the American Association for Marriage and Family Therapy (AAMFT). Founded in 1942, the goal of this 23,000-member organization is the promotion of marriage and family therapy as a distinct mental health discipline (Shields, Wynne, McDaniel, & Gawinski, 1994).

The professional home for counselors is the American Counseling Association (ACA). Since 1986, the ACA has maintained a division for those members whose professional practice involves family therapy. This division is the International Association of Marriage and Family Counselors (IAMFC). The IAMFC's goals are

1. To promote ethical practices in marriage and family counseling/therapy.
2. To encourage research in marriage and family counseling/therapy.
3. To share knowledge and emphasize adherence to the highest quality training of marriage and family counselors/therapists.
4. To provide a forum for exchange on relevant issues related to marriage and family counseling/therapy.
5. To examine ways to intervene in systems.
6. To help couples and families cope more successfully with life challenges.
7. To use counseling knowledge and systemic methods to relieve the problems confronting marriages and families. (IAMFC, 1995, unpaginated)

Currently, the IAMFC has more than 8,000 members. Other organizations with a family therapy focus include the American Family Therapy Academy (AFTA), Division 43 of the American Psychological Association (APA), and the Family Therapy Section of the National Council on Family Relations (NCFR).

Licensure/Certification

Currently, thirty-one states have enacted certification or licensure laws for mental health professionals who practice family therapy (AAMFT, 1994). Over the next decade, additional states are expected to enact such laws (Gladding, 1995). At the federal level, regulations recognizing family therapy as a "core" mental health profession were set forth in the early 1990s (Shields et al., 1994).

Program Accreditation

Two organizations accredit programs that train people to practice family therapy. The Commission on Accreditation for Marriage and Family Therapy Education (COAMFTE) accredits programs that prepare MFTs. COAMFTE accreditation covers both degree-granting programs and postgraduate training institutes. Currently, sixty-nine programs possess COAMFTE accreditation.

The other accrediting body is the Council for Accreditation of Counseling and Related Educational Programs (CACREP). This organization accredits programs that prepare people to serve as professional counselors with the following specializations: (1) school counseling, (2) mental health counseling, (3) community agency counseling, (4) student affairs, and (5) marriage and family therapy. CACREP only accredits degree-granting programs. Currently, there are eleven CACREP-accredited marriage and family therapy programs.

Ethical and Legal Issues

The ethical codes of the AAMFT (1991), ACA (1995), and APA (1992) are applicable to the practice of family therapy, but the IAMFC code (1993) is perhaps the most relevant to professional counselors practicing family therapy. Elsewhere in this text (Chapter 4), Sharon Robinson Kurpius has presented the legal and ethical issues related to counseling. However, when one assumes a family systems orientation, some special issues arise. Common issues that are especially problematic for the family therapist include the following (adapted from Huber, 1994; Margolin, 1982; Patten, Barnett, & Houlihan, 1991):

> *Responsibility.* Who is the client? Is it possible to serve all members of a family even-handedly? Can you define the family system or the relationship as the client? Does insisting on seeing the whole family before treatment can begin deny treatment to those who are motivated? Is it ethical to coerce reluctant members into therapy?
>
> *Confidentiality.* Is the promise of confidentiality given to the family as a unit, or does it apply to individual family members? What should be done about information obtained from an individual prior to the involvement of other family members? Can you offer confidentiality to children when seen in a family therapy context? If family members are seen separately during family therapy,

should they be promised confidentiality? Does privileged communication exist for a family? Will a written agreement not to subpoena hold up legally? Can one member of the family waive privileged communication for all?

Therapist control. Is it appropriate for the therapist to increase the family stress in order to bring about change? Should the therapist use indirect (hypnotic, metaphoric) or paradoxical procedures that bypass conscious processes? Is the use of such techniques a violation of the concept of informed consent? In dealing with "inappropriate hierarchies," may the therapist impose his or her own values on the family? Is family therapy antithetical to the feminist perspective?

Informed consent. Who should consent to treatment? What needs to be disclosed? How can a therapist use defiance-oriented directives or paradox and also provide full disclosure?

The current context does not allow space for resolution of these issues, and in fact several of them cannot be readily resolved. The counselor who is interested in working within a family therapy perspective should, however, be aware of these issues and be prepared to grapple with them.

Research in Family Therapy

Background

The history of family therapy research is filled with contradictions. On one hand, this specialization/profession emerged from research projects such as Bateson's work on schizophrenia (Bateson et al., 1956). On the other hand, empirical research has been largely ignored in family therapy (Gladding, 1995; Lebow & Gurman, 1995; Shields et al., 1994). In a major review of family therapy research, Lebow and Gurman (1995) noted that

> *In reviewing the research base of couple and family therapy, one faces a basic dilemma. Traditional empirical research has not been the foundation for the development of these modes of practice, nor has it been the fabric of much of this work. . . . Alternative modes of investigation such as inductive reasoning, clinical observation, and deconstruction have dominated in the development of methods and treatment models. Some couple and family therapists have even been reluctant to acknowledge that empirical research has an important role. At one discouraging point, now fortunately past, there was considerable debate about whether traditional research had any relevant role in the development of family therapy. (p. 29).*

In the past decade, the growth of empirical research in family therapy has been remarkable. Thus, now mental health practitioners, health insurers, and the public at large possess the ability to compare and contrast family therapy with other types of interventions.

In terms of family therapy research, three questions that any future professional counselor should address are

1. Does family therapy work?
2. What are the professional practice patterns of family therapists?
3. How does one access family therapy research in order to enhance one's professional practice?

Each of these questions will be addressed separately.

Does Family Therapy Work?

Research that examines whether an intervention works is known as *outcome* research. In family therapy, until the late 1980s a dearth of outcome research left unanswered the question "Does family therapy work?" Only at that time had a sufficient number of studies been published so as to allow researchers to conduct meta-analyses of the family therapy research literature. Meta-analysis is a research technique by which multiple individual studies can be grouped together to empirically analyze the overall effectiveness of a particular intervention approach. Hazelrigg, Cooper, and Borduin (1987) conducted the first meta-analysis of family therapy outcome research. In their meta-analysis of twenty studies, they found that family therapy had a positive effect on clients when compared to either no treatment or an alternative treatment. Subsequent meta-analyses have confirmed that family therapy is indeed an efficacious mental health treatment approach (Hahlweg & Markman, 1988; Markus, Lange, & Pettigrew, 1990; Shadish, 1992; Shadish et al., 1993).

In addition to knowledge concerning the overall effectiveness of family therapy, strong evidence exists in the research literature concerning the effectiveness of this type of therapy with a wide range of problems. Lebow and Gurman (1995) found support for family therapy as an efficacious treatment with (1) adolescent drug abuse, (2) depression, (3) alcoholism, (4) delinquency, (5) parenting, (6) schizophrenia, and (7) agoraphobia. In addition, Alexander and Barton (1995) cited research support for family therapy as an effective intervention strategy with (1) anxiety, (2) pediatric psychopathy, and (3) adolescent behavior problems.

What Are the Professional Practice Patterns of Family Therapists?

Within the mental health service provider community, there exists a prejudice that family therapists do nothing more than "interminable marriage counseling for trivial problems" (Simmons & Doherty, 1995, p. 5). Surprisingly, little research on the practice patterns of family therapists has been conducted. Thus, research evidence that could challenge the preceding prejudice has not existed until recently. The groundbreaking study on this topic was only published in 1995. Simmons and

Doherty (1995) studied the professional practice patterns of a random sample of Minnesota MFTs. The practice variables they examined included (1) caseload, (2) presenting problem, (3) diagnosis, and (4) length of treatment.

Simmons and Doherty (1995) found that, on the average, Minnesota MFTs had thirty-nine clients in their active caseload and completed eighteen client contact hours per week. The clients served by the MFTs presented a multitude of problems at the commencement of treatment. These problems included (1) adult or child psychological problems (74 percent), (2) couples problems (59 percent), and (3) whole-family problems (42 percent). "Adjustment disorders" was the modal diagnostic category (38 percent). Other prevalent diagnostic categories included "depressive disorders" (28 percent) and "anxiety disorders" (19 percent). The median number of sessions per client was eleven, and the average fee charged per hour was $77. Simmons and Doherty's study suggests that family therapist *do* serve clients with serious problems. However, the question of whether the practice patterns of Minnesota MFTs can be extended to family therapy practitioners in other states remains open.

How Does One Access Family Therapy Research in Order to Enhance One's Professional Practice?

The vast majority of family therapy research can be found in professional journals. Both the IAMFC and the AAMFT sponsor such journals, which they send to their members. These journals are *The Family Journal: Counseling and Therapy for Couples and Families* (IAMFC) and the *Journal of Marital and Family Therapy* (AAMFT). Easy access to research is one of the major benefits of membership in a professional association. Other family therapy journals include *American Journal of Family Therapy, Child and Family Behavior Therapy, Family Process, Family Therapy, Journal of Family Psychology, Journal of Family Psychotherapy, Journal of Feminist Family Therapy*, and *Journal of Systemic Therapies*.

Summary

This chapter has attempted to introduce the reader to the contextual thinking that is the essence of family therapy. I have tried to illustrate this perspective through descriptions of family therapy diagnosis, interviewing, and treatment. In family therapy, diagnosis focuses on interpersonal rather than intrapersonal dysfunction. Sound family therapy interviewing follows a distinct eight-stage process beginning with presession planning and ending with postsession debriefing. Family therapy treatment is rich with powerful techniques. These techniques include circular questioning and ordeal prescription among others.

In addition to diagnosis, interviewing, and treatment, professional issues that are of concern to family therapists were addressed. These issues include licensure, training, professional development, and ethics. Finally, the evidence for the efficacy of family therapy was reviewed. It is my hope that this brief introduction to the concepts and techniques of family therapy will whet the reader's appetite for further exploration. If that should prove to be the case, the references below with an asterisk (*) are good starting points.

References

Ackerman, N. W. (1958). *The psychodynamics of family life.* New York: Basic Books.

Alexander, J., & Barton, C. (1995). Family therapy research. In R. H. Mikesell, D. Lusterman, & S. H. McDaniel (Eds.), *Integrating family therapy* (pp. 91–112). Washington, DC: American Psychological Association.

American Association for Marriage and Family Therapy (AAMFT). (1991). *AAMFT code of ethics.* Washington, DC: Author.

American Association for Marriage and Family Therapy (AAMFT). (1994). *AAMFT membership requirements and applications* [brochure]. Washington, DC: Author.

American Counseling Association (ACA). (1995). *Code of ethics and standards of practice.* Alexandria, VA: Author.

American Psychiatric Association. (1994). *Diagnostic and statistical manual of mental disorders* (4th ed.) (DSM-IV). Washington, DC: Author.

American Psychological Association (APA). (1992). *Ethical principles of psychologists and code of conduct.* Washington, DC: Author.

Bateson, G., Jackson, D. D., Haley, J., & Weakland, J. (1956). Toward a theory of schizophrenia. *Behavioral Science, 1,* 251–264.

Benson, M. J., Schindler, T., & Martin, D. (1991). Accessing children's perceptions of their family: Circular questioning revisited. *Journal of Marital and Family Therapy, 17,* 363–372.

Bergman, J. (1985). *Fishing for barracuda.* New York: Norton.

Bowen, M. (1991). Alcoholism as viewed through family systems theory and family psychotherapy. *Family Dynamics of Addiction Quarterly, 1,* 94–102.

*Bowen, M. (1994). *Family therapy in clinical practice.* New York: Aronson.

Carter, B., & McGoldrick, M. (1989). *The changing family life cycle: A framework for family therapy* (2nd ed.). Boston: Allyn and Bacon.

Connell, G. M., Whitaker, C., Garfield, R., & Connell, L. (1990). The process of in-therapy consultation: A symbolic-experiential perspective. *Journal of Strategic and Systemic Therapies, 9,* 32–38.

Coppersmith, E. (1985). We've got a secret. In A. Gurman (Ed.), *Casebook of marital therapy* (pp. 369–386). New York: Guilford.

Fleuridas, C., Nelson, T., & Rosenthal, D. (1986). The evolution of circular questions: Training family therapists. *Journal of Marital and Family Therapy, 12,* 113–127.

Foreman, B. D., & Cava, E. (1993). Neuro-linguistic programming in one-person family therapy. In T. S. Nelson & T. S. Trepper (Eds.), *101 interventions in family therapy* (pp. 50–54). New York: Haworth Press.

Gerson, R. (1995). The family life cycle: Phases, stages and crises. In R. H. Mikesell, D. Lusterman, & S. H. McDaniel (Eds.), *Integrating family therapy* (pp. 91–112). Washington, DC: American Psychological Association.

Gladding, S. T. (1995). *Family Therapy: History, theory, and practice.* Englewood Cliffs, NJ: Prentice Hall.

Grove, D. R., & Haley, J. (1993). *Conversations on therapy.* New York: Norton.

Gurman, A., & Kniskern, D. (Eds.). (1991). *Handbook of family therapy* (Vol. 2). New York: Brunner/Mazel.

Hahlweg, K., & Markman, H. J. (1988). The effectiveness of behavioral marital therapy: Empirical status of behavioral techniques in preventing and alleviating marital distress. *Journal of Consulting & Clinical Psychology, 56,* 440–447.

Haley, J. (1984). *Ordeal therapy.* San Francisco: Jossey-Bass.

*Haley, J. (1987). *Problem solving therapy* (2nd ed.). San Francisco: Jossey-Bass.

Haley, Jay. (1993a). How to be a therapy supervisor without knowing how to change anyone. *Journal of Systemic Therapies, 12,* 41–52.

Haley, J. (1993b). *Jay Haley on Milton H. Erickson.* New York: Brunner/Mazel.

Haley, J. (1993c). *Uncommon therapy: The psychiatric techniques of Milton H. Erickson, M.D.* New York: Norton.

Hazelrigg, M. D., Cooper, H. M., & Borduin, C. M. (1987). Evaluating the effectiveness of family therapies: An integrative review and analysis. *Psychological Bulletin, 101,* 428–442.

Huber, C. (1994). *Ethical, legal, and professional issues in the practice of marriage and family therapy.* New York: Merrill.

International Association of Marriage and Family Counselors (IAMFC). (1993). Ethical code for the International Association of Marriage and Family Counselors. *Family Journal: Counseling and Therapy for Couples and Families, 1,* 73–77.

International Association of Marriage and Family Counselors (IAMFC). (1995). *International Association of Marriage and Family Counselors* (membership brochure). Alexandria, VA: Author.

Jacobson, N. S., & Gurman, A. S. (Eds.). (1995). *Clinical handbook of couple therapy.* New York: Guilford.

*Kerr, M., & Bowen, M. (1988). *Family evaluation.* New York: Norton.

Kershaw, C. J. (1992). *The couple's hypnotic dance.* New York: Brunner/Mazel.

Lankton, C. (1988). Task assignments: Logical and otherwise. In J. Zeig & S. Lankton (Eds.), *Developing Ericksonian therapy* (pp. 257–279). New York: Brunner/Mazel.

Lebow, J. L., & Gurman, A. S. (1995). Research assessing couple and family therapy. *Annual Review of Psychology, 46,* 27–57.

LeCroy, C. W., Carrol, P., Nelson-Becker, H., & Sturlaugson, P. (1989). An experimental evaluation of the Caring Days technique for marital enrichment. *Family Relations, 38,* 15–18.

Margolin, G. (1982). Ethical and legal considerations in marital and family therapy. *American Psychologist, 37,* 788–801.

Markus, E., Lange, A., & Pettigrew, T. F. (1990). Effectiveness of family therapy: A meta-analysis. *Journal of Family Therapy, 12,* 205–221.

*McGoldrick, M. & Gerson, R. (1985). *Genograms in family assessment.* New York: Norton.

Minuchin, S. (1982). Reflections on boundaries. *American Journal of Orthopsychiatry, 52,* 655–663.

*Minuchin, S., & Fishman, C. (1981). *Family therapy techniques.* Cambridge, MA: Harvard University Press.

Minuchin, S., Montalvo, B., Gurney, B., Rosman, B., & Schumer, F. (1967). *Families of the slums.* New York: Basic Books.

Minuchin, S., & Nichols, M. P. (1993). *Family healing.* New York: Free Press.

Minuchin, S., Rosman, B., & Baker, L. (1978). *Psychosomatic families.* Cambridge, MA: Harvard University Press.

Moran, A., Brownlee, K., Gallant, P., Meyers, L., Farmer, F., & Taylor, S. (1995). The effectiveness of reflecting team supervision: A client's experience of receiving feedback from a distance. *Family Therapy, 22,* 31–47.

*Nelson, T. S., & Trepper, T. S. (Eds). (1993). *101 interventions in family therapy.* New York: Haworth Press.

Patten, C., Barnett, T., & Houlihan, D. (1991). Ethics in marital and family therapy: A review of the literature. *Professional Psychology: Research and Practice, 22,* 171–175.

Ritterman, M. (1986). Exploring relationships between Ericksonian hypnotherapy and family therapy. In S. de Shazer & R. Kral (Eds.), *Indirect approaches in therapy* (pp. 35–47). Rockville, MD: Aspen Publications.

Satir, V. (1964). *Conjoint family therapy.* Palo Alto, CA: Science & Behavior Books.

*Satir, V. (1983). *Conjoint family therapy* (3rd ed.). Palo Alto, CA: Science & Behavior Books.

Sauber, S. R., L'Abate, L., Weeks, G. R., & Buchanan, W. L. (1993). *The dictionary of family psychology and family therapy* (2nd ed.). Newbury Park, CA: Sage.

Shadish, W. R. (1992). Do family and marital psychotherapies change what people do? A meta-analysis of behavioral outcomes. In T. D. Cook, H. M. Cooper, D. S. Cordray, H. Hortmann, L. V. Hedges, J. Light, T. A. Louis, & F. Mosteller (Eds.), *Meta-analysis for explanation: A Casebook.* New York: Russell Sage Foundation.

Shadish, W. R., Montgomery, L. M., Wilson, P., Wilson, M. R., Bright, I., & Okwumabua, T. (1993). Effects of family and marital therapies: A meta-analysis. *Journal of Consulting & Clinical Psychology, 61,* 992–1002.

Shields, C. G., Wynne, L. C., McDaniel, S. H., & Gawinski, B. A. (1994). The marginalization of family therapy: A historical and continuing problem. *Journal of Marital and Family Therapy, 20,* 117–138.

Sieburg, E. (1985). *Family communication.* New York: Gardner Press.

Simmons, D. S., & Doherty, W. J. (1995). Defining who we are and what we do: Clinical practice patterns of marriage and family therapists in Minnesota. *Journal of Marital and Family Therapy, 21,* 3–16.

Stanton, D. (1988). The lobster quadrille: Issues and dilemmas for family therapy research. In L. Wynne (Ed.), *The state of the art in family therapy research: Controversies and recommendations* (pp. 5–32). New York: Family Process Press.

Walsh, W. M., & McGraw, J. A. (1996). *Essentials of family therapy.* Denver: Love Publishing.

Weber, T., & Levine, F. (1995). Engaging the family: An integrative approach. In R. H. Mikesell, D. Lusterman, & S. H. McDaniel (Eds.), *Integrating family therapy* (pp. 45–71). Washington, DC: American Psychological Association.

*Whitaker, C., & Bumberry, W. (1988). *Dancing with the family: A symbolic-experiential approach.* New York: Brunner/Mazel.

Whitaker, C., & Keith, D. (1981). Symbolic-experiential family therapy. In A. Gurman & D. Kniskern (Eds.), *Handbook of family therapy* (pp. 187–225). New York: Brunner/Mazel.

Whitaker, C., & Malone, T. (1953). *The roots of psychotherapy.* New York: Blakiston.

Wynne, L. (1988). An overview of the state of the art. In L. Wynne (Ed.), *The state of the art in family therapy research: Controversies and recommendations* (pp. 249–266). New York: Family Process Press.

Chapter *18*

Counseling Gay, Lesbian, and Bisexual Clients

Reese M. House, Ed.D. *Jennie L. Miller, M.A.*

There are at least 20 to 25 million gay, lesbian, and bisexual individuals in the United States, figures based on the estimate that approximately 10–15 percent of the adult population is gay (Betz & Fitzgerald, 1993; Fassinger, 1991; Kinsey, Pomeroy, Martin, & Gebhard, 1953; Kinsey, Pomeroy, & Martin, 1948; Singer & Deschamps, 1994). These figures may actually underestimate the true number of gay, lesbian and bisexual individuals in society, as many individuals do not report same-gender activity, because of the stigma attached to being gay in our society. Recently, some studies have questioned the 10–15 percent figure and found the number of reported gay individuals closer to 5 percent (Singer & Deschamps, 1994). However, as Singer and Deschamps stated, "Gross underreporting in many studies, especially those that involve face-to-face interviews with researchers, is pervasive" (p. 9).

Whatever the exact number of gays, lesbians, and bisexuals in the United States, they are becoming more visible and active in their pursuit of equal rights. Before the 1970s, sexual orientation was a fairly invisible aspect of the American population. This invisibility was, to a large extent, by choice. The stigmatization of homosexuality in our society caused most gays, lesbians, and bisexuals to avoid the risks associated with disclosing their sexual orientation. "Hostility and discrimination at the hands of an unaccepting society created a climate of secrecy that did not permit challenges to the prevailing stereotypes" (Blumstein & Schwartz, 1983, p. 9). In the last twenty years, great numbers of gays developed a community identity to counter negative reactions from society. This "coming out" of gays has provoked considerable backlash and antigay sentiment throughout the United States. In some states (Oregon, Idaho, Colorado, Maine) and cities (Cincinnati, Miami), antigay initiatives have been placed on the ballot.

However, there is increasing legal support for the civil rights of gays, lesbians, and bisexuals, as demonstrated by the 1996 Supreme Court decision that ruled that Colorado's antigay Amendment 2 was unconstitutional. And, at least one state has been forced to consider legalizing same-sex marriage. A 1990 lawsuit in Hawaii, still under review when this chapter was written, challenged the denial of a marriage license application made by three same-sex couples.

As more and more people identify themselves as gay and become more visible, all members of society, including counselors, will be forced to address issues involving sexual orientation. All counselors have clients who are gay. Some of these clients will be self-identified as gay, and some will hide their gay identity and pass as heterosexual. Some counselors may say, "I don't know anyone who is gay or lesbian," or "No gay people will come to me, because I work as a high school counselor or pastoral counselor," or "I have no gay clients on my caseload." These perceptions are inaccurate. Whether a counselor has a private practice, works for an agency, school, church, business, or in the military, he or she will have gay, lesbian, and bisexual clients. This chapter provides an introduction to basic facts and issues about being gay that will help counselors become effective when working with gay clients and their families and friends.

Who Is Gay, Lesbian, or Bisexual?

The initial challenge for counselors may be in determining a client's sexual orientation. There is no "typical" gay, lesbian, or bisexual. Contrary to prevailing stereotypes, not all gay males are hairdressers with platform shoes and excessive jewelry. Neither do all lesbians wear flannel shirts and blue jeans. There is no description that is completely inclusive, and describing the "typical" gay male, lesbian, or bisexual is impossible. Gay, lesbian, and bisexual people come from a cross section of races, nationalities, religions, socioeconomic levels, family backgrounds, geographical locations, and cultures. There are gay parents, spouses, children, teenagers, couples, grandparents, uncles, aunts, and cousins. Similarly, the sexual orientation of an individual cannot be determined by occupation. Gays are business owners, ministers, teachers, lawyers, truck drivers, members of the armed services, and industrial workers. The following examples illustrate the diversity of gay clients:

1. Sally and Jennifer are a lesbian couple who have been living as partners in the same small community for ten years. They are 31 and 34. Sally is a nurse, and Jennifer works as a counselor in a drug treatment program. Sally and Jennifer decided they wanted to have a child together, and Sally was artificially inseminated. Their son Kevin is now 7 and attends public school. As coparents, the two women attend school functions and work with Kevin's teachers on his academic and social progress. Sally and Jennifer face the same issues as any couple in raising a child. However, some teachers are uncomfortable working with Sally and Jennifer as co-parents, and some children tease Kevin about having two mothers.

2. Chet is a 33-year-old male lawyer who has entered a twenty-eight-day treatment program for cocaine abuse. He is a successful attorney, practicing in a large law firm. He is gay and lives with his lover of three years. No one at work knows that he is gay. As a closeted individual, he is reluctant to discuss his sexual orientation in the treatment program. However, the issue of being gay and closeted, which requires leading a "double" life, causes him stress and exacerbates his abuse of cocaine. Chet must face his abuse issues in treatment and also needs to address the issues surrounding his gay life, or the treatment is not likely to be successful.

3. Joe is a 19-year-old freshman in college who was a star football player in high school. Joe confronts the usual stresses of all college freshmen. In addition, he has discovered that he is attracted to men. On a visit back home, he tries to discuss his feelings with his high school football coach, whom he trusts and respects. The football coach is unclear about how to respond to Joe and seeks the advice of the high school counselor.

4. Rosalind dated boys throughout high school and college and always imagined that she would get married and have children. She was engaged at one time, but things did not work out. After college graduation, Rosalind developed a close friendship with a woman at work. The friendship moved to a more intimate level, and they engaged in a consensual sexual relationship. Rosalind did not identify as a lesbian and found that she was still attracted to both men and women. After struggling with this dual attraction, Rosalind sought counseling to explore the issue of being bisexual.

A Word about Words

Language is important for what it communicates as well as what it implies. Gay, lesbian, and bisexual individuals hear biased and offensive street language, such as "queer," "faggot," "homo," "dyke," and "queen," throughout their lives. This language affects self-esteem, stigmatizes gays and lesbians, and is just as offensive to them as ethnic slurs are to ethnic populations. Thus gays, lesbians, and bisexuals are sensitive to terminology.

Many reject the term "homosexual" because it is the term used by the dominant and often oppressing group in our culture. Although it is commonly used in the professional literature, media, and popular fiction, the term "homosexual" reflects an inaccurately narrow, clinical focus on sexual conduct. It is seen by many as archaic, imprecise, and misleading (House & Tyler, 1992). The term "homoerotic" is another clinical term that is similarly narrow and is frequently rejected as a non-inclusive term. Another term frequently questioned is "sexual preference." Preference implies that individuals choose to be gay, lesbian, or bisexual. There is increasing evidence that sexual predisposition is biologically innate; thus the term "sexual orientation" is now considered the more acceptable term ("Avoiding Heterosexual Bias in Language," 1991; Ritter & O'Neill, 1989).

As counselors work with clients, they need to be aware that clients may strongly object to certain terms. Although "gay" is often used as a general term for both men and women, not everyone will be comfortable being called "gay." Most women who use an identifying term prefer to be called "lesbian" or "gay women," and most men who identify as gay men prefer to be called "gay" rather than "homosexual." Some individuals prefer the term "bisexual." Counselors would be wise to simply ask clients their terminology preference rather than use language that might be offensive to some individuals.

Why Are People Gay, Lesbian, or Bisexual?

What causes people to be gay, lesbian, or bisexual is currently a matter of controversy. The causes of sexual orientation have not yet been determined, and it seems increasingly clear that no one factor can explain so complex and variable a trait as sexual orientation (Levay & Hamer, 1994). The most recent studies suggest that biological factors are involved in determining sexual orientation (Burr, 1993). Genetic patterns, pre- and postnatal hormonal activity, and brain structure differences are areas being explored as possible causes of sexual orientation (Levay & Hamer, 1994; Money, 1987). Several researchers support the idea that genes may influence or predispose individuals, but emphasize that environmental cues and social learning play a key role in creating the broad continuum of sexual orientation (Byne, 1994; Johnston & Bell, 1995; Levay & Hamer, 1994; Money, 1987).

Whatever the causes of sexual orientation, counselors need to recognize "that persons with diverse sexual orientations exist and that the existence of this diversity is not pathological" (Dworkin & Gutierrez, 1989, p. 7). Same-gender sexual orientation is a "valid developmental outcome for many adults" (Morin & Rothblum, 1991, p. 947), and counselors need to assist gays, lesbians, and bisexuals in a non-biased and professional manner.

Definition of Gay, Lesbian, and Bisexual

Stein and Cohen (1986), define homosexuality as "an attraction for a person of the same sex within one or more of the dimensions of affection, fantasy, or erotic desire" (p. 28). However, it is not always easy to define who is gay, lesbian, or bisexual. A significant number of people in society have same-sex relations. How do we know which of these individuals is lesbian, gay, or bisexual? What about the adolescent male who fantasizes about another boy in the classroom? Or the individual who has had a few same-sex experiences as a teenager? What about the woman who feels an occasional attraction to another woman? Or the person who has sexual desires for a person of the same gender but never acts on the desire? What

Table 18-1   The Kinsey Scale of the Continuum of Human Sexual Experience

Kinsey Rating	Description
0	Exclusively heterosexual in psychological response and behavior
1	Predominantly heterosexual; incidental homosexual behavior
2	Predominantly heterosexual; more than incidental homosexual behavior
3	Equally heterosexual and homosexual in psychological response and behavior
4	Predominantly homosexual; more than incidental heterosexual behavior
5	Predominantly homosexual; incidental heterosexual behavior
6	Exclusively homosexual in psychological response and behavior

about the married man with children who identifies as heterosexual, but has sex with men outside of marriage?

The answers to these and many other questions about sexual orientation are often confusing and unclear. And, as Krajeski (1986) noted, the terminology used in professional writing about homosexuality has often been imprecise. Part of the confusion results from the "popular misconception that homosexuality and sex are one and the same" (Blumenfeld & Raymond, 1988, p. 85). The fact that an individual engages in specific sexual conduct does not define that person's sexual orientation.

Kinsey et al. (1948) were the first to indicate that the labels "homosexuality" and "heterosexuality" do not describe most people. They concluded that people's orientation were not exclusive and that homosexuality and heterosexuality are poles on a continuum (see Table 18-1). This continuum suggests that people have a range in both sexual attractions and sexual behavior. Some people are always attracted to a person of the opposite gender. Others are always attracted to a person of the same gender. However, many people are attracted to and act sexually with both genders.

The term "bisexual" has existed as a concept since the process of psychosexual development was conceptualized by Freud and his contemporaries, but not until recently have bisexuals been included in theory or research about sexual orientation (Fox, 1995). "Bisexuality has been continually attacked as a nonentity, a transitional stage from heterosexuality to homosexuality or vice-versa, and as a denial of one's homosexuality" (Wolf, 1992, p. 175).

Klein (1993) found that the Kinsey continuum did not adequately explain the complexity of sexual orientation, and in addressing the issue of bisexuality, asked such questions as "What does it mean to be a Kinsey 2 or 3"? (p. 15). He developed seven distinct variables (Figure 18-1) that can be used with clients to help clarify the complexity of sexual orientation.

It is important to understand that *sexual attraction* is not synonymous with *sexual behavior*. A person can be attracted to one gender and yet have sex with another. This may or may not be the case with Rosalind, described earlier in this chapter,

---

1. Sexual attraction
2. Sexual behavior
3. Sexual fantasies
4. Emotional preference
5. Social preference
6. Heterosexual or homosexual lifestyle
7. Self-identification

Figure 18-1   Seven Variables of Sexual Orientation

who is questioning her sexual behavior with both men and women. Asking about *sexual fantasies* is often a helpful tool in counseling, and many believe that one's fantasies and dreams are the most important criterion in determining sexual orientation (Klein, 1993). Sexual fantasies can change over the life span, and these changes provide important information for counselors. The fourth variable, *emotional preference,* focuses on which gender an individual prefers to be emotionally involved with. *Social preference* addresses the degree to which a person likes to socialize with members of his or her own gender, or the opposite gender. *Heterosexual or homosexual lifestyle,* the sixth variable, concerns whether the person lives in the heterosexual or homosexual social world. Does he or she have mostly bisexual, lesbian, or gay friends, or mostly heterosexual friends and acquaintances? *Self-identification* asks the individual to state whether they identify themselves as gay, lesbian, bisexual, or heterosexual. Using these seven variables, Klein developed the Sexual Orientation Grid (Figure 18-2) to help develop a profile in clarifying sexual orientation.

It is important to differentiate between "act" and "identity" when discussing sexual orientation. Individuals who focus only on the "act" believe that sexual acts or behaviors define the person. When using this concept, labels are given to the behaviors in question rather than to the person engaging in the behavior (Blumenfeld & Raymond, 1988). However, this behavior-based definition fails to recognize a holistic view of the person. For example, a male teenager who experiments with same-sex behavior does not necessarily have a gay identity. The experimental behavior is just that, and labeling someone as "homosexual" or "gay" because of such experimentation does not take into account the developmental nature of sexuality.

Those who ascribe to the identity theory assert that sexuality is "more than merely a behavior but is rather an aspect of personal identity which strongly influences the ways people live their lives and view the world at large" (Blumenfeld & Raymond, 1988, p. 77). Under this approach, being gay is associated with a lifestyle, not just sexual desires or behavior.

Being gay is not merely the ability and willingness to engage in homosexual behavior. Indeed, being gay is being different, having a distinct identity, frequently

Variable	Past	Present	Ideal
Sexual attraction*			
Sexual behavior*			
Sexual fantasies*			
Emotional preference*			
Social preference*			
Hetero/homo lifestyle**			
Self-identification**			

People rate themselves on a seven-point scale from 1 to 7 as follows:

(*) 1 = other sex only   (**) 1 = heterosexual only

2 = other sex mostly   2 = heterosexual mostly

3 = other sex somewhat more   3 = heterosexual somewhat more

4 = both sexes equally   4 = heterosexual or gay/lesbian equally

5 = same sex somewhat more   5 = gay/lesbian somewhat more

6 = same sex mostly   6 = gay/lesbian mostly

7 = same sex only   7 = gay/lesbian only

Source: Adapted from Klein (1993).

Figure 18-2   Klein Sexual Orientation Grid

in a way that is felt even before it is consciously or sexually expressed. Gayness is a special affinity and a special feeling toward people of the same gender; it is not the inability to love and to relate to others, nor is it a denial of the opposite sex. Rather it is a special capacity and need to love and to express one's love for people of the same gender in all the meanings of the term "love." (Woodman & Lenna, 1980, p. 11)

When society categorizes an individual using only one dimension of humanness, a significant part of that person is omitted. This omission leads to stereotyping and labeling, which have a significant and detrimental impact on the individual. The following examples illustrate such stereotyping and labeling: "He is a dumb jock; what is he doing with a philosophy major?" "She's a woman; she shouldn't do that kind of work." "He's gay; he should not be working with children." "She is married; she couldn't possibly be bisexual." All these statements focus on only one aspect of the individual. By focusing on an isolated aspect, the person in each of these examples is minimized and reduced to that one aspect—an unfair and inaccurate characterization of the whole person. The more holistic approach to human behavior focuses on the integration of all aspects of the individual, including the emotional, social, intellectual, spiritual, and physical dimensions of each person. This approach recognizes that individuals are unique and emphasizes the importance of looking at the whole person rather than determining someone's worth based on a single characteristic.

Counselors who work with gays, lesbians, and bisexuals need to consider the more holistic view and realize that while sexual activity is a part of many relationships, it is frequently not the primary focus of relationships. Not all gay, lesbian, and bisexual clients come to counseling to address issues related to sexual orientation. Counselors need to address the issues that are presented and not make sexual orientation the problem.

Homophobia and Heterosexism

Cultural Homophobia

We live in a homophobic culture. The term *homophobia* was first defined by Weinberg (1973) as a fear, dread, or loathing of gays and lesbians. Perhaps it would be more accurate to describe homophobia as a fear of individuals who are "perceived" to be gay, lesbian, or bisexual. People who are homophobic rely on their own preconceived ideas of sexuality and often make a point of condemning, punishing, and even outlawing gays and lesbians (Forstein, 1986; Rubenstein, 1993).

People who are homophobic downgrade, deny, or stereotype the existence of gays, lesbians, and bisexuals. These phobic and negative responses range from individuals who tell "fag" or "queer" jokes to the extreme examples of violence against and murder of gays, lesbians, and bisexuals. Documented hate crimes including physical violence and harassment against gays and lesbians have increased dramatically over the past few years (National Gay & Lesbian Task Force, or NGLTF, 1995). As Mel White (1995) stated, "there is a war raging against gay and lesbian people in our country right now. Our civil rights are on the line. Our freedom is at stake. The homophobic lies of the religious right are murdering the souls and threatening the civil rights of gay and lesbian Americans" (p. 284).

Cultural homophobia is also manifested in the widespread discrimination faced by gays. Gay individuals are discriminated against in employment, housing, and within religious organizations. Certain career positions such as teaching, the military, police, and public office are frequently available only to those who keep their sexual orientation hidden. Likewise, those who are known or perceived to be gay are frequently denied housing. Gays, lesbians and bisexuals are also denied the sanctuary of religious organizations on the basis of their sexual orientation. In a recent edict, Pope John Paul II denounced homosexual activity as "an intrinsic moral evil" and called on churches to dissociate themselves from gays. As a result, many gay Catholic organizations have been evicted from church property and denied open participation in church activities.

Cultural Heterosexism

Cultural heterosexism assumes that heterosexuality is or should be the only acceptable sexual orientation. Heterosexism "is so ubiquitous that it is hardly noticeable. Even a cursory survey of American society reveals that homosexuality is largely hidden and when publicly recognized, it is usually condemned or stigmatized" (Herek, 1993, p. 90). Although closely aligned with homophobia, it is less blatant and overt and does not usually involve active aggression against gays and lesbians. However, heterosexism demands heterosexuality in return for first-class citizenship. There are a myriad of subtle and indirect ways that the system reinforces heterosexuality as the only acceptable and viable life option; for example, (1) parental expectations that their children will marry a person of the opposite sex; (2) media portrayals of positive and satisfying relationships as exclusively heterosexual; (3) the presumption by teachers that all their students are straight; and the exclusion of any discussion of homosexuality in most classes (Blumenfeld & Raymond, 1988). Cultural heterosexism is a more insidious form of discrimination and occurs by neglect, omission, and/or distortion, while homophobia is discrimination by intent and design (Blumenfeld & Raymond, 1988).

Heterosexism, along with homophobia, is the societal norm in the United States against which gays, lesbians, and bisexuals must struggle and results in prejudice, discrimination, harassment, and antigay violence (Jung & Smith, 1993). These societal norms exclude openly gay, lesbian, and bisexual individuals from social, religious, and political power and force them into silence concerning their lives (Mollenkott, 1985). Gays are also denied legal recognition as couples, leading to limitations on visitations in hospitals, custody rights, survivorship benefits, and the denial of the right to participate in a variety of other benefits available only to married couples.

In spite of these efforts to blame and silence them, lesbians, gay men, and bisexuals have made tremendous social and political gains in the past twenty-five years. These advances include securing passage of protective state and local legislation and gaining considerable status as a minority community in American society (Herek, 1994). Congress recently passed the Hate Crimes Statistics Act of 1990, which mandates collection of statistics on bias crimes of all kinds, including antigay crimes. "This has been heralded by activists as a significant victory for gay rights" (Fassinger, 1991, p. 163).

As counselors work with gays, lesbians, and bisexuals, they need to be sensitive to the effects of homophobia and heterosexism on their clients. Individuals may question their sexual orientation and experience it as a source of pain, danger, and punishment rather than love, intimacy, and community. "Being the target of discrimination often leads to feelings of sadness and anxiety; it can also lead to an increased sense that life is difficult and unfair, and dissatisfaction with one's larger community" (Herek, 1994, p. 336). In addition, hate crimes perpetuated against individuals may result in more severe psychological consequences.

Internalized Homophobia

Internalized homophobia represents an internalization of the negative attitudes and assumptions of societal homophobia by an individual (Sophie, 1987). Internalized homophobia results from the combination of negative attitudes apparent in cultural homophobia and an individual's own fear of being gay, lesbian, or bisexual. Gay individuals learn to fear their sexual orientation from the negative attitudes expressed by others in society. "Bisexuals, lesbians, and gay males live in a world that teaches that same-sex activity is morally repulsive, psychologically damaging, or that it does not exist at all" (Blumenfeld & Raymond, 1988, p. 264). This negative information about their sexuality comes from credible sources such as friends, family, church, school, and mass media. When this information is internalized, it creates substantial dissonance. Such dissonance often results in low self-esteem, threatens the development of identity, and becomes a major source of distress for gay clients.

Homophobia and Heterosexism in Counselors

Counselors are raised in the same homophobic and heterosexist culture as everyone else. Counselors may believe that they are not afflicted with homophobia or heterosexism and that they are immune from negative responses toward gays. However, such immunity seems unlikely. Counselors who have not confronted their homophobic beliefs and behaviors provide inadequate, improper, and harmful services to gay clients and those related to or dependent on them (Moses & Hawkins, 1985). Ethical codes of the counseling profession emphasize that discrimination on the basis of sexual orientation is not ethical or acceptable. As Buhrke (1989) states "it is the ethical counselor who respects the worth, dignity, potential, and uniqueness, of heterosexual, bisexual, and lesbian and gay people" (p. 77).

Figure 18-3 identifies personal homophobia assessment questions, developed by the National Association of Social Workers, or NASW (1985, pp. 153–154) to help counselors identify and address their own homophobia. The questions may also be used in counseling sessions with clients who are dealing with homophobia issues.

Changing Attitudes

The struggle for equality by gays is currently at the center of political and social struggles in American life. This struggle will likely continue. When President Bill

1. Do you stop yourself from doing or saying certain things because someone might think you are gay, lesbian, or bisexual? If yes, what kinds of things?

2. Do you ever intentionally do or say things so that people will think you are not gay? If yes, what kinds of things?

3. Do you believe that gays or lesbians can influence others to become gay or lesbian? Do you think someone could influence you to change your sexual orientation?

4. If you are a parent, how would you (or do you) feel about having a lesbian, gay, or bisexual daughter or son?

5. How do you think you would feel if you discovered that one of your parents or parent figures, or a brother or sister, were gay, lesbian, or bisexual?

6. Are there any jobs, positions, or professions that you think lesbians, gays, and bisexuals should be barred from holding or entering? If yes, why so?

7. Would you go to a physician whom you knew or believed to be gay, lesbian, or bisexual if that person were of a different gender from you? If that person were of the same gender as you? If not, why not?

8. If someone you care about were to say to you, "I think I'm gay," would you suggest that the person see a therapist?

9. Have you ever been to a gay or lesbian bar, social club, party, or march: If not, why not?

10. Would you wear a button that says, "How dare you assume that I'm heterosexual"? If not, why not?

11. Can you think of three positive aspects of a gay, lesbian, or bisexual lifestyle? Can you think of three negative aspects of a heterosexual lifestyle?

12. Have you ever laughed at a "queer" joke?

Figure 18-3   Personal Homophobia Assessment Questions

Clinton directed the change in military policy toward lesbians and gays, a heated backlash and debate erupted. This is only one example of the emerging presence of gay issues that are increasingly visible in newspapers, radio, TV, magazines, and movies. Americans are being forced to take a stand on an issue that they previously had ignored or denied. With this attention, there have been an increased number of surveys and opinion polls asking Americans their views on gay issues.

General trends in these surveys indicate that the American public is becoming more accepting of gays and lesbians. In 1983, a survey by *Newsweek* magazine reported that 66 percent of the U.S. population felt that homosexuality was an unacceptable lifestyle (Blumenfeld & Raymond, 1988). *Newsweek* conducted a similar poll in 1992 and found that 53 percent of the public thought homosexuality was an unacceptable lifestyle (Wilson, 1992). In 1989, the *San Francisco Examiner,* which conducted the most extensive poll ever of attitudes toward gay people, concluded that Americans are becoming more accepting of gay people and gay rights ("A Special Report," 1989). In this national poll, the *Examiner* found that only 48 percent of the people surveyed believed that homosexuality was an unacceptable lifestyle.

There is also a growing consensus that gays, like other minorities, deserve protection from job discrimination. Between 1982 and 1992 there was a 15 percent increase in public support for giving gays equal protection on the job—from 59 percent to 74 percent (Singer & Deschamps, 1994). But according to the same 1993 Gallup poll, acceptance of homosexuality as a lifestyle has increased only marginally from 34 percent to 38 percent. Despite these increases in acceptance of gays, there still remain sizable groups that fight against the rights of gays and lesbians and believe that gay lifestyles are improper. Homophobia and heterosexism remain at the core of these negative attitudes in our society.

Developing an Identity

In human development theories, the development of a distinct identity and positive self-worth are primary tasks identified as necessary for a healthy state of being. People develop and define their identities and sense of self-worth through an interactive process between themselves and their environment. The ability to give and accept affirmation and love accompanies this positive view of identity and self-worth.

Coming Out

This process of developing an identity as a gay person is called "coming out." Coming out and identifying oneself as gay is frequently a reason why gay individuals find themselves in counseling. There are many stages in the coming-out process. The first step is to acknowledge feelings of attraction for the same gender. Then individuals need to decide whether to share the fact of their sexual orientation with others such as parents, friends, children, employers, and co-workers. Clients need to understand why they wish to share information with others and the possible consequences.

Several "coming-out" models provide a framework for understanding this process of identity development (Cass, 1984; Coleman, 1985; Falco, 1987; Lewis, 1984; Sophie, 1987; Troiden, 1989). The authors' model in Table 18-2 draws on each of these systems to identify the client's experiences and counselor's tasks for six coming-out stages. It is important to remember that these stages do not necessarily occur in the order listed. After going through one stage, individuals frequently find themselves circling back to the same stage again when new thoughts, feelings, or actions occur.

The coming-out process may occur at any age. Some individuals have indicated that they knew they were attracted to the same sex as early as age 6 or 7. If people come out during the teenage years, then development of sexual identity is congruent with adolescent development. However, coming out as a teenager can be particularly difficult because adolescents seek and need approval and support

Table 18-2   The Coming-Out Stages

Stages	Client Experience	Counselor Task
Predisclosure		
Precoming out (Coleman, 1985); being different (Lewis, 1984); identity confusion (Cass, 1984); recognizing and accepting lesbian feelings (Sophie, 1987); senitization (Troiden, 1989).	Awareness of being different—may be vague. May not be able to talk about feelings. Confused, alienated, defensive, and beginning to wonder about the possibility of being gay. Probably has not disclosed to anyone feelings of being different.	Helps client identify both internal and external conflicts. Assists client in talking about thoughts and feelings without judging or labeling. Helps client understand that feelings and thoughts are acceptable. Helps client look at consequences of acting on thoughts and feelings. Is open to client's awareness.
Disclosure		
Coming out (Coleman, 1985); dissonance (Lewis, 1984); identity comparison (Cass, 1984); coming out to self (Sophie, 1987); identity confusion (Troiden, 1989).	Acknowledges same gender feelings and identifies self as possibly gay. Faces and copes with resultant conflict with heterosexual lifestyle, including homophobia and heterosexism. Experiences confusion, questions values, roles, and self-concept. Concerned about possible loss of friends and family. Expresses strong attraction to individuals of the same gender.	Accepts client's acknowledged feelings and thoughts. Helps client understand that same-sex feelings and thoughts are acceptable. Helps client through grieving process, work through denial, shame, anxiety, alienation, and self-esteem issues. Encourages client to reevaluate expectations and goals. Helps client develop positive image of gays and lesbians. Helps client value his or her personhood. Helps client sort through issues of sex role identification. Provides client with gay community resources, such as publications, support groups, and spiritual groups. Asks client questions about coming out, such as How will people react to your coming out? Who in your life will be affected by your coming out? Have you acted on your sexual thoughts?
Exploration/ Experimentation		
Exploration (Coleman, 1985); relationships (Lewis, 1984); identity tolerance (Cass, 1984); coming out to others (Sophie, 1987).	Experiments with social and sexual relationships. Decides who to come out to, in what setting, to how many people, how much, and what to say. Feels intense emotion and is uncertain of social skills. Needs to find supportive community and gain a positive self-concept.	Helps client to decide about coming out. Helps cope with the consequences of coming out. Helps client establish support network while continuing to accept feelings and thoughts. Helps client develop self-esteem and interpersonal skills. Assists client in understanding the intensity of feelings and the awkwardness in social relationships. Helps client develop a model for pursuing relationships, including dating, courtship, and sexual behavior.

(continued)

Table 18-2   *(continued)*

Stages	Client Experience	Counselor Task
Identity Development		
First relationships (Coleman, 1985); stable identity (Lewis, 1984); identity acceptance (Cass, 1984); identity assumption (Troiden, 1989).	Develops and learns to live in same-sex relationships. Begins to attribute value to being gay by taking part in gay subculture. Develops skill of "passing" as heterosexual, and decides when it is appropriate to be "out." Feels more positive about being gay.	Helps client with continuing issues of self-esteem. Helps client with frustration and pain of being rejected by some people. Is supportive of relationship issues. Helps client with communication skills and role development in relationships. Helps client understand that some relationships may not last, and to learn from such loss.
Identity Prizing		
Identity pride (Cass, 1984).	Values the gay, lesbian, or bisexual experience above the heterosexual. Accepts self as valuable and contributing member of society. Enjoys and values gay subculture and friends gained as a gay person. Comes out to more people. Experiences anger and rejection from members of society, yet maintains a positive sense of self.	Assists client in continuing decisions about self-disclosure. Helps client express thoughts and feelings and understand actions in addressing the conflicts and joys in life. Finds ways to support client in maintaining a positive self-image despite some continuing societal rejection.
Identity Integration		
Integration (Coleman, 1985, Lewis, 1984); identity synthesis (Cass, 1984); commitment (Troiden, 1989).	Integrates internal and external experiences into a healthy self-view. Being gay or lesbian takes much less energy and attention. Public and private identities merge into one unified and integrated self-image. Relationships are more successful and are characterized by honesty, mutual trust, and intimacy. Client proceeds on with age-appropriate issues and developmental tasks.	Affirms view that being gay is only one aspect of total self. Helps client continue to adapt to new identity. Assists with continuing self-disclosure and self-labeling. Helps client with ongoing development of personal relationships.

from both peers and adults. Teenagers take the risks both of being thrown out of their homes by parents if they identify themselves as gay (Blumenfeld, 1992; Silberman & Hawkins, 1988) and of experiencing rejection from their friends (Anderson, 1995). Many individuals do not come out until later years and may not "enter their true adolescence until their chronological adolescence has long passed" (Coleman, 1985, p. 36). Some individuals "come out" as senior citizens. Whenever gays come out, they address an identity crisis and need assistance in sorting through the coming-out issues and developing a positive sense of self.

Because gays are not usually born into gay families, the process of coming out is more difficult than it otherwise would be. Most gays and lesbians have few role models and no self-validating and visible culture on which to pattern themselves (Fassinger, 1991; Forstein, 1986; Garnets & Kimmel, 1993). Bisexuals have even fewer role models and are caught in the middle of two worlds (Wolf, 1992). Generally, gays, lesbians, and bisexuals who have not come out suffer oppression alone, without benefit of advice or emotional support from relatives or friends. Since the development of a defined and positive gay identity is frequently not encouraged or supported by friends and family or by society, it is essential for counselors to be positive and supportive as clients work through the coming-out process.

There are many issues to be addressed in the development of identity and the coming-out process. The alternatives open to the individual and the ramifications of choices must be explored and clarified. It is important that the counselor remain aware of the process and the interrelationship between developing an identity and coming out. Clients may need assistance in looking at both the positive and negative aspects of coming out. Counselors will need to use personal history assessment techniques to determine how to assist the client in the decision-making process about coming out. The client who is anticipating self-disclosure concerning sexual orientation may benefit from practicing the disclosure through role playing. Using the empty chair technique, allowing the client to play different parts, can help the client experience expected reactions such as fear, abuse, and abandonment.

Deciding Whether to Come Out

Each person must decide whether to identify him- or herself publicly as gay, lesbian, or bisexual. Not identifying oneself publicly and living a secret life is termed living in the "closet." Secrecy about feelings and self-perceptions supports internalized homophobia. Closeted gays blanket their entire lives with self-constriction, constantly monitoring their thoughts, emotions, and responses. Such hiding does irreparable harm to their sense of integrity and leaves them in a stressful and dissonant position, detracting from their mental health and well-being.

Coming out is a never-ending process, and decisions about whether to come out occur on a daily basis. The stresses of addressing the issue of sexual orientation affect the function and quality of life no matter how far out of the closet gays are, or how carefully cloistered and defended they are about their lifestyle (Riddle & Sang, 1978; Weston, 1991). Gays, lesbians, and bisexuals experience constant pressure both to stay in and to come out of the closet. For example, after a weekend when co-workers are discussing what they did, does the gay person share with whom he or she spent time, or make up an appropriate other-gender partner? At holiday times, does the gay person bring his or her partner to the family dinner, or go alone and feign being unattached? Does a bisexual married woman come out to her family and friends?

As counselors work with clients who are addressing coming-out issues, they need to remember that self-disclosure is necessary for self-acceptance and self-regard. Disclosing your sexual orientation and perceived identity is necessary for

1. What kind of reactions do you expect when you tell family members, friends, co-workers, and so on?
2. How can you determine what the reactions might be?
3. What would be the worst possible reaction?
4. What can you do to prepare yourself against that reaction?
5. What happens when or if you tell your parents?
6. Should you tell your parents together or individually?
7. Should you tell both of your parents?
8. What happens if you do not tell certain people?
9. Is it necessary to tell everyone?
10. What are the best ways to tell people?
11. Can you think of alternative ways to tell people?
12. Are you aware that responses may change over time?

Figure 18-4   Consequences of Coming Out—Questions to Ask Clients

affirmation of self-worth and enhancement of personal integrity (Garnets & Kimmel, 1993). Choosing to stay in the closet and not publicly identify oneself as gay frequently supports shame and guilt and perpetuates a negative self-image. However, it is important that each person decide whether to publicly identify as gay and how far to come out of the closet. Counselors need to counsel about this question, rather than give answers (Norton, 1995). Circumstances vary, and counselors need to assist clients in this difficult decision-making process by assessing the issues involved. Counselors who are not familiar with the emotional constellation involved in coming out may give clients some very inappropriate advice (Markowitz, 1991). Joe, the college freshman identified earlier in the chapter, faces some difficult choices. What will be the effect on his relationship with family and friends? If he comes out, will his parents continue financial support for college? If they do not, does he have alternatives to finance his education? If the decision is to stay in the closet, how will this affect Joe? Questions listed in Figure 18-4 can help clients determine the consequences of coming out.

Identity Dysfunctions

Individuals who do not develop a positive self-view in the coming-out process frequently develop an identity dysfunction. Identity dysfunctions lead the person to initiate friendships or work relationships that support the continuation of a negative self-view. The resulting behaviors manifest themselves in difficulties with intimacy and maintaining relationships. Dysfunctions of identity are confusion, conflict, and denial. Counselors need to understand and identify the dysfunctional roles taken on by the client and explore with the client alternative ways of enhancing the self rather than denying the self.

Identity Confusion

When people are not accepted by the culture, they experience rejection. For example, teenagers are expected to attend high school dances with members of the opposite sex. If gay teenagers want to take someone of the same gender to a senior prom, they do not conform to the expectations of parents and peers. The majority of gay teenagers are reared in nongay families, which seldom provide the support needed in accepting and affirming a nonsanctioned identity (Fassinger, 1991). The resulting rejection may be perceived as rejection of the self or emotional abandonment and thus disaffirms an individual's sense of worth (Colgan, 1987). The rejection and resulting low self-worth creates identity confusion for the individual.

Bisexuals may experience even more identity confusion than gay men and lesbians because of the inherent complexity of bisexuality. The following questions are often asked by individuals who are confused about identity issues: Who am I in this society? Why don't I fit into the roles defined by society? What can I do to be accepted in society? Where can I find support? Counselors need to assist clients in responding to such questions about how to fit into a society that is nonaccepting. Answering such questions will help clients address the confusion that they are experiencing.

Identity Conflict

Gay, lesbian, and bisexual clients with identity conflicts often have low self-worth and place the needs of others above their own. Identity conflict frequently involves overattachment or overidentification with another person. An individual may become lost in the self of others. This response stems from previous rejection and emotional isolation. An individual may become obsessed with another person and do whatever the partner wants, to avoid further rejection. As a result, the individual may become victimized and possibly sexually dysfunctional (Colgan, 1987; Island & Letellier, 1991). People in identity conflict may experience feelings of unworthiness and blame themselves each time a relationship is terminated. Another common feature of overidentification is for a person to immerse him- or herself in community organizations, thus placing the needs of the community above self needs. Counselors need to address the low self-esteem issues of such clients, to help them learn to value themselves and seek balance in their relationships.

Identity Denial

When individuals deny their sexual orientation and negate their identity, they sometimes detach from their emotions. For example, they might disconnect their emotions during sexual performance; insulate themselves from feelings by drug and alcohol abuse, or adopt the role of "rejector" or "suitor" in relationships. The rejector acts from a sense of anger and hostility, whereas the suitor is constantly in search of the right man or woman who will bring immediate fulfillment (Silverstein, 1981). All these behaviors are forms of self-denial and deaden the pain the individual is feeling from the loss of the self.

Community Identity

As counselors work with gay, lesbian, and bisexual clients, especially those addressing identity issues, it would be helpful to have knowledge of gay and lesbian community organizations. Gays and lesbians have established communities to support each other because of their invisibility and oppressed status (D'Augelli & Garnets, 1995). Both social and professional groups have been established in most urban areas, and many people find folks in kindred communities away from home. Social organizations are formed around common interests such as hiking, bowling, bridge, and square dancing. Other local and national organizations have been established to serve political and advocacy functions for gays. Groups exist that address a wide range of issues such as health, legal concerns, aging, youth, religious, and political needs. Bookstores, with gay and lesbian periodicals, books, and newspapers exist in most large cities. Most large cities have gay, lesbian, and bisexual counseling centers that serve as a community resource.

Counselors need to be aware of the gay community resources and make this information available to their clients. It should be noted that there are not as many resources available for the bisexual community, and counselors need to take extra care to find appropriate resources for their bisexual clients. Counselors located in rural communities need to be aware of national resources available by mail and the resources in the nearest large city. A sample of community and national sources is listed in the appendix at the end of the chapter.

Special Situations in Counseling

Relationships

Unlike ethnic minorities, lesbians and gay men were not measured by the U.S. census until 1992, making it extremely difficult to obtain accurate demographic information on living patterns in the gay community. The studies that have been conducted contradict the popular perception that the majority of gays and lesbians do not live with a partner or maintain a monogamous relationship. In studies conducted between 1977 and 1983, 40 to 60 percent of gay men indicated they were in a steady relationship. A 1992 study found that 56 percent of gay men and 71 percent of lesbians were in steady relationships (Singer & Deschamps, 1994). A more recent survey of gays and lesbians found that 87 percent of women and 52 percent of men were in monogamous relationships (Lever, 1995). With the continuation of the AIDS pandemic into the foreseeable future, it is likely that even more gays will choose to live with partners in a monogamous fashion (Driggs & Finn, 1990).

With increased attention being paid to homosexuality in the popular media, there is more awareness of lesbian and gay couples (Peplau, 1993). This, along with study by social scientists, has begun to provide a few models on which gay and lesbian couples can base their relationships. However, lesbian and gay couples frequently base their expectations on heterosexual modeling that may include one partner taking care of the other, or one partner being more feminine or masculine (McWhirter & Mattison, 1984). As products of society, gay men and women share the expectations and rules of opposite-sex couples and assume roles in relation to each other that are most often based on sex role expectations for heterosexual couples (Murphy, 1992).

> *Lesbians are socialized as women first, and gay men are socialized as men first. Men are taught to be assertive, competitive, and aggressive and to initiate sexual activity. Women are taught to be compliant, passive, and sexually exclusive. Given this conditioning, it is not uncommon for gay male couples to experience competition as a difficulty in relationships or for lesbian couples to have trouble with fusion and difficulty in separating. (Silberman & Hawkins, 1988, p. 106)*

Sex role expectations are changing dramatically, yet there are still only a few visible role models on which gay and lesbian couples can base their relationship. Gay and lesbian couples frequently express curiosity about how other same-sex couples deal with their everyday lives and address issues such as finances, outside relationships, family, and sex. Although the lack of modeling for gay and lesbian couples creates uncertainty about how to behave as a couple, the lack of societal guidelines for same-sex couples allows for creativity in establishing the ground rules in the relationship.

Most often, gay and lesbian couples bring concerns to counseling that are no different from the issues in heterosexual relationships. These may include differences in socioeconomic and family backgrounds, level of education, religious and value differences, communication problems, previous relationships, illness, financial issues, individual emotional problems, sexual dysfunction, and jealousy. Even though gay and lesbian couples confront the very same day-to-day concerns as any two people living together, "they do not have the social, legal or moral sanctions that sustain opposite-sex couples. Thus the development and maintenance of same-sex couples involves a commitment to a difficult process with many destructive internal and external forces in its path" (Forstein, 1986, p. 105).

Lesbian and gay male couples who live together as same gender partners do experience relationship problems unique to sexual orientation. McWhirter & Mattison (1984) identify ignorance, prejudice, oppression, and homophobia as issues that every gay couple must address. To fight these, counselors must assess the depth of these issues and the effect on the self-concept of the individuals involved. It may be helpful to suggest to clients that they gain accurate information about homosexuality through reading, videotapes, attendance at lectures, and other sources to help them fight these issues in society. As a corollary to these concerns, couples frequently disagree about how open to be about their sexual orientation. If one member of the couple is more out of the closet than the other, that presents problems for the relationship that need to be addressed in counseling.

Lesbian Couples

Lesbians typically seek out relationships that are characterized by deep emotional bonds and the sharing of intimacy at various levels. It is common for lesbian couples to go through a developmental process with each stage representing a continued commitment to generativity and collaboration (Clunis & Green, 1993; Slater, 1995). Partners strive to develop equity within the relationship, which is viewed by them as atypical of heterosexual relationships (Slater, 1995). Lesbian relationships show these relationship-nurturing traits because of the cultural messages women receive about the value of coupling and relationship bonding (Clunis & Green, 1993), the lack of sex role definition within lesbian relationships, and the freedom to establish roles without prescription.

Although there are many positive aspects regarding lesbian couples, there are also negative aspects of which the counselor needs to be aware when dealing with lesbian couples. Since lesbian relationships are not recognized socially or legally, problems are magnified when a lesbian couple has children (Browning, Reynolds, & Dworkin, 1991; Slater, 1995). Recall our chapter opening: Sally and Jennifer may face teachers who are uncomfortable working with or hostile toward two mothers. When couples break up, custody disputes arise, and the nonbiological mother may not be allowed visitation rights even though the couple may have been together for several years.

One of the major difficulties lesbian couples experience is the issue of intimacy versus autonomy (Browning et al., 1991). Lesbian couples can become so close that they experience fusion, and conflicts may arise regarding individual needs as opposed to relationship needs. Another common problem lesbian couples may experience is dealing with stage differences in "coming out" or individual development of identity. When one partner is totally open and the other one has not told her family, many conflicts can arise. Other stressors include monogamy versus nonmonogamy issues, sexual issues regarding desire and absence of, racial/cultural differences, and parenting issues (Browning et al., 1991).

Gay Male Couples

The custody issues, the degree of "outness," and the stresses identified for lesbian couples also apply for gay male couples. Another issue for gay male couples is the common fear that the relationship will not last and that gay men are incapable of intimacy. The lack of societal support for gay male relationships may be one reason that some relationships end prematurely. However, surveys have found that these stereotypes are not true and that indeed gay male couples do establish lasting intimate relationships (Blumstein & Schwartz, 1983; McWhirter & Mattison, 1984). Gay couples who do stay together in the face of the odds likely do so because they truly care for each other (Driggs & Finn, 1990).

McWhirter and Mattison (1984), in their pioneering effort, developed a descriptive and developmental model of gay male relationships in which they identify six stages that describe the tasks a male couple encounters as the relationship develops:

Stage 1.   Blending (year 1)
Stage 2.   Nesting (years 2 and 3)
Stage 3.   Maintaining (years 4 and 5)
Stage 4.   Building (years 6 through 10)
Stage 5.   Releasing (years 11 through 20)
Stage 6.   Renewing (beyond twenty years)

This model provides a basis for understanding that, although each relationship has a life of its own, a gay male relationship passes through predictable developmental stages. Counselors might use this model in counseling with gay couples to assess whether the couple is on "task" or whether one member of the couple has moved at a faster pace than the other. The accumulation of data and development of concepts pertinent to working with gay male couples is a recent phenomenon, and counselors would benefit from a careful perusal of the data as they develop.

Violence in Lesbian and Gay Male Couples

One serious problem that is being recognized in lesbian and gay couples is physical violence, abuse, and battering. There is limited research on this phenomena, but some suggest that there is approximately the same amount of battering in gay and lesbian couples as there is in heterosexual couples (Font, 1995). The dynamics within the abusive gay or lesbian relationship are similar to heterosexual relationships in that there is a loss of personal power, self-esteem, and control (Clunis & Green, 1993). However, violence between same-gender couples seems to concern authorities less, and because of the invisibility and lack of social support, it is difficult for those involved to seek intervention (Carl, 1992; Conley, 1995).

Gay men and lesbians batter because they want to exercise power over their partners. Individuals who batter have learned that violence is effective in getting their partners to comply with their wishes (Hart, 1989). The impact of battering on the victim can be profound, as a sense of fear, mistrust, and disillusionment takes over and closeness and equality in the relationship disappears. As in any issues of violence, the safety of the victim takes precedence over supporting the relationship or taking care of the current emotional needs (Hammond, 1989). Counselors need to be sensitive to these issues and help restore the integrity and self-worth of the victim in addition to examining issues with the abuser. Island and Letellier (1991) outline the following guidelines in helping victims of partner abuse:

1. Couple counseling is inappropriate and dangerous.
2. The counselor must understand domestic violence issues.
3. The counselor must be gay sensitive and/or gay affirmative.
4. The counselor must not use any theories to excuse or justify battering behavior.
5. The counselor must not view violence (especially male) as innate and natural.

Gay and Lesbian Families

Gays and lesbians are coupling, creating new families, having and rearing children and challenging society's definition of what "family" means. Sally and Jennifer, identified at the beginning of this chapter, are examples of a growing phenomenon in the United States. It is estimated that there are as many as 5 million lesbian mothers and 3 million gay fathers in the United States (Martin, 1993). Gay men and lesbians are choosing to have children and to raise them in redefined families. "The lesbian and gay baby boom is creating a culture of its own, evolving new definitions of family relationships" (Martin, 1993, p. 6).

Most of the difficulties of gay and lesbian parenting are similar to the stresses felt in heterosexual marriage and may include such issues as jealousy, time spent with children, privacy, and communication. However, gay and lesbian parents often confront added stressors. Coparenting a child is frequently exacerbated by the couple's inability to become legal stepparents. Gay and lesbian couples who wish to adopt children will find it difficult; currently very few gay or lesbian couples in the United States have been granted legal adoptions of children. In some divorce situations, concerns arise about custody and visitation rights of the gay parent to his or her child. Many states discriminate against gay individuals in awarding child custody, and in some states being gay is reason enough to be considered an unfit parent. On a positive note, Alaska, Oregon, Washington, California, Michigan, Indiana, South Carolina, New York, Connecticut, New Jersey, and Massachusetts laws state that sexual orientation is not relevant in custody disputes (Singer & Deschamps, 1994). The laws concerning the rights of gay and lesbian parents are filled with contradictions, and efforts need to be mobilized to change some of the existing laws (Benkov, 1994). Counselors, at the least, need to be aware of the statutes in their states and help clients find supportive legal assistance. Some counselors may want to consider being more proactive and assisting gay and lesbian clients to obtain more legal rights.

Other issues that arise for gay parents include concerns about coming out to the wife or husband, to children, and to other family members. Issues of coming out are also pertinent to the children of gay and lesbian parents. These children will need to grieve the loss of their heterosexual parent, resolve conflicts between their love for their parent and social standards, examine their own fears about being gay or lesbian, and decide whether to tell their friends. Some children may choose to hide their parent's sexuality from friends because they fear a negative response. These issues of coming out are very delicate and intricate, as described in an earlier section, and must be considered in the framework of the developmental history of the individual.

Religious Issues

Gays and lesbians who are raised in families affiliated with a religious denomination often confront conflicting values between their sexual orientation and their religion. Since the twelfth century, there has been hostility directed toward individuals of same-gender orientation (O'Neill & Ritter, 1992). Frequently religious beliefs include the idea that sex between people of the same gender runs counter to God's plan. Such religious doctrine makes it difficult for the gay person to live authentically in the religious world. If a gay person is unable to actively participate in spiritual and religious dimensions of life without oppression and confusion, then this issue may need to be addressed in counseling (Fortunato, 1983).

Gay clients frequently come to counseling with the belief that there is no place for them in their religion and that they are "sinners," "black sheep," or "unwanted." Some have been excommunicated from the church; others have not been allowed to marry; some have been denied ordination. Client distress manifests itself in anger toward the church, and feelings of personal shame and guilt. Clients need an opportunity to discuss the options available to them and to decide whether to remain affiliated with the religion of their family, seek a new religious affiliation, or pursue other avenues to meet their spiritual needs. Gays who remain in a nonaccepting church need to learn how to balance the negative views of the church and their sexual orientation.

Most major denominations now have gay church groups affiliated with them (see the chapter appendix). These groups include Dignity (Catholic), Integrity (Episcopal), Affirmation (United Methodist), Affirmation (Mormon), Evangelicals Concerned, Friends for Lesbian and Gay Concerns (Quakers), Kinship (Adventist), Lutherans Concerned (Lutheran), Seventh Day Adventist Kinship International, Gay Synagogue (Jewish), and Unitarian Universalists for Lesbian/Gay Concerns. The Metropolitan Community Church is a nondenominational gay church that has services nationwide. Also, many individuals in church groups are striving to rectify the homophobia within their church by establishing "affirming" or "welcoming" congregations that are inclusive of gays, lesbians, and bisexuals.

As counselors work with clients about religious beliefs and sexual orientation, they must be aware of their own religious value system and beliefs. Counselors who have been raised in a denomination that discriminates against gays will have to either move beyond these homophobic and heterosexist beliefs or refer to counselors who are gay supportive to help clients address these difficult issues.

Drug and Alcohol Abuse

There is a widely held assumption by mental health professionals that drug and alcohol abuse is quite high in the gay and lesbian community. Some have stated that alcoholism is the number one health problem among gay men and lesbians (Kus, 1987). The research in this area is sparse and contains methodological limitations (Paul, Stall, & Bloomfield, 1991). However, the available research does suggest that approximately 20–30 percent of gay men and lesbians are chemically dependent on alcohol or drugs (Clunis & Green, 1993; Kus, 1990; Lohrenz, Connely, Coyne, & Spare, 1978; Paul et al., 1991).

Research has shown that internalized homophobia may explain the etiology and the high incidence of alcoholism in gay American men (Kus, 1987) and lesbians (Browning et al., 1991). Gays and lesbians tend to misuse alcohol or drugs to ameliorate their feelings related to societal rejection, alienation, and stress (Deevey & Wall, 1992). Although the substance abuse may result from a lack of a positive identity, counselors cannot help resolve the underlying problem until the substance abuse has stopped. Chet, the lawyer who entered a treatment program for cocaine abuse, must be clean and sober in order to address the issues that surround leading a double life.

The sexual orientation of the client should not affect the quality of treatment services provided by chemical dependency professionals. With such a high incidence of chemical abuse among gay, lesbian, and bisexual clients, treatment centers need to address sexual orientation issues with clients. One suggested method is to ask clients about their sexual orientation in a routine and nonjudgmental manner during the treatment intake session. Asking gives the clients the choice about whether to reveal sexual orientation. Asking the question also allows clients to be less worried about when they will be "found out," because it sends a message that sexual orientation is a legitimate issue (Finnegan & McNally, 1987). Gay, lesbian, and bisexual clients who come to treatment may be experiencing heightened shame and guilt. Therefore it is important to approach questions about sexuality in routine ways that indicate to clients that any answers are acceptable. "If the question is not posed, the gay or lesbian client may feel heterosexuality is assumed and homosexuality is possibly unacceptable in this setting" (Finnegan & McNally, 1987, p. 61). Not asking about sexual orientation may indicate that the agency is not sensitive to gay issues and the underlying feelings of gay clients.

Similarly, too often lesbians, gay men, and bisexuals have sought treatment for relationship difficulties, depression, or anxiety and never reported their chemical abuse, nor have they been asked (Faltz, 1992). Intake and assessment procedures with all gay clients should include questions about drinking and using.

Self-help groups, a necessary adjunct to counseling chemically dependent individuals, are available for gays and lesbians in most cities. These include Alcoholics Anonymous, Narcotics Anonymous, Valium Anonymous, and Cocaine Anonymous. Counselors need to know about local gay-friendly self-help groups and make appropriate referrals.

AIDS

Acquired immunodeficiency syndrome (AIDS), first identified in 1981, is a usually fatal disease for which there is no known cure or immunization. Gay men were initially the hardest hit group in the United States. As a result, homophobia and stigma became intertwined with the first responses to AIDS. Initially, AIDS was popularly referred to as the "gay disease" and as the Wrath of God, or WOG (McLaughlin, 1989). One writer observed that "in some quarters the misapprehension exists that AIDS is caused by homosexuality, not a retrovirus" (Brandt, 1988, p. 165). Today this is still true to some extent, and the association of AIDS with gay men has created a secondary epidemic of prejudice, fear, and ignorance (House, Eicken, & Gray, 1995). These continuing responses have led to discrimination against those with AIDS and those who are suspected of having AIDS. Such discrimination is found nationwide in housing, insurance, employment, child custody, and health care (Cohen & Wiseberg, 1990; NGLTF, 1995).

Counselors need to recognize that these external factors have a profound impact on all gays and to also understand the individual behavioral manifestations caused by AIDS. Significant psychological reactions such as depression, anxiety, and anger often result from finding out that you are HIV positive. Fears of death and dying, isolation, disclosure of sexual orientation to family and community, contagion issues, hopelessness, loss of self-esteem, and an increase in internalized homophobia are common responses to the diagnosis of AIDS (Lima, Lo Presto, Sherman, & Sobleman, 1993). There are often efforts to keep the HIV/AIDS diagnosis a secret from particular family members or from people outside the family due to fears of rejection.

It is also important to note that all gay men have been profoundly affected by the AIDS epidemic. Uninfected gay men, the survivors, face severe psychological stress as they have spent the last fifteen years wrapped up in the epidemic. "In many cases, HIV-negative gay men have a psychological experience—a personal and social identity—that is more like that of a sick or dying man" (Odets, 1995, p. 14). Denial, guilt, loss, depression, and anxiety are common reactions of surviving gay men who have lost countless friends and acquaintances to AIDS.

Counselors are in a pivotal position to address the current issues related to AIDS by acting as agents of change in schools, churches, community agencies, government programs, treatment centers, and private practice. They can assess and assist with the "enormous emotional needs" of the friends and family of PLWAs—people living with AIDS (Greif & Porembski, 1989, p. 79). Counselors can also provide accurate information about AIDS to clients and family members, professional colleagues, and the communities where they live and work. To do this effectively, counselors need to present the message that it is an individual's behavior, not belonging to a particular group, that puts a person at risk. This message must also be presented in way that is "completely affirming of gay sexuality and the gay client's identity" (Klotz, 1995, p. 231).

Counselors must be prepared to take risks as advocates for PLWAs and their families in order to guarantee competent and compassionate treatment. Such risks include (1) nonjudgmental confrontation of beliefs based on ignorance and behavior grounded in prejudice and bigotry, (2) taking the leadership in AIDS education and prevention strategies, (3) challenging misstatements about AIDS and gays whenever they occur, (4) providing accurate factual information, (5) encouraging the reconsideration of uninformed opinions, and (6) educating clients by discussing safer sex practices and the dangers of sharing needles during drug use.

AIDS has caused people to talk about sex and death, two subjects that people in our society avoid. It has helped bring gays, sex, and death out of the closet. "The multiple threats of significant health problems, issues of death and dying, coping with the fear associated with AIDS, and social backlash related to AIDS present complex and difficult issues for which counselor support is critical" (House et al., 1995, p. 5). Compassionate and gay-affirmative counselors can help sort through the myriad of issues presented by AIDS.

Loneliness, Guilt, Depression, and Suicide

Many gays experience loneliness, depression, anxiety, guilt, anger, and/or suicidal thoughts as a result of the dissonance between their feelings and society's proscriptions. These conflicts are much the same as those experienced by all members of society. But many gays experience a greater depth of feeling and an absence of hope of resolving the conflicts (Fortunato, 1983). Great anxiety and loneliness come from realizing that there may never be support from parents, siblings, family members, or loved ones. Life can be extremely painful to gays who have lost friends or a job or their church membership because of their sexual orientation. These feelings of loss must either be avoided, fought, or worked through. Counselors need to assist gay clients in working through the stages of loss that are inherent to being gay in a heterocentric culture. The following stages provide a structure when assisting clients with these issues.

Denial/Bargaining

Gay clients in this stage remain closeted and secretive. Frequently they have feelings of paranoia, are depressed, have phobic reactions, and are alcohol or drug abusers. They may recognize societal oppression, but refuse to deal with it. They will bargain with themselves about being gay, make excuses for their behavior, and deny their sexual orientation even though they may be engaging in same-sex behavior. They are caught in a codependent phase, making excuses for their behavior and defending the people who are oppressing and rejecting them. Counselors need to confront the denial and direct the focus to the source of the oppression.

Anger

Clients who are in the anger stage frequently address their anger outwardly in the form of protests, marches, letter writing, or circulating petitions. This can be a very positive use of anger. However, if they simply express their anger without addressing the source of the anger, they may become rigid, defensive, and closed. Anger can also be directed toward oneself and is often related to the shame and guilt that the individual feels about being gay. This inward expression of anger is often associated with loneliness and suicidal ideation. Counselors need to work carefully with clients in this stage, help them express their anger in appropriate ways, and eventually work through the anger.

Depression

Individuals who are in extreme denial and live totally in the closet isolate themselves from other gays and have minimal social and sexual contacts. These individuals have ingested the fear of being gay and internalized the oppression of society. Gays who are depressed may be suicidal, drink and use too much, and engage in self-pity. They see society as "right" and themselves as "wrong." Counselors need to address the feelings of shame and guilt and encourage clients to take responsibility for themselves rather than blaming society and the people in their life for the awful state of "their world." It is also important to note that the depression may not be related to sexual orientation and may be caused by other issues or events in the client's life.

Acceptance/Integration

In this stage, individuals begin to accept and integrate sexual orientation into their life. In this process, individuals need to stop asking "Why me?" stop denying their sexual orientation, and relate to others in an open and caring manner. Individuals in this stage begin to look beyond the expectations that other people will affirm them, and look for self-affirmation. This involves taking a public step and proactively assuming responsibility for their lives. When these steps are taken, "energy that has been locked within can be released and reinvested elsewhere" (O'Neill & Ritter, 1992, p. 145). Counselors need to be encouraging and supportive in this process.

Reformulating/Transformation

After taking a public step, individuals often experience a new-found freedom. The energy that has been consumed by their maintaining a false public self is now available for more creative endeavors. This new centeredness permits individuals to live more spontaneously and move beyond their loss (O'Neill & Ritter, 1992). This reformulating and transformation expands insight and vision and allows individuals to lead more productive and fulfilling lives.

Moving from a lonely or depressed state to healing and productivity is a complex process, and counselor support is crucial. Counselors need to be warm, accepting, and nonjudgmental as gay, lesbian, and bisexual clients work through these processes.

Professional Directions

The attitudes of counseling professionals toward gay men and lesbians have changed dramatically over the years. In 1973, the American Psychiatric Association stopped labeling homosexuality as a form of mental illness. The American Psychological Association did the same in 1975. The assumption associated with these changes was that counseling practices would be modified to reflect a view of homosexuality as an acceptable lifestyle (Corey, Corey, & Callanan, 1988). Today more and more counselors hold positive attitudes toward gays, lesbians, and bisexuals, but a 1990 study found that a large and diverse sample of psychologists held negative biases and misinformation about gays and lesbians (Garnets & Kimmel, 1993). Some counselors believe "that homosexuality necessarily indicates the presence of psychopathology" (Hancock, 1995, p. 400). These negative stances toward gays, lesbians, and bisexuals oppose the current ethical standards and practices of the profession.

Counselors should deliberately create a gay-affirmative approach that validates sexual orientation; recognizes the oppression of gays, lesbians, and bisexuals; and actively helps them overcome its external and internal effects (Fassinger, 1991). To be gay affirmative is to value homosexuality and heterosexuality equally as natural or normal attributes (Fassinger, 1991; Krajeski, 1986). This approach is proactive in nature and helps restore options to our clients.

Many professional organizations have developed a gay and lesbian task force, committee, or division to provide support for counseling professionals and a positive direction for counseling with gays and lesbians. Division 44, the Society of the Psychological Study of Lesbian and Gay Issues of the American Psychological Association (APA), and the Association of Gay, Lesbian, and Bisexual Concerns of the American Counseling Association (ACA) are examples of efforts to support gay and lesbian concerns within professional organizations.

Until recently it was assumed that heterosexuality was the only suitable orientation for therapists (Rochlin, 1985). However, publicly identified gay male and lesbian mental health professionals are growing in number. Gay professionals who come out serve as an important resource both for the gay community and for other counselors. They also provide a role model for gays, lesbians, and bisexuals and security for those who want to see a gay professional (Woodman & Lenna, 1980). Since identification with the therapist is one of the key elements that produces change in clients, it is important for gay, lesbian, and bisexual counselors to publicly identify themselves.

Conclusion

Before counselors can work effectively with gay, lesbian, and bisexual clients, they must confront the cultural homophobia and heterosexism in our society. Many counselors have absorbed misinformation and myths about homosexuality. For example, many counselors function under the myth that all clients are heterosexual. A question such as "When did you first know you were gay?" has a heterosexual bias. It could just as easily be asked, "When did you first know you were straight?" When counselors believe and act on myths about gays, they do a disservice to gay, lesbian, and bisexual clients.

The lack of practical knowledge about gays and the gay lifestyle is a major obstacle to satisfactory counseling. Therefore the first responsibility for counselors is to educate themselves about the unique concerns of gays, lesbians, and bisexuals. This step includes learning about laws, policies, and practices that affect lesbian, gay, and bisexual people and educating yourself about gay and lesbian culture and community norms. Counselors can do this most easily by meeting and talking with gay people. Such face-to-face meetings will likely dispel the myths and preconceived ideas about gays. It is also important for counselors to read gay-affirmative books and periodicals and learn about available resources for gays. The reference list at the end of this chapter and the resource list in the appendix offer current sources of information.

It is crucial that therapists recognize that they may be seen as the representatives of a hostile society, or as authority figures with a heavily weighted opinion. Some gay men, lesbians, and bisexuals avoid counseling because they fear rejection if they reveal their sexual orientation. Each counselor must counter these expectations with an expressed awareness of the issues facing the gay or lesbian client and an openness to the concerns expressed. Counselors have the responsibility to let clients know that they will listen. They can do this by having books about gays, lesbians, and bisexuals visibly placed on bookshelves, posting supportive articles about gay issues on bulletin boards, seeing that gay articles get placed in the school newspaper, and by rejecting and challenging antigay language and jokes.

It is also important to be an ally for gays, lesbians, and bisexuals by promoting the acceptance and understanding of gays and lesbians (Dworkin & Gutierrez, 1992; Washington & Evans, 1991). As allies in the communities in which they live, counselors can support public and institutional policy decisions that affect gays, lesbians, and bisexuals. They can encourage tolerance in educational and religious settings, and advocate for nondiscriminatory measures. Counselors must not ignore the cultural and societal context in which their clients live, and they need to support clients in their struggles to transcend cultural homophobia and heterosexism.

Professional counselors are in a powerful position to help gays recognize and accept their sexual identity, improve their interpersonal and social functioning, and value themselves while living in a predominantly heterocentric society. Counselors who are sensitive to sexual orientation issues, who have examined and challenged the heterosexist and homophobic assumptions of our culture, and who have confronted their own values, can assist all clients, whatever their sexual orientation.

Summary

In the last twenty-five years, individuals who identify themselves as gay, lesbian, or bisexual have become increasingly visible in our society. These individuals face specific stresses resulting from the hostility and negative attitudes regarding homosexuality that many in our society still hold. With the increasing visibility, there has also been an increasing polarization of attitudes toward the gay community. Some individuals and groups have instigated antigay measures to deny the civil rights of gays, lesbians, and bisexuals. These prejudicial attitudes regarding homosexuality include cultural homophobia, which can be defined as a fear or dread of individuals who identify themselves as gay, lesbian, or bisexual, and cultural heterosexism, which is the assumption of social normality and superiority by heterosexuals. The stresses of living with this hostility and anger must be understood and responded to by counselors. To do this effectively, counselors must first be aware of and address their own prejudices regarding homosexuality.

For gay, lesbian, and bisexuals clients, their sexual orientation may or may not be the main issue they wish to address in counseling. These individuals face the same life problems as anyone else and may not appreciate a counselor's assumption that the issue of sexual orientation is of more significance than other personal issues. However, for many clients, their sexual orientation does create intensified stresses and conflicts that they may wish to address with a counselor. The issue of coming out, or deciding to make public their sexual orientation, is a process that can be particularly stressful. Counselors can assist clients struggling with such decisions by helping the client to understand the stages of the coming-out process and the risk and problems associated with each stage.

Counselors working with gay, lesbian, and bisexual clients should be sensitive to concerns such as relationship issues, identity dysfunctions, drug and alcohol abuse, AIDS, and family issues. Gays, lesbians, and bisexuals are creating families of choice and may need assistance in understanding how to address the issues of living in their communities. To do this, counselors need to gain knowledge of sexual orientation issues and the community resources available for gay, lesbian, and bisexual clients. Gay-supportive counselors not only accept their gay, lesbian, and bisexual clients, but they also advocate for them in their communities.

References

A special report: Gays in America. (1989, June.) *San Francisco Examiner*, pp. 1–78.

Anderson, D. A. (1995). Lesbian and gay adolescents: Social and developmental considerations. In G. Unks (Ed.), *The gay teen: Educational practice and theory for lesbian, gay, and bisexual adolescents* (pp. 17–28). New York: Routledge.

Avoiding heterosexual bias in language. (1991). *American Psychologist, 46,* 973–974.

Benkov, L. (1994). *Reinventing the family: The emerging story of lesbian and gay parents.* New York: Crown Publishers.

Betz, N. E., & Fitzgerald, L. F. (1993). Individuality and diversity: Theory and research in counseling psychology. *Annual Review of Psychology, 44,* 343–381.

Blumenfeld, W. J. (1992). *Homophobia: How we all pay the price.* Boston: Beacon.

Blumenfeld, W. J., & Raymond, D. (1988). *Looking at gay and lesbian life.* Boston: Beacon.

Blumstein, P., & Schwartz, P. (1983). *American couples.* New York: Morrow.

Brandt, A. M. (1988). AIDS: From social history to social policy. In E. Fee & D. M. Fox (Eds.), *AIDS: The burdens of history* (pp. 147–171). Berkeley: University of California.

Browning, C., Reynolds, A. L., & Dworkin, S. H. (1991). Affirmative psychotherapy for lesbian women. *Counseling Psychologist, 19,* 177–196.

Buhrke, R. A. (1989). Incorporating lesbian and gay issues into counselor training: A resource guide. *Journal of Counseling and Development, 68,* 77–80.

Burr, C. (1993, March). Homosexuality and biology. *Atlantic Monthly, 271,* 47–65.

Byne, W. (1994, May). The biological evidence challenged. *Scientific American, 270,* 50–55.

Carl, D. (1992). *Counseling same-sex couples.* New York: Norton.

Cass, V. C. (1984). Homosexual identity formation: A concept in need of definition. *Journal of Homosexuality, 10,* 105–126.

Clunis, D. M., & Green, G. D. (1993). *Lesbian couples.* Seattle: Seal Press.

Cohen, R., & Wiseberg, L. S. (1990). *Double jeopardy—threat to life and human rights: Discrimination against persons with AIDS.* Cambridge, MA: Human Rights Internet.

Coleman, E. (1985). Developmental stages of the coming out process. In J. C. Gonsiorek (Ed.), *A guide to psychotherapy with gay and lesbian clients* (pp. 31–43). New York: Harrington Park Press.

Colgan, P. (1987). Treatment of identity and intimacy issues in gay males. *Journal of Homosexuality, 14,* 101–123.

Conley, B. (1995, October). Battering in same-sex couples. *In the Family, 1*(2), 23–24.

Corey, G., Corey, M. S., & Callanan, P. (1988). *Issues and ethics in the helping profession* (3rd ed.). Pacific Grove, CA: Brooks/Cole.

D'Augelli, A. R., & Garnets, L. D. (1995). Lesbian, gay, and bisexual communities. In A. R.

D'Augelli & C. J. Patterson (Eds.), *Lesbian, gay, and bisexual identities over the lifespan: Psychological perspectives* (pp. 295–320). New York: Oxford University Press.

Deevey, S., & Wall, L. J. (1992). How do lesbian women develop serenity? *Health Care for Women International, 74,* 239–247.

Driggs, J. H., & Finn, S. E. (1990). *Intimacy between men: How to find and keep gay love relationships.* New York: Dutton.

Dworkin, S. H., & Gutierrez, F. (1989). Introduction to special issue. Counselors be aware: Clients come in every size, shape, color, and sexual orientation. *Journal of Counseling and Development, 68,* 6–8

Dworkin, S. H., & Gutierrez, F. (1992). Epilogue: Where do we go from here? In S. Dworkin & F. Gutierrez (Eds.), *Counseling gay men and lesbians: Journey to the end of the rainbow* (pp. 335–339). Alexandria, VA: American Counseling Association.

Falco, K. (1987). *Psychotherapy with lesbian clients: A manual for the psychotherapist.* Unpublished doctoral dissertation, Oregon Graduate School of Professional Psychology, Pacific University, Forest Grove.

Faltz, B. G. (1992). Counseling chemically dependent lesbians and gay men. In S. Dworkin & F. Gutierrez (Eds.), *Counseling gay men and lesbians: Journey to the end of the rainbow* (pp. 245–258). Alexandria, VA: American Counseling Association.

Fassinger, R. E. (1991). The hidden minority: Issues and challenges in working with lesbian women and gay men. *Counseling Psychologist, 19,* 157–176.

Finnegan, D. G., & McNally, E. B. (1987). *Dual identities: Counseling chemically dependent gay men and lesbians.* Center City, MN: Hazelden Educational Materials.

Font, R. (1995, October). Commentary on battering in same-sex couples. *In the family, 1*(2), 24–25.

Forstein, M. (1986). Psychodynamic psychotherapy with gay male couples. In T. S. Stein & C. J. Cohen (Eds.), *Contemporary perspectives on psychotherapy with lesbians and gay men* (pp. 103–137). New York: Plenum Press.

Fortunato, J. E. (1983). *Embracing the exile: Healing journey of gay Christians.* New York: Seabury.

Fox, R. C. (1995). Bisexual identities. In A. R. D'Augelli & C. J. Patterson (Eds.), *Lesbian, gay, and bisexual identities over the lifespan: Psychological perspectives* (pp. 48–86). New York: Oxford University Press.

Garnets, L. D., & Kimmel, D. C. (1993). Introduction: Lesbian and gay male dimensions in the psychological study of human diversity. In L. D. Garnets & D. C. Kimmel (Eds.), *Psychological perspectives on lesbian and gay male experiences* (pp. 1–51). New York: Columbia University Press.

Greif, G. L., & Porembski, E. (1989). Implications for therapy with significant others of persons with AIDS. *Journal of Gay and Lesbian Psychotherapy, 1,* 79–86.

Hammond, N. (1989). Lesbian victims of relationship violence. In E. D. Rothblum & E. Cole (Eds.), *Lesbianism: Affirming nontraditional roles.* New York: Haworth Press.

Hancock, K. A. (1995). Psychotherapy with lesbians and gay men. In A. R. D'Augelli & C. J. Patterson (Eds.), *Lesbian, gay, and bisexual identities over the lifespan: Psychological perspectives* (pp. 398–432). New York: Oxford University Press.

Hart, B. (1989). Lesbian battering: An examination. In K. Lobel (Ed.), *Naming the violence: Speaking out about lesbian battering.* Seattle: Seal Press.

Herek, G. M. (1993). The context of antigay violence: Notes on cultural and psychological heterosexism. In L. D. Garnets & D. C. Kimmel (Eds.), *Psychological perspectives on lesbian and gay male experiences* (pp. 89–107). New York: Columbia University Press.

Herek, G. M. (1994). Psychological heterosexism in the United States. In A. R. D'Augelli & C. J. Patterson (Eds.), *Lesbian, gay, and bisexual identities over the lifespan: Psychological perspectives* (pp. 321–346). New York: Oxford University Press.

House, R. M., Eicken, S., & Gray, L. A. (1995). A national survey of AIDS training in counselor education programs. *Journal of Counseling and Development, 74,* 5–11.

House, R. M., & Tyler, V. (1992). Group counseling with gays and lesbians. In D. Capuzzi and D. Gross (Eds.), *Introduction to group counseling* (pp. 183–204). Denver: Love Publishing.

Island, D., & Letellier P. (1991). *Men who beat the men who love them: Battered gay men and domestic violence.* New York: Haworth Press.

Johnston, M. W., & Bell, A. P. (1995). Romantic emotional attachment: Additional factors in the development of the sexual orientation of men. *Journal of Counseling and Development, 73,* 621–625.

Jung, P. B., & Smith, R. F. (1993). *Heterosexism: An ethical challenge.* Albany: State University of New York Press.

Kinsey, A., Pomeroy, W. B., & Martin, C. E. (1948). *Sexual behavior in the human male.* Philadelphia: Saunders.

Kinsey, A., Pomeroy, W. B., Martin, C. E., & Gebhard, R. H. (1953). *Sexual behavior in the human female.* Philadelphia: Saunders.

Klein, F. (1993). *The bisexual option.* New York: Harrington Park Press.

Klotz, D. E. (1995). Safer sex maintenance and reinforcement for gay men. In W. Odets & M. Shernoff (Eds.), *The second decade of AIDS: A mental health practice handbook.* New York: Hatherleigh Press.

Krajeski, J. P. (1986). Psychotherapy with gay men and lesbians: A history of controversy. In T. S. Stein & C. J. Cohen (Eds.), *Contemporary perspectives on psychotherapy with lesbians and gay men* (pp. 9–25). New York: Plenum Press.

Kus, R. J. (1987). Alcoholics Anonymous and gay American men. *Journal of Homosexuality, 14,* 253–276.

Kus, R. J. (1990). *Keys to Caring: Assisting your gay & lesbian clients.* Boston: Alyson Publications.

Levay, S., & Hamer, D. H. (1994, May). Evidence for a biological influence in male homosexuality. *Scientific American, 270,* 44–49.

Lever, J. (1995, August 22). The 1995 Advocate survey of sexuality and relationships: The women. *Advocate,* pp. 23–30.

Lewis, L. A. (1984). The coming out process for lesbians: Integrating a stable identity. *Journal of the National Association of Social Workers, 29,* 464–469.

Lima, G., Lo Presto, C., Sherman, M., & Sobleman, S. (1993). The relationship between homophobia and self-esteem in gay males with AIDS. *Journal of Homosexuality, 25(4),* 69–76.

Lohrenz, L. J., Connely, J. C., Coyne, L., & Spare, K. E. (1978). Alcohol problems in several midwestern homosexual communities. *Journal of Studies on Alcohol, 39,* 1959–1963.

Markowitz, L. M. (1991, January–February). Homosexuality: Are we still in the dark? *Family Networker, 15(1),* 27–35.

Martin, A. (1993). *The lesbian and gay parenting handbook: Creating and raising our families.* New York: HarperCollins.

McLaughlin, L. (1989). AIDS: An overview. In P. O'Malley (Ed.), *The AIDS epidemic: Private rights and the public interest* (pp. 15–35). Boston: Beacon Press.

McWhirter, D. P., & Mattison, A. M. (1984). *The male couple: How relationships develop.* Englewood Cliffs, NJ: Prentice Hall.

Mollenkott, V. R. (1985). *Breaking the silence, overcoming the fear: Homophobia education.* Available from the Program Agency, United Presbyterian Church, U.S.A., 475 Riverside Drive, Room 1101, New York, NY 10015.

Money, J. (1987). Sin, sickness, or status? Homosexual gender identity and psychoneuroendocrinology. *American Psychologist, 42,* 384–399.

Morin, S. F., & Rothblum, E. D. (1991). Removing the stigma: Fifteen years of progress. *American Psychologist, 46,* 947–949.

Moses, A. E., & Hawkins, R. O. (1985). Two-hour in-service training session in homophobia. In H. Hidalgo, T. Peterson, & N. J. Woodman (Eds.), *Lesbian and gay issues: A resource manual for social workers* (pp. 152–157). Silver Springs, MD: National Association of Social Workers.

Murphy, B. C. (1992). Counseling lesbian couples: Sexism, heterosexism, and homophobia. In S. Dworkin & F. Gutierrez (Eds.), *Counseling gay men and lesbians: Journey to the end of the rainbow* (pp. 63–79). Alexandria, VA: American Counseling Association.

National Association of Social Workers (NASW). (1985). *Lesbian and gay issues: A resource manual for social workers.* Washington, DC: Author.

National Gay & Lesbian Task Force (NGLTF). (1995, March). *Antigay/lesbian violence in 1994: National trends, analysis and incident summaries.* (Code No. 060). Washington, DC: Author.

Norton, J. (1995). The gay, lesbian, bisexual populations. In N. A. Vacc, S. Devaney, & J. Wittmer (Eds.), *Experiencing and counseling multicultural and diverse populations* (3rd ed., pp. 147–177). Bristol, PA: Accelerated Development.

Odets, W. (1995). *In the shadow of the epidemic: Being HIV-negative in the age of AIDS.* Durham, NC: Duke University Press.

O'Neill, C., & Ritter, K. (1992). *Coming out within: Stages of spiritual awakening for lesbians and gay men.* San Francisco, CA: Harper.

Paul, J. P., Stall, R., & Bloomfield, K. A. (1991). Gay and alcoholic: Epidemiologic and clinical issues. *Alcohol Health & Research World, 15*(2), 151–160.

Peplau, L. A. (1993). Lesbian and gay relationships. In L. D. Garnets & D. C. Kimmel (Eds.), *Psychological perspectives on lesbian and gay male experiences* (pp. 395–419). New York: Columbia University Press.

Riddle, D. I., & Sang, B. (1978). Psychotherapy with lesbians. *Journal of Social Issues, 34*(3), 84–100.

Ritter, K. Y., & O'Neill, C. W. (1989). Moving through loss: The spiritual journey of gay men and lesbian women. *Journal of Counseling and Development, 68,* 9–15.

Rochlin, M. (1985). Sexual orientation of the therapist and therapeutic effectiveness with gay clients. In J. C. Gonsiorek (Ed.), *A guide to psychotherapy with gay and lesbian clients* (pp. 21–29). New York: Harrington Park Press.

Rubenstein, W. B. (Ed.). (1993). Lesbians, gay men, and the law. New York: New Press.

Silberman, B. O., & Hawkins, R. O., Jr. (1988). Lesbian women and gay men: Issues for counseling. In E. Weinstein & E. Rosen (Eds.), *Sexuality counseling: Issues and implications* (pp. 101–113). Pacific Grove, CA: Brooks/Cole.

Silverstein, C. (1981). *Man to man: Gay couples in America.* New York: Morrow.

Singer, B., & Deschamps, D. (Eds.). (1994). *Gay and lesbian stats: A pocket guide of facts and figures.* New York: New Press.

Slater, S. (1995). *The lesbian family life cycle.* New York: Free Press.

Sophie, J. (1987). Internalized homophobia and lesbian identity. *Journal of Homosexuality, 14,* 53–65.

Stein, T. S., & Cohen, C. J. (1986). *Contemporary perspectives on psychotherapy with lesbians and gay men.* New York: Plenum Press.

Troiden, R. R. (1989). The formation of homosexual identities. In G. Herdt (Ed.), *Gay and lesbian youth* (pp. 43–73). New York: Harrington Park Press.

Washington, J., & Evans, N. J. (1991). Becoming an ally. In N. J. Evans & V. A. Wall (Eds.), *Beyond tolerance: Gays, lesbians and bisexuals on campus* (pp. 195–204). Alexandria, VA: American Association for Counseling and Development Press.

Weinberg, G. (1973). *Society and the healthy homosexual.* Garden City, NY: Anchor Books.

Weston, K. (1991). *Families we choose: Lesbians, gays, kinship.* New York: Columbia University Press.

White, M. (1995). *Stranger at the gate: To be gay and Christian in America.* New York: Penguin.

Wilson, J. D. (1992, September 14). Gays under fire. *Newsweek, 120,* 35–41.

Wolf, T. J. (1992). Bisexuality: A counseling perspective. In S. Dworkin & F. Gutierrez (Eds.), *Counseling gay men and lesbians: Journey to the end of the rainbow* (pp. 175–187). Alexandria, VA: American Counseling Association.

Woodman, N., & Lenna, H. (1980). *Counseling with gay men and women.* San Francisco: Jossey-Bass.

Appendix: Resources on Gay, Lesbian, and Bisexual Issues

Professional Organizations

Association for Gay, Lesbian, and Bisexual Issues in Counseling (AGLBIC)
P.O. Box 216
Jenkintown, PA 19046

Association of Lesbian and Gay Psychologists
2336 Market Street, #8
San Francisco, CA 94114

Committee on Lesbian and Gay Issues
National Association of Social Workers
750 First Street, NE
Washington, DC 20002
(202) 408–8600 Ext. 287

National Association of Lesbian and Gay Alcoholism Professionals (NALGAP)
204 West 20th Street
New York, NY 10011

Society for the Psychological Study of Lesbian and Gay Issues
c/o American Psychological Association
750 First Street, NE
Washington, DC 20002
(202) 366–6037

Information and Referral

Federation of Parents and Friends of Lesbians and Gays, Inc. (PFLAG)
P.O. Box 27605
Washington, DC 20038
(202) 638–4200

Gay and Lesbian Outreach to Elders
1853 Market Street
San Francisco, CA 94103
(415) 552–1997

Gay Men's Health Crisis
Box 274
132 West 24th Street
New York, NY 10011
(212) 807–7660

Human Rights Campaign
1101 14th Street NW, Suite 200
Washington, DC 20005
(202) 628–4160

Lambda Legal Defense and Education Fund
132 West 43rd Street
New York, NY 10036
(212) 995–8585

National Gay and Lesbian Task Force
Gay Organizations Mailing List
2320 17th Street NW
Washington, DC 20009
(202) 332–6483

National Gay and Lesbian Families Project
1517 U Street, NW
Washington, DC 20009
(202) 332–6483

Religious Organizations

Affirmation (Gay and Lesbian Mormons)
Box 46022
Los Angeles, CA 90046
(213) 255–7251

Affirmation (United Methodists for Gay and Lesbian Concerns)
Box 1021
Evanston, IL 60204
(708) 475–0499

American Baptists Concerned
872 Erie Street
Oakland, CA 94610–2268
(510) 465–8652

Dignity, USA
1500 Massachusetts Avenue, NW, Suite 11
Washington, DC 20005
(202) 861–0017

Evangelicals Concerned
c/o Dr. Ralph Blair
311 East 72nd, #1G
New York, NY 10021
(212) 517–3171

Friends for Lesbian and Gay Concerns (Quakers)
Box 222
Sumneytown, PA 18084
(215) 234–8424

GBF (Gay Baha'i Fellowship)
P.O. Box 2623
Ashville, NC 28802
(704) 274–5671 (fax)

GLAD Gay and Lesbian Affirming Disciples)
Christian Church (Disciples of Christ)
Box 19223
Indianapolis, IN 46219–1223
(206) 324–6231

Integrity (Episcopalian)
P.O. Box 19561
Washington, DC 20036–0561
(201) 868–2485

Lutherans Concerned/North America
Box 10461
Chicago, IL 60610–0461

National Gay Pentecostal Alliance
P.O. Box 1391
Schenectady, NY 12301–1391
(518) 372–6001

Presbyterians for Gay/Lesbian Concerns
Box 38
New Brunswick, NJ 08903–0038
(908) 249–1016

Seventh Day Adventists–Kinship International, Inc.
Box 3840
Los Angeles, CA 90078
(213) 876–2076

Unitarian Universalists for Lesbian/Gay Concerns
25 Beacon Street
Boston, MA 02108
(617) 742–2100

United Lesbian and Gay Christian Scientists
Box 2171
Beverly Hills, CA 90212–2171
(310) 850–8258

*World Congress of Gay and Lesbian Jewish
    Organizations*
P.O. Box 3345
New York, NY 10008

Metropolitan Community Church
Usually listed in the white pages of the local
    telephone directory, or contact
*Universal Fellowship of Metropolitan Community
    Churches*
5300 Santa Monica Boulevard #304
Los Angeles, CA 90029
(213) 464–5100

Bookstores

A Different Light
New York, San Francisco, West Hollywood
(800) 343–4002

Chosen Books
940 West McNichols
Detroit, MI 48203
(313) 864–0458 or (800) 225–5300

Giovanni's Room
345 South 12th Street
Philadelphia, PA 19107
(800) 222–6996

Glad Day Bookshop
673 Boylston Street
Boston, MA 02116
(617) 267–3010

Lambda Rising
1625 Connecticut Avenue
Washington, DC 20009
(800) 621–6969

Oscar Wilde Memorial Bookstore
15 Christopher Street
New York, NY 10014
(212) 255–8097

The Naiad Press
P.O. Box 10543
Tallahassee, FL 32302
(800) 533–1973

Publications

The Advocate
6922 Hollywood Boulevard, 10th Floor
Los Angeles, CA 90028
(800) 827–0561

Gay Community News
167 Tremont Street, Fifth Floor
Boston, MA 02111
(617) 426–4469

Gayellow Pages
Renaissance House
Box 292, Village Station
New York, NY 10014
(212) 674–0120

In the Family
(A magazine for lesbians, gays, bisexuals, and
    their relations)
P.O. Box 5387
Takoma Park, MD 20913
(301) 270–4771

Children of Lesbians & Gays Everywhere
2300 Market St. #165
San Francisco, CA 94114
(415) 583–8029

Hot Lines

Gay Men's Health Crisis, Inc. (New York)
(212) 807–7517

National Center for Missing and Exploited Children
(800) 843–5678

U. S. Public Health Service AIDS HOTLINE
(800) 342-AIDS

Chapter 19

Counseling Ethnic Minority Clients

Linda G. Matthews, M.A.   *Donald R. Atkinson, Ph.D.*

There has been a growing interest in the role of race and ethnicity in counseling process and outcome over the past twenty-five years. This interest is exemplified in the counseling literature by a proliferation of research articles, theoretical papers, and books that serve to assist practitioners in learning to work capably with ethnic minority populations—that is, African American, American Indian, Asian American, and Hispanic American men and women. These extensive works cover a range of content areas including, but not limited to, descriptions of the cultural characteristics of specific ethnic minority populations, insights on how to train counselors to develop effective competency in multicultural counseling, and discussion of culture-specific theory regarding the identity development of ethnic minority people. The current chapter attempts to highlight and organize this literature in order to present the reader with an overview of multicultural counseling, including its history, the current status of multicultural counseling research and training, and guidelines for counseling practice.

In this chapter we focus on ethnic minority clients, but we recognize that the counselor may be either a European American or a member of an ethnic minority group. Thus at one level, this chapter covers the problems and issues relevant to the dyad of the European American counselor working with an ethnic minority client. This focus is important because, in terms of sheer numbers, European Americans predominate in the counseling profession. Also, as members of the dominant culture, some European American counselors may hold ethnocentric or racist attitudes toward ethnic minority clients. Such attitudes can create serious barriers to counseling.

Compared to European American counselors, many ethnic minority counselors may share experiences, communication/cultural styles, and beliefs with their culturally diverse clients and therefore may be more culturally sensitive to them. Yet we do not make the assumption that ethnic minority counselors necessarily have all the beliefs, knowledge, and skills needed to be successful with all culturally diverse clients. The lack of theory and research focused on the counseling process when the counselor and client are from the same or different ethnic minority backgrounds limits our knowledge of the characteristics or skills that either facilitate or impede counseling effectiveness within these dyads. Consequently, as the dynamics related to the culturally diverse client being paired with a European American or an ethnic minority counselor remain critical to our discussion of research and training, we emphasize that efforts to acquire the beliefs, knowledge, and skills necessary to work with culturally diverse populations should serve as a primary goal for *all* counselors.

The Ethnic Minority Populations

Similar to other American subcultures, individuals within each of the ethnic minority populations tend to share cultural characteristics (such as languages/dialects, communication styles, values, belief systems, and so on) that are based on their racial/ethnic group heritages. Articles and books in cultural anthropology and in counseling have documented how these characteristics have distinct meaning for members of a cultural group in terms of how they generally perceive their work, raise children, establish group norms and rituals, and assume familial roles. Thus unique cultural characteristics distinguish each ethnic group from other subcultures of the larger society.

Another factor that distinguishes ethnic minority populations from other American subcultures is the common experience of oppression. Ethnic minority men and women share a history of physical, economic, and sociopolitical oppression in the United States (in fact, it is in this sense that we refer to them as a minority, that is, a group of people singled out for differential and inferior treatment). For example, history reveals that African Americans have endured racial injustices since their initial presence in America. These injustices have ranged from chattel slavery and Jim Crow to the more subtle and institutionalized acts of racism prevalent today, such as the limited inclusion of culture-relevant content in school curricula and the limited opportunity for the advancement of blacks into high-level career positions. American Indians, who have been denied rights of self-determination continually since the arrival of Europeans in the Western hemisphere, have likewise suffered from massacres, incarcerations, and legalized exploitations that have greatly contributed to many contemporary problems, including high rates of alcoholism and low life expectancy (Richardson, 1981). Asian Americans also have been the victims of exploitation and discrimination. For example, Chinese Americans were used for cheap labor, assaulted, and killed by white mobs during the "yellow peril" mania of the late nineteenth century, and Japanese Americans were relegated to concentration camps during World War II. Despite achieving higher educational gains than European Americans, both Chinese and Japanese Americans still lag behind European Americans in economic prosperity (D. W. Sue, 1973). Similarly, Latinos have been singled out for discrimination. Many first-generation Mexicans and other Latin Americans migrate to the United States with little or no English-speaking proficiency and with limited skills to enter a competitive and technologically oriented American workforce. Because of language differences and restrictive work skills, these immigrants continue to be relegated to low-paying, low-status jobs, which often leave them vulnerable to further exploitation. Although it is difficult to find agreement concerning the reasons these groups have been victims of oppression, some critics conclude that these experiences may be caused by differences in the cultural patterns, languages, and skin color of ethnic minority and European American populations.

Both the cultural characteristics of ethnic minorities and the common experience of oppression in America have implications for counseling practice (referred to as the "cultural deterministic" and "ethnic minority status" perspectives, respectively; S. Sue, Akutsu, & Higashi, 1985). From a cultural deterministic perspective, S. Sue and D. W. Sue (1977) describe how counseling practices tend to be characterized by the values, attitudes, and behaviors of European American, middle-class society, which may conflict with the cultural characteristics of ethnic minority clients. For example, traditional counseling practices tend to focus on individualistic goal setting and expressiveness of personal issues by the client. However, many Asian Americans tend to value the interdependence of the family structure over the attainment of individual goals. Moreover, restraint of feelings and emotions is more likely to be preferred among some Asian Americans than open expression of emotions. Time orientation is another area in which European American values conflict with some ethnic minority values. European American culture generally has a future orientation, whereby people place an inordinate amount of time on preparing for what will hopefully occur later in life, whereas others, such as African Americans and American Indians, generally possess a present orientation, with emphasis on what occurs in the present. As a result, counseling goals that are future oriented may not be consistent with the needs of culturally diverse clients.

From an ethnic minority perspective, counseling may be perceived as an experience to approach with mistrust and suspicion, particularly with European American counselors (Vontress, 1981). Some authors argue that mistrust and suspicion may be considered healthy to some degree, as mistrust and suspicion have served to protect ethnic minorities (specifically African Americans) from psychological and physical harm (Grier & Cobbs, 1968; Ridley, 1984; Thomas & Sillen, 1972). Depending on the extent of mistrust, however, the interaction between a European American counselor and a culturally diverse client may negatively influence rapport building, presumed to be a necessary precondition to counseling effectiveness (Jourard, 1964).

Another experience common to some culturally diverse clients as a function of their ethnic minority status is the stress related to cultural conflict. Cultural conflict occurs when immigrants and their descendants attempt to maintain some of their indigenous cultural practices and values in the face of internally and/or externally imposed pressures to acculturate into mainstream society. The experience related to such conflict has been characterized in the literature as "acculturative stress" (Mena, Padilla, & Maldonado, 1987; Saldana, 1994; Smart & Smart, 1995b; Williams & Berry, 1991) and has been examined most commonly among Hispanic and Asian American immigrant populations. Although cultural conflict may be most evident among second- and third-generation immigrants, acculturative stress can also be an issue among individuals whose ancestors have been in the United States for many generations. Thus Anderson (1991) discusses the relevance of acculturative stress among African Americans, a population for whom immigration occurred (in most cases) many generations ago.

D. W. Sue (1981) pointed out the psychological implications of being a "marginal" person, that is, an individual caught between two cultures. Although some individuals eventually reconceptualize the position in the more positive framework of biculturalism, many others experience it as a source of stress throughout their lifetime. The problem is exacerbated by the fact that even those individuals who choose to acculturate fully often find that they are never completely accepted by the dominant society as an assimilated person. Smart and Smart (1995b) discuss acculturative stress in terms of the loss of social support, self-esteem, and identity experienced by immigrants. They discuss significant experiences of immigrants from Latin America, including discrimination based on skin color, that contribute to acculturative stress among Hispanic Americans.

Research findings suggest a relationship between acculturation and acculturative stress. In a study of Hispanic American undergraduate students, Sanchez and Fernandez (1993) found that even among individuals who indicated high ethnic identity, an inverse relationship existed between identification with mainstream identity and level of stress. Saldana (1994) also reported a relationship between level of acculturation and psychological distress in a study of Hispanic American students in predominantly European American universities. Other recent articles have suggested that acculturative stress is related to depression, diminished occupational functioning, and strained or ineffective counselor–client relationships (Shin, 1994; Smart & Smart, 1995a).

Diversity between and within Ethnic Minority Populations

Although ethnic minority populations do have some common experiences, it would be a serious mistake to not recognize the numerous cultural differences that exist between and within these populations. Most of us have enough familiarity with African American, American Indian, Asian American, and Hispanic American cultures to recognize the cultural differences among these groups; it is also important to acknowledge that by using these broadly encompassing labels, we are glossing over some very important subgroup differences. For example, among American Indians there is evidence that over 500 different tribes, each with its own unique cultural patterns, existed at the time that Columbus arrived in the Western hemisphere. Some of these distinct cultural patterns have survived to the present day (in spite of earlier efforts to eliminate them) and account for differences within the American Indian population. For example, the religious beliefs and practices of Hopis and Navajos are quite different, despite the fact that they frequently share some of the same geographic area. Similarly, cultural distinctions exist among African Americans, Asian Americans, and Hispanic Americans, all of whom can trace their cultural backgrounds to the many ethnic/cultural groups in Africa, Asia, and Latin America, respectively.

Nor are cultural differences between individuals limited to differences between ethnic/cultural groups within these larger categories that we use for the sake of convenience. Within each culturally diverse group are differences that are a function of such factors as geographic area, economic background, gender, acculturation, and ethnic identity development. We will have more to say about within-group differences when we review research on multicultural counseling.

Criticisms of the Profession: A Historical Perspective

Until the mid-1960s, little attention was given to the unique experiences of ethnic minorities and their special counseling needs. Gilbert Wrenn's 1962 article discussing the culturally encapsulated counselor is generally recognized as the first to suggest that practitioners were providing counseling from their own narrow cultural perspective. Wrenn urged counselors to broaden their monocultural perspectives in order to be more responsive to the needs of clients from culturally different backgrounds. Only in this manner, he argued, would counselors be effective with all their clients, regardless of client background.

Although the counseling profession was slow in responding to Wrenn's charge of cultural encapsulation, by the late 1960s a groundswell of professional criticism was beginning to emerge. Influenced by the civil rights era of the 1950s and 1960s, critics began to accuse the predominantly European American mental health profession of being ethnocentric and racist in all phases of service delivery, including diagnoses, treatment decisions, counseling process, and outcome. Initially these charges were based on the personal observations and inferences of counselors and observers, with little hard data to back them up. It was not until the mid-1970s that researchers began to collect the kind of data that could support or refute some of the criticisms being levied against the profession. In this section we discuss these criticisms and present some of the research data that bear on them.

A common theme in the criticism of the counseling profession is that the services provided by the profession are biased against ethnic minority clients. The possibility of bias seems very real, given that the majority of counselors are European American who were raised in a basically racist social structure. The fact that prior to Wrenn's 1962 article so little attention was given to the special needs of culturally diverse clients offers some support for the hypothesis of counselor bias. By the mid-1970s, however, more direct evidence relevant to the issue of counselor bias began to appear in the form of research on differential diagnosis and treatment. Reviews by Sattler (1977), Abramowitz and Murray (1983), and Atkinson

(1985) of archival research concluded that there is evidence of both differential diagnoses and differential treatment being applied to ethnic minority clients. In her recent review of African American patients in the mental health system, Worthington (1992) offered additional support for these conclusions. Furthermore, she cautioned mental health care providers not only to be aware of cultural biases in diagnosis and treatment but also to consider the "holistic and spiritual approach that [racial/ethnic] minority group members may take to [mental health] care." Solomon (1992) suggested that misdiagnoses of racial/ethnic minorities may be due to a failure on the part of clinicians to consider the "cultural realities" of these individuals and a tendency to apply diagnostic criteria that reflect a Western bias in terms of normative experiences.

Another criticism of counseling and mental health services is that they simply are not addressing the needs of ethnic minority clients. Because counseling theories and services were developed by and for middle-class European American clients, these critics argued, they simply do not address the type of concerns that culturally diverse clients are likely to have. Smith (1977) noted that the intrapsychic nature of some counseling theories and the concomitant practice of insight-oriented therapy may overlook significant factors related to a "sick" society. For instance, a culturally diverse client's problem related to personal adjustment may be compounded by his or her difficulty in dealing with racial discrimination at work. Or an unemployed ethnic minority client may experience difficulty with securing adequate employment to support his or her family. Traditionally, counselors and psychotherapists do not become involved in the day-to-day survival needs of their clients, yet the resolution of these concerns may be equally or perhaps more relevant to the client than an attainment of insight into inner conflicts.

Although no one has yet empirically demonstrated that contemporary counseling theories fail to address ethnic minority needs, some studies provide data that support such an inference. If culturally diverse clients see counseling services as irrelevant to their needs, then one would assume that they would not use these services. Research on ethnic minority use of mental health services has yielded mixed results. Earlier studies and reviews provided consistent evidence of underuse among ethnic minorities (Abramowitz & Murray, 1983; Leong, 1986; Sattler, 1977). Much of this research, however, was limited to out-patient mental health services or did not distinguished between out-patient and in-patient services (Snowden & Cheung, 1990). More recently, Snowden and Cheung (1990) found that blacks were overrepresented and Asian Americans were underrepresented as patients in community mental health centers and mental institutions; representation of Hispanics and Native Americans varied by setting. In another study (Cheung & Snowden, 1990), the authors reported that blacks and Native Americans were more likely and Asian Americans less likely to be hospitalized than were whites. Other researchers have provided further evidence of this utilization trend in in-patient settings (Hu, Snowden, Jerrell, & Nguyen, 1991; S. Sue et al., 1991). With regard to out-patient settings, the research findings consistently suggest that *some* ethnic minority groups underutilize mental health services. Hu et al. (1991) found that blacks were less likely than whites to use public out-patient services and that Asian Americans were more likely than whites to do so. In a recent study with ethnic minority women, Padgett, Patrick, Burns, and Schlesinger (1994) found evidence of underuse of out-patient mental health services among black and Hispanic women.

Analysis of these studies and reviews also is complicated because some of them include allocation (generally under the therapist's control) of mental health services with use (generally under the client's control) of mental health services. Analysis is further complicated by the fact that some reviews have focused on archival studies, whereas others have relied on surveys of expectations about use of services. These limitations notwithstanding, the data do suggest that *some* ethnic minorities (particularly blacks and Hispanics) are less likely to self-refer for counseling and more likely to drop out prematurely from counseling in out-patient settings than are European Americans.

The underrepresentation of ethnic minority counselors has been viewed as an explanation for the underuse in those instances where underuse has been documented. Numerous studies have found that ethnic minorities are underrepresented among both professional counselors and among counselor trainees (see review by Atkinson, 1985), the latter finding suggesting that underrepresentation is likely to continue to be a problem in the future. Young, Chamley, and Withers (1990) found that the percentage of racial/ethnic minorities among faculty in counselor education programs is significantly lower than their percentage in the U.S. population. Furthermore, the authors reported a lower hiring rate of racial/ethnic minority faculty in such programs than is seen in the minority population nationwide. Other studies support the hypothesis that perceived unavailability of ethnically similar or sensitive counselors does contribute to the underuse of and/or premature termination from mental health services by racial/ethnic minorities (Atkinson, Jennings, & Liongson, 1990; Romero, 1985). In a study involving African American, Native American, Latino/Latina American, and Filipino American students, Atkinson et al. (1990) found this to be particularly true for individuals who reported stronger ethnic identification rather than biculturalism or mainstream identification.

Also supporting the hypothesis that the lack of ethnic minority counselors may be a reason for underuse in out-patient settings is the research on preference for counselor ethnicity. Preference for counselor race/ethnicity has been one of the most commonly used dependent variables in cross-cultural counseling research. Minority subjects are typically asked to express a preference between an ethnically similar counselor and an ethnically dissimilar counselor. Harrison (1975), Sattler (1977), and Atkinson (1983) all concluded from their reviews of research that African American subjects rather consistently preferred African American counselors. Lopez, Lopez, and Fong (1991) conducted a series of studies with Mexican Americans and found a clear preference for ethnically similar counselors. In a recent examination of research on racial/ethnic minorities and their perceptions of and preferences for ethnically similar counselors and European American counselors, Coleman, Wampold, and Casali (1995) found that minorities did prefer counselors of similar ethnicity. They further noted that perceptions of and preferences for counselors were influenced by respondent level of cultural affiliation. Another recent review (Atkinson & Lowe, 1995) concluded that "in general, ethnically similar counseling dyads are associated with more positive counseling process and outcome than are ethnically dissimilar counseling dyads." (p. 405).

Although not all ethnic minority clients prefer a racially, ethnically similar counselor, it seems clear that the unavailability of such counselors is a factor that deters many culturally diverse clients from seeking counseling services.

In the absence of culturally similar counselors, the counseling relationship may be fraught with barriers that result from cultural differences. In a landmark article, D. W. Sue (1981) elaborated on the misunderstandings that may occur from cultural variations in verbal and nonverbal communication. These misunderstandings, in turn, may impede the formation of an effective counseling relationship. Three major impediments were identified by D. W. Sue (1981): (1) language barriers between the counselor and client; (2) class-bound values that tend to characterize treatment approaches; and (3) culture-bound values that are used to judge normality and abnormality in clients (p. 420). For each of the three types of impediments, S. Sue and D. W. Sue (1977) describe how generic characteristics of counseling reflected European American, middle-class values and characteristics, whereas the values and characteristics of ethnic minority clients may be notably different. For example, language barriers are reflective of counseling situations characterized by a monolingual orientation; culturally diverse clients may tend to have bilingual orientations. Class-bound characteristics inherent in generic counseling include an emphasis on verbal communication as well as emotional and behavioral expressiveness, the attainment of insight, and the willingness to disclose intimate details of one's personal life. These characteristics and others (for example, adherence to time schedules and the valuation of long-range goals) represent aspects of middle-class values that may differ from the values of ethnic minority clients. Lastly, the authors explain that culture-bound factors include an emphasis on an individual (versus a family) approach to treatment and an emphasis on cause-and-effect relationships. Again, these factors may contribute to barriers to facilitating an effective counseling relationship.

The Current Status of Multicultural Counseling

The counseling profession has begun to respond to the criticisms that it does not address the needs of ethnic minority clients, although many would argue that the response has been both slow in pace and inadequate in scope. Clearly, culturally diverse clients are recognized by the profession as a growing and important population that counselors, regardless of their own racial/ethnic background, must be prepared to serve. In this section, we examine recent developments in training culturally sensitive counselors, conducting multicultural counseling research, and building culturally relevant psychological theories.

Training

In response to criticisms regarding the lack of training in multicultural counseling, professional organizations have begun to develop policies that address this concern. In fact, the Vail conference, sponsored by the American Psychological Association (APA) and held in 1973, set forth the recommendation that conducting therapy or counseling without cultural sensitivity should be declared unethical. This conference and subsequent national conferences (the Austin conference in 1975 and the Dulles conference in 1978) also yielded recommendations that spurred the creation of several policies and boards to resolve such important issues as increasing the representation of ethnic minority populations in psychology graduate programs and establishing standards and guidelines for graduate training programs to prepare students for working with culturally diverse populations. It was further suggested that all professional psychologists obtain training and continuing education in the special issues of different religious, ethnic, sexual, and economic groups. Moreover, in order for programs to become accredited by the APA, programs have to adhere to criteria that include the need for cultural diversity among faculty and students (Casas, 1984; Altmaier, 1993). The APA also issued guidelines by which psychological service providers should assess and understand "the role that culture and ethnicity/race play in the sociopsychological and economic development of culturally diverse populations" (APA, 1993, p. 45).

A number of workshops and conferences have been organized at the national level to address the issue of multicultural counseling training, including the annual Winter Roundtable at Teachers' College, Columbia University, New York, and an NIMH-funded project at Howard University (Chunn & Dunston, 1980, cited in Casas, 1985). These efforts have led to a number of proposed training models and course curricula geared toward increasing culture sensitivity, stimulating self-awareness of racial/ethnic issues and stereotypes, and providing the necessary tools for effective counseling with people of different racial/ethnic origins. The literature continues to offer a variegated selection of training models that can be implemented within existing programs (in curricula) and as workshops and specialized training programs. The following are examples of some of these models.

Corvin and Wiggins (1989) proposed an antiracism training model to engage European American professionals in self-exploration and to help them examine their own racism. The authors use Standard 2 of the proposed ethical standards for counselor practice by Ibrahim and Arredondo (1986) as the basis of their model. This model assumes that in order for a person to be able to develop cross-cultural expertise or competence, "one must (1) recognize, assess, and understand oneself as a member of a particular racial group; (2) become aware of one's own racism, and (3) take active steps to effect change" (Corvin & Wiggins, 1989, p. 107).

S. Sue et al. (1985) offered training suggestions for nonminorities to work with ethnic minority groups. Their training model proposed three important elements to training therapists in providing culturally consistent forms of treatment. The first of these elements is a knowledge of culture and status, whereby the trainee becomes aware not only of the client's culture (or the cultural-deterministic perspective) but also of the perceptions and behaviors of ethnic minority groups as a function of the interaction of cultural patterns and institutions in the United States, to which they refer as the ethnic minority group perspective. A second element proposed by the authors is experiential in nature, requiring that students work with clients from ethnic communities to complement the intellectualization and abstraction in discussing such issues in the classroom. Lastly, these authors propose the use of innovative strategies in working with racial/ethnic group clients. They argue that because of cultural deterministic and minority status issues, traditional forms of treatment may not be effective.

Carney and Kahn (1984) proposed a developmental model for trainees in multicultural counseling. This model conceptualizes five stages through which trainees pass in expanding their ability to work with culturally diverse clients. Each stage evaluates trainees' knowledge of cultural groups, attitudinal awareness, cross-cultural sensitivity, and specific cross-cultural counseling skills. Next, the authors propose that a paradigm for training should include essential *challenges* and *supports* that will successfully move trainees on to increasing their competence in multicultural counseling. Challenges are defined as gains in knowledge, attitudes, and counseling skills that are new to trainees, and supports include a training atmosphere that promotes personal sharing and reduces threat in the learning environment, both of which are essential to growth from one stage to the next.

Johnson (1987) has criticized current multicultural training models for teaching trainees only to "know that" cultural differences exist. What these models lack is a component that teaches students to "know how" to conduct their work with individuals from culturally diverse backgrounds. According to Johnson (1987), "knowing how" constitutes the skills necessary for becoming expert in working with diverse groups; "knowing that" only addresses an awareness that cultural differences exist. Based on the conceptualizations of Ivey (1977), who defines the culturally effective individual as an effective communicator in more than one cultural content, and Pederson's (1978) triad model for multicultural counseling, Johnson developed the Minnesota Multiethnic Counselor Education Curriculum, or MMCEC (Johnson, 1982). The MMCEC represents an effort to infuse content from two categories of cultural experts (ethnic minority psychologists and experienced ethnic minority clients) into the training of counselors.

In a review of the literature, McRae and Johnson (1991) discussed the need to emphasize self, information and knowledge, relationship, and performance in cross-cultural counseling training. They assert the necessity for trainees to (1) possess awareness and knowledge of themselves as cultural beings; (2) demonstrate ability to appropriately relate with individuals representing diverse cultural backgrounds; (3) possess cognitive ability to promote correct perceptions of cultural groups, their environments, and their social systems; and (4) perform satisfactorily in multicultural situations. In the past several years, models that address these necessities have surfaced in the literature on training in multicultural counseling. Sabnani, Ponterotto, and Borodovsky (1991) proposed a stage model of cross-cultural counselor training that incorporates white racial identity (Helms, 1990) as an integral component of training for European American counselors. This model describes the attitudes associated with the stages of white racial identity (contact, disintegration, reintegration, pseudo-independence, immersion/emersion, and autonomy) and discusses strategies for training European American counselors in cross-cultural counseling as well as facilitating their movement through the model.

There currently exist numerous models and guidelines that have been constructed to promote multicultural program development within counselor training programs. The Multicultural Program Development Pyramid (Ridley, Mendoza, &

Kanitz, 1994) outlines five levels of development and serves as a guide for counseling programs to formulate their own multicultural programming. Ponterotto, Alexander, and Grieger (1995) devised the Multicultural Competency Checklist, or MCC for counseling training programs. The MCC is a programmatic guide for the development of cultural awareness and multicultural training competence. Six themes are reflected in the MCC: (1) minority representation, (2) curriculum issues, (3) counseling practice and supervision, (4) research considerations, (5) student and faculty competency evaluations, and (6) physical environment.

There is evidence that a growing number of counselor education programs are providing some training in multicultural counseling. Hills and Strozier (1992) surveyed the directors of forty-nine counselor training programs and found that almost all (forty-three out of forty-nine) of the programs offered at least one course in multicultural issues and that coursework in multiculturalism was required for twenty-nine of these programs. However, Arredondo (1985) speculated that although many programs may provide the theoretical knowledge on cultural differences, the necessary skills development is desperately lacking. A subsequent study found that relatively few counselor education programs require practicum experience in cross-cultural counseling (Ibrahim & Arredondo, 1986).

Bernal and associates have examined multicultural training in clinical psychology programs. Bernal and Padilla (1982) reported that only 41 percent of the clinical psychology programs responding to their survey offered one or more courses "that might contribute to the students' understanding of minority or other cultures" (p. 782). This study also found that while clinical program directors tended to agree that multicultural training is "somewhat important," relatively few have implemented efforts to address the multicultural training in their graduate programs. In a more recent study, Bernal and Castro (1994) examined the changes in the training of clinical psychologists based on data collected during the periods of 1979–1980 and 1990–1991. The authors report evidence of an increase in some key aspects of multicultural training, but they assert that two critical changes need to be implemented: (1) a shift from providing minimal exposure to culture to engaging in active training for cultural competence and (2) a significant increase in ethnic minority faculty representation, which may only occur as a consequence of an increase in the number of ethnic minority students being admitted into counseling programs. Quintana and Bernal (1995) examined multicultural training in counseling and clinical psychology programs to determine whether it met the standards of ethnic minority training proposed by such researchers as Bernal and Castro (1994) and Ridley et al. (1994). They found that counseling programs were slightly more involved in multicultural training than were clinical programs, but that very few of these counseling programs meet the standards for producing culturally proficient psychotherapists.

Support for Arredondo's (1985) concern that multicultural training may be restricted to theory and Bernal and Castro's (1994) concern that it may not focus on application can be found in a study by Mintz, Bartels, and Rideout (1995). In a survey of psychology interns' perceptions of their graduate-level training for cross-cultural counseling, these authors found that interns perceive their preparation for multicultural counseling to be mediocre; few respondents indicated that they had taken courses in counseling ethnic minorities, and most agreed that issues of multi-culturalism were not incorporated into core courses. The majority of the interns did report the presence of experts on issues of cross-cultural counseling and the encouragement to examine their biases during training. None of the recent studies have examined the nature or extent of actual cross-cultural counseling experiences during practicum.

The research on multicultural training received *during* internship has also yielded ambiguous results. Murphy, Wright, and Bellamy (1995) surveyed training directors of fifty-three university counseling centers and found that about 96 percent of the programs included training in multicultural issues, most commonly didactic instruction presented during seminars. More than half (58.5 percent) of the sites offered development programs on multicultural issues to staff members. Only 5.7 percent of the sites, however, required that interns have ethnic minority clients in their caseloads. This latter finding is particularly disconcerting, as research indicates that supervised experience in cross-cultural situations is significantly related to increased multicultural competence (Pope-Davis, Reynolds, Dings, & Ottavi, 1994).

Given the evidence that counseling graduate programs may not adequately train students in multicultural counseling, there appears to be some justification to Casas, Ponterotto, and Gutierrez's (1986) criticisms of the profession. According to these authors, "continued apathy by the counseling profession toward racial and ethnic minorities will result in a significant number of counselors working from what should be regarded as an unethical position, one that could eventually result in the ethical indictment of the profession." (p. 348).

Research

The call for additional research on issues related to multicultural counseling by ethnic minority critics in the late 1960s has resulted in a steady increase in empirical investigations. In 1970, Sattler published a review of research on racial "experimental effects" in experimentation, testing, interviewing, and psychotherapy and reported that he found only three studies that included counselor or client race as an independent variable. By 1980 multicultural counseling research was beginning to appear regularly in some professional journals. In a survey of research published in the *Journal of Counseling Psychology*, Ponterotto (1988b) found that while racial/ethnic research accounted for an average of only 4.1 percent of the articles published between 1976 and 1980 (inclusive), for the six-year period from 1981 to 1986 this figure had increased to an average of 7.3 percent. More recent reviews of the literature have suggested a *decline* in the number of research publications pertaining to ethnic minorities. Graham (1992) reported a decrease in the representation of African Americans in the publications of six American Psychological Association (APA) journals (including the *Journal of Consulting and Clinical Psychology*, the *Journal of Counseling Psychology*, and the *Journal of Applied Psychology*) from 1970 to 1989. Furthermore, in an examination of the research in ten APA journals during the same time period, Santos de Barona (1993) reported a decrease in the number of journal articles presenting information relevant to ethnic minorities.

In our earlier discussion of the criticisms directed at the counseling profession, we examined some of the research reviews on multicultural counseling. Our examination of these research reviews suggests that, in general, ethnic minorities (1) use counseling services differently (based on survey and archival data), (2) receive different diagnoses from European Americans (archival data), (3) receive different and often less preferred types of treatment (archival data), (4) prefer an ethnically similar counselor (based on survey and analogue research), and (5) are underrepresented in the counseling profession. An interesting feature of all the multicultural counseling research published prior to 1980 (and the majority of research published since then) is that one client variable—client race/ethnicity—has served as the sole or primary independent variable. A general criticism of this substantial body of research on client race/ethnicity is that although it may have important implications for mental health service and training policy (documenting, for example, the need to select unbiased counselor trainees), it offers little to guide the practicing counselor when working with an ethnic minority client.

The practice of comparing various ethnic minority groups on a variety of counseling-related dependent variables also is subject to the following criticisms. First, by lumping all individuals of a particular racial/ethnic group together for statistical purposes, we fail to recognize those intragroup differences that could, in effect, mask any between-group differences that may exist. Second, this method confuses race/ethnicity with culture (S. Sue & Zane, 1987; Johnson, 1990). Unless we group people on the basis of culture rather than race/ethnicity, we are left with the generally unacceptable finding that differences between the groups sampled are somehow a function of skin color and physical characteristics. Third, by examining mean differences between racial/ethnic groups on some criterion measure without recognizing intragroup differences, we risk the possibility of perpetuating stereotypes for an entire racial/ethnic group that may be true only for a minority of individuals in the group. Fourth, the very process of comparing various racial/ethnic groups to the majority group (variously identified as European American, white, Anglo, Caucasian) reinforces the view that the latter group is the standard of measure on the criterion involved.

Recently, researchers have begun examining the relationship between within-group, culture-specific variables and counseling process and outcome variables. Three variables—acculturation, cultural mistrust, and ethnic identity development—appear to be particularly fruitful within-group variables that deserve further research. In a series of studies with Asian Americans, acculturation was found to be related to attitudes toward mental health services and ratings of counselor credibility, although not always in the hypothesized direction. Atkinson and Gim (1989) reported that the most acculturated Asian American university students were (1) most likely to recognize personal need for professional psychological help, (2) most tolerant of the stigma associated with psychological help, and (3) most open to discussing their problems with a psychologist. A later study by Gim, Atkinson, and Whiteley (1990), however, found that the Asian American college students who reported low and medium levels of acculturation were more willing to see a counselor for their concerns than were their highly acculturated peers. Also, Atkinson, Lowe, and Matthews (1995) found no relationship between acculturation and willingness to see a counselor in a recent study of Asian American university students.

Potentially conflicting findings were also reported for two studies examining the relationship between Asian American acculturation and ratings of counselor credibility. Gim, Atkinson, and Kim (1991) reported that Asian American students' level of acculturation interacted with counselor ethnicity and counseling style when the students rated counselor credibility; college students with low acculturation consistently gave the lowest credibility ratings to European American counselors who portrayed a "culture-blind" counseling style. Contrary to their initial hypothesis, Atkinson and Matsushita (1991) found that bicultural Japanese American university students rated European American counselors as more attractive than did their Western-identified counterparts.

Five studies have examined the relationship between one aspect of acculturation, cultural commitment (or what Padilla, 1985, refers to as "cultural loyalty"), and selected counseling process variables. Four of these studies were conducted with American Indian participants. Examining a college student sample, M. E. Johnson and Lashley (1989) found a direct relationship between commitment to American Indian culture and the importance that Native American students assigned to having an ethnically similar counselor. This relationship was also found among Native American high school students (Big Foot-Sipes, Dauphinais, LaFromboise, Bennett, & Rowe, 1992). In a paired-comparison study, Bennett and Big Foot-Sipes (1991) found that Native Americans with the strongest commitment to Native American culture expressed the greatest preference for an ethnically similar counselor. An inverse relationship was found between Native Americans' cultural commitment and their ratings of counseling and confidence in mental health professionals (Price & McNeill, 1992). In the one study with Mexican American college students that related cultural commitment to counseling process, Sanchez and Atkinson (1983) found that participants with a strong commitment to the Mexican American culture had less favorable attitudes toward using professional counseling services than did subjects with a weak commitment to Mexican American culture. Cultural commitment also was found to be related to preference for counselor ethnicity. Participants with a strong commitment to the Mexican American culture expressed a greater preference for a Mexican American counselor than for a European American counselor.

Three studies with Mexican American participants have also examined the relationship between more global measures of acculturation and counseling process variables. Lopez et al. (1991) found a relationship between level of acculturation and preference for ethnically similar counselors; they found that participants indicating medium levels of acculturation reported stronger preference for ethnically similar counselors than did their low-acculturation counterparts. Neither Ponce and Atkinson (1989) nor Atkinson, Casas, and Abreu (1992) found a relationship between Mexican American college students' level of acculturation and the ratings they gave to Mexican American or European American counselors.

In general, these studies suggest that cultural commitment (or cultural loyalty) on the part of ethnic minority individuals is directly related to their preference for an ethnically similar counselor and inversely related to their attitudes toward mental health services. The relationship between ethnic minority scores on more comprehensive acculturation measures and counseling process variables remains ambiguous.

The construct of *cultural mistrust* was first introduced in an article written by Terrell and Terrell (1981) and has since been examined as a within-group variable in the counseling literature involving African Americans. Terrell and Terrell (1984) found that black clients with a high level of mistrust who were seen by a white counselor had a significantly higher rate of premature termination (failure to show for a second, scheduled appointment and to contact facility within three months after the initial interview) from counseling than did highly mistrustful black clients seen by a black counselor. Findings from this study also revealed a main effect for trust level, with highly mistrustful clients having significantly higher rates of premature termination, regardless of the race of counselor. Watkins and Terrell (1988) found that highly mistrustful blacks who were assigned to white rather than black counselors tended to have diminished expectations for counseling. A subsequent study (Watkins, Terrell, Miller, & Terrell, 1989) revealed that in comparison to blacks low on mistrust, highly mistrustful blacks regarded the white counselor as less credible and less able to help them with four problem areas: general anxiety, shyness, inferiority feelings, and dating difficulties. A recent study suggests that highly mistrustful blacks express more negative attitudes toward seeking help from facilities staffed primarily by European Americans and anticipate less satisfaction with counseling services (Nickerson, Helms, & Terrell, 1994). In a study of counseling process, Thompson, Worthington, and Atkinson (1994) found an interaction between mistrust and counselor ethnicity, such that less mistrustful African Americans were more self-disclosing with a black counselor.

Black *identity development* is another intragroup variable that is beginning to be the subject of a number of studies. This research is covered briefly in the next section, in which we discuss Cross's (1972, 1978, 1995) model of nigrescence.

Emerging Theoretical Frameworks

Although existing counseling theories have been criticized for being oriented toward European American, middle-class clients, no new counseling theories specially designed for ethnic minority clients have emerged to date. What has emerged in the past twenty-five years, however, is a number of theories of psychological development specific to ethnic minority populations that have important implications for counseling practice. These include, but are not limited to, Cross's (1972) model of psychological nigrescence (the process of achieving black racial consciousness), Jackson's (1975) Black Identity Development (BID), Atkinson, Morten, and D. W. Sue's (1979) Minority Identity Development model (MID), and S. Sue's Cultural Identity Model (1977).

Unfortunately, empirical investigations that either substantiate or extend these theories to counseling process and outcomes have not been forthcoming, with one notable exception. Cross's theory of nigrescence has been subjected to a systematic program of research by Janet Helms and Thomas Parham that relates racial identity development to mental health and counseling variables. Therefore, we have elected to discuss Cross's (1972) model of psychological nigrescence in some detail in this section. The selection of this model also was based on (1) its similarity to the other models and, hence, its representative nature and (2) the promise that subsequent elaborations to the original model appear to have.

Cross's (1972) theory of psychological nigrescence describes the stages through which black people proceed in coming to terms with their blackness. Influenced by the oppressive forces experienced by the generations of African Americans, this theory espouses that black people differ in their worldviews; these differences essentially reflect how white people and black people are perceived. In an extension of this model, Parham (1989) notes that black racial identity is influenced by these oppressive forces:

> *The development of an individual's racial identity is not simply a reaction to oppressive elements within a society, although certainly those elements are very influential. This extended model assumes that Black/African self-identity is an entity independent of socially oppressive phenomena: Black/African identity is actualized through personal thoughts, feelings, and behaviors that are rooted in the values and fabric of Black/African culture itself. Identity development is, however, influenced by an interaction between internal (individual) and external (environmental) influences. (p. 195)*

Progression through the stages of racial identity development is a lifelong process; individuals may go from one stage to the next or may experience a recycling, whereby former stages may be revisited any number of times (Helms, 1985; Parham, 1989). Transcendence from one stage to the next involves a combination of factors, including personal readiness, prior cultural-socialization experiences, and educational experiences (Helms, 1985).

According to the original theory of psychological nigrescence, the black person in the first stage of black racial identity development, the *preencounter stage,* thinks, acts, and behaves in ways that are prowhite and antiblack. He or she honors aspects of white people or of European American culture, while spurning that which is related to black people or to black culture. In a revision of the original theory, Cross (1995) pointed out that black self-hatred in this stage has been overstated and that a general outlook downplaying the significance of race is the underlying characteristic of preencounter blacks. The transition from the preencounter stage to the *encounter stage* is stimulated by some significant event or events that shake the individual's worldview. According to Helms (1985), this transition is characterized either by a strongly negative experience with white people or a strongly positive experience with black people. The *immersion–emersion stage* is characterized by a reactive psychological withdrawal into blackness and a proactive positive acceptance of blackness (Helms, 1989, p. 237). The individual immerses himself or herself into all that is related to blackness in an attempt to rid the self of all traces of the previous identity. Finally, the *internalization stage* is characterized by a resolution of conflict whereby the individual achieves inner security and self-confidence about his or her blackness (Parham, 1989). He or she internalizes positive acceptance of blackness and considers the oppression of all people as significant.

Significantly, the theory of psychological nigrescence suggests that the development of racial identity may positively impact mental health. The inference is that therapists need to address issues of racial identity development with their black clients in order to facilitate healthy psychological adjustment. According to theoretical formulations on counselor–client pairings, the movement through the stages of racial identity may be best accomplished with counselors in higher stages of identity development than their clients, thus defining a progressive relationship (Helms, 1984, 1990). These formulations apply not only to white counselors (using a model of white racial identity development) but also to black counselors.

The first published study investigating Cross's theory examined black students' preferences for counselor by race (Parham & Helms, 1981). Their findings revealed that among black student participants, preencounter attitudes significantly, positively related to preferences for a white counselor, whereas encounter and internalization attitudes significantly, positively related to preference for a black counselor. A study by Helms and Carter (1991) provided further evidence of the relationship between racial identity development and counselor preference. Results of their study indicated that preencounter attitudes were directly related to preference for white male counselors.

Other studies have generally tested and partly substantiated the original theoretical model (Cross's model of psychological nigrescence). Parham and Helms (1985a) examined the relationship between racial identity attitudes and self-actualization and found that both preencounter and immersion attitudes were negatively related to mentally healthy self-actualizing tendencies. In contrast, encounter attitudes were positively related to self-actualization tendencies and negatively related to feelings of inferiority and anxiety. In a later study, Parham and Helms (1985b) found that racial identity attitudes also related to self-esteem. Although preencounter and immersion attitudes were significantly related to low self-regard among black college students, awakening racial identity (encounter attitudes) was positively associated with self-esteem. In another study of African American college students, Carter (1991) found that preencounter attitudes were significantly positively related to such experiences as anxiety, paranoia, and global psychological distress.

Several studies have tested variables of the psychological nigrescence model on counseling-related variables. Using a paired-comparison technique, Ponterotto, Alexander, and Hinkston (1988) did not find a relationship between racial identity stages and preferences for counselor characteristics. However, the authors acknowledged that their reliance on the racial identity categories based on the peak scores of respondents was not methodologically consistent with the developmental nature of the construct or with instructions of the developers of the Racial Identity Scale (Parham & Helms, 1981), the instrument they used to assess racial identity in the study. Another study (Pomales, Claiborn, & LaFromboise, 1986) found an interaction between racial identity and cultural sensitivity, such that respondents classified in the encounter stage rated the culturally sensitive counselor as the most expert and culturally competent. As racial identity of the respondents was determined by peak score, this study shared some of the same methodological limitations as were expressed by Ponterotto et al. (1988). Employing a methodology more consistent with the developmental nature of the racial identity construct, Austin, Carter, and Vaux (1990) found that preencounter attitudes were significantly associated with the most knowledge about the counseling center and a belief in its effectiveness as a source of help; emersion/immersion attitudes were significantly related to perceptions of less effectiveness and utility.

The research findings from studies investigating racial identity development appear to provide partial support for Cross's model. The studies that have been conducted to date suggest that attitudes toward oneself and toward other people vary from stage to stage. These investigations not only provide new developments to the previous theory, but also stimulate intriguing implications for counseling blacks and, possibly, other racial/ethnic group populations.

Perhaps because the model is relatively recent, there have been few studies conducted using the psychological nigrescence model. Moreover, there have been few studies reflecting the racial identity development of non-black racial/ethnic group populations. Leong's (1986) review concludes pointedly that this process of development may be a critical research variable in the study of Asian Americans. Phinney (1992, 1993) has attempted to address the need for racial/ethnic identity development with other ethnic minority groups. Phinney (1992) devised a multi-group ethnic identification measurement scale reflecting elements of racial identification that are common across various ethnic groups; she administered this scale to African American, Asian American, Hispanic American, Native American, and mixed-background college students, as well as African American, Asian American, Hispanic American, and mixed-background high school students. The reliability of the scale was established in this study, and the author recommended its use as a measure of racial identification among diverse groups. Phinney (1993) also constructed a three-stage model of identification based on existing models and empirical studies with minority adolescents from various ethnic groups. The following stages were proposed: (1) unexplored ethnic identification, (2) ethnic identification search/moratorium, and (3) ethnic identification achievement.

More research is needed that directly investigates the contribution of racial identity development theory to counseling-related outcomes. Also, other assessments of racial identity development are needed to capture this development beyond attitudes. These assessments are particularly important if researchers are to attempt investigations of the differing types of interactions of counselors and clients based on racial identity attitudes (see Helms, 1985).

Guidelines for Multicultural Counseling Practice

D. W. Sue et al. (1982) developed a list of cross-cultural counseling competencies that we believe still serve as the best guidelines for multicultural counseling practice available today. Basically, they identified three types of minimal competencies that should be incorporated into all counselor-training programs. These three areas of competence are beliefs/attitudes, knowledges, and counseling skills. We provide our own discussion of these competence areas but refer the reader to the original authors for further elaboration of the specific competencies.

Beliefs/Attitudes

To begin with, counselors who plan to work with ethnic minority clients need to examine and evaluate their attitudes toward members of culturally diverse populations. Counselors should question whether they experience feelings of discomfort, anxiety, anger, or guilt toward ethnic minorities, in general, and evaluate how these feelings may influence their effectiveness as culturally competent counselors. Further exploration may lead the counselor to uncover some of the sources of his or her attitudes. For example, one's attitudes about ethnic minorities may stem from negative personal experiences and/or from one's ethnocentric views toward the dominant culture. This is a particularly challenging task for European American counselors, because the larger society constantly reinforces European American ethnocentrism. When counselors find that they are unable to give up on their ethnocentric criteria for evaluating culture-specific aspects of a client's behavior, they should refer the client to a counselor who can be accepting of the client's values.

Evaluations of one's stereotypic and prejudicial attitudes may also lead counselors to training opportunities that will involve systematic efforts toward attitude change. For European American counselors, these efforts may entail a process of developing their levels of white racial identity development, defined as the process through which a white person proceeds in coming to an understanding of his or her status in the dominant cultural group (Helms, 1984). This process involves an intellectual, affective, and cognitive transcendence culminating with an acceptance of culturally diverse individuals as equals. The development of white racial identity development and other levels of awareness are crucial features of such training models proposed by Corvin and Wiggins (1989), Katz and Ivey (1977), Ponterotto (1988a), and Sabnani et al. (1991).

Some ethnic minority counselors may be motivated to work with culturally diverse clients because they feel committed to ensuring that these clients receive culturally responsive services. These counselors may also feel that they are capable of providing culturally responsive services because they have formulated counseling theories and practices for ethnic minority clients either on their own or through training programs they have sought out. Nevertheless, some ethnic minority counselors may need to evaluate their stage of racial/ethnic identity development or acculturation level to determine how these stages or levels may influence their efficacy as counselors for culturally diverse clients. Similar to some European American counselors, some ethnic minority counselors may harbor negative or stereotypic attitudes toward certain or all ethnic minority clients. Naturally, these attitudes can influence the counseling relationship, process, and /or outcome. Again, we point out that these factors have quite different implications for the training of ethnic minority versus European American counselors and for their impact on treatment issues. Currently, there are no training models in the literature that specifically elaborate on how ethnic minority counselors can be most effective with culturally diverse clients.

Knowledges

In addition to an ongoing examination of beliefs and attitudes about cultural issues, culturally sensitive counselors continually seek to expand their knowledge relevant to multicultural counseling. D. W. Sue et al. (1982) have identified four types of knowledge that counselors should possess. The first type is knowledge of how the sociopolitical system in the United States treats ethnic minorities. An examination of the history of oppression of culturally diverse groups is helpful in gaining this knowledge. This knowledge is perhaps best gained in a group where discussions focus on such topics as past and present patterns of oppression, personal experiences of oppression, and the effects of past and present discrimination on client attitudes and behaviors.

Knowledge of specific cultures is a second type of knowledge that the culturally sensitive counselor needs to possess. Although it is probably not possible to know all aspects of all ethnic minority cultures, the counselor should attempt to learn all that he or she can about the culture of any client with whom the counselor is working. This includes learning about the beliefs, values, behaviors, and history of the culture.

The third type of knowledge involves an understanding of which counseling theories and techniques are based on ethnocentric principles and which are generic enough to be applied to all cultural groups. Some aspects of counseling may be incongruent with the values of a particular culture and should be avoided. For example, client self-disclosure is considered to be an essential ingredient for a number of approaches to counseling. Yet self-disclosure of intimate feelings may be an anathema in some cultures. Reading books and articles on cross-cultural and multicultural counseling can facilitate knowledge about these incongruencies.

The final type of knowledge is an awareness of the institutional barriers that contribute to ethnic minority underuse of mental health services. This includes an awareness of how such factors as location, language, and structured appointments can contribute to underuse. This awareness probably is best developed by discussing institutional barriers with representatives of the various ethnic minority populations.

Counseling Skills

As with the critique of any professional behavior, we know much more about what is wrong with the counseling services provided ethnic minority clients than we do about what are appropriate counseling skills. Much has been written about the need for culturally sensitive counselors, but beyond defining the attitude of tolerance for diversity and the knowledge of various cultures as prerequisites for effective multicultural counseling, little has been written about the specific, unique skills needed to work with culturally diverse clients. A number of authors have discussed the need for counselors to use healing techniques from the client's indigenous culture, but these recommendations seem only appropriate for those situations where the client is completely (or almost completely) monocultural and his or her problem requires remediation rather than facilitation from a psychotherapist/healer. To the extent that counseling by definition is a facilitative, educational, preventive process that focuses on client decision making, the use of indigenous healing techniques appears to have limited application.

It can reasonably be argued that any counseling procedure that is helpful in multicultural counseling also can be applied effectively with European American clients. This argument should not deter us, however, from attempting to identify specific skills that may need to be employed with greater regularity and more intensely when the client is a member of an ethnic minority population than when the client is European American. With this caveat in mind, we identify three types of counseling skills that are needed when working with ethnic minority clients: (1) assessment of cultural influences; (2) credibility building; and (3) culturally relevant strategies. It should also be noted prior to the following discussion that the ongoing examination of beliefs/attitudes and the acquisition of knowledge about cultures are essential prerequisites to developing and using these three types of skills.

Assessment of Cultural Influences

When a counselor is working with an ethnic minority client, it is imperative that the counselor assess the influence of the indigenous and dominant cultures on the life of the client. To conduct this assessment, the counselor must be knowledgeable about the relevant indigenous culture, the process of acculturation and/or ethnic identity development, and the potential for conflict between the indigenous and dominant cultures. The goals of the assessment are to determine (1) where the client is on the acculturation and/or ethnic identity development continuum and (2) whether cultural conflict is playing a role in either the client's presenting or underlying problem.

The assessment of where the client is on the acculturation and/or ethnic identity development continuum must be done without an acculturation or development bias. If the counselor has a preconceived notion about acculturation and identification, it is a good indication that the counselor is still operating from an ethnocentric value structure and that further self-examination is needed in the area of beliefs/attitudes. The purpose of this assessment is to understand the client better, build credibility with the client, and determine what counseling strategies might be most effective. Although the concepts of cultural identification and acculturation apply to all racial/ethnic groups, they are most readily applied to American Indians, Asian American, and Hispanic Americans because a body of literature exists about acculturation among these groups. Recent research, however, has introduced the concept of African American acculturation into the literature (Landrine & Klonoff, 1994, 1995). Similarly, although the concept of racial/ethnic identity development can be applied to other racial/ethnic groups (Leong, 1986; Phinney, 1993) it applies most readily to African Americans due to the earlier work on black identity development.

The assessment of client acculturation or identity development can be done either reactively or proactively, whichever is more consistent with the counselor's own approach to counseling. A reactive assessment involves careful listening for client-initiated information about the client's cultural values and ethnic identification. A proactive assessment involves sensitive queries about the client's cultural/ethnic identification. Overly aggressive questions about the client's cultural/ethnic identification may be perceived by the client as intrusive and unnecessary, particularly if the client feels his or her identification is unrelated to the problem.

Assessment of the role that cultural conflict plays in the client's presenting or underlying problem also can be reactive (careful listening) or proactive (sensitive queries). In our opinion, however, the counselor should remain in a reactive mode initially, at least until the client has provided some information that suggests cultural conflict as a factor. The possibility of cultural conflict playing a role in the problem may not be apparent to the client immediately, and the counselor may have to make this connection for the client after sufficient data have been collected in the interview. For example, an ethnic minority client may present homework procrastination and poor grades in college as a major concern, but in the course of the counseling session may reveal that expectations of his or her ethnic community determined enrollment in a major that the client finds uninteresting. A culturally sensitive counselor does not attempt to solve the conflict but rather helps the client identify it as a possible issue and then facilitates the client's resolution of the conflict.

Credibility Building

S. Sue and Zane (1987) assert that counselor credibility is a particularly relevant consideration in working with culturally diverse groups. A counselor is viewed as a credible source of help when the client perceives the counselor to be an expert and trustworthy helper. According to S. Sue and Zane, counselor credibility is enhanced through ascribed status (the position one is assigned by others) and achieved status (status one earns as a result of one's skills). These authors go on to suggest that use of counseling services by ethnic minorities primarily may be a function of ascribed credibility, and premature termination by ethnic minorities primarily may be a function of achieved credibility.

The obvious implication of this discussion is that counselors should attempt to optimize their ascribed and achieved credibility with culturally diverse clients in order to increase the chances that they will enter and remain in counseling. Although ascribed status may be a function of rather inflexible characteristics such as age, sex, and professional degree and how these characteristics are viewed by the client's culture, counselors can do something about their achieved status. S. Sue and Zane (1987) hypothesize that by conceptualizing client problems in a way that is consistent with the client's belief system, interacting with the client in ways that are consistent with the client's cultural values, and defining goals for counseling that are consistent with the client's perception of the problem, the counselor can enhance his or her credibility. In contrast, by adhering strictly to a conceptualization of client problems based on a particular theory, placing demands on clients to interact in ways that they find repugnant or irrelevant, and devaluing the client's stated goal by focusing on a hypothesized underlying goal, the counselor may lose credibility. This discussion once again emphasizes the importance of gaining knowledge about, and an appreciation for, the client's culture.

Culturally Relevant Strategies

Basically, two approaches to providing culturally relevant strategies for ethnic minority clients have been espoused. One approach, frequently cited for Asian, Hispanic, and Native Americans, is to adopt the healing techniques that are part of the client's indigenous culture. As suggested earlier, however, the blanket recommendation that healing techniques from the client's indigenous culture should be used with a culturally diverse client seems unjustified, given that some fully acculturated clients may prefer mainstream counseling techniques. A second approach is to adapt current counseling strategies to the client's culture. The counseling strategies that frequently are cited as culturally appropriate for ethnic minority clients are directive counseling strategies. For example, it is recommended that for low-income African American clients, counseling that is characterized by a directive approach is more effective than an approach that is introspective and insight oriented (MacKinnon & Michels, 1971). Similar prescriptions have been advised for Asian, Hispanic, and Native American clients. However, these recommendations appear to be based more on class-bound issues than on issues that are relevant to culture. For example, Vontress (1981) notes that a directive approach to counseling may be as appropriate for poor Appalachian clients of European descent as it is for poor ethnic minority clients. In addition to the concern that preferences for directive counseling approaches are related to class issues, some directive strategies may actually hinder the counseling relationship. Richardson (1981) noted that advice giving should be avoided in counseling with American Indians. He argued that advice giving by non-Indians may be perceived as authoritarian and demeaning to the client. Similar concerns may hold for other ethnic minority clients; ethnic minority clients may perceive that counselors who offer excessive advice are viewing and treating them as childlike or unequipped to make decisions for themselves. As one might imagine, there are many dangers to overgeneralizing approaches with certain groups that depend on a number of significant factors.

A recent examination (Zane, Hatanaka, Park, & Akutsu, 1994) of ethnic-specific mental health services provided for Asian Americans found few significant differences in client outcome and premature or early termination between Asian American and European American clients. This finding appears to suggest that ethnic-specific or culture-relevant counseling strategies may make counseling more amenable to and/or effective for ethnic minority clients.

In our opinion, the counselor must have a thorough knowledge of the client's culture before attempting to either adopt indigenous healing techniques or adapt directive (or any other) counseling strategies to meet the needs of the client. We also believe that the need for culturally relevant strategies can be conceptualized as a continuum ranging from no need for the fully acculturated ethnic minority client to considerable need for the fully traditional culturally diverse client. Another factor that will influence the need for culturally relevant strategies is the purpose of counseling. If the purpose is to facilitate client decision making, healing techniques based on the indigenous belief system may be of little value. In contrast, if the purpose is to remediate a psychological disorder, use of a healing technique consistent with the client's belief system may be imperative.

In our judgment, a counselor should apply prescriptive strategies only if he or she first has acquired the appropriate beliefs/attitudes and knowledge. Rather than indiscriminately applying a prescriptive approach to counseling all ethnic minority clients, the culturally competent counselor first assesses (1) the client's level of acculturation (or stage of identity development), (2) the extent to which barriers to establishing rapport are present within the relationship, (3) the extent to which culture-specific issues may influence the problem or facilitate the treatment process, and (4) whether the goal is remediation or prevention. Given this information, the counselor can then determine whether it is most appropriate to adopt a healing technique from the client's culture or adapt counseling approaches to the client's level of acculturation/identity development.

Summary

Some issues relevant to counseling ethnic minority clients are the acknowledgment and appreciation of the unique cultural characteristics of ethnic minority groups and the consideration of the common experience of oppression. Ethnic minority populations are defined by experiences that ethnic minorities share in common—discrimination and cultural conflict. Although American Indians, African Americans, Asian Americans, and Hispanic Americans share some common experiences, it is important to recognize the differences among and within the four groups. Some criticisms that have been leveled against the profession are the presence of biases in the delivery of services to ethnic minority clients, the failure of the profession to address the needs of ethnic minority clients, and the underrepresentation of ethnic minority counselors in the field of mental health. Although the profession has initiated some measurable changes in the areas of training and research, there is considerable room for improvement.

With respect to guidelines for practice, counselors should begin by examining and evaluating their attitudes and beliefs toward ethnic minorities through identity development. This process is different for European American and ethnic minority counselors. European American counselors should examine their status in the dominant culture, as well as their level of acceptance of culturally diverse populations as equal. Ethnic minority counselors should consider their identity development in terms of their level of acculturation to the dominant culture, as well as their attitudes toward their own ethnic group and other culturally diverse populations. Also crucial in becoming culturally competent is the need to acquire knowledge related to the sociopolitical conditions affecting ethnic minorities, specific cultures, counseling theories and techniques based on ethnocentric principles, and the barriers to service use. Finally, culturally appropriate counseling skills include skills in assessing cultural influences, building credibility, and providing culturally relevant strategies.

References

Abramowitz, S. I., & Murray, J. (1983). Race effects in psychotherapy. In J. Murray & P. R. Abramsom (Eds.), *Bias in psychotherapy* (pp. 215–255). New York: Praeger.

Altmaier, E. M. (1993). Role of Criterion II in accreditation. *Professional Psychology: Research & Practice, 24*(2), 127–129.

American Psychological Association (APA). (1993). Guidelines for providers of psychological services to ethnic, linguistic, and culturally diverse populations. *American Psychologist, 48*, 45–48.

Anderson, L. P. (1991). Acculturative stress: A theory of relevance to Black Americans. *Clinical Psychology Review, 11*(6), 685–702.

Arredondo, P. (1985). Cross-cultural counselor education and training. In P. Pederson (Ed.), *Handbook of cross-cultural counseling and therapy* (pp. 281–290). Westport, CT: Greenwood Press.

Atkinson, D. R. (1983). Ethnic similarity in counseling psychology: A review of the research. *Counseling Psychologist, 11*(3), 79–92.

Atkinson, D. R. (1985). A meta-review of research in cross-cultural counseling and psychotherapy. *Journal of Multicultural Counseling and Development, 13*, 138–153.

Atkinson, D. R., Casas, A., & Abreu, J. (1992). Mexican-American acculturation, counselor ethnicity and cultural sensitivity, and perceived counselor competence. *Journal of Counseling Psychology, 39*(4), 515–520.

Atkinson, D. R., & Gim, R. H. (1989). Asian-American cultural identity and attitudes toward mental health services. *Journal of Counseling Psychology, 36*, 209–212.

Atkinson, D. R., Jennings, R. G., & Liongson, L. (1990). Minority students' reasons for not seeking counseling and suggestions for improving services. *Journal of College Student Development, 31*(4), 342–350.

Atkinson, D. R., & Lowe, S. M. (1995). The role of ethnicity, cultural knowledge, and conventional techniques in counseling and psychotherapy. In J. G. Ponterotto, J. M. Casas, L. A. Suzuki, & C. M. Alexander (Eds.), *Handbook of Multicultural Counseling* (pp. 387–414). Thousand Oaks, CA: Sage.

Atkinson, D. R., Lowe, S., & Matthews, L. (1995). Asian-American acculturation, gender, and willingness to seek counseling. *Journal of Multicultural Counseling & Development, 23*(3), 130–138.

Atkinson, D. R., & Matsushita, Y. J. (1991). Japanese-American acculturation, counseling style, counselor ethnicity, and perceived counselor credibility. *Journal of Counseling Psychology, 38*(4), 473–478.

Atkinson, D. R., Morten, G., & Sue, D. W. (1989). *Counseling American minorities.* Dubuque, IA: Brown.

Austin, N. L., Carter, R. T., & Vaux, A. (1990). The role of racial identity in black students' attitudes toward counseling and counseling centers. *Journal of College Student Development, 31*(93), 237–244.

Bennett, S. K., & Big Foot-Sipes, D. S. (1991). American Indian and White college student preferences for counselor characteristics. *Journal of Counseling Psychology, 38*(4), 440–445.

Bernal, M. E., & Castro, F. G. (1994). Are clinical psychologists prepared for service and research with ethnic minorities? Report of a decade of progress. *American Psychologist, 49*(9), 797–805.

Bernal, M. E., & Padilla, A. M. (1982). Status of minority curricula and training in clinical psychology. *American Psychologist, 37*, 780–787.

Big Foot-Sipes, D. S., Dauphinais, P., LaFromboise, T. D., Bennett, S. K., & Rowe, W. (1992). American Indian secondary school students' preferences for counselors. *Journal of Multi-cultural Counseling and Development, 20*(3), 113–122.

Carney, C. G., & Kahn, K. B. (1984). Building competencies for effective cross-cultural counseling: A developmental view. *Counseling Psychologist, 12,* 111–119.

Carter, R. T. (1991). Racial identity attitudes and psychological functioning. *Journal of Multi-cultural Counseling and Development, 19*(3), 105–114.

Casas, J. M. (1984). Policy, training, and research in counseling psychology: The racial/ethnic minority perspective. In S. D. Brown & R. W. Lent (Eds.), *Handbook of counseling psychology* (pp. 785–831). New York: Wiley.

Casas, J. M. (1985). A reflection on the status of racial/ethnic minority research. *Counseling Psychologist, 13,* 581–598.

Casas, J. M., Ponterotto, J. G., & Gutierrez, J. M. (1986). An ethical indictment of counseling research and training: The cross-cultural perspective. *Journal of Counseling and Development, 64,* 347–349.

Cheung, F. K., & Snowden, L. R. (1990). Community mental health and ethnic minority populations. *Community Mental Health Journal, 26*(3), 277–291.

Coleman, H. L. K., Wampold, B. E., & Casali, S. L. (1995). Ethnic minorities' ratings of ethnically similar and European American counselors: A meta-analysis. *Journal of Counseling Psychology, 42*(1), 55–64.

Corvin, S. A., & Wiggins, F. (1989). An antiracism training model for white professionals. *Journal of Multicultural Counseling and Development, 17,* 105–114.

Cross, W. E., Jr. (1972). The Negro-to-black conversion experience: Toward a psychology of black liberation. *Black World, 20*(9), 12–37.

Cross, W. E., Jr. (1978). The Cross and Thomas models of psychological nigrescence. *Journal of Black Psychology, 5,* 13–19.

Cross, W. E., Jr. (1995). The psychology of nigrescence: Revising the Cross model. In J. G. Ponterotto, J. M. Casas, L. A. Suzuki, & C. M. Alexander (Eds.), *Handbook of multicultural counseling* (pp. 91–122). Thousand Oaks, CA: Sage.

Gim, R. H., Atkinson, D. R., & Kim, S. J. (1991). Asian-American acculturation, counselor ethnicity and cultural sensitivity, and ratings of counselors. *Journal of Counseling Psychology, 38*(1), 57–62.

Gim, R. H., Atkinson, D. R., & Whiteley, S. (1990). Asian-American acculturation, severity of concerns, and willingness to see a counselor. *Journal of Counseling Psychology, 37*(3), 281–285.

Graham, S. (1992). "Most of the subjects were white and middle class": Trends in published research on African Americans in selected APA journals, 1970–1989. *American Psychologist, 47*(5), 629–639.

Grier, W. H., & Cobbs, P. M. (1968). *Black rage.* New York: Bantam Books.

Harrison, D. K. (1975). Race as a counselor–client variable in counseling and psychotherapy: A review of the research. *Counseling Psychologist, 5,* 124–133.

Helms, J. E. (1984). Toward a theoretical explanation of the effects of race on counseling: A black and white model. *Counseling Psychologist, 12,* 153–165.

Helms, J. E. (1985). Cultural identity in the treatment process. In P. Pederson (Ed.), *Handbook of cross-cultural counseling and therapy* (pp. 239–245). Westport, CT: Greenwood Press.

Helms, J. E. (1989). Considering some methodological issues in racial identity counseling research. *Counseling Psychologist, 12,* 227–252.

Helms, J. E. (1990). *Black and white racial identity: Theory, research, and practice.* New York: Greenwood Press.

Helms, J. E., & Carter, R. T. (1991). Relationships of white and black racial identity attitudes and demographic similarity to counselor preferences. *Journal of Counseling Psychology, 38*(4), 446–457.

Hills, H. I., & Strozier, A. L. (1992). Multicultural training in APA-approved counseling psychology programs: A survey. *Professional Psychology: Research & Practice, 23*(1), 43–51.

Hu, T., Snowden, L. R., Jerrell, J. M., & Nguyen, T. D. (1991). Ethnic populations in public mental health: Services choice and level of use. *American Journal of Public Health, 81*(11), 1429–1434.

Ibrahim, F. A., & Arredondo, P. M. (1986). Ethical standards for cross-cultural counseling. Counselor preparation, practice, assessment, and research. *Journal of Counseling and Development, 64*, 349–351.

Ivey, A. (1977). Cultural expertise: Toward systematic outcome criteria in counseling and psychological education. *Personnel and Guidance Journal, 55*, 296–302.

Jackson, B. (1975). Black identity development. *Journal of Educational Diversity, 2*, 19–25.

Johnson, M. E., & Lashley, K. H. (1989). Influence of Native-Americans' cultural commitment on preferences for counselor ethnicity and expectations about counseling. *Journal of Multicultural Counseling and Development, 17*(30), 115–122.

Johnson, S. D., Jr. (1982). *The Minnesota Counselor Education Curriculum: The design and evaluation of an intervention for cross-cultural counselor education.* Unpublished doctoral dissertation, University of Minnesota, Minneapolis.

Johnson, S. D., Jr. (1987). Knowing that versus knowing how: Toward achieving expertise through multicultural training for counseling. *Counseling Psychologist, 15*, 320–331.

Johnson, S. D. (1990). Toward clarifying culture, race, and ethnicity in the context of multicultural counseling. *Journal of Multicultural Counseling and Development, 18*(1), 41–50.

Jourard, S. M. (1964). *The transparent self.* Princeton, NJ: Van Nostrand.

Katz, J. H., & Ivey, A. G. (1977). White awareness: The frontier of racism awareness training. *Personnel and Guidance Journal, 55*, 485–489.

Landrine, H., & Klonoff, E. A. (1994). The African American Acculturation Scale: Development, reliability, and validity. Special Section: Africentric values, racial identity, and acculturation: Measurement, socialization, and consequences. *Journal of Black Psychology, 20*(2), 104–127.

Landrine, H., & Klonoff, E. A. (1995). The African American Acculturation Scale II: Cross-validation and short form. *Journal of Black Psychology, 21*(2), 124–152.

Leong, F. T. L. (1986). Counseling and psychotherapy with Asian-Americans: A review of the literature. *Journal of Counseling Psychology, 33*(2), 196–206.

Lopez, S. R., Lopez, A. A., & Fong, K. T. (1991). Mexican Americans' initial preferences for counselors: The role of ethnic factors. *Journal of Counseling Psychology, 38*(4), 487–496.

MacKinnon, R. A., & Michels, R. (1971). *The psychiatric interview in clinical practice.* Philadelphia: Saunders.

McRae, M. B., & Johnson, S. D. (1991). Toward training for competence in multicultural counselor education. Special Issue: Multiculturalism as a fourth force in counseling. *Journal of Counseling and Development, 70*(1), 131–135.

Mena, F. J., Padilla, A. M., & Maldonado, M. (1987). Acculturative stress and specific coping strategies among immigrant and later generation college students. Special Issue: Acculturation research. *Hispanic Journal of Behavioral Sciences, 9*(2), 207–225.

Mintz, L. B., Bartels, K. M., & Rideout, C. A. (1995). Training in counseling ethnic minorities and race-based availability of graduate school resources. *Professional Psychology: Research & Practice, 26*(3), 316–321.

Murphy, M. C., Wright, B. V., & Bellamy, D. E. (1995). Multicultural training in university counseling center predoctoral psychology internship programs: A survey. *Journal of Multicultural Counseling and Development, 23*(3), 170–180.

Nickerson, K. J., Helms, J. E., & Terrell, F. (1994). Cultural mistrust, opinions about mental illness, and black students' attitudes toward seeking psychological help from white counselors. *Journal of Counseling Psychology, 38*(4), 446–457.

Padgett, D. K., Patrick, C., Burns, B. J., & Schlesinger, H. J. (1994). Women and outpatient mental health services: Use by black, Hispanic, and white women in a national insured population. Special Issue: Women's mental health services. *Journal of Mental Health Administration, 21*(4), 347–360.

Padilla, A. M. (1985). Acculturation and stress among immigrants and later generation individuals. *Spanish Speaking Mental Health Research Center Occasional Papers*, (20), 41–60.

Parham, T. A. (1989). Cycles of psychological nigrescence. *Counseling Psychologist, 17,* 187–226.

Parham, T. A., & Helms, J. E. (1981). The influence of black students' racial identity attitudes on preference for counseling race. *Journal of Counseling Psychology, 28,* 250–257.

Parham, T. A., & Helms, J. E. (1985a). Attitudes of racial identity and self-esteem of black students: An exploratory investigation. *Journal of College Student Personnel, 26,* 143–146.

Parham, T. A., & Helms, J. E. (1985b). Relation of racial identity attitudes to self-actualization and affective states of black students. *Journal of Counseling Psychology, 32,* 431–440.

Pederson, P. B. (1978). Four dimensions of cross-cultural skill in counseling training. *Personnel and Guidance Journal, 56,* 480–484.

Phinney, J. S. (1992). The multigroup ethnic identity measure: A new scale for use with diverse groups. *Journal of Adolescent Research, 7*(2), 156–176.

Phinney, J. S. (1993). A three-stage model of ethnic identity development in adolescence. In M. E. Bernal, & G. P. Knight (Eds.), *Ethnic identity: Formation and transmission among Hispanics and other minorities* (pp. 61–79). Albany: State University of New York Press.

Pomales, J., Claiborn, C. D., & LaFromboise, T. D. (1986). Effects of black students' racial identity on perceptions of white counselors varying in cultural sensitivity. *Journal of Counseling Psychology, 33,* 57–61.

Ponce, F. Q., & Atkinson, D. R. (1989). Mexican-American acculturation, counselor ethnicity, counseling style, and perceived counselor credibility. *Journal of Counseling Psychology, 36,* 203–208.

Ponterotto, J. G. (1988a). Racial consciousness development among white counselor trainees: A stage model. *Journal of Counseling and Development, 16,* 146–156.

Ponterotto, J. G. (1988b). Racial/ethnic minority research in the *Journal of Counseling Psychology:* A content analysis and methodological critique. *Journal of Counseling Psychology, 35,* 410–418.

Ponterotto, J. G., Alexander, C. M., & Grieger, I. (1995). A Multicultural Competency Checklist for counseling training programs. *Journal of Multicultural Counseling and Development, 23*(1), 11–20.

Ponterotto, J. G., Alexander, C. M., & Hinkston, J. A. (1988). Afro-American preferences for counselor characteristics: A replication and extension. *Journal of Counseling Psychology, 35,* 175–182.

Pope-Davis, D. B., Reynolds, A. L., Dings, J. G., & Ottavi, T. M. (1994). Multicultural competencies of doctoral interns at university counseling centers: An exploratory investigation. *Professional Psychology: Research & Practice, 25*(4), 466–470.

Price, B. K., & McNeill, B. W. (1992). Cultural commitment and attitudes toward seeking counseling services in American Indian college students. *Professional Psychology: Research & Practice, 23*(5), 376–381.

Quintana, S. M., & Bernal, M. E. (1995). Ethnic minority training in counseling psychology: Comparisons with clinical psychology and proposed standards. *Counseling Psychologist, 23*(1), 102–121.

Richardson, E. (1981). Cultural and historical perspectives in counseling American Indians. In D. W. Sue (Ed.), *Counseling the culturally different: Theory and practice.* New York: Wiley.

Ridley, C. (1984). Clinical treatment of the nondisclosing black client: A therapeutic paradox. *American Psychologist, 39,* 1234–1244.

Ridley, C. R., Mendoza, D. W., & Kanitz, B. E. (1994). Multicultural training: Reexamination, operationalization, and integration. *Counseling Psychologist, 22*(2), 227–289.

Romero, D. (1985). Cross-cultural counseling: Brief reactions for the practitioner. Special Issue: Cross-cultural counseling. *Counseling Psychologist, 13*(4), 665–671.

Sabnani, H. B., Ponterotto, J. G., & Borodovsky, L. G. (1991). White racial identity development and cross-cultural counselor training: A stage model. *Counseling Psychologist, 19*(1), 76–102.

Saldana, D. H. (1994). Acculturative stress: Minority status and distress. *Hispanic Journal of Behavioral Sciences, 16*(2), 116–128.

Sanchez, A. R., & Atkinson, D. R. (1983). Mexican-American cultural commitment, preference for counselor ethnicity, and willingness to seek counseling. *Journal of Counseling Psychology, 30,* 215–220.

Sanchez, J. I., & Fernandez, D. M. (1993). Acculturative stress among Hispanics: A bidimensional model of ethnic identification. *Journal of Applied Social Psychology, 23*(8), 654–668.

Santos de Barona, M. (1993). The availability of ethnic materials in psychology journals: A review of 20 years of journal publication. *Contemporary Educational Psychology, 18*(4), 391–400.

Sattler, J. M. (1970). Racial "experimenter effect" in experimentation, testing, and interviewing, and psychotherapy. *Psychological Bulletin, 73,* 137–160.

Sattler, J. M. (1977). The effects of therapist–client racial similarity. In A. S. Gurman & A. M. Razin (Eds.), *Effective psychotherapy: A handbook of research* (pp. 252–290). New York: Pergamon Press.

Shin, K. R. (1994). Psychosocial predictors of depressive symptoms in Korean-American women in New York City. *Women & Health, 21*(1), 73–82.

Smart, J. F., & Smart, D. W. (1995a). Acculturative stress: The experience of the Hispanic immigrant. *Counseling Psychologist, 23*(1), 25–42.

Smart, J. F., & Smart, D. W. (1995b). Acculturative stress of Hispanics: Loss and challenge. *Journal of Counseling and Development, 73*(4), 390–396.

Smith, E. J. (1977). Counseling black individuals: Some stereotypes. *Personnel and Guidance Journal, 55*(7), 390–396.

Snowden, L. R., & Cheung, F. K. (1990). Use of inpatient mental health services by members of ethnic minority groups. *American Psychologist, 45*(3), 347–355.

Solomon, A. (1992). Clinical diagnosis among diverse populations: A multicultural perspective. Special Issue: Multicultural practice. *Families in Society, 73*(6), 371–377.

Sue, D. W. (1973). Ethnic identity: The impact of two cultures on the psychological development of Asian-in-Americans. In S. Sue & N. Wagner (Eds.), *Asian-Americans: Psychological perspectives* (pp. 140–149). Palo Alto, CA: Science and Behavior Books.

Sue, D. W. (1981). *Counseling and culturally different: Theory and practice.* New York: Wiley.

Sue, D. W., Bernier, J. E., Duran, A., Feinberg, L., Pederson, P., Smith, E. J., & Vasquez-Nuttal, E. (1982). Position paper: Cross-cultural counseling competencies. *Counseling Psychologist, 10*(2), 45–52.

Sue, S. (1977). Psychological theory and implications for Asian Americans. *Personnel and Guidance Journal, 55,* 381–389.

Sue, S., Akutsu, P. O., & Higashi, C. (1985). Training issues in conducting therapy with ethnic minority group clients. In P. Pederson (Eds.), *Handbook of cross-cultural counseling and therapy* (pp. 275–281). Westport, CT: Greenwood Press.

Sue, S., Fujino, D. C., Hu, L. and Takeuchi, D. T. (1991). Community mental health services for ethnic minority groups: A test of the cultural responsiveness hypothesis. *Journal of Consulting & Clinical Psychology, 59*(4), 533–540.

Sue, S., & Sue, D. W. (1977). Chinese-American personality and mental health. *Amerasia Journal, 1,* 36–49.

Sue, S., & Zane, N. (1987). The role of culture and cultural techniques in psychotherapy: A critique and reformulation. *American Psychologist, 42,* 37–45.

Terrell, F., & Terrell, S. (1981). An inventory to measure cultural mistrust among blacks. *Western Journal of Black Studies, 5,* 180–184.

Terrell, F., & Terrell, S. (1984). Race of counselor, client sex, cultural mistrust level, and premature termination from counseling among black clients. *Journal of Counseling Psychology, 31,* 371–375.

Thomas, A., & Sillen, S. (1972). *Racism and psychiatry.* New York: Brunner/Mazel.

Thompson, C. E., Worthington, R., & Atkinson, D. R. (1994). Counselor content orientation, counselor race, and black women's cultural mistrust and self-disclosures. *Journal of Counseling Psychology, 41*(2), 155–161.

Vontress, C. E. (1981). Racial and ethnic barriers in counseling. In P. B. Pederson, J. G. Draguns, W. J. Lonner, & J. E. Trimble (Eds.), *Counseling across cultures* (2nd ed., pp. 87–107). Honolulu: University of Hawaii Press.

Watkins, C. E., Jr., & Terrell, F. (1988). Mistrust level and its effects on counseling expectations in black client–white counselor relationships: An analogue study. *Journal of Counseling Psychology*, *35*, 194–197.

Watkins, C. E., Jr., Terrell, F., Miller, F., & Terrell, S. (1989). Cultural mistrust and its effects on expectational variables in black client–white counselor relationships. *Journal of Counseling Psychology*, *36*, 447–450.

Williams, C. L., & Berry, J. W. (1991). Primary prevention of acculturative stress among refugees: Application of psychological theory and practice. *American Psychologist*, *46*(6), 632–641.

Worthington, C. (1992). An examination of factors influencing the diagnosis and treatment of black patients in the mental health system. *Archives of Psychiatric Nursing*, 6(3), 195–204.

Wrenn, C. G. (1962). The culturally encapsulated counselor. *Harvard Educational Review*, *32*, 444–449.

Young, R. L., Chamley, J. D., & Withers, C. (1990). Minority faculty representation and hiring practices in counselor education programs. *Counselor Education & Supervision*, *29*(3), 148–154.

Zane, N., Hatanaka, H., Park, S. S., & Akutsu, P. (1994). Ethnic-specific mental health services: Evaluation of the parallel approach for Asian-American clients. Special Issue: Asian American mental health. *Journal of Community Psychology*, *22*(2), 68–81.

Chapter **20**

Counseling Clients
with Disabilities

Hanoch Livneh, Ph.D.   *Elizabeth T. Wosley-George, Ph.D.*

Counseling people with disabilities is quantitatively rather then qualitatively different from counseling able-bodied clients. The prime difference lies in the prominence with which certain themes (such as independence versus dependence, personal loss, coping with crisis situations) emerge during the counseling process. This chapter focuses on the application of various concepts and counseling interventions to working with clients who sustained a disability.

The chapter is organized into three main sections. First, a general overview of the principal goals and interventions for clients with disabilities is provided. Next the reader is familiarized with particular concerns facing clients who have specific disabilities and with appropriate strategies to counsel them. Finally, we offer a brief description of recommended academic education for counselors who intend to work with clients with disabilities, followed by a presentation of program accreditation and professional certification and membership issues.

Overview of Goals and Interventions
Applied to Clients with Disabilities

It has been suggested (Cowen, 1973; Hershenson, 1990; Leventhal & Hirschmann, 1982; Livneh, 1995) that the provision of human services may be conveniently categorized into three temporally ordered phases—prevention, intervention, and postvention. In prevention, often termed *primary intervention,* the focus is on education or the creation of public awareness as to the likelihood of certain activities or situations (such as smoking, job stress) causing physical (such as lung cancer) or psychological (such as burnout) problems. In other words, the emphasis is on preventing diseases and stressful situations before they are likely to occur. Intervention, the second phase, emphasizes the direct and time-limited strategies, adopted by practitioners, when dealing with crisislike situations, such as myocardial infarction or spinal cord injury (in the medical field) or suicide threats, panic attacks, and family crisis (in the psychotherapeutic field). Here emphasis is placed on early detection of signs of disease or crisis situations followed by an immediate intervention. Finally, the postvention or tertiary intervention phase is geared toward assisting people with permanent or long-lasting physical, psychiatric, and mental disabilities to cope successfully and adjust to life with the functional limitations imposed by the particular disabling condition. The focus is on restoring the client to optimal functioning. This latter phase is also known as *rehabilitation.*

The ultimate rehabilitation goals are improving quality of life (Crewe, 1980; Livneh, 1988) or adaptation to life with a disability. Life, however, does not proceed in a vacuum. Therefore, the abstract goal of improving quality of life may be concretized by anchoring it in two environmental contexts, namely, community and labor force memberships. The goal of community membership, or reintegration of people with disabilities, encompasses improving life quality via independent living, self-support, or self-sufficiency in both the home and the community at large. The goal of labor force reintegration, in contrast, pertains to the improvement of life through economic independence as typically manifested in successful gainful employment or related productive endeavors.

Rehabilitation goals may be further subdivided as to their adjustment domains—physical and psychosocial. The domain of physical adjustment concerns the body's capability to function successfully within its surroundings. It is assessed through the performance of activities of daily living (ADL), mobility, and the negotiation of the physical environment. Psychosocial adjustment concerns the capacity to function appropriately in the personal and interpersonal spheres. It often includes coping with the adverse effects of the disabling conditions and maintaining social competence in the face of negative attitudes and restrictions imposed by others.

Similarly, rehabilitation intervention strategies may also be conceived to be associated with community and labor force contexts and to focus on the physical and psychosocial domain. Moreover, rehabilitation interventions can be further classified into person-aimed (internal focus) and environment-aimed (external focus) strategies (Livneh, 1989; Scofield, Pape, McCracken, & Maki, 1980). Person-aimed interventions are those that envision the client as their prime target and seek to modify his or her emotions, perceptions, cognitions, behaviors, and/or skills. Examples of these types of interventions include personal adjustment counseling, behavioral modification, vocational counseling, and ADL skill development.

Environment-aimed interventions, in contrast, are those that consider the external environment as the target of interest and hence strive to modify it in order to meet client needs and goals. Among the latter interventions are removal of architectural barriers, use of assistive aids (such as hearing aids and prostheses) to restore lost perceptual and motoric functions, placement of the client in a group home, job tasks modification, and so on.

As is evident from this cursory classification of rehabilitation goals and interventions, counseling is just one modality adopted by practitioners who work with clients with disabilities. Indeed, personal adjustment counseling strategies occupy a single rehabilitation intervention component that belongs in the community context, focuses on the psychosocial adjustment domain, and emphasizes client-aimed interventions. This chapter is primarily concerned with applying counseling theories to personal (psychosocial) adjustment to life with a disability. The interested reader may refer to Anthony (1979), Coulton (1981), Livneh (1989), and Scofield et al. (1980) for further discussion of environment-aimed interventions and the various work-related rehabilitation modalities.

Application of Counseling Interventions to Specific Groups of Clients with Disabilities

People with disabilities share several common problems. The problems that affect the personal domain include (1) lack of motivation, frequently associated with secondary gain; (2) reluctance to participate in rehabilitation tasks; (3) depression; (4) damaged body image; (5) damaged self-concept; (6) loss of control; (7) loss of reward and pleasure source; (8) loss of physical and economic independence; (9) difficulty in accepting and adjusting to disability; and (10) inability to access the environment. Problems that impact the interpersonal domain include (1) dependence (medical, psychosocial, and/or financial); (2) impaired social and vocational roles; (3) changing family dynamics and relationships; (4) disruption of social life; (5) negative attitudes toward disability; (6) societal rejection and social isolation; (7) disuse or lack of appropriate social skills; and (8) decreased sexual activity (Auvenshine & Noffsinger, 1984; Backman, 1989; Lubkin, 1995; Medis, 1982; Thomas, Thoreson, Butler, & Parker, 1992; Vash, 1981; Wright, 1980).

In order to cope successfully with these issues, most authors recommend intervention strategies that emphasize the mastery of independent living and coping skills. Training modules aimed at achieving these goals typically stress the need for the client to acquire the physical, social, emotional, and cognitive skills necessary to successfully adapt to the disability. Moos and Tsu (1977) recommend the following adaptive tasks as part of coping with disability: (1) dealing with pain and incapacitation, (2) dealing with the management of stress in both institutionalized and community environments, (3) managing negative feelings elicited by the disability, (4) managing a positive self-image, (5) developing a sense of competence and mastery, (6) changing lifestyle, (7) fostering independence, (8) managing relationships with family and friends, and (9) preparing the client for an uncertain future when additional losses are anticipated. Other adaptive tasks may include the provision of information on available opportunities for regaining personal and economic independence; development of assertiveness skills; acquisition of decision-making, problem-solving, and goal-setting skills; value clarification; and dealing with motivational problems (Marshak & Seligman, 1993, Vash, 1981).

Since a client's personal needs and counseling goals invariably spring directly from the nature, duration, and severity of the disability, this section acquaints the reader with the most important disability-associated issues and psychological interventions applicable to counseling clients with disabilities. Counselors work with a large number of disabling conditions, only the most common of which are discussed in this chapter. The eight disabilities are blindness, deafness, spinal cord injury, cardiac impairment, epilepsy, cancer, traumatic head injury, and psychiatric disorders. Each condition is first considered as related to its impact on the person's life (functional limitations, psychosocial implications), and then recommendations for counseling and related interventions are provided.

Counseling Clients Who Are Blind

Impact of Blindness

It is estimated that almost 2 million Americans are blind or significantly visually impaired. Approximately two-thirds are 65 years or older, and less than 10 percent are below the age of 45 (Kirchner, 1988; Kirchner & Lowman, 1978). The following represent the major functional limitations associated with blindness.

Physical Impact

Obviously, the chief problem faced by a person who is blind is associated with mobility limitations. Lack of freedom of movement creates considerable obstacles for people who are blind. These obstacles compromise the capacity to live independently in the community and have direct implications for social and vocational functioning.

Psychosocial Impact

The individual who is blind frequently faces a dependence–independence conflict (Lindemann, 1981). Socially, such a person is almost completely dependent on the environment, yet emotionally he or she may not be prepared to accept this dependence. Hence, interpersonal relations are marked by self-restraint, insecurity, and cautiousness (Falvo, 1991; Gloor & Bruckner, 1980). Future goals and aspirations are strongly affected, as are relationships with the physical and social worlds. Related psychosocial difficulties may include underdeveloped socialization skills, lack of assertiveness, feelings of isolation, and increased anxiety level (Panek, 1992; Vander Kolk, 1983). Finally, a person who is blind often faces negative societal attitudes (rejection, social stereotyping, pity, fear, patronization) that further impede his or her integration into the community.

Recommendations for Intervention

The initial and undoubtedly foremost intervention modality with blind and visually impaired clients includes sight substitutes. Sight substitution methods include mobility training (cane travel and use of a guide dog) and compensatory communication training (large-type printer, special magnifying lenses, Braille use, Braille typewriters, Kurzweil reading machine use). The acquisition of such knowledge and skills brings about renewed positive self-esteem, a sense of independence and control of the environment.

The following recommendations are noted in the literature concerning the psychosocial adjustment to blindness (Cull, 1973; Falvo, 1991; Vander Kolk, 1983):

1. Assist the client to view disability functionally (emphasize remaining abilities) rather than anatomically (merely in terms of loss of sight).
2. Help the client understand the emotional responses (such as anxiety and depression) that follow adventitious blindness and accept this condition. Carroll (1961) argues that blind people need to reach a phase of acceptance of dying as a sighted person and rebirth as a blind person.
3. Explore feelings with regard to attitudes held by family and peers.
4. Help the client to understand feelings of family and peers that result from changes associated with the condition.
5. Be understanding and accepting of client's emotional responses and the psychological defenses used, and offer supportive counseling accordingly.
6. Avoid fostering unnecessary dependence in the client.
7. Help the client adjust his or her self-concept and personal goals so that realistic limits imposed by the disability are not ignored.
8. Teach the client self-care, socialization, assertiveness, and independent living skills.

Two counseling approaches that appear to be particularly suited for clients who are blind (see, for example, Vander Kolk, 1983) are behavioral therapy and Gestalt therapy. The former technique emphasizes modeling of adaptive behaviors via the senses of touch and hearing, reinforcement of appropriate behaviors, and rehearsal of newly acquired behaviors. The latter stresses acting out feelings and attitudes, and role-playing various inner conflicts associated with loss of sight. Finally, counselors must be aware that clients who are blind rely almost exclusively on auditory cues. The customary eye contact with the client is thus rendered ineffective. Similarly, long periods of silence that traditionally are judged to be constructive in allowing for reflective thinking may be interpreted by the client as signs of disinterest, distress, or rejection on the part of the counselor.

Counseling Clients Who Are Deaf

Impact of Deafness

More Americans have a hearing impairment than any other chronic physical or sensory disability. However, although approximately 20 million Americans have some form of unilateral or bilateral hearing impairment, only 2 million are classi-fied as having profound hearing loss (Kerman-Lerner & Hauck, 1993; Schein, 1981). The principal functional limitations associated with deafness are discussed next.

Physical Impact

Since people who are deaf are restricted in their information intake to primarily visual channels, the paramount problem they encounter is communicative. Although fundamentally a social problem, loss of or impaired hearing poses nu-merous environmental obstacles that might have a direct effect on the person's safety and security. For example, the inability to readily respond to honking horns, police or ambulance sirens, children crying, a yell for help, a phone ringing, or a tree falling could create decidedly life-threatening situations in the lives of people who are deaf.

Psychosocial Impact

As mentioned, deafness creates a cardinal communicative handicap. The impact of deafness extends to include sociocultural deprivation, experiential depreciation, and isolation from family and friends. The entire processes of enculturation and environmental adaptation are negatively affected (Ostby & Thomas, 1984). Several authors (Costello, 1973; Eleventh Institute on Rehabilitation Services, 1974; Falvo, 1991; Kerman-Lerner & Hauck, 1993; Lindemann, 1981) suggest that the following issues are often noted among people who are deaf.

1. A tendency to deny that there is anything wrong with one's hearing
2. Suspiciousness concerning other people's motivations and intentions
3. Conceptual and language limitations due to misunderstanding of many id-iomatic phrases
4. Maladaptive behavioral patterns (withdrawal, passive-aggressiveness) that prevent effective relationships with their hearing peers
5. Social and emotional immaturity
6. Difficulties in understanding and appreciating humor
7. Frustrations due to inadequate communication and isolation from the hearing population
8. Grief reactions, and at times full-blown depression, if onset of disability is sudden
9. Embarrassment at not being able to follow conversation
10. Overprotective, dependency-fostering parents and significant others

Recommendations for Intervention

When surgical or sound amplification methods (use of a hearing aid) fail to im-prove auditory functioning, treatment of the person who is deaf must resort to compensatory communication skills training. Among the most commonly used training methods are speech (lip) reading, speech therapy (especially for prelingual hearing loss), finger spelling, sign language, and the use of adaptive equipment (teletypewriters, television decoders, and telephone aids such as telecommunication devices for the deaf—TDD). Counselors who work with clients who are deaf should become proficient, yet remain flexible, in the use of these communicative methods (Falvo, 1991; Levine, 1977) and should be able to use body language and other nonverbal modes of communication (Eleventh Institute on Rehabilitation Services, 1974; Ostby & Thomas, 1984). In addition, the counselor should acquire sufficient knowledge about people who are deaf, their subculture, and the psychosocial, educational, and vocational ramifications of deafness.

The following counseling guidelines (adapted from Bolton, 1976) can enable the practitioner to better serve clients who are deaf:

1. Involve parents and family members in the counseling process, paying special attention to their attitudes toward the person who is deaf.
2. Adopt a situation-specific and practical counseling approach (emphasize the here-and-now). Avoid highly verbal and abstract levels of communication, especially when clients have become deaf prelingually.
3. Allow time and be patient, since clients who are deaf will generally require longer periods of time for services.
4. Realize that deaf clients often require various supportive services (such as interpreting, letter writing, and explanations of agency's rules and regulations).
5. Prepare clients for an acceptable level of overall functioning in the community (socialization skills, sex education, parenting skills, and work-related issues).
6. Become more aware of possible fatigue associated with lengthy communication periods.
7. Be direct and repeat whenever necessary.
8. Use paper and pencil to stress verbal messages.

Two counseling approaches that are of particular importance to the counselor who works with clients who are deaf are cognitive-behavioral and group counseling. In the former, the focus is on exposure to reality, learning the consequences of one's actions and choices, and the acquisition of socialization skills. Structured group counseling, in contrast, emphasizes realization of common problems shared by participants, goal setting, and the acquisition of vocational skills (Danek, 1983).

Counseling Clients Who Have Spinal Cord Injuries

Impact of Spinal Cord Injury

The National Spinal Cord Injury Data Research Center (Young, Burns, Bowen, & McCutchen, 1987), estimates that there are 150,000 individuals (paraplegics and quadriplegics) in the United States who have suffered spinal cord injury. Of these injuries, 70 percent occurred as a result of trauma, and the remaining 30 percent were associated with various diseases. Most people with spinal cord injury are young at the time of the accident (mean age = 28 years) and are males. The incidence of spinal cord injury in the United States is approximately 6,000 to 10,000 new injuries per year (Donovan, 1981). The functional limitations attributed to spinal cord injury are summarized next.

Physical Impact

Impaired mobility is obviously the cardinal limitation associated with spinal cord injury. However, in addition to restricted ambulation, individuals with spinal cord injury, depending on the degree and severity of their injury, might also have functional impairements in personal hygiene (for example, grooming and bathing activities), eating and drinking, dressing, toileting, writing, driving an automobile, and, especially in men, performing sexually). Further complications may arise from muscle spasticity, contractures (loss of range of motion), pressure sores, pain, cardiopulmonary and urinary system infections, and body temperature regulation (Donovan, 1981; Falvo, 1991; Hu & Cressy, 1992).

Psychosocial Impact

Two emotional responses often associated with the onset of spinal cord injury include denial of the injury's permanency or its degree of severity and depression and its predecessor, learned helplessness—the belief that one is powerless in controlling rewards and punishments (Crewe & Krause, 1987; Seligman, 1975).

Changes in body image invoke perceptual distortions that may result in diminished ability to acquire new physical skills and adapt to environmental requirements. Since social, occupational, and financial problems are rather common, disruption of family life and social roles may occur. Possible long-term psychological reactions to the traumatization are passivity, dependency (including secondary gain), passive-aggressiveness, frustration, and feelings of social inadequacy and embarrassment (Cull & Hardy, 1975). Increased substance abuse has also been observed among people with spinal cord injury (Heinemann, 1993; Hu & Cressy, 1992). Finally, attitudinal barriers and public misunderstanding may create additional obstacles, impeding the person with spinal cord injury from reintegrating into the physical, social, and vocational environments.

Recommendations for Intervention

For the most part, medical interventions for spinal cord injury include (1) surgery (to relieve pressure on the cord), (2) stabilization of the vertebral column, (3) medication (to relieve autonomic disturbances), (4) skin care, (5) bladder and bowel function training, (6) proper dietary control, (7) sexual functioning retraining, and (8) physical and occupational therapy to improve ambulation, mobility, and proper use of extremities (Hu & Cressy, 1992).

Counseling with people who have a spinal cord injury should address problems created by the injury in any area of life, including self-concept, acceptance of disability, independent living issues, sexual and marital adjustment, social relationships and vocational concerns (Brucker, 1983; Crewe & Krause, 1987; Cull & Hardy, 1975; Hu & Cressy, 1992). Two important concerns for clients with spinal cord injury are sexual functioning and socialization. Since the fertility rate for men is low and orgasmic capability is often lost in women (Crewe & Krause, 1987), these problems are of major concern to the client. Counselors should be, therefore, ready to deal with these and related sexual and marital concerns at any time during the counseling process. Clients may also need to be taught new interpersonal skills (knowing when to refuse unnecessary help or request assistance without feeling inadequate, embarrassed, or guilty).

Several authors view the goal of spinal cord injury rehabilitation as behavioral change of the client. Hence they recommend appropriate counseling methods to achieve this goal. Crewe and Krause (1987), for instance, suggest a cognitive-behavioral approach to identify client belief systems and then help them to better understand how their emotions and behaviors are shaped by their self-verbalization. They further recommend teaching clients to alter their beliefs in the direction of increased internal locus of control over life events. Romano (1976) reports on social skills and assertiveness training programs successfully employing behavioral rehearsal, modeling, and feedback to clients with spinal cord injuries.

Group and peer counseling modalities are particularly suited for counseling clients with spinal cord injury (Treischmann, 1988). In these settings, emphasis has been placed on issues such as problem solving, increased self-understanding, and gaining insight into the process of coping with disability and improved feelings of self-regard (Manley, 1973; Miller, Wolfe, & Spiegal, 1975).

Counseling Clients with Cardiac Impairment

Impact of Heart Impairment

Cardiovascular diseases are the leading cause of disability and death in the United States. A total of 30 million Americans have some form of heart and blood vessel disease. It is estimated that approximately 1 million Americans survive major cardiac events (such as heart attacks and coronary artery bypass surgery) annually (Houd, 1978; Rey, 1993). The major cardiovascular diseases include (1) high blood pressure (hypertension); (2) congestive heart failure (the heart's inability to pump sufficient blood to meet the body's requirements); (3) arteriosclerotic heart disease (buildup of lipid deposits on the inner walls of the arteries, leading to narrowing or blocking of the passages and resulting in a heart attack or coronary thrombosis); (4) heart attack or myocardial infarction (complete occlusion of the coronary artery, resulting in a portion of the heart muscle being deprived of blood supply); (5) rheumatic heart disease (a childhood disease resulting from rheumatic fever, which damages the heart muscle and valves); and (6) various congenital heart defects (Brammell, 1981; Falvo, 1991; Rey, 1993).

Physical Impact

The functional limitations associated with heart impairment are various. Chief among them are angina pectoris (chest pain), dyspnea (shortness of breath on exertion), diet restriction, difficulties in tolerating extremes of temperature, and limitations of vocational (such as restricted walking and lifting ability) and avocational (such as limited ability to engage in various sports activities) pursuits. The nature and degree of these limitations are linked directly to the severity and duration of the particular impairment involved (Johnson & Getzen, 1992; Rey, 1993).

Psychosocial Impact

Individuals affected by cardiac impairments are likely to exhibit reactions of fear and anxiety during the acute illness phase (following a heart attack) and long-term depressive reactions. Anxiety and depression are often magnified because of fears of recurrent attacks, forced dependency, other life stresses, sexual dysfunction, marital conflicts, financial worries, returning-to-work issues, and reduction in preimpairment activities (Falvo, 1991; Thoreson & Ackerman, 1981).

In addition, the client may deny impairment. Denial may take one of the following forms: (1) total denial of being ill or disabled, (2) denial of major incapacitation, (3) minimization of effects of disability, or (4) admission of illness in the past, but denial of its present incapacitation (Brammell, 1981). Further psychological reactions are feelings of helplessness, dependency, anger, and frustration (Thoreson & Ackerman, 1981).

Family reactions to the stress generated by the life-threatening impairment are of utmost importance. Because the majority of adult onset heart disorders, especially heart attacks, occur among employed males, the spouse's attitudes and support bear significantly on the success of the rehabilitation program. Frequently encountered spouse affective and behavioral responses, such as anxiety concerning the husband's survival, anxiety about the future (children's education, health insurance), added household and occupational responsibilities, and the like may strongly affect the husband's psychological adaptation (Thoreson & Ackerman, 1981).

Recommendations for Intervention

The goals of cardiac rehabilitation are to prolong the patient's life and improve life quality, both psychosocially and vocationally. These goals are accomplished via educating the client on the nature of the impairment and its risk factors, modifying lifestyle (for example, diet and alcohol and tobacco consumption), maintaining psychosocial integrity, and sustaining existing vocational abilities (Brammell, McDaniel, Niccoli, Darnell, & Roberson, 1979; Falvo, 1991). Medical methods geared toward life extension include (1) surgical procedures (coronary artery bypass, coronary angioplasty, electronic pacemaker implantation, cardiac transplantation), (2) restrictions on existing diet practices (reducing fat intake, restricting salt), (3) building exercise tolerance, (4) avoiding tobacco usage, and (5) medication (such as nitroglycerin, anticoagulants, and diuretics) to manage vessel dilation, chest pain, high blood pressure, and so forth (Falvo, 1991; Johnson & Getzen, 1992).

Psychosocial management to improve quality of life can be affected by numerous physical, psychological, social, vocational, and financial factors. It is incumbent on the counselor who works with heart patients to construct a comprehensive psychosocial rehabilitation program that incorporates the following elements (Backman, 1989; Nunes, Frank, & Kornfeld, 1987; Rey, 1993):

1. Provide the client with information on the nature of and functional limitations linked to heart disease.
2. Train the client in progressive muscle relaxation procedures, to relieve emotional stress.
3. Encourage the client to ventilate his or her pentup anxieties, concerns, and other negative emotions in a supportive, therapeutic environment.
4. Assist the client in cognitive restructuring, with the goal of modifying irrational emotional reactions and thoughts.
5. Apply behavioral modification procedures to enable the client to acquire appropriate behaviors necessitated by present physical conditions. Clients may be taught new adaptive behaviors through thought stopping of stress-inducing themes, behavioral prescriptions, role-playing exercises, and behavioral rehearsals of new and adaptive behaviors. These methods may be of particular importance when counseling type A individuals, who possess hard driving, competitive, and deadline-oriented personalities (Brammell et al., 1979; Gentry, 1978).
6. Pay attention to sexual concerns and misperceptions such as fear about coital death and impotence (Lindemann, 1981).
7. Discuss with client issues related to returning to work. Explore and analyze vocational interests, assets, and limitations, with the goal of achieving successful and functionally appropriate vocational placement.
8. Be cognizant of the symbolic significance of the human heart. Of all organs, it is arguably the one most closely associated with life itself. In their role as providers of health and quality of life improvement services, counselors should pay particular attention to the psychological importance of the heart and the dynamics, conscious or otherwise, associated with the process of adaptation to a chronic and life-threatening disability.

Counseling Clients with Epilepsy

Impact of Epilepsy

It is estimated that the incidence of recurring seizures or epilepsy in the general population is between 1 and 3 percent (Hauser & Hesdorffer, 1990). The reasons for this wide spread include different definitions and case-finding techniques (Hermann, Desai, & Whitman, 1988) and the unwillingness, among people affected and their families, to disclose this often misunderstood problem. Epileptic seizures, traditionally classified as *petit mal, grand mal, focal* or *Jacksonian,* and *psychomotor,* are currently termed *absence, generalized tonic-clonic, simple partial,* and *complex partial seizures,* respectively. They affect equally both genders and people of all age and ethnic groups. Approximately 75 percent of all people with epilepsy have developed seizures prior to the age of 21. With appropriate medication, 60 percent of those who have epilepsy can become seizure free and an additional 15–20 percent experience a reduction in their seizure frequency (Fraser, 1993; Hylbert & Hylbert, 1979).

Physical Impact

Epilepsy is a brain disorder. Its most prominent functional limitations, depending on the nature and type of seizure, is a temporary loss of consciousness (Wright, 1980). During the seizure-free periods, people with epilepsy are fully functioning members of society. Although ability to drive an automobile is usually not affected, differing states' laws require of them certain seizure-free periods (that may range from six to twenty-four months) before a driving license is issued. A second cluster of functional limitations often arises from the adverse side effects of anticonvulsant medication. These medications, especially when reaching toxic levels, can cause the user to have a wide array of symptoms, ranging from skin rash, gum bleeding, hand tremor, coordination difficulties, and vision problems to nausea, vertigo, fatigue, and drowsiness (Fraser, 1993).

Psychosocial Impact

The individual with epilepsy is confronted with numerous unresolved problems. He or she feels healthy at times and at other times feels him- or herself to be a person with epilepsy. The person with epilepsy must continuously face questions such as

"Since the epilepsy is a brain disorder, am I physically or mentally ill?"

"Since epilepsy has no cure or real end to it, what is the prognosis for my becoming seizure free? in remission? and for how long?"

"Is epilepsy inherited, or would the low threshold for the brain's abnormal electrical discharge be genetically transmitted to my offspring?"

"Will the seizure occur in social or work situations? And, if it does, how would people react to the seizure?"

Obviously, the anxiety and stress associated with the anticipation of seizures, the lack of a cognitively structured environment for the person with epilepsy, and the perceived discrediting attribute of epilepsy result in an immensely taxing psychosocial world. Attempts at concealing the condition lead to further stress and anxiety. These, in turn, are associated with increased seizures, resentful feelings of embarrassment, shame and guilt, and finally social isolation.

Ososkie (1984) and DeLoach and Greer (1981) underscore the negative impact that stigmatizing public attitudes have on the life of the person with epilepsy. The way family members and society at large react to the person with epilepsy has a decidedly large effect on the person's self-concept and adjustment. Parental over-protection and the imposition of many unnecessary restrictions foster dependency and isolation. Coupled with the frequently attached stigma by employers, ignorant of the factual basis of the disorder, many people with epilepsy find the world of work alien and frightening.

Lastly, as previously described, because of the side effects of high toxic levels of anticonvulsant medications many people with epilepsy also demonstrate periodic signs of impairment in various mental processes, including memory, attention, and judgment (Fraser, 1993; Ward, Fraser, & Troupin, 1981).

Recommendation for Intervention

Medical treatment of epilepsy consists of drug therapy and, in a small number of cases, brain surgery. Commonly used anticonvulsant medication, such as carbamazepine (Tegretol), phenytoin (Dilantin), phenobarbital (Lumanil), valproic acid (Depakene), and primidone (Mysoline), prevent either hypersynchronic neuron discharge or spread of discharge. Surgical intervention generally consists of removing a portion of the temporal lobe (temporal lobectomy) and is done when seizures are still uncontrollable after medication use (Fraser, 1993; Hermann et al., 1988). In addition, clients are advised to avoid excessive fatigue-created activities and emotional turmoil and assure themselves of adequate rest and a balanced diet.

General counseling goals include (1) examining the nature of the epileptic seizures and their effect on the client, (2) dispelling the misperceptions held by client and family regarding epilepsy and its functional implications, (3) discussing with client and family ways of coping with the adverse effects of epilepsy, and (4) minimizing the number of areas affected by the existence of epilepsy and assuming responsibility for, and independence of, one's own life. The counselor should seek to help the client accept the seizure condition, its unpredictability, and the feelings associated with it (Fraser & Clemmons, 1983). Denial of epilepsy is not an infrequent occurrence. Because denial is manifested in failure to comply with medication schedules, ignoring requests to avoid alcohol intake, and/or pursuit of vocational and avocational hazardous activities, this repudiation of reality must be dealt with by the counselor.

Awareness training Gestalt therapy techniques and supportive confrontational procedures are appropriate to combat unyielding denial. Clients who exhibit anxious or depressive reactions, who experience self-defeating thoughts, or who shun social interactions can benefit from cognitive and rational-emotive therapy methods. Here, clients are assisted in identifying the specific situation, the activities and beliefs that lead to the irrational, negative, and self-defeating cognitions and their resultant painful emotions, such as anxiety and depression (Fraser & Clemmons, 1983).

Behavioral modification (for example, positive and negative reinforcement, and time out) and self-management (for example, relaxation exercises) procedures have also been shown to be effective interventions with seizure-prone clients. Furthermore, their applications along with EEG biofeedback training were found to be positively associated with decreased seizure frequency (Kaplan & Wyler, 1983).

Group counseling approaches are recommended to enable clients to combat social isolation, deal with concealment or denial of impairment, and reach a state of disability acceptance (Ososkie, 1984). Similarly, group-based skill training classes are highly valuable in assisting participants to better understand and accept their condition as well as to share in the group's joint endeavors (Fraser & Clemmons, 1983). Finally, family counseling may help participants to deal with issues such as overprotection, covert or overt rejections, and guilt associated with perceived causation of impairment.

Counseling Clients with Cancer

Impact of Cancer

It is estimated that one in three to four individuals, or approximately 65 to 85 million Americans now living, will at one point contract cancer (Dunham, 1978; Elmayan, 1992). Approximately 1.1 million new cancer cases are detected each year in the United States, and there are, at present, over 3 million people (40 percent of those who were diagnosed with cancer) who have survived cancer for five or more years (Elmayan, 1992; Freidenbergs & Kaplan, 1993). Cancer is not a single disease entity. There are more than 100 different types of diseases termed *cancer* (often referred to as *malignancy* or *neoplastic disease*). Skin cancer is the overall most frequent type of cancer. However, breast and prostate cancers are the most frequent cancers for women and men, respectively. Among females, breast and uterine cancers are the chief causes of fatality, whereas lung and prostate cancers are the most common causes of death among males. Although cancer can strike at any age group, it is more common in older individuals (Freidenbergs & Kaplan, 1993; Healey & Zislis, 1981).

Physical Impact

Because of the variety of cancer types, it is virtually impossible to cogently discuss all the functional limitations associated with the disorder. Hence only the most prominent physical limitations resulting from the onset of cancer will be delineated. (The interested reader may refer to Falvo [1991] and Freidenbergs & Kaplan [1993] for a more detailed treatment of the topic.) Limitations on activities of daily living (grooming, bathing, dressing, feeding, toiletry) are more commonly associated with cancers affecting the brain, the larynx, head and neck, breast, lung, and upper extremities. Ambulation difficulties result more often from cancers of the lower extremities and the brain. Speech and communication are affected by cancers of the brain, the larynx, and the head and neck. Most cancers, with the possible exception of leukemia, lymphoma, and cancers of the lung and spinal cord, have an adverse effect on the person's sexual functioning and cosmesis. Finally, most forms of cancer are, at one point or another, associated with organic pain, feelings of fatigue, and general weakness (Elmayan, 1992; Healey & Zislis, 1981).

Psychosocial Impact

The diagnosis of cancer exerts an immense impact on the client and his or her family. Anxiety is one of the initially experienced reactions to the diagnosis of cancer. Several types of fear and anxiety have been mentioned in this regard. More commonly divulged fears include fear of losing one's future, fear of pain and mutilation associated with the cancerous growth, fear of losing integrity of the body, fear of being separated from loved ones, fear of creating a burden on family members, concern about how the family will care for itself, fear of losing self-control, fear of losing identity (self-image), and fear of losing one's independence (Allen & Sawyer, 1984; Carey, 1976; Falvo, 1991; Pattison, 1977).

A second reaction to cancer onset is denial. Denial of the condition, or its implications, may delay necessary treatment and have an adverse affect on the client and his or her family. Depression, yet another common reaction to life-threatening disorders, is a natural concomitant of cancer and is manifested by feelings of helplessness, hopelessness, vulnerability, and the like. Depressive themes may range from mourning of the anticipated loss of one's life to struggling with guilt feelings triggered by the belief that cancer may have been a punishment for past wrongdoings. Lastly, feelings of anger and bitterness are also prevalent and may be an indication of (1) inability to tolerate daily routine (medical regime, family reactions), (2) jealousy directed at others, or (3) blame projected onto others for the perceived onset of the condition or its lack of improvement.

Recommendations for Intervention

Medical treatment of cancer is accomplished through surgery, radiation therapy, and/or chemotherapy. Whereas surgery and radiation therapy are relatively straightforward procedures, chemotherapy—due to its generalized effects on many of the body systems—carries with it a host of related side effects (such as nausea, hair loss, fatigue, and weakness). Counselors who work with cancer clients should thoroughly familiarize themselves with these added problems and their psychosocial and social-familial implications (Elmayan, 1992; Falvo, 1991).

Immediately following the diagnosis of cancer, the counselor's main role is to assist the client with cancer to effectively cope with the ensuing anxiety and stress. The counselor should provide the client with accurate and useful information about the disease, its course, and the prognosis, so that irrational fears and misperceptions may be alleviated and realistic hope instilled. Hope frequently increases the client's motivation, sense of meaning, productivity, and adherence to the medical regime and successfully contributes to coping with the psychological impact of the disease (McAleer & Kluge, 1978; McCollum, 1978). Counselors, however, should be cautious in drawing a fine balance between optimism and realism. Issues of disease recurrence following treatment; the ambiguity surrounding the cause, treatment, and prognosis of the disease; the effects of treatment and its associated side effects; and the financial burdens of hospital and treatment cost should all be dealt with early in the counseling process (McAleer & Kluge, 1978).

The overriding goal of rehabilitation is restoring the client to the highest possible level of physical, psychological, social, and vocational functioning. Nowhere is this goal more important than in cancer rehabilitation. Similarly, enhancing the quality of life (even if time limited) becomes a primary concern of the counselor (Allen & Sawyer, 1984). Perhaps one of the first issues to be jointly explored by client and counselor should be that of *meaning* of the involved organ (loss of breast or leg, facial disfigurement) and the resulting pain and suffering to the client (Cobb, 1973). Uncovering the client's feelings regarding these issues may, then, serve as a predecessor toward finding a sense of meaning in one's life and the inevitability of death.

Obviously, one of the most painful tasks facing the counselor and client is dealing with the issue of death, dying, and the grieving process. As the disease progresses, and if no cure is found, and the certainty of impending death looms larger, most counseling sessions should focus on the acceptance of death. Counseling for the acceptance of death (Cobb, 1973; McAleer & Kluge, 1978) should focus on issues such as facing the agony of separation from loved ones, preparation of the family for the separation, taking pride in one's past accomplishments ("leaving a a mark" on this world), and the like. In order to successfully cope with these painful topics, the counselor should provide the client with emotional support and a sense of personal security, increase the client's feelings of personal worth and dignity, create an atmosphere where the client and family can openly and honestly express their emotions and ultimately serve as a "silent companion" to all involved people (Allen & Sawyer, 1984; Cobb, 1973; Kübler-Ross, 1969).

Insofar as an increasingly larger number of clients with cancer survive the disease, they should be allowed to assume gradual control over their lives and be given a significant role in participating and contributing to their own treatment program. They should be routinely consulted about setting goals and making decisions concerning situations affecting personal and family welfare. In this context, family counseling assumes particular importance. Decisions concerning family role redefinitions and role modifications must be faced. McAleer and Kluge (1978) recommend teaching the family problem solving and family management skills geared toward acceptance of disability-linked residual functional limitations (amputation, medication side effects), sexual activities, financial management, vocational readjustment, and recreational activities. Freidenbergs and Kaplan (1993) recommend a three-prong approach to counseling cancer patients that includes (1) educational interventions (such as clarifying the patient's medical condition), (2) counseling interventions (such as offering the patient reassurance and verbal support, and (3) environmental interventions (such as referring the patient for further health services).

Of the various counseling approaches, two that seem to address many of the aforementioned issues are Gestalt and cognitive-behavioral therapy. Gestalt therapy may benefit clients in resolving unfinished life issues that, due to the impending death, may never be resolved (saying farewell to loved ones and, in general, gaining awareness of personal feelings toward death and dying, pain and suffering). Behavioral interventions, in contrast, through the application of muscle relaxation techniques, systematic desensitization, thought stopping, and guided imagery can reduce muscle tension associated with anxiety, stress, and pain and allow clients to focus their thought on nonthreatening and pleasant scenes (Dolan, Allen, & Bell, 1988; Fleming, 1985; Lyles, Burish, Krozely, & Oldham, 1982).

Counseling Clients with Head Injury

Impact of Head Injury

Each year, approximately 500,000 people in the United States incur traumatic head injury (THI) requiring hospitalization. Of these individuals, 80 percent survive the head injury. However, 75,000 to 100,000 of these survivors sustain mental and physical impairments severe enough to render normal life virtually impossible (Kraus, 1987). THI affects primarily young adults in their late teens and twenties. Males outnumber females by a ratio of 2 or 4 to 1 (Dixon, Trexler, & Layton, 1993; Twelfth Institute on Rehabilitation Issues, 1985). THI is defined as "brain damage from a blow or other externally inflicted trauma to the head that results in significant impairment to the individual's physical, psychosocial and/or cognitive functional abilities" (Twelfth Institute of Rehabilitation Issues, 1985, p. 3). Hence THI differs from conditions emanating from internal brain traumas such as stroke or brain tumors.

Physical Impact

Since THI results from either direct and localized damage to the brain, or from more diffuse insult (concussion, brain swelling, intracranial fluid pressure), its physical manifestations are widely varied (Falvo, 1991). Physical correlates of THI typically include various perceptual-spatial deficits, such as visual-motor incoordination, visual dysfunction, muscle spasticity, seizures and aphasia, and might also be associated with headaches, dizziness, lack of energy, and fatigue (Dixon et al., 1993; Novack, Roth, & Boll, 1988; Torkelson-Lynch, 1983). Almost all clients will initially be affected in their ability to read, write, eat, dress, ambulate, drive, and attend to personal hygiene (Anderson, 1981).

Psychosocial Impact

The effects of THI on personality may be conveniently classified into three general categories—cognitive, affective, and behavioral. The cognition consequences of head trauma encompass all intellectual deficits resulting from the injury. These include impairments of verbal processes, learning, memory, recognition, abstract reasoning, judgment, attention, and concentration. Affected are speech and language abilities (communicative and symbolic processing), insight, organizational skills, problem-solving and decision-making skills, and processing of information (Dixon et al., 1993; Falvo, 1991; Novack et al., 1988; Rosenthal, 1987; Torkelson-Lynch, 1983).

The affective consequences of THI relate to the emotional reactions directly associated with the onset of injury. The most common emotional reactions include anxiety, denial, depression, and agitation. Anxiety is manifested through paniclike and catastrophic reactions to the impairment and persistent irritability (Prigatano, 1989). Denial of the disorder is a rather common reaction among head-injured people. It may range from minimizing the consequences of the injury and its permanence to unawareness of existing problems and to failure to acknowledge the injury itself (Rosenthal, 1987). Depression, which usually sets in following initial acknowledgment of the injury and its consequences, is manifested by low self-regard, feelings of worthlessness, social withdrawal, and generally diminished or blunted affect. Finally, agitation (usually considered a by-product of lower tolerance for frustration) is typified by emotional lability (frequent and easily triggered changes in temperament), anger, irritability, loss of control over emotions, self-centeredness, lack of concern for others' welfare, suspiciousness, and impatience (Falvo, 1991; Greif & Matarazzo, 1982).

The behavioral components of THI include impulsivity, aggressive behavior, behavioral restlessness, social disinhibition (including sexually aggressive remarks), decreased initiative and motivation, and diminished goals-directed behaviors. These correlates of psychomotor agitation are often traced to temporal lobe damage (Falvo, 1991; Greif & Matarazzo, 1982).

Recommendations for Interventions

A wide range of interventions is available for helping clients with THI. Since a substantial number of the THI survivors manifest behavioral disorders, the goals of most rehabilitation programs have been geared toward decreasing these behavioral disturbances, increasing socially appropriate behaviors and preparing the individual to enter the community after the acquisition of independent living and when feasible, educational and vocational skills. Prigatano et al. (1986) further describe the goals of psychotherapy with THI clients as (1) providing a model that helps clients understand what has happened to them, (2) helping clients deal with the meaning of the brain injury in their life, (3) helping clients achieve a sense of self-acceptance and forgiveness for themselves and others who have caused the accident, (4) helping clients make realistic commitments to interpersonal relations and work, (5) teaching clients how to behave in different social situations, (6) providing specific behavioral strategies for compensating for neuropsychological deficits, and (7) fostering a sense of realistic hope.

Behaviorally oriented treatment approaches appear to be particularly useful when counseling clients who have sustained head injury. Behavioral management—based on operant conditioning principles such as negative reinforcement (to modify or extinguish maladaptive behaviors), positive reinforcement in the form of social praise and tangible rewards (to increase appropriate social behaviors), behavioral shaping (reinforcing approximations of desired responses), and token economies—is often used with THI clients (Greif & Matarazzo, 1982; McMahon & Fraser, 1988; Wood, 1984).

Another treatment approach frequently used is based on cognition remediation principles. Using intensive teaching, cognitive retraining, and extensive rehearsal, clients are taught to improve their mental functions and gradually ameliorate their perceptual, verbal, thought-processing, and problem-solving deficits (Ben-Yishay & Diller, 1983; Harris, 1984). In order to achieve these targets, counselors adopt a variety of highly structured activities to facilitate learning. These include the use of memory aids such as written or tape-recorded reminders and diaries, repeated explanations, and multiple examples to gradually instill confidence in the client in the ability to cope with the cognitive challenges of everyday life activities, such as problem solving, money, and time management (Greif & Matarazzo, 1982; Novack et al., 1988).

A rather unique approach is provided by Torkelson-Lynch (1983), who uses a modified three-phase Carkhuffian model to counsel clients with THI. In her approach, Torkelson-Lynch first explores with the client his or her feelings toward each established goal (such as improved grooming or job exploration). Second, during the understanding and knowledge-gaining phase, instructions and explanations are related to the client as clearly and explicitly as possible. Finally, in the action skill building phase, the counselor facilitates cognitive retraining using structural skill modules, memory retraining, language and communication exercises, and social skill exercises.

Cicerone (1989) identifies increasing the client's capacity for self-observation as one goal of THI rehabilitation. Accordingly, he recommends the use of informative and educational counseling approaches to help clients who are unaware of their deficits. The use of videotape to provide clients with the necessary feedback on their present communication and interpersonal skills, repeated observations to assess their performance in a nonthreatening setting, and real-life community-based activities to avoid the artificial treatment settings are all marshaled to increase the client's level of awareness and attentiveness.

Two final approaches, to be briefly mentioned, are family and group counseling. Personal adjustment counseling of family members (McMahon & Fraser, 1988) serves to educate the members about the implications of THI and to secure its participation throughout the treatment program. Family members learn how to provide realistic hope, structure, and protection to the client without fostering false hope or unnecessary dependence. Concomitantly, family members are also provided with the opportunity to explore their own feelings toward the injury and the injured party (such as guilt and rejection) and to resolve those "unfinished business" issues that have surfaced following the onset of disability. Group counseling is another beneficial treatment approach to clients with THI. It offers participants several advantages. Notable among them are socialization with people facing similar problems, expanding one's repertoire of interpersonal behaviors, alleviating isolation and demoralization, seeing how others have progressed in overcoming their difficulties and engaging in supportive, goal-oriented group activities (Cicerone, 1989; Novack et al., 1988).

Counseling Clients with Psychiatric Disorders

For the purposes of this chapter, three major groups of psychiatric conditions will be discussed: schizophrenia, bipolar disorder, and major depression.

Schizophrenia

Schizophrenia represents a heterogenous group of disorders with certain core clinical features (Hyman, Arana, & Rosenbaum, 1995). Described as the most chronic and disabling of the severe mental disorders, schizophrenia typically develops in the late teens or early twenties. This illness curtails career plans, ends relationships, and torments not only the people directly affected but also their families and friends. The DSM-IV (American Psychiatric Association, 1994) specifies five major subtypes of the illness: Paranoid, Disorganized, Catatonic, Undifferentiated, and Residual. According to a National Institute of Mental Health (NIMH, 1995a) report, more than 2 million Americans are affected by schizophrenia in any given year, and only one in five recovers completely. Even with available treatment, most people continue to suffer persistently or episodically from their illness throughout a large part of their lives. One measure of the anguish of schizophrenia may be inferred from its lethality: an estimated 1 of every 10 people with the illness commits suicide (NIMH, 1995a).

Psychosocial Impact of Schizophrenia

Schizophrenia is known to have two main categories of symptoms, the "positive" symptoms, which are prominent during the active phase of the illness, and the "negative" symptoms, which are prominent during the prodromal and residual phases. Both categories of symptoms have significant psychosocial impact. It is, however, the "positive" symptoms that typically lead to psychiatric treatment or hospitalization. These "positive" symptoms reflect an excess or distortion of normal functions and include hallucinations, disorganized speech, and grossly disorganized or catatonic behavior (American Psychiatric Association, 1994). The "negative" symptoms of the illness are equally disabling and include affect flattening, alogia, avolition, anhedonia, withdrawal, social isolation, and a decreased motivation for self-care. The psychosocial impact of the illness on people with schizophrenia is costly. The significant cognitive deficits impair interpersonal relationships. Common problems in thinking—which include poor memory, concentration difficulties, distorted or inaccurate perceptions, and difficulty grasping concepts—become evident in completion of tasks that were easy to accomplish prior to onset of the illness. Accompanying this decline are marked impairment in social functioning, vulnerability to stress, and difficulty in coping with normal activities of daily living. People who suffer from schizophrenia lead restricted lives, and many of those who were institutionalized become homeless following release to the community.

Recommendations for Intervention

A wealth of evidence has accumulated over the last several decades and documents the fact that schizophrenia has strong biochemical elements (Torrey, 1988). Despite the biochemical nature of the illness, it is also known that environmental factors can have an important influence on the course of the illness. Stressful life events, such as the death of a loved one and emotionally charged living environments, have been found to increase the chances that a person with schizophrenia will have a symptom relapse requiring hospitalization. The treatment of schizophrenia requires thoughtful integration of biological, psychological, and environmental factors (Kane, 1989). Antipsychotic drugs remain the mainstay treatment for schizophrenia, especially in alleviating the "positive" symptoms of the illness. Unfortunately, the older antipsychotic medications have noxious extrapyramidal and anticholinergic side effects that contribute to noncompliance with treatment. The extrapyramidal (motor-related) side effects could, in addition, leave people with a permanent physically disfiguring condition, such as tardive dyskinesia (involuntary stereotypical movements following prolonged dopamine block).

Clozapine (Clozaril), one of the newer medications, was originally introduced into the United States in 1990 (Hyman et al., 1995) and has shown to result in few extrapyramidal side effects. People who are prescribed clozapine, however, need to have their blood monitored on a weekly basis, as the side effect of agranulocytosis (depletion of white blood cells) is potentially lethal. The newest medication on the market, risperidone (Risperdal) lacks anticholinergic side effects, examples of which are dizziness, blurred vision, urinary retention, and fecal impaction. However, at large doses it may produce extrapyramidal side effects.

Traditional insight-oriented therapy may not only be ineffective, but also might indeed worsen symptoms of schizophrenia (Torrey, 1988). Supportive, behavioral, and rehabilitative approaches are generally more effective than confrontational or analytic models (Kaplan & Sadock, 1981). The overall goal of psychiatric rehabilitation is to ensure that people with psychiatric disability can perform those physical, emotional, social, and intellectual skills needed to live, learn, and work in the community, with the least amount of support necessary from agents of the helping professions (Anthony, 1979). The major methods by which this goal is accomplished involve either teaching the person the specific skills needed to function effectively or providing community-based environmental resources needed to support or strengthen present levels of functioning (Anthony, Cohen & Cohen, 1983; Liberman & Evans, 1985). The goals of psychiatric rehabilitation are to increase the adaptive functioning of people with schizophrenia and to decrease maladaptive behavior through restoring the individual's ability for independent living, socialization, and effective life management. The resultant reduction in hospital use, as subjects participate in psychiatric rehabilitation activities and case management services, is well documented (Bell & Ryan, 1984; Bond, 1984; Bond, Miller, Krumweid, & Ward, 1988).

Bipolar Disorder

Bipolar disorder, also known as *manic-depressive disorder,* is an illness involving episodes of serious mania and depression. Its symptoms range from persistently elevated or expansive mood (such as inflated self-esteem and grandiose delusions) to feelings of helplessness, and hopelessness, with periods of normal mood in between (Hilliard, 1990). Typically beginning in adolescence or early adulthood, the illness is chronic but may often go unrecognized for several years. According to an NIMH report (1993), at least 2 million Americans suffer from manic-depressive illness. The median age of onset for the illness is 29 years for men, and 34.5 years for women (Kaplan & Sadock, 1989).

Psychosocial Impact of Bipolar Disorder

In bipolar disorder, depressive episodes alternate intermittently with manic ones, marked initially by heightened energy and mood, sharpened and usually creative thinking, irritability, and increased self-confidence. In full mania, these symptoms progress to grandiose delusions and psychotic, disruptive behavior (NIMH, 1993). The psychosocial impact is devastating for many people, including their family and friends. For those afflicted with the illness, it is extremely disruptive and distressing. During the manic phase of the illness, family members often have to cope with serious behavioral problems, such as wild spending sprees, running up of credit card accounts, and drug abuse. Also, an increased sexual drive may lead to risky sexual behavior and poor judgment. Frequently, there is obnoxious, provocative, or intrusive behavior, and the denial that anything is wrong (NIMH, 1993). Other problems that families, friends, and co-workers may have to deal with include extreme irritability and distractibility of the individual, excessive "high" or euphoric feelings, increased activity, restlessness, racing thoughts, and rapid speaking. People in the manic phase of the illness have been known to make long-distance phone calls at odd hours, to various destinations, often running up the family's phone bills.

This decreased need for sleep and these unrealistic beliefs about one's abilities and powers are quickly replaced during the depressed phase by persistent feelings of sadness, hopelessness, pessimism, guilt, worthlessness, helplessness, and a lost interest or pleasure in ordinary activities, including decreased sexual drive. The individual has decreased energy, feelings of fatigue or of being "slowed down," difficulty concentrating, and problems with memory and decision making. These symptoms are accompanied by sleep disturbances, loss or gain of appetite and weight, chronic pain, or other persistent bodily symptoms that are not caused by other physical disease. Thoughts of suicide or suicide attempts could also ensue during this phase.

Recommendations for Intervention

Most people affected by bipolar disorder can obtain substantial relief from their mood swings. At the present time, lithium, a naturally occurring substance, still constitutes the mainstay treatment for people with bipolar disorder. Augmentation of lithium with the anticonvulsants carbamazepine (Tegretol), valproic acid (Depakene), or divalproex sodium (Depakote) has proved to be effective for the treatment of rapid cycling bipolar disorder, or for individuals who do not respond well to lithium alone. For the depressed phase of the illness, several types of antidepressants can be useful when combined with lithium. These include tricyclics, heterocyclics, monoamine oxidase (MAO) inhibitors, selective serotonin reuptake inhibitors, and other antidepressants such as bupropion (Wellbutrin). Careful monitoring of antidepressant therapy is, however, necessary, because antidepressants may precipitate a switch into mania (Hyman et al., 1995). During the manic phase of the illness, therapists should approach the individual with empathy and nonconfrontational attitude but should not support inappropriate behavior. The therapist needs to be flexible and yet set limits, be directive, and promote reality testing (Perry, Frances, & Clarkin, 1985). During the depressed phase the therapist needs to be structured and present oriented and establish clear and realistic goals while encouraging hope and an increased activity level. Family and group therapies have been found to also be successful in promoting compliance, stabilization, and socialization (Schatzberg & Cole, 1991; Seligman, 1990) and in helping affected families to handle past and current problems (Schatzberg & Cole, 1991). The relatively high level of functioning of people with bipolar disorder suggests that only minor clinical emphasis must be placed on social skills. Safety is an issue of importance during manic episodes and can be monitored with family support and good case management. Participation in self-help groups and activities is also seen as a helpful procedure for people with bipolar disorder.

Major Depressive Disorder

Depression is a common and costly mental illness that affects approximately 17.6 million Americans each year. Estimates for the cost of depression to the nation in 1990 ranged from $30 to $44 billion. Depression also has an astronomical cost in lost work, estimated to be as high as 200 million days each year. In addition, there is an impact on productivity, due to the nature of the symptoms, and an immeasurable disruption to personal and family life (NIMH, 1995b). The lifetime risk for major depressive disorder in community samples has varied from 10 to 25 percent for women and from 5 to 12 percent for men. Cultural background often influences the experience and communication of symptoms of depression (American Psychiatric Association, 1994).

Psychosocial Impact of Major Depressive Disorder

The psychosocial impact of major depression is evident on close examination of the symptoms of the illness. These symptoms include persistent sad or "empty" mood, loss of interest in pleasurable activities, decreased sexual drive, and increased fatigue. These symptoms often lead to major problems in interpersonal relationships. Very often, the person with depression is misunderstood and blamed for being lazy. On the job, the individual may frequently be tardy or absent, as motivation and energy levels compounded by feelings of hopelessness make work seem meaningless. Irritability, lack of interest, and crying spells make co-workers, family, and friends uncomfortable. Insomnia or hypersomnia and a disturbed sleep pattern, coupled with poor memory and concentration difficulties, often affect decision making and general performance at work and at home. Frequent suicidal ideation and attempts put friends and family on edge, further increasing feelings of guilt already being experienced by the affected individual. In certain cases, the symptoms are accompanied by psychotic features, such as command auditory hallucinations, further increasing the risk for suicide.

Recommendations for Intervention

Effective pharmacologic and psychological treatments for people diagnosed with major depression are available and are frequently used concurrently. Medications include the traditional tricyclics, heterocyclics, and monoamine oxidase (MAO) inhibitors, which, in addition to causing sedation, weight gain, and orthostatic hypotension, typically have many anticholinergic side effects such as dizziness, blurred vision, constipation, urinary retention, and fecal impaction. The sedation caused by these medications may make it especially difficult to drive or to operate machines on the job. Furthermore, the use of MAO inhibitors calls for a strict avoidance of foods containing tyramine, examples of which are aged cheeses, beer, red wines, smoked fish, dry or fermented sausages, caviar, yeast extracts, liver (beef and chicken), and overripe fruits (Hyman et al., 1995; Kaplan & Sadock, 1990; Schatzberg & Cole, 1991). Fortunately, the newer antidepressants fluoxetine (Prozac), fluvoxamine (Luvox), sertraline (Zoloft), and paroxetine (Paxil), also known as selective serotonin reuptake inhibitors (SSRIs), lack the anticholinergic side effects and potential cardiotoxicity of the tricyclics. In addition, they are less sedating and do not cause weight gain. Venlafaxine (Effexor) the newest antidepressant, introduced into the United States in 1994, inhibits the uptake of the neurotransmitters norepinephrine and serotonin. Electroconvulsive therapy (ECT) is usually reserved for acute disabling episodes of depression and for cases that are refractory to other therapies.

Psychotherapies that have been found effective include both individual and group behavioral therapies (Lewinsohn, Sullivan, & Grosscup, 1980; Rehm, 1984), cognitive-behavioral therapies (Beck, Rush, Shaw, & Emery, 1979; Emmelkamp, 1986) as well as interpersonal therapy, or IPT (Klerman, Weissman, Rounsaville, & Chevron, 1984). Since 15 percent of people with recurrent depression commit suicide (Klerman et al., 1984), it is important to assess for (1) suicidal ideation, including the existence of definite plans; (2) homicidal ideation, a frequently overlooked concomitant (Rosenbaum & Bennett, 1986); (3) severity of illness, as measured by symptoms; and (4) degree of functional impairment. It is also important to assess for presence of (1) medical disorders, since certain illnesses may share common symptoms with psychiatric symptomatology; (2) psychotic symptoms, which could be mood congruent (for example, delusions of guilt, disease, or punishment) or mood incongruent (such as thought insertion or persecutory delusions without depressive themes). Command auditory hallucinations need to be taken very seriously, especially commanding harm to self or others.

Kornblith, Rehm, O'Hara, and Lamparski (1983) and Lewinsohn and Hoberman (1982) reviewed cognitive-behavioral approaches to the treatment of depression and found several ingredients that are instrumental in producing positive change. According to their findings, the ingredients include (1) the presentation of a concrete rationale for depression and treatment, as well as a vocabulary for defining and describing the problem; (2) a highly structured approach that offers clear plans for change, while giving clients a sense of control; (3) the provision of feedback, so that clients can perceive change, receive reinforcement, and attribute improvement to their own efforts; and (4) teaching of skills that increase personal effectiveness and independence. Whichever model (behavioral, cognitive-behavioral, or IPT) a therapist chooses to follow, it is important to promote a realistic appraisal of alternatives and goal setting, a sense of mastery and improved self-esteem, better reality testing, clearer boundaries between self and others, a repertoire of problem-solving skills, and coping mechanisms (Seligman, 1990).

It is necessary to maintain a network of psychosocial support for people with depression. Access to support from family, friends, and mental health providers is necessary in between depressive episodes, and in times of crisis. It is especially important to have phone numbers for crisis lines and area emergency services readily available for use should suicidal ideation persist.

Training and Qualifications of Counselors Who Work with Clients with Disabilities

Academic Training and Program Accreditation

Academic training of counselors whose interest lies in working with clients with disabilities is accomplished almost invariably through rehabilitation counselor education (RCE) programs. These training programs are typically graduate (master's level) programs and are offered by counselor education or counseling psychology departments. Completing the programs normally requires two years of academic and clinical training when pursued full time.

The curriculum content in most of these training programs has been developed and verified by the Council on Rehabilitation Education (CORE). CORE was established in 1971 as an accreditation body to oversee the academic and clinical training of rehabilitation counselors and to promote effective delivery of rehabilitation services to people with disabilities. Of the approximately 100 RCE programs in the United States, 84 are currently CORE accredited. These programs must show evidence of a graduate-level curriculum that provides its trainees with a course of study that includes, but is not limited to, the following knowledge and/or skill areas: (1) history and philosophy of rehabilitation; (2) rehabilitation legislation; (3) organizational structure of the rehabilitation system (public and private, nonprofit and for-profit service delivery); (4) counseling theories, approaches, and techniques; (5) case management; (6) career development and vocational counseling theories and practices; (7) vocational evaluation, occupational information, job analysis, and work adjustment techniques; (8) job development and placement; (9) medical aspects of disability; (10) psychosocial aspects of disability; (11) knowledge of community resources and services; (12) rehabilitation research; (13) measurement and testing; (14) legal and ethical issues in rehabilitation counseling; (15) independent living; and (16) special topics in rehabilitation (such as transition from school to work, supported employment, rehabilitation engineering).

In addition, rehabilitation counseling trainees are required to participate in supervised practicum and internship experiences for a total of a minimum of 600 clock hours in approved rehabilitation sites and under the supervision of a certified rehabilitation counselor.

Certification and Licensure

The Commission on Rehabilitation Counselor Certification (CRCC) is the primary certifying body of rehabilitation counselors in the United States. It offers the following national certifications: Certified Rehabilitation Counselor (CRC), Certified Insurance Rehabilitation Specialist (CIRS), Certified Case Manager (CCM), and Certified Alcohol Counselor (CAC). There are at present nearly 11,000 counselors who are rehabilitation certified.

The main purpose of CRCC is to assure that professionals who practice counseling with clients with disabilities (rehabilitation counseling) meet acceptable standards of professional expertise. CRCC, founded in 1973, was the first national certification organization to be sponsored by an American Counseling Association (ACA) division (formerly known as the American Association for Counseling and Development), namely, the American Rehabilitation Counseling Association (Emener & Cottone, 1989). In accordance with the knowledge and skill areas required by CORE for program accreditation purposes, CRCC tests rehabilitation applicants on the following content subjects: (1) rehabilitation philosophy, history, structure, and legislation, (2) medical and psychosocial aspects of disability, (3) counseling theories and techniques, (4) occupational information, (5) job development and placement, (6) evaluation and assessment, (7) vocational adjustment, (8) research utilization, and (9) ethical issues.

The duration of the certification is five years. At the end of the five-year period, the Certified Rehabilitation Counselor (CRC) who has not accumulated a total of

100 approved contact (clock) hours of continuing education must retake and successfully pass the CRC exam to maintain his or her certification.

State-regulated licensure of counselors who work with clients with disabilities is usually accomplished through the enactment of omnibus state legislation that governs the practice of various professional counselor groups (mental health, marriage and family, community, rehabilitation). These state laws regulate individuals in the use of the title ("professional counselor"), as well as the practice of the profession.

Professional Associations

At present, the following national professional organizations offer membership to counselors who seek to specialize in working with clients with disabilities: (1) the American Rehabilitation Counseling Association (ARCA), Division of ACA; (2) the National Rehabilitation Counseling Association (NRCA), Division of the National Rehabilitation Association (NRA); (3) the Rehabilitation Psychology Division (Division 22) of the American Psychological Association (APA); and (4) the National Association of Rehabilitation Professionals in the Private Sector (NARPPS).

ARCA and NRCA are organizations representing professional rehabilitation counselors and others concerned with improving the lives of people with disabilities (educators, researchers, administrators). These two organizations, established about the same time period (1956–1957), have as their mission the provision of leadership to promote excellence in rehabilitation counseling practice, training, research, consultation, and professional growth. They further emphasize the importance of modifying environmental and attitudinal conditions and barriers so that more opportunities become available to people with disabilities in employment, education, and community activities. The membership of ARCA and NRCA is composed of rehabilitation counselors and other practitioners employed in both the public and private sectors (divisions of vocational rehabilitation, commissions for the blind and visually impaired, hospitals and rehabilitation units, mental health centers, rehabilitation workshops, university services for students with disabilities, self-help organizations and private rehabilitation organizations).

The Rehabilitation Psychology Division of the APA represents members (mainly psychologists) who are interested in the psychosocial consequences of disability and rehabilitation (personal adjustment and growth, coping strategies, social and attitudinal barriers) in order to better serve people with disabilities. This division is equally interested in the development of high standards and practices for professional psychologists who serve clients with disabilities. Most of the division members are educators, researchers, and practicing psychologists whose clientele is composed mainly of people with physical, psychiatric, and cognitive impairments.

Finally, NARPPS is an organization whose members are invariably committed to the advancement of rehabilitation practices in the private for-profit rehabilitation sector. Although traditional counseling activities make up only a minor portion of the job tasks performed by private rehabilitation professionals, they nonetheless offer individual and group counseling services to clients as may be required for achievement of sound vocational choice and successful job placement. Members of NARPPS typically include rehabilitation counselors, rehabilitation nurses, vocational evaluators, and job placement specialists.

Summary

The purpose of this chapter was to acquaint the beginning counseling student with (1) the impact of various disabling conditions on the client, (2) the intervention strategies most commonly adopted by counselors who work with clients with disabilities, and (3) the academic programs, their accreditation procedures, certification and licensure considerations, and the professional organizations of counselors who serve clients with disabilities. Counselors who intend to pursue the career of rehabilitation counseling and specialize in working with clients with disabilities may find it advantageous to directly contact the following organizations: (1) ARCA/ACA, 5999 Stevenson Avenue, Alexandria, VA 22304; (2) NRCA/NRA, 8807 Sudley Rd. #102, Manassas, VA 22110; (3) CORE, 1835 Rohlwing Rd., Suite E, Rolling Meadows, IL 60008; (4) CRCC, 1835 Rohlwing Rd., Suite E, Rolling Meadows, IL 60008; and (5) the National Council on Rehabilitation Education (NCRE), Administrative Office, Department of Special Education & Rehabilitation, Utah State University, Logan, UT 84322.

References

Allen, H. A., & Sawyer, H. W. (1984). Individuals with life-threatening disabilities: A rehabilitation counseling approach. *Journal of Applied Rehabilitation Counseling, 15*(2), 26–29.

American Psychiatric Association. (1994). *Diagnostic and statistical manual of mental disorders* (4th ed.) DSM-IV. Washington, DC: Author.

Anderson, T. P. (1981). Stroke and cerebral trauma: Medical aspects. In W. C. Stolov & M. R. Clowers (Eds.), *Handbook of severe disability* (pp. 119–126). Washington, DC: U.S. Department of Education.

Anthony, W. A. (1979). *Principles of psychiatric rehabilitation.* Baltimore: University Park Press.

Anthony, W. A., Cohen, M., & Cohen, B. (1983). The philosophy, treatment process and principles of the psychiatric rehabilitation approach. *New Directions in Mental Health, 17,* 67–69.

Auvenshine, C. D., & Noffsinger, A. L. (1984). *Counseling: An introduction for the health and human services.* Baltimore: University Park Press.

Backman, M. E. (1989). *The psychology of the physically ill patient: A clinician's guide.* New York: Plenum Press.

Beck, A. T., Rush, A. J., Shaw, B. F., & Emery, G. (1979). *Cognitive therapy of depression.* New York: Guilford Press.

Bell, M. D., & Ryan, E. R. (1984). Integrating psychosocial rehabilitation into the hospital psychiatric service. *Hospital and Community Psychiatry, 35,* 1017–1023.

Ben-Yishay, Y., & Diller, L. (1983). Cognitive deficits. In M. Rosenthal, E. Griffith, M. Bond, & J. Miller (Eds.), *Rehabilitation of the head-injured adult* (pp. 167–182). Philadelphia: Davis.

Bolton, B. (Ed.). (1976). *Psychology of deafness for rehabilitation counselors.* Baltimore: University Park Press.

Bond, G. R. (1984). An economic analysis of psychosocial rehabilitation. *Hospital and Community Psychiatry, 35,* 356–362.

Bond, G. R., Miller, L. D., Krumweid, R. D., & Ward, R. S. (1988). Assertive case management in three DMHCs: A controlled study. *Hospital and Community Psychiatry, 39,* 411–418.

Brammell, H. L. (1981). Cardiovascular diseases. In W. C. Stolov & M. R. Clowers (Eds.), *Handbook of severe disability* (pp. 289–308). Washington, DC: U.S. Department of Education.

Brammell, H. L., McDaniel, J., Niccoli, S. A., Darnell, R., & Roberson, D. R. (1979). *Cardiac rehabilitation.* Denver: Webb-Warring Lung.

Brucker, B. S. (1983). Spinal cord injuries. In T. G. Burish & L. A. Bradley (Eds.), *Coping with chronic disease* (pp. 285–311). New York: Academic Press.

Carey, R. G. (1976). Counseling the terminally ill. *Personnel and Guidance Journal, 55,* 124–126.

Carroll, T. J. (1961). *Blindness.* Boston: Little, Brown.

Cicerone, K. D. (1989). Psychotherapeutic interventions with traumatically brain-injured patients. *Rehabilitation Psychology, 34,* 105–114.

Cobb, A. B. (Ed.). (1973). *Medical and psychological aspects of disability.* Springfield, IL: Thomas.

Costello, P. M. (1973). Educational and social factors in the rehabilitation of hearing disabilities. In A. B. Cobb (Ed.), *Medical and psychological aspects of disability* (pp. 303–328). Springfield, IL: Thomas.

Coulton, C. J. (1981). Person–environment fit as the focus in health care. *Social Work, 62,* 26–35.

Cowen, E. L. (1973). Social and community interventions. *Annual Review of Psychology, 24,* 423–472.

Crewe, N. M. (1980). Quality of life: The ultimate goal in rehabilitation. *Minnesota Medicine, 63,* 586–589.

Crewe, N. M., & Krause, J. S. (1987). Spinal cord injury: Psychological aspects. In B. Caplan (Ed.), *Rehabilitation psychology desk reference* (pp. 3–35). Rockville, MD: Aspen.

Cull, J. G. (1973). Psychological adjustment to blindness. In A. B. Cobb (Ed.), *Medical and psychological aspects of disability* (pp. 336–348). Springfield, IL: Thomas.

Cull, J. G., & Hardy, R. E. (1975). *Counseling strategies with special populations.* Springfield, IL: Thomas.

Danek, M. (1983). Rehabilitation counseling with deaf clients. *Journal of Applied Rehabilitation Counseling, 14*(3), 20–25.

DeLoach, C., & Greer, B. G. (1981). *Adjustment to severe physical disability: A metamorphosis.* New York: McGraw-Hill.

Dixon, T. M., Trexler, L. E., & Layton, B. S. (1993). Brain injury: Trauma and stroke. In M. G. Eisenberg, R. L. Glueckauf, & H. H. Zaretsky (Eds.), *Medical aspects of disability* (pp. 76–91). New York: Springer.

Dolan, J. D., Allen, H. A., & Bell, T. T. (1988). Neoplastic disease: Considerations for the rehabilitation profession. In S. E. Rubin & N. M. Rubin (Eds.), *Contemporary challenges to the rehabilitation counseling profession* (pp. 183–196). Baltimore: Brookes.

Donovan, W. H. (1981). Spinal cord injury. In W. C. Stolov & M. R. Clowers (Eds.), *Handbook of severe disability* (pp. 65–82). Washington, DC: U.S. Department of Education.

Dunham, C. S. (1978). Cancer. In R. M. Goldenson (Ed.), *Disability and rehabilitation handbook* (pp. 305–317). New York: McGraw-Hill.

Eleventh Institute on Rehabilitation Services. (1974). *The rehabilitation of the deaf.* Fayetteville: University of Arkansas, Arkansas Rehabilitation Research & Training Center.

Elmayan, M. M. (1992). Cancer. In M. G. Brodwin, F. Tellez, & S. K. Brodwin (Eds.), *Medical, psychosocial and vocational aspects of disability* (pp. 233–249). Athens, GA: Elliott & Fitzpatrick.

Emener, W. G., & Cottone, R. R. (1989). Professionalization, deprofessionalization, and reprofessionalization of rehabilitation counseling according to criteria of professions. *Journal of Counseling and Development, 67,* 576–581.

Emmelkamp, P. M. G. (1986). Behavior therapy with adults. In S. L. Garfield & A. E. Bergin (Eds.), *Handbook of psychotherapy and behavior change* (3rd ed., pp. 385–442). New York: Wiley.

Falvo, D. R. (1991). *Medical and psychosocial aspects of chronic illness and disability.* Gaithersburg, MD: Aspen.

Fleming, V. (1985). Relaxation therapy for far-advanced cancer. *American Journal of Nursing, 77,* 1585–1588.

Fraser, R. T. (1993). Epilepsy. In M. G. Eisenberg, R. L. Glueckauf, & H. H. Zaretsky (Eds.), *Medical aspects of disability* (pp. 192–207). New York: Springer.

Fraser, R. T., & Clemmons, D. (1983). Epilepsy rehabilitation: Assessment and counseling concerns. *Journal of Applied Rehabilitation Counseling, 14*(3), 26–31.

Freidenbergs, I., & Kaplan, E. (1993). Cancer. In M. G. Eisenberg, R. L. Glueckauf, & H. H. Zaretsky (Eds.), *Medical aspects of disability* (pp. 105–118). New York: Springer.

Gentry, W. D. (1978). Behavior modification of the coronary-prone behavior pattern. In T. M. Dembroski, S. M. Weiss, J. L. Shields, S. G. Haynes, & M. Feinleib (Eds.), *Coronary-prone behavior.* New York: Springer.

Gloor, B., & Bruckner, R. (Eds.). (1980). *Rehabilitation of the visually disabled and the blind at different ages.* Baltimore: University Park Press.

Greif, E., & Matarazzo, R. G. (1982). *Behavioral approach to rehabilitation.* New York: Springer.

Harris, J. (1984). Method of improving memory. In B. A. Wilson & N. Moffatt (Eds.), *Clinical management of memory problems* (pp. 46–62). Rockville, MD: Aspen.

Hauser, W. A., & Hesdorffer, D. C. (1990). *Epilepsy: Frequency, causes, and consequences.* New York: Demos.

Healey, J. E., & Zislis, J. M. (1981). Cancers. In W. C. Stolov & M. R. Clowers (Eds.), *Handbook of severe disability* (pp. 363–376). Washington, DC: U.S. Department of Education.

Heinemann, A. W. (1993). Prevalence and consequences of alcohol and other drug problems following spinal cord injury. In A. W. Heinemann (Ed.), *Substance abuse and physical disability* (pp. 63–78). New York: Haworth Press.

Hermann, B. P., Desai, B. T., & Whitman, S. (1988). Epilepsy. In V. B. Van Hasselt, P. S. Strain, & M. Hersen (Eds.), *Handbook of developmental and physical disabilities* (pp. 247–270). New York: Pergamon Press.

Hershenson, D. B. (1990). A theoretical model for rehabilitation counseling. *Rehabilitation Counseling Bulletin, 33,* 268–278.

Hilliard, J. R. (Ed.). (1990). *Manual of clinical emergency psychiatry.* Washington, DC: American Psychiatric Press.

Houd, H. (1978). Cardiac disorders. In R. M. Goldenson (Ed.), *Disability and rehabilitation handbook* (pp. 318–330). New York: McGraw-Hill.

Hu, S. S., & Cressy, J. M. (1992). Paraplegia and quadriplegia. In M. G. Brodwin, F. Tellez, & S. K. Brodwin (Eds.), *Medical, psychosocial and vocational aspects of disability* (pp. 369–391). Athens, GA: Elliott & Fitzpatrick.

Hylbert, K. W., & Hylbert, K. W. (1979). *Medical information for human service workers.* State College, PA: Counselor Education Press.

Hyman, S. E., Arana, G. W., & Rosenbaum, J. F. (1995). *Handbook of psychiatric drug therapy* (3rd ed.). Boston: Little, Brown.

Johnson, J., & Getzen, J. (1992). Cardiovascular disease. In M. G. Brodwin, F. Tellez, & S. K. Brodwin (Eds.), *Medical, psychosocial and vocational aspects of disability* (pp. 317–333). Athens, GA: Elliott & Fitzpatrick.

Kane, J. M. (1989). Schizophrenia: Somatic treatment. In H. I. Kaplan & B. J. Sadock (Eds.), *Comprehensive textbook of psychiatry* (Vol. 1, 5th ed., pp. 727–792). Baltimore: Williams & Wilkins.

Kaplan, B. J., & Wyler, A. R. (1983). Coping with epilepsy. In T. G. Burish & L. A. Bradley (Eds.), *Coping with chronic disease* (pp. 259–284). New York: Academic Press.

Kaplan, H. I., & Sadock, B. J. (1981). *Modern synopsis of psychiatry* (Vol. 3). Baltimore: Williams & Wilkins.

Kaplan, H. I., & Sadock, B. J. (Eds.). (1989). *Comprehensive textbook of psychiatry* (Vol. 1, 5th ed.) Baltimore: Williams & Wilkins.

Kaplan. H. I., & Sadock, B. J. (1990). *Pocket handbook of clinical psychiatry.* Baltimore: Williams & Wilkins.

Kerman-Lerner, P., & Hauck, K. (1993). Speech, language, and hearing disorders. In M. G. Eisenberg, R. L. Glueckauf, & H. H. Zaretsky

(Eds.), *Medical aspects of disability* (pp. 208–230). New York: Springer.

Kirchner, C. (1988). *Data on blindness and visual impairments in the U.S.* (2nd ed.). New York: American Foundation for the Blind.

Kirchner, C., & Lowman, C. (1978). Sources of variation in the estimated prevalence of visual loss. *Journal of Visual Impairment and Blindness, 72,* 329–333.

Klerman, G. L., Weissman, M. W., Rounsaville, B. J., & Chevron, E. S. (1984). *Interpersonal psychotherapy of depression.* New York: Basic Books.

Kornblith, S. H., Rehm, L. P., O'Hara, M. W., & Lamparski, D. M. (1983). The contribution of self-reinforcement training and behavioral assignments to the efficacy of self-control therapy for depression. *Cognitive Therapy and Research, 7,* 499–528.

Kraus, J. F. (1987). Epidemiology of brain injury. In P. R. Cooper (Ed.), *Head injury* (pp. 1–19). Baltimore: Williams & Wilkins.

Kübler-Ross, E. (1969). *On death and dying.* New York: Macmillan.

Leventhal, H., & Hirschmann, R. S. (1982). Social psychology and prevention. In G. S. Sanders & J. Suls (Eds.), *Social psychology* of *health and illness* (pp. 183–226). Hillsdale, NJ: Erlbaum.

Levine, E. (1977). *The preparation of psychological service providers to the deaf.* Monograph No. 4. Silver Spring, MD: Professional Rehabilitation Workers with the Adult Deaf.

Lewinsohn, P. M., & Hoberman, H. M. (1982). Behavioural and cognitive approaches. In E. S. Paykel (Ed.), *Handbook of affective disorders* (pp. 338–345). New York: Guilford Press.

Lewinsohn, P. M., Sullivan, J. M., & Grosscup, S. J. (1980). Changing reinforcing events: An approach to the treatment of depression. *Psychotherapy: Theory, Research and Practice, 17,* 322–334.

Liberman, R. P., & Evans, C. C. (1985). Behavioral rehabilitation for chronic mental patients. *Journal of Clinical Psychopharmacology, 5,* S8–S14.

Lindemann, J. E. (1981). *Psychological and behavioral aspects of physical disability.* New York: Plenum Press.

Livneh, H. (1988). Rehabilitation goals: Their hierarchical and multifaceted nature. *Journal of Applied Rehabilitation Counseling, 19*(3), 12–18.

Livneh, H. (1989). Rehabilitation intervention strategies: Their integration and classification. *Journal of Rehabilitation, 55,* 21–30.

Livneh, H. (1995). The tripartite model of rehabilitation intervention: Basics, goals, and rehabilitation strategies. *Journal of Applied Rehabilitation Counseling, 26*(1), 25–29.

Lubkin, I. M. (Ed.). (1995). *Chronic illness: Impact and interventions.* Boston: Jones and Bartlett.

Lyles, J. N., Burish, T. G., Krozely, M. G., & Oldham, R. K. (1982). Efficacy of relaxation training and guided imagery in reducing the aversiveness of cancer chemotherapy. *Journal of Consulting and Clinical Psychology, 50,* 509–524.

Manley, S. (1973). A definitive approach to group counseling. *Journal of Rehabilitation, 39,* 38–40.

Marshak, L. E., & Seligman, M. (1993). *Counseling persons with physical disabilities: Theoretical and clincal perspectives.* Austin, TX: Pro Ed.

McAleer, C. A., & Kluge, C. A. (1978). Counseling needs and approaches for working with a cancer patient. *Rehabilitation Counseling Bulletin, 21,* 238–245.

McCollum, P. S. (1978). Adjustment to cancer: A psychosocial and rehabilitative perspective. *Rehabilitation Counseling Bulletin, 21,* 216–223.

McMahon, B. T., & Fraser, R. T. (1988). Basic issues and trends in head injury rehabilitation. In S. E. Rubin & N. M. Rubin (Eds.), *Contemporary challenges to the rehabilitation counseling profession* (pp. 197–215). Baltimore: Brookes.

Medis, N. (1982). Counseling strategies with handicapped students. In C. W. Humes (Ed.), *Counseling the handicapped client: A series of training modules* (pp. 33–48). Falls Church, VA: American Personnel and Guidance Association.

Miller, D., Wolfe, M., & Spiegel, M. (1975). Therapeutic groups for patients with spinal cord injuries. *Archives of Physical Medicine and Rehabilitation, 56,* 130–135.

Moos, R. H., & Tsu, V. D. (1977). The crisis of physical illness: An overview. In R. H. Moos (Ed.), *Coping with physical illness* (pp. 3–21). New York: Plenum Press.

National Institute of Mental Health (NIMH). (1993). *Bipolar disorder.* NIMH Publication No. 93–3679. [on-line]. Mental Health Fax4U Document No. 933679. Available from Rockville, MD, phone (301) 443–5158.

National Institute of Mental Health (NIMH). (1995a). *Facts about depression* [on-line]. Mental Health Fax4U Document No. 953477. Available from Rockville, MD, phone (301) 443–5158.

National Institute of Mental Health (NIMH). (1995b). *Mental illness in America: The National Institute of Mental Health agenda* [on-line]. Mental Health Fax 4U Document No. 955005. Available from Rockville, MD, phone (301) 443–5158.

Novack, T. A., Roth, D. L., & Boll, T. J. (1988). Treatment alternatives following mild head injury. *Rehabilitation Counseling Bulletin, 31,* 313–324.

Nunes, E. V., Frank, K. A., & Kornfeld, D. (1987). Psychologic treatment for the type A behavior pattern and for coronary heart disease: A meta-analysis of the literature. *Psychosomatic Medicine, 48,* 159–171.

Ososkie, J. N. (1984). Epilepsy: Implications for rehabilitation. *Journal of Applied Rehabilitation Counseling, 15*(2),12–15.

Ostby, S., & Thomas, K. R. (1984). Deafness and hearing impairment: A review and proposal. *Journal of Applied Rehabilitation Counseling, 15*(2), 7–11.

Panek, W. C. (1992). Visual disabilities. In M. G. Brodwin, F. Tellez, & S. K. Brodwin (Eds.), *Medical, psychosocial and vocational aspects of disability* (pp. 217–230). Athens, GA: Elliott & Fitzpatrick.

Pattison, E. M. (1977). *The experience of dying.* Englewood Cliffs, NJ: Prentice Hall.

Perry, S., Frances, A., & Clarkin, J. (1985). *A DSM-III casebook of differential therapeutics.* New York: Brunner/Mazel.

Prigatano, G. P. (1989). Bring it up in milieu: Toward effective traumatic brain injury rehabilitation interventions. *Rehabilitation Psychology, 34,* 135–144.

Prigatano, G. P., et al. (1986). *Neuropsychological rehabilitation after brain injury.* Baltimore: Johns Hopkins University Press.

Rehm, L. P. (1984). Self-management therapy for depression. *Advances in Behavior Research and Therapy, 6,* 83–98.

Rey, M. J. (1993). Cardiovascular disorders. In M. G. Eisenberg, R. L. Glueckauf, & H. H. Zaretsky (Eds.), *Medical aspects of disability* (pp. 119–146). New York: Springer.

Romano, M. (1976). Social skills training with the new handicapped. *Archives of Physical Medicine and Rehabilitation, 57,* 302–303.

Rosenbaum, M., & Bennett, B. (1986). Homicide and depression. *American Journal of Psychiatry, 143,* 367–370.

Rosenthal, M. (1987). Traumatic head injury: Neurobehavioral consequences. In B. Caplan (Ed.), *Rehabilitation psychology desk reference* (pp. 37–63). Rockville, MD: Aspen.

Schatzberg, A. F., & Cole, J. O. (1991). *Manual of clinical psychopharmacology* (2nd ed.). Washington, DC: American Psychiatric Press.

Schein, J. D. (1981). Hearing impairments and deafness. In W. C. Stolov & M. R. Clowers (Eds.), *Handbook of severe disability* (pp. 395–407). Washington, DC: U.S. Department of Education.

Scofield, M., Pape, D., McCracken, N., & Maki, D. (1980). An ecological model for promoting acceptance of disability. *Journal of Applied Rehabilitation Counseling, 11*(4), 183–187.

Seligman, L. (1990). *Selecting effective treatments: A comprehensive, systematic guide to treating adult mental disorders.* San Francisco: Jossey-Bass.

Seligman, M. (1975). *Helplessness: On depression, development, and death.* San Francisco: Freeman.

Thomas, K., Thoreson, R., Butler, A., & Parker, R. M. (1992). Theoretical foundations of rehabilitation counseling. In R. M. Parker & E. M. Szymanski (Eds.), *Rehabilitation counseling: Basics and beyond* (2nd ed., pp. 207–247). Austin, TX: Pro Ed.

Thoreson, R. W., & Ackerman, M. (1981). Cardiac rehabilitation: Basic principles and psychosocial factors. *Rehabilitation Counseling Bulletin, 24,* 223–255.

Torkelson-Lynch, R. (1983). Traumatic head injury: Implications for rehabilitation counseling. *Journal of Applied Rehabilitation Counseling, 14*(3), 32–35.

Torrey, F. E. (1988). *Surviving schizophrenia: A family manual* (Rev. ed.). New York: Harper & Row.

Treischmann, R. B. (1988). *Spinal cord injuries: Psychological, social, and vocational rehabilitation* (2nd ed.). New York: Demos.

Twelfth Institute on Rehabilitation Issues. (1985). *Rehabilitation of the traumatic brain injured.* Menomonie: Research and Training Center, Vocational Rehabilitation Institute, University of Wisconsin-Stout.

Vander Kolk, C. J. (1983). Rehabilitation counseling with the visually impaired. *Journal of Applied Rehabilitation Counseling, 14*(3),13–19.

Vash, C. L. (1981). *The psychology of disability.* New York: Springer-Verlag.

Ward, A. A., Fraser, R. T., & Troupin, A. S. (1981). Epilepsy. In W. C. Stolov & M. R. Clowers (Eds.), *Handbook of severe disability* (pp. 155–168). Washington, DC: U.S. Department of Education.

Wood, R. L. (1984). Behavior disorders following severe brain injury: Their presentation and psychological management. In N. Brooks (Ed.), *Closed head injury: Psychological, social and family consequences* (pp. 195–219). London: Oxford University Press.

Wright, G. N. (1980). *Total rehabilitation.* Boston: Little, Brown.

Young, J. S., Burns, P. E., Bowen, A. M., & McCutchen, R. (1987). *Spinal cord injury statistics: Experience of the regional spinal cord injury systems.* Phoenix, AZ: Good Samaritan Medical Center.

Index

ABC method, 141
Abramowitz, S. I., 437, 438
Abreaction, 128
Abreu, J., 446
Absence of seizures, 474
Abuse or Neglect, Problems Related to, 251
ACA Press, 24
Accord through opposition, 154
Accreditation, 25–27
   disabled clients, programs for counselors of, 487–488
   of family therapy programs, 390
Accreditation Standards and Procedures Manual (CACREP), 27
Acculturation Problem, 251
Acculturative stress, 436
Accuser/defender role, 155
Achievement tests, 225–226
Ackerman, M., 472
Ackerman, N. W., 368–369
Acquired immunodeficiency syndrome (AIDS). *See* AIDS
Action skills, 81
Activating events, 130, 131
Active listening, 70
   older adults, counseling of, 360
Active Living Model, 162
Activities of daily living (ADL), 464
Acute Stress disorder, 247, 248
Adjustment Disorders, 236, 241, 250
Adjustment Disorder with Depressed Mood, 236, 241
Adler, A., 9, 52, 53, 56, 57, 58, 114, 115
Adolescents. *See also* Children; Family therapy
   approaches with, 336–340
   attachment/automony related issues, 336
   behavior modification for, 336
   brief family consultation, 341–344
   coming out, 408, 410
   difficulties with counseling, 333
   disorders first diagnosed in, 244–245
   focus of treatment, 333
   games in play therapy for, 276–277
   group counseling for, 339–340
   intervention with, 160–162
Adult Antisocial Behavior, 243
Advanced empathy, 77–78
Advertising services, 91
Affect, 113
African Americans. *See* Minorities
Age-Related Cognitive Decline, 251
Aging. *See* Older adults
Agoraphobia, 247
AIDS, 34, 36, 420–421
   adolescents facing, 336

career counseling and, 200
confidentiality and, 93–94
guidance/psychoeducational groups for, 170
monogamous relationships and, 414
school counseling, 291, 305
Akutsu, P. O., 435, 455
Albertson, Ralph, 8
Alcohol abuse, 37
   homosexuality and, 419–420
Alcoholics Anonymous, 246, 420
Alexander, C. M., 443, 449
Alexander, F., 144
Alexander, J., 392
Allan, J., 257, 258, 259–261
Allen, H. A., 477, 478, 479
Allen, L., 282
Alliance for the Guidance of Rural Youth, 11
Allport, G. W., 51, 56, 57, 58, 117
Alpha IQ intelligence tests, 10
Altekruse, M., 25–26
Altmaier, E. M., 441
Alzheimer's disease, 245
Amatea, E. S., 160
American Association for Counseling and Development (AACD), 18, 22–23
American Association for Marriage and Family Therapy (AAMFT), 27, 30, 315, 389
American Association of Collegiate Registrars, 11–12
American Association of Retired Persons (AARP), 350
American Association of Sex Educator Counselors and Therapists, 30
American College Counseling Association, 23
American College Personnel Association (ACPA), 314
American Council of Guidance and Personnel Associations (ACGPA), 11, 18
American Counseling Association (ACA), 18, 315, 389. *See also Code of Ethics and Standards of Practice* (ACA)
   development of, 19–23
   divisions of, 24
   regional structure of, 23–24
American Educational Research Association (AERA), 223
American Family Association, 33
American Family Therapy Academy (AFTA), 389
American Indians. *See* Minorities
American Journal of Family Therapy, 393
American Mental Health Counselors Association (AMHCA), 22, 25, 239, 312–316

credentialing by, 316–320
   successes of, 324–325
   War Chest grant, 318–319
American Personnel and Guidance Association (APGA), 18, 19, 312
   AMHCA and, 313–316
American Psychiatric Association (APA), 423
American Psychological Association (APA), 9, 31, 223, 389, 423
   training standards, 13
American Rehabilitation Counseling Association (ARCA), 20, 488, 489
American School Counselors Association (ASCA), 19–20, 25, 314
Americans with Disabilities Act (ADA), 17
   career counseling and, 200
Amerikaner, M., 259
Amnestic Disorder, 245
Amster, F., 275
Anastasi, A., 216, 219, 224, 227, 229, 230
Anchor, K. N., 184
Anderson, D. A., 410
Anderson, J. D., 182, 183, 184
Anderson, L. P., 436
Anderson, T. P., 479
Anorexia Nervosa, 249
   Restricting Type, 241
Anthony, W. A., 465, 483
Antidepressants, 485, 486
Antigay initiatives, 398
Antiracism training model, 441
Antisocial Personality Disorder, 251
Anxiety, 127
   in career counseling client, 209
   DSM-IV diagnoses, 247–248
   short-term anxiety provoking psychotherapy, 144–145
   in time-limited therapy, 148
APGA Guidepost, 312–313
Applied Psychology: An International Review, 199
Appraisal
   defined, 215–216
   in school counseling, 294
Approaches to Art Therapy (Rubin), 262
Appropriateness of test, 219–220
Aptitudes of career counseling client, 205–206
Aptitude tests, 226–227
Arana, G. W., 482
Arbitrary inference, 337
Arbona, C., 197, 198, 200
Arbuckle, D., 175
Aristotle, 56
Arousal Disorder, 249
Arredondo, P. M., 443
Artistic people, 195